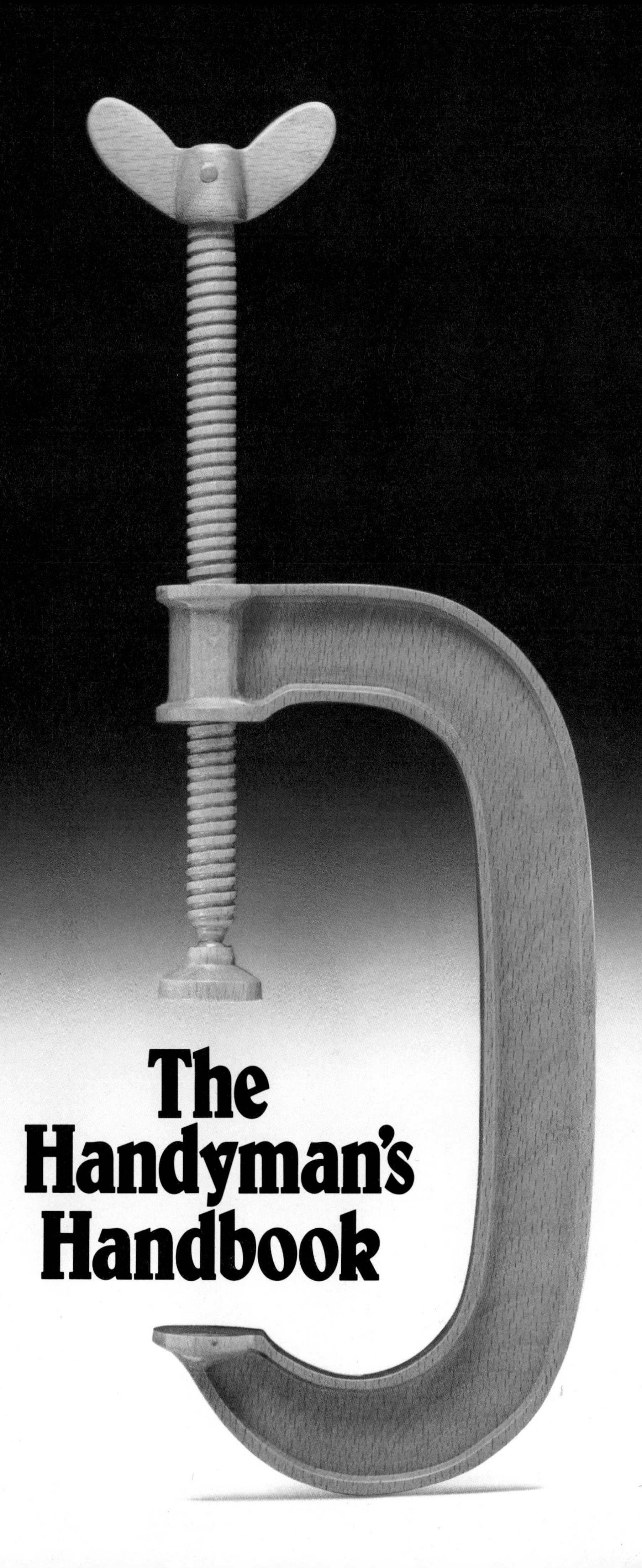

# The Handyman's Handbook

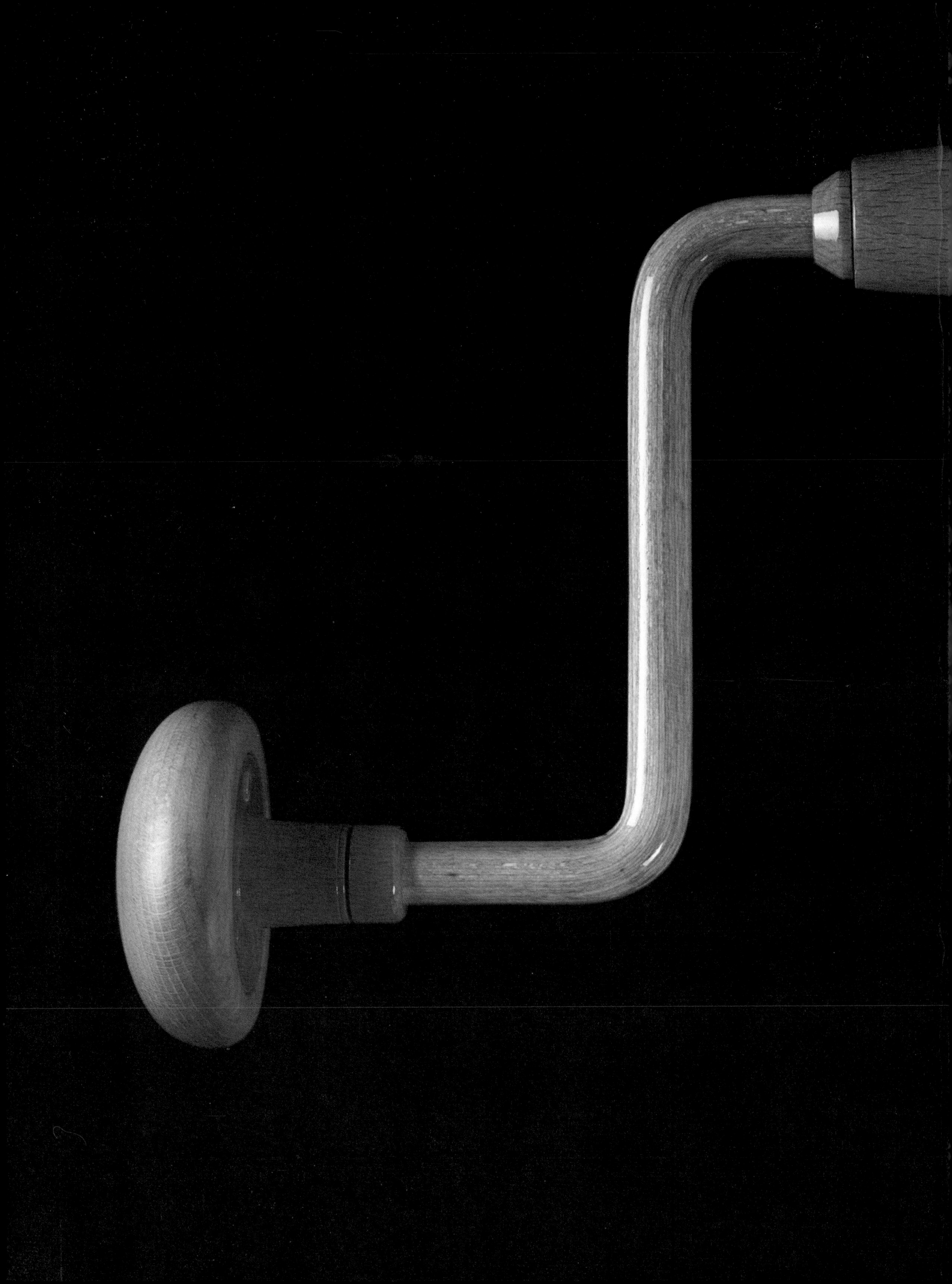

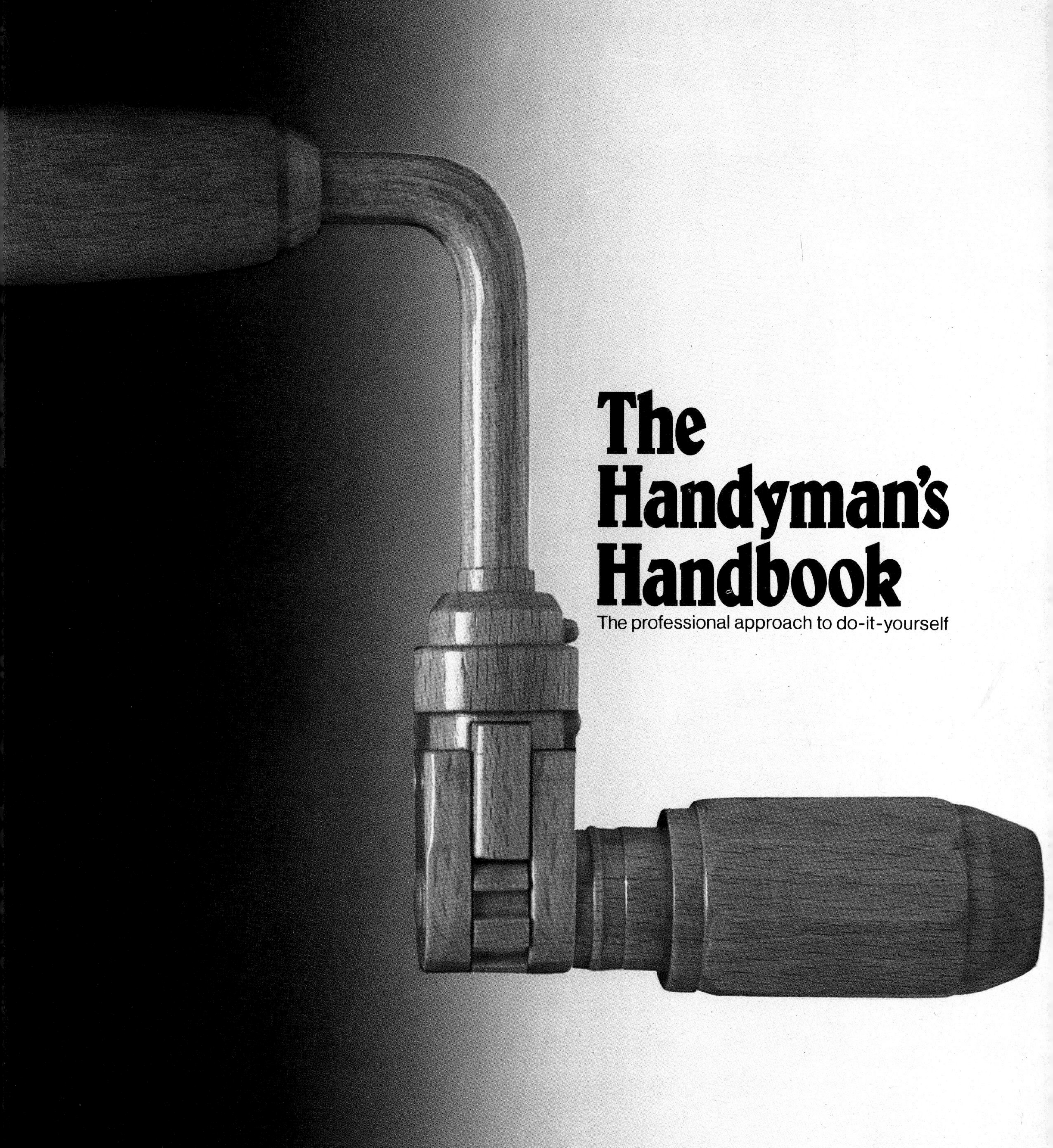

# The Handyman's Handbook

The professional approach to do-it-yourself

Mitchell Beazley Publishers Limited, London

**Major Projects designed by Sampson Fether**

Peter Sampson DESRCA FSIA
Ben Fether FSIA
Richard Miles BA
Mike Nuttall BA MDESRCA
Tony Rostron BA

**Additional designs by**
Nick Hawker, Peter Parkinson, John Pennicott, Amanda Webb



**Tips compiled by James Bush with the assistance of**
Bill Sutton (builder)
Colin Murray (carpenter)
Eric Griffiths (carpet specialist)
Ian Simpson (electrician)
Sid Holmes (joiner)
Ron West-Webbe (painter and decorator)
Bill Davis (plumber)

**Technical consultants**
Christopher Jones, Garry Porter

**Art Editor**
Mel Petersen

**Assistant Art Editor**
John Ridgeway

**Designer**
Ayala Kingsley

**Art Assistant**
Keith Savage

**Artist**
Harry Clow

**Photographers**
Nigel Messett, James Jackson

**Editors**
Jeremy Harwood, Lawrence Clarke

**Editorial Researchers**
Elspeth Graham, Cynthia Hole

**Editorial Assistant**
Michael Alexander

**Production**
Hugh Stancliffe

**Publisher** James Mitchell
**Executive Editor** Iain Parsons
**Production Director** Mike Powell

The Handyman's Handbook was edited and designed by Mitchell Beazley Publishers Limited, Mill House, 87–89 Shaftesbury Avenue, London W1V 7AD


First edition published 1978, reprinted 1980


Typeset by Key Film (Trendbourne Ltd.), London
Reproduction by Gilchrist Bros. Ltd., Leeds
Printed and bound in Spain by
Printer Industria Grafica SA, Barcelona 1980
Depósito Legal B. 48197-1977

ISBN 0 85533 096 1 (Hardback edition)
ISBN 0 85533 259 8 (Paperback edition)

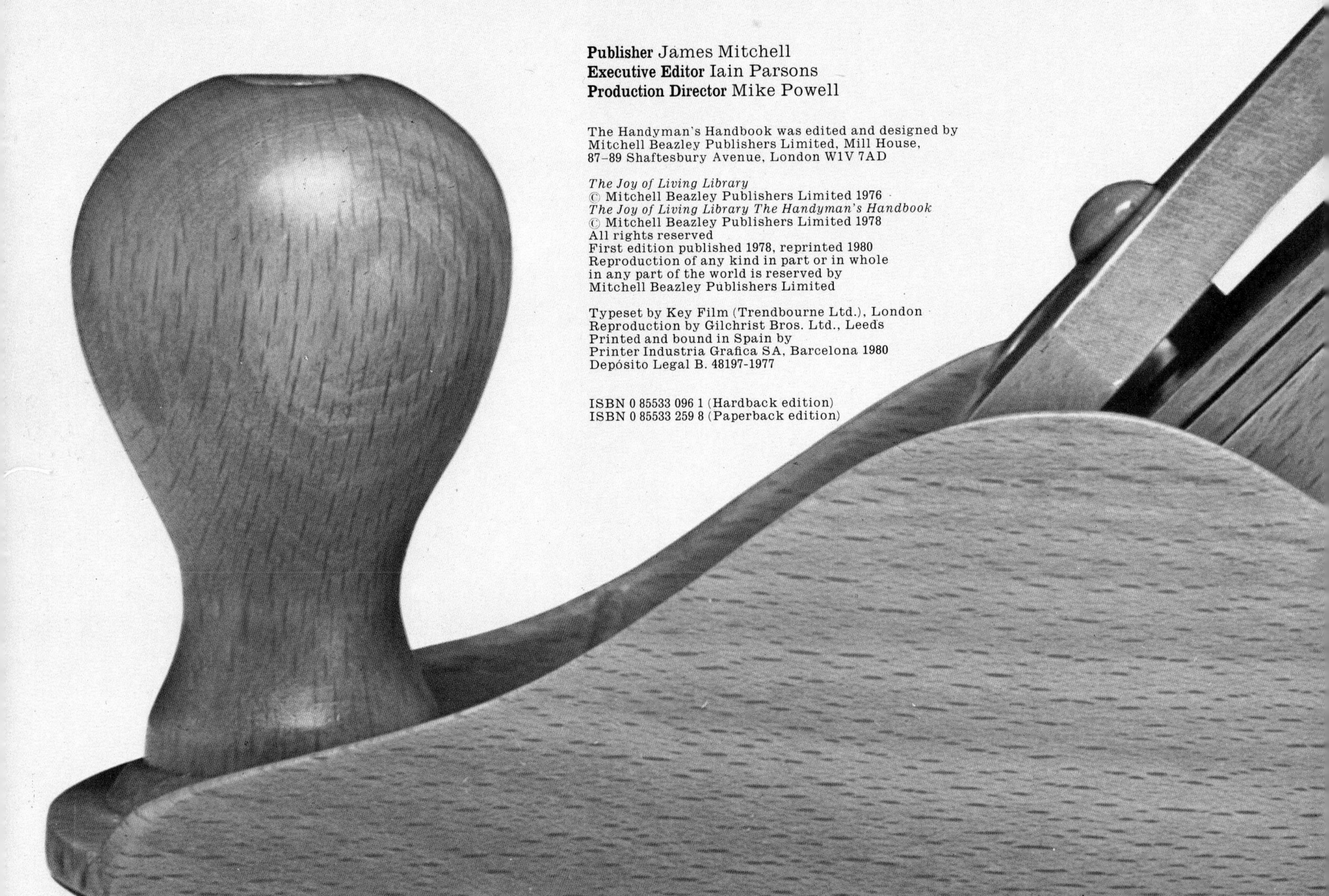

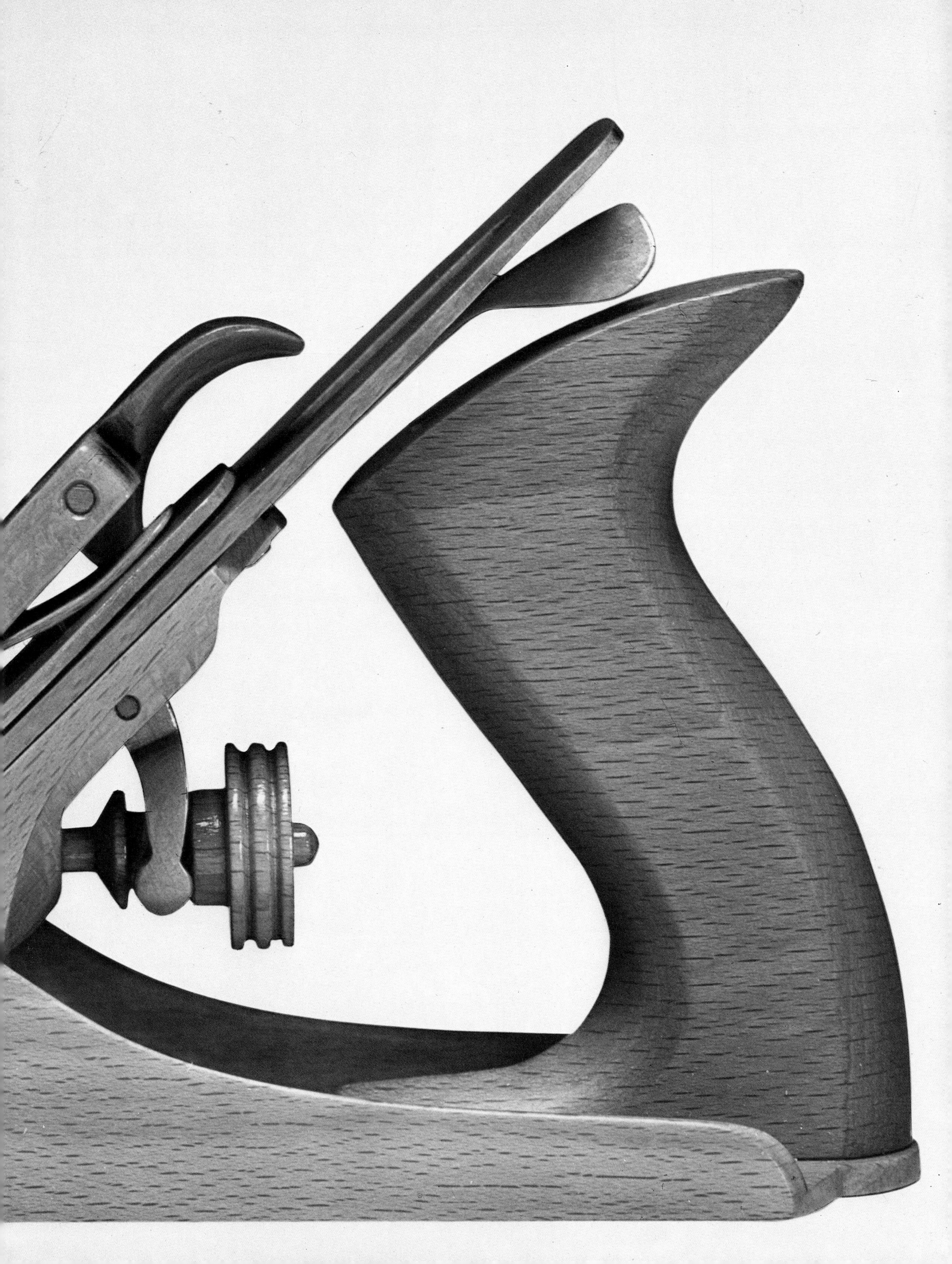

# Introduction

*The Handyman's Handbook* is planned so that the home handyman can swiftly locate the precise information that is so often the key to quickly and efficiently carrying out jobs about the home. The book's 700 tips and hints single out the essence of any job. They provide the essential information and techniques that will enable both the novice and the experienced do-it-yourself enthusiast to undertake tasks in and around the home with the complete confidence of the professional. In addition, the book contains twenty-six projects—each one conceived by a specialized designer. They are distinctive and original, but involve only simple construction techniques, enabling the handyman to build decorative objects with the same high degree of finish normally achieved only by skilled craftsmen.

When ordering materials, remember it is always worth consulting the supplier for advice.

## How to use the book

The book's 700 tips and twenty-six projects are in numerical order, the advice on tools and do-it-yourself safety being presented separately in the margins of each page. Each tip and project is keyed with its own number, making reference to and from the comprehensive Contents/Index fast and simple.

## The Contents/Index

In the Contents/Index, all the tips and projects are listed in three main sections—Projects, Materials and Work Areas. Under Projects are brief descriptions of each project, together with illustrations. Materials and Work Areas are divided into sections under headings, such as Adhesives, Paint, Ceilings, Floors, etc., within which each relevant tip is listed alphabetically with its number. Where appropriate, the main headings are further sub-divided.

## Locating a tip

Most tips can be located in two different ways. Tips dealing with floor tiles, for instance, appear in the Materials section under Tiles and in the Work Areas section under Floors. Thus, **Laying Ceramic and Vinyl Floor Tiles 534** comes under the main heading Tiles, sub-heading Fitting and Laying, in the Materials section; in the Work Areas section it appears under the main heading Floors, sub-heading Tiles.

## The Project pages

Each project is presented in two ways. It is shown first in colour photographs in its completed form, with the relevant project number at the top of the page. Then, immediately following, comes all the information required to make it. This includes an exploded drawing, or drawings, showing the construction in detail, a materials list—where appropriate—and a step-by-step explanation of how the project is built. Cross-references to relevant tips are also listed.

## The Glossary

Occupying the last 15 pages of the book, this lists 210 entries, arranged alphabetically and selected to provide further information on those materials, techniques and methods covered in the main section of the book.

## Metric and Imperial

In all but two special cases, metric and Imperial measurements have been given side by side. All the materials used in the projects are available in standard metric sizes. These are not usually based on exact metric conversions. In timber sizes, for example, the standard metric equivalent for 1in is 25mm—not 25.4mm, which is the exact conversion figure. However, all cutting instructions in the projects are based on an exact metric conversion; for example, the conversion for a 6ft 3in length of timber, 1905mm, is based on 25.4mm.

When buying timber, remember that all planed wood will be approximately 4mm/$\frac{5}{32}$in less in width and thickness than the sawn size; this planed size is known as nominal. Thus, a length of 50mm/2in by 25mm/1in timber will in reality measure about 46mm/1$\frac{27}{32}$in by 21mm/$\frac{27}{32}$in. All standard wood sizes given in the projects are nominal. If in doubt, always consult the supplier. Remember that timber merchants, for example, will usually cut wood to specified requirements.

# Contents/

# 1

## Projects

Contents/Index pages 3-4

# Index

## Materials

Contents/Index pages 5-13



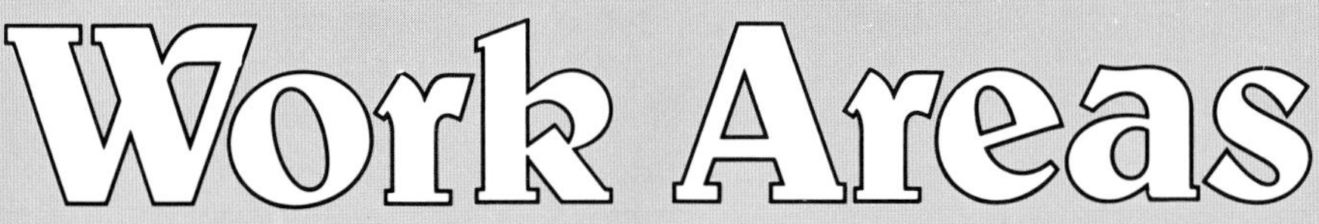

## Work Areas

Contents/Index pages 14-20

# Contents/Index

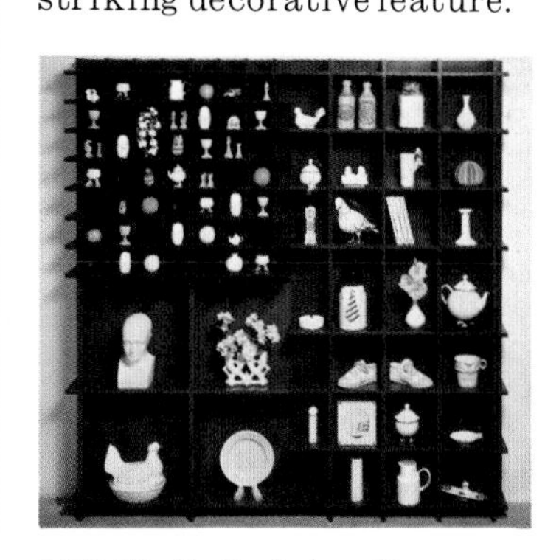

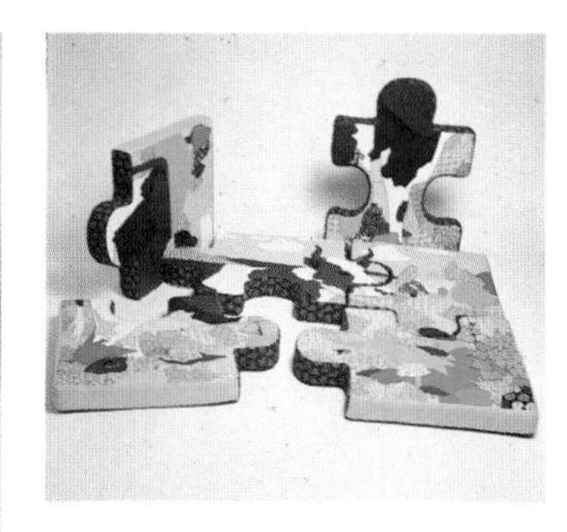

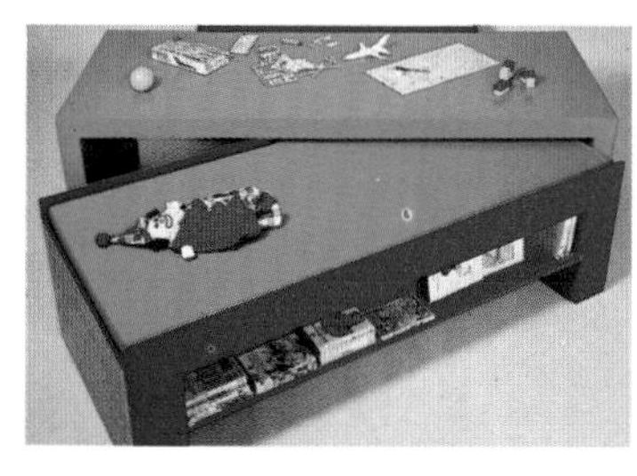



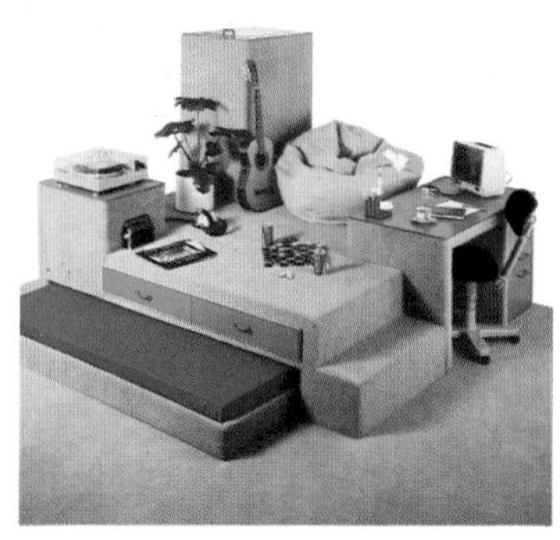



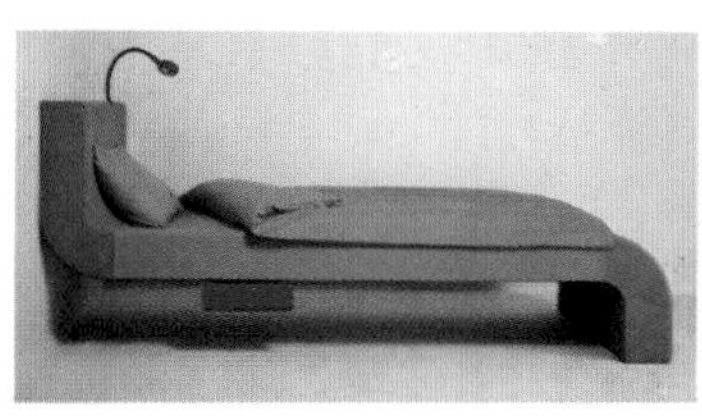

# Projects

**292 Fitted hi-fi**
This hi-fi rack solves space problems while the speaker finish improves the look.

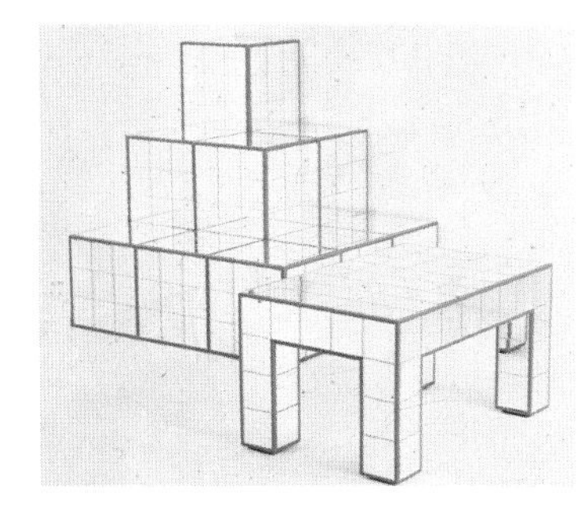

**293 Tiled furniture**
Ideal for display, these plinths and tables utilize ceramic and mirror tiles.

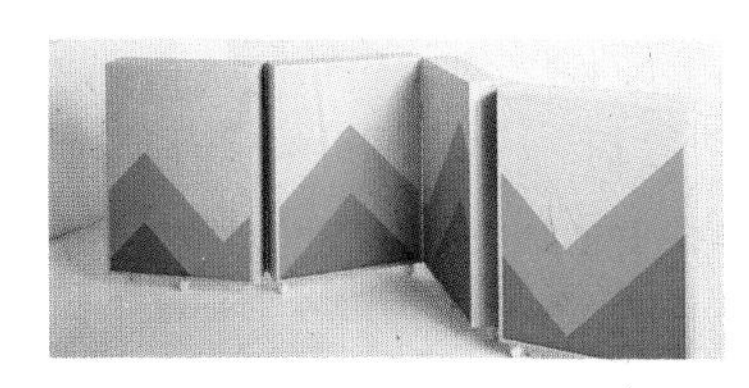

**294 Storage screen/1**
This set of compact, movable, fold-out cupboards provides attractive storage.

**295 Storage screen/2**
Shelves and sections can be added as required to this room-dividing screen.

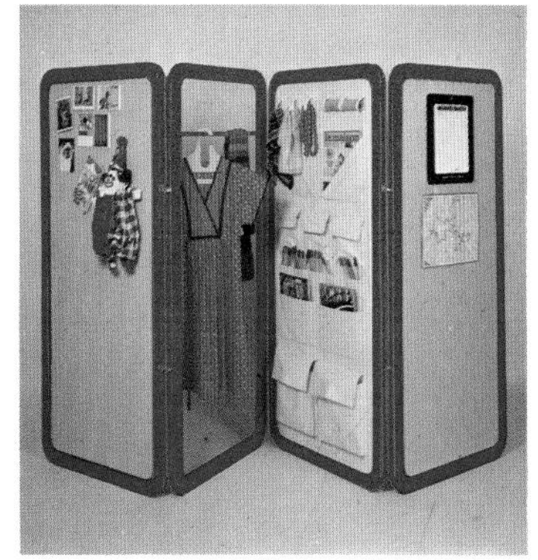

**296 Storage screen/3**
Planned for clothes storage, this screen can be folded up when not in use.

**297 Drawer units**
Canvas is the unusual drawer and finishing material for this unit.

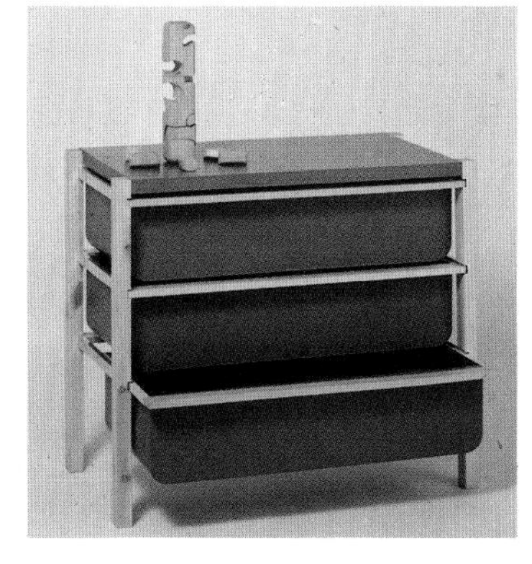

**298 Drawer units**
These curved, plywood drawers are light and easy to move.

**576 Decorative finishes/1**
Four ways of giving a home-made fitted kitchen a professional finish.

**577 Decorative finishes/2**
Unmatched furnishings can be unified by careful decoration and arrangement.

**597 Decorative finishes/3**
These easily cast fibreglass feet add a dash of style to simple furniture.

**598 Decorative finishes/4**
Unconventional finishing can totally transform the appearance of furniture.

**599 Picture framing**
The skills of producing an attractive picture frame are easily acquired.

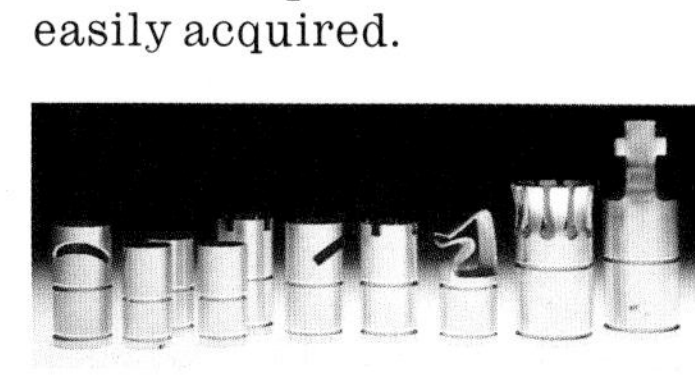

**600 Chess and draughts**
Metal and acrylic is the basis of this striking chess and draughts set.

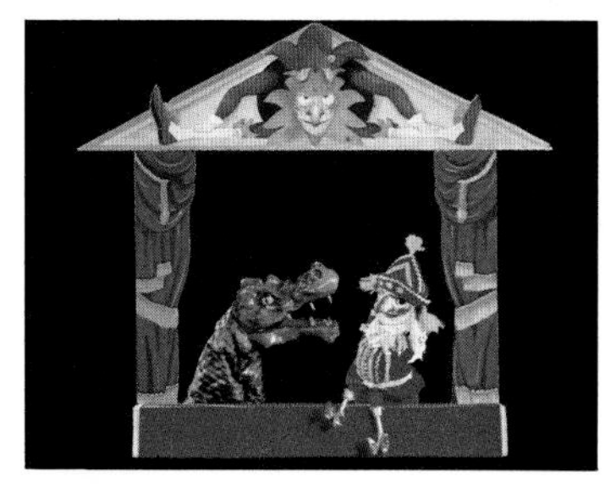

**601 Glove puppets**
These distinctive fibreglass puppets are both simple and fun to make.

**602 Modular toy kit**
This kit of crafted parts can be combined to build up many different toys.

# Contents/Index

## Adhesives



## Bricks and mortar

# Materials

# Carpets

## Estimating and preparation



## Fitting



## Renovating and repairing



## Underlay



## Safety



## Tools



# Concrete and cement

## Estimating



## Fastening and fixing



## Finishing



## Laying



## Mixing and storing



## Paving



## Preparation



## Repairing and maintaining



## Safety



## Tools

# Contents/Index

## Glass and mirrors



## Metals

# Materials

## Paint and varnish

# Contents/Index

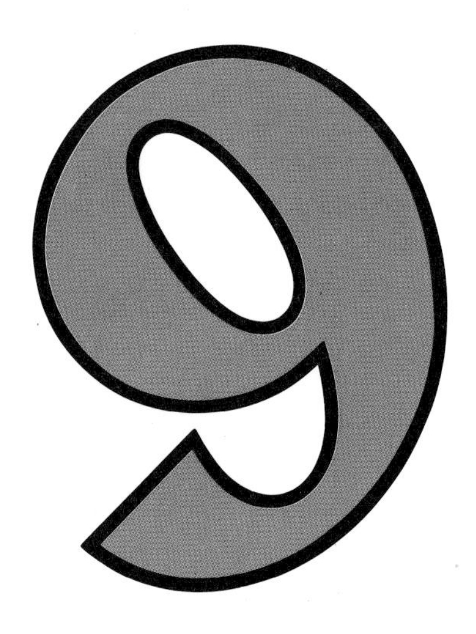

## Paint and varnish (Continued)

# Materials

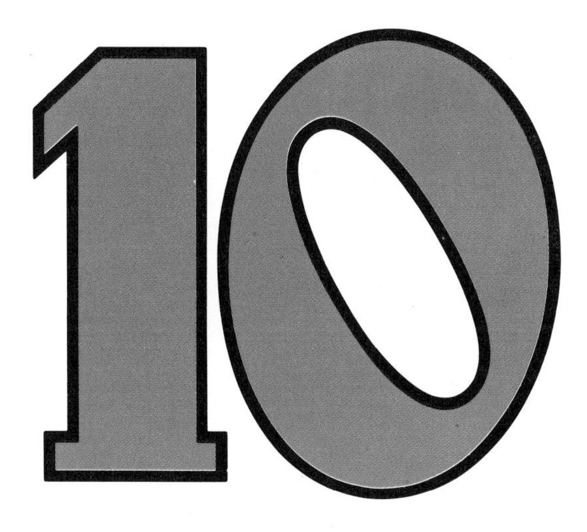

# Plaster



# Tiles, linoleum and vinyl sheeting

# Contents/Index

# 11

## Wall and ceiling paper



## Wood

# Materials

# Contents/Index

# 13

## Wood (Continued)

# Materials/Work Areas

# 14



## Bathrooms



### Safety

# Contents/Index

# 15

## Ceilings



### Safety



## Doors



## Electrics



### Safety

# Work Areas

# 16

## Fences



## Floors

### Carpeting



### Concrete



### Marble



### Tiles, linoleum and vinyl sheeting



### Wood and board



### Safety

# Contents/Index

# 17

## Furniture

### Finishing



### Preparing and fitting



### Renovating and repairing



### Shelving



## Heating



### Safety

# Work Areas

# 18

## Paths



### Safety



## Pipes and taps



### Safety



## Roofs



### Safety

# Contents/Index

# 19

## Stairs



### Safety



## Walls

### Exterior preparation, laying and finishing



### Exterior renovation and repair



### Interior preparation and decoration



### Interior renovation and repair

# Work Areas

## Windows

# Work bench

# 1

Combining stout construction with a high degree of finish, this compact work-bench will solve two of the home handyman's most difficult problems—storing tools and materials out of the way but conveniently to hand, and fitting an essentially practical and normally cumbersome work-surface into the home. Free-standing—and portable—or fixed to a wall, it is suitable for any area of the home or for the garage, where it will still leave room for a car.

# 1

When making this workbench, remember that the optimum height of the worktop is about 74 cm/29 in. The overall dimensions of the unit illustrated are 1295 mm/51 in by 1219 mm/48 in by 203 mm/8 in. The frame and drawers can be assembled using butt-joints throughout in preference to those joints used in the original.

**Basic frame:** Made from 25 mm/1 in thick plywood. The outer vertical supports are 1295 mm/4 ft 3 in by 203 mm/8 in; the top central support is 584 mm/1 ft 11 in by 178 mm/7 in, the bottom 673 mm/2 ft 2½ in by 178 mm/7 in. The top is 584 mm/1 ft 11 in by 1168 mm/3 ft 10 in and the base and central horizontal support 1168 mm/3 ft 10 in by 165 mm/6½ in.

**Back panel:** Use 6 mm/¼ in plywood, 1219 mm/4 ft by 1295 mm/4 ft 3 in.

**Doors, worktop:** Made from 25 mm/1 in plywood. Each door is 584 mm/1 ft 11 in by 686 mm/2 ft 3 in; the top is 610 mm/2 ft by 1168 mm/3 ft 10 in.

**Internal components:** Cut from 12 mm/½ in thick plywood. A 6 mm/¼ in thick pegboard is also required and swan neck bolts, 76 mm/3 in hinges and a lock.

**Assembling the frame**

Mark the recesses for the hinges of the doors and top on the two vertical supports and the central horizontal support and cut them out. Decide upon the positions for the shelves and drawers and mark and cut the supports accordingly, using stopped housing joints on the outer vertical supports and housing joints on the central supports. Assemble the basic frame; dovetail joints can .be used.

**Fitting the interior**

Size the shelves and cut out the stopped housing joints. Add vertical separators where required, and assemble by gluing in place. Disguise the through housing joints by gluing and pinning edging strips along the full lengths. Assemble the drawers. If a pegboard is required, mount it on battens 19 mm/¾ in clear of the basic frame.

Complete the workbench by fitting a lock and hinges and attaching bolts to the doors to hold the lowered worktop in place. Glue and screw plywood lengths as handles. Finally recess the back panel and glue and pin it into the frame and shelves and fit the doors and worktop.

## 2 Making a stopped housing joint

For a neat finish to any shelving unit use a stopped housing joint. Taking the width of the shelf as a guide, mark up the support pieces. If the shelf is to be flush with the front of the support, saw a third of the way into the thickness of the upright, stopping about 12mm/½in from the front edge. Pare the recess clean with a chisel. Notch the front of the shelf to fit the groove and glue it in place.

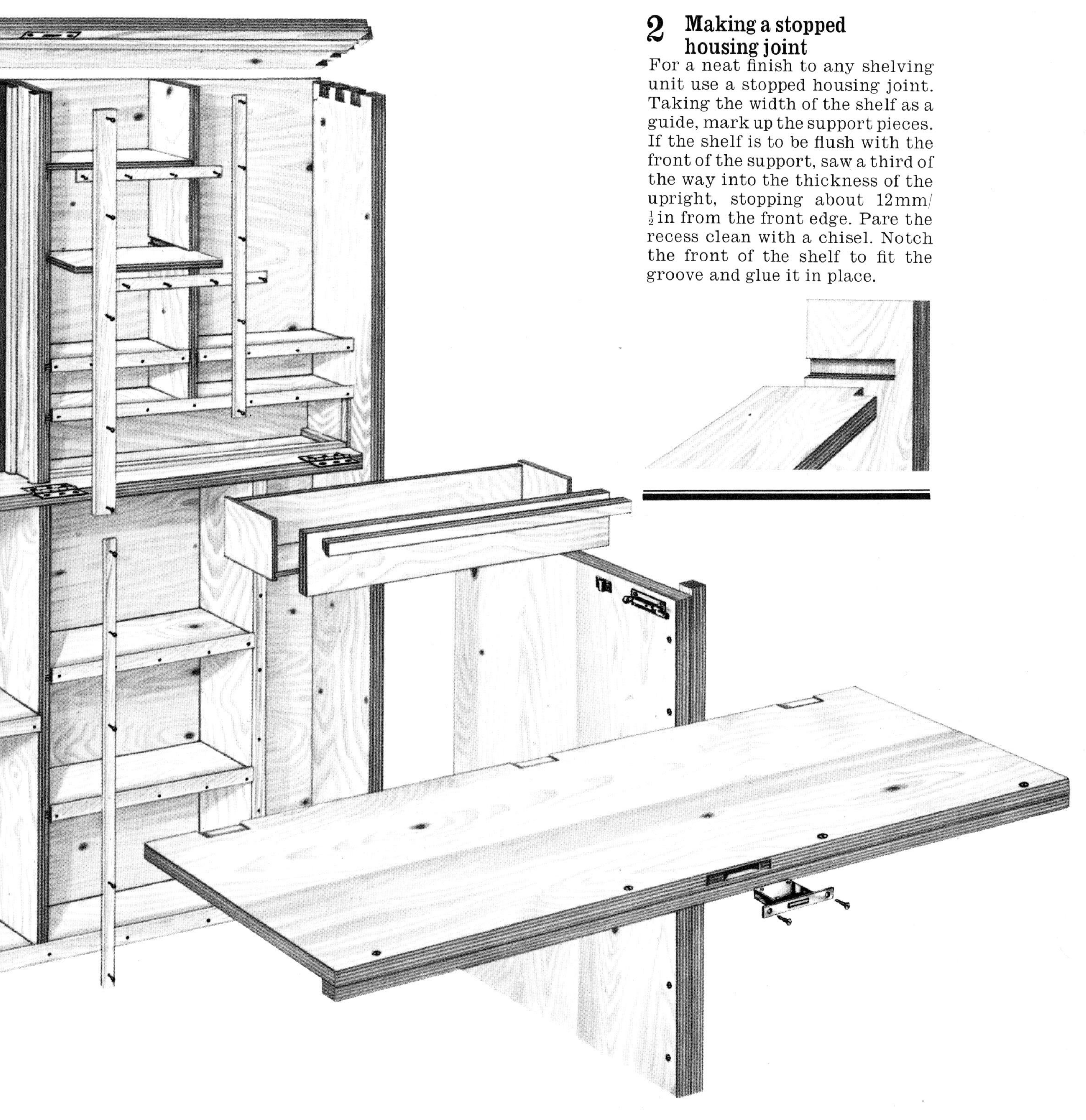

*See also Tips on*
Preparation 174, 551
Marking up 253, 520
Adhesives 81
Cutting 370
Joints 2, 243
Fixing 245, 261, 565
Finishing 77, 175, 203, 536

# Murals and enlargements

The creation of a personal mural can be almost as straightforward as painting a wall. Any subject, taken from patterns and shapes or photographs and paintings, can be reproduced in any place, from an outside brick wall to a cupboard door, for a dramatic visual effect. Often the best results are achieved with bold images and flat colour. When using photographs or other tone originals as a base, simplify the images by first tracing over the outline.

The only limitation on the enlargement from the original subject to the chosen surface is the space available—for complete coverage an image can be sized and cropped to fit. But, whatever the enlargement, the method of reproducing it—by superimposing a grid on the image and transferring it—remains the same.

**The maximum enlargement**
First measure the wall and mark the measurements up on tracing paper; for an easy reduction, change the metres or feet dimensions to millimetres or inches. Place the wall tracing over the image, aligning the left-hand corners, and draw a diagonal line over the tracing through the top right-hand corner of the image. The point of maximum enlargement is where the line meets the edge of the marked-up wall.

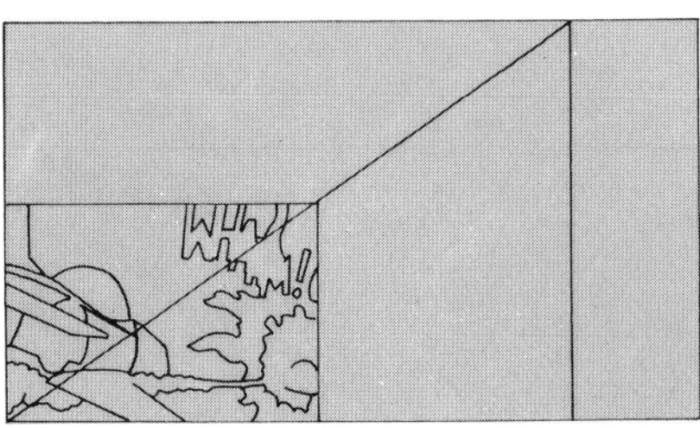

**Complete coverage of a surface**
If an image is to cover a complete area, it may have to be cropped. First mark up the wall measurements on tracing paper as before. Draw a diagonal line from the bottom left to the top right-hand corner. Position the paper over the image. At the point where the diagonal crosses the edge of the image draw a line at right angles to that edge to establish the area that can be used. Move it over the image to decide on the crop.

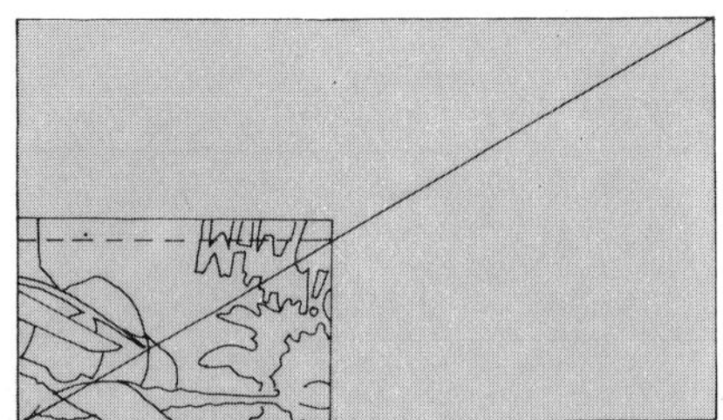

### Using a grid

Choose a square grid size that is suited to the image—the more detailed the image the smaller the grid. As a guide, each square on the wall grid should be about 152 mm/6 in. Draw the grid over the image; then draw the proportionately enlarged grid on the wall. Number matching squares along two sides of each grid. Then simply mark the wall grid where the outline of the image crosses a grid line, and join up the marks.

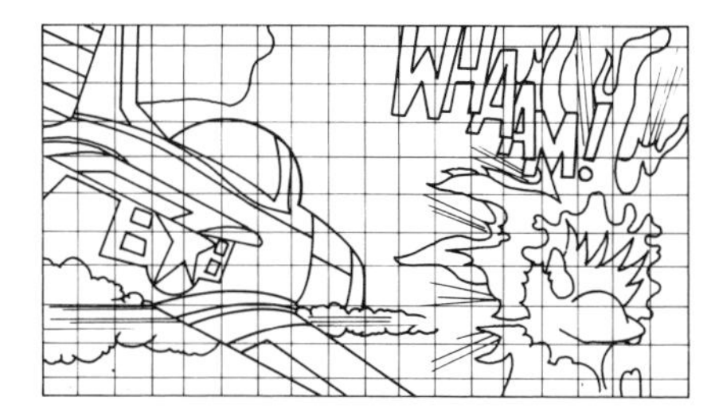


### Enlarging and finishing

If unusual patterns or shapes are required, mark them out on a distorted grid (below). Alternatively, for simple enlargements over a relatively small area, take a colour transparency of the design or use an existing colour snap; project it on to the wall and draw over the image.

The most suitable paint for most surfaces is acrylic. When mixing the colours, check to see how they look in both artificial and natural light.

Experiment to achieve different textures when applying the paint. Try using a rag, sponge, comb or palette knife. For a clean edge, use transparent self-adhesive masking film, available from graphic art shops. Stick the film over the wall drawing and cut away the area for painting. Use stencils for repeating patterns. Once completed, protect the mural with a coat of colourless matt varnish.

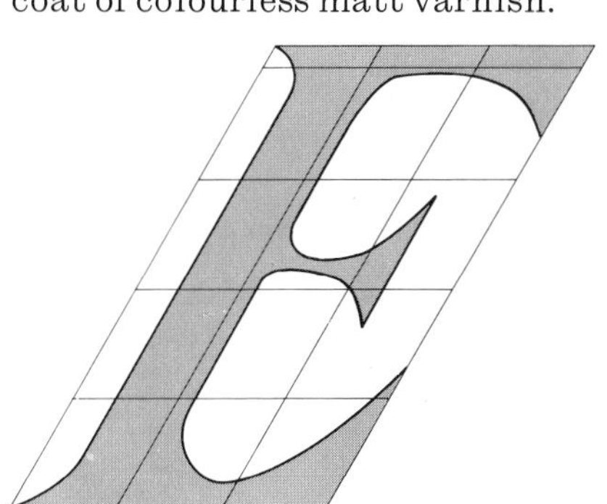

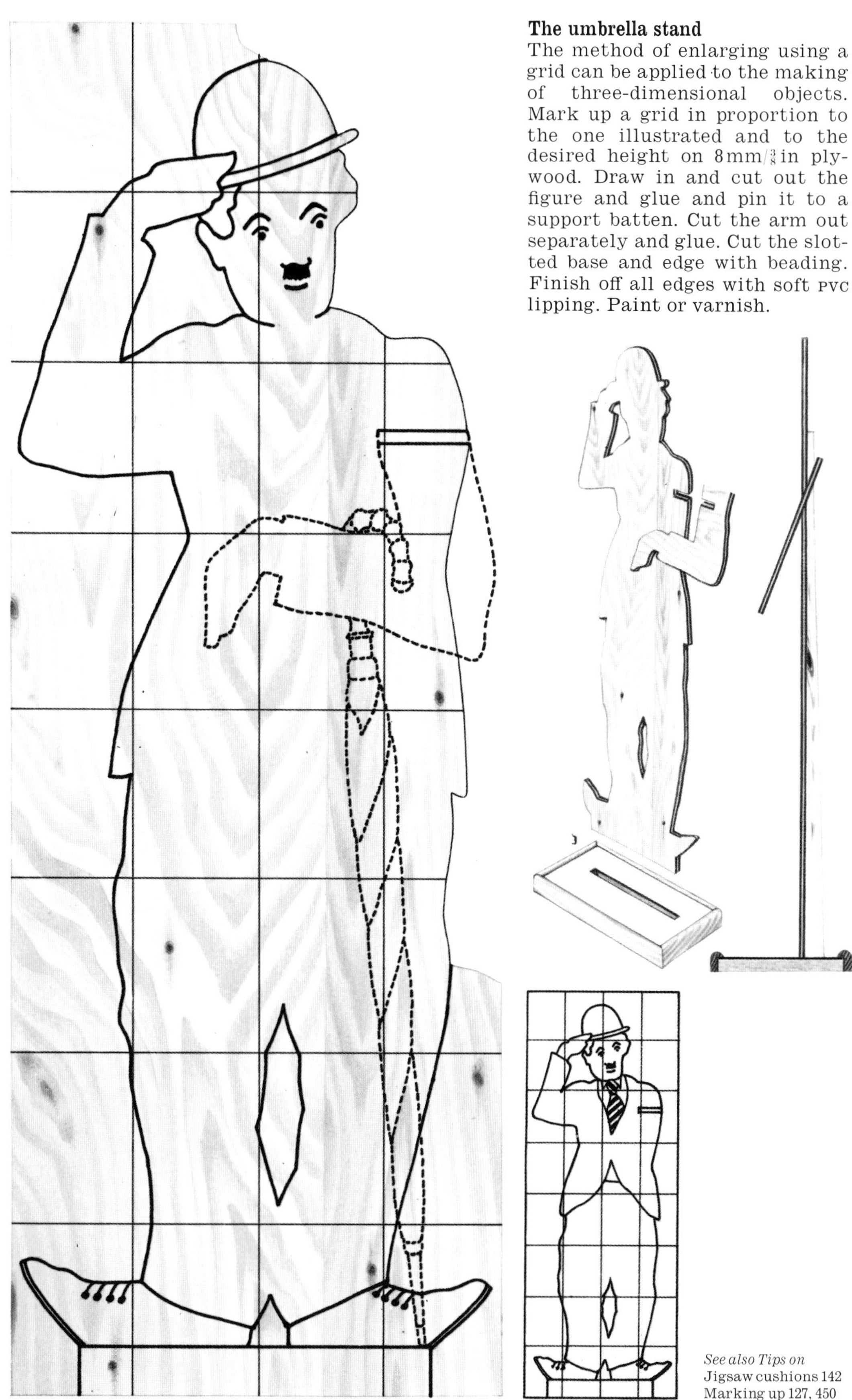

### The umbrella stand

The method of enlarging using a grid can be applied to the making of three-dimensional objects. Mark up a grid in proportion to the one illustrated and to the desired height on 8 mm/⅜ in plywood. Draw in and cut out the figure and glue and pin it to a support batten. Cut the arm out separately and glue. Cut the slotted base and edge with beading. Finish off all edges with soft PVC lipping. Paint or varnish.

*See also Tips on*
Jigsaw cushions 142
Marking up 127, 450

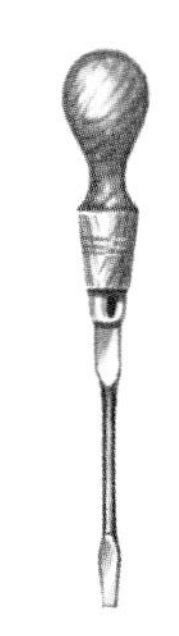

## 4 Screwdriver

Always make sure that the tip of a screwdriver is the same size as the slot of the screw it is being used to tighten. If not, the tip may score into the timber or damage the screw slot.

## 5 Concrete paths

Never use a metal trowel to smooth off the surface of a newly laid concrete path. Too smooth a finish will make the path dangerous to walk on in wet weather. Use a wooden float, which will slightly roughen the concrete.

## 6 Straightening a warped cupboard door

Warped cupboard doors can often be straightened out by wedging them in a reverse warp. Fit a sash cramp to pull in the outwardly bowed section of the door and wedge a block behind the inward bow to force it out. However, if it is impossible to fit a cramp to the door, wedge it back into position by nailing a block of wood to the framework, or by using a heavy weight, such as a bucket of sand. With both methods, leave the door to settle in the warp for at least a week before removing the cramp or block. If necessary repeat.

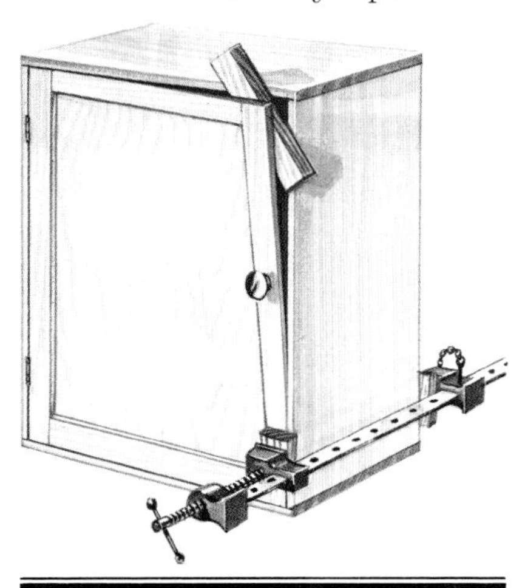

## 7 Concealing screw holes in hardwood

When cutting hardwood, save the sawdust—mixed with glue it makes an ideal matching filler for screw holes.

## 8 Adapting pliers to make handling easier

Fit a short length of rubber tubing to the handles of a pair of pliers or metal grips to provide a spring action to close the teeth when the pliers or grips are released. This is a particularly helpful aid when only one hand is free to use the tool, as when working on a repair from the top of a ladder.

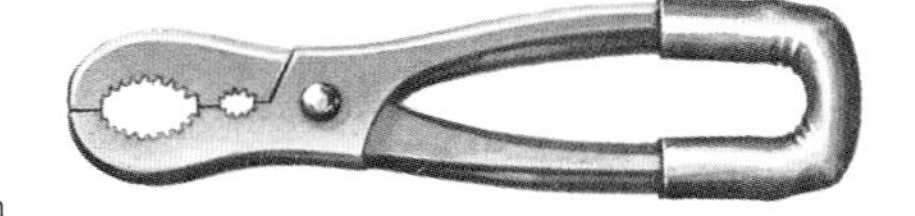

## 9 Bending pipes without a bending spring

To maintain the circular section when bending a copper pipe use a bending spring—a specialized tool which can be hired from a do-it-yourself shop. Make sure that the spring is the same size as the internal diameter of the pipe.

If, however, a bending spring is not available, an acceptable alternative is to plug one end of the pipe and pack it tightly with damp sand. When the pipe is full, plug the other end. The pipe can now be bent without any risk of it buckling or "crimping".

## 10 Removing paint from intricate mouldings

The easiest way to remove paint from mouldings or awkwardly shaped pieces of wood, such as the grooved bottoms of stair balusters and the rounded legs of kitchen chairs, is to thoroughly soak a pad of wire wool in paint remover. Wearing rubber gloves for protection, rub the pad over the surface and well into the crevices. Allow the paint remover to soak into the surface for about fifteen minutes and then go over it again with the pad, keeping the wire wool well soaked. Repeat the procedure until the paint has been removed.

## 11 Concealing nails in hardwood or softwood

To conceal a nail in woodwork, use a sharp chisel to raise a sliver of the wood at the point where the nail is to be fixed. Hammer in the nail and then carefully glue the sliver back in position, using a PVA adhesive.

## 12 Planing a flat surface accurately

Before planing a piece of wood, lightly scribble on it with a soft pencil. Pencil marks will remain on any low spots, thus providing an accurate guide to the amount of additional planing necessary to get a flat surface. Finally, after removing all the marks, run a careful check with a try square to make sure the surface is true.

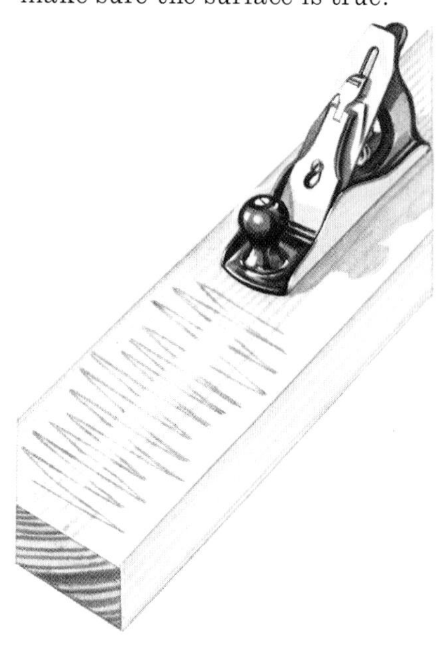

## 13 The right mix for fixing glass bricks

The best mix for fixing glass bricks—these have good sound- and heat-insulation qualities—is made up from one part cement, one part lime and four parts soft sand. The mix must be fairly dry or the weight of the bricks will squeeze wet mortar out of the joints.

## 14 The first stage before painting with a roller

Before painting a ceiling with a roller, always start by touching in corners and a thin strip around the edges with a 38mm/1½in brush, using it edge-on. It is awkward—and often impossible—to use a roller in corners effectively, and if one is used along the edges it can smear paint on the adjacent walls. Repeat when painting walls.

## 15 Cutting laminated safety glass

The main problem when cutting laminated safety glass—in which two sheets of glass are bonded together with a plastic interlayer—is to separate the glass from its interlayer. The usual method is to use a trimming knife after the glass has been cut, but this method can leave ragged edges on the plastic and shell the edges of the glass.

The best way is to burn the interlayer away with the aid of methylated spirit. Wearing protective gloves and goggles, score both sides of the glass along the cut line. Complete the cuts by bending first one side of the sheet and then the other over a length of batten. This stage of the process is completed when a shiny, reflective line appears along the full length of the score lines on both sides of the glass.

Position the sheet of laminated glass on a bench with its cut lines just overhanging the edge and gently work the strip that is to be cut off in an up-and-down movement. Occasionally brush out the very small splinters of glass that flake off the edges, or they may become lodged within the cut and shell the glass.

Continue bending the strip until it moves freely through an angle of about 70°. Keeping the cut open, pour a small amount of methylated spirit into it—preferably from a plastic bottle that has a pin-hole pierced in the cap. Take care not to use too much methylated spirit or the flames may flare too high. Aim for about a teaspoonful for every 450 mm/18 in to 600 mm/24 in of cut line.

Put a match to the methylated spirit and, holding the off-cut strip, gently move it up and down again, pulling it away as the interlayer burns. The off-cut strip will come away from the glass within a matter of seconds. The heat is neither intense nor long-lasting enough to harm the glass.

## 16 Thawing frozen taps and supply pipes

An easy way to thaw a frozen tap is to pour boiling water on to a rag wrapped round the tap. The rag retains the hot water, giving it time to act.

If the supply pipe is frozen, work backwards from the outlet tap. Keep the tap open—as the ice thaws, the water pressure will help to dislodge any obstinate pieces.

## 17 Levelling and cementing crazy paving

Crazy paving should always be laid on a prepared surface. To ensure that the crazy paving is level, place three or four pats of mortar, each about the size of an egg, on the surface to serve as a base. This makes it easier to adjust the level of each slab. Use a mix of one part of cement to six parts of sand and tap the stones down lightly with a mallet.

Fill any gaps in the paving with a thin cement mix. To reduce mess, pour some of the mix into a strong plastic bag. Cut off one of the corners of the bag, and squeeze the cement into the gaps.

## 18 Giving a smooth finish to chipboard edges

Use a fine-grain filler to get a smooth finish on rough edges of manufactured boards, such as chipboard. First spread the filler along the edges of the board, pushing it well into the wood with a filler knife. Allow the filler to dry hard and then smooth the edge with wet-and-dry paper. If the edge needs to be shaped, plane the edges to the curve required. Then proceed as before.

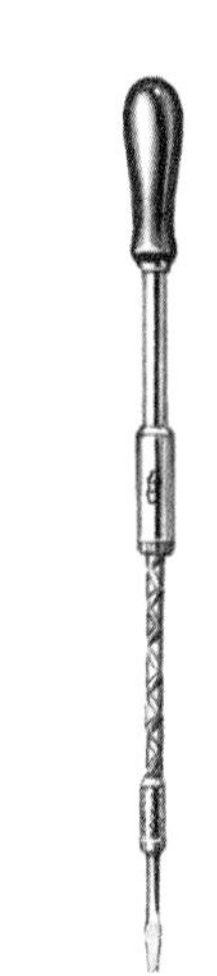

## 19 Ratchet screwdriver

The pressure needed to "pump" a ratchet screwdriver can cause it to slip off a screw and damage the surface of the surrounding wood. Only use one on rough work or where the finished joint will not be seen.

## 20 Diluting acids

Never add water to acid when making up a diluted solution. Always pour the acid into the full amount of water being used. If this procedure is not followed, the first few drops of water coming into contact with the acid will cause a violent reaction in which the acid will splash.

## 21 Notched spreader

To counteract any unevenness in the surface of a wall, use a notched spreader when applying adhesive before fixing tiles. The notches raise the adhesive 3mm/⅛in from the surface. Press the tiles firmly against the adhesive—not hard against the wall—to ensure an even alignment.

## 22 Electric switches in a bathroom

Never use conventional electric switches in a bathroom—use a pull-cord switch or locate the switch outside the bathroom. This avoids the possibility of someone with wet hands operating a switch and receiving a shock.

## 23 Replacing a washer on a leaking tap

To replace a washer on a leaking tap, turn off the water supply and open the tap fully. Pull off or unscrew the protective shield and loosen the retaining nut with a wrench or spanner. If the nut is stiff, protect it with a piece of cloth. Remove the top of the tap from the body. Remove the washer—unscrewing it from the jumper if necessary—and replace it. Reassemble the tap, close it and turn on the water supply again.

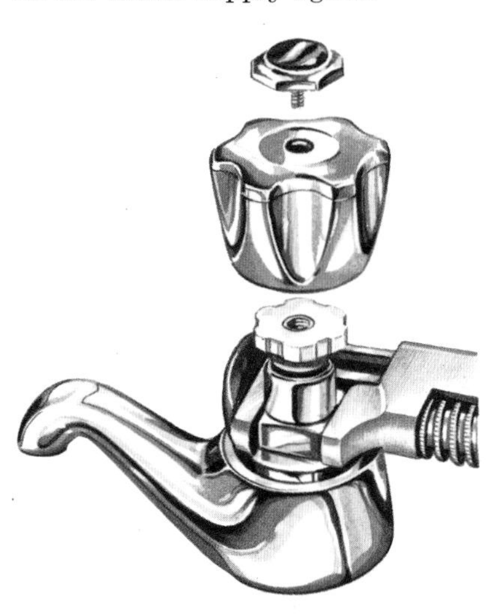

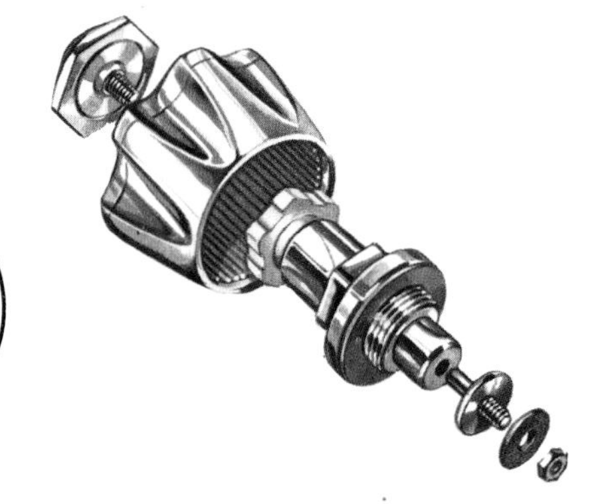

## 24 Fixing into joists in old houses

As the ceiling plaster in old houses is often fragile, use screws—never nails—to attach fixing blocks to joists or to refix floorboards in upstairs rooms. If nails are used, the force required to hammer them home into the joists may result in the plaster on the ceiling below cracking or even breaking away.

## 25 Making strong wood joints with nails

Dovetail nailing—where two nails are driven into wood at opposite angles—makes a much stronger joint than conventional nailing.

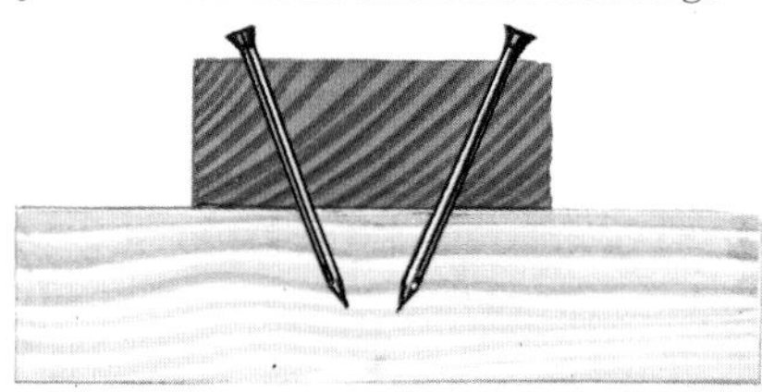

## 26 Selecting and applying paint for walls

Although most modern paints will not leave distinguishable marks so that it is possible to see where work has been resumed, after leaving it overnight for example, it is still advisable to complete an entire wall in one session.

When applying emulsion paint, start from the top of a corner in a room and work downwards, spreading the paint in strips about 250mm/10in wide, horizontally across the wall.

Gloss paint, on the other hand, should always be applied vertically. Start from the top corner again, but work downwards in squares of about 500mm/20in. This is because gloss paint starts to dry quickly, so a bigger working area will mean that the paint will be awkward to brush out. Try and avoid overlapping the paint when joining up one section to another.

## 27 Repolishing marble floors or furniture

When repolishing marble, use four carborundum stones, coarse to medium coarse, medium and fine. Lubricating the surface with water, start by grinding with the coarse stone to remove the worst of the scratches and gradually work through the range of stones. Then, apply salts of sorrel—obtainable from builders' merchants—to the marble with a damp, coarse rag and rub it well into the surface. Wash off the salts with warm water and, after the surface has dried, polish it with beeswax.

## 28 Stopping dust settling on a newly painted door

Just before applying the top coat of paint to an outside door, sprinkle a little water on to the ground immediately in front of the door with a distemper brush or from a watering can fitted with a rose head. This is a trick used by decorators to help to lay dust that would otherwise be blown from the ground on to the wet paint—even if it is only slightly windy—and mar the surface.

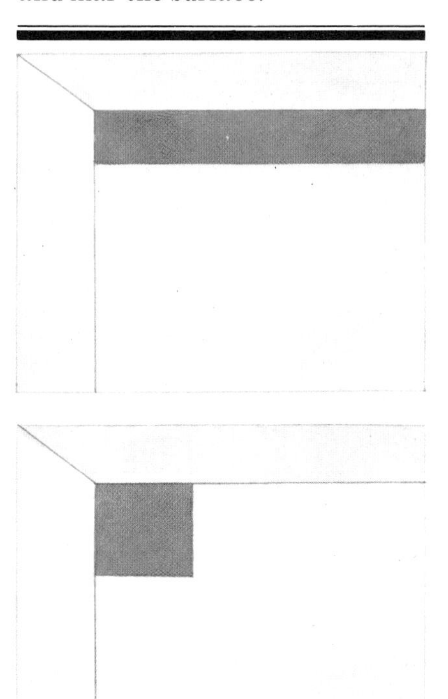

## 29 Preparing polished furniture for painting

Always make sure that all traces of polish are removed from a wood surface before applying paint or it will not adhere properly. If a silicone-based polish or ordinary wax polish has been used, rub the surface with a clean piece of coarse cloth dipped in turpentine substitute. Then clean off the surface with fine-grade glasspaper. Before starting to paint the entire surface, test on an inconspicuous area to make sure that all the polish has been removed. If not, go over it again.

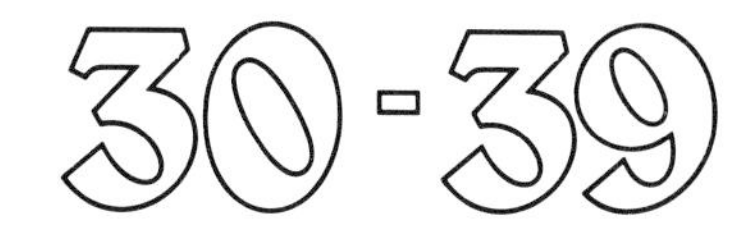

## 30 Sealing cracked or holed glass in a greenhouse

An easy way of stopping leaks or repairing cracked glass in a greenhouse roof is to fit a square of glass over the damaged area and to seal it on all sides with self-adhesive waterproof glazing tape. Use this repair when it is difficult to remove the damaged pane or where fitting replacement glass would mean disturbing the putty in adjacent panes.

## 31 Removing tile paint from brickwork

The easiest way to strip red tile-paint—frequently used on fireplace surrounds—is to burn it off the bricks with a paraffin blowlamp. This method will not destroy the original colour of the bricks.

## 32 Fitting skirting without mitring

Skirting boards can be fitted into corners easily and attractively—and without having to mitre the edges. Cut a square block of wood, slightly thicker than the skirtings and the same height. Smooth the two outer edges with a glasspaper block and slightly bevel the top, if desired. Then, glue and nail the block into the corner and butt the skirtings flush to it.

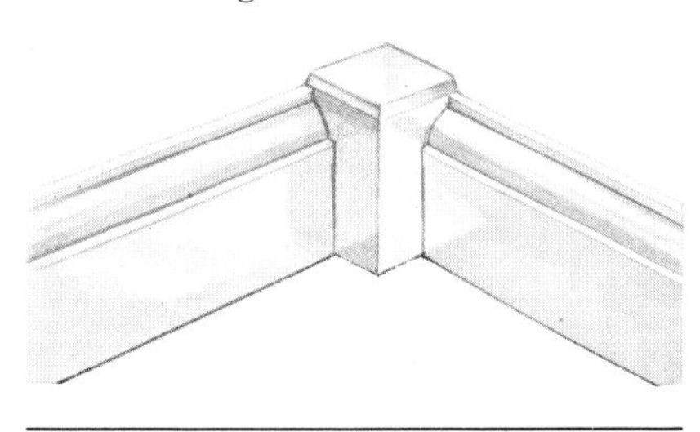

## 33 Fixing wood joints with metal dowels

One of the strongest ways of securing an end-to-end wood joint is to use a metal dowel to link the two pieces of wood together. Make a starting hole with a bradawl on both the pieces of wood to be joined. Then grip the smooth centre section of the dowel between a pair of pliers and screw the dowel into the end of one piece of wood.

Apply glue to each of the timber surfaces to be joined and then screw the second piece of timber on to the dowel. The glue helps to secure the joint.

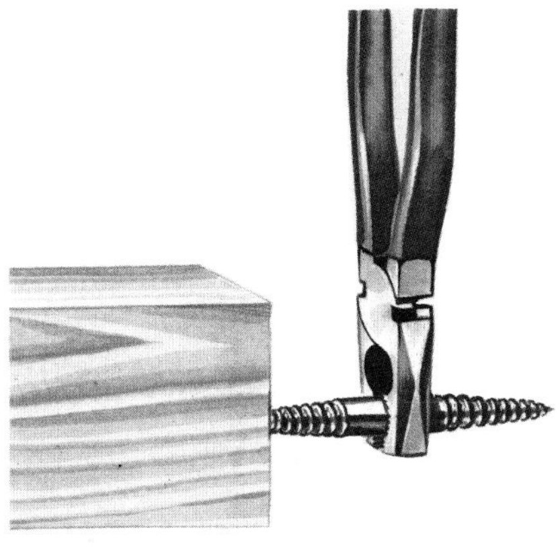

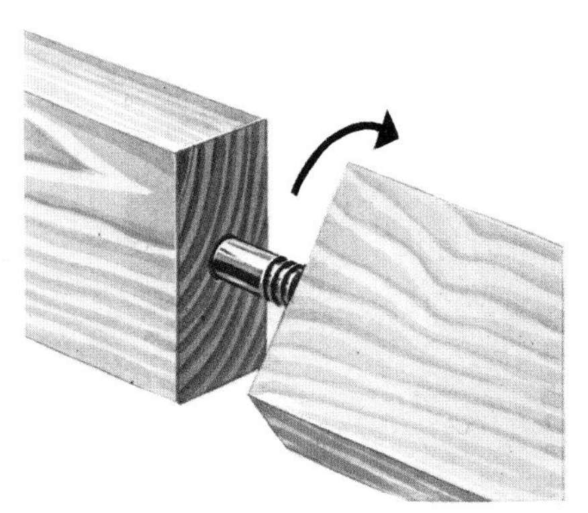

## 34 Choosing the right paint for a decoration scheme

Seeing paint over a large area makes it easier to assess its suitability for use within a decoration scheme. Cover 600 mm/24 in square panels of hardboard with the paint and place them against the walls. This check is also useful while painting, because colour shades vary in different lights.

## 35 Fixing a screw that will not tighten

If a loose screw cannot be tightened sufficiently to hold a fixing in place—and cannot be replaced with a larger screw because of the size of the screw hole—remove it and coil a length of twine tightly round the thread. Dip the screw and twine into a shellac-based polish before putting it back into the screw hole.

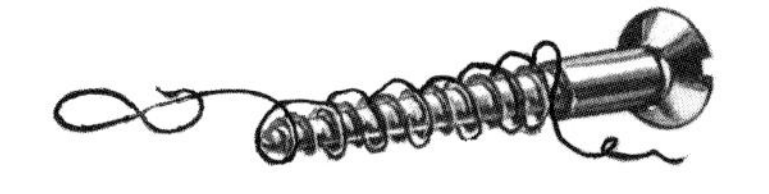

## 36 Preparing a chemically stripped surface for paint

Chemical strippers can burn skin severely, so always wear gloves when working with them to remove old paint. After using a stripper, clean the surface thoroughly with turpentine substitute. Then rub down with a medium-grade glasspaper. If the slightest trace of stripper is left on the surface, it will react with the new coat, causing it to blister.

## 37 Fitting polystyrene ceiling tiles

To avoid any air pockets that can be a potential fire risk, when fitting polystyrene tiles, spread an even layer of adhesive on the ceiling over an area large enough to take about ten tiles at one time. Use a scrap piece of smoothed wood, with a handle attached, slightly smaller in overall size than one tile, to press the tiles into place. If fingers are used they will leave unsightly marks.

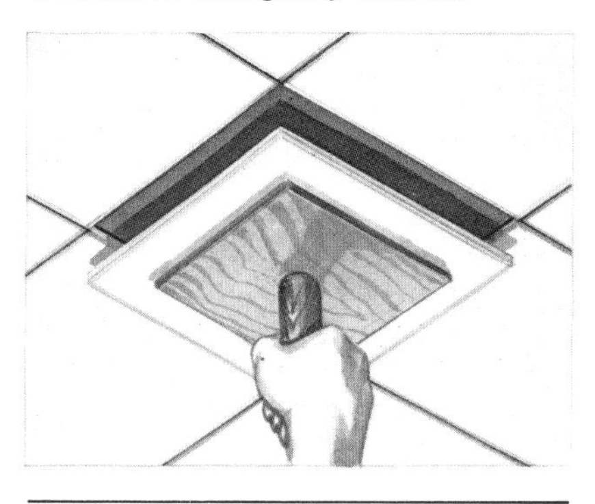

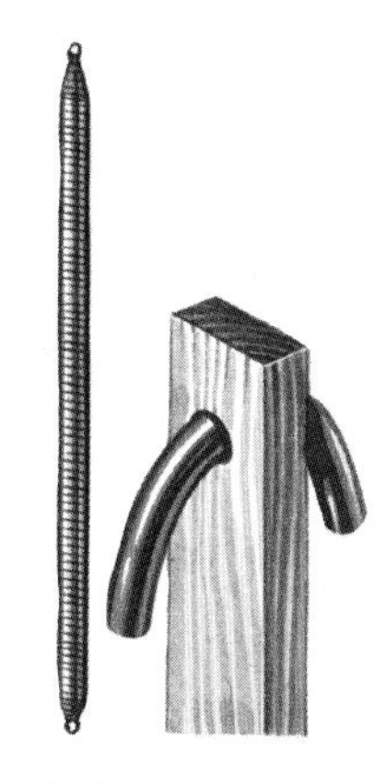

## 38 Bending spring

Use a bending spring to maintain the circular section inside a pipe while it is being bent. Pipes up to 12mm/½ in in diameter can be bent round the knee. For larger pipes, bore a hole slightly longer than the diameter of the pipe in a suitable scrap length of wood. Stand the wood upright, insert the pipe into the hole and push down firmly on each side of the pipe.

## 39 Liquids and electricity

Liquids and electricity do not mix, so never stand a container with liquid in it on a radio or television set when working in a room. If the liquid is spilt a serious fire may be started.

# 40-46

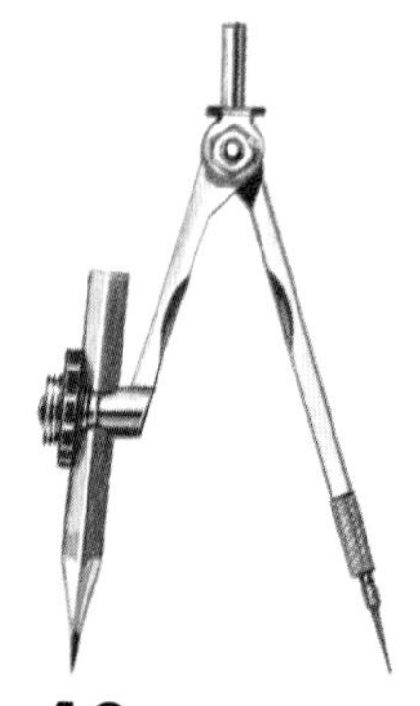

## 40
### Compass

In addition to marking out circles, a compass can also be used to scribe the cut line on a piece of wood that is to be fitted tightly against an irregular surface. Holding the wood against the surface, place the point of the compass on the surface and the pencil on the wood. Move the point along the surface to trace its irregularities.

## 41
### Checking gas pilot lights

If the gas pressure is reduced for any reason, always check the pilot lights on gas appliances. A reduction in pressure may extinguish them, creating the risk of explosion when the pressure is restored.

## 42 Weatherproofing the tops of timber posts

There are four basic methods of protecting the top of timber posts which have a porous end-grain exposed to the weather. One of these should always be adopted, or rainwater will rot the timber.

For a single bevel, saw across the top of the post at an angle of approximately 45°. If a pointed finish is required, make a double bevel by sawing from two opposite sides at the same angle. Mark lines from the mid-point of the top edge to the bottom corners on both sides of the bevel and saw down them. Smooth the sawn surfaces of both finishes—single bevelled and pointed—and then coat the timber with wood preservative.

Alternatively, make a wooden cap by cutting a square of timber 50mm/2in thick and 25mm/1in larger all round than the top of the post. Use a rasp to chamfer down the surface on all four sides and glue and nail the cap in position at the top of the post. Then apply wood preservative.

If the post is to remain unpainted, a metal cap is the ideal protection. Cut it from a piece of tin, or thin lead sheet, to a size 75mm/3in larger all round than the area of the top of the post. Mark out the outline of the area in the centre of the sheet and at each corner cut two slots at right angles to each other and meeting at the corners of the outline. Fold the cap over the top of the post and fit galvanized clout nails—these are rustless—around the edges to hold it in position.

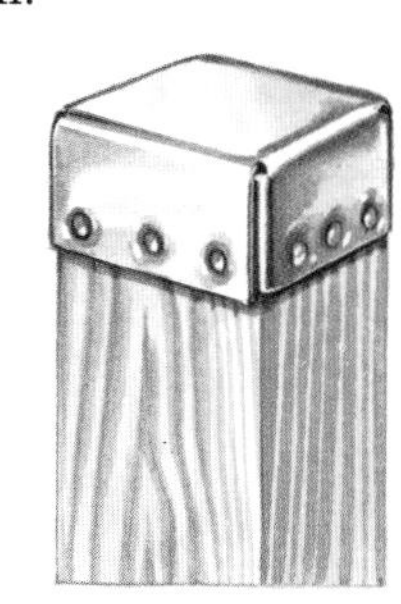

## 43 Adapting a metal float for most uses

If, when undertaking such jobs as plastering, a wooden float is unavailable, a metal float can easily be adapted to serve the same purpose. Cut a 12mm/½in thick piece of board, 25mm/1in larger all round than the metal blade, and position the float on it. Fix six 12mm/½in raised-head screws round the edge of the board to hold it in position, using large washers so that they grip the metal blade when they are tightened.

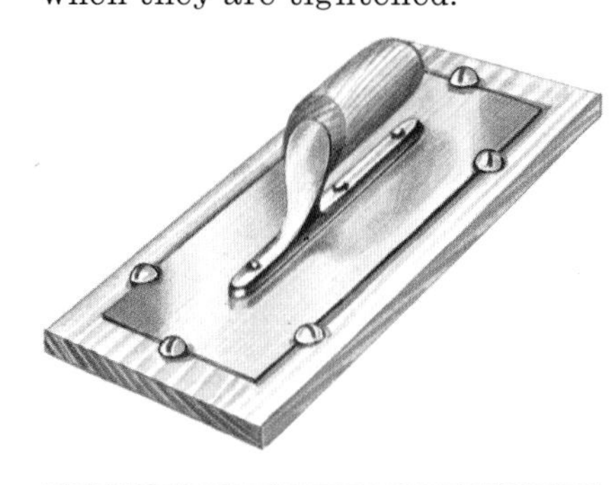

## 44 Supporting the top of a ladder used outside

Always use a ladder stay to keep a ladder clear of the gutter when working on a roof or wall of a house. If the ladder rests on the guttering, its weight can loosen gutter fixings and even split plastic guttering. When removing the ladder, make sure to lift it clear of the gutter before moving it away; if it drags against the gutter it may damage it.

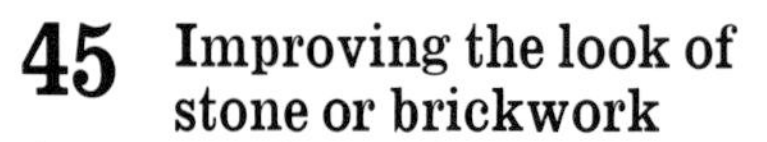

## 45 Improving the look of stone or brickwork

A matt polyurethane sealer not only brings out the colours of exterior stonework or old brickwork, but also makes them easier to clean by protecting them from dust. Brush on two coats, the first to seal the stone or brickwork, the second to enhance the colour.

## 46 Papering around a ceiling rose

Before pasting paper around a ceiling rose, switch off the electricity at the mains and remove the bulb and the light fitting. Paper the ceiling in the usual way—starting parallel to the main window and working across the ceiling—releasing the concertina-folded lengths of paper and brushing them in place.

When the ceiling rose is reached mark its position by pushing the point of a pair of scissors through the paper. With the paper supported away from the ceiling, make a rough star-shaped cut, starting with one cut running in the direction in which the paper is being laid, and finishing with a cut at right angles to the first. Reposition the paper on the ceiling, feeding the flex and bulbholder through the paper, and brush it in place.

If the rose cannot be unscrewed and the paper tucked behind it, score round the edge with the scissors and trim away the excess paper, using a trimming knife if a closer cut is required. Clean off any excess paste.

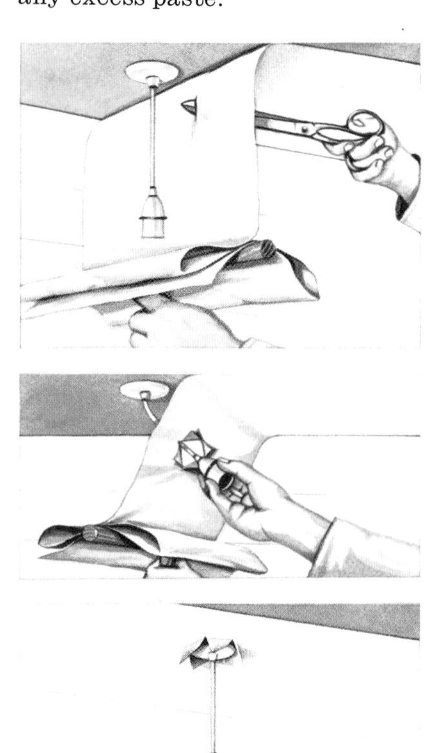

## 47 Removing moss from concrete paths or walls

To help eradicate moss growth on concrete, simply scrub the surface with a weak solution of one part of domestic bleach to approximately fifty parts of water.

## 48 Joining soft sheet metal at right angles

Use the slot-and-tab method to make a strong right-angled joint in soft sheet metal. Cut out the tabs with tinsnips, making sure that they line up with the slots which are made by lightly hammering a 10 mm/⅜ in chisel through the metal. When bending the tabs over, alternate their direction to make the joint secure.

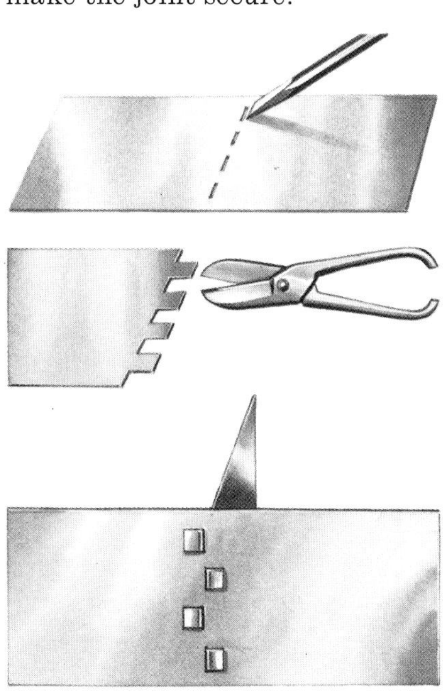

## 49 Using damp sand when making a concrete mix

When sand gets damp it increases in volume, so allow for this if it has to be used when making up cement-and-sand mixes. A standard guide is to increase the volume of sand needed by a quarter of the quantity called for. If the figure for making up a normal mix is one part of cement to four parts of sand, for instance, allow for a mix of one part of cement to five parts of damp sand.

## 50 Using tackless fittings when laying carpet

Tackless fittings are a reliable and invisible method of holding wall-to-wall carpeting in place. Nail the fittings 12 mm/½ in from the wall skirting, with the spikes facing towards the skirting. This allows the edges of the carpet to be tucked into the gap between fitting and skirting.

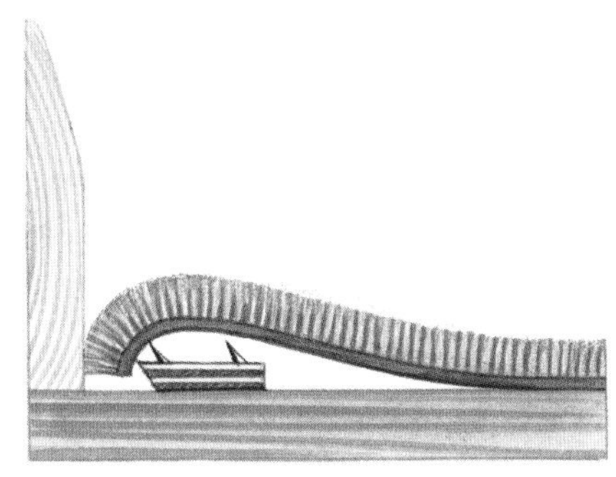

## 51 Tapering timber using a jig and circular saw

Use a simple tapering jig to make it possible to saw easy and accurate tapered cuts in long lengths of timber, when using a circular saw.

Make the jig from two 60 cm/2 ft lengths of 38 mm/1½ in by 25 mm/1 in well-seasoned and perfectly straight battens. Fit a hinge at one end to link the battens together, making sure that the hinge is smaller than the overall size of the two battens.

At the other end of the battens, fit a stop-block to the outside of one of the battens. Trim the top and bottom of the block so that it fits flush with the sides of the battens.

To set the jig to the correct angle, mark a line 30 cm/12 in from the hinged end of the jig. Decide the amount of taper that is required per 30 cm/12 in of the wood being cut and open the battens to this amount at the marked line. Nail a strip of wood across the two battens to hold the jig open in this position ready for use. With the jig resting against the saw guide, hold the timber against the jig and feed it through the saw blade, using the stop-block to help guide it along the cut line.

## 52 Weatherproofing an outside door with varnish

When varnishing an outside door, give the door at least four coats of varnish for adequate protection against the weather. If the door is particularly exposed, the procedure will have to be repeated every few years.

## 53 Sealing and finishing vinyl floor tiles

When newly laid vinyl floor tiles have set firmly in position, clean them thoroughly—taking particular care to remove any excess adhesive—and then coat them with a plastic sealant to ensure a long-lasting non-slip finish and to keep out dirt. If a high-gloss finish is required, polish them with a water-based emulsion wax polish.

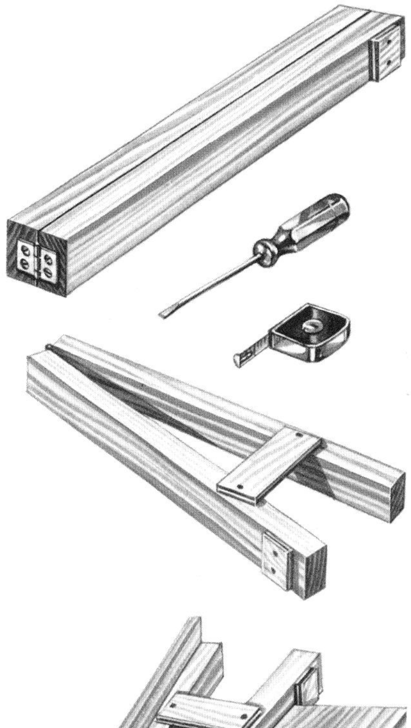

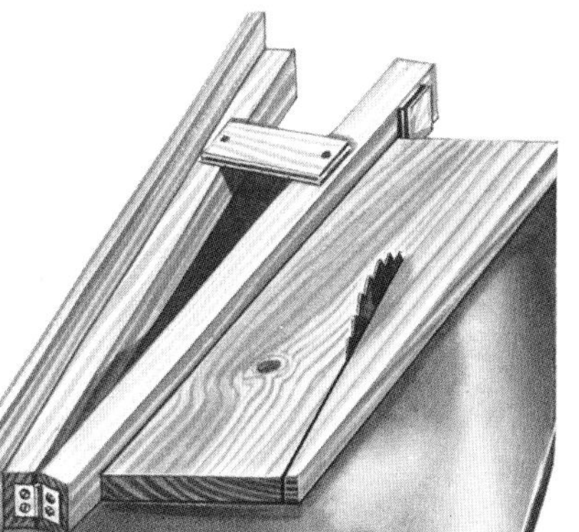

## 54 Crevice brush

To make a simple brush—ideal for reaching into awkward corners—saw the handle off a normal paint brush and fix the brush to a rod.

## 55 Working on floorboards

Always switch off both electricity and water at the mains when sawing through floorboards. There may be a heating pipe or electric cable underneath them that could be damaged, causing flooding, electric shock or a fire.

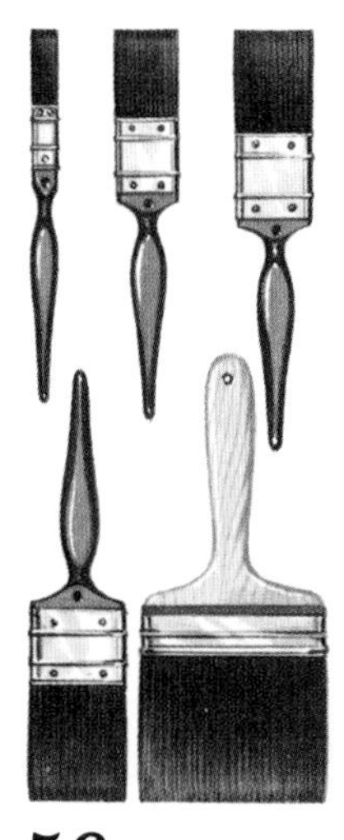

## 56
**Paint brushes**

A useful range of paint brushes to cope with most jobs around the house includes a 12mm/½in brush for glazing bars; 38mm/1½in brush for skirting boards; 50mm/2in brush for door and window frames; 75mm/3in brush for door panels; and 150mm/6in brush for walls and ceilings.

## 57
**Support on a step-ladder**

When working at the top of a step-ladder, fit a large G-cramp to provide an additional hand hold.

## 58 Freeing a nut and bolt that cannot be loosened

A nut and bolt so rusted that it cannot be undone, can easily be freed by cutting with a hacksaw and hammering with a cold chisel. Make as deep a cut as possible through the centre of the bolt head. Hold a cold chisel over the cut and hammer the chisel down to split the head open. If it is still not possible to split the head completely, hammer the cold chisel from each side of the head. Once the head is severed, the core of the bolt will fall from the hole.

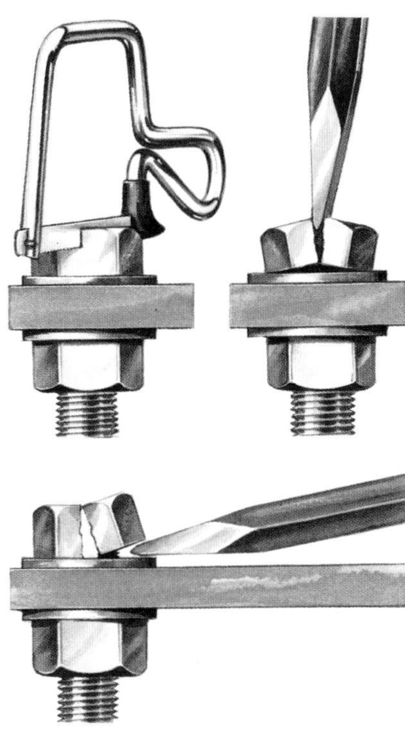

## 59 Giving hardwoods an ebony-like finish

Hardwoods, such as beech, birch and sycamore, can be given an ebony-like finish by staining with proprietary black dye. The object is to make sure the grain remains visible. Check that the wood is clean and that any holes are filled. Then smooth and finally apply the dye. Finish by lightly applying a matt polyurethane varnish; two coats may be necessary for complete protection, but try not to obscure the grain. Rub down finally with steel wool.

## 60 Checking shelving timber for straightness

Because lengths of timber are rarely perfectly straight, always look along the edge of each length to see which way the timber is bowed before using it for shelving. Fit the shelf with its concave side facing downwards so that the weight of objects on the shelf will help to straighten it out. If successful, this takes a day or two.

## 61 Testing a painted surface for gluing

When gluing to a painted wood surface, make sure that the glue will adhere to the paint. Stick a length of cellulose tape on to the paint and then pull it off sharply. If the paint comes away with the tape, the painted surface will have to be stripped. If the paint remains, smooth the surface with glasspaper and wash and dry it before applying the adhesive.

## 62 Joining new and old concrete surfaces

When laying concrete, always try and finish the job in one continuous operation. If, however, a job cannot be completed in one day, leave the last section to be laid with its edge as rough as possible. This acts as a "key" to ensure a good join between new and old work when the job is continued. Before restarting the work brush the rough edge with a "slurry" of cement and water mixed to the consistency of cream.

Where the job involves concreting to a thickness of 50mm/2in or more, insert 150mm/6in non-ferrous nails into the rough edge of the concrete. Simply press the nails at intervals of 100mm/4in into the concrete while it is still soft, leaving half of each nail exposed. This, again, will help bind the edges together.

## 63 Puttying rebates in windows

When puttying the rebate for a new pane of glass, avoid holding the putty in the palm of the hand, or it will be awkward to work. The right way to tackle the job is to "sit" the knob of putty on the knuckle of the forefinger and, working from the bottom of the rebate upwards, push the putty into the rebate with the thumb. This requires a little practice, but is quicker than the alternative of rolling the putty into strips and then pressing them into place with a putty knife. To complete the job, cut the excess putty away and brush to seal it.

When puttying the front rebate always keep the putty 3mm/⅛in below the line of the back rebate. This means that when the putty is being painted, the paint can be taken over the edge of the putty to provide a weather-proof seal that cannot be seen from the inside.

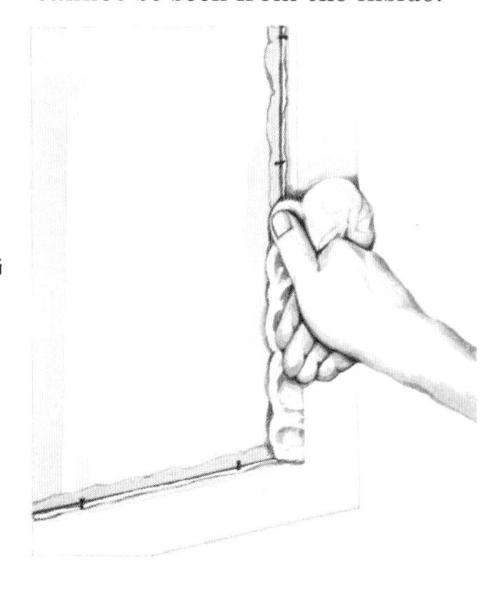

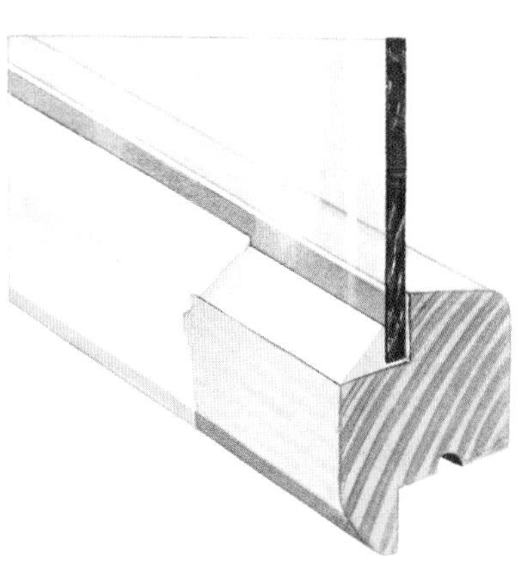

## 64 The correct proportions for mortar mixes

To make mortar, mix sand and cement, sometimes with the addition of lime, using the proportions below for specific jobs. The lime reduces the risk of the mortar cracking as it dries, and makes the mix easier to apply.

Never make up a mortar mix that will dry out harder than the bricks themselves. If the mortar is softer than the bricks, any cracks caused by settlement will follow the mortar lines and not affect the bricks. A mix of one part of cement to five or six parts of sand is usually satisfactory—but check this. For small repair jobs, use one part of cement to three parts of sand.

| | Sand | Cement | Lime |
|---|---|---|---|
| Crazy-paving base | 5 | 1 | |
| Crazy-paving pointing | 3 | 1 | |
| Brick pointing | 6 | 1 | |
| Earth-retaining walls | 9 | 2 | 1 |
| External block-laying | 6 | 2 | 1 |
| External brickwork pointing | 6 | 1 | 1 |
| Floor screeding | 4 | 1 | |
| Garden bricks/paving slabs | 3 | 1 | |
| Internal block-laying | 9 | 1 | 2 |
| Internal brickwork pointing | 9 | 1 | 2 |
| Paths | 3½ | 1 | |
| Top-coat rendering | 6 | 1 | 1 |
| Undercoat rendering | 9 | 2 | 1 |

## 65 The correct proportions for concrete mixes

To make concrete, mix sand, cement and aggregate with water, using the following proportions for specific jobs.

| | Sand | Cement | Aggregate |
|---|---|---|---|
| Brickwork foundations | 2½ | 1 | 4 |
| Fence post base | 2 | 1 | 4 |
| Path and patio foundations | 2 | 1 | 3 |

## 66 Strength in mortar and concrete mixes

Water gives mortar and concrete their bonding power. When making up either mix it is essential to use only clean, fresh water. If dirty water or rain water is used, the mix will quickly break up; with salt water, it will not set.

## 67 Mixing mortar and concrete by hand

To get an even mix when mixing the ingredients for mortar or concrete, first shovel out the amount of sand required on to a clean concrete or boarded surface. Then add the correct proportions of the remaining ingredients. Turn the mixture at least three times, finishing with a pyramid shape. Scrape out the sides of the pyramid to leave a hole in the centre.

Pour approximately three-quarters of the required amount of water into the hole. Shovelling from the outside edges of the mixture towards the centre, continue turning the mix, adding small quantities of water until the correct consistency is reached.

Never mix more mortar than can be used up within two hours, as retempering with water is unsatisfactory.

## 68 Softening a mortar mix for easier working

To make it easier to work with mortar, add a few squirts of liquid detergent to the water used to make up the mix. This mix will have a softer consistency.

## 69 Sands for mortar and concrete mixes

Use fine sand (known to the professionals as "soft" sand) for rendering outside walls and pointing, medium sand for rendering inside walls and bricklaying, and coarse sand (known as "sharp", or "hard", sand) for concreting.

## 70 Estimating amounts of aggregate for concrete

Always allow for the consolidation of all-in ballast (a mixture of sand and aggregate) when estimating the amount required for concreting. When mixed in water, all-in ballast is reduced to seven-tenths of its original volume.

The following table gives the proportions for various thicknesses of concrete spread over an area of 10 sq m/12 sq yd. The mix required for a smaller or larger area can easily be calculated from it.

Depending on the strength of the mix required, the amount of cement needed is usually three to four bags per cubic metre or cubic yard. Used to "bind" the sand and aggregate, cement is absorbed within the ballast and therefore does not affect estimates of volume.

| Thickness (over 10 sq m/12 sq yd) | Volume of All-in Ballast Required |
|---|---|
| 25 mm/2 in | 0.8 cu. m/1.0 cu. yds |
| 75 mm/3 in | 1.2 cu. m/1.4 cu. yds |
| 100 mm/4 in | 1.6 cu. m/2.0 cu. yds |
| 125 mm/5 in | 2.0 cu. m/2.3 cu. yds |
| 150 mm/6 in | 2.4 cu. m/3.0 cu. yds |

## 71 Testing the consistency of mortar and concrete

To test a mortar mix press a trowel into it—if the impression made by the trowel is retained for a minute or so, the mix is of the correct consistency. If the edges of the impression crumble, the mix is too dry; if the impression fills with water and disappears the mix is too wet. To test a concrete mix, squeeze a lump in the hand; it should cling together without too much water oozing from it.

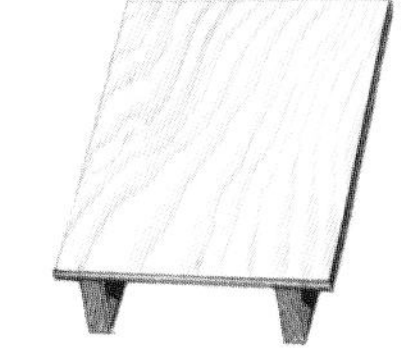

## 72 Spot board

When laying bricks, keep a supply of mortar at hand on a portable spot board. Simply nail two battens on a base board so that it will be raised off the ground and easy to lift. Always keep the surface of the board wet during use, or the moisture from the mortar will be soaked up, making the mix crumbly.

## 73 Handling mortar or cement

Always coat the hands with barrier cream before mixing, or working with, mortar or cement. This stops the materials drying out the skin.

## 74
### Try square
Used for squaring timber and for marking right-angles for cutting, a try square should be checked regularly for accuracy. Lay the square along a straight edge and draw a line down the blade. Turn the square over. If the try square is accurate, the line of the blade will coincide with the drawn line.

## 75
### Working with asbestos
Always dampen asbestos before sawing or drilling it to avoid dust being raised and inhaled. In all circumstances wear a mask and, whenever possible, work in the open air.

## 76 Sealing around toilet and bathroom fittings

Use a proprietary silicone-rubber based sealing compound to fill gaps between tiles and the tops of baths, washbasins or shower trays. The rubber in this compound means that it is flexible. However, grouting compound—a powder sold specifically for filling the gaps between tiles—has no elasticity and, in certain cases, will crack with movement.

Wash the surfaces thoroughly to remove all traces of grease and then dry them with a cloth. Apply the compound straight from the tube, squeezing it out as smoothly as possible. Always push the tube along the joint—never pull it. If the tube is pulled, it can leave gaps in the compound that will be difficult to fill neatly.

Trim off any excess with a sharp knife within a few minutes of application. Then smooth down any ridges in the compound by wetting the tip of a finger and pulling it lightly along the joint.

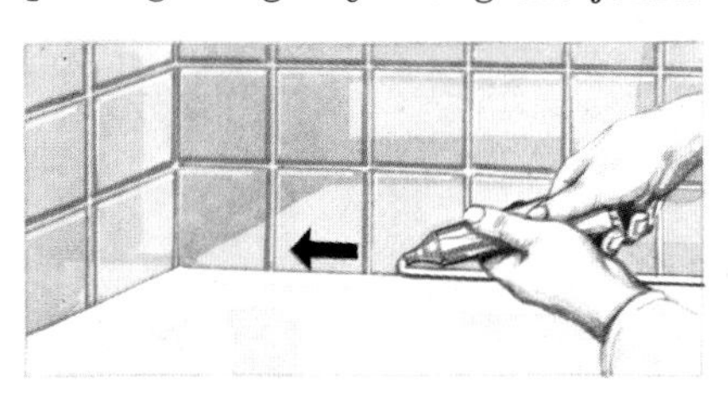

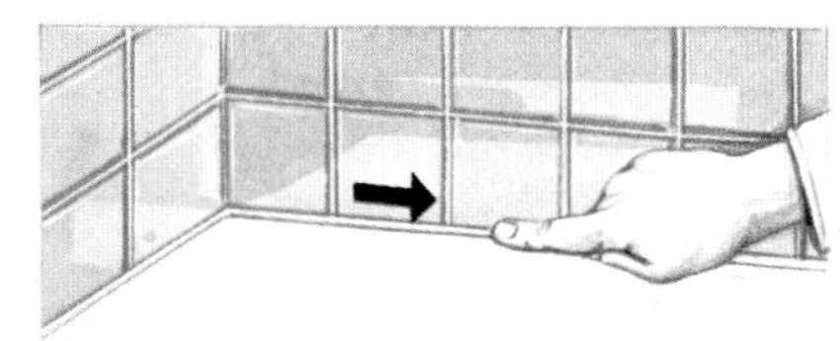

## 77 Preparing wood for varnishing

When preparing wood for varnishing, remember that even "fine" glasspaper can scratch the surface of the wood and that these scratches will show through the varnish. If, however, "fine" glasspaper is the best grade available, make it "extra fine" by rubbing two sheets of the paper together, face to face. This will remove the coarse grains that would otherwise scratch the surface.

## 78 Securing iron gates with lift-on hinges

A useful precaution to take when hanging expensive iron gates with lift-on hinges is to always fit a split pin through the top of the spigot on which the gate hangs. This lessens the chance of the gate being stolen.

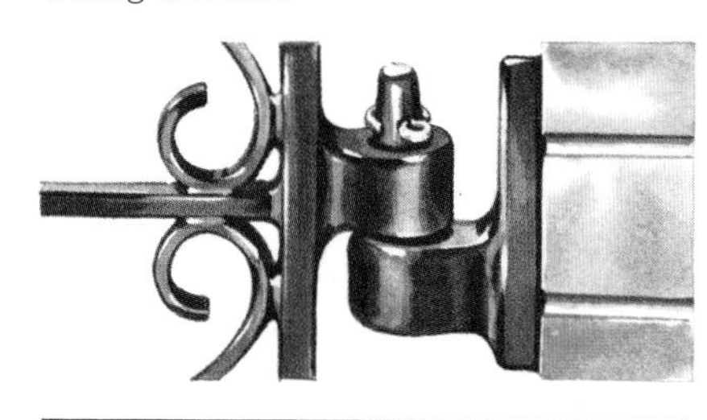

## 79 Replacing a damaged ceramic or quarry tile

To extract a damaged ceramic or quarry tile, first hammer the surface to break the tile up into small pieces, working from the centre outwards. Using a narrow cold chisel, chip away these fragments and chisel out the old adhesive. Finally, brush away all traces of dust from the cavity.

Lay the replacement tile within the hole to check that it fits. Then remove the tile, spread adhesive on the back and press it home, fitting it flush with the adjacent tiles. Clean any excess adhesive from the joints before it sets. Leave to dry. Grout a day later.

## 80 Curing a roller-blind that rewinds incorrectly

If a roller-blind will not wind itself up fully or springs back too forcefully, the probable cause is that the ratchet inside the roller needs to be tightened or loosened respectively.

If the blind is too loose, pull it down to its full extent, lift it off the support brackets and roll it up by hand. Replace the blind in position and slowly pull it downwards again. If it is still too loose, pull the blind until it is half-extended. Then remove the roller from the brackets again and repeat the hand-winding process. If the roller-blind springs back into position too forcefully, the ratchet should be loosened. Make sure the blind is fully wound, remove it, and unwind it half-way. Replace the unwound blind and test the tension. If it is still too great, repeat the process. If either method fails, fit a new ratchet.

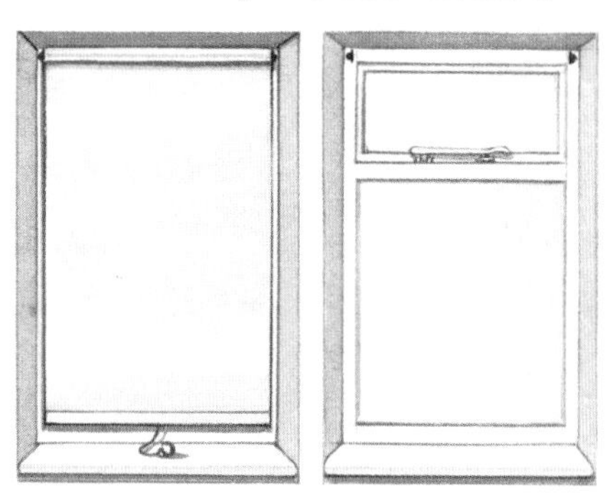

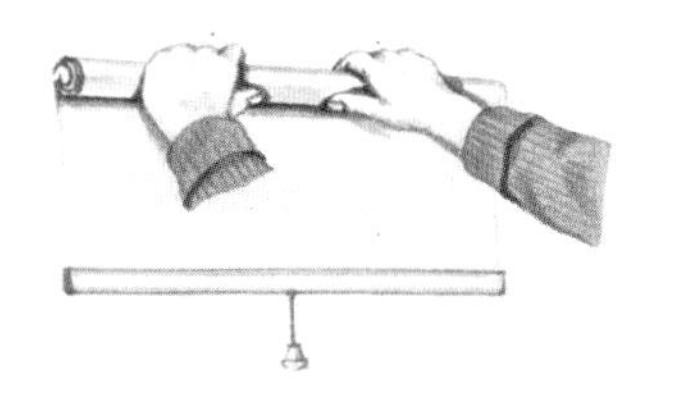

## 81 Using adhesives and sealants safely

Many adhesives and sealants give off highly flammable gases and noxious fumes. If using these materials indoors, take the precaution of making sure that the room is well ventilated and that there are no naked flames. In particular, remember the pilot light of a gas cooker or geyser, which can easily be forgotten.

## 82 Mixing ingredients for concrete in a gauge box

Always use a gauge box to make sure of the right quantities when mixing large amounts of sand and cement. Measuring quantities with a shovel or a bucket is a perfectly adequate way of tackling small tasks—but not for large ones. If each mix is not made up to the same proportions when laying a concrete path, for instance, the concrete may well dry out in a series of different shades—usually because more sand has been added to one mix than to another.

Make the gauge box by simply nailing and gluing lengths of 12mm/½in plywood together, and, so that the sand can be tipped out easily, fit it with two handles shaped from 75mm/3in by 25mm/1in timber. Make sure that the inside height of the box is 450mm/18in and that the inside base is 300mm/12in square. This means that the box will hold .042cu m/1½cu ft of sand when it is full.

As a useful addition, make a false bottom that can be dropped into the gauge box should only .028cu m/1cu ft of sand or cement be needed. The bottom should be 150mm/6in deep and should be fitted with a handle so that it can be removed easily.

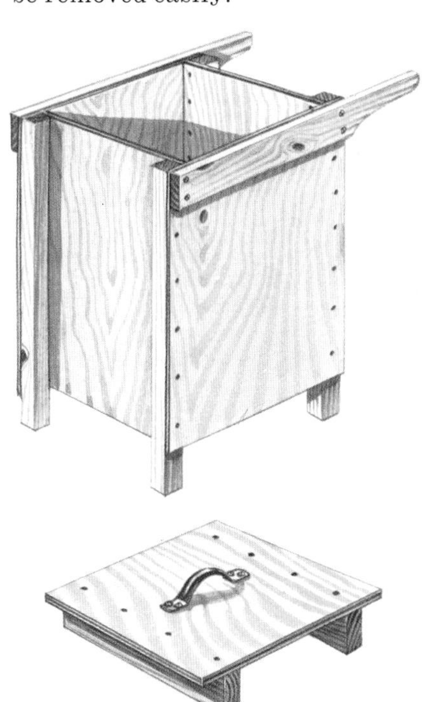

## 83 Filling corners in a concrete-panelled wall

Use a small rectangular tin to make a neat job of filling gaps in corners where concrete panels have been fitted to a wall. In one corner of the tin cut a slot to the width of the gap to be filled. Use a sharp chisel to cut notches at each side to a depth that will take a hacksaw blade. Then saw down each side of the slot and finally use the chisel again to cut across the top and bottom.

Fill the tin with a cement filling compound. Hold the tin firmly into the corner and use a trowel or a piece of wood cut slightly smaller in height and width than the slot to ram the filler in place. Work from the top downwards.

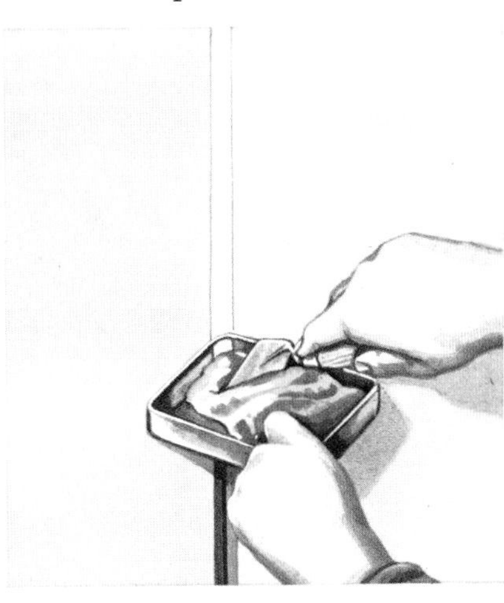

## 84 Preparing wooden floors before laying underlay

Before laying underlay for a carpet over floorboards, make sure that there are no protruding nails or tacks, and that there are no high ridges in the boards—the carpet will wear more quickly at these high spots. Punch the nails below the surface and plane off any ridges. Also fill any large cracks between the boards.

If, however, the floorboards are severely warped, cover the floor with sheets of plywood or hardboard, secured with deep-drive panel pins. If using hardboard, remember that it will have to be conditioned first to avoid the risk of possible buckling. Follow the manufacturer's instructions.

## 85 How to stop radiators from dirtying walls

To lessen the chance of dirt marks from a radiator getting on to the wall immediately above it, fit a blockboard shelf to the wall, making sure that the shelf is wide enough to overlap the radiator by about 50mm/2in and long enough to extend about 100mm/4in at each end. The shelf can either be fixed into position with mirror plates, or on angle brackets concealed behind the radiator.

For complete effectiveness, glue a strip of foam draught excluder to the back of the shelf before fixing it to the wall. Force the shelf back so that the draught excluder is squeezed up tightly.

## 86 Fixing a ceiling rose between two joists

If a light fitting needs to be fixed between two joists, a block of softwood should be fixed between them to take the weight of the fitting.

Having worked out the position for the rose, remove the relevant floorboards in the room above the ceiling and cut the block to fit between the joists. Nail two pieces of softwood into the block, flush with its ends. Mark the position of the rose and drill a hole sufficiently large to take the wiring. Then secure the block by screwing through the side pieces into the joists. Assemble the light fitting and replace the floorboards.

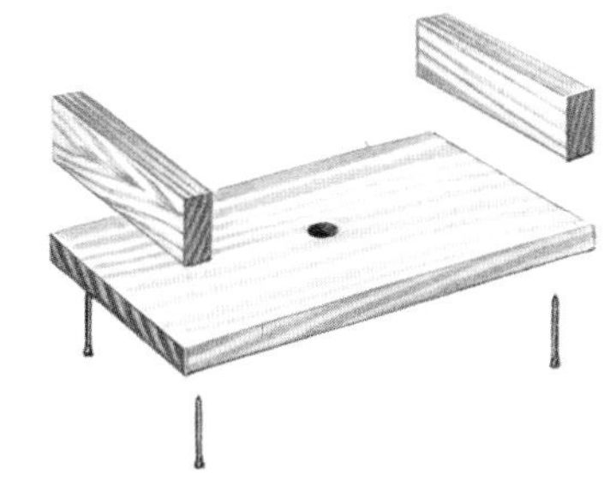

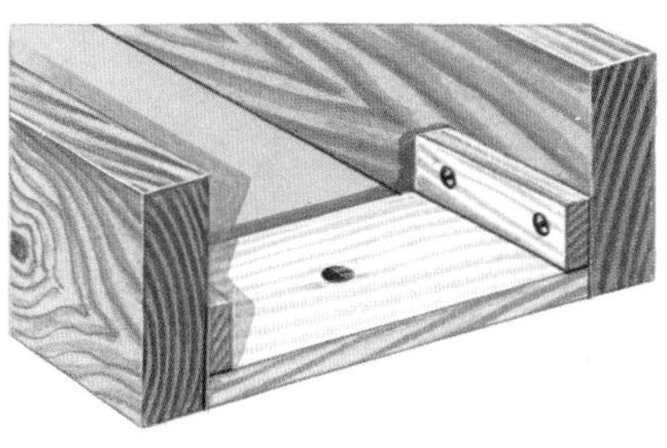

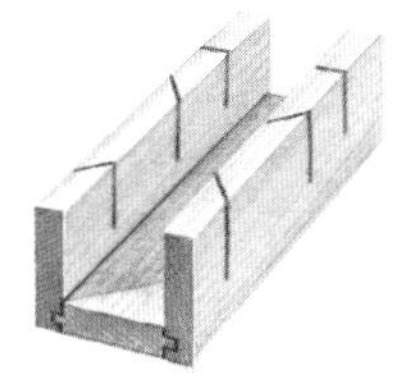

## 87 Mitre block

Use a mitre block as a guide when cutting angles in wood. Always cramp the block in a vice. This leaves one hand free to steady the piece of wood being cut.

## 88 Working with adhesives

Because some adhesives contain chemicals that are harmful to the skin, always coat the hands with barrier cream before applying them in large quantities.

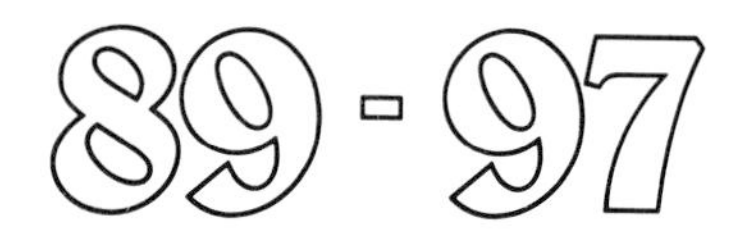

## 89
### Paint pad

When buying a large paint pad, check that it has a hollow grip. By inserting a length of broom handle into the grip, the pad can be used to paint the tops of walls and even ceilings from floor level.

## 90
### Using a cutting tool

When using a cutting tool always keep the hand holding the material behind the cutting edge of the tool. If the tool slips, no damage will occur.

## 91 Improving the bonding between laminates

One of the main difficulties in fixing one laminated plastic sheet to another is getting an adequate bond between the sheets. Scoring one surface avoids the tedious process of removing the old laminate. To make a scorer cut a 30 cm/1 ft length of 50 mm/2 in by 25 mm/1 in batten and groove it with a tenon saw to take an old hacksaw blade.

Make the groove to a depth that will leave the teeth of the blade just protruding. Rub this across the old laminate's surface to scour it sufficiently for the contact adhesive to grip.

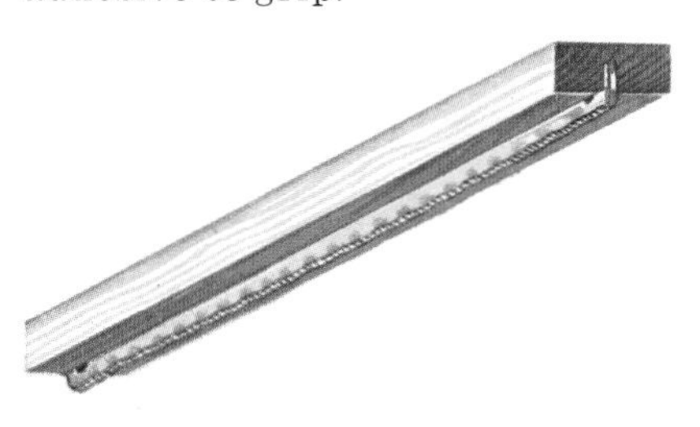

## 92 Storing varnishing brushes in frequent use

To avoid cleaning varnishing brushes that are in constant use, first drill a hole through the handles of the brushes. Then suspend them from a wooden or metal rod in equal parts of linseed oil and turpentine substitute.

The bristles of the brushes must be completely covered by the liquid without touching the bottom of the container. If the bristles rest on the bottom, they will pick up the residue of the varnish that settles there and will also become permanently curved. The mixture will need to be renewed every two to three weeks.

## 93 Storing paint brushes for use the next day

Rather than store brushes in water overnight, which involves drying them out before use, either wrap the brushes tightly in aluminium foil or place them in a tightly sealed polythene bag.

## 94 Removing a post without disturbing the ground

Lever free rather than dig out an old timber gate or fence post to avoid leaving a large hole, which would make it more difficult to fit a new post.

Leaving about 114 mm/4½ in of the nails exposed, hammer two 150 mm/6 in nails in opposite sides of the post, about 300 mm/12 in above ground level. Wind a long length of strong rope tightly round the post immediately beneath the nails. Stack bricks on each side of the post to a height just below that of the rope "cushion". Place a short but sturdy length of timber on top of the bricks and under the cushion and push down on it to lever the post upwards. Lever from each side of the post in turn and add a further brick, or bricks, as the post lifts.

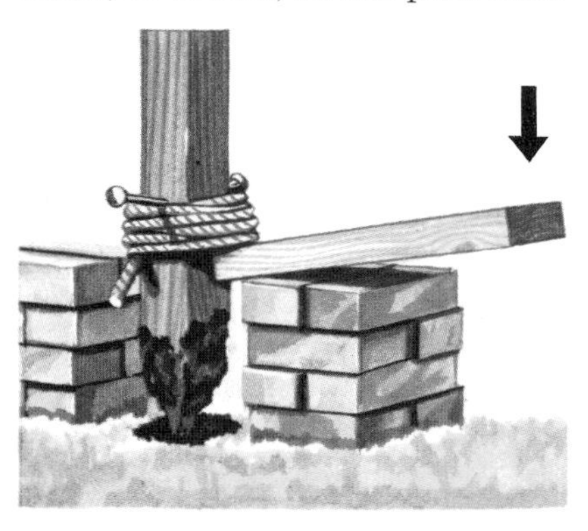

## 95 Storing paint brushes over long periods

Before storing paint brushes, make sure they are thoroughly cleaned. Use warm, soapy water to remove emulsion paint and turpentine substitute to remove oil-based paint. Shake out as much moisture as possible, then store the brushes with newspaper folded around the bristles.

## 96 Removing a damaged brick from a cavity wall

When removing a brick from a cavity wall, always take care that chippings do not fall down into the cavity. If a large piece of brick jams across the cavity it will form a bridge between the outer and inner walls along which dampness can travel.

Reduce the risk of this occurring by using a bolster chisel and a club hammer to cut a "V" down the centre of the damaged brick to a depth of about 75 mm/3 in. Hammer the bolster into the mortar on each side of the brick, angling the bolster towards the "V" to help loosen the brick. Take care not to chip adjacent bricks. Then hammer directly in the centre of the "V" until the brick splits in half. Work from each side of the brick in turn to prise it out.

## 97 Protecting a garden using wire netting

If fitting wire-netting to keep out rabbits, dig a trough at least 225 mm/9 in deep and 100 mm/4 in wide. Attach the netting to its supports, turning it inwards at the base of the trough, and replace the soil. Although rabbits can burrow down to 225 mm they will be stopped by the wire above them.

## 98 Planing the edges of timber accurately

Use a shooting board to ensure accuracy along the full length of timber when planing the edges and ends of a piece of timber.

Make the board from two pieces of timber each approximately 750mm/30in long and 15mm/⅝in thick. Cut the top board to a width about 75mm/3in narrower than the bottom board. Separate the two boards with four battens about 15mm/⅝in thick. Cut a batten for the bottom-stop to hold the board against the end of the bench, and a batten for the top-stop to hold in place the length of timber being planed. Make sure to fit the top-stop at an exact right-angle to the top section—any inaccuracy here will be duplicated down the edge of any timber being planed—and remember that, in time, the stop will need to be replaced. When fitting the components together, screw and glue to ensure a very rigid framework.

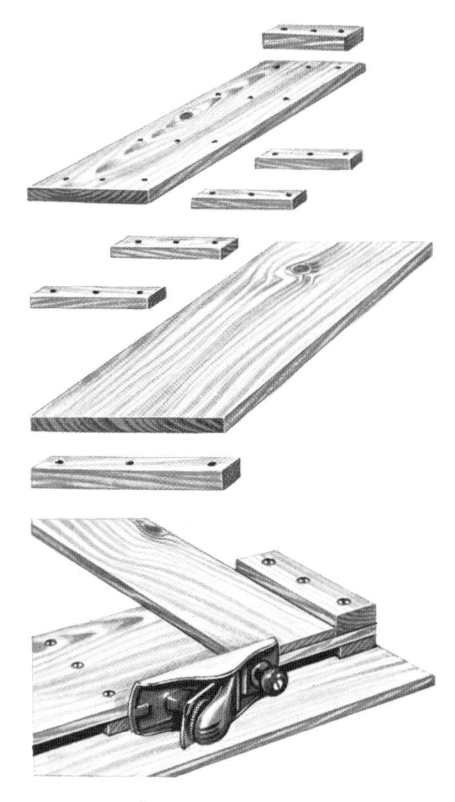

## 101 Supporting a fence post with a rotted base

Provided that the rest of the post is sound, a fence post that has rotted beneath the surface can be supported with a concrete spur. This saves having to replace the post. Dig around the post on one side to a depth of 45cm/18in. Place the spur within the hole, lining up its fixing holes with a sound part of the post. Then fill the hole with concrete. Allow at least a week for the concrete to harden. Then partly hammer coach screws through the spur into the post and tighten them with a spanner.

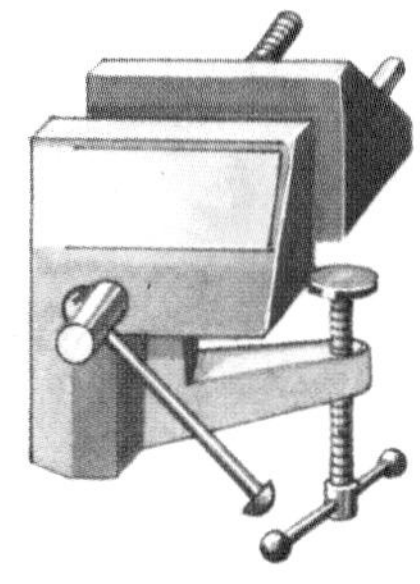

## 103 Vice

Select a vice with an offset cramp so that it can be fixed to the side of the work surface as well as the front. If it is not possible to hold narrow objects in the centre of the vice, pad the vice out with scrap wood to even out the pressure of the grip.

## 99 Checking levels over long distances

To check the levels of two points that are widely separated, use a clear flexible plastic pipe, or a hosepipe with clear plastic tubes fitted in each end. This method is especially useful for checking levels round a corner.

Fill the pipe with water and position and fix one end of it against the required level with the water in the pipe virtually flush with the pipe opening. Place the other end against a batten fixed vertically at the point where the level is being assessed and raise or lower the hosepipe until the water level is again virtually flush with the end of the pipe. Mark the level on the batten. When taking a level in this way, always have a can of water available to make good any spillages from the hosepipe during the process.

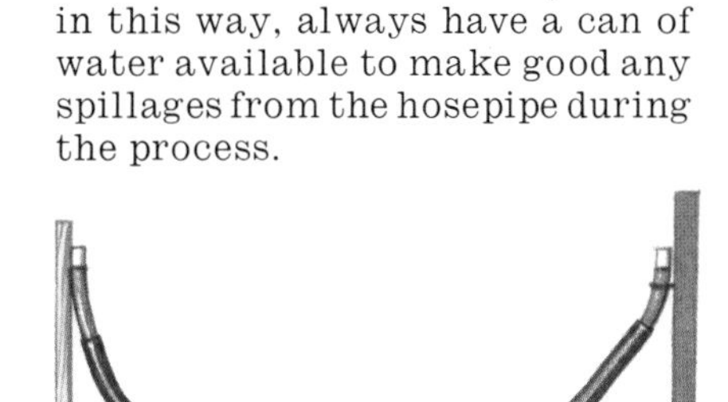

## 100 Fitting electric cables to skirting

When fitting electric cables to skirting, or around door frames, use proprietary plastic clips that are designed to fit the exact width of cable laid. First tack a clip, on one end of a long length of cable, to the skirting at the plug point—allowing at least 125mm/5in excess cable for fitting to the plug later. Then, running the cable between the thumb and forefinger, pull it hard to get it taut and fix a second clip 30cm/1ft farther along the skirting. Continue like this—pulling the cable tight and fixing clips at every 30cm/1ft—until the appliance to which the cable is to be attached is reached.

Cut off the cable, making an extra allowance for the distance from the last clip to the appliance, plus another 125mm/5in excess. Cut back the excess amounts of cable at each end and wire up.

Never work the other way round—cutting the length of cable first, wiring up and then clipping it into position. This usually leads to unsightly bulges between each clip because the cable is too slack.

## 102 Curing a creaking stair tread

A simple way of curing a creaking stair tread is to screw a strong metal angle bracket to the underside of the tread and to the riser below it. Fit one bracket each side of the staircase. If the stair still creaks fit a third bracket in the centre of the tread and riser.

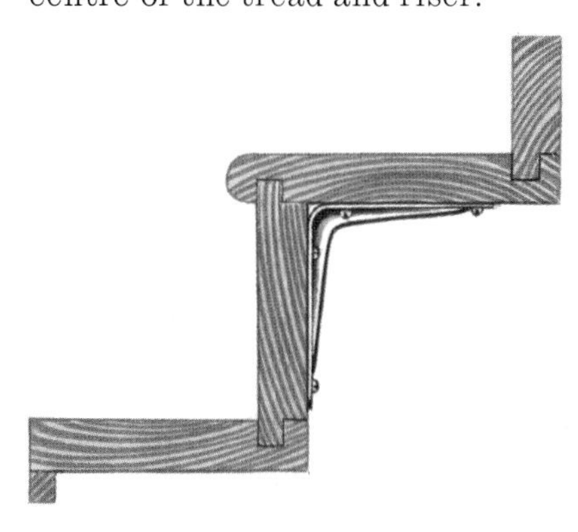

## 104 Using a paint spray

Always wear a face mask covering the nose and mouth when using a paint spray.

## 105
### Putty knife

The flexible blade of a putty knife makes it ideal for stopping up holes in woodwork, but this very flexibility can make it unsuitable for working on the putty of newly glazed windows. Adapt an old knife by cutting off the top third of the blade at a slight angle with a hacksaw. Remove any burrs with a stone or grinding wheel.

## 106
### Rubbing down lead pipes

Never use a dry abrasive paper to rub down lead pipes; the paper will raise lead dust, which is extremely harmful to health. Use well-soaked wet-and-dry paper.

## 107 Finishing off with wet-and-dry paper

Wet-and-dry paper should always be used wet to rub down painted wood and metal surfaces for a really smooth finish. Make the job easier by applying a touch of soap across the paper. This will help to soften the water used to dampen the paper and, in turn, help the paper cling to the surface being smoothed. Wash down the surface afterwards to remove the slurry.

## 108 Making a sliding door burglar-proof

To help make a sliding door burglar-proof, use a steel or metal rod that will fill the complete length of track that is visible when the sliding panel is closed. Even if a potential thief forces the door lock, he would be unable to slide the door open.

## 109 Removing stains from marble

Stains on marble can usually be bleached out with the aid of ammonia and a paste made up of hydrogen peroxide and whiting powder. First, wash the stain with ammonia and rinse. Then spread the paste on the stain and sprinkle on a few drops of ammonia.

Cover the paste with a piece of polythene to help keep it moist, and leave it for a few minutes. Then wipe off the paste, rinse the marble thoroughly with plenty of hot water, and repolish the area.

## 110 Repairing a hole in a fitted carpet

A hole in a fitted carpet can be effectively repaired by fitting a piece cut from an identical carpet. Using a trimming knife and working from the back of the carpet, cut out a neat square around the damaged area, and cut a replacement patch that fits the square exactly.

Spread a white rubber latex adhesive halfway up the edges of both the patch and the cut-out section to stop the edges from fraying. Allow at least half an hour for the adhesive to dry, then cut out a piece of hessian, or coarse sacking, that is 25mm/1in larger all round than the size of the hole. Tuck the hessian under the hole and apply rubber latex to the exposed surface. Add a further thin coating around the edge of the hole. Alternatively, use a 50mm/2in square of self-adhesive linen tape—adhesive face up—as the base for the repair. Insert the patch in position and hammer it down firmly with a block of wood.

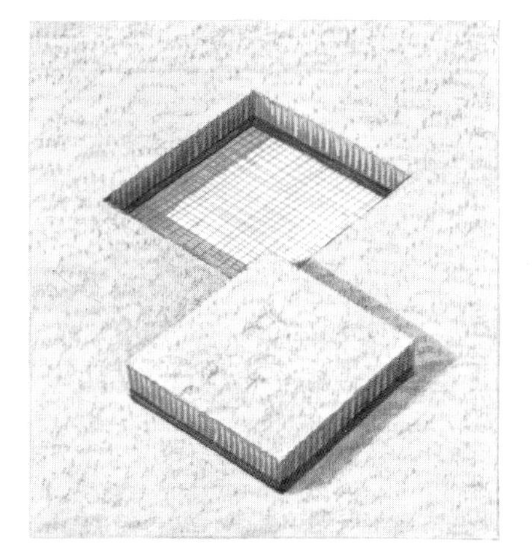

## 111 Sealing the end-grain on exterior timbers

Paint does not always adequately seal the end-grain of timber being used externally, as, say, a window sill. After priming the wood, work a proprietary filler into the grain with a glazing knife, pressing it home hard. When the filler has dried, rub down the wood with glasspaper.

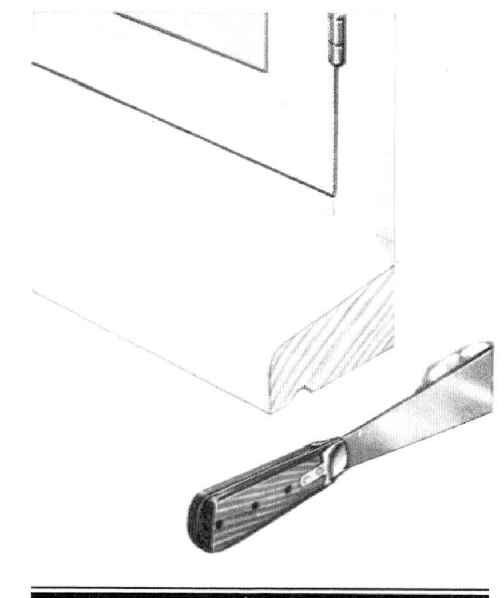

## 112 Avoiding splintering when sawing chipboard

Chipboard can be sawed with a panel or tenon saw, but it is worthwhile taking precautions to avoid it splintering on the underside when sawing it. First mark where the cut will appear and either score heavily along this line with a trimming knife, or stick tape along the line.

## 113 Removing heavily painted wallpaper

Sometimes, it is very difficult to scrape off wallpaper that has been painted with several layers of emulsion. This is because the surface of the paper has become so saturated with emulsion that water cannot soak into it.

The trick is to wet the paper and then lightly heat the surface with a blowlamp. The steam created will work its way beneath the paper, softening the paste so that the paper can be scraped off much more easily.

## 114 Fixing quadrant tiles around a bath or basin

Always work inwards from the ends towards a centre mark when fitting quadrant tiles between a wall and a bath or basin. This ensures a neat appearance and avoids the necessity of trimming either the mitred corner tiles or the round-edged end tiles, which could result in breaking the only two tiles available for completing the job.

First mark the centre of the length of the bath or basin on the wall. Fit a mitred tile into the corner, applying the adhesive recommended by the tile manufacturer. Then fix plain quadrant tiles along the length, stopping short of the centre mark. Repeat the same procedure from the other end, starting with the round-edged tile. Finally fill the gap between the two rows. If it needs a cut tile, rub the cut edge with a glasspaper block or carborundum stone.

Repeat this procedure along the width of the bath or basin, using a trimming knife to cut off any adhesive that has squeezed out from the underside of the tiles. When the adhesive is dry, grout the joints. When the joints are dry use a cloth, dipped in turpentine substitute, to wipe the tiles clean. Avoid over-soaking the cloth or the turpentine substitute may seep behind the tiles, where it will loosen the adhesive.

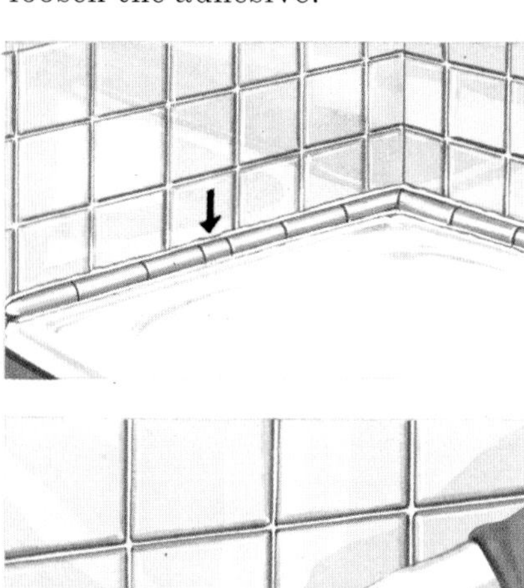

## 115 Sealing wallpaper joins with a seam roller

The pressure necessary to seal down wallpaper joins with a roller can make them shiny. To prevent this, hold a strip of paper between the roller and the join. Do not use newspaper—the print may come off. Never use a roller to seal a paper with a raised pattern, such as Anaglypta; use a brush instead.

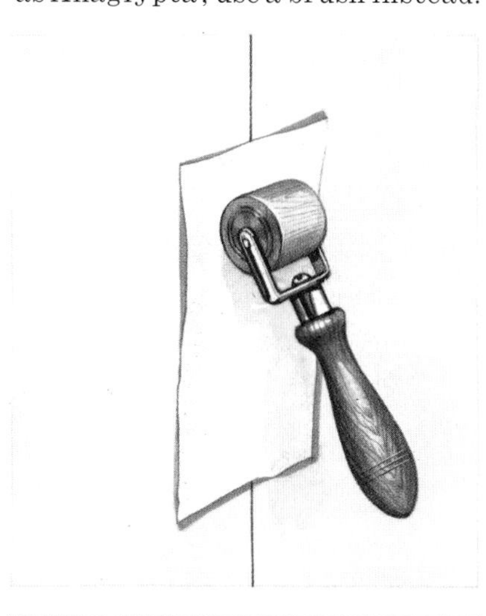

## 116 Removing hard putty from a broken window

If the putty around a broken window proves to be particularly hard to hack out from the frame, the best way to remove it is to first warm the putty with the flame of a blowlamp. The softened putty can then be easily pulled away with a shave hook.

Only use this method, however, if the window is broken—not when preparing to reputty around the edges of an undamaged sheet of glass. Otherwise, the glass could easily be cracked by the heat of the blowlamp flame.

## 117 Reducing dust from concrete floors

Concrete floors in garages and workshops should be sealed to reduce dust, which, when raised, can get into the lungs. First, brush the floor with a soft broom and then brush the concrete with two coats of PVA adhesive diluted with five parts of water.

## 118 Matching colours when filling hardwood

A convenient way of filling small holes in hardwood is to use coloured modelling clay. By working small pieces of various clay lengths together, it is always possible to match the colour of the timber.

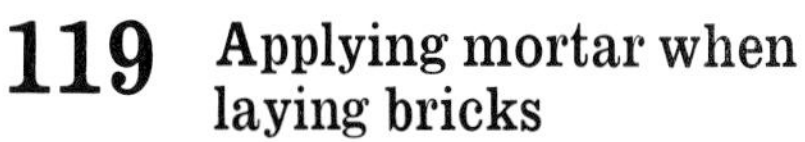

## 119 Applying mortar when laying bricks

When applying mortar for the horizontal joints in brickwork, first form it into a workable shape on the trowel so that it can be rolled off in one smooth movement. Level the mortar out to a thickness of about 12mm/½in.

Lay the next course of bricks by applying the mortar for the vertical joints to the end of the brick before it is laid. If the mortar is applied after the brick is laid it can push it out of line.

First "butter" one end of a brick with mortar and then spread it out to the same thickness as the horizontal joints. Slice off any excess mortar and tap the brick up against the brick already in position to compress the mortar thickness to 10mm/⅜in.

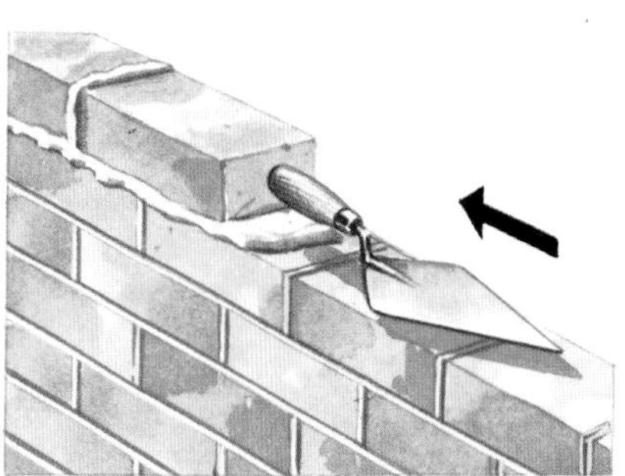

## 120 Stripping knife

A standard stripping knife is a useful all-purpose tool. Use it to strip paint off flat surfaces, scrape away patches of wallpaper, fill plaster cracks and apply adhesive for tiling.

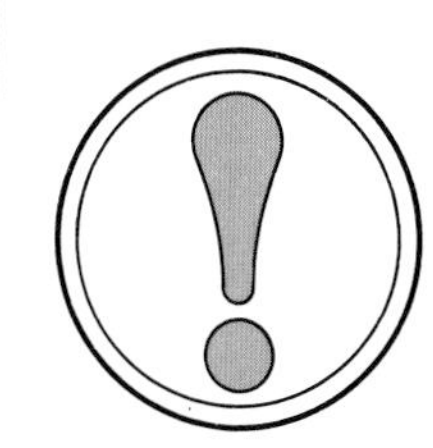

## 121 Working with step-ladders

Never use step-ladders—especially on polished floors—by simply closing the back supports to the front legs and leaning them against a wall. Either use them in the way they were intended or fix a support block against them.

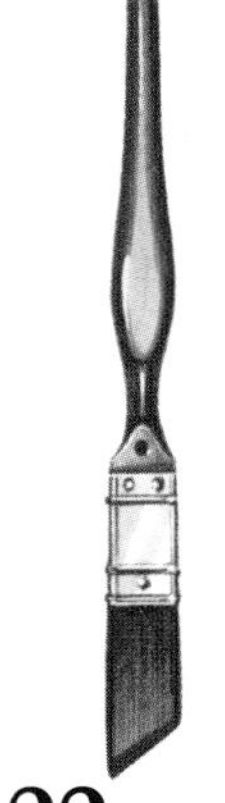

## 122 Cutting-in brush

To make a "cutting-in" brush to paint around awkward corners or narrow mouldings, first soak an ordinary 12mm ½ in brush in a water-soluble glue. When the glue is totally dry, trim the bristles off at a 45° angle and then wash out the glue.

## 123 Checking paint content

Always check the contents of paint being used on such surfaces as window sills, stair rails and nursery woodwork and furniture to make sure that they do not contain lead or other chemicals harmful to children. This particularly applies to primers.

## 124 Cutting warped timber with a circular saw

Make sure that a length of warped timber is fed through a circular saw with the concave side facing downwards. If the concave side faces upwards, the timber will rock about, making a straight cut difficult, possibly jamming the saw blade.

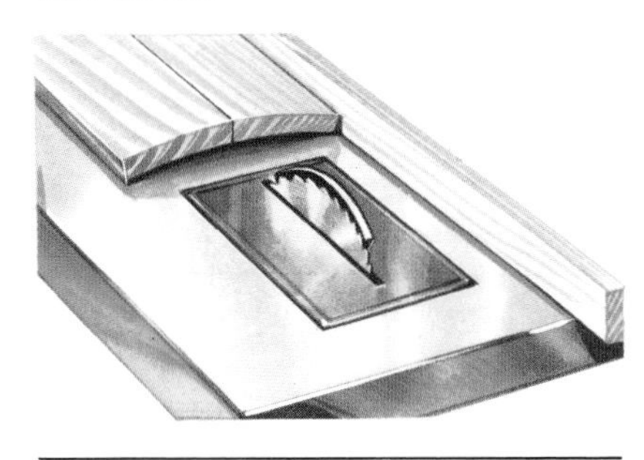

## 125 Trimming excess wallpaper

When cutting off excess wallpaper round ceiling roses, corners of window frames or light switches, leave the paper to dry for at least a day. Then make the necessary cuts with a trimming knife. Not only is it easier to make cleaner cuts on dry paper, but there is also less risk of the paper being torn.

## 126 Treating small areas of dry and wet rot

Two types of fungus—dry rot and wet rot—can affect wood in damp and poorly ventilated areas. To treat the rot cut out the affected spot and an area of at least 450mm/18in around it. Burn the infected timber. Treat the surrounding timbers with a proprietary preservative, and then fit new wood, after first treating it with preservative.

If dealing with dry rot, take especial care to avoid transmitting the spores to other areas—dry rot can be carried even on shoes. If the timber is fitted into or is adjacent to brickwork, heat the bricks with a blowlamp and then treat them with two or three coats of a strong fungicide. If, however, the rot is widespread—or reoccurs after treatment—specialist advice is essential.

## 127 Marking out circles without a compass

Circles up to 600mm/2ft in diameter can be easily marked out by adapting an ordinary wooden ruler to do the job. To mark the circle's centre fit a nail at one end. Drill holes in the centre of the ruler, at inch or centimetre intervals as required, that are large enough to take the point of a pencil. Fit a nail at one end and position it at the centre of the circle. Scribe the circle by placing a sharp pencil point through the appropriate hole.

For a larger circle, use a length of plastic curtain rail and two slider attachments. Fit a wire nail, or a bolt with the end filed to a point, into one of the sliders and fit the chosen marker into the other. Make sure that both sliders grip firmly within the track, so that they will not move out of position while the circle is being drawn.

If necessary, strengthen the track by inserting a steel rod or strip inside the top channel. Also drill out various sliders to take a variety of markers.

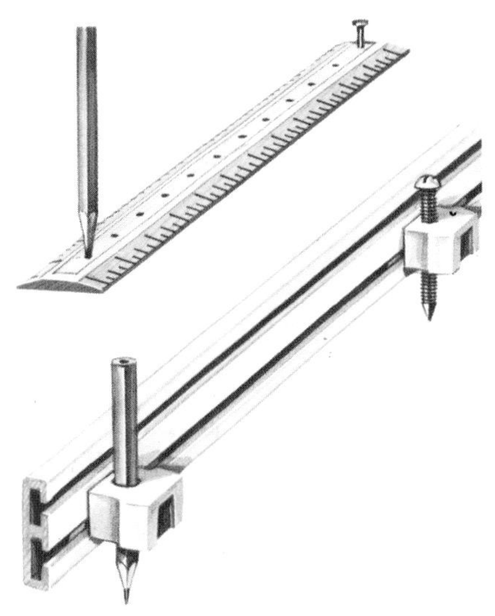

## 128 Preparing timber for creosoting

Before creosoting timber spray it with water, using a hose with a fine rose attachment. Wetting the fence will help to spread the creosote faster and reduce the amount of creosote required.

## 129 Replacing a damaged vinyl floor tile

Cut out the damaged tile with an old wide-bladed chisel, working from the centre outwards. Take care not to lift or damage the edges of adjoining tiles. Use a wide stripping knife to remove old adhesive, then brush away all traces of dust.

Apply new adhesive to the floor with a serrated spreader. Next—having immersed the tile in hot water to make it more pliable and dried it off—bend it slightly and ease it into the corners. Then press it down firmly, working from the centre outwards to remove any air bubbles.

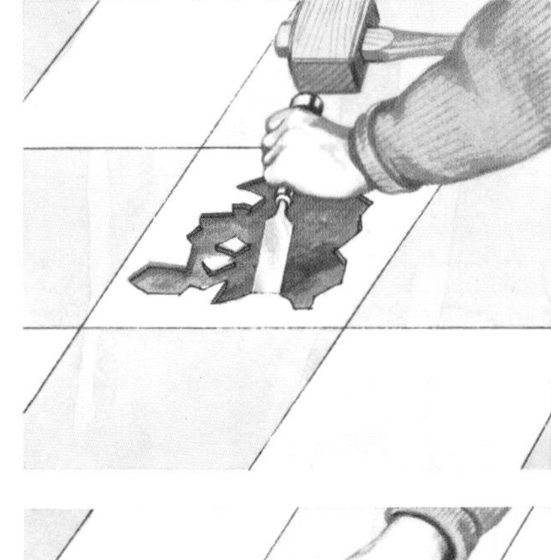

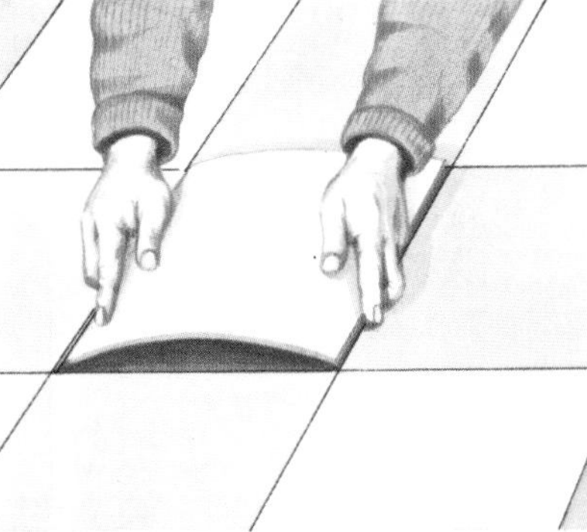

## 130 Repairing a cracked pane in a leaded light

The trick when repairing a leaded light is to cut the replacement square of glass 3mm/⅛in undersize, so that it fits into the lead "cames" of the framework without having to be forced into position. Applying additional putty around the edges will hold the new glass securely in position.

So that signs of repair are not visible from the inside, always replace the glass from the outside where possible. First, use a sharp chisel to cut into the corners of the lead on each side of the solder joints, then carefully prize back the lead to expose the edges of the glass. Remove the glass carefully and, if possible, use it as a template for the new piece of glass; otherwise cut a paper template.

Scrape out all the old putty—or "cement" as glaziers call it—from within the lead joints and brush them clean, paying particular attention to the corners, where dust and debris collect. Then apply a bed of new putty, making sure to use metal casement, rather than linseed-oil, putty. (The latter should be used only for wooden frames; it does not have the same oil content as metal casement putty, which hardens more quickly.) Because the new putty will be lighter in colour than the old, add a small amount of vegetable-black colouring powder to it so that it blends with the "cement" in the other panes.

Fit the glass in position and, using the handle of a putty knife, turn back the lead, pressing it firmly against the glass. Trim off the excess putty that will have been squeezed from beneath the lead and resolder the joints, using a flux-cored solder. Finally clean the glass with a rag lightly dipped in turpentine substitute to remove any grease or smears.

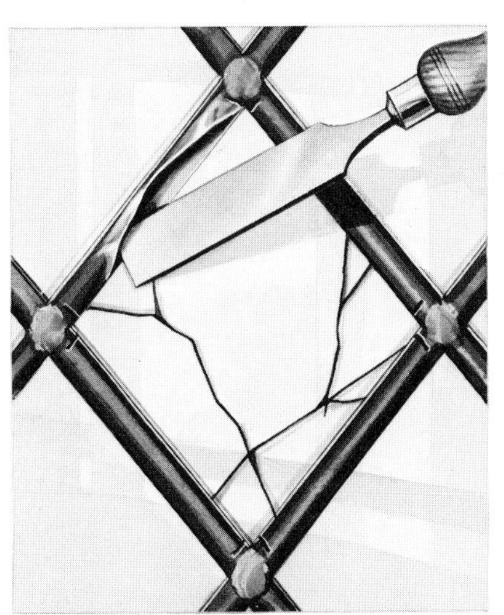

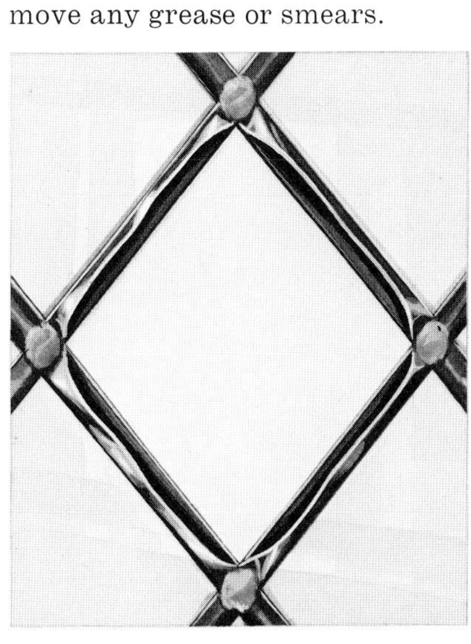

## 131 Selecting bricks for a cavity wall

When selecting bricks for a cavity wall, remember that an internal wall built of lightweight building blocks will provide better thermal insulation than one built of bricks. The lighter the blocks, the better the insulation; the lightest are made from pulverized fuel-ash taken from power station furnaces. If the wall is load-bearing, make sure that the bricks are selected accordingly.

## 132 Filling fine cracks in plaster before painting

Fine cracks in plaster should be filled before the plaster is painted, but the task can be time-consuming and laborious. Make the job easier by using a paint brush to brush a cellulose filler over the cracks. Mix the filler to the consistency of a thick paste. Wipe off any excess filler with a damp sponge before it dries and then, if necessary, rub down the cracks with fine-grade glasspaper.

## 133 Cutting a straight line in sheet metal

When cutting a clean, straight line in thin sheet metal with tin-snips, make sure the snips are long enough for good leverage. Take care not to close the jaws of the snips completely on each separate cut. If the snips are closed fully each time, they will twist the metal over as the jaws clamp together, leaving a ragged edge.

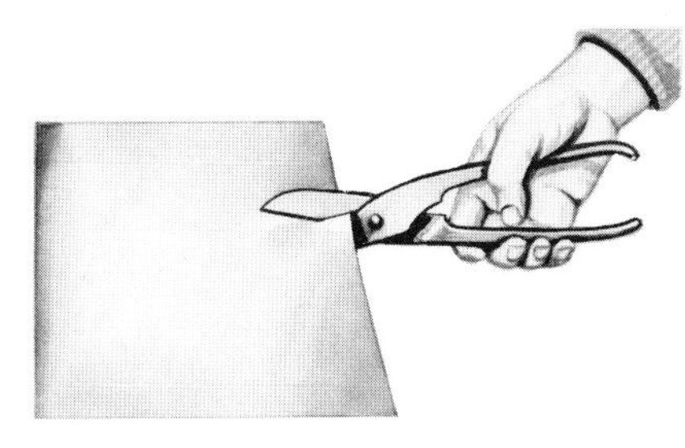

## 134 Making a cutting-in brush easier to use

One common problem that occurs when "cutting-in" paint around mouldings and glazing bars is that the bristles of the paint brush being used widen out to spread the paint on to other areas. This means that additional scraping-off work will be needed after the paint has dried. This can be awkward and time-consuming—especially on glass.

Avoid this by looping a small elastic band three or four times about 25mm/1in up from the cutting edge, so that the bristles cannot spread. Also remember to immerse the brush only as far as the elastic band when dipping it into the paint tin. If the brush is overcharged, the build-up of paint above the elastic band can be transferred to the mouldings or glazing bars.

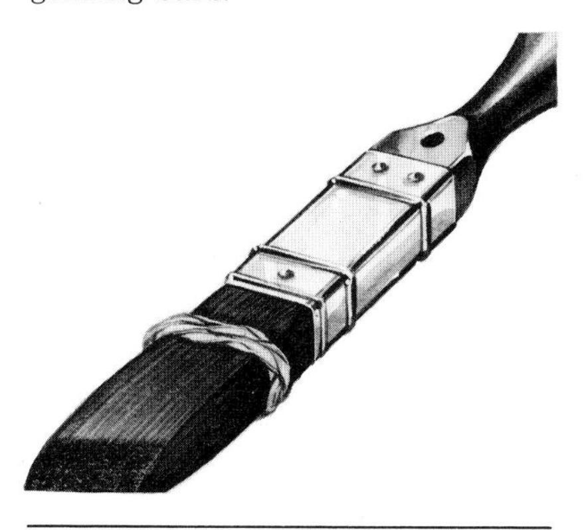

## 135 Chisel

The advantage of bevel-edge chisels over flat-edged types is that the shape of the bevel means the chisel can be used in tight corners. The most useful sizes are 6mm/¼in, 12mm/½in, 25mm/1in. When choosing the chisels, buy those with smashproof plastic handles rather than wooden ones.

## 136 Lighting a staircase

Half-landings on a staircase can be a hazard if poorly lit. Arrange for them to be lit as brightly as possible.

# Unit shelving/1

Complex in appearance but relatively easy to build, the clean lines and complete adaptability of this latticework shelving system make it suitable for use in either living- or dining-rooms. Its design was influenced in conception by the art nouveau styles of the early twentieth century.

The various units can be combined or used on their own, while the position of cupboards and shelves can also be flexible. The glossy black finish and strong contrasting colour for the fittings are especially suited to the design, which is ideal for display.

The overall height and width and the number of central supports, shelves and cabinets can be varied at will without detracting from the appearance of the unit.

The only critical dimensions are the thickness of the shelves and slats, which have to be identical—in the shelving illustrated 19mm/¾in square softwood was used. For satisfying proportions, the thickness of the upright supports should be slightly greater than that of the shelves—in this case they are 25mm/1in square.

**Preparing the supports and shelves**
Lay out the upright supports, cut to length, for one side. To ensure that the upright supports are equally spaced and exactly vertical, cut spacers to identical thicknesses and position them in the centre and at either end of the gaps.

With the width of the overall structure decided, cut the slats and shelves to size accordingly. If a stained finish is preferred, apply the stain before assembling.

Pin a slat flush with the top and bottom of the upright supports to hold them in place. Then, using a slat as another spacer, work down the complete length of the uprights, gluing and pinning each slat in place and checking the alignment with a try square.

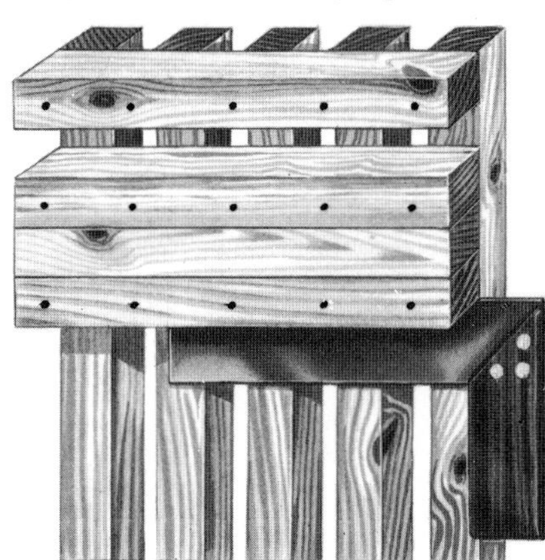

**A totally flexible system**
To make a unit that can be dismantled to be moved from room to room, use hardwood for the slats and shelves. Cramp two slats or two shelves together at a time and, using a drill stand, drill a hole centred on the join. When assembling, insert pegs into the holes between slat and shelf to hold the structure rigid.

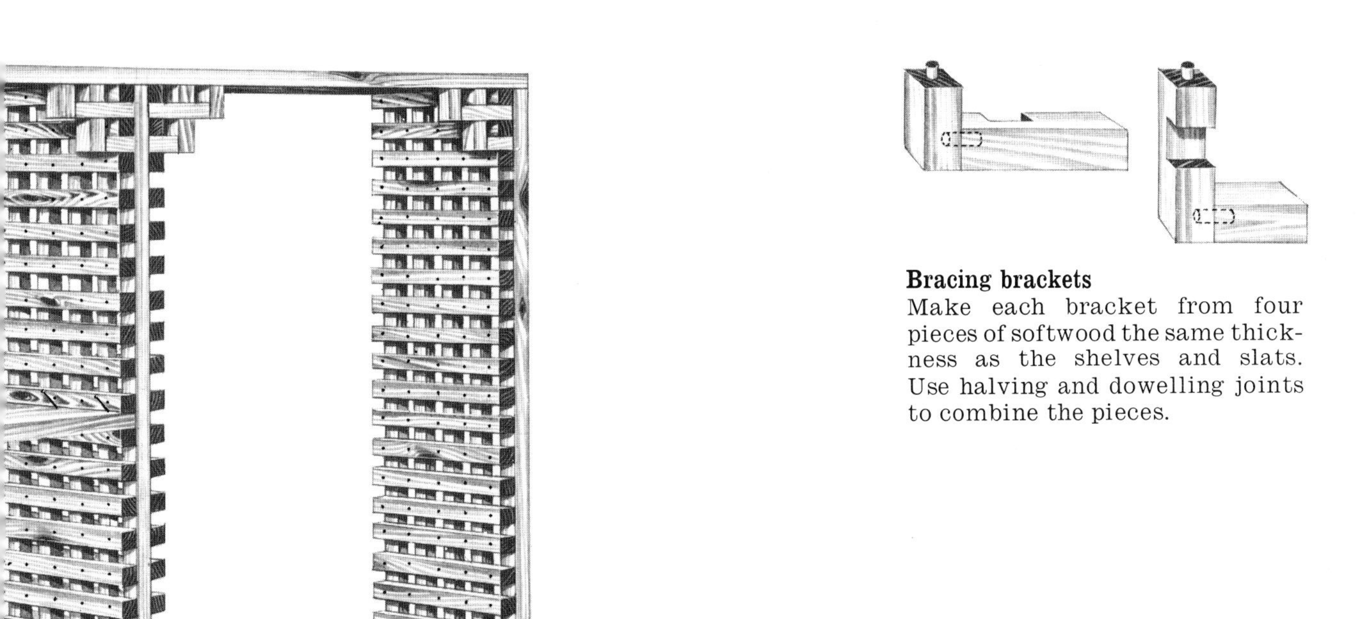

**Bracing brackets**
Make each bracket from four pieces of softwood the same thickness as the shelves and slats. Use halving and dowelling joints to combine the pieces.

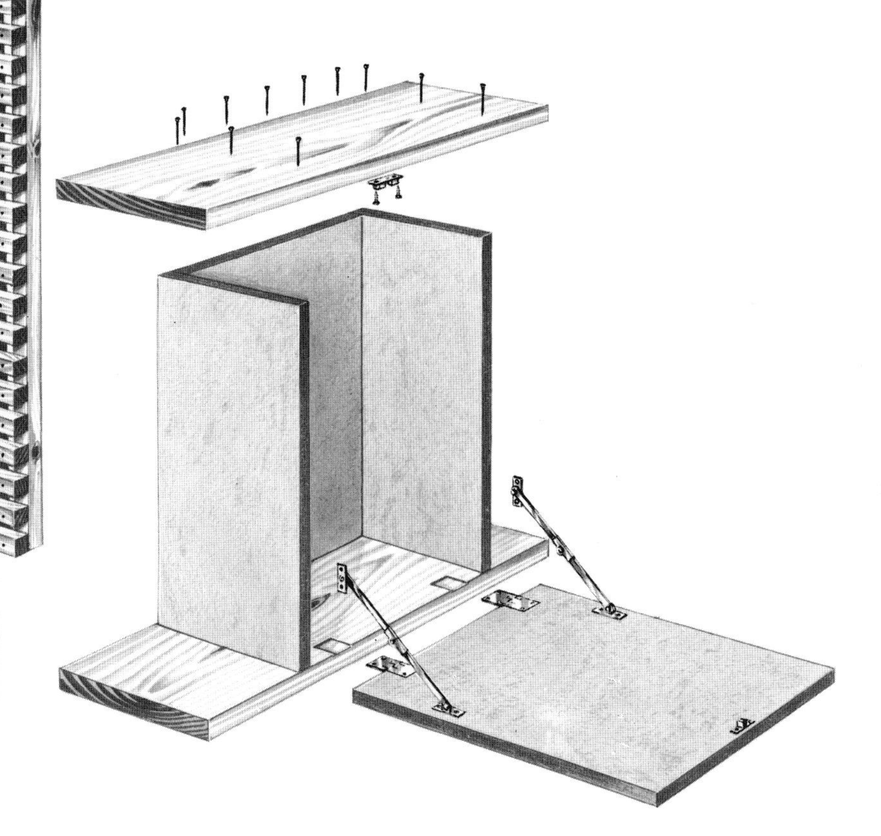

**Assembling the basic structure**
The simplest way of making the structure rigid is to secure it permanently at the top and bottom. Size the top shelf to span the complete unit and glue and pin it into the side supports. Brace the shelf with softwood brackets, gluing and dowelling them into the bottom front edge of the shelf and gluing and pinning them into the side supports.

To hold the bottom of the structure rigid, size and construct a cabinet and fit it into the shelving system. Use laminated chipboard butt-jointed in place for the sides and hinge the doors. Paint the cabinet before gluing and pinning it into the side supports.

*See also Tips on*
Preparation 174
Marking up 253, 520
Adhesives 81
Dowelling 466, 513
Fixing 261
Finishing 77, 175, 203, 522, 536
Painting 190, 706

# Unit shelving/2

Simplicity combines with versatility in this ziggurat shelving system—so-called because, like the ziggurats built in ancient Babylon, the system can be extended higher and higher, each unit being slightly smaller than the one below it. The construction is based on sandwiching sheets of chipboard between sheets of hardboard to give a smooth finish to both sides of the material. The thickness is calculated so that the proportions complement those of the unit as a whole.

The resulting arrangement is pleasing to the eye and, structurally, it is rigid enough to be free-standing and to take such fittings as a reading lamp. The units can be used individually, or a set can be placed together—run in a line or stacked to the height desired. The bottom shelf can be used, as in the units illustrated, for book, record and drink storage, while the top-most unit was specifically designed with paperback storage in mind. The decoration was carefully planned so that the colour of the paint deepens on each stage, enhancing the overall effect.

THE ATLAS OF THE EARTH

# 138

The simplicity of this attractive ziggurat design is based on achieving visually satisfying proportions with a high degree of finish. This requires a combination of chipboard and hardboard.

**Preparing the building material**

Because the ideal thickness of the components is 25 mm/1 in, it is not possible to buy standard sheets of board with a good finish on each side. The solution is to make the building material by gluing boards together. Sandwich sheets of 19 mm/$\frac{3}{4}$ in chipboard between 3 mm/$\frac{1}{8}$ in sheets of hardboard, ensuring that the shiny surface of the hardboard is uppermost to get the required finish. Apply contact adhesive to one side of the chipboard surface and to one hardboard sheet. Leave them until they are both touch dry and then bond them together. To do this, place the hardboard sheet on a flat surface and position the chipboard sheet on top of it. The weight of the chipboard should be sufficient to ensure an effective bonding. Apply adhesive to the other side of the chipboard and the remaining hardboard sheet and combine the two as before to complete the sandwich.

Depending on the number of ziggurat supports required, prepare additional sheets accordingly.

Having decided on the number of ziggurat supports, work out their individual proportions. There are four basic elements that go to make up a set of supports—the base and three uprights, small, medium and large.

To ensure both an attractive and a functional set, the suggested dimensions are: a 203 mm/8 in clearance between shelf and base for the small unit—enough to accommodate small paperbacks; a 279 mm/11 in clearance for the medium.unit to take larger books or magazines and a 355 mm/14 in clearance for the large unit to take bottles and records.

**The template**

The ziggurat pattern must interlock exactly, so it is vital that the cutting template for the stepped shape is marked up extremely accurately. The suggested height and width for each step is 50.8 mm/2 in. Make a cardboard template incorporating the number of steps required for the largest size—the base. Cut out the template and use a very sharp pencil pressed well in against the straight edges to transfer the outlines on to the prepared boards for each support. Make sure that the outlines for the support are positioned to make the most economical use of the board. Mark up the verticals for each support individually.

**Cutting out the ziggurat shape**

Cutting out each stepped shape requires patience. A jig saw is the ideal cutting tool; alternatively, a tenon saw and padsaw can be used. First cut out the rectangle enclosing each stepped shape and then saw the steps individually so that the guide line is only just removed. Rasp the edges so that, when combined, the pieces are fitting as intended.

**Cutting out the shelves**

Mark out the shelves on the prepared boards to the width of each ziggurat support. The length of each shelf should be around 457 mm/18 in to maintain the proportions. Cut out the shelves. Then stack them one above the other and check with a try square to ensure that the ends are exactly square. The smallest inaccuracy will be transferred in a magnified form down the sides of the unit to put the jointing out of line.

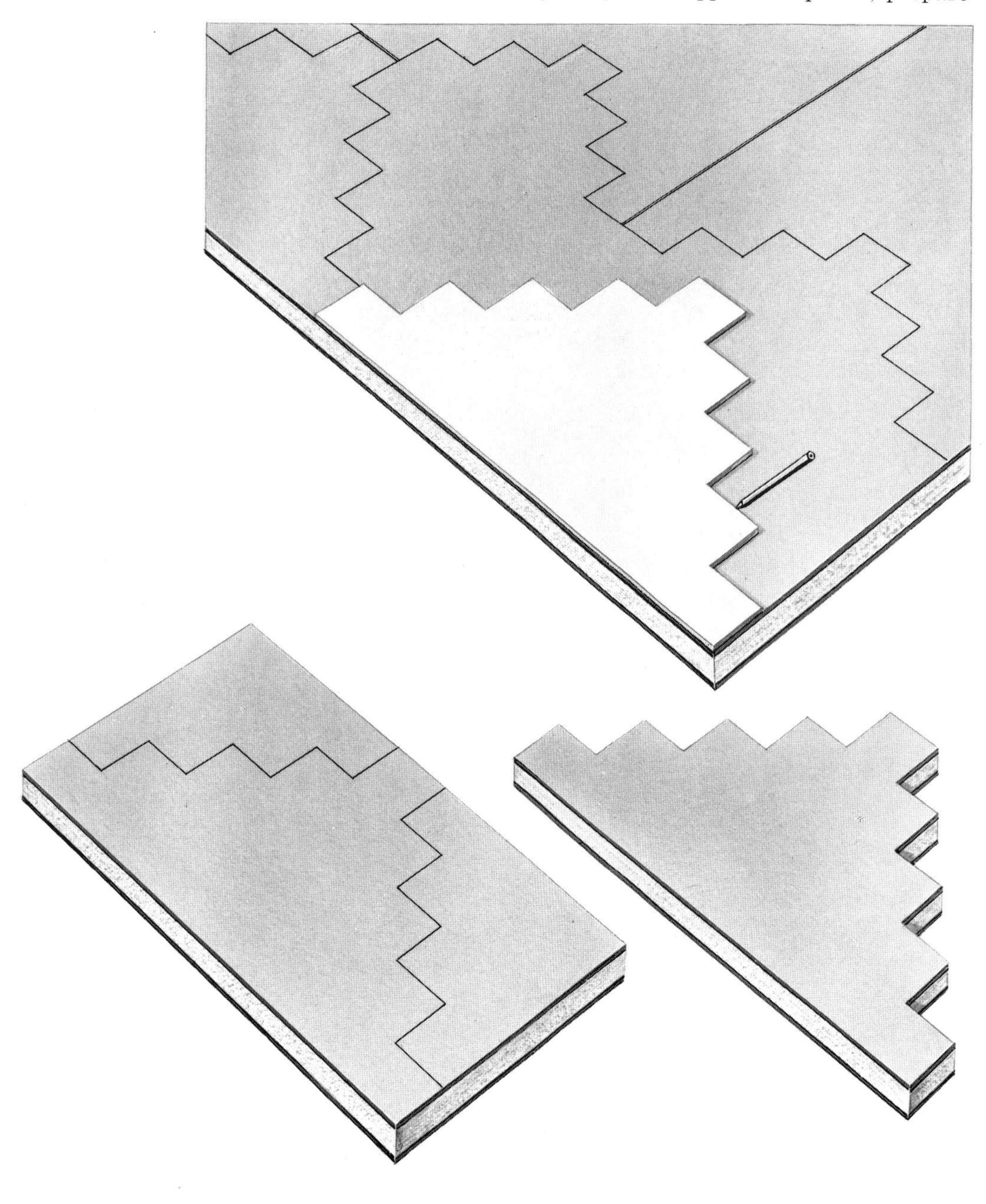

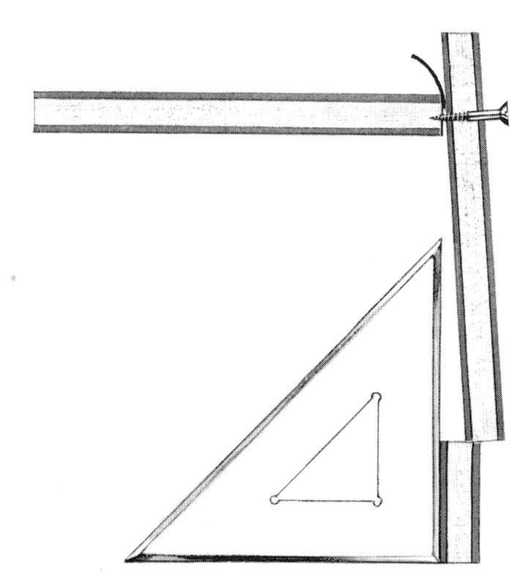

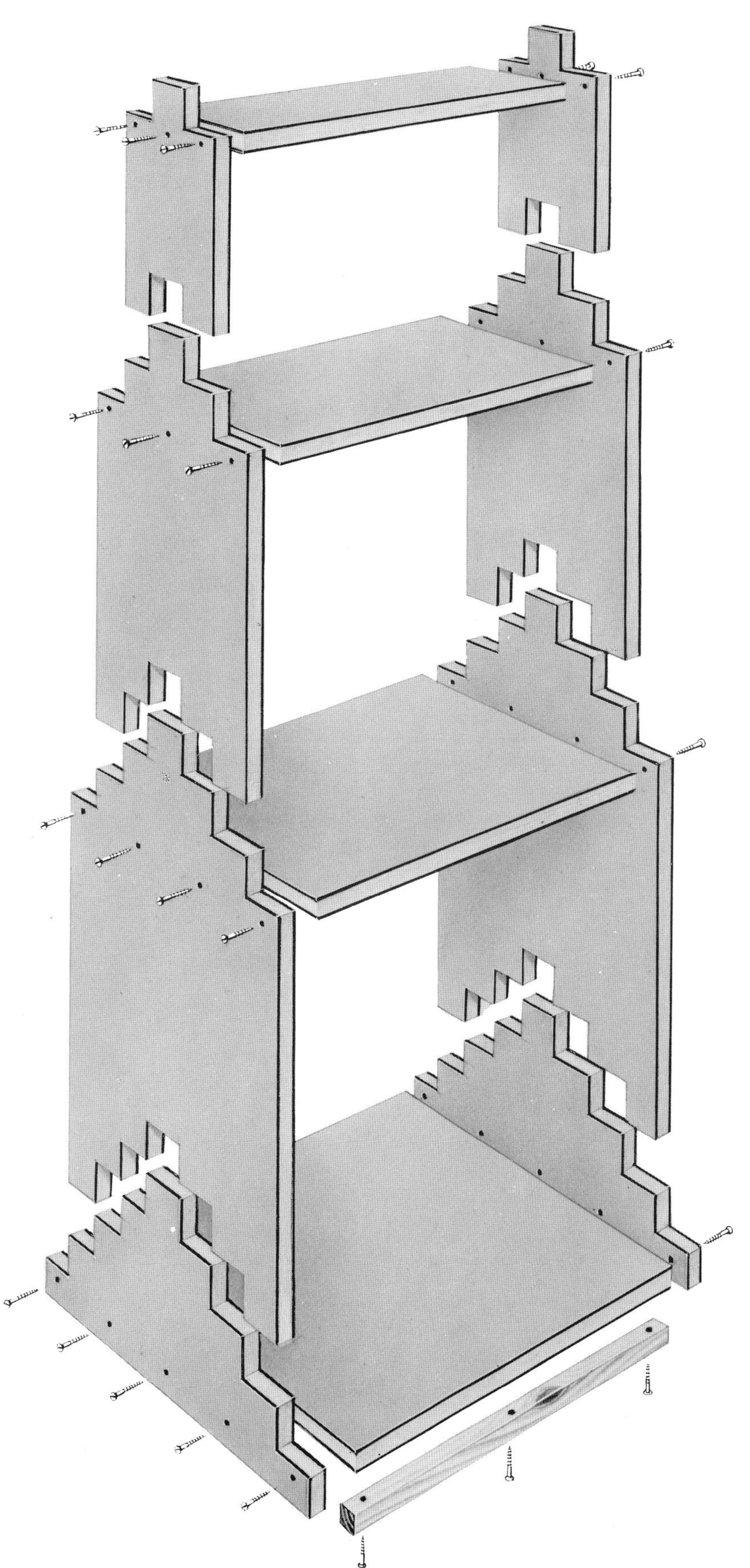

**Assembling the shelves and supports**

The shelves are held in place by a number of 50 mm/2 in no. 10 screws, screwed through the supports into the end of each shelf. Without applying glue, screw each shelf into position in order to check whether the ziggurat supports will be thrown out of line when fully assembled. Check the alignment with a set square. If, as is likely, the alignment is not exact, loosen the screws for final adjustment. To make this, pack strips of paper into the joints between the shelf ends and the sidepieces, above or below the screws, to adjust the vertical alignment. If the vertical is being thrown outside the main structure, as in the example illustrated, pack the paper above the screws. Tighten the screws and re-check the alignment. If it is exact, dismantle the shelf, apply the adhesive, reinsert the paper and screw permanently in place.

**Making the base**

Cut the base shelf to size from the prepared material. Cut two pieces of softwood the full length of the base. Screw to the under edge of the base flush with its sides, checking the alignment.

**Finishes**

Finish any exposed chipboard edges or any ends that have slightly overrun the marked lines with fine-grain filler and rub down with glasspaper. Paint each ziggurat unit by spraying, brushing or rolling. Apply several coats and leave to dry. Rub down each coat before applying the next. The units are now ready for assembly.

*See also Tips on*
Marking up 520
Adhesives 81
Cutting 112, 408
Finishing 18, 190

# Unit shelving/3

This shelving system departs from the usual rigid box frame and includes the flexibility of a series of interchangeable units, which can be constructed with related sizes of square compartments.

The vertical and horizontal members run the full height and width of each unit and are held together by halving joints. These give the system structural rigidity, making it possible to dispense with the traditional outer frame, and allowing the units to be fitted together most attractively.

# 139

In the shelving illustrated, 15mm/⅝in thick laminated chipboard was used, but plywood and chipboard are acceptable alternatives.

**Deciding the dimensions**

Before starting work, decide if several units are to be made, with a view to stacking them in a network. If so, the overall dimensions of each unit should be identical. When deciding the size of compartments required in each unit, remember that each size must be related in proportion. For example, the way to work out the right proportions of the compartments in three units is to decide what the middle unit will be used for—say, for storing paperback books—and to size the other two units accordingly.

Internal heights of the three sizes of compartment in the units illustrated are 89mm/3½in, 190mm/7½in and 394mm/15½in respectively, based on the proportions of four small compartments to one middle-sized compartment and sixteen small compartments to one large compartment. The lengths of the ends of the shelves should also vary in proportion, so that the size of each compartment is maintained when the units are combined.

**Assembling the shelves**

Having decided on the number of shelves and supports, cut them out, checking the squareness of each with a try square. Apply fine-grain filler to all rough edges and rub down with glasspaper.

Mark the positions of the cross-halving joints on one of the lengths and saw them out with a tenon saw. Use this length as a template for the remaining shelves. Note that it is essential for the joints to fit tightly together to give the structure sufficient rigidity, so prepare all the joints carefully. Glue and fit.

**Finishes**

Paint the units; this is best done with a paint spray, which ensures easy and full coverage, especially of the smaller compartments.

Both to enable the units to be fixed to a wall and to provide support for the largest units, cut out a back panel of the same material used for the shelving to the overall dimensions of each unit. Paint it and then glue and screw it into the shelving from behind.

**Sizing the ends of the shelves**

Having sized the compartments use the internal height (x) of one of the smallest as a guide to establishing the length of the ends of the shelves for each unit. As illustrated, the ends on all sides of the smallest unit and two sides of the middle and large units protrude by $\frac{1}{2}$x; the ends of the remaining two sides of the middle unit extend by $1\frac{1}{2}$x, plus 1 thickness of shelf material, and the two sides of the largest by $3\frac{1}{2}$x, plus 3 thicknesses of shelf material.

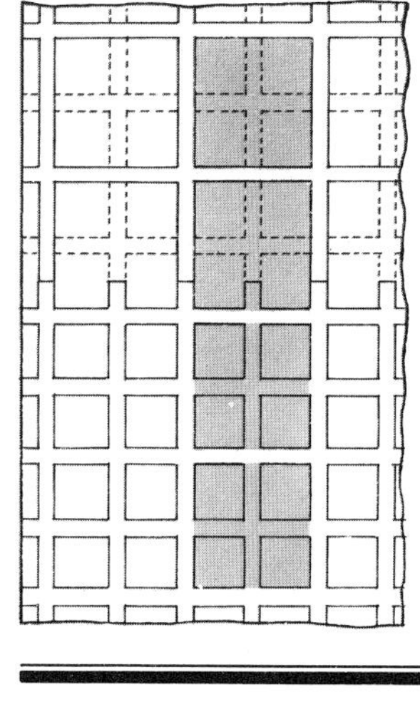

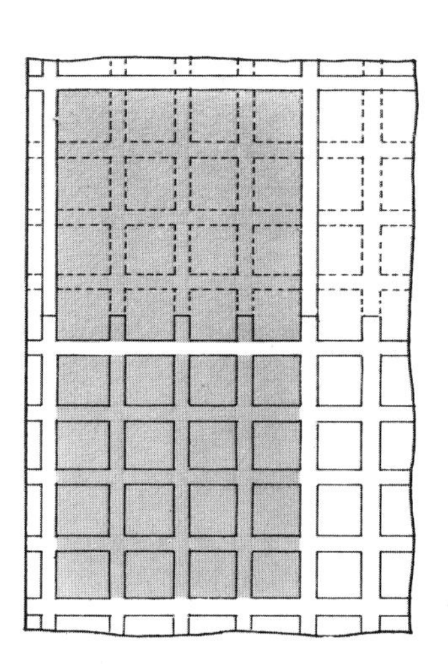

## 140 Making a cross halving joint

Using identical thicknesses of wood, lay together the pieces to be joined so that the width of each can be marked up on the other. Use a try square to continue the marks on the face down the two sides. Set a marking gauge to half the thickness of the wood and mark up the depth of the cut on each piece. Holding the wood against a bench stop, make two or more vertical cuts with a tenon saw. Place the wood in a vice and finish off at the base of the cuts with a chisel to remove the waste. Check the joint for fit, easing it in place with the chisel if necessary, and then finally glue and cramp it together.

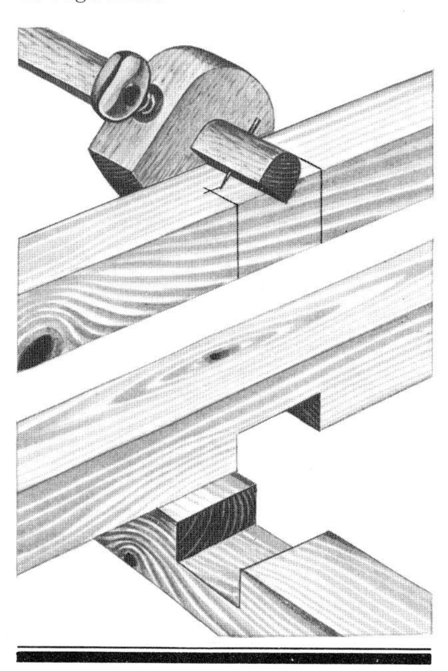

*See also Tips on*
Marking up 520
Adhesives 81
Cutting 112, 346
Joints 140
Smoothing 459
Painting 190, 706

# Display lighting

Both these kite-shaped lights are based on the same principle of diffusing light to produce a warmer, more subdued, effect than that normally produced by conventional lighting.

Simply constructed of crêpe stretched over a kite-shaped frame, the fabric-covered light is wall mounted. The acrylic light is suspended on wires from the ceiling. Its height can be varied and, when the wires are mounted on a track, it can also be moved along the wall. The almost invisible wires and the trailing tail of coiled flex allow the light to "float" against the wall.

# 141

When deciding the dimensions of the Perspex kite light, base the width on the standard sizes of strip lamp available. Always use 5 mm thick Perspex. Suspend the completed light from a pre-stretched nylon fishing line, with about 9 kg/20 lb breaking strain.

**Shaping the Perspex**

Heat makes Perspex pliable; experiment with offcuts to assess the temperature and time required. First mark guidelines about 63 mm/2½ in from each end of the Perspex. Place asbestos sheets either side of one line, leaving a gap of about 6 mm/¼ in. Place an electric fire on its back, with the asbestos and Perspex resting on the fire guard. When the Perspex is pliable, remove the asbestos, place a softwood block on the line and bend the Perspex against it.

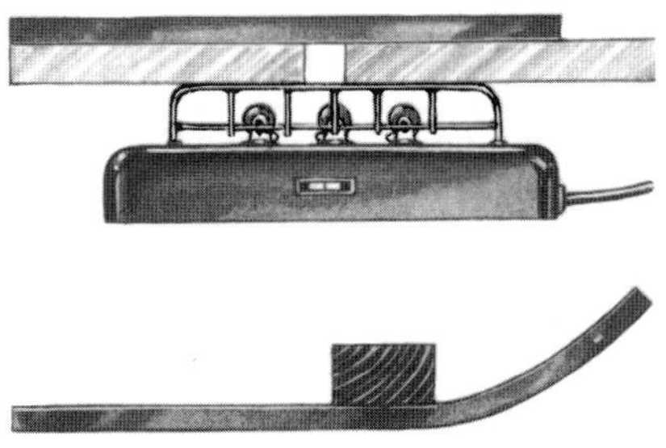

**Mounting the lamp**

Centre the lamp flush with the edge of the lower lip of the Perspex. Mark up and drill two holes for the securing bolts and one hole for the flex. Secure the lamp.

**Suspending the light**

The holes for suspending the light must be positioned so that it hangs exactly vertically. Mark on a softwood block the positions for two pins—these should be fixed so that each pin would be about 37 mm/1½ in in from either end of the Perspex. Hammer the pins partially home and snip off the heads to the same height. Place the upper lip on the pins and move it around until the light is pivoted exactly vertically. Press down on the pins to mark the Perspex. Drill the holes. Mark and drill identical holes on the lower lip and cut a slot leading into each hole. Pass the line through the top holes and attach leather eyelets to the ends. Attach the other ends to curtain glides and slot into a track. The light has two positions—with the eyelets at the top or slotted in at the bottom.

*See also Tips on*
Preparation 685
Drilling 239
Wiring up 517, 692

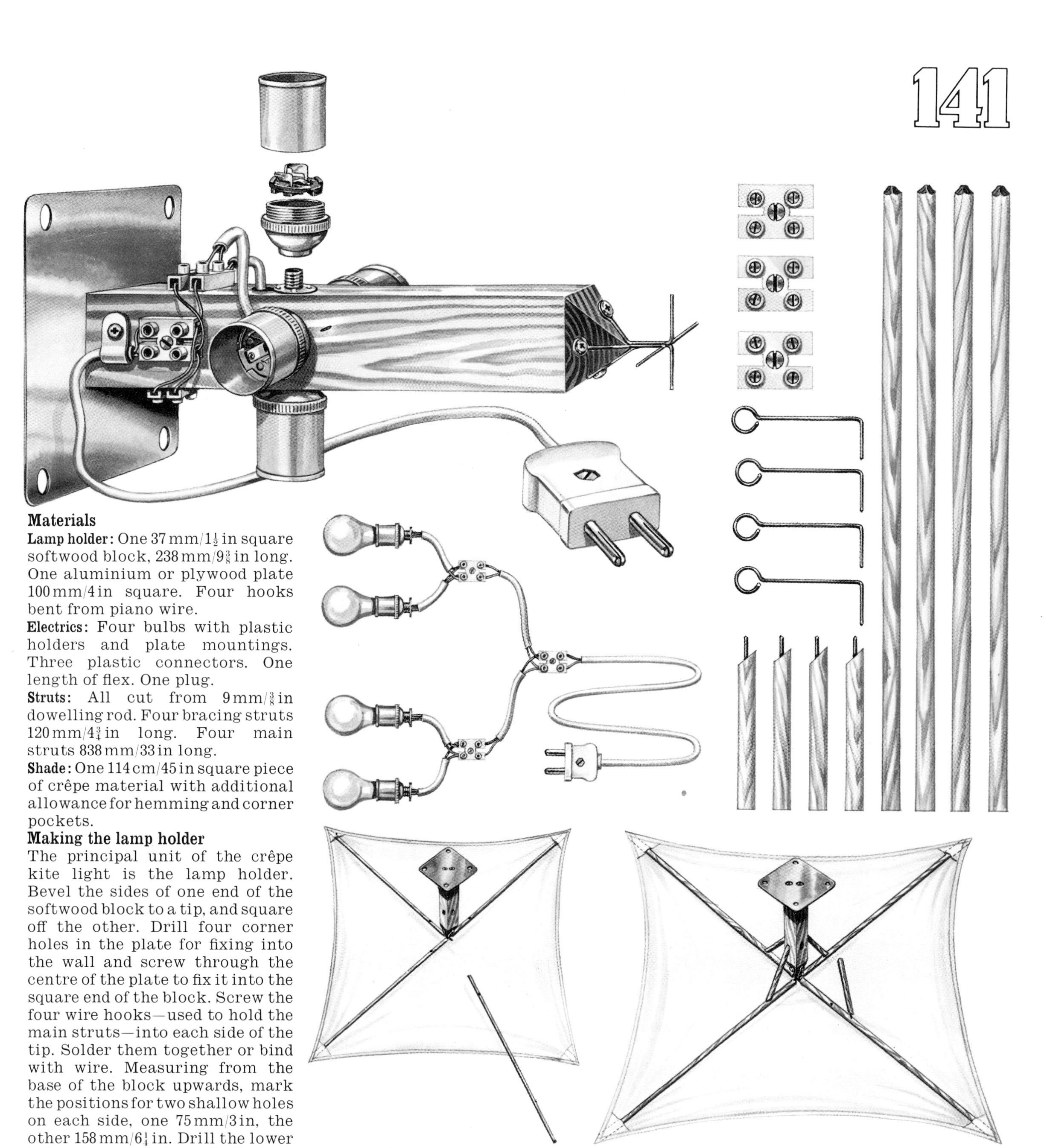

## Materials

**Lamp holder:** One 37 mm/1½ in square softwood block, 238 mm/9⅜ in long. One aluminium or plywood plate 100 mm/4 in square. Four hooks bent from piano wire.
**Electrics:** Four bulbs with plastic holders and plate mountings. Three plastic connectors. One length of flex. One plug.
**Struts:** All cut from 9 mm/⅜ in dowelling rod. Four bracing struts 120 mm/4¾ in long. Four main struts 838 mm/33 in long.
**Shade:** One 114 cm/45 in square piece of crêpe material with additional allowance for hemming and corner pockets.

## Making the lamp holder

The principal unit of the crêpe kite light is the lamp holder. Bevel the sides of one end of the softwood block to a tip, and square off the other. Drill four corner holes in the plate for fixing into the wall and screw through the centre of the plate to fix it into the square end of the block. Screw the four wire hooks—used to hold the main struts—into each side of the tip. Solder them together or bind with wire. Measuring from the base of the block upwards, mark the positions for two shallow holes on each side, one 75 mm/3 in, the other 158 mm/6¼ in. Drill the lower holes at an angle towards the base and the upper holes to the tip.

## Wiring up the electrics

Screw the bulb mountings in place over each lower hole so that the wire runs out through the hole. Follow the wiring diagram to connect up the circuit. Screw the connectors to three sides just below the mountings and insulate.

## Preparing the struts and shade

Cut a bevel and insert a steel pin at one end of each short bracing strut. Drill a hole in one end of each main strut and taper. Drill an angled hole, 95 mm/3¾ in along, to take the pin on the bracing strut. Hem the crêpe shade and sew and seam the pockets.

## Assembly

Insert the squared ends of the main struts into the shade's pockets. Insert the wire hooks on the lamp holder into the hole at the other end of each strut. Insert the pins of the bracing struts into the holes on the main struts and the ends in the holes of the holder.

# Jigsaw cushions

P

Project

Intriguing, infinitely variable in size, shape and thickness, and easy to make, these striking jig-saw cushions can be used any-where in the home. The pattern illustrated here was chosen for a child's room, but the design can be tailored to suit any décor.

The same basic principles of cutting foam, building up a decor-ative appliqué and simple sewing apply to whatever pattern or size is chosen for the cushions. They can be used scattered around a room or to form a number of low-level seats. When pieced together, they form a comfortable mattress for sleeping.

The basis for this set of jigsaw cushions is a single sheet of high-density foam; choose a sheet with a minimum depth of 100 mm/4 in to make the cushions comfortable to sit on.

Start by drawing the desired jigsaw outlines on a sheet of card the same size as the foam; if it is impossible to obtain a large enough sheet, improvise by taping a number of sheets together. To make cutting easier, make the interlocking shapes as rounded and large as possible. Place a sheet of tracing paper, on which the picture pattern will be drawn, over the card and trace the shapes. Cut out the pieces of card and transfer their shapes on to the foam by drawing round them with a suitable marker.

Next, cut the foam into its various pieces. A fine-toothed hacksaw blade or sharp bread knife can be used for this, but an electric carving knife is ideal.

Using the same pieces of card as templates, transfer each jigsaw outline to a sheet of suitable fabric, such as calico, to be used as the backing for the appliqué, and to a second sheet to be used as the cushion base. Leave a seam allowance around each outline. Cut out the pieces accordingly.

Take the marked-up tracing paper and draw the desired picture pattern. Keep the picture as simple as possible and make sure that its outlines do not coincide with those of the jigsaw. Place the tracing paper over each piece of the material for the appliqué backing and transfer the tracing. Build up the decorative appliqué over the traced outline, cutting out the pieces and pinning them in place. Finally machine or hand sew them on.

The straight strips of material covering the sides of the cushions should be slightly narrower than the full width to be covered. For example, foam 100 mm/4 in deep requires only 89 mm/3½ in of material for the sides, excluding seam allowance. This helps to ensure a tight fit and also pulls the seams round on to the vertical sides.

Complete the covering as if for box cushions. Trim seam turnings before inserting the foam. Insert the pieces, check the fit and then hand sew the final seams.

*See also Tips on*
Murals and enlargements 3
Foam rubber 490

**Marking out the material pieces**
When marking out the pieces for the appliqué backing and base material, arrange the jigsaw templates on each sheet so that there is at least a 12 mm/½ in seam allowance around each template. Mark out both the outline of the template and the seam allowance.

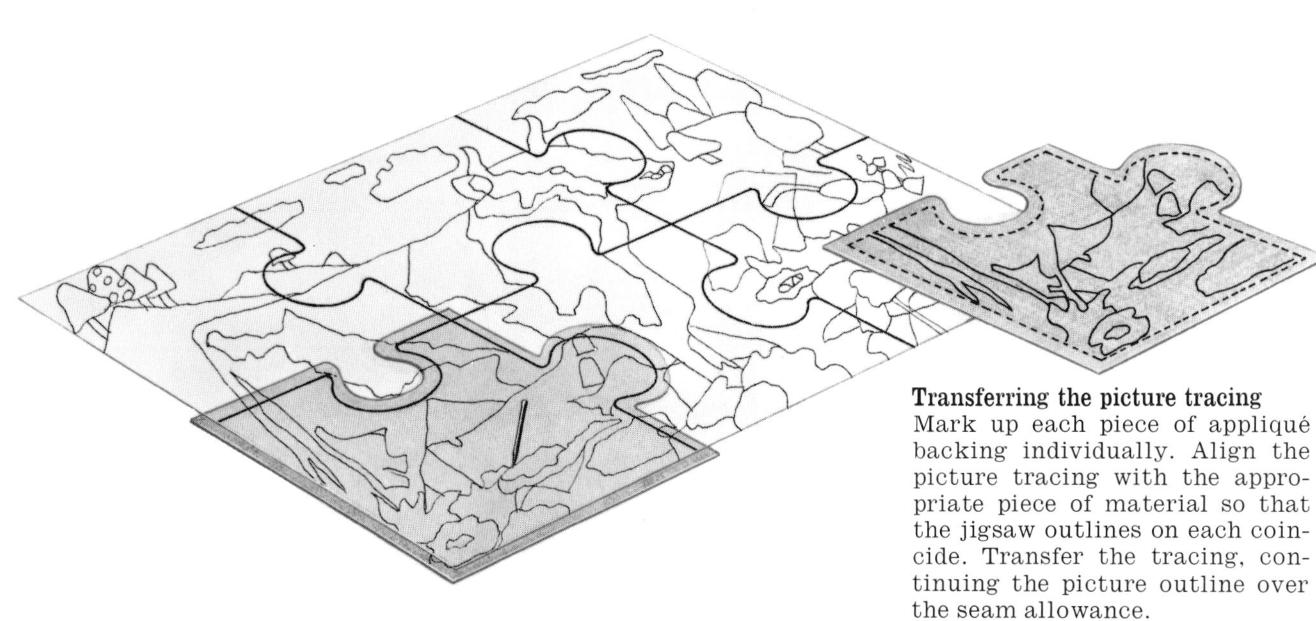

**Transferring the picture tracing**
Mark up each piece of appliqué backing individually. Align the picture tracing with the appropriate piece of material so that the jigsaw outlines on each coincide. Transfer the tracing, continuing the picture outline over the seam allowance.

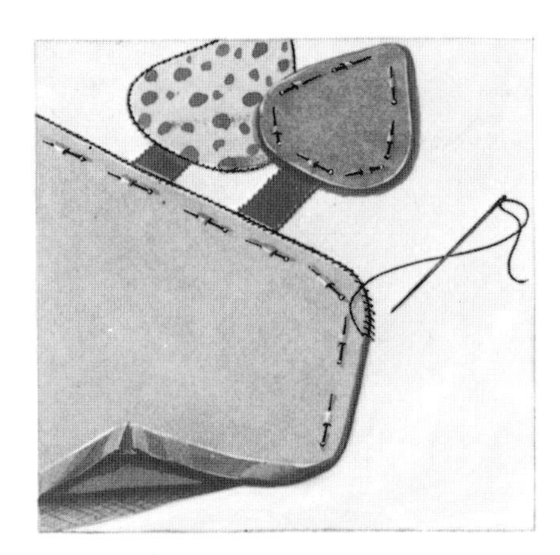

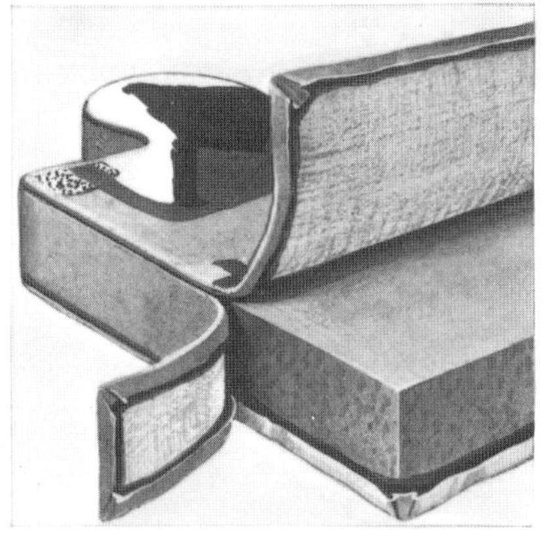

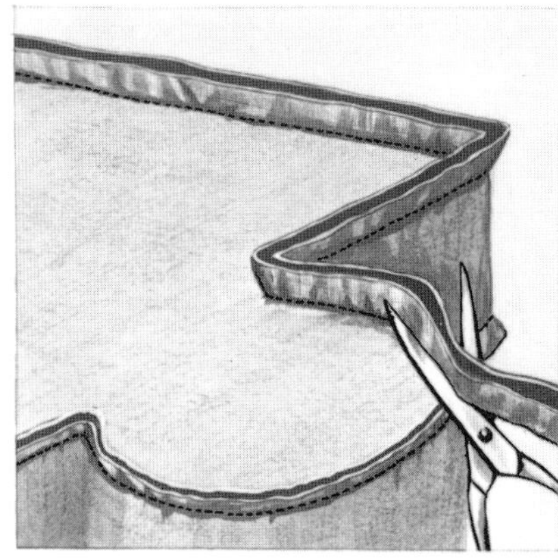

**Building up the appliqué**
Pin the various pieces of the appliqué "dry" first, so that any changes necessary in the design can be made without unpicking stitches. Where possible, hem the edges for a neater finish.

**Combining the sections**
Cut the side pieces a little undersize so that the foam is slightly compressed. Machine the pieces together with the appliqué and base material, leaving an edge unsewn to take the foam.

**Finishing off**
Turn the covering inside out. Trim off excess material around the seam turnings with a pair of sharp dress-making scissors. Turn right-side out, insert the foam and hand sew the final edge.

# Outdoor lounger

Snugly padded and easily transported, this light-weight folding lounger is especially suited for outdoor use. Its tough covering is water-resistant, its foam-based mattress makes it comfortable, its simple structure makes it easy to build. It can be used either as a low chair, when the position of its back rest and leg support can be varied for complete comfort, or laid out flat for sun-bathing. Pockets in the back provide handy storage.

**Materials**

**Panels:** Use 6mm/¼in five-ply. Two 889mm/35in by 610mm/24in for the backrest; two 356mm/14in by 610mm/24in to support the thighs and legs; and one 178mm/7in by 610mm/24in for the connecting section. Allow for smoothing.

**Padding:** Use Terylene wadding cut to ten equal lengths, 533mm/21in by 610mm/24in. Each piece sits on its own foam rubber base, 178mm/7in by 610mm/24in.

**Covering:** Choose a robust material, such as canvas, for the sleeves; two 2718mm/107in by 660mm/26in lengths are required. Choose a light waterproof material, such as kite fabric, for the top covering, 5258mm/207in by 762mm/30in.

**Preparing the sleeves and covering**

Lay one length of the canvas flat and position the five panels on top, butting them against each other. Mark up their positions on the canvas and then remove the panels. Place the second length of canvas over the first and machine down one long side, remembering to insert the handles where necessary. Trim the turnings and then turn right side out, spreading the lengths apart.

Position the top covering over the marked-up length of canvas and machine them together across their widths at 178mm/7in intervals to make the pockets for the padding. Allow about 254mm/10in in the material to get the pocket shape and make sure that the intervals coincide with the marked-up positions of the panels. Machine on pockets, if required, on the back panel material. Turn under and sew down one long side.

Turn the canvas lengths right sides together, insert the straps to take "D" rings at either end; machine the canvas ends and trim the turnings. Turn right sides out and hand sew the ends of the top covering.

To complete the sleeves, stitch through the three layers, remembering to leave the slots for the panels open.

**Assembly**

Insert the panels, smoothing them to fit, and sew the remaining long side of canvas by hand. Roll up each piece of wadding and insert it, with its foam base, into place. Finish by sewing the ends of the padded sections by hand.

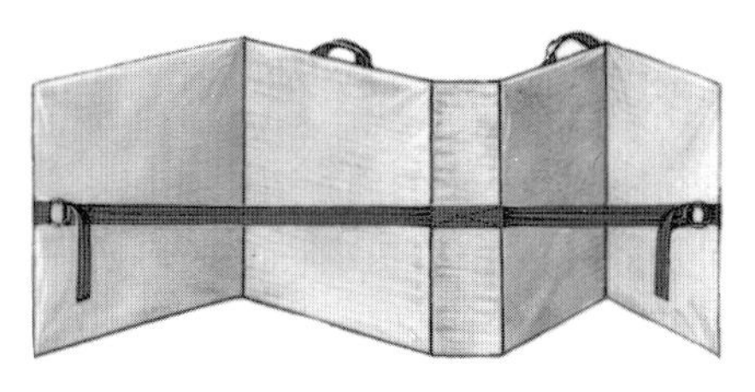

**Fitting the main strap**

Use upholsterer's webbing for the strap. Size the length needed with the lounger in the position illustrated. Machine to the underside of the connecting section.

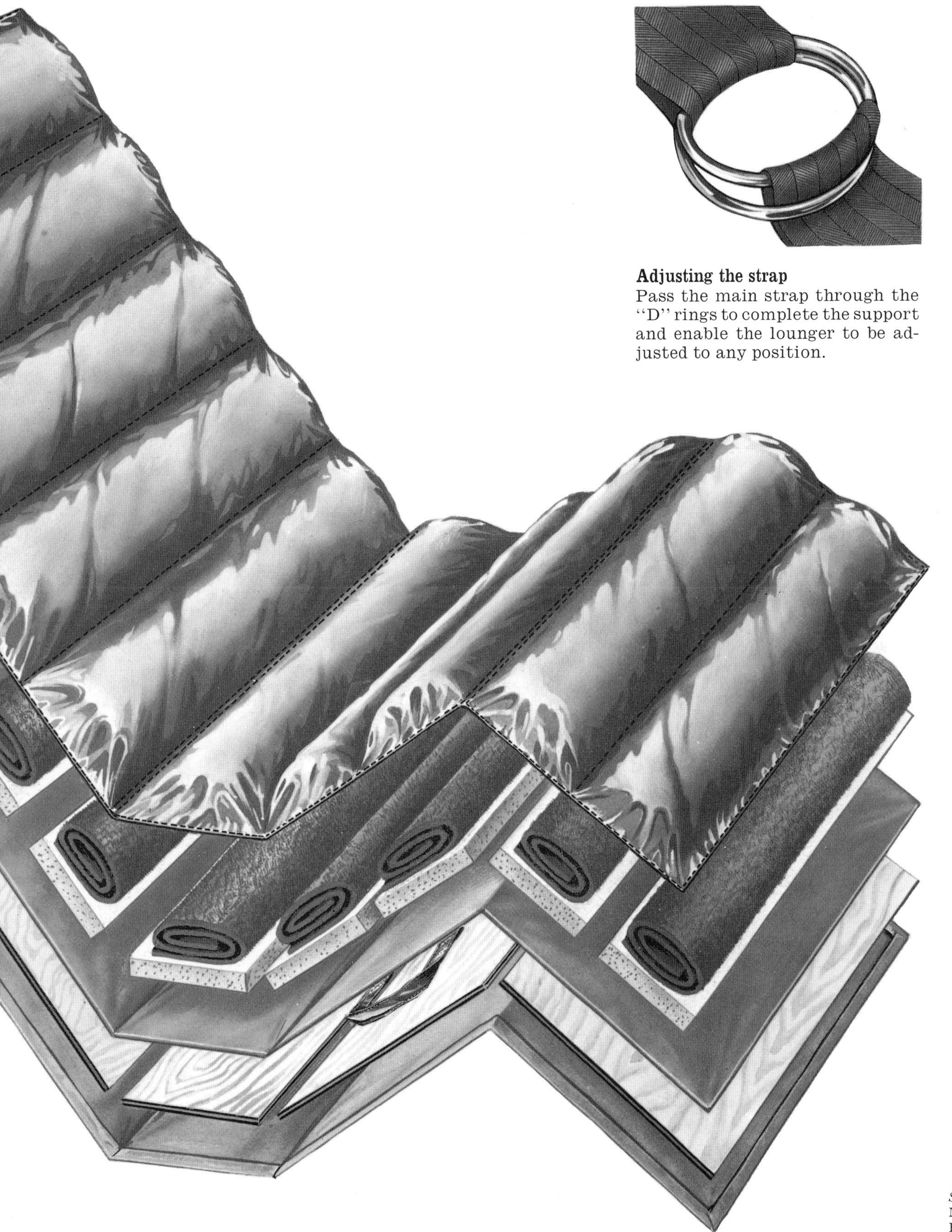

**Adjusting the strap**
Pass the main strap through the "D" rings to complete the support and enable the lounger to be adjusted to any position.

*See also Tips on*
Marking up 520
Foam rubber 490

# Room-in-one kits/1

Table, bed, bench-seat—which doubles as a spare mattress—and storage box are all neatly stacked in this colourful furniture nest, which meets all the furnishing requirements of a child's room and leaves space for playing.

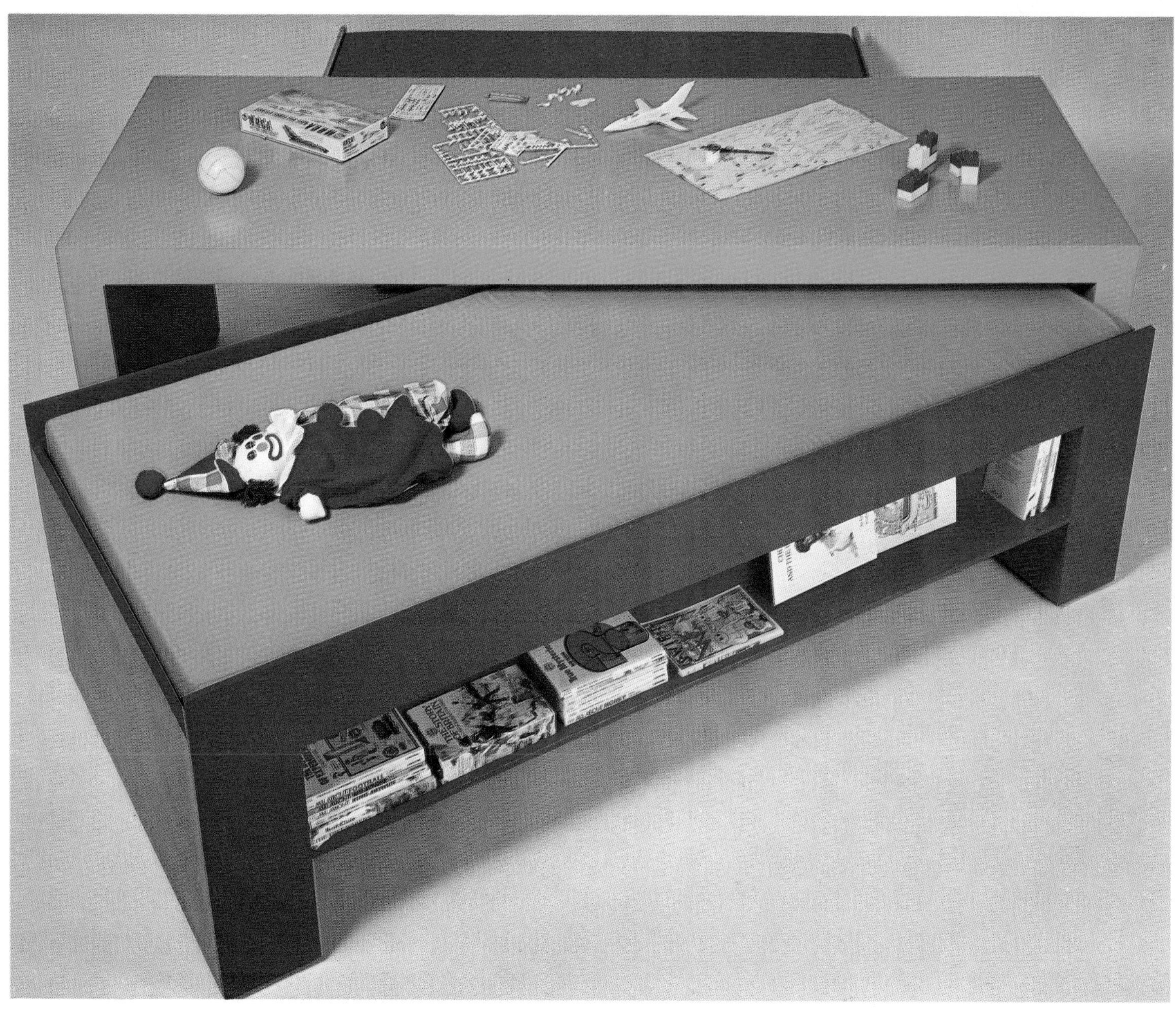

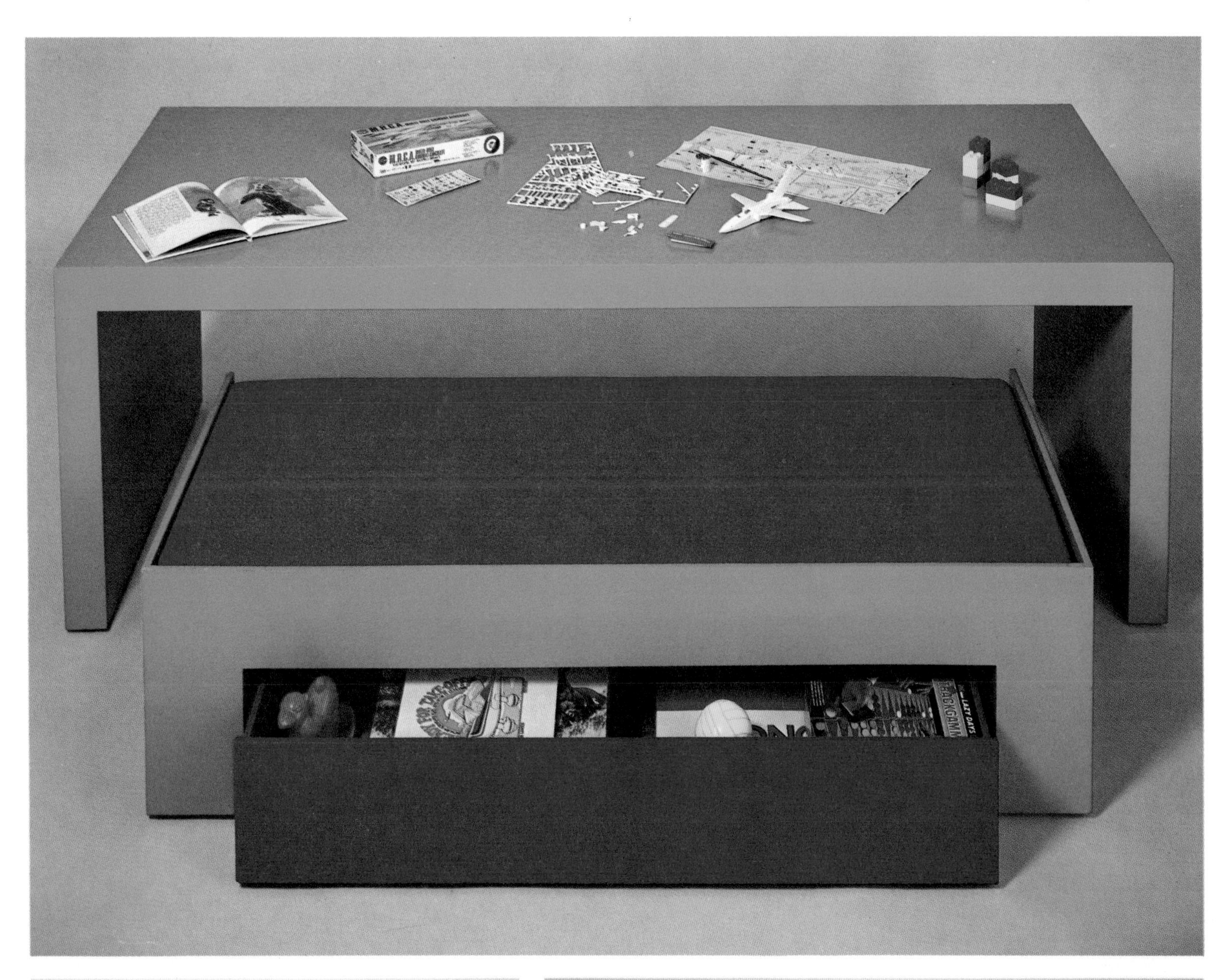

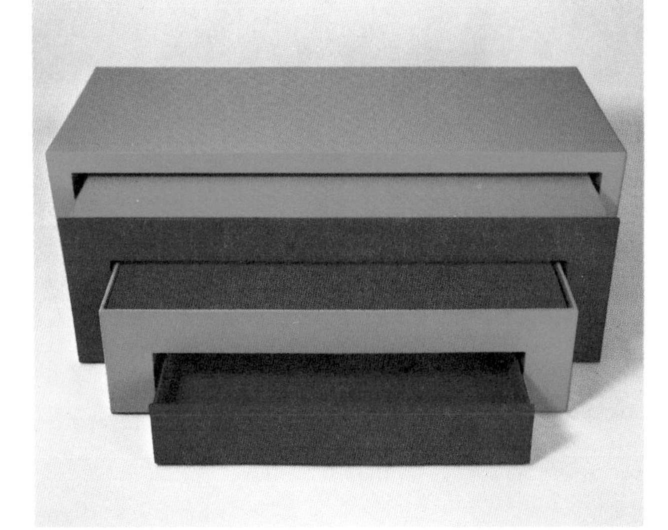

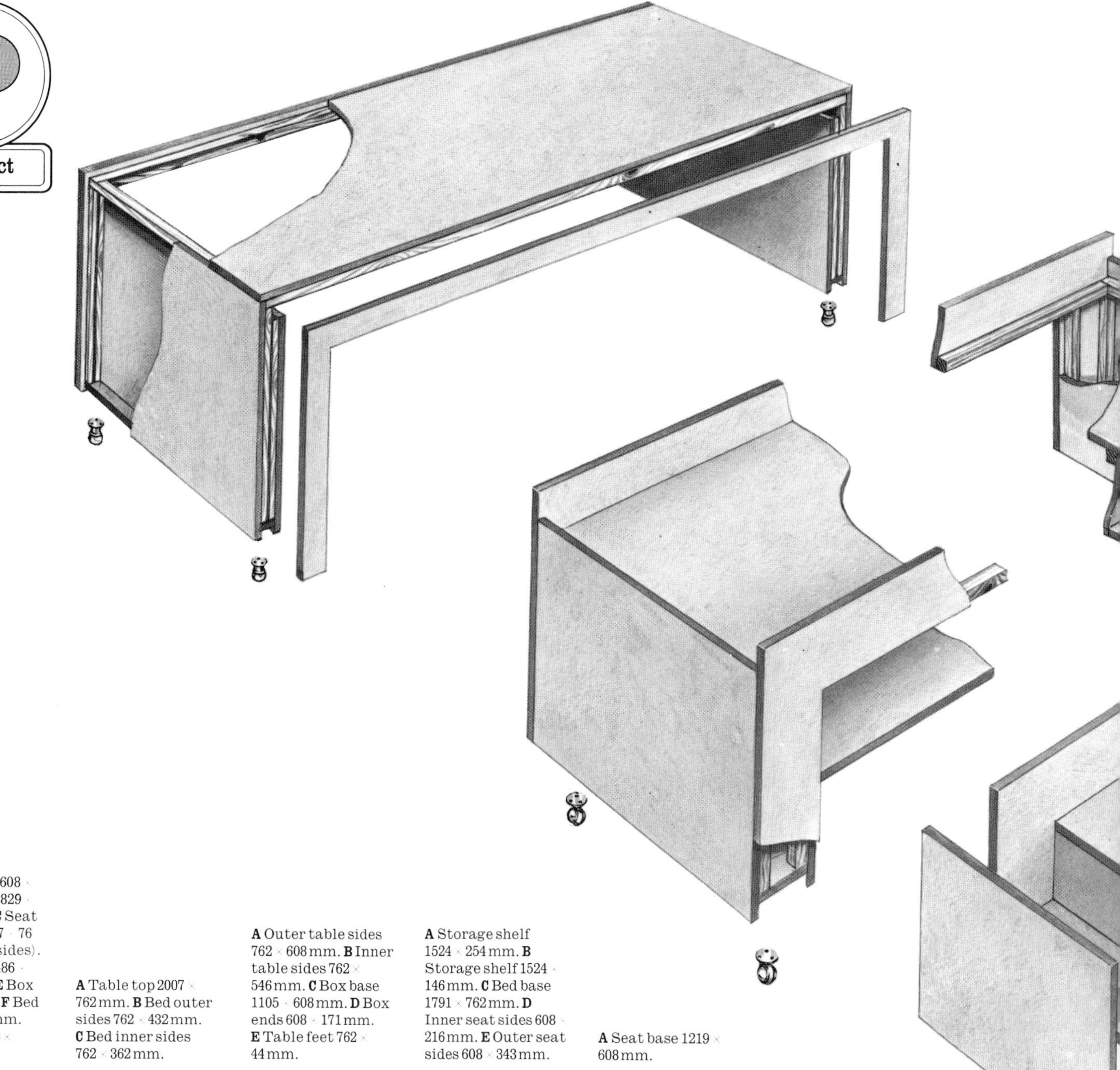

**A** Table 2007 × 608 × 76 mm. **B** Bed 1829 × 541 × 152 mm. **C** Seat front 1486 × 267 × 76 (top) 152 mm (sides). **D** Seat back 1486 × 343 × 152 mm. **E** Box 1143 × 171 mm. **F** Bed feet 762 × 114 mm. **G** Seat feet 608 × 114 mm.

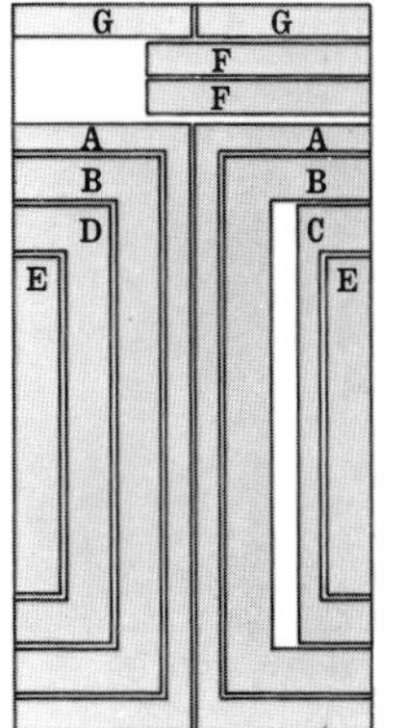


**A** Table top 2007 × 762 mm. **B** Bed outer sides 762 × 432 mm. **C** Bed inner sides 762 × 362 mm.

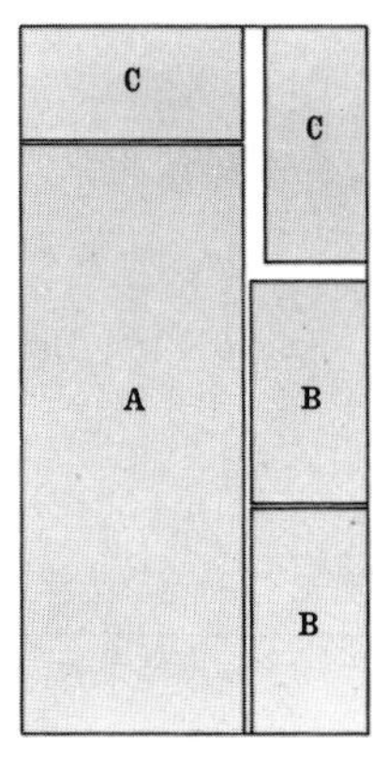


**A** Outer table sides 762 × 608 mm. **B** Inner table sides 762 × 546 mm. **C** Box base 1105 × 608 mm. **D** Box ends 608 × 171 mm. **E** Table feet 762 × 44 mm.

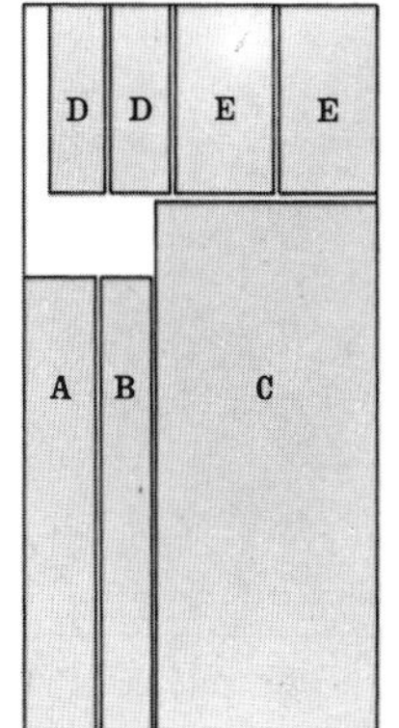


**A** Storage shelf 1524 × 254 mm. **B** Storage shelf 1524 × 146 mm. **C** Bed base 1791 × 762 mm. **D** Inner seat sides 608 × 216 mm. **E** Outer seat sides 608 × 343 mm.

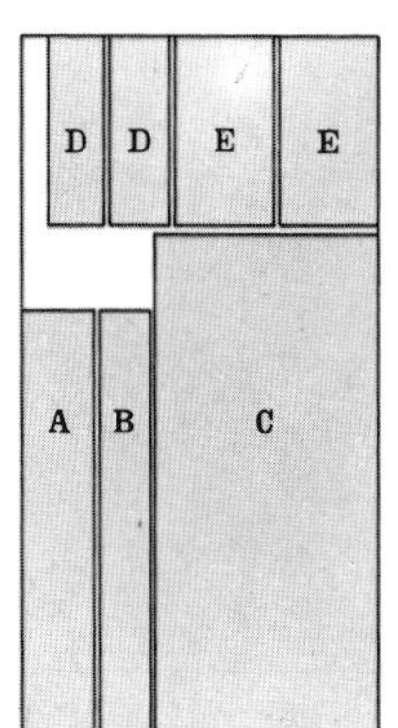


**A** Seat base 1219 × 608 mm.

# 144

The four units that go to make up the children's furniture nest—the table, bed, seat and storage box—can all be cut from four 19 mm/¾ in thick sheets of 2438 mm/8 ft by 1219 mm/4 ft chipboard, with one additional piece of 609 mm/2 ft by 1219 mm/4 ft. Follow the cutting diagram illustrated. The pieces for each unit are combined using a basic structure of supporting battens cut from 19 mm/¾ in square and 25 mm/1 in square softwood.

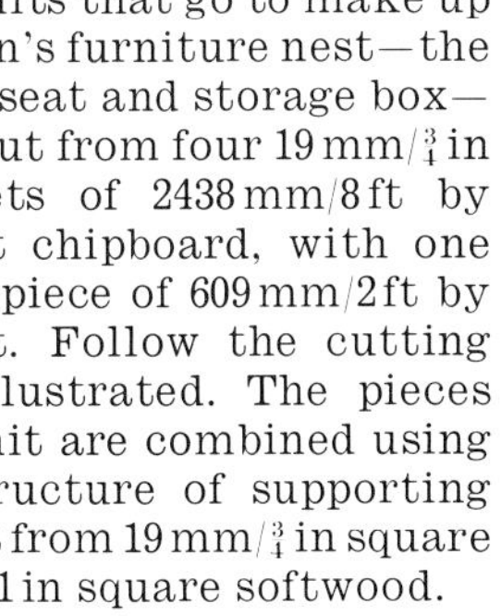

**Materials**

**Fronts, backs, sides, top, bases and feet:** Follow the cutting diagram.

**Table:** Two 1981 mm/78 in and two 723 mm/28½ in battens, 25 mm/1 in square for the top. Four 546 mm/21½ in outer leg battens and four 527/20¾ in inner leg battens, both sets 19 mm/¾ in square.

**Bed:** Three 1790 mm/70½ in battens and two 723 mm/28½ in battens, 25 mm/1 in square for the top. Eight 317 mm/12½ in outer and inner leg battens, 25 mm/1 in square. One piece of foam rubber, 1778 mm/70 in by 762 mm/30 in by 100 mm/4 in.

**Seat:** Two 1181 mm/46½ in battens, 25 mm/1 in square for the top. One 1447 mm/57 in by 584 mm/23 in by 100 mm/4 in and two 215 mm/8½ in by 584 mm/23 in by 100 mm/4 in pieces of foam rubber.

**Storage box:** Four 609 mm/24 in battens for the base, 25 mm/1 in square.

**Table**

Glue and screw the appropriate battens to the front and back chipboard pieces. Use a scrap piece of chipboard as a spacer block to ensure an even margin of 19 mm/¾ in—the thickness of the chipboard—around the edges. Use halving joints to join the two cross-battens to make a frame. Pre-drill the side and top chipboard panels and then position them against the batten supports, gluing and screwing them in place. Complete the unit by gluing the feet in position against the leg supports and pinning through the sides. Attach furniture glides to the feet. If necessary, cut back the ends of the battens to recess the feet to make the overall height to the floor 633 mm/24$\frac{13}{16}$ in. Use the same method of construction for the three remaining units.

**Bed**

Attach the batten supports to the front, back and side panels and assemble. Butt-joint the two pieces for the bookshelf, supporting the top edge against the central horizontal support and the bottom corners with two scrap support blocks. Fit the feet and castors to give a height to the floor of 514 mm/20¼ in.

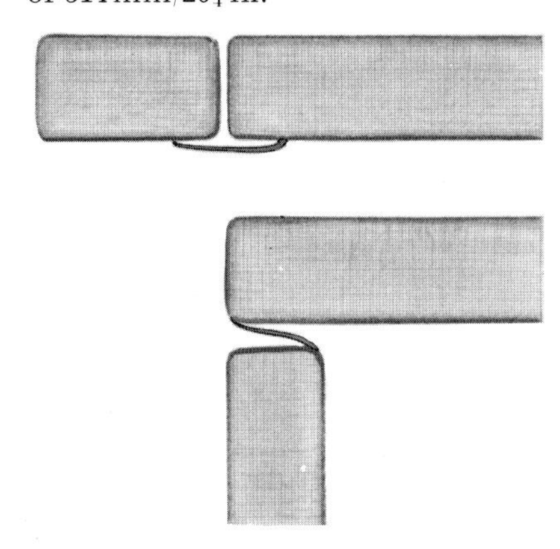

**Seat**

Cover the pieces of foam for the cushion and join them as illustrated. Attach the horizontal supports and assemble. Fit the feet and glides to give a height to the floor of 342 mm/13½ in.

**Storage box**

Butt-joint the sides and recess the base to take the castors.

**Finishing**

Finish all units by filling the end grain and pin and screw holes with fine-grain filler. Then paint.

*See also Tips on*
Marking up 253, 520
Adhesives 81
Cutting 112, 370
Joints 243
Finishing 18
Painting 706

# Room-in-one kits/2

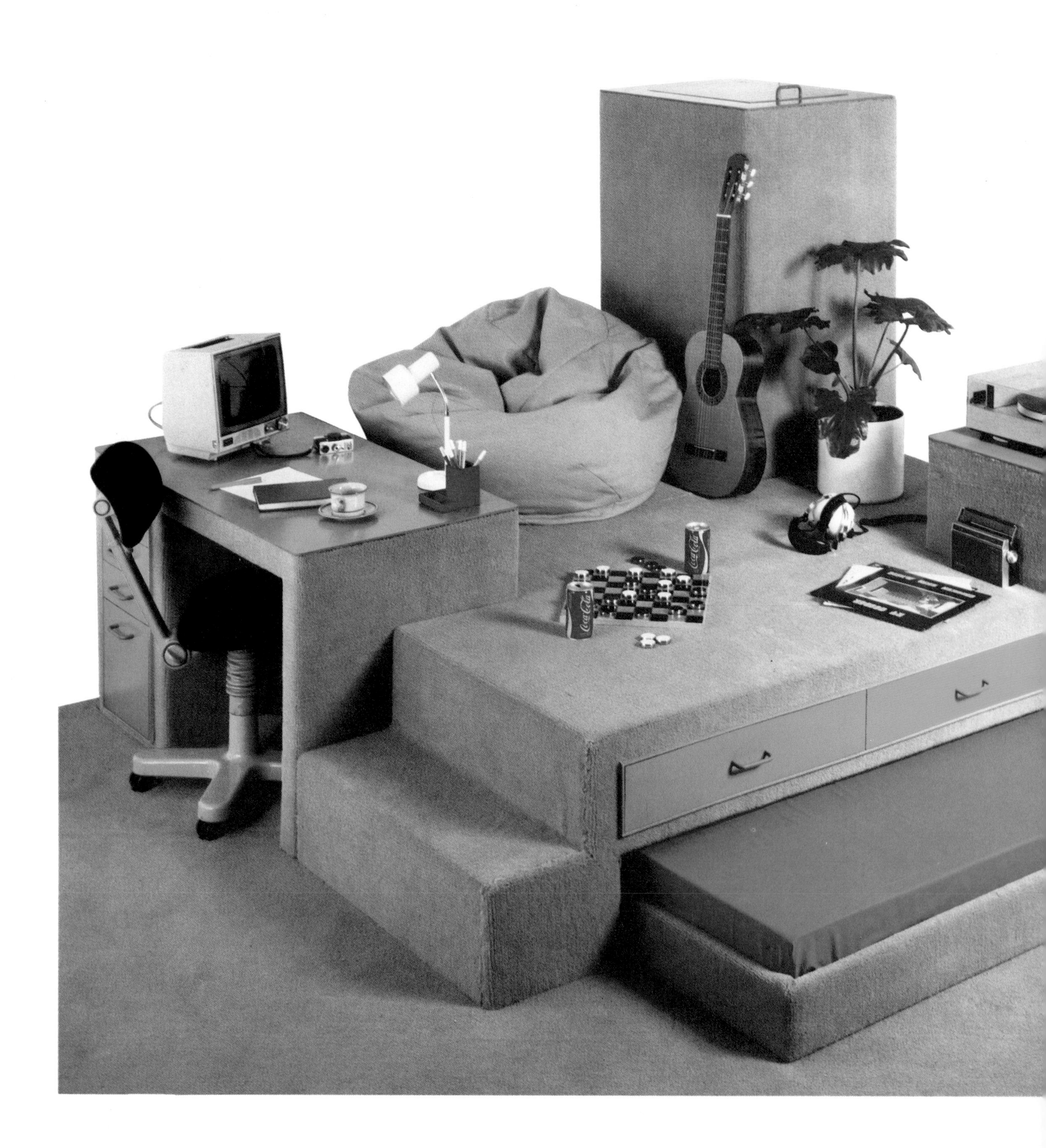

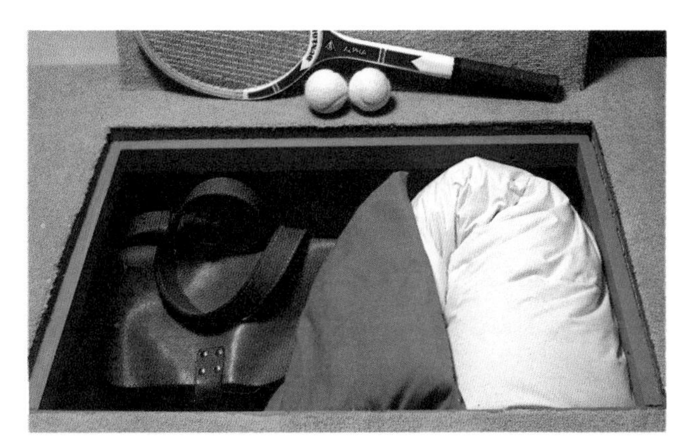

This complete room-in-one kit is especially tailored to meet the needs of the young. With a bed, work-table and ample storage everything is to hand.

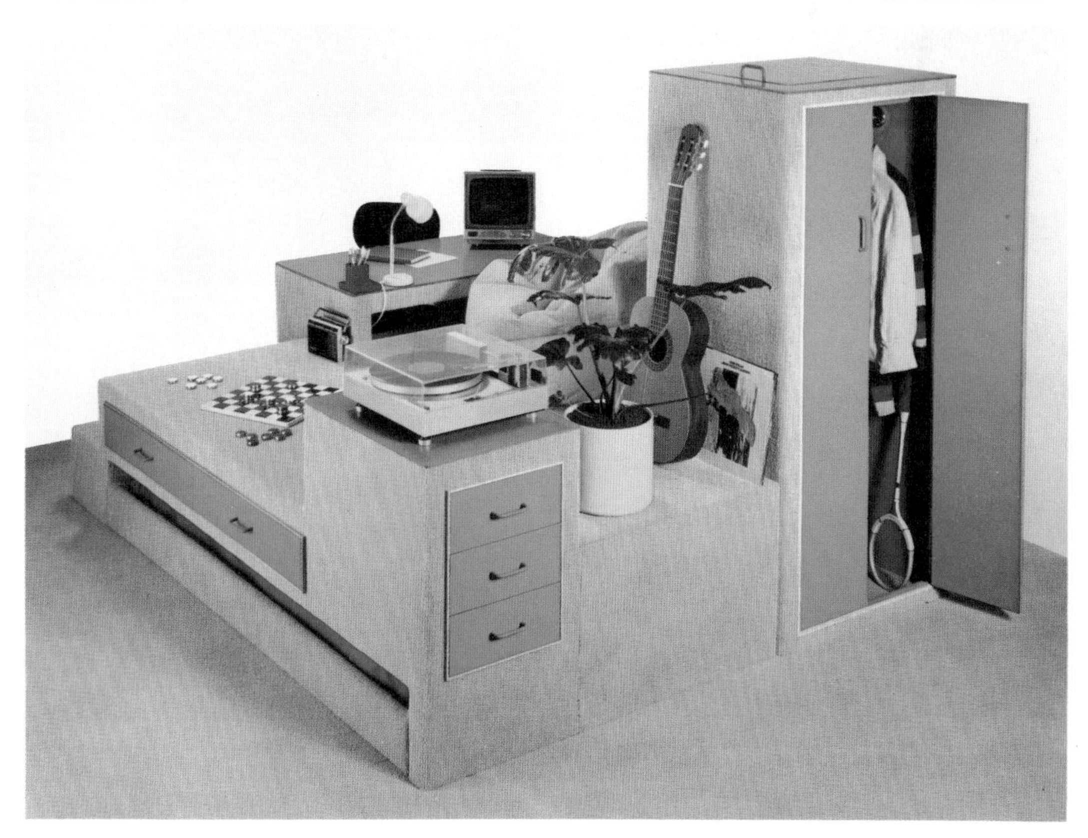

Most of the basic design elements of this teenage room unit can be adapted to suit individual needs and circumstances, but the overall height of the main plinth should be about 457 mm/18 in.

**Making the plinth**

Start by deciding on the basic shape of the plinth and then cut the sides, base and top from sheets of 12 mm/½ in chipboard. Plan the cutting carefully to make the most economic use of the material.

Secure the sides by gluing and screwing into adjoining sheets and into 50 mm/2 in square timber supports. Then, make a frame for the front—where the bed and drawers will be fitted—from the same thickness timber. Mark and cut positions for halving joints on the two supports and fit a cross-piece. Glue and screw the top rail into place and then glue and screw through the chipboard to attach the frame to the sides. Fit the chipboard base.

Next, insert the internal support panels, screwing and gluing into the existing supports and fitting additional ones where necessary. Fit strips of batten, the same thickness as the moulding, for positioning the drawers. Make the moulding by gluing together strips of mitred battening and then glue this into position in the front frame.

Make the drawers by simply butt-jointing pieces of chipboard together—but check the fit carefully. Attach handles to the fronts.

Finally, fit a hinged hatch with a fabric tab over the storage area and then fit the chipboard top. Make the step as a separate box, fitting bracing as for the plinth.

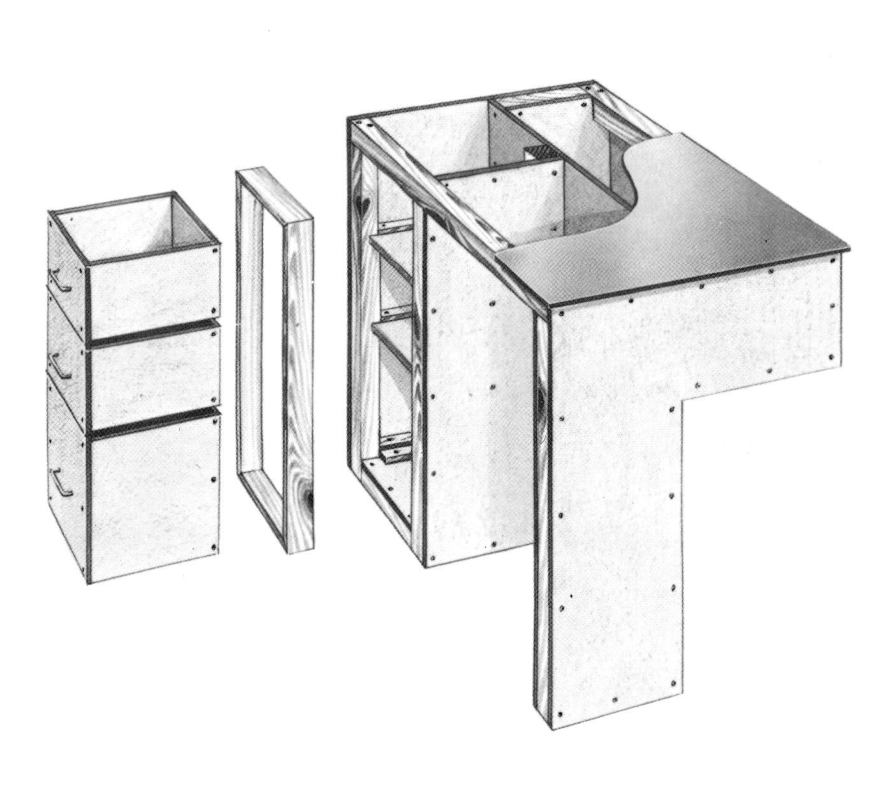

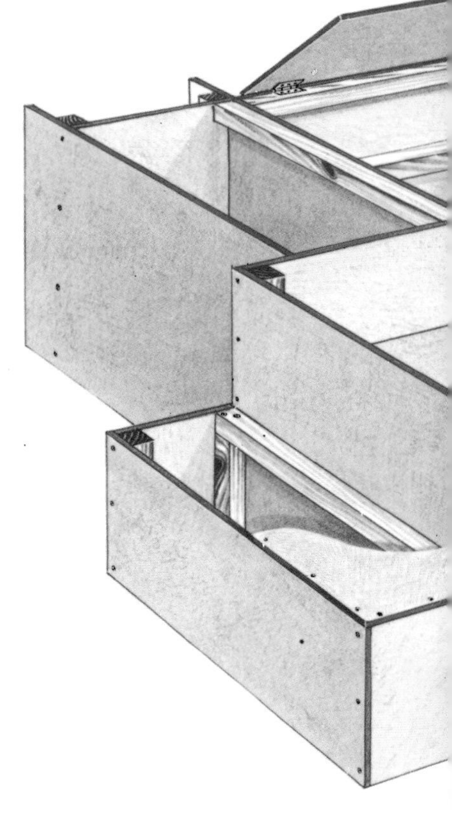

**Making the fittings**

All the fittings are constructed in basically the same manner as the plinth—by screwing, gluing and bracing pieces of chipboard. The most important point to remember is to size the chipboard carefully before cutting it, so that each fitting becomes an integral part of the whole unit; on the desk, for example, the L-shaped side and the overall width are critical factors.

When making the desk and corner unit, make a drawer frame and drawers as for the plinth. Cover each unit with a 3 mm/⅛ in thick laminated hardboard top so that it overlaps the unit by the thickness of the carpet. Glue the laminate on one side of the hardboard and then immediately glue the hardboard in place.

Fit the wardrobe with a ready-made hanging rail and the storage box with a hinged lid, which can be covered, on its inner face, with a mirror.

If fitting a bed, make a frame from lengths of 50 mm/2 in square timber. Mark up and cut halving joints for the cross-supports; fit these, and then glue a 6 mm/¼ in pegboard base in place for a mattress. Screw the chipboard sides into position. Mount the bed on furniture glides, screwed into support blocks glued into each corner.

Cover the units and plinth with foam-backed carpet, choosing one whose pile will not "open up" when fitted around right angles. Attach it with double-sided carpet tape. Try to avoid butt-joints on corners and edge all openings with 12 mm/½ in beading.

*See also Tips on*
Marking up 520
Adhesives 81, 496
Cutting 112, 370, 408
Joints 243
Smoothing 459
Finishing 18
Drawers 299
Carpeting 704

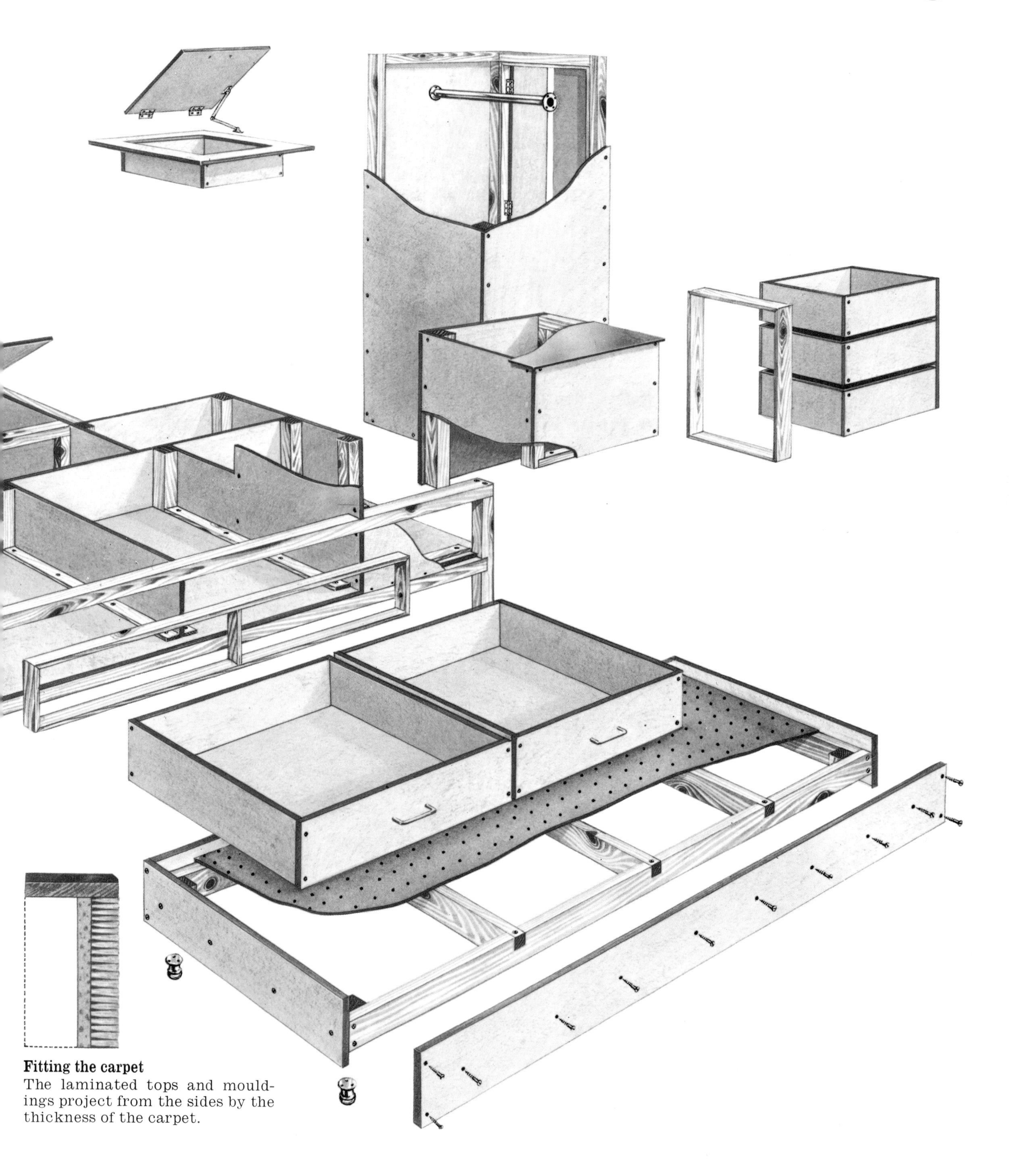

**Fitting the carpet**
The laminated tops and mouldings project from the sides by the thickness of the carpet.

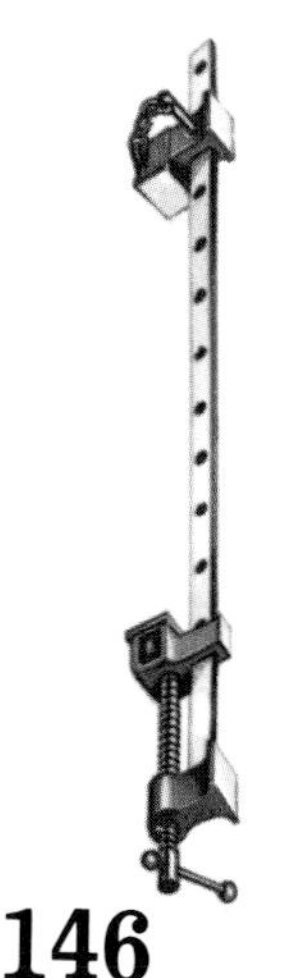

## 146
### Sash cramp

Use a sash cramp to grip the work together when undertaking major repairs. The shoe ends of the bar should always be fitted with wooden blocks about 6mm/¼in thick to avoid the risk of the cramp bruising or indenting work when it is tightened.

## 147
### Wallpaper offcuts

Fold offcuts of pasted wallpaper inwards—sticky faces together. Freshly pasted paper can be as dangerous to step on as a banana skin.

## 148 Giving exterior walls a pebble-dash finish

Pebble-dash a wall by first raking out the pointing between the bricks to a depth of about 19mm/¾in. This provides a key for the mortar. Then wet the wall thoroughly to prevent the mortar mix from drying out too quickly. Apply a mix of one part of cement, half a part of lime and three parts of sand to a depth of about 12mm/½in. While the mortar is still wet, scatter fine pebbles over the surface. Work in small areas, or the mortar will start to harden and the pebbles will fall off.

## 149 Removing heat stains from a polished surface

Remove white stains caused by hot dishes being placed on a polished surface by sprinkling cigarette ash on the stain. Rub the area of the stain gently with a soft cloth dipped in vinegar then dry and repolish.

## 150 Preventing a hammer head from slipping

Occasionally rub the head of a hammer with wire wool or emery paper. This stops the hammer head from becoming smooth, and the possibility of it slipping off a nail and marking the wood.

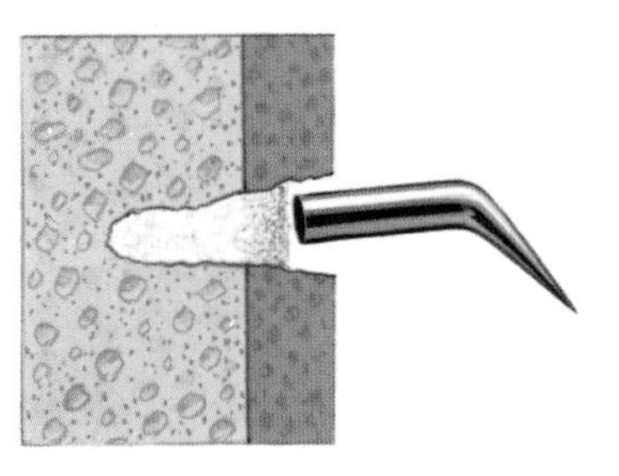

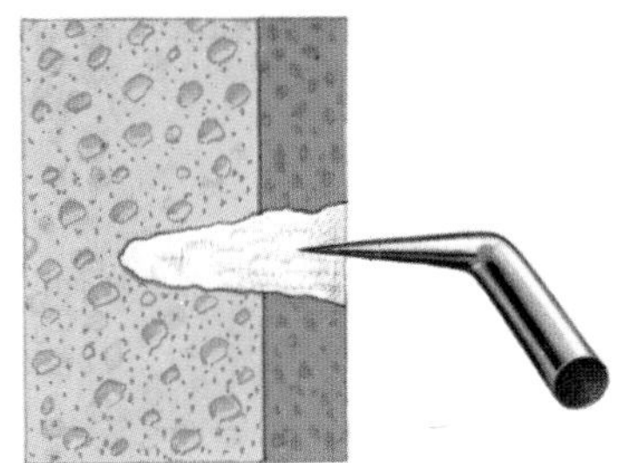

## 151 Making it easier to handle paint brushes

A paint platform is useful for keeping various-size brushes to hand and for wiping excess paint from a brush when using large tins of paint. It can be particularly useful when working from a ladder.

Make the platform from a piece of blockboard about 150mm/6in by 200mm/8in and 12mm/½in thick. Fit a 100mm/4in nail centrally along one 200mm/8in side, about 50mm/2in from the edge. Along the same side fit two hooks each side of the nail, about 25mm/1in from the edge. The two hooks catch on the lip of the tin to hold the platform in place.

Bend the nail so that the platform tilts at the required angle. Be careful, when getting near the bottom of the tin, not to lay heavy brushes at the back of the platform, or the tin may overbalance.

## 152 Painting carpeted and uncarpeted stairs

When painting uncarpeted stairs paint only every other step, so the staircase can still be used when the paint is drying. Alternatively, paint half-way across each step. When the paint has dried, complete the job. If the staircase is to be carpeted, only the visible area need be painted.

## 153 Fixing screws with asbestos compound

If, when fixing screws into a wall, the holes are too large or irregularly shaped for fibre or plastic plugs, use a non-shrink asbestos filling compound to ensure a rigid fixing.

First moisten the compound to a putty-like consistency. Then use the blunt end of the tool supplied with the filler to ram it in tightly until the hole is completely filled. Reverse the tool and press the pointed end centrally into the compound to make a starting hole for the screw. Remember to always wear a mask when working with asbestos; it is highly dangerous when inhaled.

## 154 Hammering down nail points in wood

When hammering over protruding nail points—a procedure known as clenching—always turn the points over at right-angles to the grain of the wood. Although it is easier to turn them with the grain so that the clenched ends are buried, there is a risk of the wood splitting—especially if the nails are fitted near the end of timber. If the point is too short to be bent, snip it off with pincers.

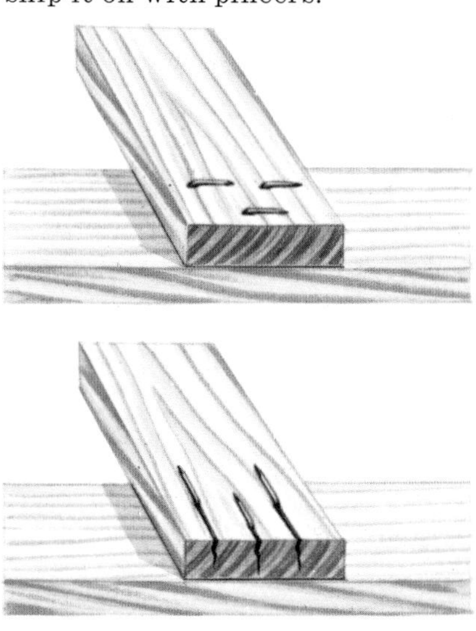

## 155 Repairing a cracked chimney stack

Having located the crack in a chimney, secure an extension ladder to the fascia board with a rope and use a ladder that hooks over the roof ridge to reach the stack.

If the crack is vertical, it is easier to pour the mortar mix down the crack rather than trowelling the mix into the cavity. First, clear all loose dust and brick and mortar chippings from the crack by scraping it out with a cold chisel and then by using a stiff brush. Wet the inside of the crack—taking care not to wet the face of the brickwork—and then press a length of wide, heavy-duty adhesive tape over the lower part of the crack. Cramp a piece of timber over the tape with a sash cramp to help hold it in place.

Mix one part of cement to three parts of sand and wet it until it has the consistency of a runny paste. Insert a funnel into the crack above the tape and pour the mix into the cavity. Allow it to set for about four hours, remove the board and tape, and repeat the process working progressively up the crack.

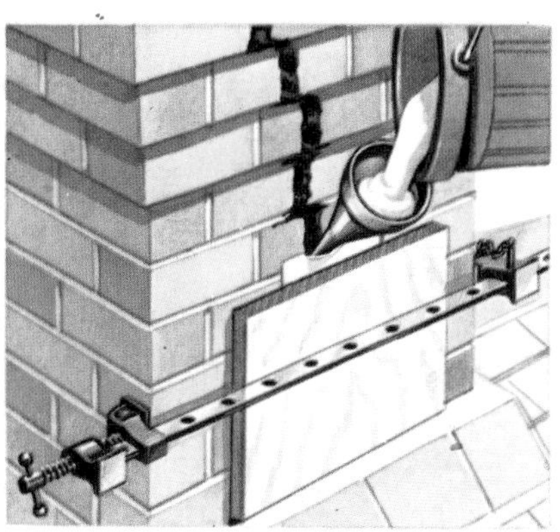

## 156 Paring a length of timber with a chisel

Always keep the chisel upright when using it for paring a piece of wood. To help ensure accuracy, always place the wood on a smooth surface, keep the head above the chisel and use the thumb of the right hand to apply the downward pressure when cutting. Guide the blade with the thumb and forefinger of the left hand. Smooth off the completed job with a file and then with glasspaper.

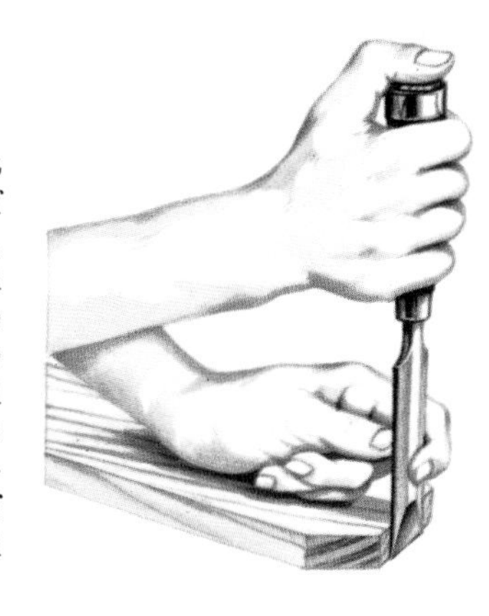

## 157 Painting plaster with emulsion

When painting plaster with emulsion, always apply a coat that has been thinned with water to the plaster first. This thinned-down coat helps seal the plaster for the second and third coats necessary for full coverage.

## 158 Nailing and screwing into concrete

Wooden dowels make good plugs for holes in concrete. Use a masonry bit to drill a hole in the concrete to match the size of the dowel. Fit the dowel and saw off any excess length. The nail or screw being used in the dowel spreads the wood so that it stays firmly in place.

## 159 Buying paint mixed to a special colour

When buying paint made up to a specified colour, make sure that the full quantity of paint needed is purchased in one order. Slight variations can occur when adding the colour pigment, even over a short time.

Always thoroughly stir the paint before using it, in case the pigments have separated out while it has been stored. In addition, if the paint has had to be made up in two or three tins, do not use the tins individually. Mix the contents together in a large container so that any colour variations that may occur between the tins will be blended.

## 160 Giving timber a rounded edge

Use a chisel as an alternative to a coping saw to cut a curve on a length of timber.

First, mark up the curve on the timber using a trimming knife and a suitable template, such as the lid of a paint tin. Cut off the corners of the timber, holding the chisel at an angle of about 45°. Then, with the chisel upright, pare the corners left by these cuts.

Continue to work round the timber, keeping the chisel's edge as close as possible to the line of the curve. Use a rasp to smooth off the exact shape of the curve and finally rub it down with a glasspaper block.

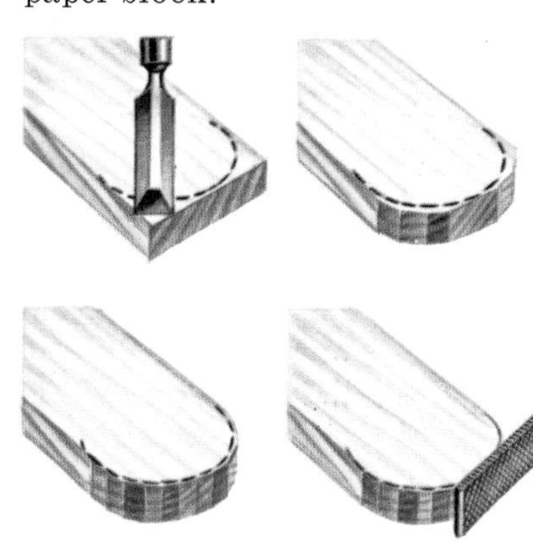

## 161 Removing saw burrs on soft metals

Remove saw burrs on soft metal tubing and sheeting, such as aluminium, copper and lead, by running the blade of a sharp penknife along the cut edges.

## 162 Keyhole saw

A keyhole saw or padsaw is often the only saw suitable for work in a very small area. Drill a hole with a diameter equal to the widest part of the saw blade as a starting point for the saw. Make sure that the hole is positioned on the inside of the proposed cutting line.

## 163 Working in a garage

Never use a naked light when working in a garage or loft—use a protected lamp on an extension lead.

# 164-168

## 164
### Wheel cutter

Always hold a glass-cutting wheel between the first two fingers, supporting it with the forefinger from above and the thumb from below. To nibble small pieces from a sheet of glass, use the appropriate notch of the cutter and wiggle it like a lever.

## 165
### Paraffin heaters

Never fill a paraffin heater to the brim of the filling hole. The fuel expands when hot and will seep out, creating a fire risk.

## 166 Reinforcing joints with brackets

When necessary, reinforce simple woodworking joints by fitting metal brackets on each side of the joints. A metal "T" can be used to join timbers at right-angles to a main framework and an "L" for reinforcing corner joints. Use angle brackets to help support shelves, and rectangular brackets to make simple household repairs, such as mending a split in a kitchen stool or chair.

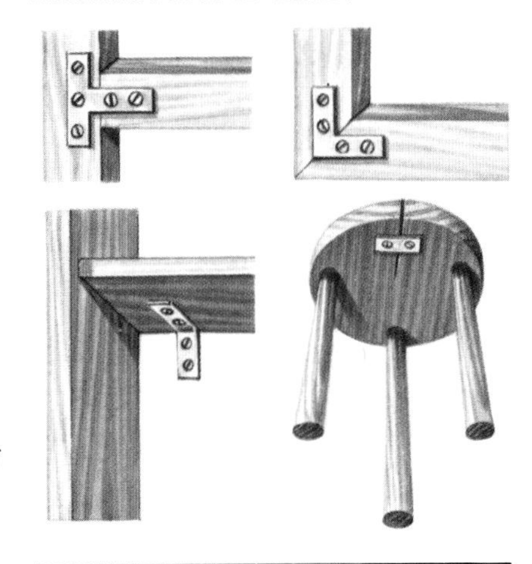

## 167 Fitting angle brackets tightly into corners

To ensure that an angle bracket fits tightly into a corner, place a piece of card under the part of the bracket to be fitted to the overlapping timber. Screw the angle bracket in place on the side frame, remove the card, and screw the bracket to the top of the frame. The gap created by the card ensures that the bracket is pulled tightly into place.

Do not place the card against the side frame, or the joint will be pulled out of place when the screws are being tightened. Make sure the brackets are rust-proof.

## 168 Cutting a large hole in a glass sheet

To cut a hole in a sheet of glass, first make a plywood template 6mm/¼in smaller than the size of the hole to be cut. This reduction allows for the distance between the wheel and the edge of the glass-cutter when it is placed against the template.

Place the glass flat on a smooth, level surface padded with thick cloth or newspapers and, holding the template firmly in position, score round it with the wheel of the glass-cutter, making sure that the start and finish of the scored line join up. From underneath the glass, tap the scored line with the head of the cutter—the wheel facing downwards—to start the cut "running". Still working from underneath, press upwards from the starting point to make the cut "run" around the entire hole. This stage is completed when a bright double line shows round the edge.

Next, score four curved lines from edge to edge of the hole and score a dozen or more small cuts within the centre area. Tap each of the curved lines from underneath as before, so that the glass is cut along these four lines as well as round the hole itself. Working from underneath again, hold the cutter upright and use the end of the pointed handle to tap the central scored lines.

Do not be afraid to strike the glass firmly. Provided that all four curved lines and the line around the hole have been made into proper cuts, any cracks will stop when they meet a cut line.

Gradually break up the centre portion of the marked-out area until the hole is large enough for the teeth of the glass-cutter to be inserted into the glass from above. Use the cutter's teeth to nibble into the edge of the glass, working in a circular movement towards the edge of the hole. Gradually, the pieces of glass within the cut lines will begin to fall away—although a few gentle downward taps from above with the handle of the cutter may be needed to remove the final pieces. Smooth off the edges using the fine face of an oilstone and working with the stone at an angle of 45°.

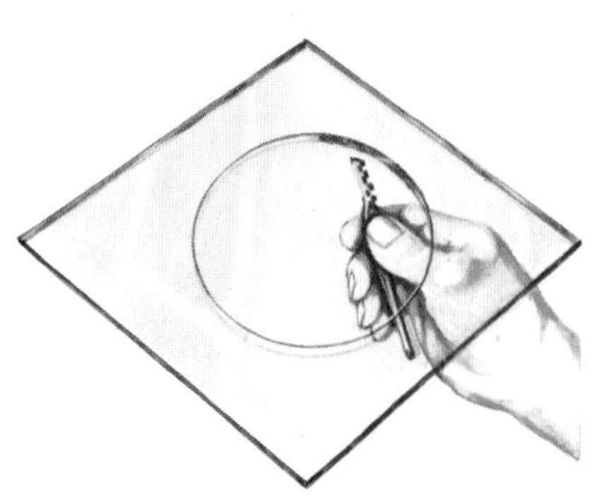

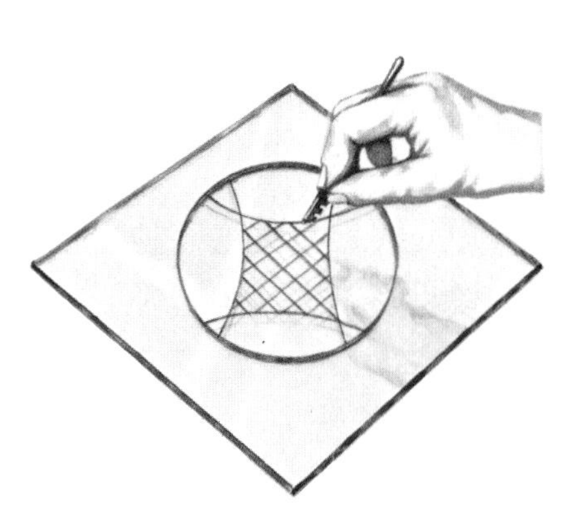

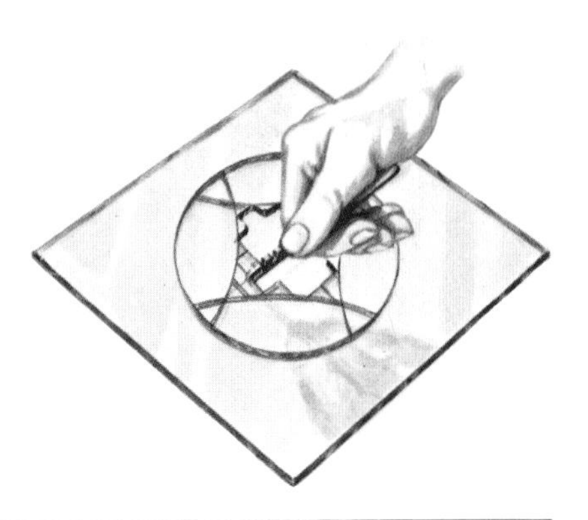

## 169 Drilling through glass and mirrors

Always use a lubricant—preferably turpentine substitute—when drilling a hole in a piece of glass or a mirror. Place the glass flat on a padded bench and mark the centre of the hole to be drilled with a wax crayon. Keep the lubricant in place by rolling out a small length of putty about 6 mm/¼ in in diameter, and forming it into a circle around the point where the hole is to be drilled. Fill the circle with the lubricant and, using a tungsten-tipped spear-pointed bit in a power drill, start drilling at slow speed, while applying steady pressure.

When the drill is about three-quarters of the way through the glass, turn the sheet over and—again using the lubricant—start drilling from this side. Make sure that the drill head is exactly centred on the original hole. Ease off the pressure on the drill just before joining up with the original hole. If the drill is forced through, it can cause pieces of glass to break away, leaving splinters around the hole.

When drilling a mirror, always start from the silvered side, so that the position of the partly drilled hole can be seen when the mirror is turned over.

## 170 Cutting patterned or frosted glass

Always cut from the smooth side when cutting patterned glass and frosted glass or the wheel of the glass-cutter will be blunted.

## 171 Making a glasspaper block for curves

Make a simple glasspaper block, for smoothing the inside surfaces of small holes or concave curves, from a 100 mm/4 in length of hosepipe cut along its full length. Cut the glasspaper large enough for its two ends to be inserted within the gap in the hosepipe.

## 172 Painting metals to prevent rusting

With the exception of galvanized metal, always give metals two coats of gloss paint after they have been primed and undercoated. This helps prevent them from rusting. Make sure that the undercoat and first coat are completely dry before applying the final coat. Because galvanized metal has more resistance to rust, it can be finished off with one coat of gloss.

## 173 Soldering aluminium to get a good bond

When soldering aluminium, first thoroughly clean the surfaces to be joined with a fine-grade emery paper. Then heat the surfaces with a blowlamp until they are hot enough to melt solder pressed against them and—wearing heat-resistant gloves—coat the joint with a special aluminium solder (obtainable from builders' merchants). Gently rub the solder with wire wool to spread it all over the surface—a process known as "tinning".

When both surfaces have been "tinned", press them together and reheat with a blowlamp to melt the solder again. When the joint has cooled, the surfaces will be bonded.

## 174 Points to watch when buying timber

The most important point to check when buying timber is that it is properly seasoned—that the timber has been allowed to dry out naturally after being felled and cut into planks. The general rule to follow is that softwoods, such as redwood and spruce, should be seasoned for at least a year, and that hardwoods, such as oak, mahogany and teak, should be seasoned for one year for every 25 mm/1 in of their thickness. Finally, when buying any type of timber, always check that the colour of the wood is even and that it has been stored level. Also watch for the presence of knots, shakes and brittle heart.

## 175 Smoothing timber without scratching it

Always rub the glasspaper in the direction of the grain when smoothing a timber surface. If the glasspaper is rubbed across the grain it will leave scratch marks. These will show up through coats of varnish and even through a thin paint finish.

## 176 Carrying large sheets of wood

Tie a length of rope into a loop—knotting it securely—to make a simple carrier for large sheets of blockboard or plywood. The rope should measure slightly more than twice the length of the board. Hook the rope around the two bottom corners of the board and grasp it in the centre.

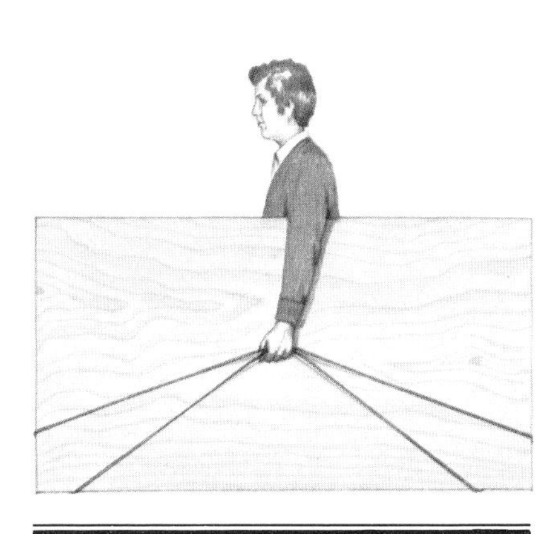

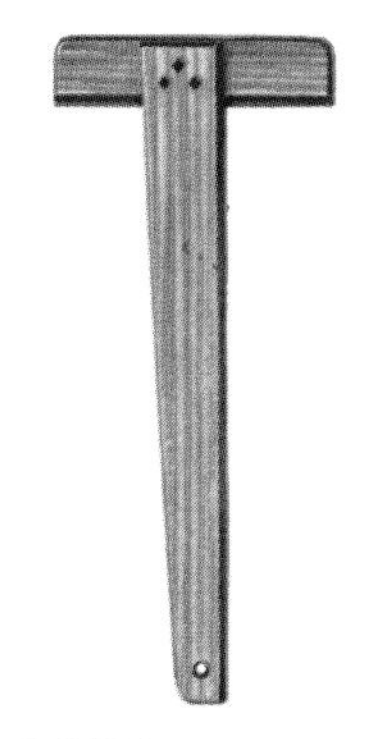

## 177 T-square

A wooden T-square can often swell out of true because of moisture in the air. To make sure that the drawing edge of the T-square is accurate, place it on a drawing board and draw a line. Turn the T-square over, and draw a line against the first line. If the square is true, the lines will "read" as a single line.

## 178 Carrying glass up ladders

Unless you are experienced, as well as confident, never carry glass up a ladder—get a professional to do the job for you.

# 179-187

## 179
### Hawk

Use a hawk to carry small quantities of plaster to a wall while working. The tool is made from a piece of 6 mm/¼ in thick plywood about 300 mm/12 in square. Nail through the board to attach a short length of broom handle.

## 180
### Working on a ladder

Never take a chance and work on a ladder in a high wind. A sudden gust can easily cause you to lose your footing.

## 181 Removing burrs from a shortened bolt

When shortening bolts, thread a nut on to the bolt past the point where the cut is to be made. Use a hacksaw to cut the bolt to the required length and then unthread the nut. This removes the burr made by the hacksaw blade during the cutting process.

## 182 Thinning wood primer to make it easy to use

If wood primer paint is difficult to use because of its thickness, thin it with equal amounts of linseed oil and turpentine substitute.

## 183 Fitting foamed-backed carpet against skirting

Lay a length of 3 mm/⅛ in thick plywood against the skirting and under the piece of carpet to be cut. If necessary, scribe the plywood to the skirting. Push the carpet against the skirting and staple it to the plywood. Turn the carpet and plywood back and, using another piece of wood as a cutting block, trim the carpet flush with the edge of the plywood. Carefully remove the staples and fit the carpet into place.

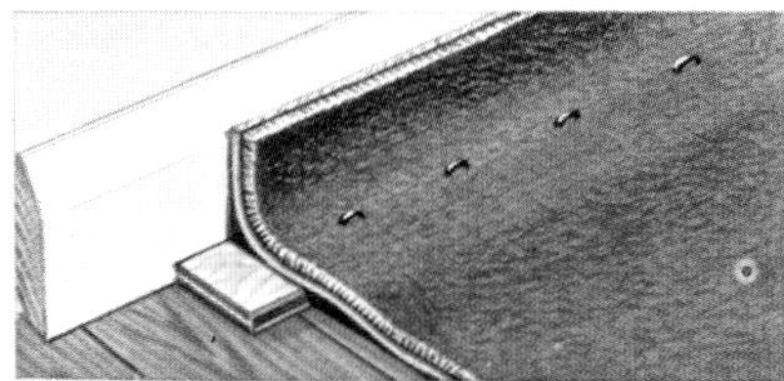

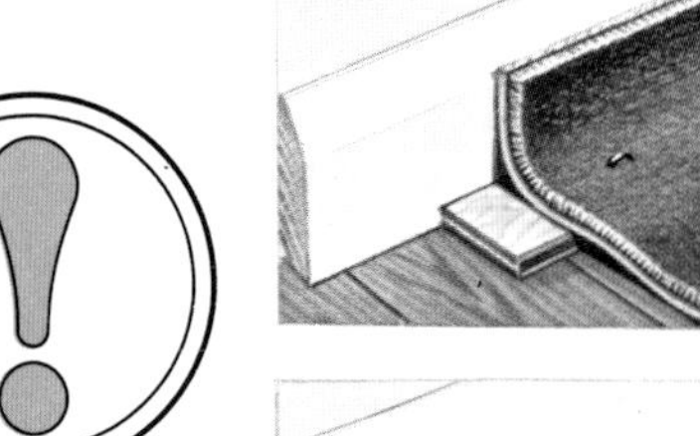

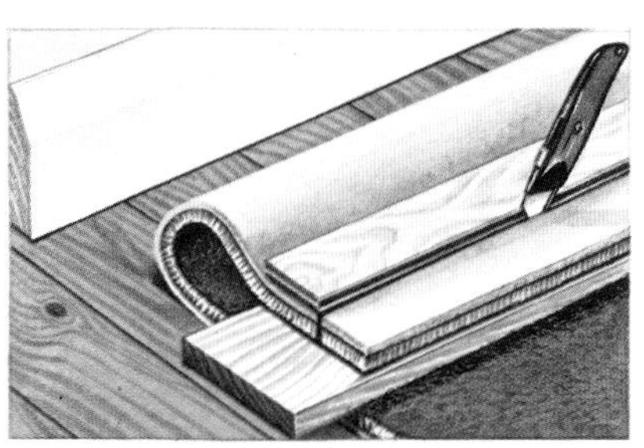

## 184 Hanging lining paper before wallpapering

When lining walls prior to wallpapering, hang lining paper horizontally. This provides a better "key" to hanging the wallpaper and avoids any possibility of fitting one butt joint over another, which makes the disguising of the joint very difficult.

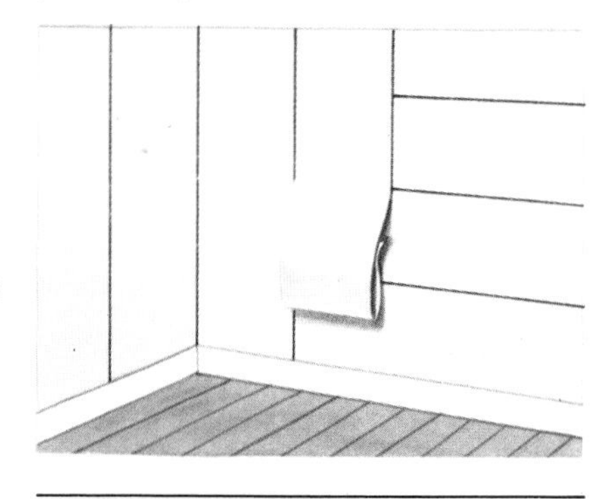

## 185 Giving timber a wax finish

Use a silicone wax for a durable finish on most timbers. The darker the wood usually the more suited it is to waxing. For the best finish always seal the timber first. Work one coat of the sealer well into the grain using a brush or cloth, and then smooth the surface down. If necessary repeat the procedure. Apply the wax generously with a cloth, again working well into the surface. Complete the application by lightly rubbing with the grain. Leave the wax to harden for several hours. Rub the wax finish up with a soft brush and buff with a cloth, again with the grain. Finally apply two further coats, leaving at least a day between each coat.

## 186 Checking reground chisel and plane bevels

To make the best use of a chisel or plane blade, regularly check that the bevel of each has been reground to the correct angle by measuring the bevel's depth. This should be 2½ times the thickness of the blade at its square edge—the bevel of a 6 mm/¼ in blade, for instance, should be 15 mm/⅝ in deep for the angle to be correct.

## 187 Sharpening chisel and plane blades

Chisel and plane blades should be sharpened before use. The right way to sharpen them is to grind the bevel of the blade to an angle of 25°, and to hone the cutting edge to an angle of 30°. Shape the bevel on an abrasive wheel, regularly dipping the blade in water and working it from side to side to ensure even wear on the wheel.

Use an oilstone to shape the cutting edge. Make sure the stone is kept well oiled with a thin oil, and use a honing guide to maintain the correct angle on the blade. Hone the blade away from you in long strokes down the full length of the stone, keeping the edge pressed firmly against the stone. This process will raise a slight burr of metal along the edge. Remove this by turning the blade over, and, keeping it perfectly flat, making one stroke down the stone. Repeat the process until the burr is removed.

## 188 Tiling kitchen and bathroom walls

Take special care when marking out a kitchen or bathroom wall for ceramic tiling. This is necessary because floor levels are seldom exactly true, so they should never be relied upon as an accurate starting point.

First, fix a horizontal batten the height of a tile above what appears to be the lowest point on the floor or skirting, making sure that it is positioned accurately by laying a spirit level along its length. Check, by sliding a tile along the floor or skirting, that the tile height is not exceeded at any point along the batten. This is important, because it is preferable to fit the bottom row of tiles by cutting them rather than to leave small gaps that will be awkward if not impossible to fill. If the floor does drop more than the height of a tile, lower the batten so that the biggest gap left does not exceed one tile width.

Next, calculate the number of full tiles needed to cover the full width of the wall and mark where the exact centre of this row of tiles will fall. Fix a vertical batten at this centre point—again checking with a spirit level that its position is exactly true.

Begin tiling from the left-hand corner created by the two battens, working horizontally and building upwards. Apply the adhesive directly to the wall with a serrated spreader, working in areas about 300 mm/12 in square and finishing off by spreading the adhesive in horizontal lines. Press the tiles into position and, unless they are fitted with spacer lugs, place matchsticks between each tile to get an even spacing for grouting. Every two or three rows check that the horizontal and vertical are still accurate, because tiles tend to "creep" out of alignment. Once this half of the wall has been tiled, remove the battens and tile the rest of the wall by eye. Leave the job to dry for twenty-four hours—longer, if necessary.

When the adhesive has dried, grout the tiles. Remove the matchsticks and, working with the palm of the hand and fingers or a small piece of sponge, rub grouting compound into all the joints. The compound should be mixed to the consistency of a fairly thick cream.

As the compound dries, rub off the surplus with a dry cloth and then finish the joints by running a rounded stick down them to get an even, slightly concave, finish to the grouting.

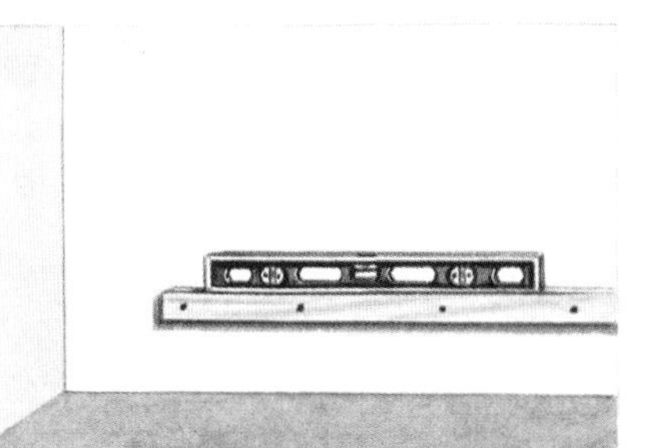

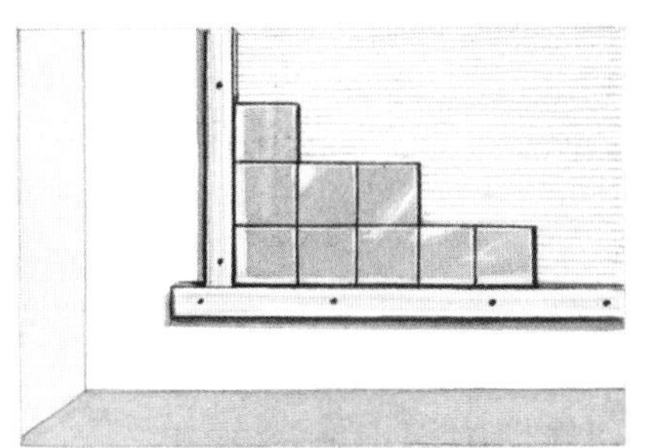

## 189 Preparing damp inner walls for papering

Line the inside of damp walls with aluminium foil, using a proprietary adhesive, before wallpapering. First, remove any old paint and wash the surface down with a solution of one part of ammonia to eight parts of water. Leave it to dry and then apply the foil, smoothing it down carefully to avoid creasing.

## 190 Painting furniture with a brush or spray gun

Spread sheets of newspaper over the floor and stand each leg of the chair or table in the lid of a tin before painting. If the legs stand directly on the paper, they will stick to it as the paint dries and the finish may be spoiled. For speedier coverage use a paint spray gun. Hold a card behind the legs to block most of the spray.

## 191 Working with a chisel over large areas

Whenever possible, chisel from side to side, at an angle, rather than force the chisel straight ahead. This extends the life of the cutting edge. Keep the bevel face down for the rough cut and reverse it for paring.

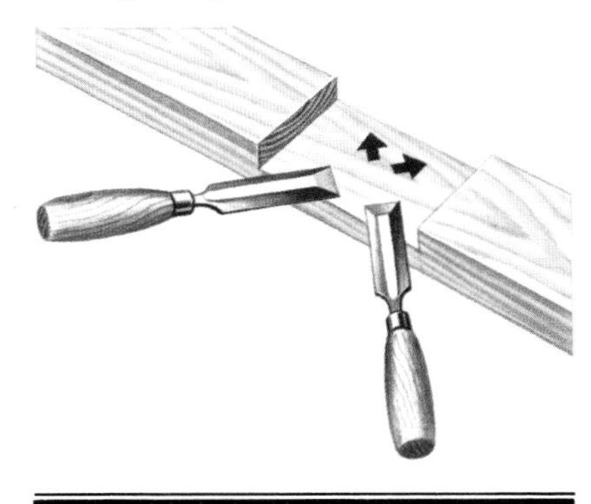

## 192 Repairing the surface of a concrete path

Resurface cracked concrete paths with a strong mortar mix of one part of cement to three parts of sand. First, break up the whole path into small pieces with a heavy hammer. Make sure the pieces are well rammed down and then wedge boards into position with wooden pegs at 1 m/3 ft intervals on each side of the path, extending them above the existing surface by 25 mm/1 in. Coat the surface with a PVA bonding agent, obtainable from builders' merchants. This stops the existing concrete absorbing too much moisture from the new mix.

After hosing the path to wet it thoroughly, pour the mortar mix over the path up to the height of the boards. Allow it to harden for at least a week before removing the boards and cover it with damp sacking to slow the drying time.

## 193 Scratcher

Use a scratcher to roughen the surface of a plaster undercoat or mortar screed before applying the final coat of plaster. Make one by hammering nails into the edge of a block of wood, leaving about 25 mm/1 in of nail protruding. Snip off the heads with pincers.

## 194 Climbing a ladder

Always grip the sides—not the rungs—when climbing a ladder. If a rung is loose, it may be pulled out completely.

# 195-202

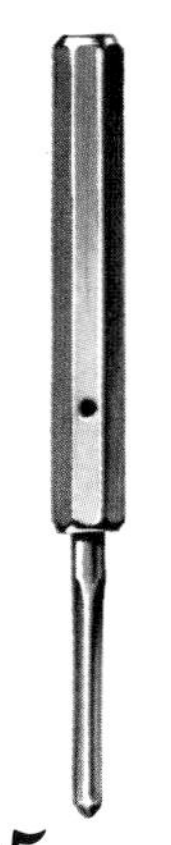

## 195
**Masonry punch**

When making holes in brickwork with a masonry punch, twist the punch round after each hammer stroke. This clears the powdered debris from the face of the hole, helping the punch to "bite" deeper on the next hammer stroke and preventing it from becoming firmly embedded in the wall.

## 196
**Electric cables in plaster**

Never bury an electric cable in plaster without enclosing it in plastic conduit, because there may be a hairline crack in the cable's insulation. Plaster takes a long time to dry out and can act as a conductor of electricity. Conduit also helps to protect cable—and handyman—if a nail is accidentally driven into the wrong place in the wall.

## 197 Wallpapering around a light switch

Hold the length of paper in position before pasting and press it lightly over the switch button, where a small hole should be made with a sharp trimming knife. Lay the paper flat and make four diagonal cuts extending from the centre of the hole to just beyond the corners of the light switch. Paste the paper and let it soak.

Switch the electricity off at the mains. Loosen the screws holding the switch and gently pull the switch plate forward away from its socket. Hang the paper on the wall, easing the loose switch plate through the four diagonal cuts. Turn back the edge of each and trim the paper with scissors to leave a square hole that just overlaps the switch socket. Refit the switch plate, carefully butting together the four cut marks.

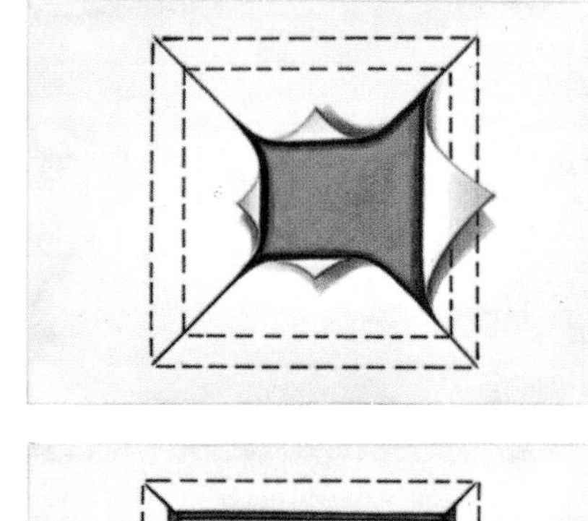

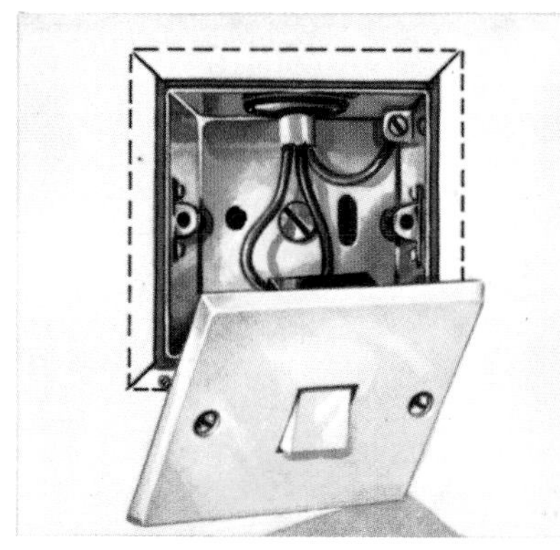

## 198 Protecting dowels in a vice

Before putting wooden dowelling or thin tubing in a vice, fit two clothes pegs on to it. This gives the vice a square edge to grip and makes sure that the rod will not be marked by the pressure exerted on it by the vice.

## 199 Replacing a clay brick in a wall

When replacing a clay brick in a wall, soak the brick in clean water for at least twenty minutes and thoroughly wet the surrounding bricks and mortar. This helps the new mortar to adhere properly when the brick is positioned.

## 200 Door and window fittings and painting

A useful precaution to take before painting doors or windows is to remove all fittings, such as stays, handles and locks. Apart from the possibility of getting paint on the edges of fittings, excess paint may cause the paint to run both underneath and down the side of the fittings.

## 201 Distinguishing the finishes on furniture

To test whether the surface of furniture is french-polished or cellulose-lacquered (the two basic types of furniture finishes), rub an inconspicuous area of the surface with a cloth dipped in methylated spirit. Within a few minutes, as the polish is dissolved by the spirit, a french-polished surface becomes soft and leaves a stain on a finger rubbed across the area, whereas a cellulose finish is not affected by the spirit.

Alternatively, scrape the surface with a sharp knife. French polish will come away from the surface in small shavings that crumble to a brown dust; cellulose produces a white dust.

## 202 Casting home-made concrete paving slabs

Paving slabs can be made with the aid of a simple wooden frame made from 50 mm/2 in deep strips of softwood laid on a level surface. Lay 12 mm/½ in of damp sand in the bottom of the frame and cover it with a mix of one part of cement to three parts of sand. Smooth off any surplus with a straight-edge.

Leave the concrete for 1½ hours and then cut through it with a trowel held firmly against a long straight-edge to cut the slabs to the size required. Leave the slabs to harden for a week; then remove the framework and lift them out with a spade.

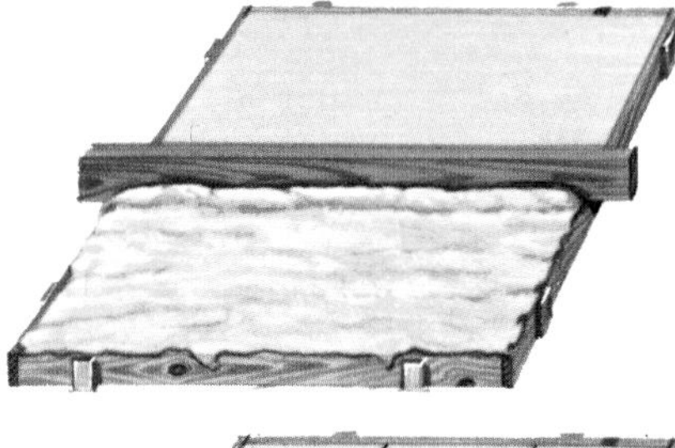

## 203 Smoothing lengths of wood with a plane

Always try to plane a long piece of wood in a series of single strokes to produce long ribbon-like shavings. Make sure that the wood is resting on a level surface and keep it steady throughout the operation. At the start of a stroke, apply pressure to the front of the plane; but, when the middle of the stroke is reached, make sure that the pressure is applied equally to both the front and the handle. When approaching the end of a stroke, transfer the bulk of the pressure to the handle.

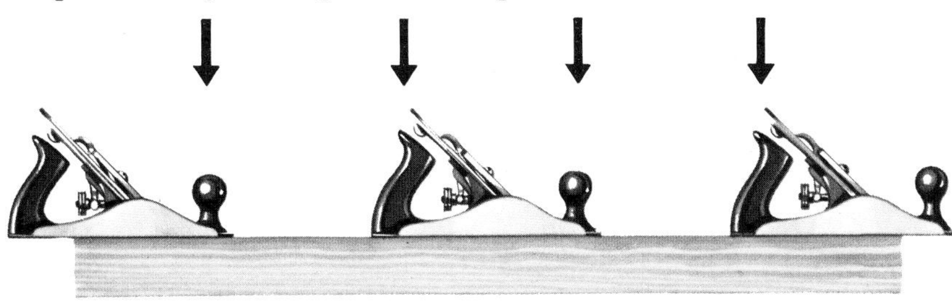

## 204 Strengthening fixings in chipboard edges

To make a firm fixing into the edges of chipboard, fit pieces of solid timber to allow the screws to bite. If the fixing is near a corner of the chipboard, drill a hole in the adjoining edge, insert a length of dowelling and glue it into place. On long edges, chisel out a slot and glue and nail a piece of timber into place to take the weight of the fixing.

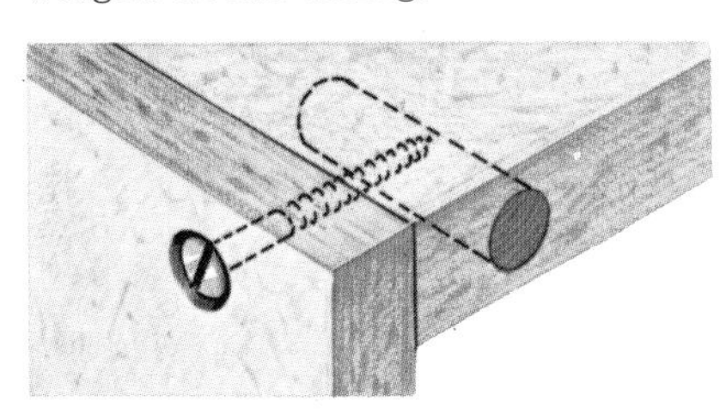

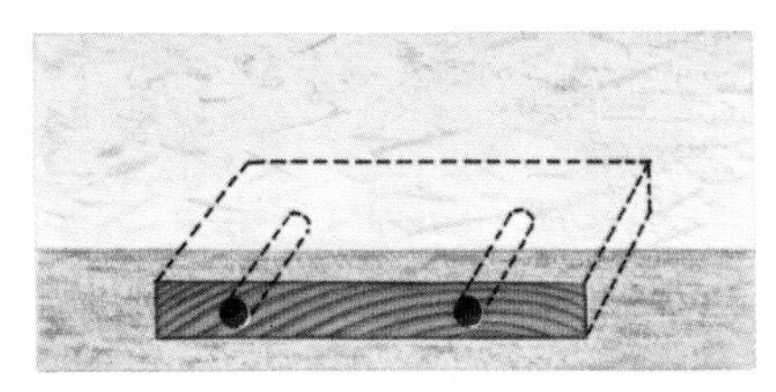

## 205 Painting exterior and interior woodwork

Apply a primer, at least one undercoat and one top coat of gloss paint to outside woodwork. For a more hard-wearing surface, add an extra top coat. Prime new inside woodwork whenever possible, as the primer seals the wood.

## 206 Matching patterned wallpaper

Simplify the task of matching large patterns of wallpaper by using alternate lengths of paper from two rolls. This eliminates the excessive wastage that can otherwise occur when trying to get an exact match for the pattern using only one roll.

## 207 Estimating patterned wallpaper needs

When calculating the amount of wallpaper needed, allow at least 600mm/2ft for wastage on each roll of large patterned paper. This will compensate for the waste in matching large patterns.

## 208 Locating fixing plugs after wallpapering

Clearly mark the holes of fixing plugs for pictures and mirrors before wallpapering a room, particularly when using heavy wallpapers. This saves a great deal of time that would otherwise be wasted in finding their original position. Do this by wedging the ends of wooden toothpicks into the holes, leaving about 6mm/¼in of toothpick protruding. These will pierce the lengths of wallpaper as they are being hung. Remove them just before reinserting picture hooks or any other fixings that have been removed.

## 209 Fixing mirrors to a wall

The weakest parts of a mirror are the areas between the screw holes and the edges. To lessen the chances of the mirror cracking, tighten the fixing screws until they hold the mirror firmly—then undo them half a turn. If the wall surface is uneven, fit rubber washers between the back of the mirror and the wall to help cushion the mirror.

## 210 Freeing sticking sash windows

Sash windows often stick because layers of paint have built up within their grooves over the years. Apply two or three coats of paint stripper, then reprime the woodwork, undercoat it and finally give it a top coat.

## 211 Removing nails without damaging wood

If removing a long or partially driven nail from a piece of wood, use the claw of a claw hammer and work in a series of pulls. Whenever possible, place a piece of scrap wood under the hammer head to take the pressure of levering and so avoiding bruising.

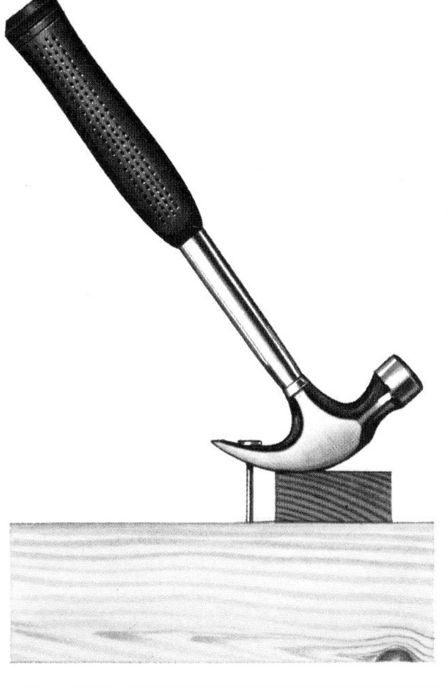

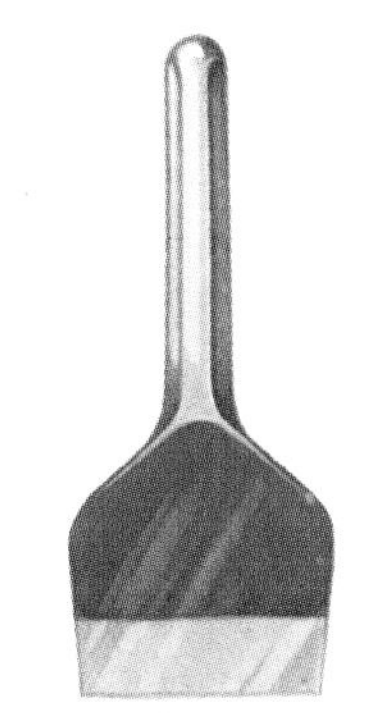

## 212
**Bolster**

Use a bolster preferably with a club hammer to cut a brick, though a steel-shafted hammer can be used as an alternative. Only cut sound bricks. A sub-standard brick can easily shatter when hit.

## 213
**Electric cables and skirting**

Never use staples to secure an electric cable or flex to the top of a skirting board; the staples may cut into the insulation and cause a short circuit. Use, instead, purpose-made C-shaped clips.

# 214-222

## 214 Fine-gauge drill

A home-made fine-gauge drill can be made by cutting off the head of a small nail and filing the point on three sides. The drill should be used on narrow mouldings, before nailing, where there is a danger of the wood splitting.

## 215 Wallpaper and electricity

When soaking and stripping off wallpaper or applying wallpaper around a light switch or power socket, turn off the electricity at the mains.

## 216 The correct way to make a lapped joint

A lapped joint is one of the easiest joints to make, requiring the marking up and cutting of only one of the pieces of wood being joined. Mark the wood to be cut with a gauge to the exact width and thickness of the interlocking piece. Cut the width of the joint with a tenon saw and then make some extra cuts within the joint itself. Roughly chisel these cuts out with the bevelled edge of the chisel facing the inside of the cut. Finally, trim them to their exact measurements by using the chisel with its flat side facing the inside of the cut. Spread adhesive over the joints and screw the two pieces together.

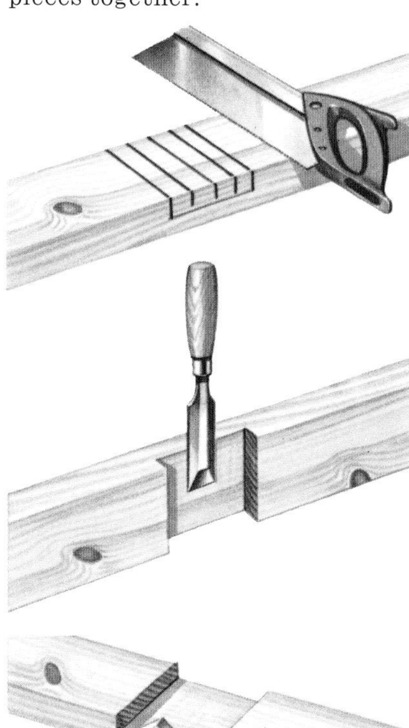

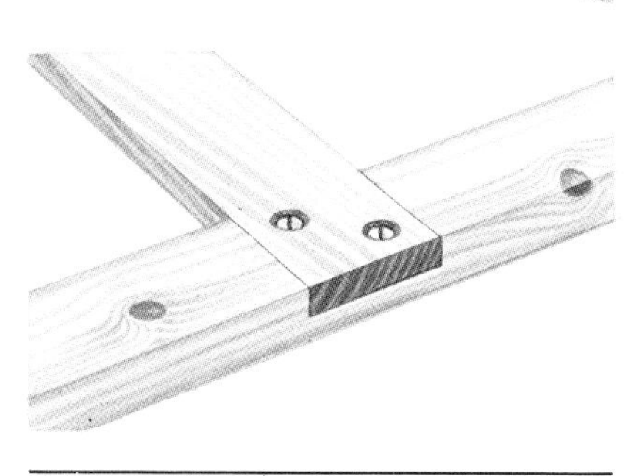

## 217 Fitting panes of glass in a greenhouse

Always lay a matchstick within each overlap, over the top of the lower of two panes, when fitting panes in a greenhouse. The gap created by the matchsticks prevents capillary attraction drawing water up between the two panes, leaving dirt marks that are impossible to remove.

## 218 Making it easy to sharpen a gimlet

To sharpen a gimlet, first drill in a scrap of hardwood a hole 19mm/¾in deep and with a diameter slightly less than the shaft of the gimlet. Alternatively, if it is not too blunt, bore the hole with the gimlet itself.

Fill the hole with fine carborundum powder and oil and insert the gimlet into the hole, boring down a further 12mm/½in.

Repeat the procedure in a scrap of softwood, this time using the abrasive without the addition of any oil.

## 219 The correct spacings for double glazing

When fitting double glazing, remember that the ideal cavity between the two sheets of glass for sound insulation is 200mm/8in. The most efficient cavity for thermal insulation is 19mm/¾in.

## 220 Preparing wooden forms for concrete

Brush oil, such as used motor oil, on the sides of boards used in forms for concrete, before pouring the concrete into place. The oil stops the concrete sticking to the wood as it hardens and makes the supports easy to remove.

## 221 Sharpening a drill's centre bit

Before sharpening a centre bit push the centre point into a block of wood to hold the bit steady. Lightly rub the cutting edge of the bit and the nicker, which scores the circle, with a file—preferably a fine needle file—held at a constant angle. Try to remove as little metal as possible.

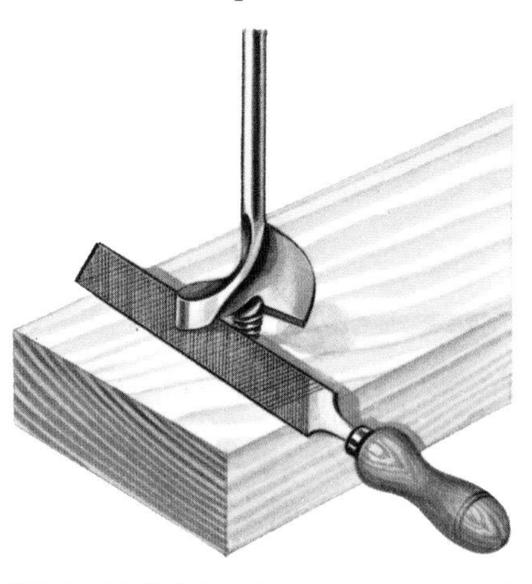

## 222 Fitting glazing sprigs to rebates

Always use the side of a purpose-made chisel to fit sprigs (headless tacks) to rebates to hold glass in position. Resting the chisel flat against the pane of glass slide it backwards and forwards across the glass to push the sprig home. Hold the chisel lightly against the pane to avoid scratching the glass.

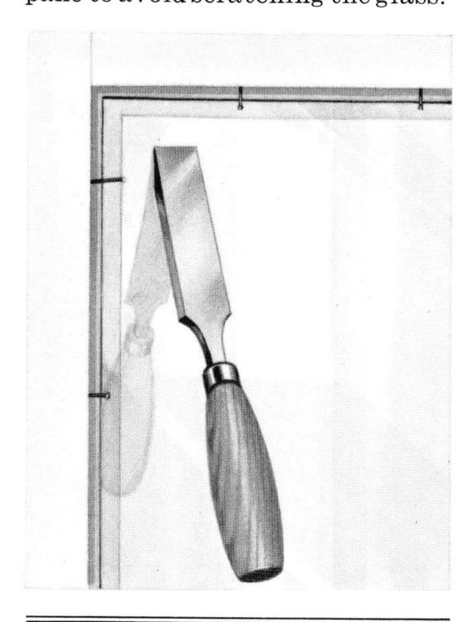

## 223 Taking a dovetail joint apart

To take apart a dovetail joint that needs to be reassembled later, such as in an old piece of furniture where the glue is not water-resistant, first remove any nails—punching them clear, if possible. Then cut into the glued joint with a trimming knife. Pour a little boiling water over the cuts and allow it to soak into the glue to soften it. Lightly tap the joint apart using a wooden mallet. If the joint does not begin to move after a few taps, the glue has not softened sufficiently and more boiling water should be applied.

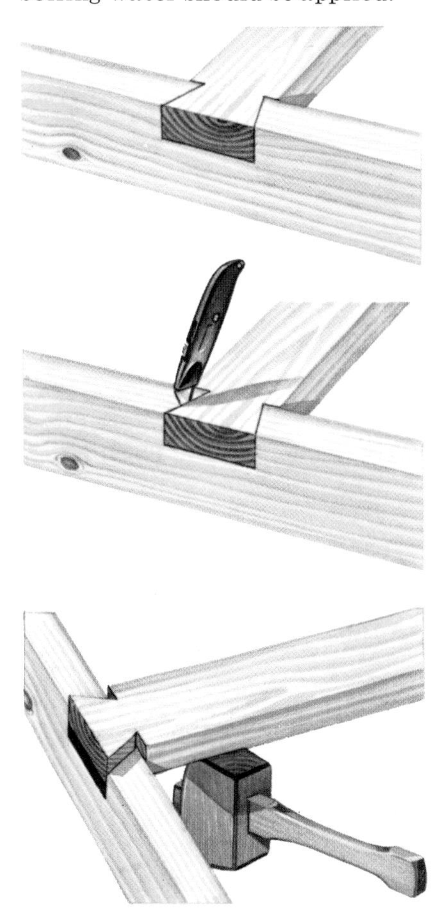

## 224 Fitting patterned glass sheets

Always fit patterned glass with the rough side facing inwards. If the rough side is on the outside, the glass will quickly become grimy as dirt in the air lodges in the crevices of the pattern.

## 225 The correct procedure for stirring paints

Thixatropic paints must not be stirred; unlike most other paints they do not "settle" in the same way. When using liquid paints, however, always stir them thoroughly first so that the particles settled in the bottom of the tin are distributed evenly.

If using a paint-stirring attachment on an electric drill, use it at a slow speed and remember to switch the drill on and off while the stirrer is still immersed in the paint. If stirring paint by hand, use a length of clean hardwood batten, turning it in a circular lifting motion. Make sure, too, that the stirring-stick is pushed well down into the edge around the bottom of the tin.

When finished, replace the lid firmly and stand the tin upside-down. The next time the paint is needed the skin will be at the bottom of the tin.

## 226 Restoring the bonding qualities of dried glue

Restore the bonding qualities of a glue that has dried on a laminated surface by ironing the surface with a warm iron.

## 227 Temporarily repairing a split pipe

An easy way of temporarily repairing a small-bore pipe that has split badly after being frozen is to cut out the damaged section of the pipe and link the two ends with a length of rubber garden hose. Make sure the hose stays firmly in place by fitting jubilee clips over each end of the hose, and also remember to turn on the water supply at only half pressure until a permanent repair can be made.

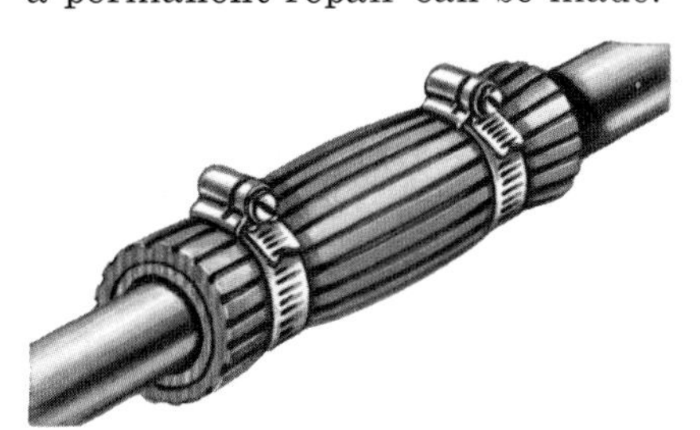

## 228 Working around the edge of a carpet

If it is necessary to move a carpet back to reach a work area on the edge of a room, first prise up the tacks and then pull back the four corners of the carpet and turn back the four side edges. If the carpet is simply rolled up it is more likely to stretch out of shape and will rarely fit properly when rolled out again.

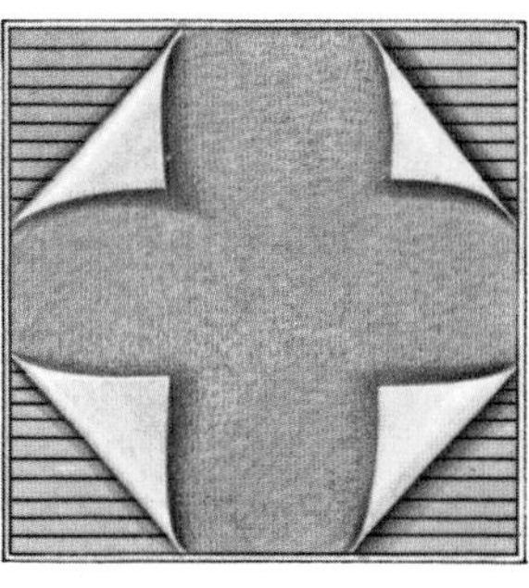

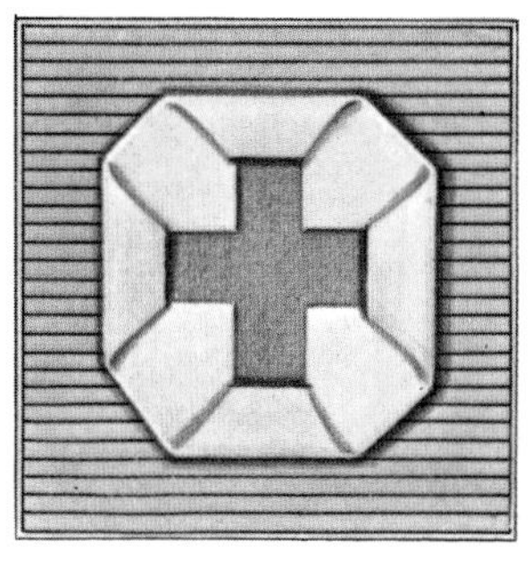

## 229 Finding where doors and windows stick

To locate the points where doors and windows stick insert a piece of carbon paper between the opening and the frame. The surfaces that bind together and need to be planed are those where the carbon leaves a smudged impression.

## 230 Recognizing and confirming dry rot

The most common early-warning signs of dry rot are a "mushroom" odour, the sudden appearance of reddish brown spores on the affected floor, window ledge or piece of furniture, and a softening of the timber. Push a penknife into the suspected area. Dry rot is present if the blade sinks deeply with little effort.

## 231 G-cramp

Only tighten a G-cramp by hand, not with a tool such as a wrench—turning the cramp too tightly will cause dents in the surface of the timber being gripped. As an additional safeguard, place a piece of scrap wood beneath each of the cramp jaws.

## 232 Electric fires in a bathroom

Never use a portable electric fire in a bathroom. Use only the infra-red ray type of heater, fitted to the wall and controlled by a pull-cord switch. Position the heater so that it cannot be switched on or off, or adjusted, from the bath.

# 233 - 242

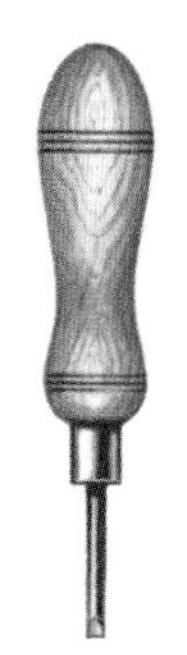

## 233
### Bradawl

Make the starting holes for screws measuring up to 4 mm/$\frac{5}{32}$ in diameter with a bradawl — preferably one with a squared tip. However, the starting holes for screws measuring over 4 mm/$\frac{5}{32}$ in diameter should always be drilled.

## 234
### Carrying glass

When carrying two or more sheets of glass, interleave them with sheets of newspaper and protect the hands with pads of paper or canvas gloves. When carrying a single pane in windy weather, remember that a single gust of wind can easily snap it.

## 235 Restoring silvering on the back of a mirror

A black spot appearing on a mirror is usually a warning that the silvering on the back of the mirror is beginning to break up. It can be temporarily disguised by sticking a piece of burnished silver paper over the damaged part with adhesive tape.

Do not try to unpeel the tape once it has been positioned, as this could pull off more of the silvering from the mirror.

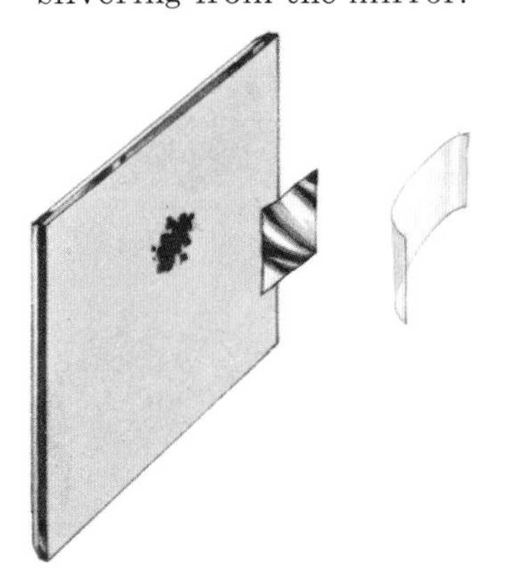

## 236 Painting putty fitted around windows

Always wait between seven to ten days before painting new putty fitted around windows. Otherwise the paint will seal in the putty's linseed oil and so prevent the putty from hardening properly.

## 237 Laying a concrete path beside a wall

To allow a tamping beam to be used lengthways to level a concrete path being laid alongside a wall, lay the concrete in alternate bays. Start by laying a framework the full length of the path, placing dividing boards between each section and inserting a 19 mm/$\frac{3}{4}$ in strip of asphalt-impregnated fibreboard against the wall. This forms an expansion joint.

After laying the first set of bays, leave the concrete to harden for at least forty-eight hours. Then remove the dividing boards and fill in the other bays. Remove the rest of the framework when the entire path has set.

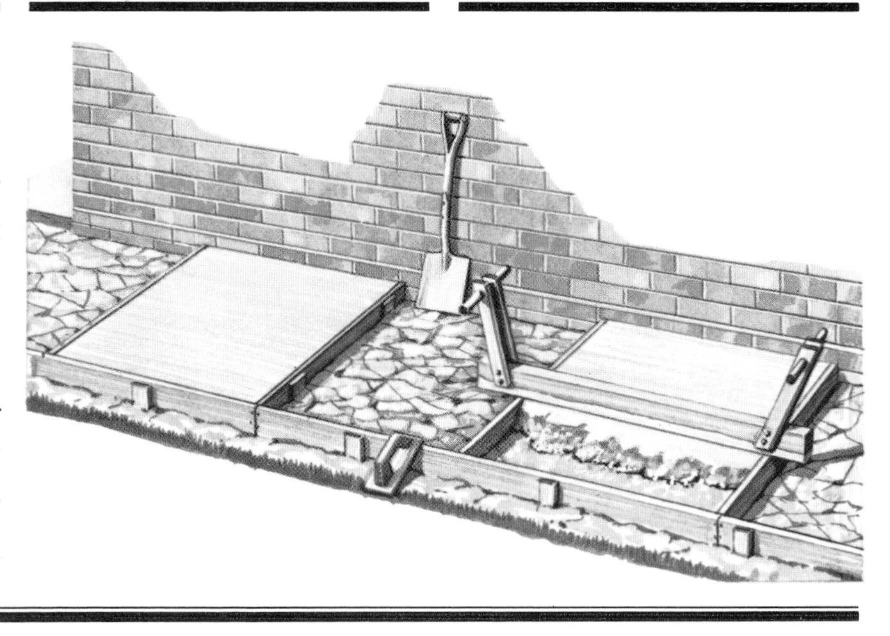

## 238 Checking that timber is not twisted

To check whether a piece of timber is twisted, place two metal straight-edges upright across the width of the timber. Line up the top edges of the straight-edges by looking down the timber. If they match up exactly, the timber is level and suitable for use. Repeat this check at 450 mm/18 in intervals on long lengths of timber.

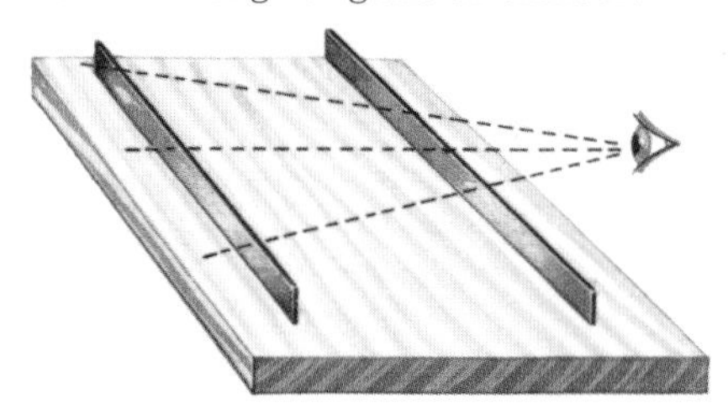

## 239 Drilling holes in soft metals

Use the point of a nail to mark the centre point when drilling a hole in soft metal. This stops the head of a twist drill from wandering off-centre before it can bite into the surface of the sheet.

## 240 Making a plane smoother to use

Rub candlewax on the sole of a plane to help it slide more easily over timber surfaces.

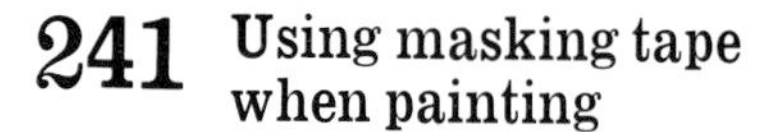

## 241 Using masking tape when painting

Apply masking tape to protect surfaces when painting awkward angles, such as glazing bars in windows. Peel off the tape before the paint has dried hard; otherwise the edges of the newly painted surface will be damaged.

## 242 Securing a stepladder at the top of stairs

Always make stepladders secure when working at the top of stairs by first tying the legs of the ladder together. Then screw a batten into the floorboards in front of the ladder so that it cannot slip, or rest heavy weights against its feet.

## 243 Butt-jointing timber securely

Because of the strength of modern adhesives, glued butt-joints are strong enough for most joining jobs—as, for instance, when making drawers. Nail or screw the joints if necessary for strength.

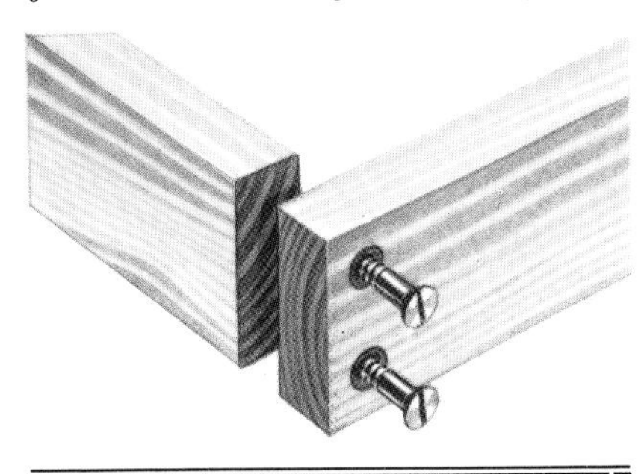

## 244 Fasteners for securing fixings in plasterboard

Secure fixings in plasterboard can be made with three types of fasteners—a spring toggle bolt, a sleeve bolt and an anchor bolt.

If using a spring toggle bolt remember to attach any fasteners required before fixing the bolt. The toggle, which opens out after it is pushed through the hole, will be lost if the bolt is removed.

Use a sleeve bolt—in which a rubber sleeve is compressed against the plasterboard as the head of the bolt is tightened—as a useful waterproof joint. These bolts are also especially suited for fastening plastic or metal sheeting.

An anchor bolt expands to grip the wall as it is tightened, giving a strong fixing for heavy objects.

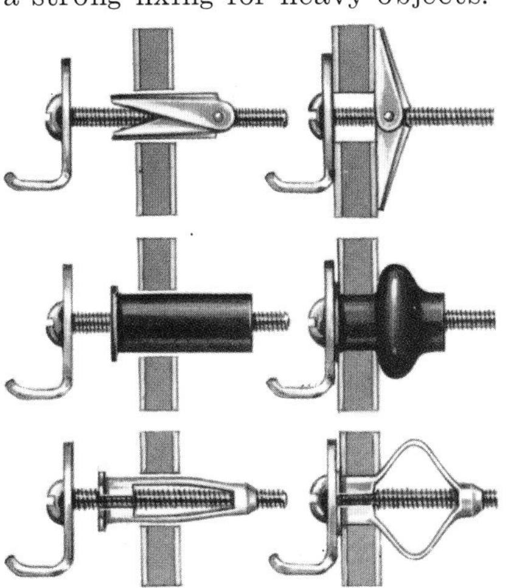

## 245 Nailing narrow wood mouldings

Always blunt the point of a panel pin before nailing a narrow hardwood moulding to prevent the wood from splitting. Blunt the pin by lightly hammering it against a concrete surface.

## 246 Fitting screws in awkward places

To hold a screw in position while tightening it in a place that is difficult to reach, fit a piece of rubber tubing about 25mm/1in long firmly over the end of a screwdriver. Push the screw, head-first, into the end of the tube.

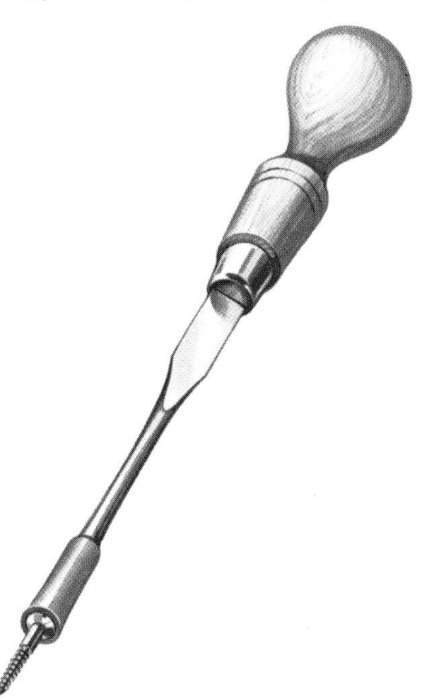

## 247 Stripping obstinate wallpaper

Water often fails to loosen firmly stuck patches of wallpaper. Lightly brush a thin mix of wallpaper paste on to the patch, and, when the patch has almost dried, wet the surface by brushing it with hot water. The layer of paste will help "hold" the hot water, letting it soak the paper. Alternatively, score the surface of the paper with a sharp trimming knife or old hacksaw blade before soaking it with hot water.

## 248 Strengthening weak window-frame joints

Strengthen a weak joint in a window frame invisibly by sinking a metal plate in the outside edge of the frame.

Make a series of cuts with a tenon saw 5mm/$\frac{3}{16}$in deep on each side of the joint. Chisel these out and screw the plate in position. Glue a strip of plain softwood, about 3mm/$\frac{1}{8}$in thick, over the plate, and insert filler into the gaps. When the glue and filler have thoroughly dried, plane and sand the wood strip with glasspaper so that it fits perfectly flush with the framework.

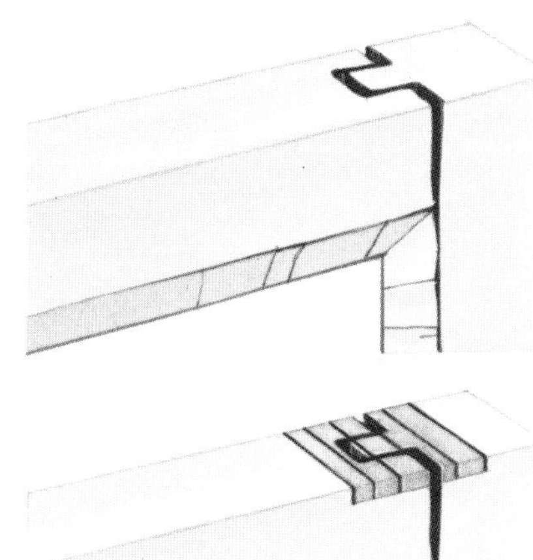

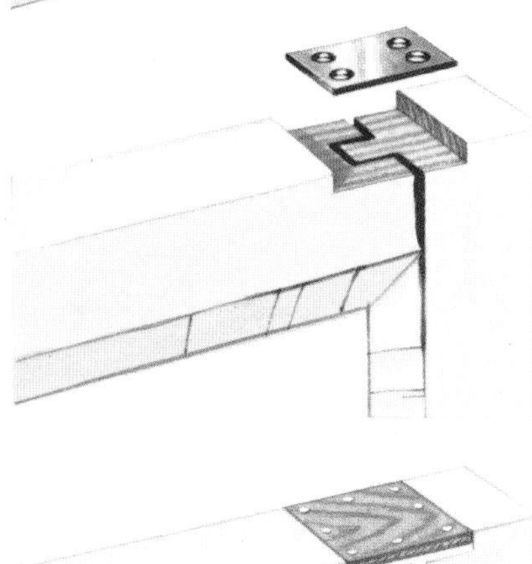

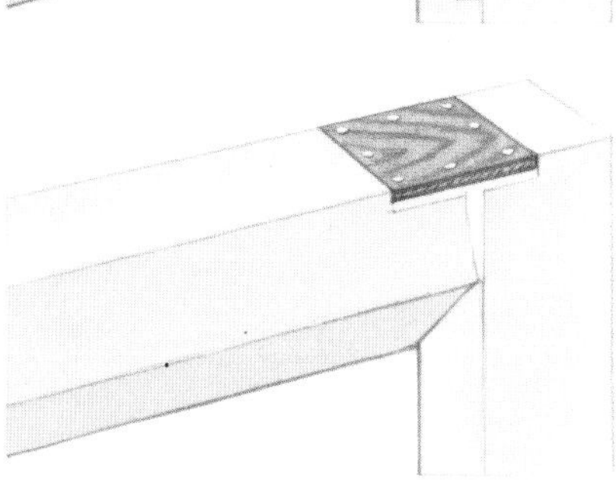

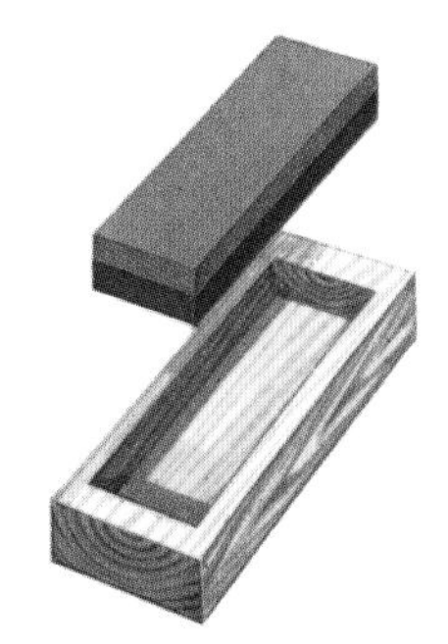

## 249 Oilstone

Use an oilstone to sharpen blades. Always keep it in a hardwood box, recessed so that the edges of both oilstone and box are exactly flush. This ensures that the full length of the stone can be used when blades are being sharpened.

## 250 Electrical repairs

Always switch off the electricity at the mains when changing any type of fuse, or replacing a switch plate or socket outlet. Always switch off at the appliance when changing a plug or a light bulb.

# 251-260

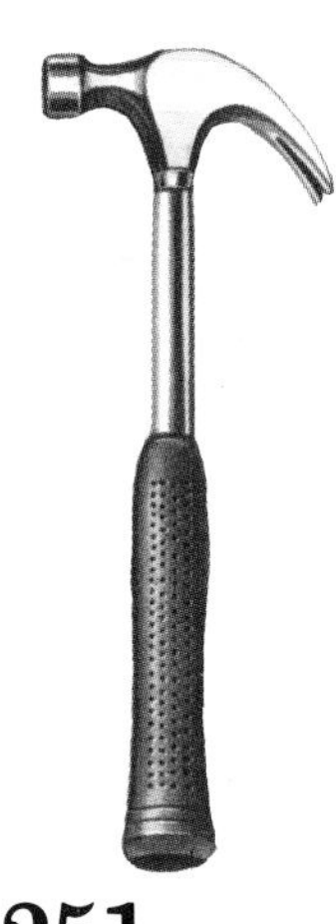

## 251
### Claw hammer

A claw hammer is an essential tool because it can be used to extract as well as drive nails. Those with steel shafts are far stronger than wooden-handled versions, but the rubber or plastic grip can become slippery. Avoid this by washing the grip with warm, soapy water. Rinse and dry thoroughly.

## 252
### Power tool leads

When using any type of power tool, such as an electric drill or a floor sander, loop the lead over one shoulder so that it is out of the way. Otherwise it may be severed.

## 253 Marking wood to ensure a square cut

Make sure of a square cut when sawing timber by marking the timber out with a try square. Start off by marking across one broad surface, then first down one short side, then the other, followed by the last broad surface. Avoid making the mark in one continuous line around the edges. If this is done, the slight variations that occur in the squareness of the timber sides will be compounded, and the line may finish as much as 6 mm/¼ in away from where it started.

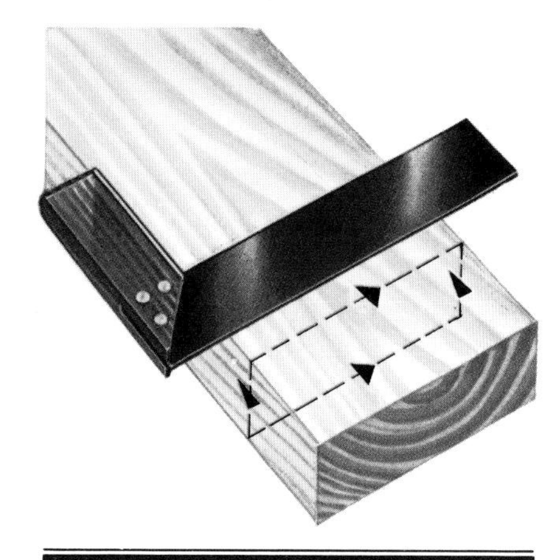

## 254 Finding the centre of a circle

The simplest way to find the centre of a circle when, for example, marking up a vinyl tile for cutting, is to draw a straight line which intersects the circle at two points, dividing it into a large and small segment. Measure and mark the centre of that part of the line that is within the circle. Place the edge of a set square exactly on this line with the right angle at the centre point. Draw the bisecting line, so that it, too, cuts through the circle at two points. The centre of the circle lies midway between these two points.

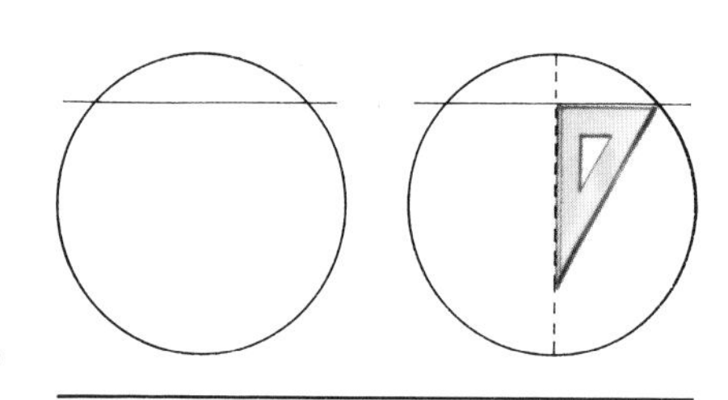

## 255 Making wide cuts in metal with a hacksaw

If a hacksaw blade is too narrow for the required cut, make a wider one by fitting an additional blade to the hacksaw. Make sure that the extra blade has the same ratio of teeth—either 14, 18, 24 or 32 every 25 mm/1 in—and that the blade is fitted in the correct way, with the teeth facing away from the handle. Lubricate the blades with oil while cutting.

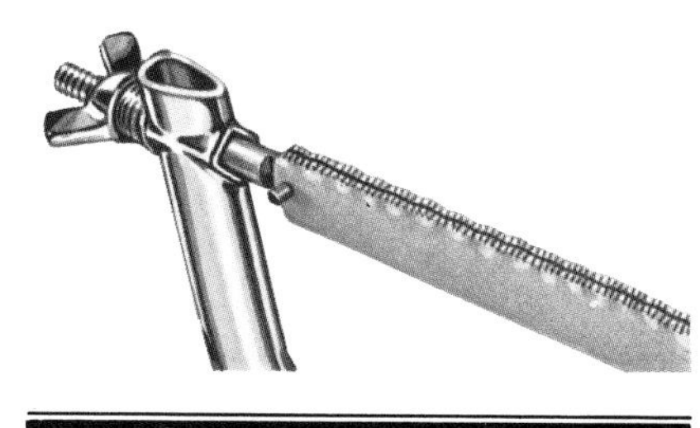

## 256 When and how to use ready-mixed concrete

Buy ready-mixed concrete for areas that require more than $3\,m^3$/$4\,yd^3$ rather than mix it yourself—the time and labour saved by not having to mix the concrete by hand more than justifies the additional cost. Remember to have helpers standing by when the concrete arrives; $3\,m^3$ of cement weighs six tons—the equivalent of about 60 barrow loads—and it must be laid within 2½ hours, or less if the weather is extremely hot. Also make sure that all preparation work—such as laying and levelling out the hardcore, clearing access for the lorry and fitting all the necessary formwork in position—has been completed well in advance of pouring.

## 257 Using a hacksaw blade for the first time

If a hacksaw blade snaps half-way through a cut, fit a new blade to the saw and, making sure the blade is taut, start a fresh cut from the other side. Never continue along the existing cut. A worn blade makes a slightly thinner cut than a new one, and the replacement blade will bind and may break if used in the original cut line. When sawing, avoid too much pressure.

## 258 Choosing the right straight-edge

Use a length of aluminium angle as a straight-edge when cutting such materials as vinyl, cork and hessian. A wooden straight-edge may not only slip on the hard surface of a vinyl tile, for example, but can also be damaged by a trimming knife.

## 259 Cleaning the joints between glazed tiles

The simplest way to clean dirty joints between tiles is to rub them gently with an ordinary pencil eraser. If this method fails, scrape out the old compound with a sharp nail. Mix new grouting compound and refill the joints, finishing them off by scraping them with a rounded stick.

## 260 Removing protruding staples from a surface

Remove protruding staples by pushing a nail through the loop of the staple head. Then position a claw hammer under the nail and prise the staple free. To avoid any risk of damage, place a piece of card under the hammer.

# 261-270

## 261 Hammering nails or pins into place

Hold small nails or panel pins in position for hammering by pushing them through a thin piece of card. Pull the card off once the nail has been hammered home. A comb can be used instead.

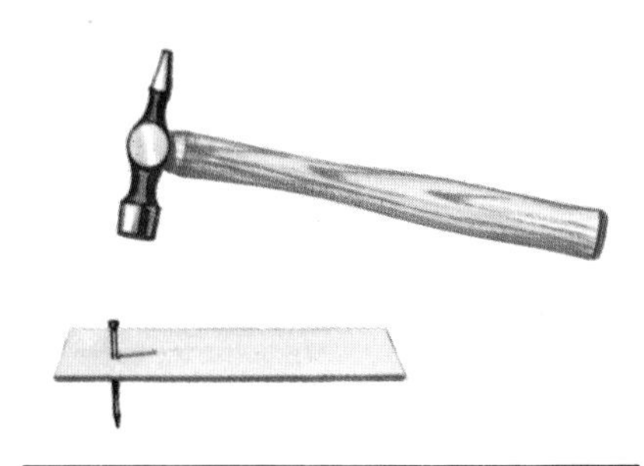

## 262 Giving a fence post firm support

Support a wooden fence post by screwing two battens—each about 600 mm/2 ft long and at right angles to each other—to the bottom of the post. Use non-ferrous screws.

Dig a hole for the post and two trenches for the battens. Steep the battens and the bottom of the post in wood preservative, then place them in position. Pack broken bricks tightly round the battens, check the vertical with a level and then pack the earth into place.

## 263 Keeping cement dry during storage

Store bags of cement on a slatted wood platform about 100 mm/4 in off the ground so that air can circulate underneath to keep the cement dry.

## 264 Marking out tiles to fit around a pedestal

Make a simple template from a piece of thin card cut to the same size as the tile to be fitted around the pedestal. Cut strips about 6 mm/¼ in apart along one edge of the card. They should be long enough to accommodate the pedestal when the card is placed in the position that the tile will occupy. Place the card in that position and press down the strips round the edge of the pedestal; where they turn up is the cutting line for the tile. Transfer the shape of the folds from the template to the tile by lightly marking with a felt-tip pen.

## 265 Removing air bubbles in dried-out wallpaper

Remove an air bubble from behind dried-out wallpaper by making a vertical and horizontal cut with a trimming knife across the bubble, making sure that the cuts stretch slightly beyond the bubble's extremes. Fold back the corners of the cuts and repaste the paper. Allow a few minutes for the paste to soak the paper, and then press the flaps back into position, using a firm pressure and wiping off any excess paste squeezed from them with a sponge.

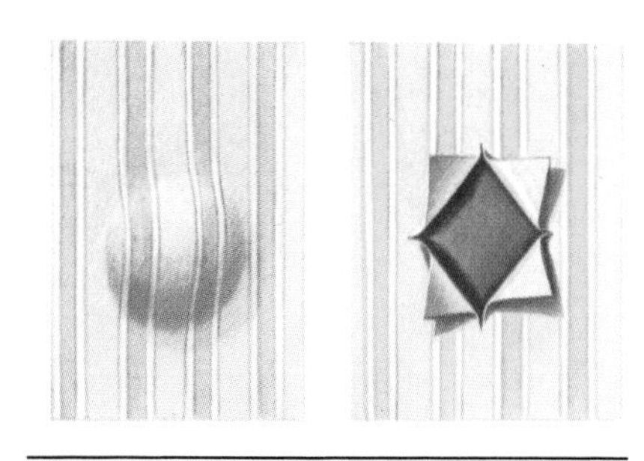

## 266 Hanging bold-patterned wallpaper

The chimney breast is the focal point of the room. Thus, when papering a chimney breast above a fireplace with a bold-patterned paper, always position the first length of the paper centrally.

## 267 Rust-proofing tools stored in a damp place

Tools which have to be stored in a damp work-shed or garage can be protected from rusting by spraying them lightly with oil. This forms a protective skin over the metal, which prevents rust.

## 268 Finding a true horizontal

Never work on the basis of measurements taken from floors and ceilings—these are rarely level. When fitting shelves into an alcove, for example, measuring up from the floor invariably leads to the shelf being fitted at an angle. The only way to make sure of a perfect horizontal is to mark the position required for the shelf on the back of the alcove. Hold a straight-edge against this line, and, checking with a spirit level, rotate the straight-edge until the exact horizontal has been established. Mark this point and carry out the same procedure on the insides of the alcove to establish where the shelf should be fixed.

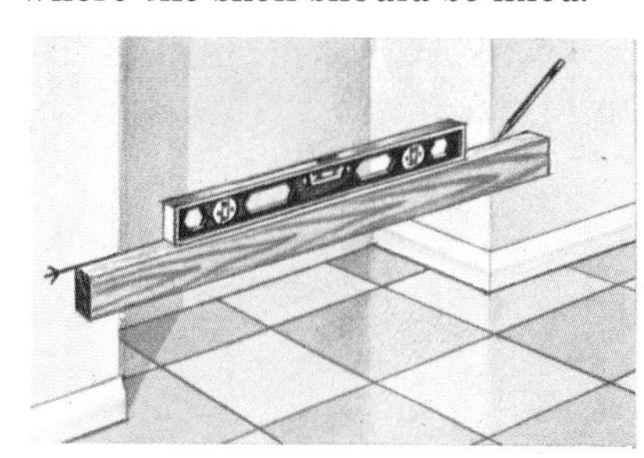

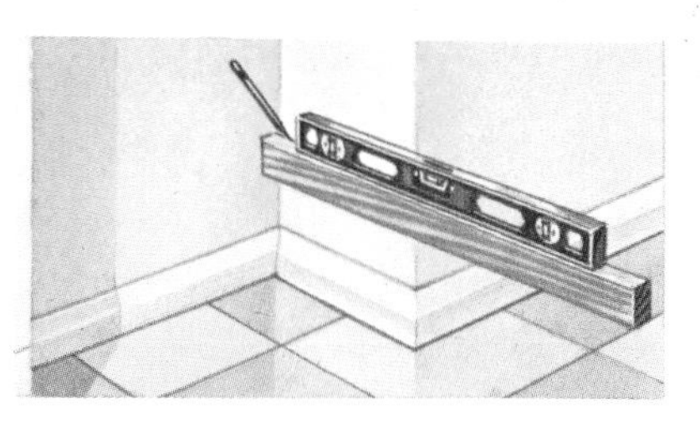

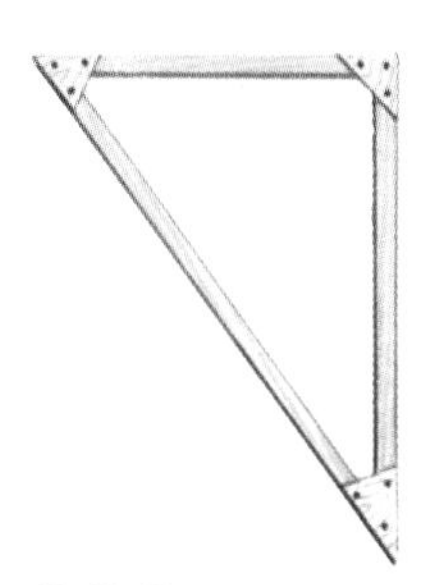

## 269 Builder's square

A vital tool for accurate laying-out work, a builder's square can be made from three pieces of 50 mm/2 in by 12 mm/½ in battening. Construct it on the 3-4-5 principle, joining the 900 mm/3 ft base and the 1,200 mm/4 ft upright by a 1,500 mm/5 ft length of batten. Provided these measurements are exact, a true right angle will be created.

## 270 Mixing detergents

Never mix detergents. Some types—particularly powder and liquid chemicals—create poisonous vapours when mixed.

# 271-280

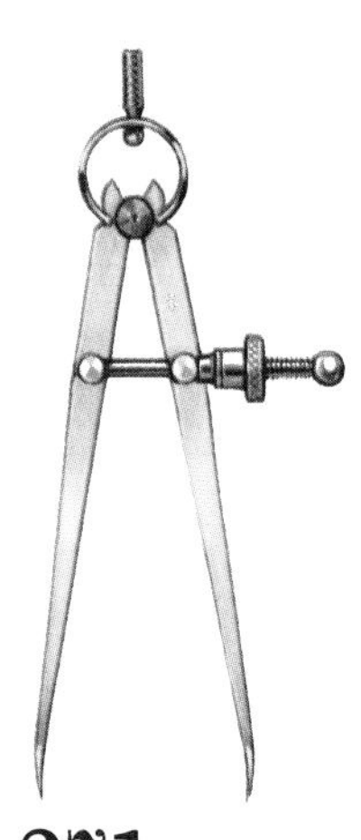

## 271
**Dividers**

Dividers are a useful tool for marking out a series of measurements quickly and accurately. They are also especially suited for scribing circles on wood, as they actually cut into the surface to provide a cutting guide. Remember, however, to hold a piece of wood or card at the centre point to avoid making an unwanted hole.

## 272
**Working in confined spaces**

Wear a skull cap or a similar close-fitting hat when using a power tool in a confined space, for example under a car or between floor joists. The cap will prevent hair from becoming entangled in the mechanism.

## 273 The correct footwear to use on ladders

Always wear shoes when working from a high ladder. Boots make it difficult to "feel" the rungs; while soft-soled shoes may help this, they do not prevent feet from becoming sore if working for any length of time. Take care not to overreach to the side as this can cause the ladder to slide in the opposite direction.

## 274 Ensuring the strength of adhesive joints

Sprinkle strands of wire wool over an adhesive joint. These help bond the glue and so make the joint much stronger.

## 275 Preparing timber edges for paint

Before painting a piece of timber, rub down the edges to a slight bevel to get a better adhesive surface for the paint. Use a glasspaper block with a fine- or medium-grade paper.

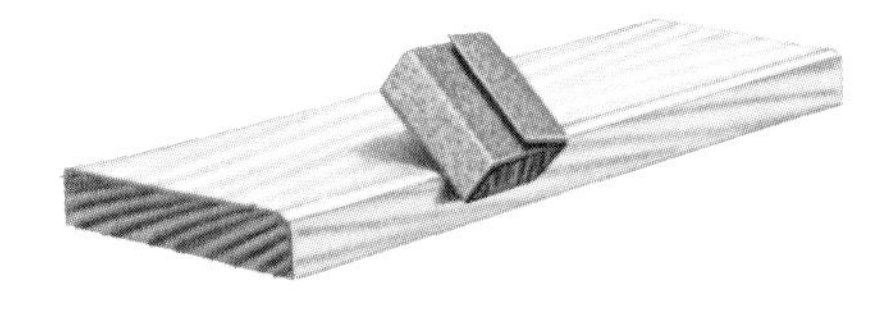

## 276 Sawing narrow strips off the ends of timber

Cramp a waste piece of wood under a piece of timber when sawing a very thin strip off the end. This removes the danger of the timber splitting. Make sure the waste extends past the proposed cutting line to give adequate support to the strip being cut.

## 277 Bending a soft metal bar to a right angle

Bend a soft metal bar to a right angle by making two or three shallow saw cuts in the bar at the point where it is to be bent. Place the bar in a vice with the saw cuts on the inside of the proposed bend and hammer the end over with a rubber mallet—or, if the bar is thin enough, force it over by hand. The saw cuts will prevent the bar distorting.

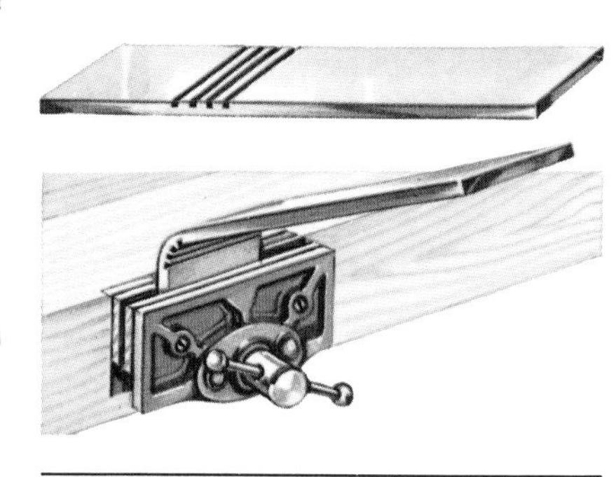

## 278 Cutting a rectangular hole in timber

To cut a rectangular hole in timber, first drill four holes, one in each corner of the proposed rectangle. Use a padsaw to start a cut from one of the holes and for the verticals; if the rectangle is large enough, finish off the sawing with a panel saw. The width of the panel saw's blade makes for greater accuracy when joining up with the cuts at each of the corners. If, however, the rectangle required is not large enough to accommodate a panel saw, use a padsaw for the entire job.

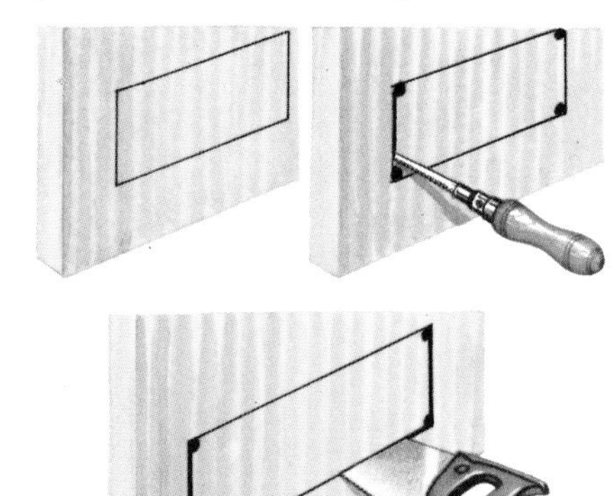

## 279 Drilling holes in a ceiling

Fit the cap of a detergent bottle over the twist bit of a power drill to prevent dust dropping into the eyes when drilling holes in a ceiling. Use one hand to grip the top of the drill and at the same time steady the cap.

## 280 Making a through housing joint

Use through housing joints to provide secure joints for shelving. First, draw a line square across the inner face of the upright. Hold the shelf against the line and mark the exact depth of the shelf on the upright. Then use a depth gauge to mark the depth lines for the cut. These should not be more than one-third of the thickness of the upright, or the joint will be weakened. Working just on the waste side of the line, saw down to the depth lines with a tenon or a dovetail saw, and then chisel out the cut. Start with the chisel at an angle of 30° and gradually reduce this until the centre is chiselled away. During this stage of the job, check the cut several times with a straight-edge to make sure it is flat and the depth constant. Plane the end of the cross-member and glue the joint into place. Where possible, screw, pin or nail it for extra strength.

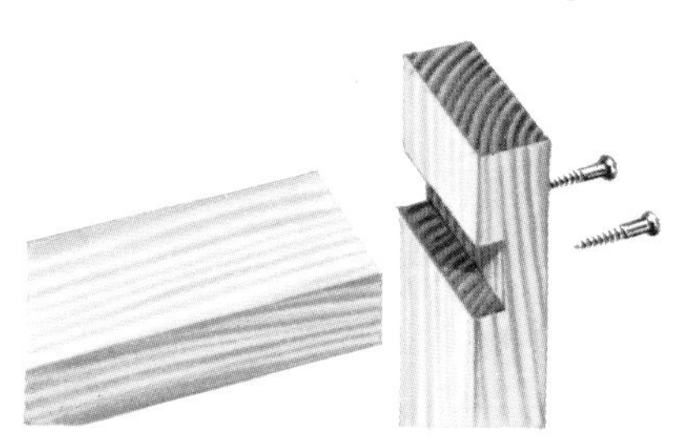

## 281 Tiling the underside of an opening in a wall

To tile the underside of a door or window opening in a wall, cut a thin strip of 6mm/¼in ply the same width as the opening and three lengths of timber 6mm/¼in less than the height of the opening to act as props for the strip. Size the area to be tiled, as full-width tiles may not fit the opening. If it is necessary to cut the tiles, either use a trimmed tile in the centre or have odd tiles at each end to achieve a balance. Always use the second method if the tiles have to fit in with an existing tiled pattern on the wall. Use round-edge tiles, with the round edges facing outwards.

Start by spreading adhesive along the area to be tiled and then press the first tile into position. Put the strip in place under this tile and support it with one of the vertical props. Taking care not to dislodge the prop, spring the strip down and place the second tile in position. Put the second prop under it. Pull the strip back again and insert a third tile, this time moving the second prop along under the third tile.

Continue the process until either the middle or the end of the reveal is reached, depending on the starting point. Then, keeping the second prop at this point, start working with the third. Move this prop along under each tile until the tiling has been completed. Leave the strip and its supports in position until the adhesive has thoroughly dried. Then grout the joints.

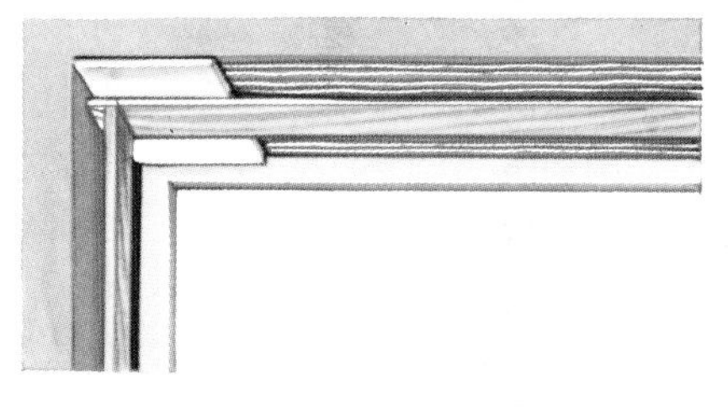

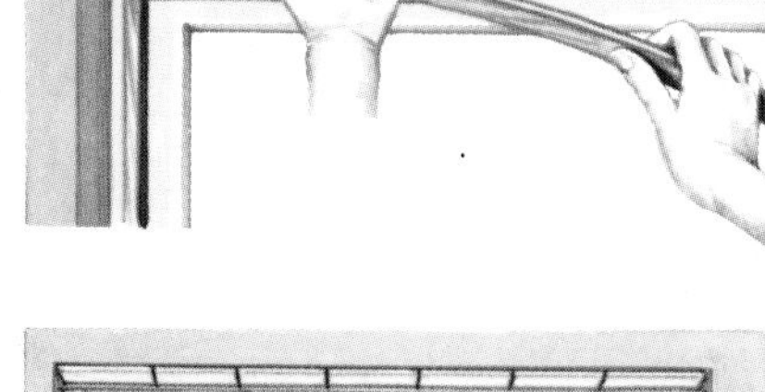

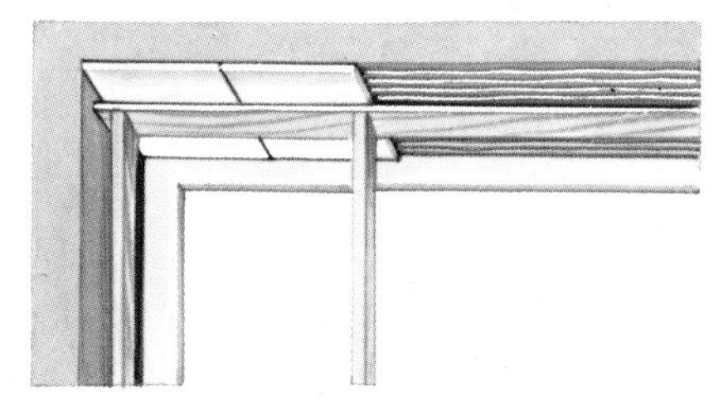

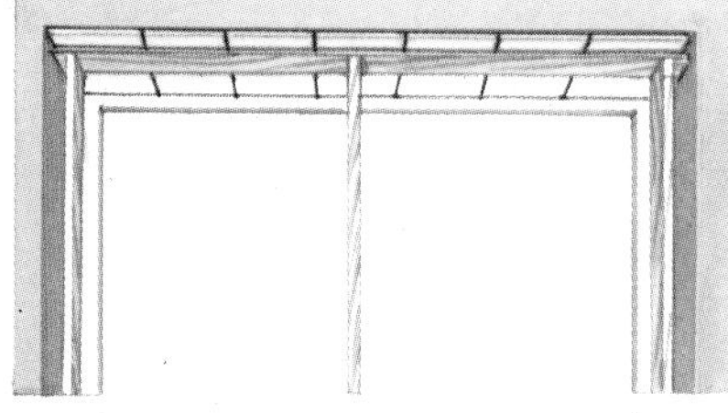

## 285 Cutting awkward shapes in ceramic tiles

The simplest way of cutting an awkward shape in a ceramic tile is to score the outline of the shape to be cut out through the glaze using a tile cutter with a tungsten carbide tip. Do not use a glass cutter as it will become blunt. Using a pair of pincers carefully nibble away small pieces of the tile until the score line has been reached. Smooth off the cut edge with glasspaper if necessary.

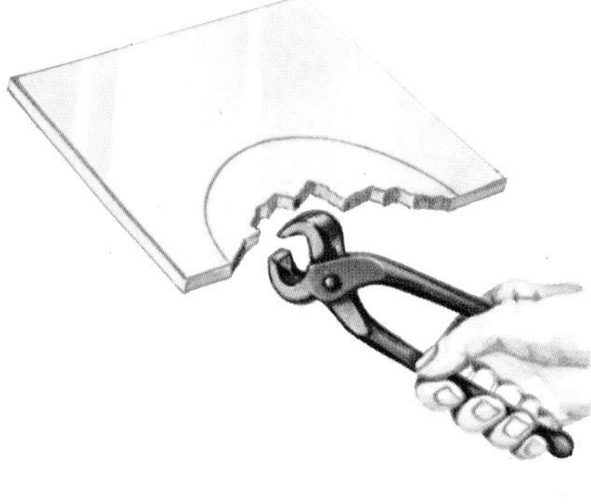

## 286 Painting mouldings in two colours

To lessen the risk of mess and to ensure a perfect finish when painting intricate mouldings in two colours, always paint the whole of the moulding first in the colour that will appear on the recessed areas. Leave this to dry and then paint the raised surfaces of the moulding.

## 288 Hacksaw

A hacksaw blade cuts only one way—forwards. Make sure to fit a new blade to the saw with the teeth facing away from the handle. After making the first few cuts with a new blade, which will stretch the blade slightly, tighten the screw holding the blade by one more turn.

## 282 Preventing concrete ponds from cracking

Leave a well-inflated car tyre inner tube in a garden pond during cold weather. The floating tube takes up the expansion of the water as it freezes and so reduces the risk of the sides of the pool cracking under heavy pressure.

## 283 Protecting the surface of newly laid asphalt

Cover newly laid asphalt with a sprinkling of sharp, dry, clean sand for three or four days. This stops it sticking to shoes.

## 284 Fitting a masonry nail into brickwork

Hammering a masonry nail into brickwork can be dangerous, as the nail could snap and fly into the face or the eye with considerable force.

A simple precaution is to cut a piece from the end of a drinking straw and fit it over the nail to reduce the danger of this happening. The straw automatically frees itself as the nail is hammered home into the brick.

## 287 Fitting shelving against a wall

Ensure a perfect fit for shelving against an irregular wall by resting the shelf against the wall and marking the profile of the wall on the shelf with a pencil by pushing a narrow block along the wall.

## 289 Acids and poisons

Never keep acidic or poisonous fluids in bottles that children associate with lemonade or similar drinks.

# Sculptured bed

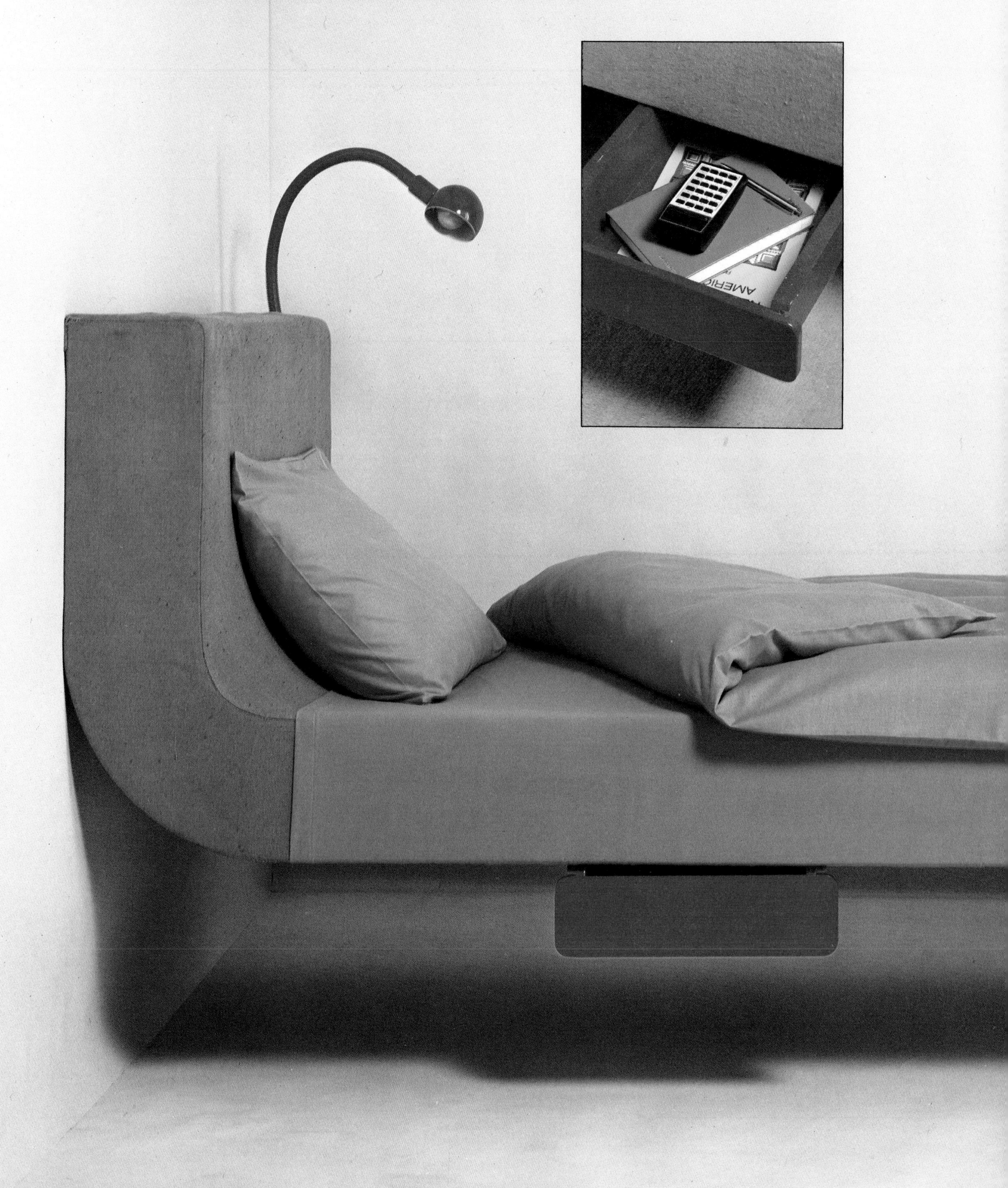

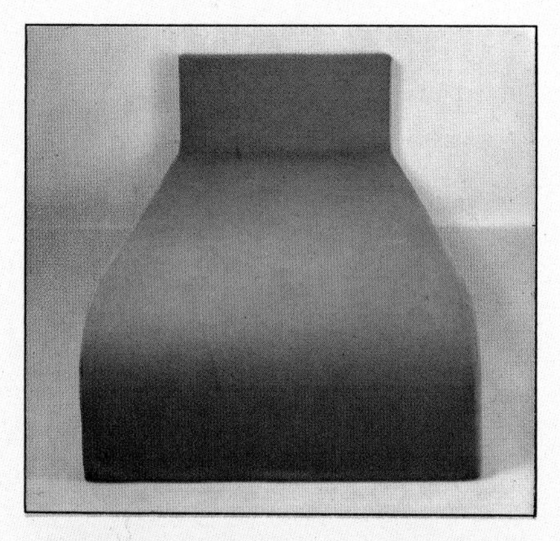

The graceful undulating lines of this bed give it a clean, sculptured look. A continental quilt and fitted bottom sheet, cunningly and neatly secured by a length of nylon fastening strip, make it simple to keep the bed tidy. The moulded look is achieved by building up layers of foam on a pegboard base to form a comfortable mattress. The whole structure is then encased in a simple-to-sew fabric cover.

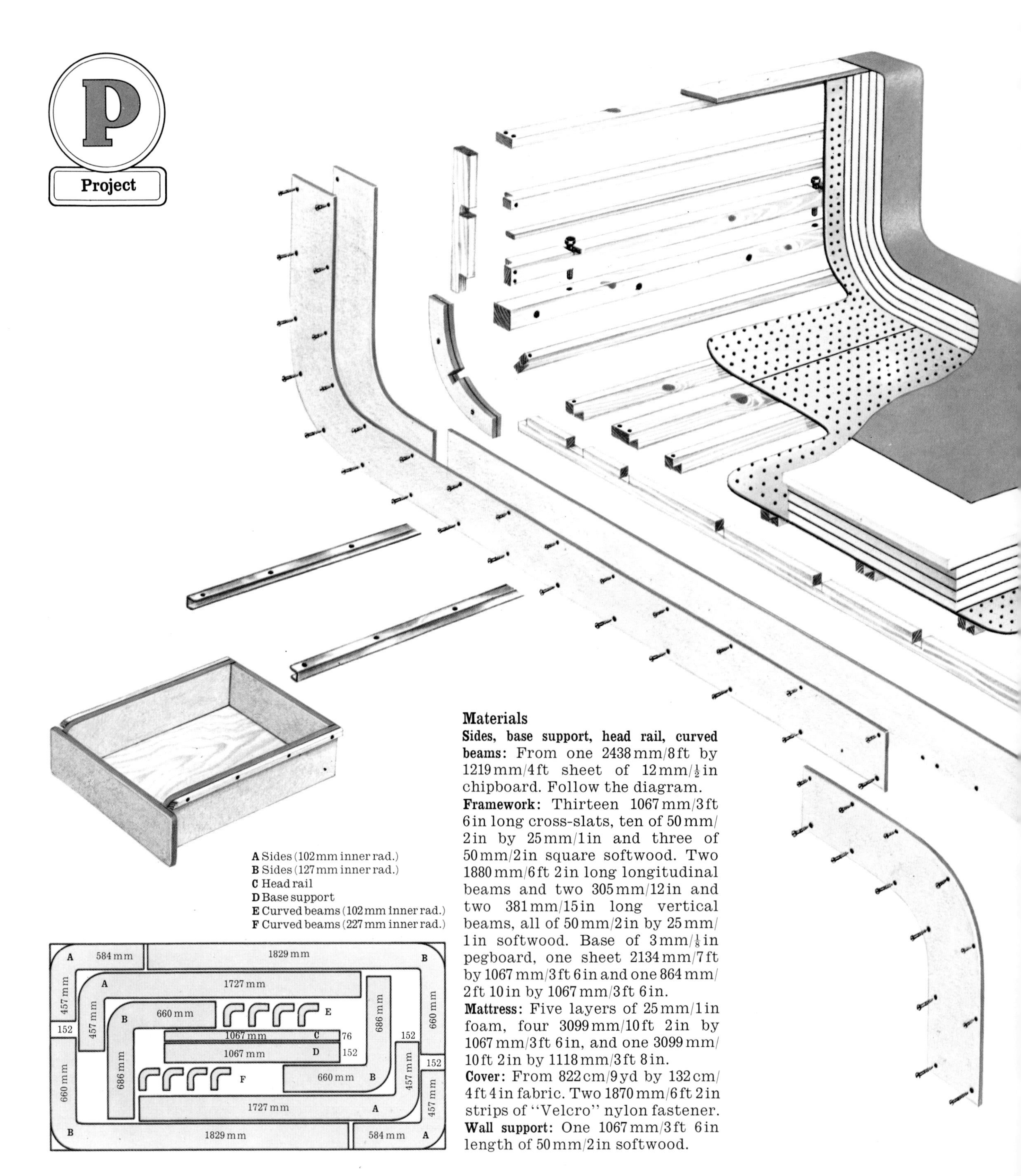


## Materials

**Sides, base support, head rail, curved beams:** From one 2438 mm/8 ft by 1219 mm/4 ft sheet of 12 mm/½ in chipboard. Follow the diagram.

**Framework:** Thirteen 1067 mm/3 ft 6 in long cross-slats, ten of 50 mm/2 in by 25 mm/1 in and three of 50 mm/2 in square softwood. Two 1880 mm/6 ft 2 in long longitudinal beams and two 305 mm/12 in and two 381 mm/15 in long vertical beams, all of 50 mm/2 in by 25 mm/1 in softwood. Base of 3 mm/⅛ in pegboard, one sheet 2134 mm/7 ft by 1067 mm/3 ft 6 in and one 864 mm/2 ft 10 in by 1067 mm/3 ft 6 in.

**Mattress:** Five layers of 25 mm/1 in foam, four 3099 mm/10 ft 2 in by 1067 mm/3 ft 6 in, and one 3099 mm/10 ft 2 in by 1118 mm/3 ft 8 in.

**Cover:** From 822 cm/9 yd by 132 cm/4 ft 4 in fabric. Two 1870 mm/6 ft 2 in strips of "Velcro" nylon fastener.

**Wall support:** One 1067 mm/3 ft 6 in length of 50 mm/2 in softwood.

The overall dimensions of the bed illustrated are 241 cm/7 ft 11 in by 1117 mm/3 ft 8 in. In no circumstances should the width exceed 1219 mm/4 ft. The unit can accommodate drawers.

First check that there is sufficient space to fit the bed and that the wall is sound enough to take its weight.

**The sides**

Cut out the chipboard pieces and smooth their edges with glasspaper. Glue and screw the side pieces together as illustrated.

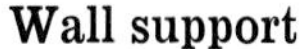

**Wall support**

Cramp together one of the three 50 mm/2 in square softwood cross-slats and the block for the wall support. Drill two holes through both pieces to take 127 mm/5 in coach bolts. Uncramp the pieces and enlarge the holes on the wall support block. Chisel slots through the holes on the cross-slat to take the heads of the coach bolts.

**Framework**

Mark up halving joints on the two longitudinal beams at 305 mm/12 in centres and on seven of the thirteen cross-slats. Centre the wall-support cross-slat 381 mm/15 in from the head of the bed, and the remaining 50 mm/2 in cross-slats, one 183 cm/6 ft from the front edge of the foot of the bed to take the joins of the pegboard base, and the other 12 mm/½ in from the foot. Mark halving joints on the four vertical beams and on the remaining cross-slats. Cut the joints and pre-drill them.

Glue and screw a longitudinal beam flush with the bottom of each side. Continue the beam around the curves of each side by gluing and screwing the curved chipboard sections in place. Similarly glue and screw the four vertical beams at either end.

Assemble the framework by gluing the slats onto the beams and screwing through the holes.

Wet the pegboard on its rough side along the lines of the curve. Glue and pin the boards to the 50 mm/2 in square cross-slat, and then, working along the framework, glue and pin the sides into the longitudinal beams, bending the boards to fit the curves.

Complete the framework by gluing and screwing the chipboard base support in place, with a scrap softwood stiffener running the full length, and similarly fix the head rail.

**Mattress and cover**

Position and patch glue each of the five layers of foam together with the larger overlapping the top sides.

Cut the fabric cover into three pieces to fit the sides and top. Stitch it along the bed's top edges. Attach it to the under edges of the sides with glue and staples or tacks. Fit the strips of "Velcro" nylon fastener under each edge. Cut the sheet to fit the length of the bed and attach the other half of the fastener to its edges.

**Fixing to the wall**

Mark a line on the wall 58 cm/23 in up from the floor. Position the top edge of the wall support block on the line and fix it to the wall. Drop the coach bolts through the holes in the cross-slat and cap the block with a glued scrap of softwood. Bring the bed up against the wall, aligning the block and cross-slat so that the bolts can be dropped through to secure the bed.

**Drawer**

Fix two metal runners to a pair of cross-slats and cut the drawer from chipboard or softwood, using screwed and glued butt-joints to complete it. Round the edges of the front panels.

*See also Tips on*
Preparation 174
Marking up 520
Adhesives 81
Cutting 112, 370
Smoothing 18, 171
Drawers 299

# Upholstered furniture

Achieving the professional look in a large piece of soft furniture such as the sofa illustrated may seem complex, but the construction principles are very simple. The method used to build this sofa can be applied to any type or size of furniture. The whole concept is based on the careful planning and construction of the arms and cushions—and this could equally well be applied to chairs or a smaller sofa unit. Comfort and shape are achieved by using Terylene wadding over blocks of foam built, where necessary, around a wooden frame. The removable covering can be either stretch or non-stretch fabric.

## Materials for the base unit

All chipboard is 18 mm/¾ in thick.
**Frame and top:** Two 2159 mm/7 ft 1 in and three 711 mm/2 ft 4 in beams and four 50 mm/2 in by 107 mm/4 in corner blocks—all of 50 mm/2 in by 100 mm/4 in softwood. One 2235 mm/7 ft 4 in by 1067 mm/3 ft 6 in chipboard top.
**Corners:** Sixteen sections each of five layers of 114 mm/4½ in square chipboard off-cuts.
**Side panels:** Four 203 mm/8 in, two 711 mm/2 ft 4 in, two 381 mm/15 in, one 1168 mm/3 ft 10 in and one 152 mm/6 in long; all from 95 mm/3¾ in wide chipboard.
**Cushion bases:** From chipboard. Two 914 mm/3 ft by 406 mm/16 in; two 584 mm/23 in by 406 mm/16 in; one 1372 mm/4 ft 6 in by 584 mm/23 in; one 406 mm/16 in by 355 mm/14 in.

## Assembling the frame and top

Butt-joint the frame, using glue and screws. Cut the corner sections to the required radius; notch them as illustrated and glue and screw in place. Glue and screw the side panels into the notched corner sections. Shape the chipboard top to cover the frame, apply glue to the top surfaces of the frame and screw the top into the beams. Shape the cushion bases to fit, rounding the corners on the underside, and position dry on the top. Drill holes to take T-nuts.

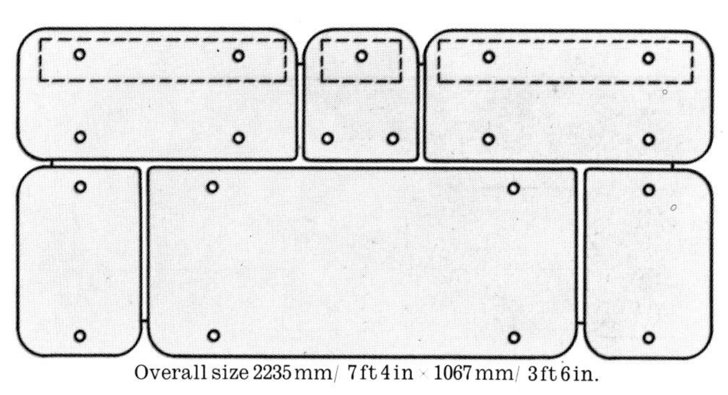
Overall size 2235 mm/ 7 ft 4 in · 1067 mm/ 3 ft 6 in.

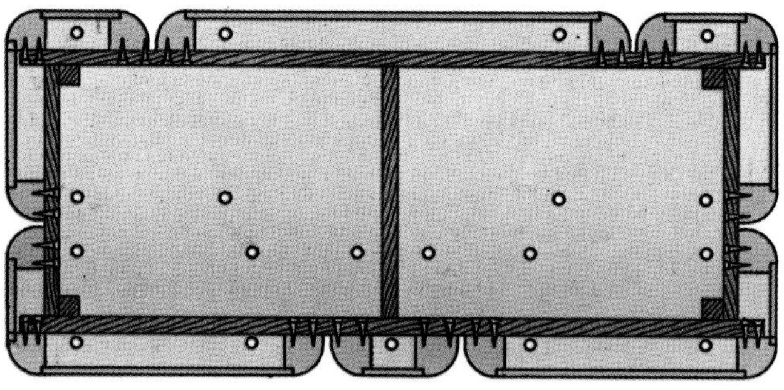

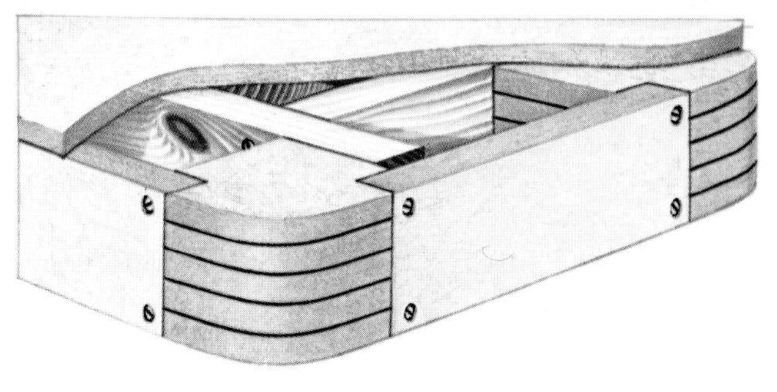

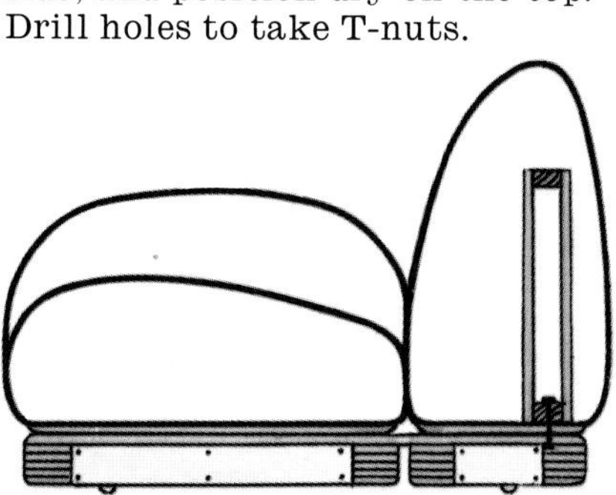

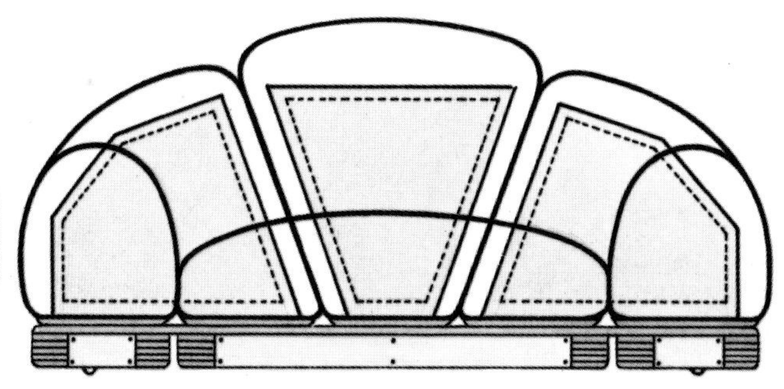

## Constructing the back sections

Each back section has a strengthener of two shaped chipboard sides cut to a maximum height of 635 mm/25 in and separated by a 50 mm/2 in by 25 mm/1 in softwood frame with a 50 mm/2 in batten at the base. Glue and screw three of the sides together. Align the batten with the holes on its cushion base, and glue and screw. Drill through the holes into the batten to take the T-nuts. Insert the T-nuts into all the bases—back and front—then fix the remaining side to the back strengtheners.

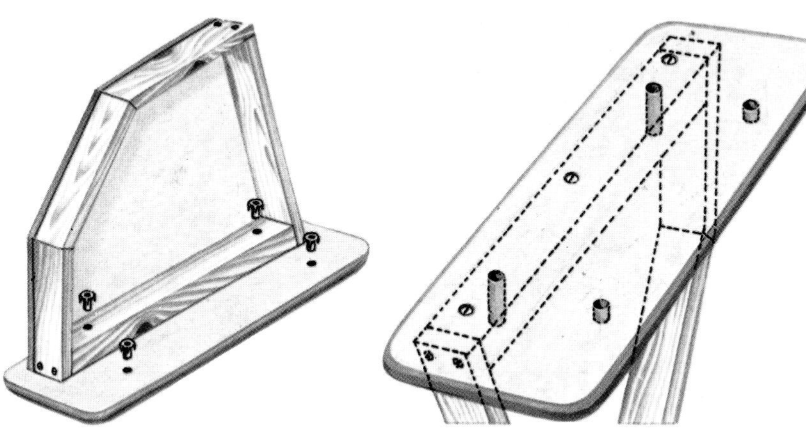

*See also Tips on*
Marking up 253, 520
Adhesives 81
Cutting 112, 370
Foam rubber 490
Finishing 18

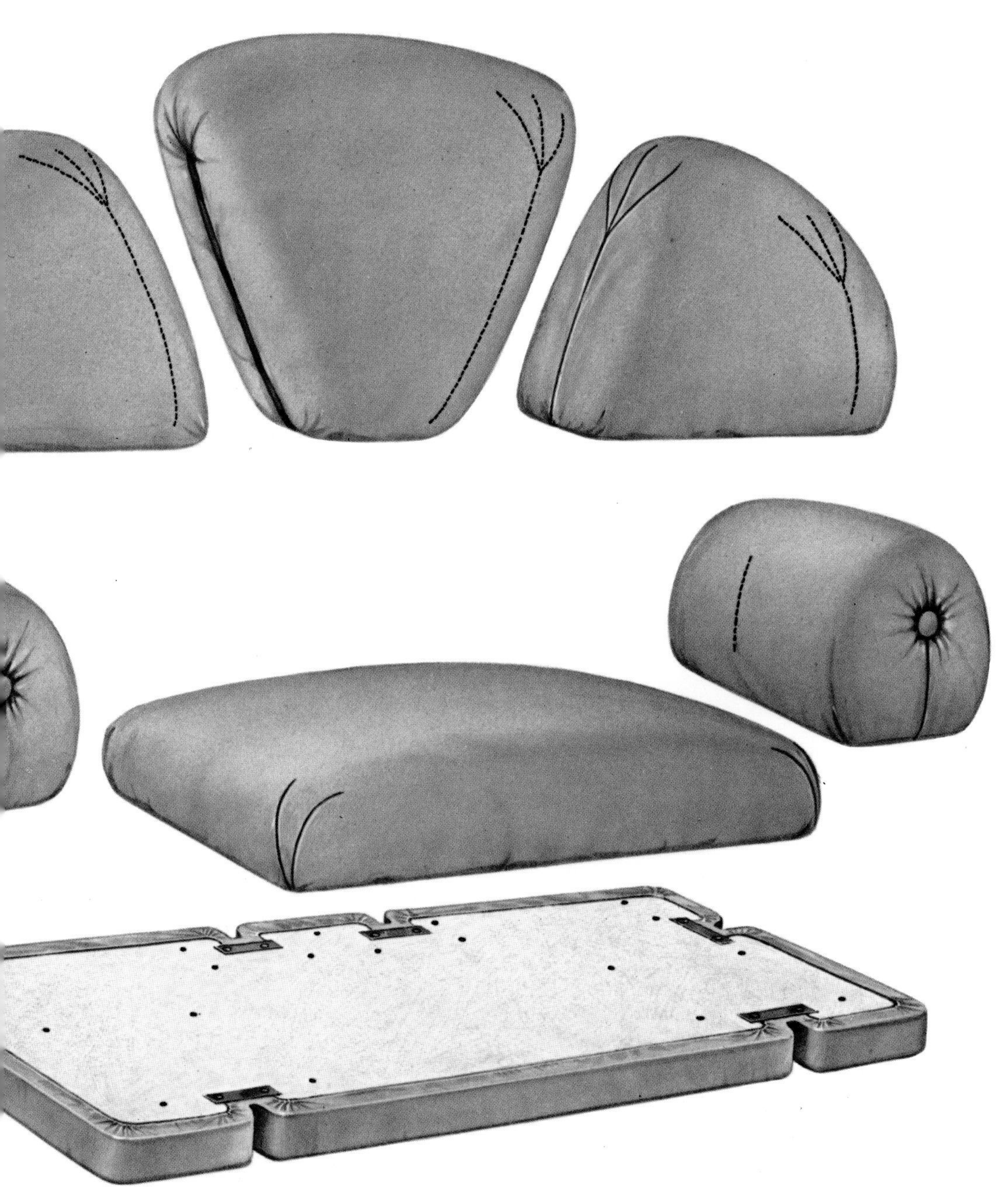

## Covering

A total length of 11m/12yd by 147cm/58in is required for both the cotton undercover and the fabric top. Use a stretch fabric.

First cut the cotton undercover as a large pocket following the seams indicated (centre left). Where the material has to be gathered, snip the edge of the cotton until it lies flat. Untack the material and use it as a template for the fabric top, making a hemming allowance. Tack and machine the undercover. Fit it over the foam, filling with extra wadding if necessary. Staple to the underside of the base. Tack and machine the fabric pieces, using a button to cover the gathered ends, and hem the base edges to take a length of elastic; use a "Velcro" strip fastener for one side of the rear centre section to enable the cover to be removed.

## The main frame and assembly

Glue a 25mm/1in thick layer of foam to the edges of the main frame. Cut a length of fabric to size; fit elastic and "Velcro" strip fasteners at the points where the corners turn inwards, and fit the "Velcro" in matching positions on the base. Fit castors to the inner corner blocks. Bolt the units into the T-nuts.

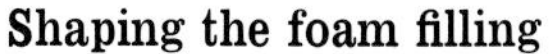

## Shaping the foam filling

Glue foam plastic blocks, 457mm/18in thick, to the bases of the arms, and 279mm/11in thick to the seat base. Carve one arm first and make a template from it for the other. Glue on Terylene wadding to finish off the shape. Glue foam strips, 50mm/2in thick, along the frame of the side strengtheners, 228mm/9in thick to the top, and 50mm/2in thick to the sides of the centre strengthener. Glue slabs of foam either side of each strengthener to fit flush with the base edges and finish as before.

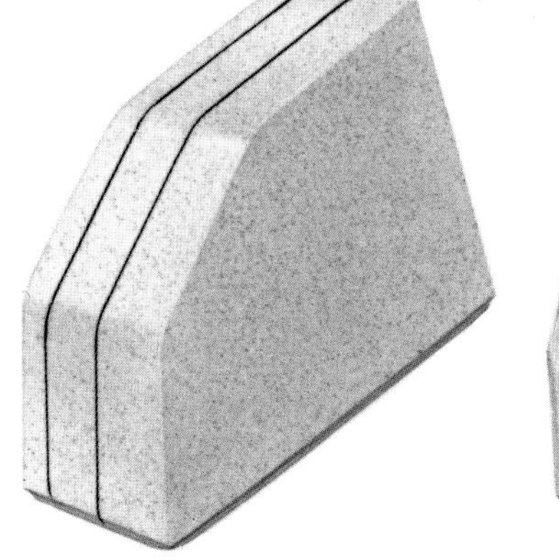

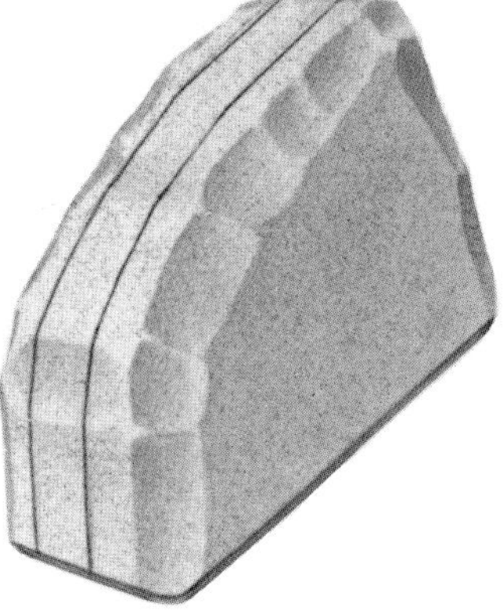

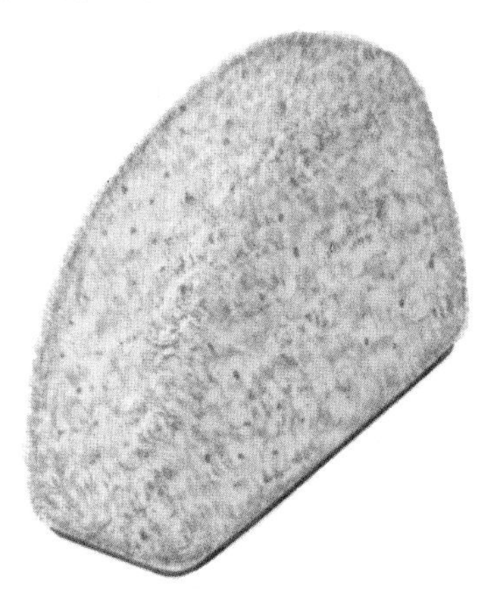

# Fitted hi-fi

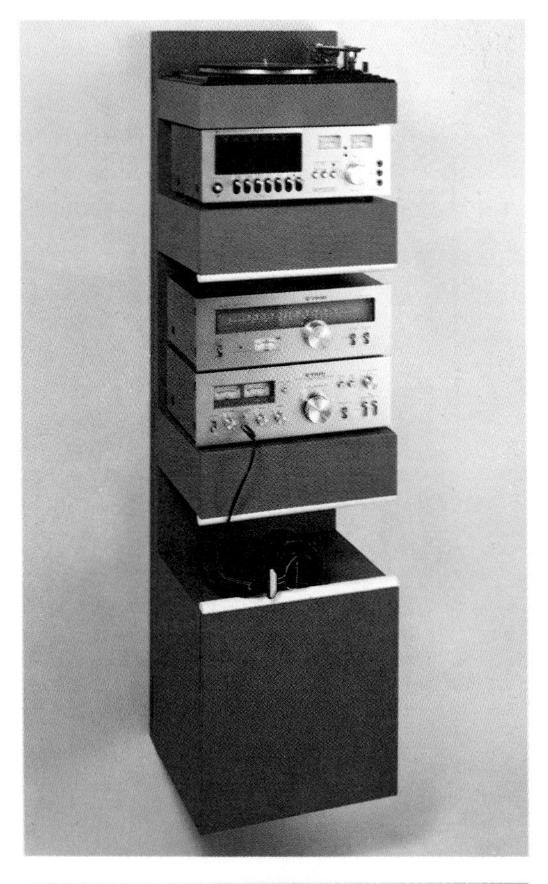

The pleasingly functional good looks of most modern hi-fi equipment makes it worth displaying. However, when laid out side by side, the various units involved tend to take up too much room. The solution is to stack the components vertically.

This wall rack, with its neutral finish, provides an attractive way of doing this and hides the inevitable tangle of wires. Drawer and cabinet are sized to provide storage for records and cassettes. For an unusual—but highly attractive—finish, the speakers can be covered with a fabric chosen for acoustic suitability and to match the neutral finish of the rack, or to blend in with an existing decor. They are raised off the floor to improve sound quality.

### Speaker finishes

Covering a pair of speakers with fabric and supporting them on simple frames turns them into attractive pieces of furniture.

Ideally, proprietary speaker cloth should be used. If using a conventional fabric, however, check its suitability by holding it to the light. If it is reasonably transparent it should not baffle the sound.

Supporting the speakers on frames should reduce any "boominess" in the bass register. The optimum height is usually with the tweeter at the ear level of a seated listener.

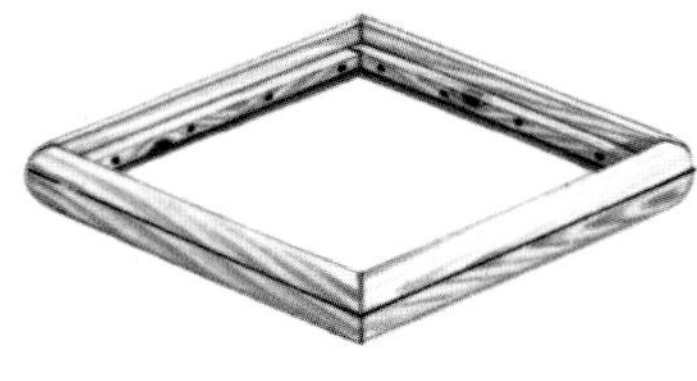

### The frame

Use 37mm/1½in square softwood for the butt-jointed box frame.

### Material finishes

A speaker and frame can be covered together as one glued and screwed unit, or the two can be covered individually. If using a stretch material, stitch a single seam to form a sleeve and pull it into place. A non-stretch material can be stapled into position.

To finish the cover at the top of the speakers, first glue and pin a quarter-round beading along the edge. Pull the fabric tight over the speaker and staple or tack it in place. Conceal the fasteners by positioning a mirror, cut to fit within the beading, on the top. Construct a beading frame for terminal panels so that the fabric can be hemmed around them.

### Moulding finishes

The covered speakers can be finished with a variety of mouldings. The two suggestions illustrated here—the first for a speaker and frame covered individually, the second for a combined unit—use quarter-round mouldings.

Construct a frame with the same dimensions as the speaker base from 12mm/½in square softwood. Make up half-round moulding strips. Mitre the ends of the strips and glue and pin them to the frame. Round off the corners with glasspaper and then paint.

To make a plinth, size the smallest tier so that it fits tightly against the side of the frame and build up accordingly. Mitre the corners, glue and pin into softwood battens, positioned as illustrated, and paint.

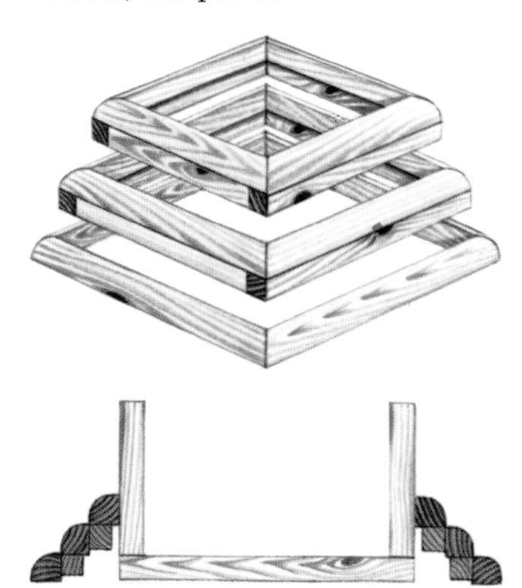

### Hi-fi rack

Convenient operating heights for the various pieces of equipment determine the vertical dimensions of the hi-fi rack. The rack is wall-mounted to avoid floor vibrations, so, before starting work, check that the wall is sound enough to take its weight.

### The frame

Use 50mm/2in by 25mm/1in softwood supports for three sides of the outer frame, cutting them to the height and width of the complete rack. Use a 25mm/1in square support for the upright which will take the hinged inner frame. Dowel and glue. Cut a sheet of laminated chipboard to fit flush with the frame's edge and glue and screw it in place.

Drill regularly spaced screw holes into the chipboard, so that the shelves can be fixed at differing levels, and a series of larger oval holes as wiring outlets. Cut a notch in the base of the frame to serve as the main outlet for the various electrical leads.

Cut the inner frame from 50mm/2in by 25mm/1in softwood, to fit flush within the outer frame. Dowel and glue.

Mark up and cut the positions for the hinges on the frames, then paint them. Attach the hinges and fit a magnetic catch to keep the unit closed. Mount the unit by screwing through the inner frame.

### Record deck

Cut the sides of the deck support from laminated chipboard and butt-joint them together. Glue and pin a hardboard base. Screw a 50mm/2in square softwood block into the back inside surface and screw metal L-brackets against it in both corners. Drill a hole through the softwood and chipboard to take the wiring.

### Drawers

To make the frame for the drawers, cut the two sides and top and bottom pieces from laminated chipboard and butt-joint them. Glue and screw a 50mm/2in square softwood block flush with the back inside edge of the top.

Construct the four sides of the drawer from butt-jointed chipboard and fit a plywood base, gluing and pinning throughout. Finish the front of the drawer by sizing a piece of laminated chipboard to fit flush with the outside

*See also Tips on*
Marking up 520
Adhesives 81
Cutting 346
Dowelling 466, 513
Joints 243, 381
Fixing 245
Smoothing 459
Painting 706

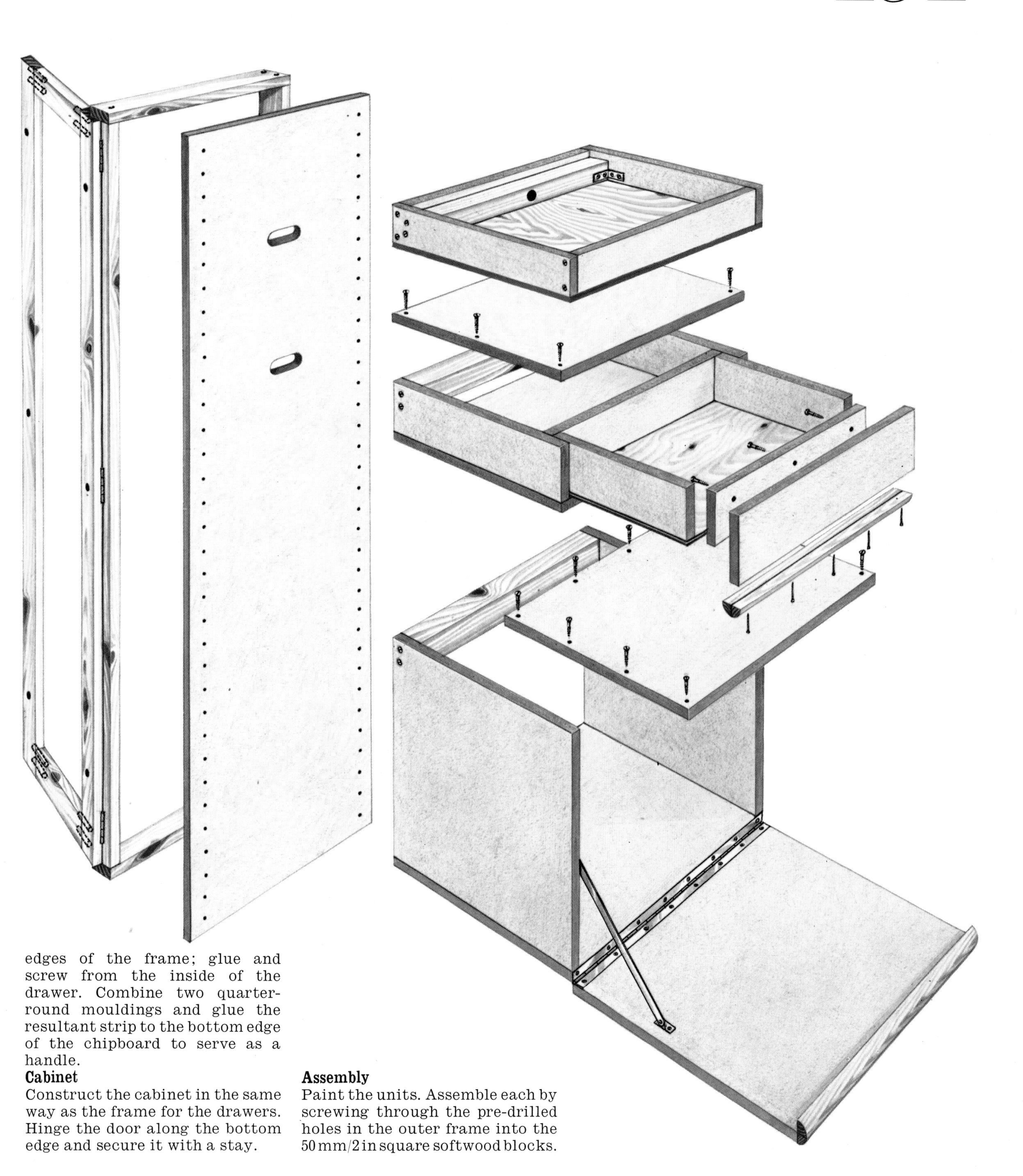

edges of the frame; glue and screw from the inside of the drawer. Combine two quarter-round mouldings and glue the resultant strip to the bottom edge of the chipboard to serve as a handle.

**Cabinet**

Construct the cabinet in the same way as the frame for the drawers. Hinge the door along the bottom edge and secure it with a stay.

**Assembly**

Paint the units. Assemble each by screwing through the pre-drilled holes in the outer frame into the 50 mm/2 in square softwood blocks.

# Tiled furniture

Ordinary mirror or ceramic tiles fixed on wooden frames are the basis for these striking matching tables and plinths. The crisp shapes and finishes of the tiles are enhanced by decorative beading and grouting. The corner units are especially suited for plant display, while the tables can be used both in and out of doors.

The key to making both these pieces of tiled furniture is to mark up all the dimensions "dry" first, as these are dictated by the size of tiles chosen and the number of tiles required. Lay out on the construction material the tiles and beading that will cover it before starting each stage. All beading should be the same thickness as the tiles. Either ceramic or mirror tiles can be used; if mirror tiles are chosen, remember to buy enough tiles at one time for the complete job, as otherwise it may prove impossible to match them so that they fit. It is also important that they lie flush with the beading to eliminate projecting, rough glass edges, so the best type to buy are the ones fitted with pads.

Use sheets of 12mm/½in thick chipboard for the sub-frames.

**Making the table**

Make the table top by gluing and pinning lengths of chipboard together to form a shallow box. The legs are made in two right-angled sections, braced with support blocks. Each side is as wide as a tile width plus two internal dimensions of a right-angle bead.

Fit the legs to the top by gluing and screwing through the sides and down through the top. Attach a dome glide—obtainable from a D-I-Y shop—to the base of each leg, fitting another internal block to hold it. Alternatively, use rubber pads.

Glue on the beading, mitred where necessary at the corners, and secure it with veneer pins or very small panel pins. Smooth down the edges with glasspaper and fill any holes. Then paint the beading with emulsion or gloss paint, according to choice. Allow the paint to dry and then fit the tiles, using the recommended adhesive.

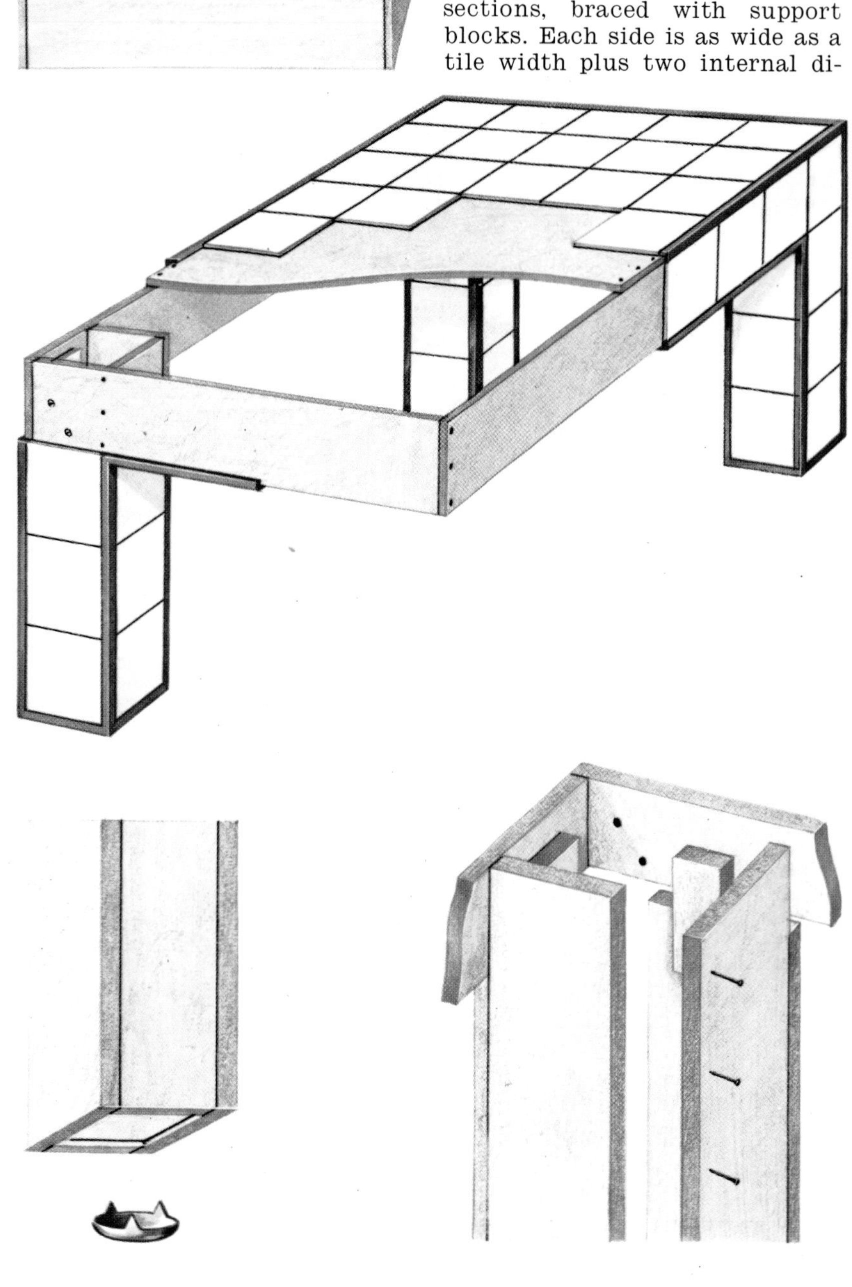

**Making the stands**

If the stands are to form a corner unit, as illustrated, only the visible surfaces need be tiled. The stands can be designed to form a central unit and stacked to any desired height, but follow the plan (right) for arranging the tiles on the upper surfaces.

When making the stands, work from the topmost unit downwards to make it easier to position the central strips of beading on the lower units accurately. Having marked up the top unit, cut it out and glue and pin it together to form a cube. Fit the beading, mitred where necessary, and secure it with pins. Smooth down the edges and fill any holes. Paint the beading, allow it to dry and then fit the tiles.

Place the cube on another sheet of chipboard and lay the next set of tiles and beading around it. This will form the top of the next stand. Use chipboard and cover in the same way as the cube.

Follow the same procedure for subsequent stands and for the base. When making the base, strengthen it with internal cross-pieces, linked with halving joints; glue and screw through support blocks fitted into the central internal angles.

**Finishing**

If using ceramic tiles, fill the gaps between them with standard waterproof grouting. This can be coloured, if desired. Simply paint the grouting with a fine brush. The grouting will absorb the paint; wipe away any surplus on the tiles with a damp cloth.

*See also Tips on*
Marking up 520
Adhesives 81
Cutting 112
Joints 243
Fixing 641
Grouting 481

293

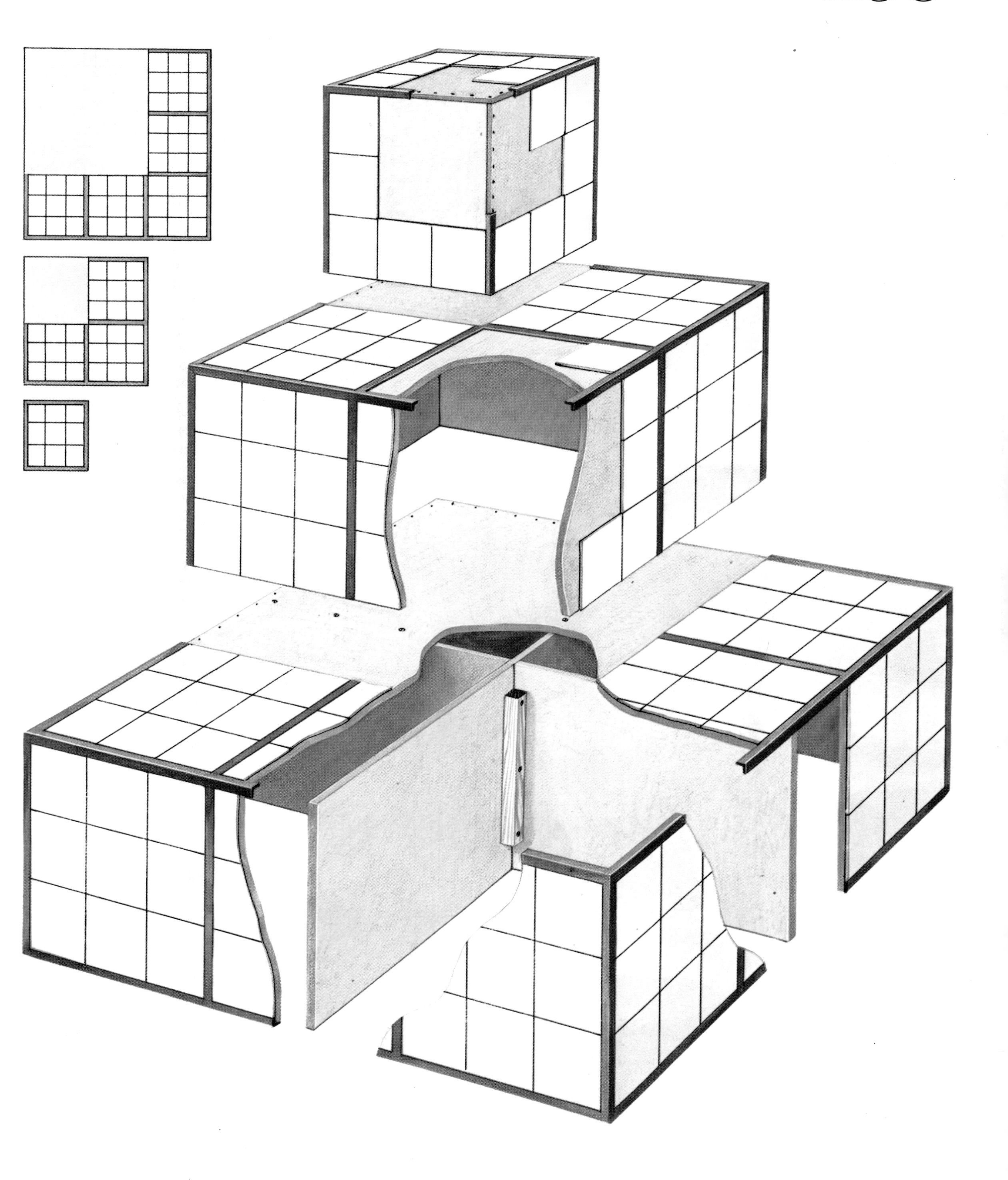

# Storage screen/1

This series of compact fold-out cupboards doubles as a storage/ display unit and as a low-level room divider. The interior can be tailored to any use—this one, with its drawers, cupboards and shelves, has been neatly designed to take some of the multitude of things that most young flat-dwellers like to have within reach, but not necessarily in view. Each of the units is hinged and set on castors, making it easy to open out or move about.

# 294

Each unit of this storage screen is 838mm/2ft 9in high and 635mm/2ft 1in wide. The units are hinged together so that the screen can be folded away and are fitted with castors so that it can be moved easily. The overall dimensions can be varied if desired.

**Materials for one unit**
Two 808mm/2ft 7¾in by 152mm/6in uprights and two 635mm/2ft 1in by 152mm/6in horizontal sections, cut from 15mm/⅝in thick laminated chipboard. Four strips of 12mm/½in square batten for the back edges, together with an 808mm/2ft 7¾in by 603mm/1ft 11¾in sheet of 6mm/¼in hardboard for the back panel.

**Hinges and castors:** Two steel butt hinges and three furniture castors for each unit.

**Shelves, drawers and doors:** Cut from the same thickness chipboard as that used for the main structure; 6mm/¼in thick plywood is required for the sides and backs of the drawers.

**Making the units**
Make up each frame by butt-jointing the appropriate lengths of board together, using a PVA woodworking adhesive and countersinking screws into the joints. Fill the cut edges and screw holes with fine-grain filler and rub them down with glasspaper. Glue and pin the strips of batten around the back of each frame, recessing them 12mm/½in from the back edge. Glue and pin the back panel to the battens.

Stack the completed units together, edges flush. Mark up positions for the hinges and chisel out recesses for them.

**Fitting out the screen**
Notch out 12mm/½in from the inside corners of each shelf so that they will fit around the battens and glue and pin them into place through the side framework. The angled shelves are made from two pieces of laminated chipboard, butt-jointed at right angles and secured by gluing and pinning.

Remember to allow for the additional thickness of the doors when fitting shelves inside cupboards. When fitting the doors, make sure to recess the hinges, so that they do not project when the doors are closed. Drill 37mm/1½in holes for finger pulls. Paint the units and then fit the hinges and castors.

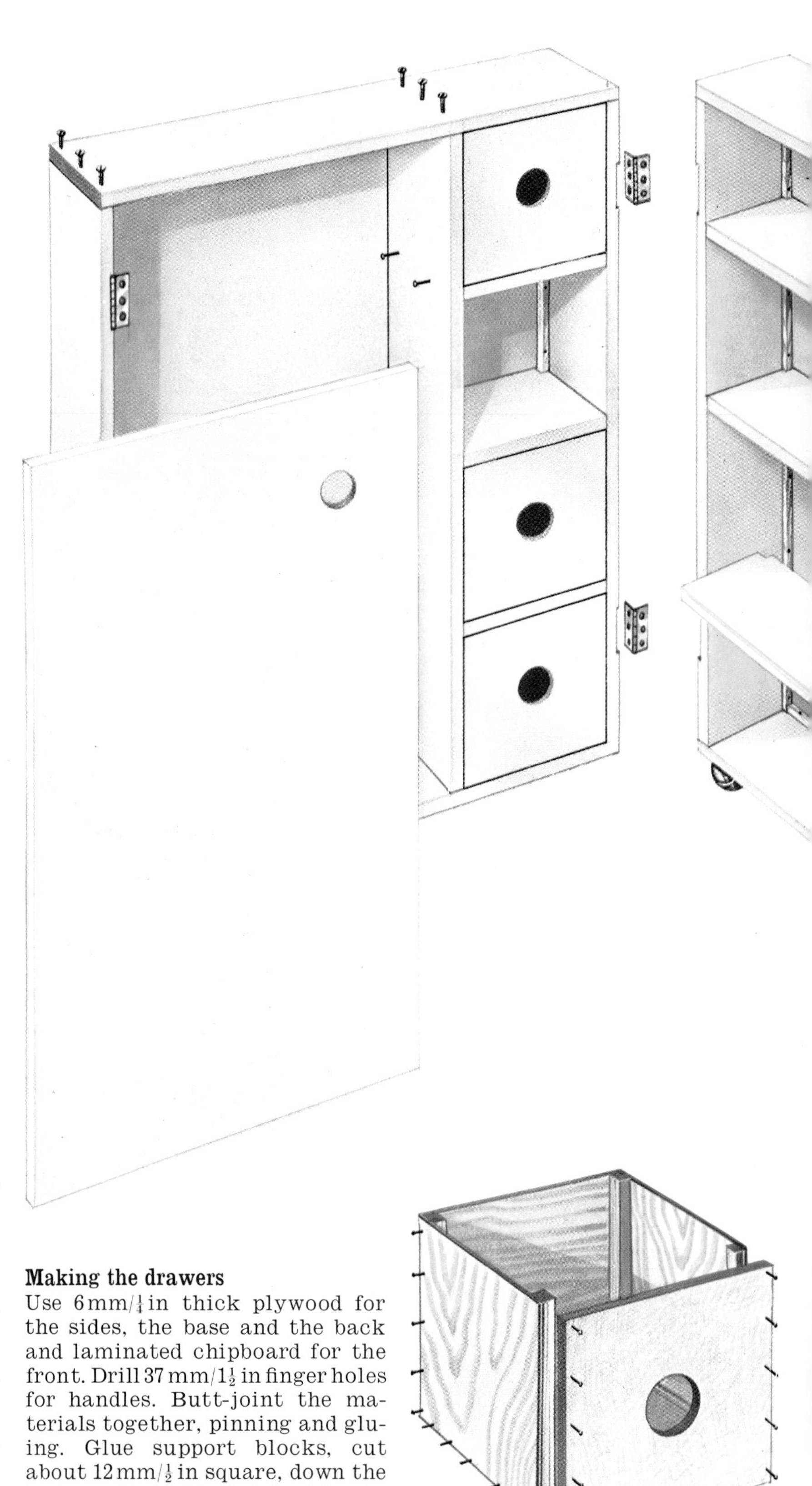

**Making the drawers**
Use 6mm/¼in thick plywood for the sides, the base and the back and laminated chipboard for the front. Drill 37mm/1½in finger holes for handles. Butt-joint the materials together, pinning and gluing. Glue support blocks, cut about 12mm/½in square, down the full length of the joints. Fit the completed drawers in position between two shelves.

**Panels and castors**
Paint a pattern on the back panels before assembly. Space them with 30 mm/1¼ in wide blocks, mark up and paint, using masking tape to achieve a clear definition. Fit the castors on each unit as shown.

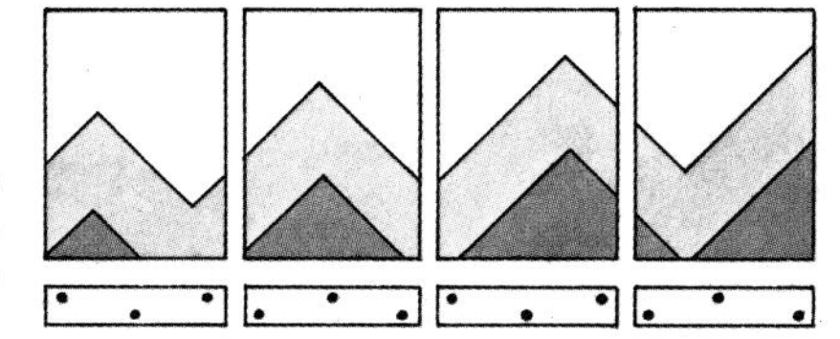

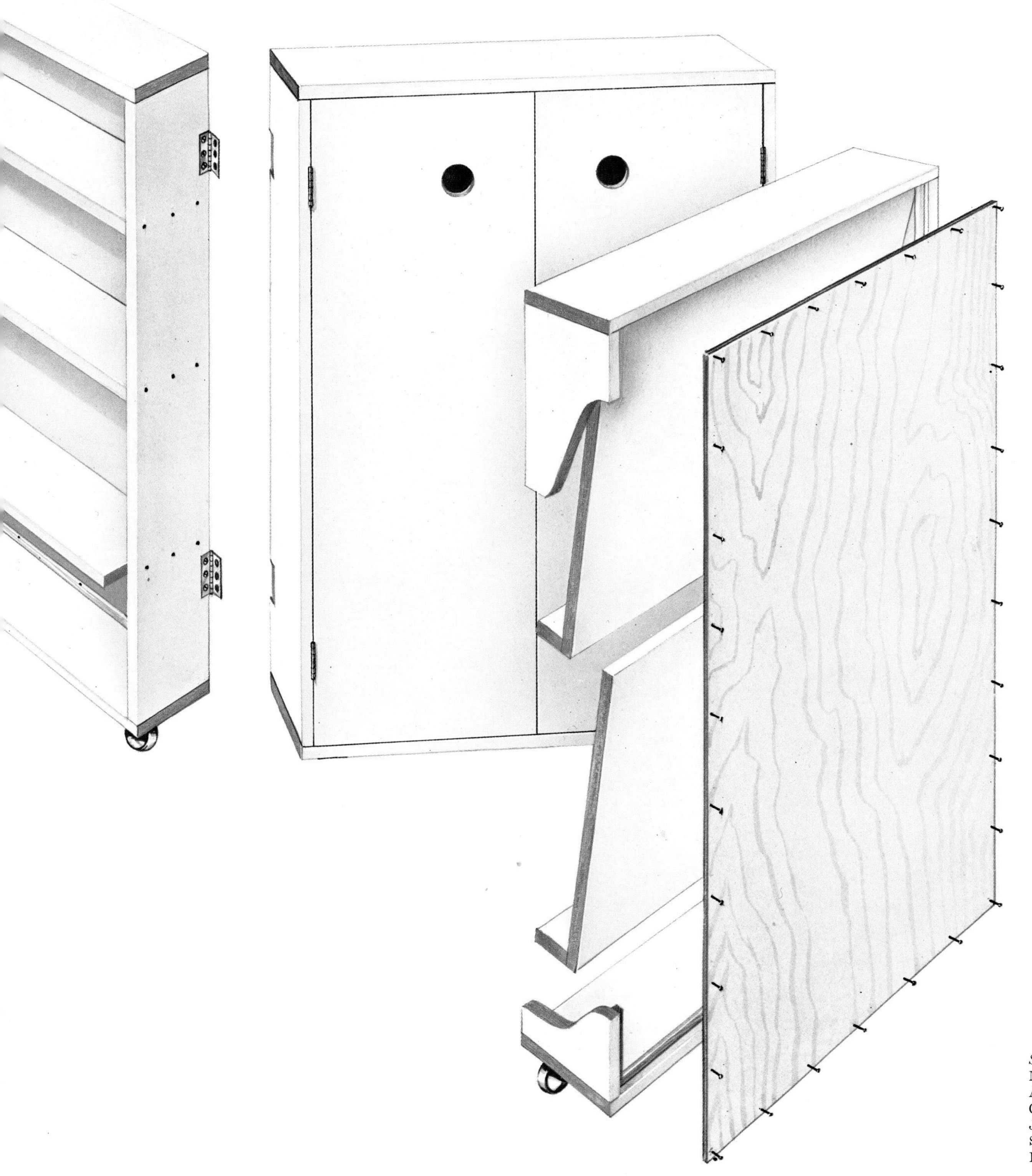

*See also Tips on*
Marking up 520
Adhesives 81
Cutting 346, 370
Joints 243
Smoothing 459
Painting 241, 706

# Storage screen/2

This shoulder-high screen makes an ideal room partition at seated eye-level. Designed as a decorative unit, the screen is particularly suited for plant display. Its size and use are completely flexible because any number of sections can be added; these can be quickly opened out in a variety of patterns. In addition, any number of shelves can be used, at any height, on both sides. Those sections left free on the ends can be arranged most attractively.

The screen is sturdy and can be easily dismantled so that both screen and shelves can be stored when not in use.

The construction principle is simplicity itself; sandwiching sheets of hardboard together and linking them with canvas hinges. Pre-drill regularly spaced holes to make it easy to fix the shelves in a variety of positions.

This display shelving screen is an effective room divider at seated eye level. It is constructed from 3mm/⅛in hardboard cut into 1524mm/5ft by 304mm/1ft panels, a series of which are hinged together with strips of canvas.

**Making the screen**

The screen is built up by sandwiching the canvas hinges between the panels. First bevel all edges of the hardboard panels, using a coarse glasspaper block. The bevels give the edges an attractive finish. Then carefully mark out on one panel the positions of the screw holes, through which the shelves will eventually be fixed. Drill the holes and then redrill them on the outside of each panel with a countersink bit. Paint the outside face of each panel.

**Fitting the hinges**

Use strips of stout, unpainted canvas as hinges for the sections of the screen. Each strip should be about 154mm/6in wide, and positioned so that each section can fold back flat against another.

Place a panel—painted face downwards—on a clean, flat surface and glue a strip of canvas in place with contact adhesive, remembering to allow the necessary overlap. Spread adhesive over the exposed surface of the board and the upper surface of the canvas. Then apply adhesive to the inside face of another hardboard panel and position it face to face with its partner, making sure that the screw holes are precisely aligned. Position the next panel with the canvas overlapping and continue until all the sections of the screen are hinged together.

**Making the shelves**

Make the shelves from lengths of 50mm/2in by 25mm/1in softwood, cut to form a triangular frame—with two short sides of identical length—and surfaced with a piece of hardboard. The length of the two sides is the width of a folding section of the screen. Once complete, mark guidelines down the centre of two sides of each shelf for screw holes to correspond to the holes drilled in the screen. Position the shelf against the screen—it will be level when the line is visible through both screw holes in the screen. Screw each shelf into position from the opposite side of the screen.

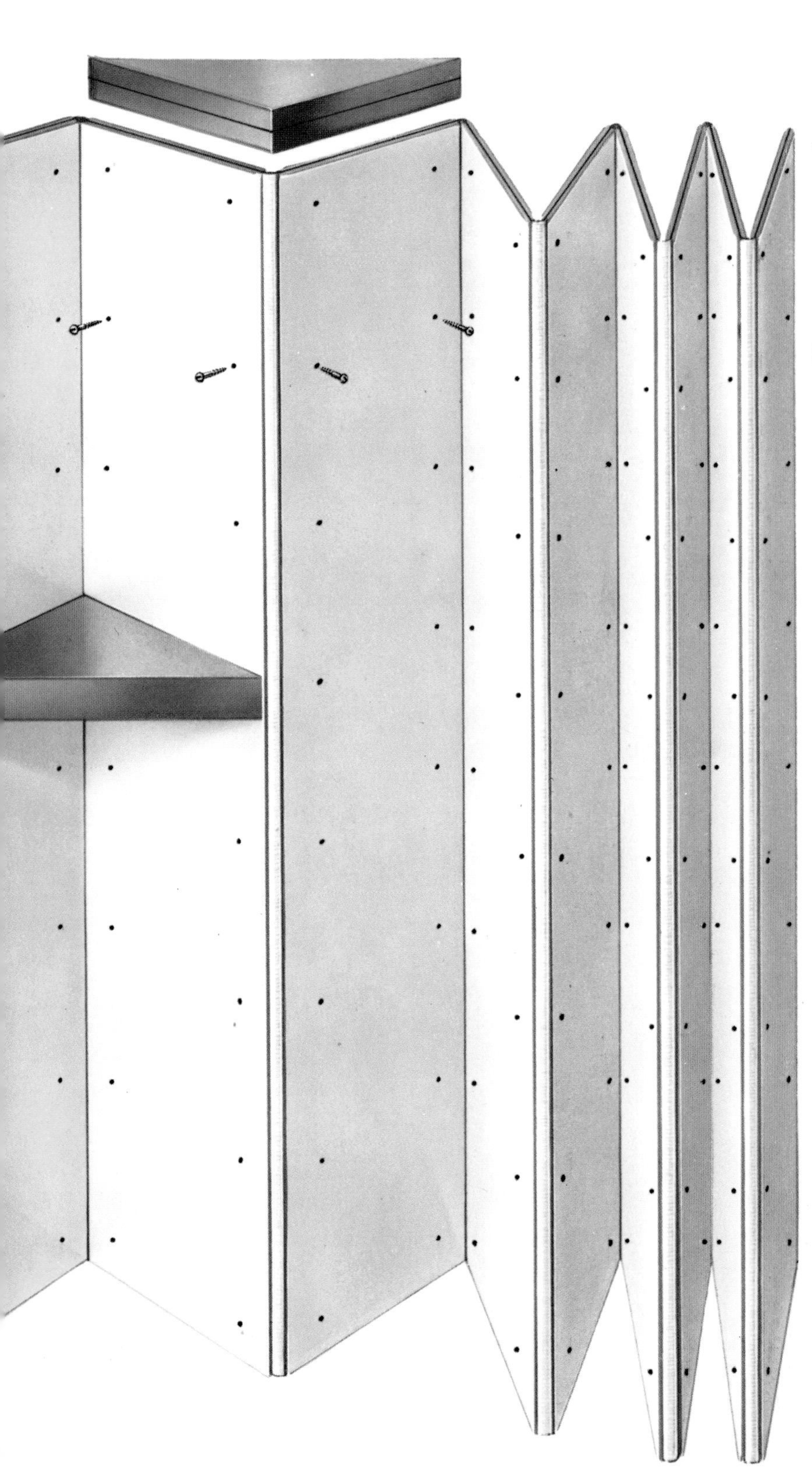

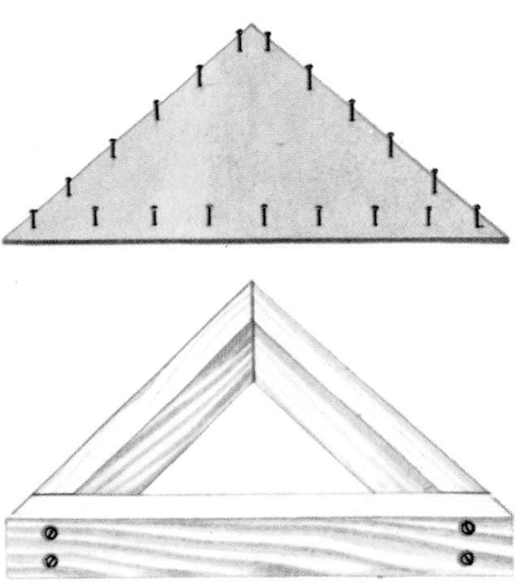

**Assembling the shelves**
Glue and screw the sides of each shelf together and pin the hardboard top in place. Then smooth down the edges of the hardboard flush with the wood and conceal the screw and pin holes. Paint the completed shelves before marking up for assembly.

**Drilling the screw holes**
Mark up the positions of the screw holes for the shelves on a single sheet of hardboard, a fair distance from the edge and equally spaced along the sheet. Cramp this marked-up sheet on the others and use it as a template to drill all the screw holes.

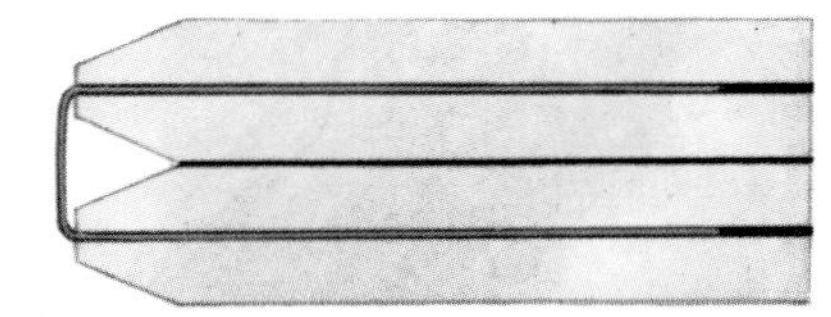

**Fixing the hinge width**
Assemble two panels of the screen "dry" as if folded. Sandwich a canvas strip between each panel and measure how much material is required to allow the section to fold.

*See also Tips on*
Marking up 520
Adhesives 81
Cutting 370, 408
Fixing 386
Painting 706

# Storage screen/3

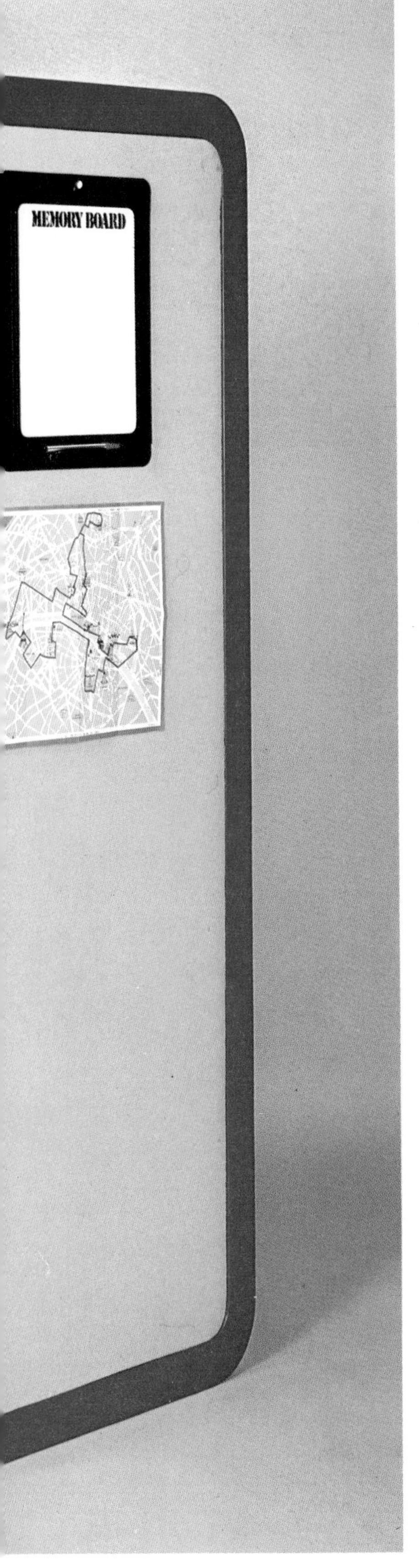

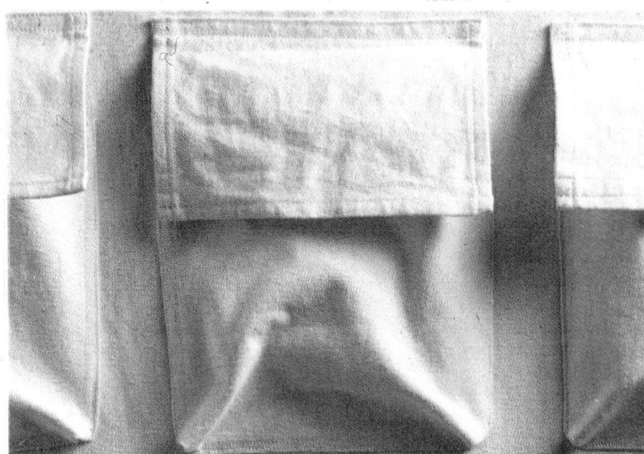

This tall, folding screen with its pockets, hooks and hanging rail provides attractive and unusual storage space. It can be used as a room divider, to create privacy within a large room, or it can be arranged to brighten up awkward corners. The pinboard used in the screen illustrated adds a colourful decorative touch, though a full-length mirror could just as easily be inserted into this, or indeed any other frame. Folded flat, the screen takes up little space and can easily be stored away when it is not required.

The storage screen can be fitted out to suit most requirements. Hanging rails, mirrors, pinboards or pocket panels can all be included.

**Materials for one frame**

**Basic framework:** Two 1829 mm/6 ft uprights of 63 mm/2½ in by 37 mm/1½ in thick softwood, joined by two 800 mm/2 ft 7½ in by 63 mm/2½ in softwood crosspieces of the same thickness. Two sets of battens, cut from 25 mm/1 in by 12 mm/½ in timber—one being 1651 mm/5 ft 5 in and the other 660 mm/2 ft 2 in. Four 37 mm/1½ in square softwood cubes for the inner curves.

**Panels:** One 1651 mm/5 ft 5 in by 660 mm/2 ft 2 in softboard panel and one hardboard panel of the same dimensions.

**Hinges:** Each frame is linked by two "soss" hinges.

**Making the framework**

Use glued dowelling joints to assemble the frames. If a hanging rail is required, remember to drill a hole in the side of each upright of the chosen frame to take a length of dowelling rod and to insert the rail during assembly.

Tap the joints tight with a mallet; while the glue dries, either cramp the frames, or bind them tightly together with tape.

As a guide to help round the outer corners accurately, use a template made to a 100 mm/4 in radius. Cut away the waste to just short of the marked line with a tenon saw and finish off with a rasp and glasspaper.

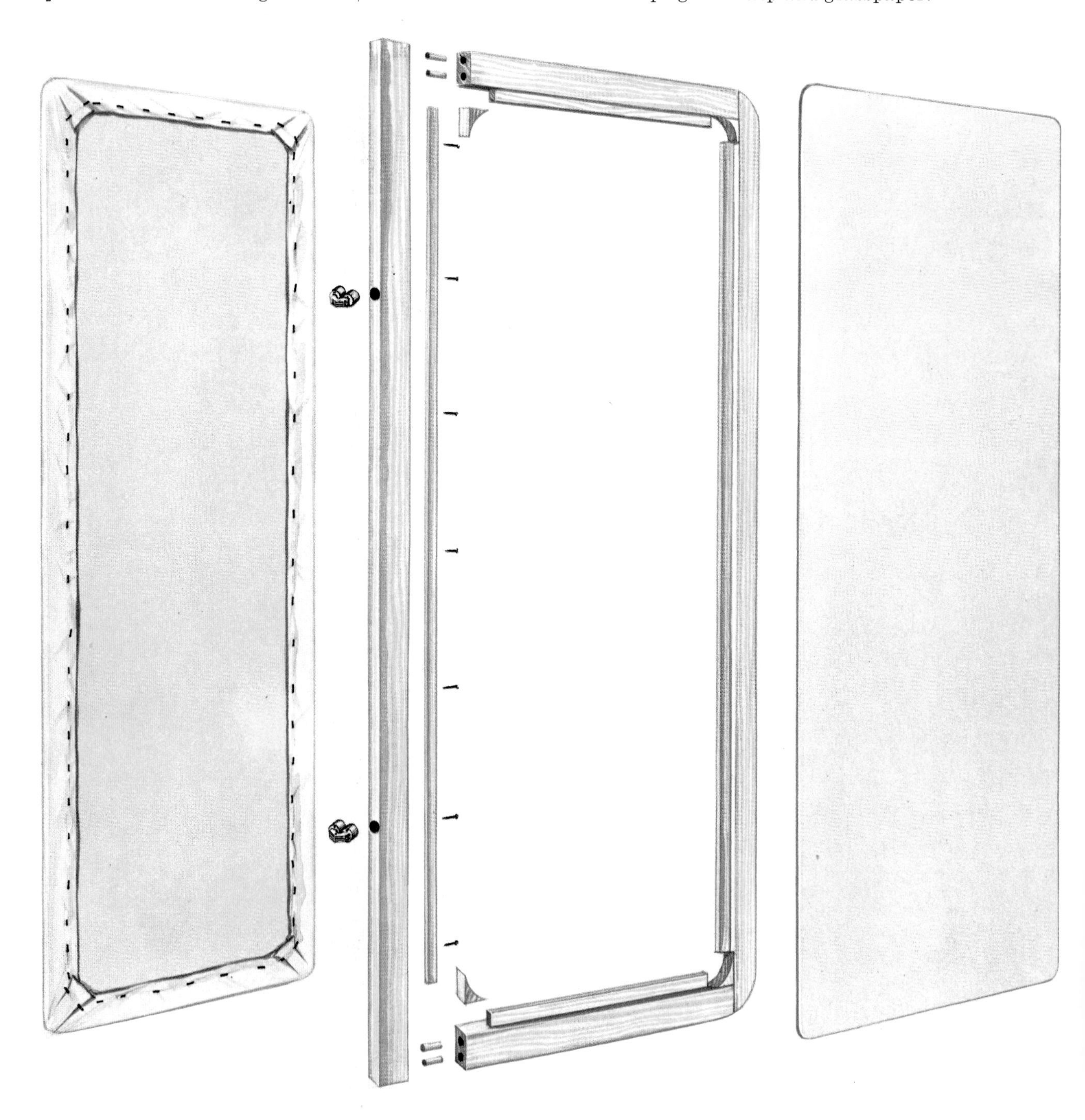

*See also Tips on*
Marking up 520
Adhesives 81
Cutting 370, 408
Dowelling 513, 466
Drilling 718
Smoothing 171

Make the inner curves from the four softwood cubes. Again, use a template, cut to a 37 mm/1½ in radius. Saw away the waste and finish as before. Glue and pin each completed curve to the inside corners of the frames.

Glue and pin the batten supports for the panels to the inside of the frame, positioning them off centre with a 12 mm/½ in clearance on one side. This allows for the different thickness of the softboard and hardboard.

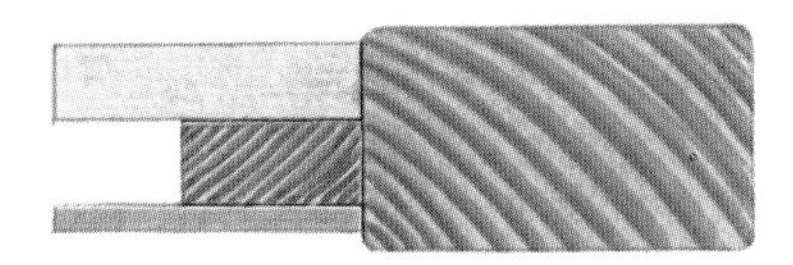

Smooth off all outer edges of the frame with glasspaper and finish with fine-grain filler. Paint.

**Making the panels**

Round the corners of the softboard and hardboard panels, using the same template as for the inner curves of the frame. If desired, the softboard panels can be covered with canvas, presewn with pockets of varying sizes. When covering the panels, first smooth down their edges to allow for the fabric thickness. Then stretch the material over the edges and glue and staple it to the inside surface. Paint the hardboard panel.

Glue and pin the softboard panels firmly to the battens, as these are the panels designed to be load-bearing. Finally, glue the hardboard panels into place.

**Fitting the hinges**

Stack the assembled frames with their edges flush. Mark up the positions of the hinges in identical places on each frame, positioning them a fair distance in from each end of the uprights. Drill the hinge holes and fit the hinges.

**Hinges and panels**

If selecting different hinges to the ones used on the screen illustrated, remember that they must have a sufficiently large span to allow the sections of the screen to fold flat against each other.

Similarly, if two softboard or two hardboard panels are preferred, remember that the thickness of two panels plus one batten support should be slightly less than that of the frame.

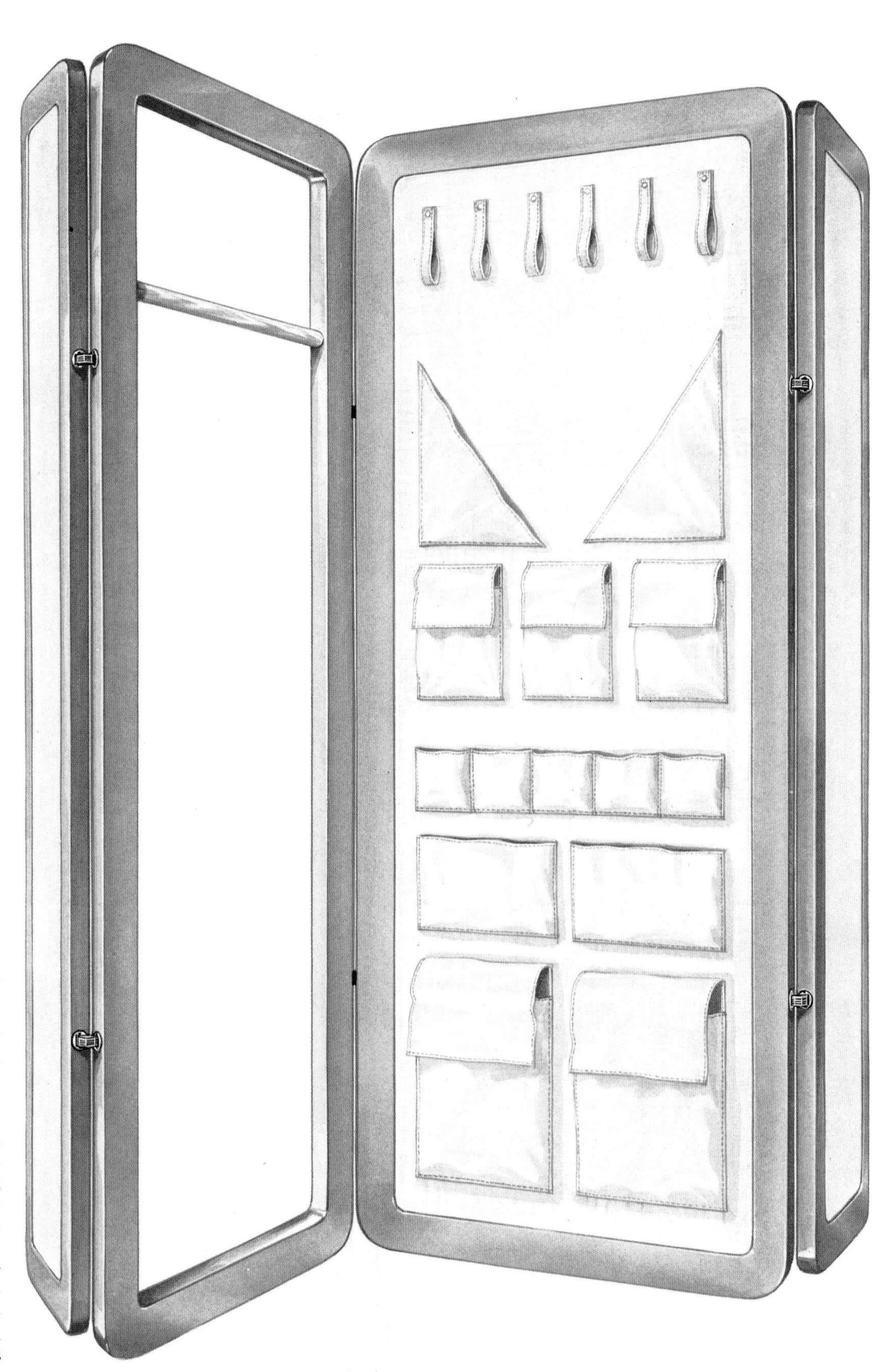

# Drawer units

The deep drawers of these two attractive drawer units provide plenty of storage space, yet both units are light enough to be easily moved around. Set in simply constructed but solid wooden frames, the drawers themselves make surprising and effective use of canvas and plywood.

In the first unit, canvas is both the chosen drawer and covering material. In the second, thin plywood is bent to form the attractively curved shape of the drawers; the matt paint was applied with a roller to add an unusual texture.

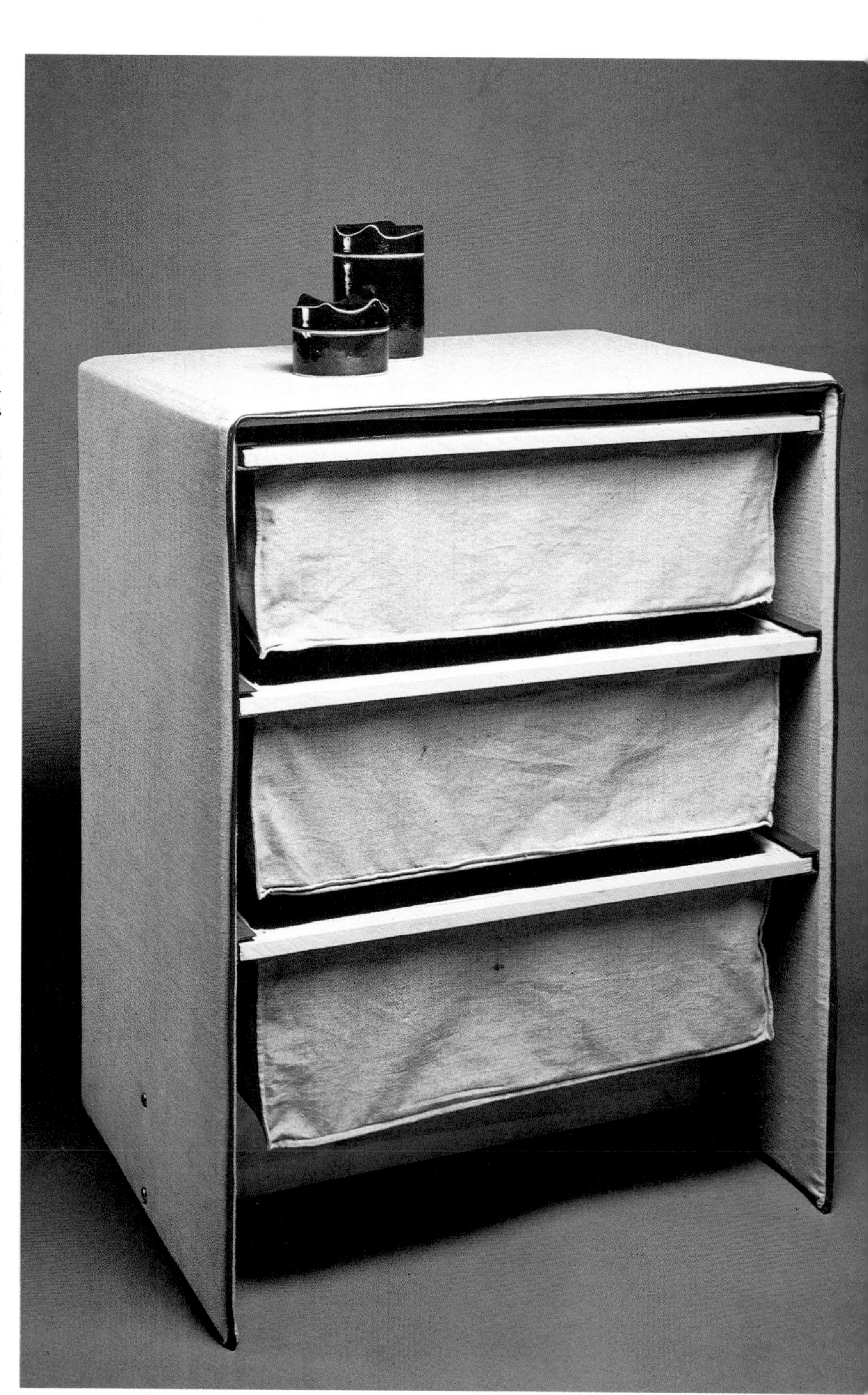

# 297/298

# 297

**Materials**

**Frame:** Made of three 12 mm/$\frac{1}{2}$ in plywood panels. The two side panels are 435 mm/17 in by 770 mm/30 in and the top panel is 597 mm/23$\frac{1}{2}$ in by 770 mm/30 in. The panels are held by a crosspiece of 25 mm/1 in softwood, 583 mm/23 in long and 120 mm/4$\frac{3}{4}$ in deep.

**Frame covering:** Each panel has a layer of 6 mm/$\frac{1}{4}$ in thick foam on the outside surfaces. The outer sleeve covering is cut from a 640 cm/7 yd by 121 cm/48 in length of heavy upholstery canvas and edged with leather piping, of which a total length of 533 cm/17 ft 6 in is required.

**Drawers:** Each drawer has a base of 6 mm/$\frac{1}{4}$ in thick hardboard and a top frame of 19 mm/$\frac{3}{4}$ in by 12 mm/$\frac{1}{2}$ in softwood. Use the same type of upholstery canvas in lengths of 535 mm/21 in. Secure it by metal corner brackets and strips of 6 mm/$\frac{1}{4}$ in softwood. Cut 460 mm/18 in long runners from 19 mm/$\frac{3}{4}$ in square plastic channel, and drawer stops from 12 mm/$\frac{1}{2}$ in square softwood.

**Making the main frame**

Cut the panels for the frame to their exact size. Cut a double-bevel along all edges and then glue the foam into place. Mark two screw holes for the crosspiece in central positions. Drill the holes, using the first marked-up panel as a template for the other.

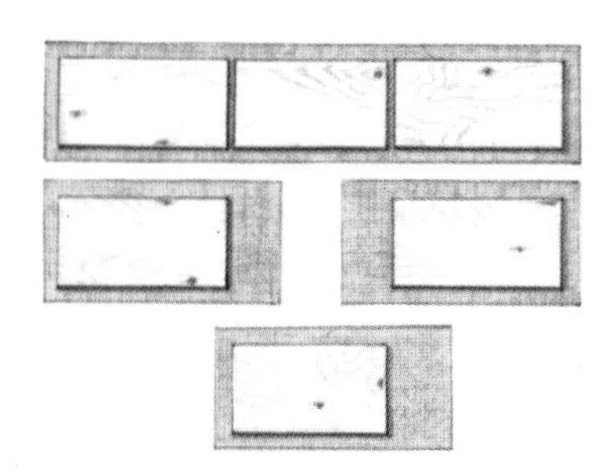

**Fitting**

The key to making this canvas chest of drawers is to ensure that the boards for the frame fit tightly in their sleeves. Follow, in order, the illustrations below for positioning, pinning and machining. Lay the long canvas length on the floor and position the panels end to end on it. Place the appropriate pocket on each panel.

Pin the outside edges of the pockets to the outside edge of the bottom sheet, making sure that the pockets fit as tightly as possible against the edges of the panels. Mark the positions of the pins with tailor's chalk on both surfaces. Remove the pins.

Fold the leather piping together, right sides out, and machine the entire length. Then, using the chalk line as a guide, machine the leather on to the right side of the large canvas sheet. Ease the material around the corners, trimming off any excess.

Next, pin the two larger covering sheets, right sides together, to the outside edges of the base sheet. Turn the leather piping inwards and enclose it within the seam. Tack and machine. Follow the same procedure for the two outside edges of the centre pocket.

Turn inside out. Try fitting the panels; if they are loose, take in the appropriate seams.

The centre pocket still has two edges unsewn—one with 25 mm/1 in of seam allowance and the other with 89 mm/3$\frac{1}{2}$ in. Turn in the 25 mm width and topstitch. Leave the other edge open, so that the plywood can be inserted, but topstitch a matching line on to the base sheet at the hinge.

Insert the panels, folding and tucking the 87 mm widths around and under their exposed ends.

**Final fittings**

Pre-drill countersunk screw holes into the runners, spacing them at even intervals. To fit the runners, first position the runner for the top drawer 37 mm/1$\frac{1}{2}$ in from the top edges and position the next two sets of runners 200 mm/8 in apart. Start the holes in the covered panels with a bradawl. First screw the back ends of each runner to the frame through a wooden block. Insert the other screws. Finally, fit the crosspiece, using screw cups to minimize damage to the fabric. Check that all screws are secured tightly.

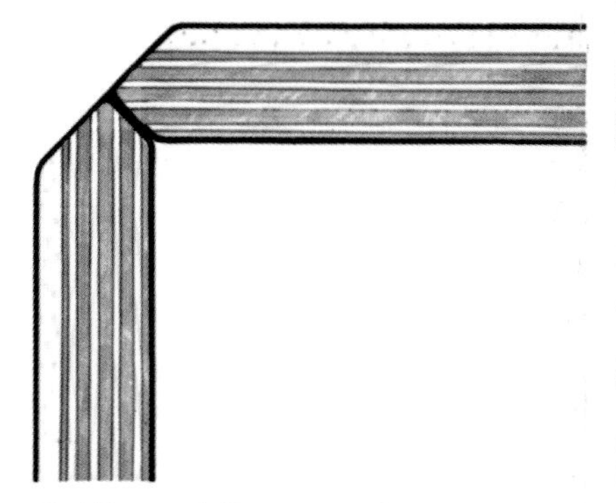

**Cutting out the canvas**

Lay the panels end to end lengthways down the heavy canvas. Cut around all three together, leaving 25 mm/1 in of seam allowance on the sides. Next, cut out the covering pockets. Lay each of the panels in turn on the canvas and cut out, leaving 25 mm/1 in of seam allowance on three sides and 89 mm/3$\frac{1}{2}$ in allowance on one of the 435 mm/17$\frac{3}{4}$ in sides.

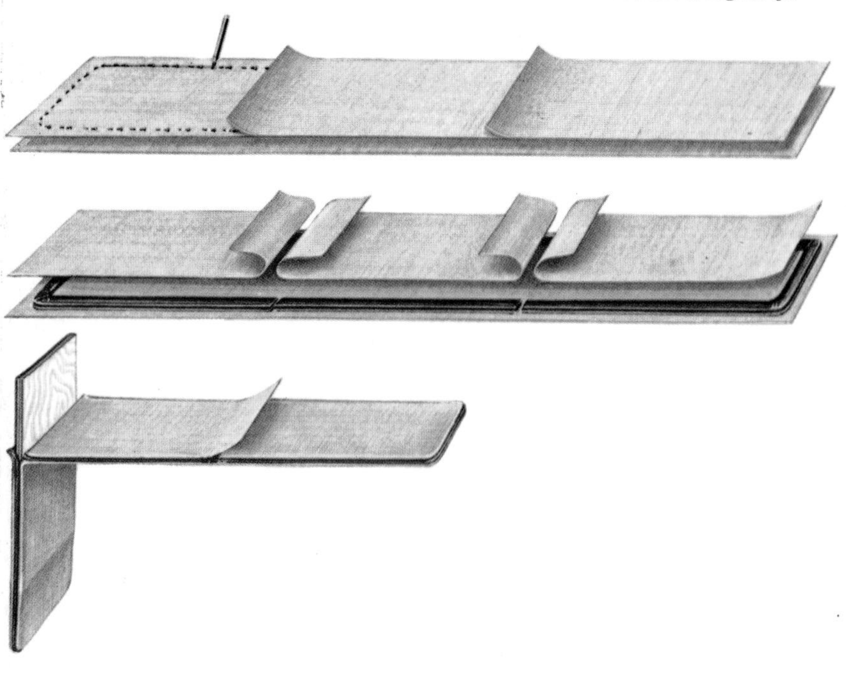

**Making the drawers**
Mark up and cut out the canvas sections for each drawer. Machine together corner seams, right sides together. Trim the seam turnings, pin the seams together—wrong sides in to enclose raw edges—and then topstitch.

The hardboard drawer base is enclosed in a canvas envelope. To make this, place another piece of fabric over the existing base and machine on three sides and then topstitch the base seam. Leave one end open so that the hardboard can be inserted.

Link the wooden frames by dowelling and gluing the corners. Sandwich the corners of the drawer material between the metal brackets and the frame. Staple the remaining material in place and secure by pinning the softwood strips to the frame.

Turn each completed drawer upside down and pull the fabric pouch through the frame to conceal its fixings. Fit each drawer into its runners to complete the chest of drawers.

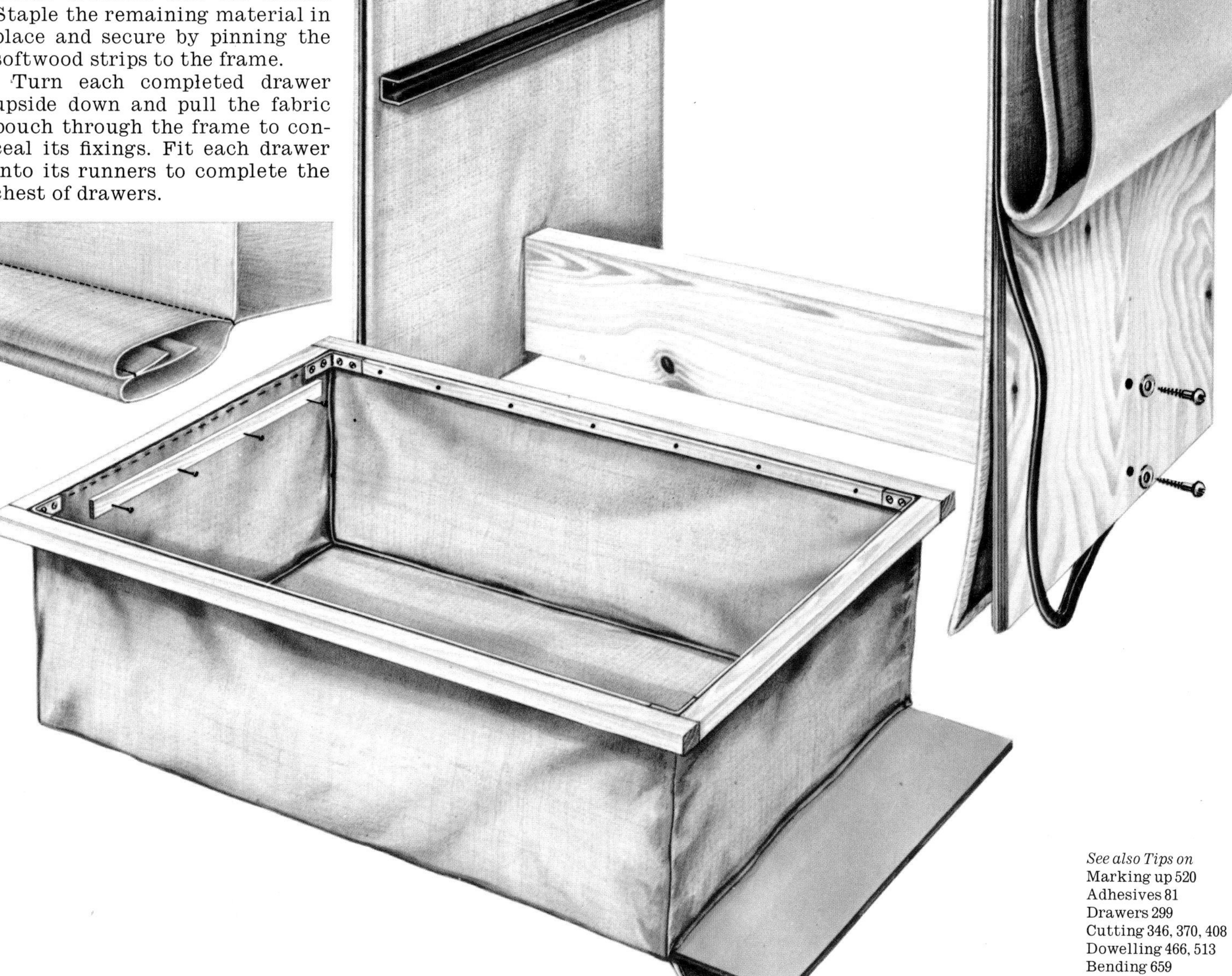

*See also Tips on*
Marking up 520
Adhesives 81
Drawers 299
Cutting 346, 370, 408
Dowelling 466, 513
Bending 659
Smoothing 459

The unit illustrated is 737mm/29in by 864mm/34in by 457mm/18in and takes three 184mm/7¼in by 819mm/32¼in by 368mm/14½in drawers.

**Materials**

**Legs, crossbeams and tops:** Four 737 mm/29in lengths of 50mm/2in by 37mm/1½in softwood for the legs and three 819mm/32¼in lengths of 50mm/2in by 19mm/¾in softwood for the crossbeams. Two 15mm/⅝in thick sheets of laminated chipboard for the top, 457mm/18in by 800mm/31½in.

**Runners:** Six 457mm/18in lengths of 25mm/1in by 12mm/½in aluminium runner.

**One drawer:** Two 752mm/29½in by 185mm/7¼in front and back panels of 15mm/⅝in laminated chipboard and one 1125mm/44¼in by 370mm/14½in sheet of 2mm thick plywood (aeroply) for the base. Two 370mm/14½in lengths of 19 mm/¾in square softwood for the glides and one 816mm/32⅛in length of 50mm/2in by 19mm/¾in softwood for the handle.

**Making the frame**

Cramp the legs together and mark up halving joints to take the runners. Cut out the joints. Then drill two screw holes at the front of the runners and two holes at the back to take dowels. Slot the runners into their recesses and drill through the holes into the

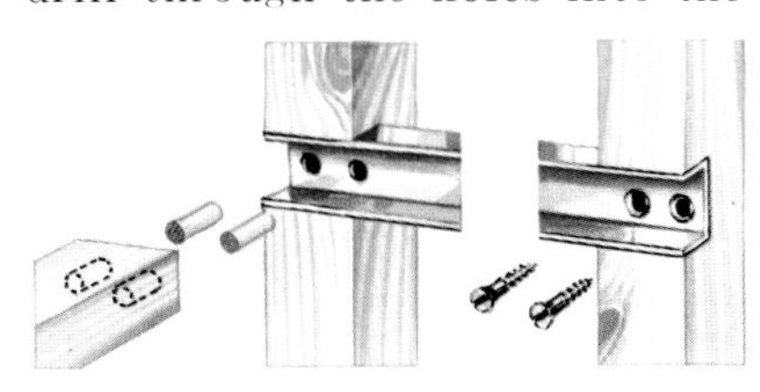

legs. Screw the runners home from the inside at the front. Mark up and drill positions for the dowels on the crossbeams and glue the crossbeams into position at the back of the unit.

To form the top, dowel and glue together two sheets of laminated chipboard. Drill screw holes for attachment to the legs, fill the holes with a plug and screw into it.

**Making the drawers**

Round the bottom corners of the laminated chipboard used for the front and back panels to a 37mm/1½in radius. Square up the plywood base at one end. Apply glue to the panel edges and secure. Glue and fix the glides and handles.

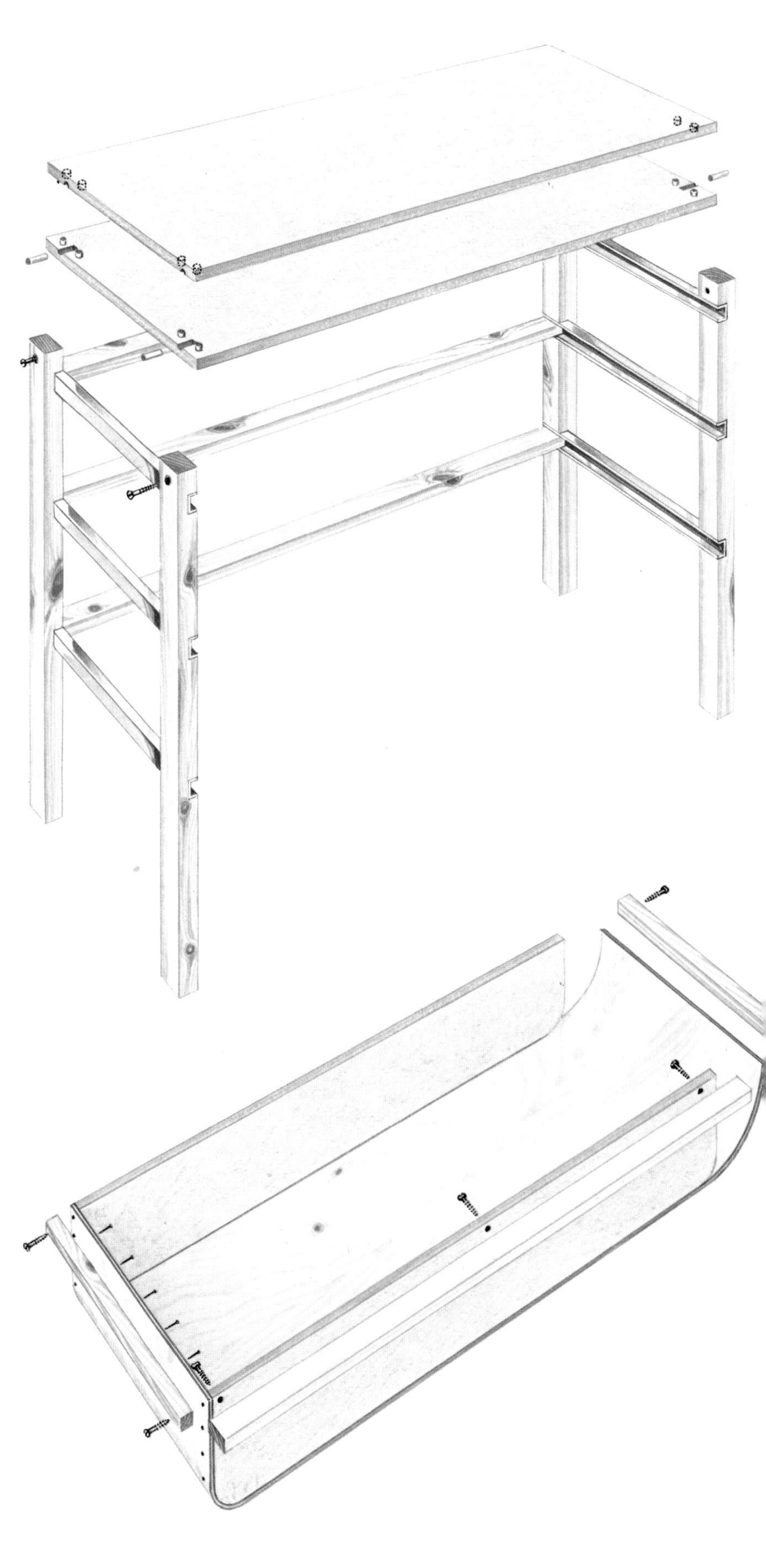

*See also Tips on*
Marking up 520
Adhesives 81
Drawers 299
Cutting 346, 370, 408
Dowelling 466, 513
Bending 659
Smoothing 459

## 299 Fitting drawers the easy way

The two major points to remember when making drawers are to make sure that the sides are parallel and that the joints are strong enough to hold the drawers rigid. Glued and screwed butt joints are usually adequate, but remember to fit a false front to conceal exposed end grain.

Various techniques can be used to ensure that the drawer slides smoothly. In the rail technique, a framework of battens is built up to take the drawer. As the battens under the drawer act both as supporting rails and runners, the base must be recessed so that the drawer can slide easily.

To fit drawers using the cleat and groove technique, fix a single cleat on each side of the supporting framework to slot into a groove cut in the side of the drawer. Cut the groove to not more than half the thickness of the wood with a combination plane, or the drawers will stick. In the three cleat method, attach one cleat to the drawer and two to the frame, above and below it.

Top hanging is a method used for fitting a drawer underneath a table. Combine two cleats to form an L-shape and attach to the underside of the table. Then screw a single cleat to the top of the drawer's sides to slot into the angle.

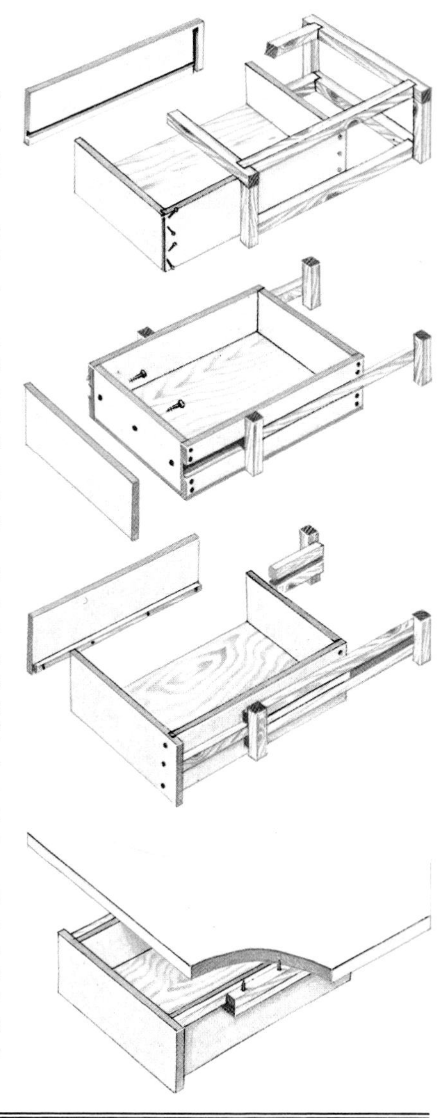

## 300 Using central heating economically

Avoid switching a central heating system off at night during cold weather. Maintaining a flow of heat to ensure that the overall temperature does not fall below 10°C (50°F) saves fuel when compared to that used in restarting a cold system.

## 301 Removing coffee or tea stains from carpet

White coffee or tea spilt on carpets can usually be removed by sponging with tepid water and detergent. To remove black coffee, rub the stain with glycerine first.

## 302 Storing oil for window hinges

Old nail-varnish bottles make useful storage containers for oil. Because they have a built-in brush fitted to the screw cap, they are very handy for small oiling jobs around the house.

## 303 Removing smoke stains from walls

To remove persistent smoke stains on painted walls rub them with half a lemon. Or, as a last resort, use carbon tetrachloride, but beware of the fumes. If working inside, wear a mask and make sure there is plenty of ventilation.

## 304 The right way to cut a brick

Use a bolster and club hammer to split a brick. First score a cutting line around the four sides of the brick with a nail. Then lay the brick in a bed of sand to cushion it and hammer the blade of the bolster into the score line all round the brick, cutting deeply on each of the four corners. Finally stand the brick on one side and, with the bolster resting in the cut on the other side, strike it firmly with the hammer.

## 305 When and how to use a nail punch

If possible, always punch the heads of nails below the surface of timber with a nail punch. These are usually about 100 mm/4 in long with diameters ranging from about 1.5 mm/$\frac{1}{16}$ in to 4.5 mm/$\frac{3}{16}$ in. The best type to buy is a punch with a square shank, as this is less likely to roll off a bench than one with a round shank. Choose a punch slightly smaller in diameter than that of the nails. Tap the head of the punch with a hammer to drive the nail head just below the surface. Then fill the hole proud with a proprietary filler and rub it down with a fine-grade abrasive paper.

## 306 Lifting heavy paving slabs

The way to raise a heavy paving slab that has sunk below the level of adjoining slabs is to first lever it free with a crowbar. Then slide it clear by resting its edge on a length of iron pipe or on the handle from an old broom. Never try to bodily lift a slab free; it can lead to a severe strain.

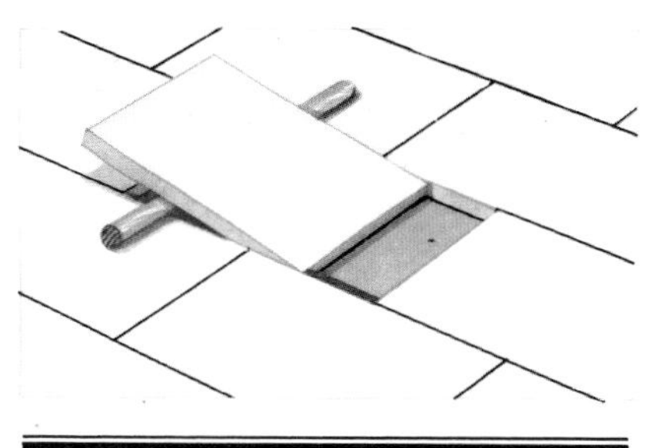

## 307 Dusting brush

After rubbing surfaces down with glasspaper, brush them thoroughly with a dusting brush before painting. This prevents the finish from becoming pitted.

## 308 Using a wrench

Whenever possible, always pull a wrench —never push it. If it has to be pushed, do it with the hand open, so that, if the wrench slips, the hand is out of the way.

# 309-320

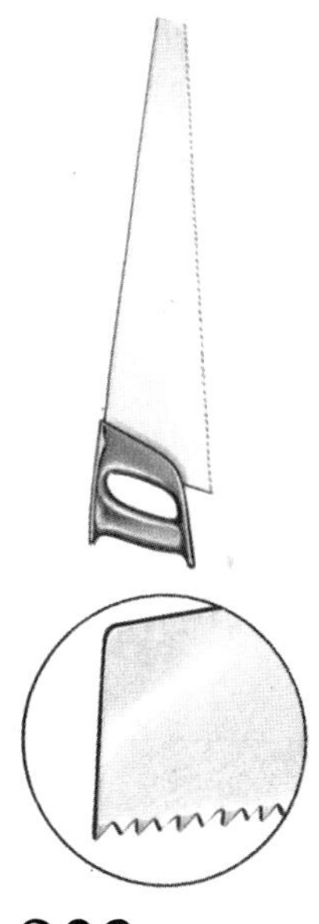

## 309
### Crosscut saw
A crosscut saw has between seven and twelve teeth to each 25 mm/1 in and is used for cutting across the grain of timber. Always make the first stroke by pulling the saw towards you and guide the blade with the knuckle of the thumb until the cut has started. Keep the blade at a 45° angle to the timber throughout the job.

## 310
### Fitting glass to windows
Never press the middle of a pane of glass when fitting it to a window. The middle is the weakest part and any excessive pressure can break the glass.

## 311 Strengthening a single-brick wall
A single-brick wall more than twelve courses high must be strengthened by building piers at regular intervals of approximately 3m/10ft. Make sure that the piers bond in with the wall, with no continuous vertical joints.

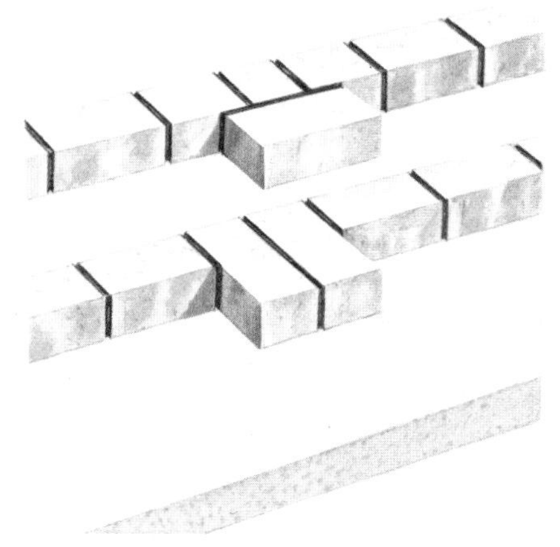

## 312 Estimating brick requirements
Allow 50 standard bricks for each 1sq m/11sq ft of brickwork when building a single-brick wall. This figure leaves a dozen bricks or so over in case of accidents, such as breakages in cutting. Double the figure when ordering bricks for a cavity wall.

## 313 Strengthening a corner joint
When fitting a timber block on the inside of a joint's internal angle to strengthen the joint, chamfer the corner of the block that fits into the angle. Otherwise glue may be squeezed out, so preventing the block from sticking securely in the angle. If necessary, reinforce the joint with nails.

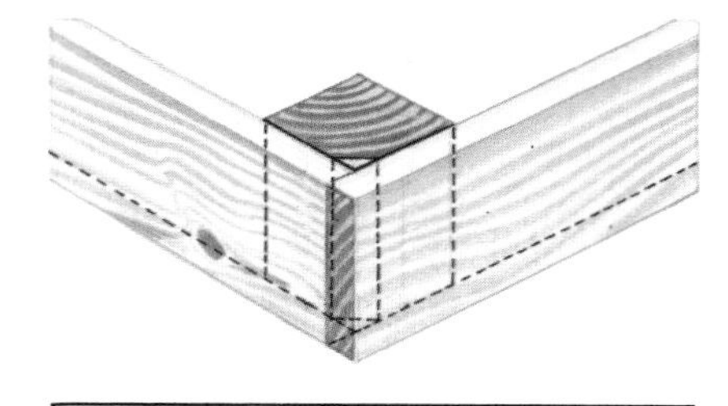

## 314 Removing stains from vinyl tiles
Remove old adhesive marks and splashes of paint from vinyl tiles or vinyl sheeting by rubbing them with a cloth dipped in turpentine substitute. But always work quickly—the turpentine substitute can dissolve the vinyl surface if the job is prolonged.

## 315 Cleaning files with a wire brush
Always work down the grain of a file when cleaning it with a wire brush. Otherwise, the edges of the teeth can become blunted, making it ineffective for metalwork.

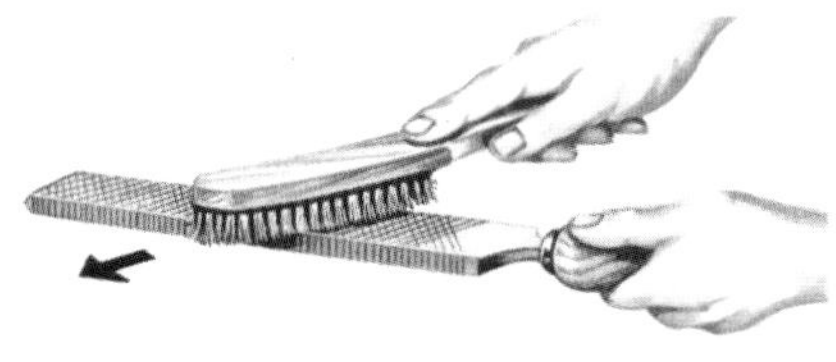

## 316 Strengthening a wall's foundation
When building a low wall, lay the first course crossways along the foundation and then build up the subsequent courses. Bricks laid in this way are known in the trade as "headers", and provide additional strength for the base of the wall.

When building up the subsequent courses of the wall, always make sure that the vertical joins in one course do not coincide with the course immediately above it. They should line up with those in the next but one course. This technique is known as bonding.

## 317 Preventing metals from tarnishing
Stop metals such as brass and copper tarnishing after they have been polished by giving the surface two coats of a thin varnish. The varnish prevents the metal surface from coming into contact with moisture in the air, which causes the tarnishing. Use a soft brush—preferably one with camel hair bristles—which is less likely to leave brush marks.

## 318 Laying foundations for brickwork
To ensure a level finish when laying foundations for brickwork, insert a series of wooden pegs about 600mm/2ft apart into the earth at the base of the trench. Leave each peg protruding above the ground to the exact depth of the concrete foundation—this should normally be 100mm/4in for single-brick walls and 150mm/6in for double-brick walls. Lay a straight-edge across the pegs, two at a time, and use a spirit level to check that they are all at the same height. Pour a mix of one part of cement, two parts of sand and four parts of aggregate—or one part of cement and six parts of "all-in" aggregate, obtainable from builders' merchants—into the trench until it is level with the top of the pegs.

## 319 Painting narrow surfaces tidily
If possible use the correct width of paint brush when painting a narrow surface, such as the edge of a door. Using a brush wider than the surface not only leads to paint runs down the surface, but also wears the brush down in the middle. If the right width of brush is not available, however, use the brush sideways on to the surface to save wear on the bristles and lessen the possibility of drips and runs.

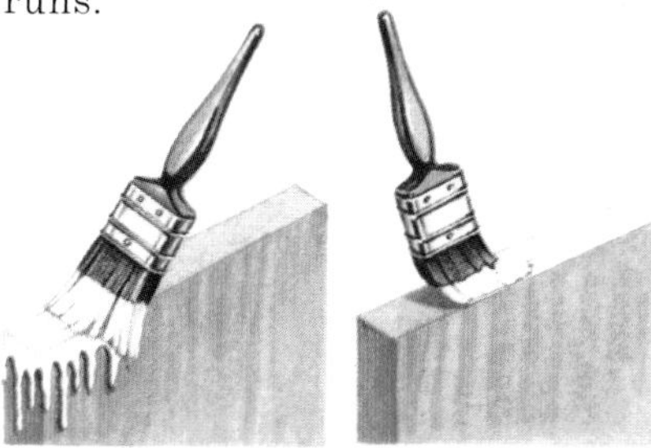

## 320 Protecting newly laid concrete while it dries
Cover newly laid concrete with damp sacking to help retard the drying time and so increase the concrete's durability. Drying takes between four and ten days, depending on the weather.

## 321 Planing the end grain of timber

Do not try to plane along the whole length of timber when planing the end grain of a piece of wood, as this will tear away the edge of the wood. Either plane from each end to the centre or fix a waste strip flush with the wood and plane against this. Hold the plane at an angle of approximately 30° to the cutting direction. Support the wood in a vice, if possible, to make the job easier.

## 322 Repointing with coloured mortar

Coloured mortar can be used as a decoration, and also to disguise the newness of repointed joints. To give a grey tone to the mortar, when working on a small area, rub dirt into the mix. If the area is large, use a vegetable dye, obtainable from a builders' merchant.

When using vegetable dyes, remember that the colour will be much lighter after the mix has dried than it was when it was first made up. To get the right colour, experiment with previously measured quantities of powder and mortar and allow them to dry. Then working in equal proportions, make up the full quantity.

When repointing part of a brick wall with coloured mortar, always rub the surrounding mortar joints with candlewax. This stops the existing joints soaking up the colour.

## 323 Bonding new and old concrete securely

Always undercut the edges of a hole being repaired in a concrete path or floor. This provides a secure key for new concrete and stops it lifting from the surface. Use a bolster to cut into the concrete and hammer it at an angle of 45° inside the edge. Make sure that all traces of cracked concrete or dust are cleared from the hole; then coat the surfaces to be repaired with PVA bonding agent to increase the adhesion qualities between the new concrete and the old. Finally, fill the hole with the new mix and cover the repair with sacking or a polythene sheet to allow it to cure. If using sacking, keep it moist.

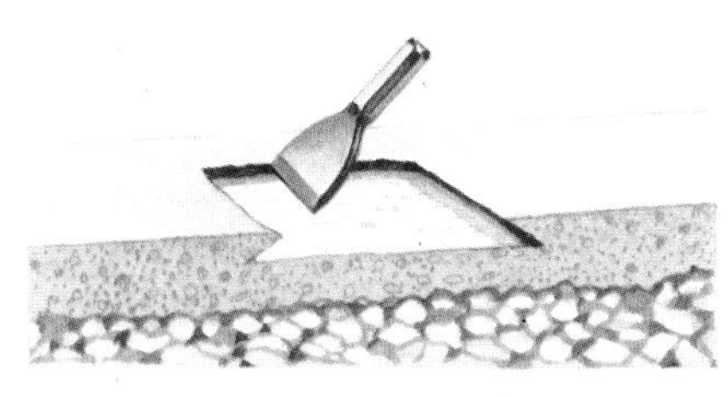

## 324 Painting flush doors

Mentally divide flush doors into three horizontal sections when painting them. Working from the top section downwards, paint vertically down the left-hand side of the first section, then down the right-hand side, and finally join the two with horizontal strokes. Finish the whole section with vertical strokes, working from the bottom upwards. Follow this procedure for the other two sections; work quickly so that all the sections dry together.

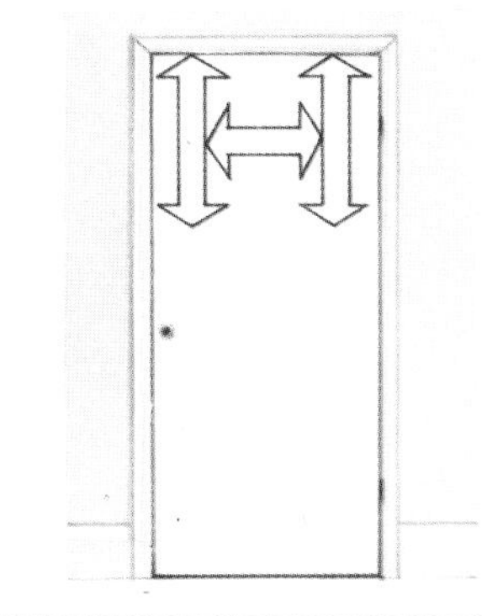

## 325 Cutting large sheets of glass

Always use a T-square when cutting large sheets of glass; it is difficult keeping a firm grip on a normal straight-edge while cutting. If making the T-square, cut a notch in the cross-piece flush with the main cutting edge to enable the cut to be completed cleanly.

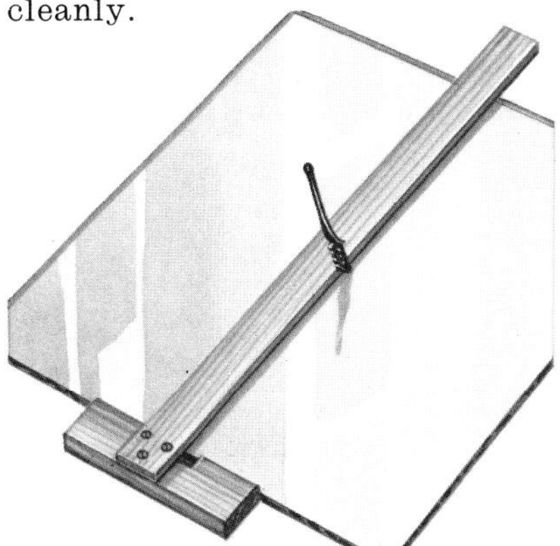

## 326 Checking the slope of a retaining wall

When building a small retaining wall in a garden, ensure that it has a uniform slope along its length by using a plumb line held in a simply made frame to check the angle of the slope. Fit three lengths of 75mm/3in by 25mm/1in batten together, setting the back upright at the angle required, and fitting the top and bottom battens square and parallel with each other. Drill a hole through the top batten for the plumb line and mark where it lines up on the bottom batten. Place the frame against the wall, check the position of the plumb bob against the mark and repeat the process at intervals along the wall. If the angle is uniform, the plumb bob should line up with the mark on each occasion.

## 327 Hammer

To help produce a clean hammer stroke, the hammer should be correctly balanced. A wooden-shafted claw hammer is well balanced if it remains upright when stood on the claw.

## 328 Kitchen floors

When choosing a floor covering for a kitchen, always use a non-slip material, such as vinyl sheeting or quarry tiles, which will prevent skidding even when wet.

# 329-338

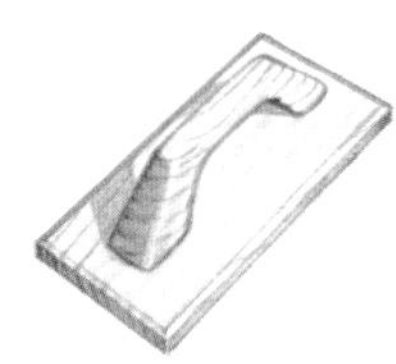

## 329
**Wooden float**

Rub over the surface of a plaster undercoat with a wooden float to give a rough finish. This helps the final coat to bond securely.

## 330
**Polystyrene tiles and sheeting**

Never fit polystyrene sheeting to tiles above fireplaces or gas water heaters. Otherwise there will be a risk of fire.

## 331 Using beading to make timber mouldings

Lengths of beading can make effective composite mouldings when glued and pinned together. Glue the beading to the wood with a contact adhesive and pin it at 300 mm/12 in intervals. Punch the heads of the pins below the surface and fill the holes with a proprietary filler.

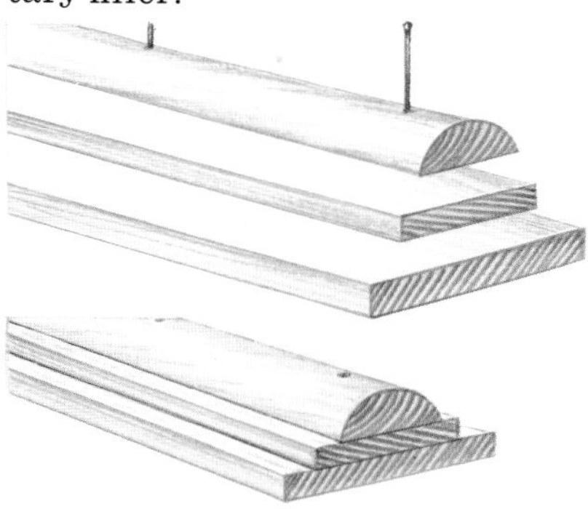

## 332 Straining old paint before using it

Make sure that old paint is free of lumps by straining it through a fine mesh—such as an old stocking—before using it up. Wrap the mesh round a paint kettle and strain the paint from the tin into the kettle. The ideal working depth of paint in a kettle is about 25 mm/1 in.

## 333 Protecting wooden ladders stored outside

Varnish wooden ladders—especially if stored in the open—to protect them from the weather. Never paint them—any faults or deterioration of the wood may then be hidden, creating dangerous conditions for subsequent use.

## 334 Storing tins of paint over long periods

Tins of paint that need to be stirred before use should be stored upside down, with the lid firmly secured. The skin that settles on top of the paint will then be at the bottom when the tin is next opened, making the paint far easier to stir.

## 335 Fixing corrugated sheeting to a roof

Always position the nails or screws used to fix corrugated sheeting to a roof at the top of the corrugation. If the nails or screws are fitted in the hollows where the rainwater runs, the roof will leak. Fit a rubber, nylon or fibre washer, which is moulded to the shape of the curve, under the head of each nail or screw.

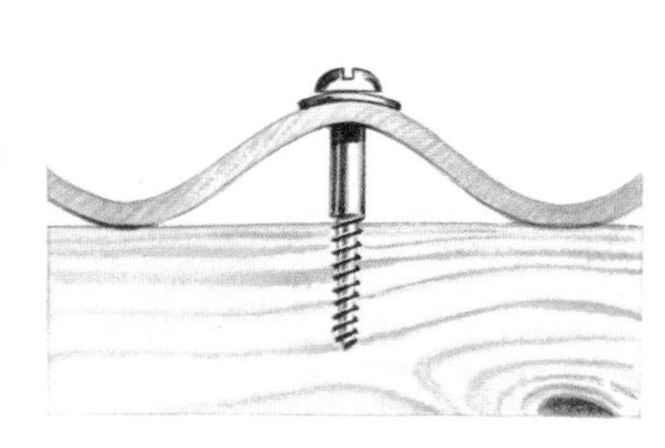

## 336 Keeping a bricked-up chimney ventilated

Always fit an air brick within the brickwork when bricking up a fireplace—or a ventilation grill if boarding up the opening. This lets air circulate in the chimney. Without such ventilation, any moisture will not evaporate completely and, as a result, dampness may affect the chimney breast.

## 337 Preparing and painting a gloss-painted surface

When painting over existing gloss paint, first wash the surface thoroughly. When dry, rub the surface with fine glasspaper. This helps the new paint to adhere. Brush the surface thoroughly before painting to remove all traces of dust from the smoothing.

## 338 Replacing tongued-and-grooved flooring

First locate the joists at either end of the damaged area—parallel rows of nail heads across the floor indicate their position. Drill a hole in the board at each end of the damaged area, flush with the joists. Mark a cutting line from the outside edge of the holes and cut across the board's width with a keyhole saw. If the board cannot be prised apart, split it down its length by hammering a chisel along a line on either side of the damaged area. Remove the centre section and then simply pull away the two outside pieces.

To fit the replacement board, first nail two offcuts of wood to the joists, ensuring that they are flush with the top of the joists. Cut the new board to fit and then chisel off the lower part of the grooved edge. Slot the tongue of the new board into place, drop the board down, and nail it to the offcuts.

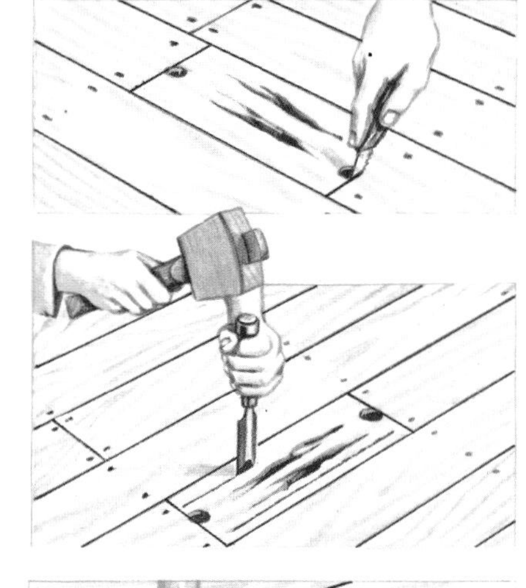

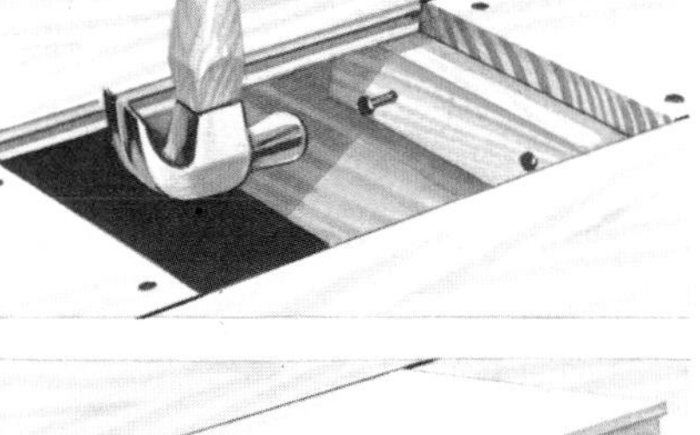

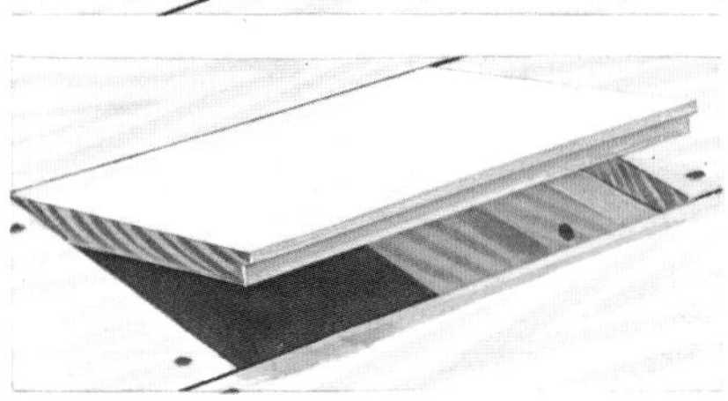

## 339 Joining aluminium tubing easily

A simple method of joining aluminium tubing is to cut a scrap 50mm/2in long section of tube with the same diameter as the tubes to be joined. Saw a slit down this section, squeeze it together with a pair of grips and insert it inside the two lengths of tube. Then push the tubes together over the join. The section will spring open sufficiently to hold the tubes in place—though the joint can be made more permanent by fitting it with self-tapping screws to secure the section in place.

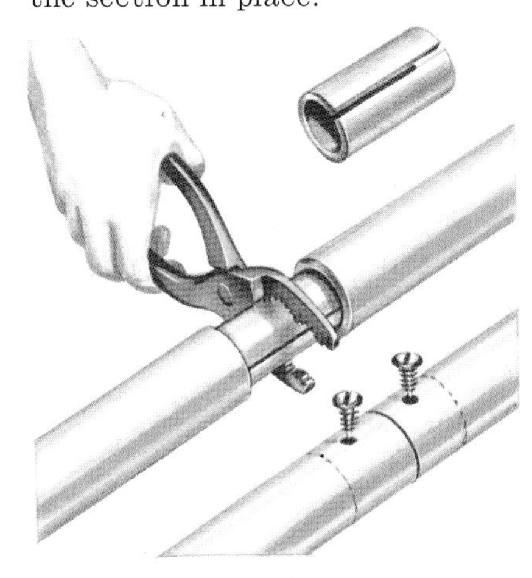

## 340 The right time of year to paint outside

Whenever possible, try to do outside painting in late summer, following a dry spell, and starting after the dew has cleared. At other times of the year, damp will cause the new paint to peel, excess sun will make it blister, while frost makes gloss paint go flat.

If the job has to be done during a wet spell, wipe over the surface of woodwork with a dry cloth first, and always work on the driest part of the house.

## 341 Keeping an asbestos roof free from moss

Lay a length of thick copper wire across the highest point of an asbestos roof to prevent moss growth. When it rains, copper salts will be dispersed down the roof, stopping moss from growing.

## 342 Joining aluminium sheets strongly

Instead of a drill, use nails to make screw holes when joining aluminium sheets with self-tapping screws. The torn edges left by the nails give the screws more metal to bite on and make the joint stronger.

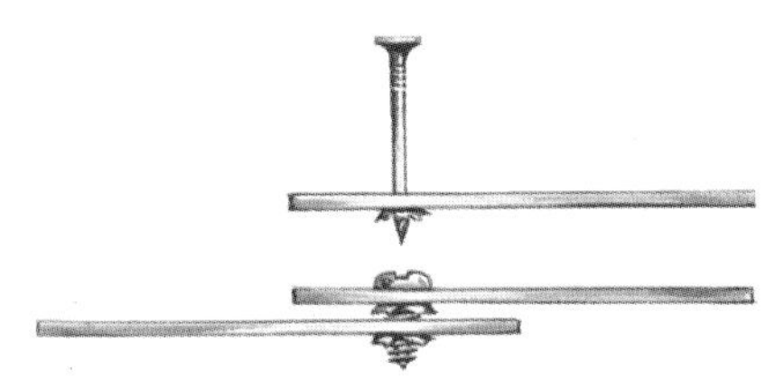

## 343 Replacing damaged plain-edged flooring

Remove a damaged section of plain-edged board by first drilling a hole about 25mm/1in from the set of nails in the joists at each end of the section. Cut across the board's width with a padsaw, working from the holes. Either nail offcuts to the sides of the joists and nail the replacement piece into them, or, with a bolster chisel, prise up the board on each joist, slide a rod underneath, remove the nails and saw along the nail line. Nail the board back and fit the replacement piece in place on the joist.

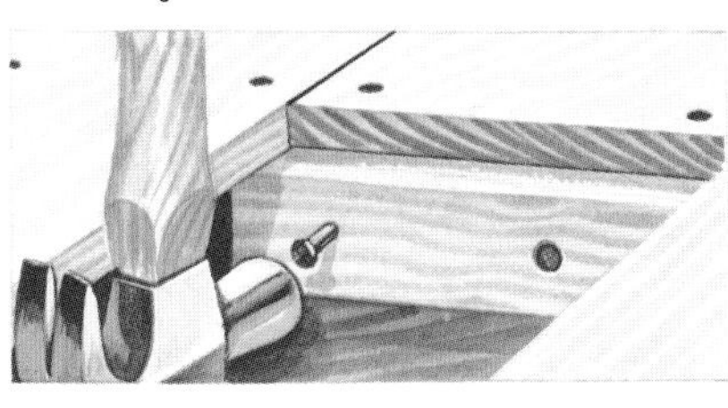

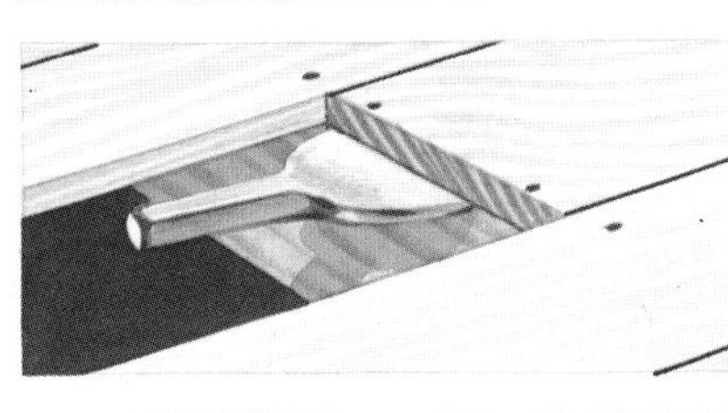

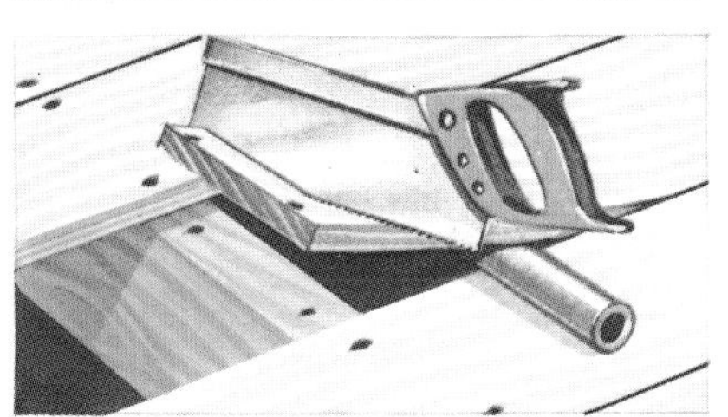

## 344 Plugging and filling large holes in plaster

Holes in plaster less than a thumbnail in area can easily be filled with a proprietary filler, instead of having to make up a plaster mix. However, larger holes need to be plugged first. Do this by soaking newspaper in water, screwing it up to the approximate size of the hole and then soaking it in plaster mixed to a creamy consistency. Push the plug into the hole so that it fits flush. When it has dried, fill the rest of the hole with filler and finally smooth down the surface.

## 345 Checking the level of a large work area

If the level over a large work surface needs to be checked, use a spirit level screwed to a long length of straight, squared up timber to do the job.

## 346 Cutting laminated chipboard cleanly

To simplify the task of cutting laminated chipboard cleanly, make a guide from two lengths of wood about 100mm/4in longer than the width of the sheet. Also cut two small blocks the same thickness as the chipboard. Cramp the guides in position where the saw cut is to be made and, using a tenon saw held upright against the edge of the guide, saw approximately half-way through the board. Turn the board over and repeat the procedure. At the half-way mark, the saw blade will meet the original cut, completing the job without leaving the rough edges and splits that can disfigure the edge.

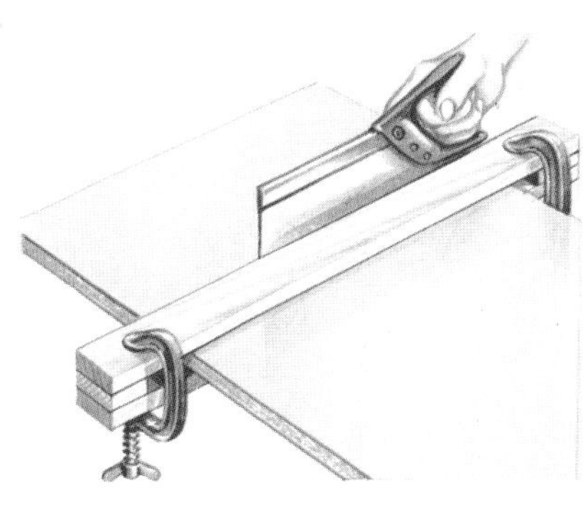

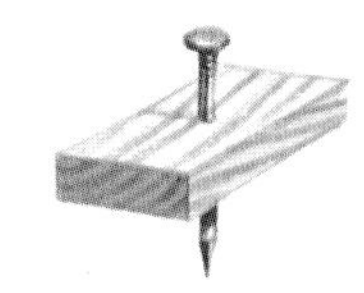

## 347 Scriber

Use a scriber as a cutting guide for fitting tiles or flooring. It can be made from a piece of wood about 150mm/6in by 38mm/1½in, with a nail driven into it about 50mm/2in from one end.

## 348 Mirrors above fireplaces

Never stretch to look into a mirror above a fire. If a person wearing flowing clothing, such as a nightdress, does this there is a danger of the clothing catching fire.

# 349-358

## 349
### Marking gauge

A dowel inserted through the hole of a cotton reel makes a simple and perfectly adequate gauge for marking proposed cutting lines on timber. Hammer a fine panel pin through the dowel so that the point protrudes 5mm/$\frac{3}{16}$in. Drill a hole into the reel and insert a small hook that can be tightened to lock the dowel when the correct marking distance has been established.

## 350
### Electric extension leads

Never run an electric appliance from an extension lead rolled round a reel for more than a few minutes. Prolonged use may cause heat to be generated in the cable and ultimately cause smouldering. Undo all the cable from the reel.

## 351 Fitting round-head rivets simply

Riveting is an inconspicuous, strong and reliable method of joining metals together permanently. When fitting round-head rivets, make sure that the shank of the rivet projects through both pieces of metal by a distance equal to 1¼ times the diameter of the rivet. This ensures that the right amount of metal is left exposed for shaping the head.

Rest the head of the rivet on a metal block, close the plates with a rivet set and strike the other end of the shank with the flat of a ball-peen hammer. Once the shank begins to spread, use the ball-peen of the hammer to finish shaping the head. If a perfect round head is required, form it with a rivet snap.

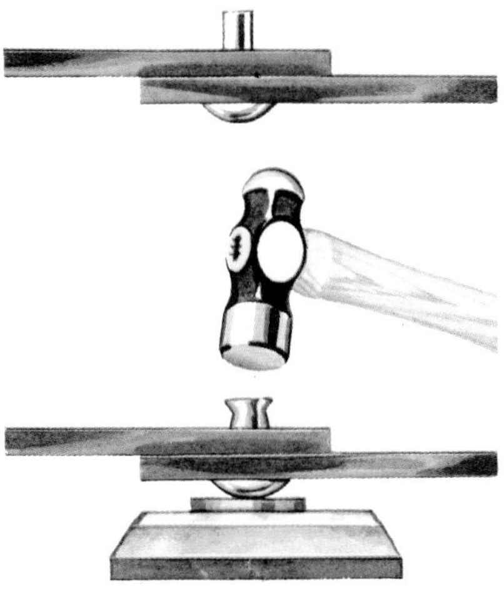

## 352 Gluing easily and without mess

To prevent glue from sticking on a surface where it is not required, give the surface a thin coating of wax.

## 353 Making it easier to cut metal tubing

Before cutting a metal tube with a hacksaw, score the surface of the metal with the edge of a file at the point to be cut. This helps to guide the blade along its correct cutting line.

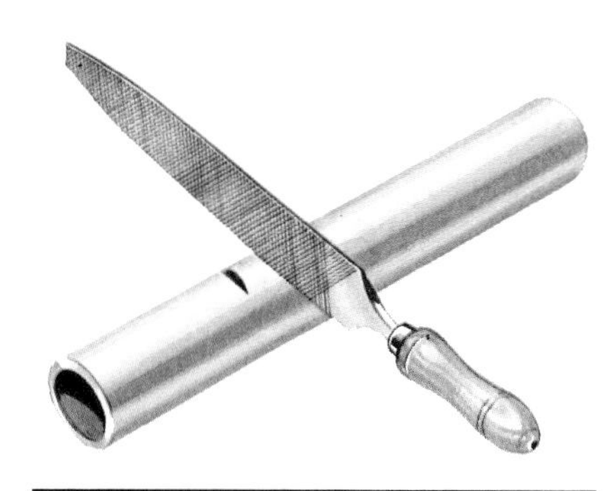

## 354 Giving a newly sanded floor protection

Protect the newly sanded surface of a wooden floor by sealing it with three coats of clear polyurethane. For an extra-smooth finish, dilute the first coat with one part of turpentine substitute to five parts of polyurethane; this lessens the risk of the polyurethane becoming tacky. When it is thoroughly dry, smooth the surface with fine-grade glasspaper. After the last two coats have dried, apply a wax floor polish.

## 355 Positioning heavy panels for fixing

When fixing heavy panels such as plasterboard just above floor-level, use a foot lever adapted from two blocks of wood to help lift and hold the panels in position until they have been secured.

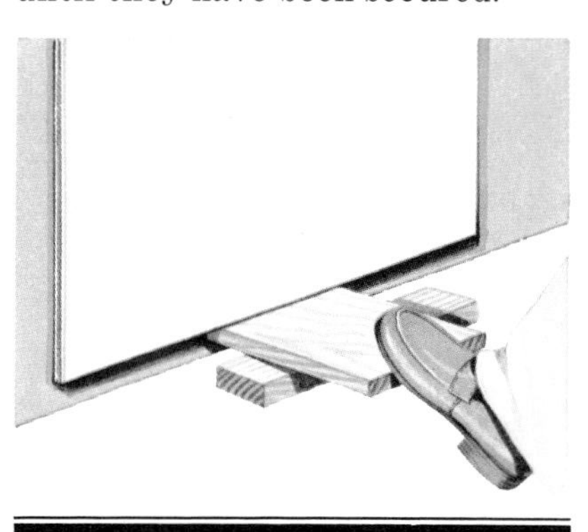

## 356 Laying foundations for concreting

Always lay concrete on a solid foundation, or it will crack. First, make sure that the ground is level by pummelling it down hard and then pack the aggregate for the sub-base down tightly on it. Lay out a frame using timbers at least 25mm/1in thick and subdivide this into 3m/10ft square sections, using softwood boards. Wedge both the frame and boards.

Remove the boards and frame once the concrete has set and fill the gaps with asphalt. Because the asphalt remains pliable beneath its hard surface, the concrete is able to expand without cracking.

## 357 Cutting awkward shapes in vinyl tiles

Lightly warm a vinyl or thermoplastic tile by putting it in an oven or in boiling water for a few minutes. The heat will slightly soften the tile, making it easier to cut awkward shapes in it.

## 358 Fixing screws firmly into hardwood

Before fixing screws into wood, always pre-drill the wood. The holes should be slightly smaller in diameter than that of the actual screws being used, otherwise the screws may not bite into the wood. If brass screws are being used in hardwood, fit a steel screw of the same size first to form the hole, or the brass—which is softer than steel—may shear.

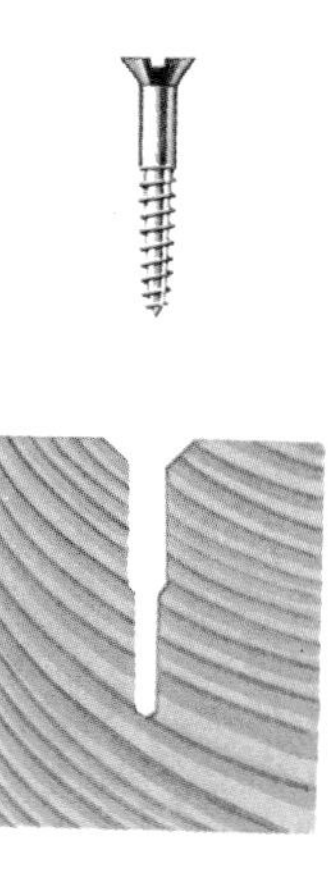

## 359 Finding the size of a window pane

To estimate the size of new glass for a cracked or broken window, measure across the full width and height of the frame (dotted) and deduct 6mm/¼in from this measurement to allow the glass to fit the opening. Alternatively, measure across the full width and height of the exposed glass, making an adequate allowance for the glass covered by the rebates.

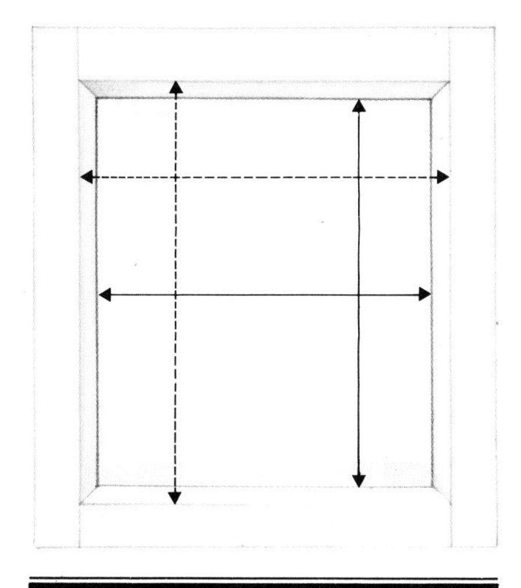

## 360 Supporting a ladder on hard ground

Help support a ladder on hard ground by standing it on a board, having glued and screwed a length of timber approximately 75mm/3in by 50mm/2in to its front edge to act as a stop. Drive three 150mm/6in nails through the board along its back edge to prevent the board from slipping. When the ladder is being used on dry concrete or paving-stone surfaces in dry weather, remove the nails and glue a square of rubber to the underside of the board.

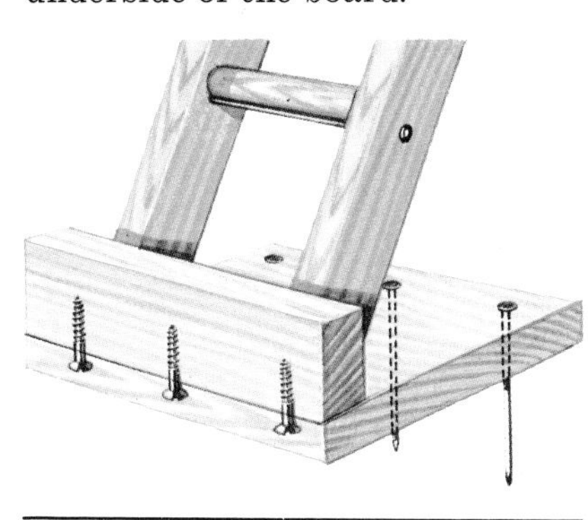

## 361 Marking the positions of hinges on a new door

Mark the position of hinges when fitting a new door by first propping the door in place on two wedges. To establish the position for the top hinge, make a mark on both the door and frame 150mm/6in from the top of the door, and for the bottom hinge 200mm/8in from the bottom. Fit the hinges inside these marks, with the top edge of the higher hinge flush with the top mark, and the bottom edge of the bottom hinge flush with the bottom mark.

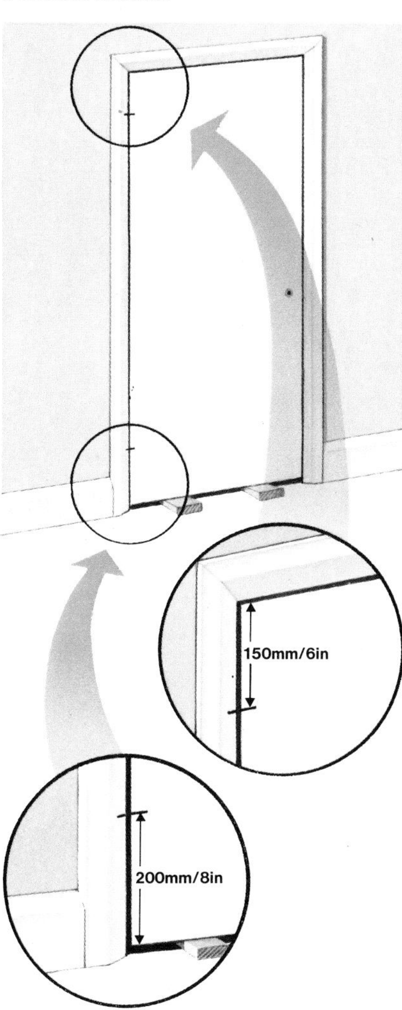


## 362 Storing remnants of putty or mastic

Small amounts of left-over putty or mastic will keep for a considerable period if they are kept in a screw-top jar full of water.

## 363 Freeing a rusted nut from a bolt in timber

Help free a rusted nut from a bolt fitted vertically through timber by building up a ring of putty around the nut to create a moat. Fill the moat with penetrating oil and leave it to soak into the thread of the bolt for a day.

## 364 Making very small steel screws easy to fit

Because they are difficult to hold and screw, very small steel screws can be awkward to fit into position. However, if they are kept in a box containing a magnet, they will pick up magnetic induction, which will make them "self-stick" to the screwdriver.

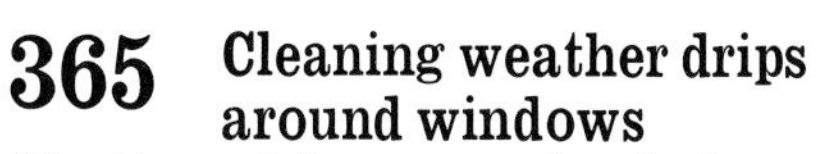

## 365 Cleaning weather drips around windows

Weather drips around windows and along the underside of sills can be awkward to clean out before repainting because there is no tool custom-made to fit all the different curves of the drip. The simple solution is to insert a screw with the appropriately-sized head into a length of dowelling and to use the head as a scraper to remove the paint.

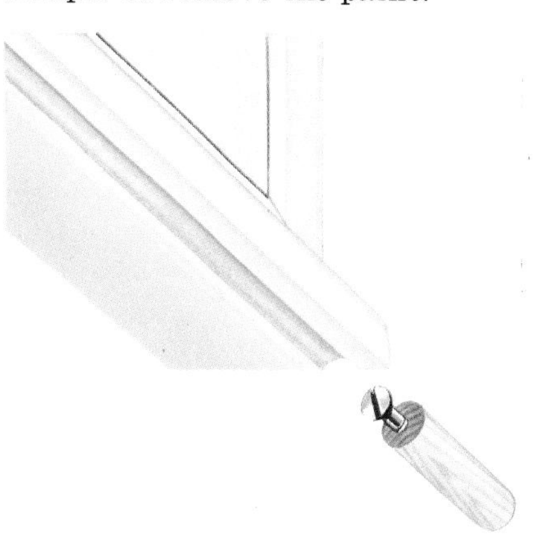

## 366 Gimlet

Used for making a starting hole for screws up to number six gauge, a gimlet is worked in a continuous clockwise direction. When removed its screw thread leaves a protruding rim of wood, which should be smoothed down.

## 367 Steps and stairs

Always repair a broken step, or a loose stair tread or riser as soon as possible. All are hazards that can cause serious falls.

## 368 Smoothing brush

When buying a wallpaper smoothing brush, check the amount of "spring" in the bristles. If the bristles are too weak they will fold over when the paper is being brushed and the wooden handle may catch the paper and tear it.

## 369 Working on a roof

When working on a roof, tie a lifeline around the waist whenever possible and make sure that it is secured to a solid object, such as a chimney stack. Use a bowline to secure the line—it is a safe and non-slip knot.

## 370 Cutting large sheets of board

A step-ladder, opened out and laid on its side, makes an excellent support when sawing up large sheets of hardboard or block-board.

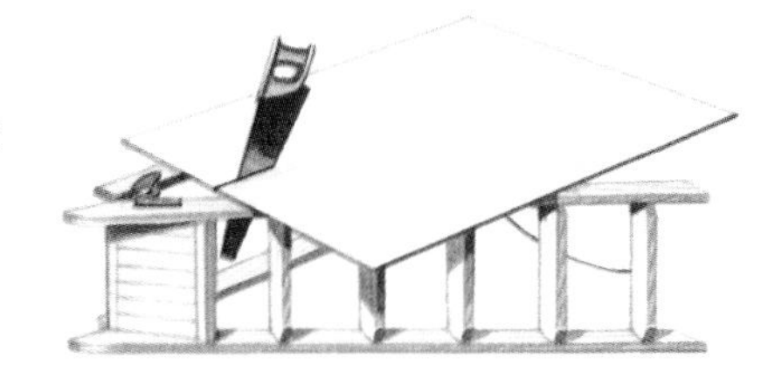

## 371 Digging out a trench for foundations

When digging out a trench for foundations, always dig it deep enough to remove all large pieces of vegetable matter in the soil. If any tree or shrub roots, for instance, are left in the ground they will gradually rot away and the soil surrounding them will eventually fall into the cavities they have left, leaving the foundations unsupported. These may eventually sink and will almost certainly crack. Fill any additional depth created with an extra layer of hardcore; this is obtainable from builders' merchants.

## 372 Shaping a bend in soft metal bars

The way to accurately shape a bend in a bar of soft metal such as aluminium, is to hold the bar over a length of iron pipe gripped firmly in a vice. Tap the bar with a rubber or wooden mallet to bend it to the required shape.

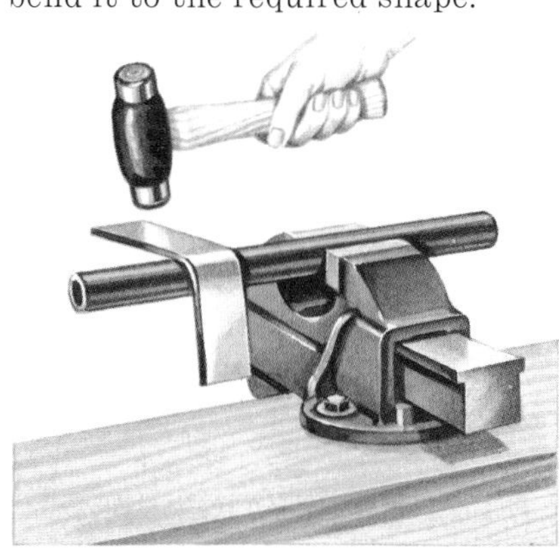

## 373 Decorating a stairwell safely

As the first priority, always make sure that the working platform is secure when decorating a stairwell. This makes it possible to decorate both the head wall (the highest part of the staircase) and the well wall (the wall next to it) with complete safety.

Start by taking up the stair carpet and then rest a ladder against the head wall, making sure that it is positioned at a safe working angle. Wrap cloths, or place old socks, around the tops of the ladder to prevent damage.

If there is only one landing stand a hop-up or strong box on it—testing that the box will take your weight—and lay a plank from the hop-up to the ladder. If there is more than one, place a step-ladder against the well wall on the first landing and screw a batten to the floor to stop it slipping. Finally, stand a hop-up or a box on the top landing. Lay a plank from the hop-up to the step ladder and then lay another one across to the head wall ladder. In both cases, place a second scaffold board over the first if the distance between the main supports is greater than 1,800 mm/6 ft. This removes the risk of the single board "bouncing" when it is walked on.

If papering the stairwell, remember that there is a danger that the weight of the paste may damage the long lengths of paper needed, so always work with a helper supporting the paper from below. Turn the first length of paper about 12 mm/½ in from the well wall on to the head wall. If painting the wall, treat each area separately. Start off with the upper part of the well wall and work downwards to complete it. Then tackle the head wall. Try to complete the job in one operation so that there will be no join lines in the finished paintwork.

## 374 The correct order for papering a stairwell

Start papering a stairwell by hanging the longest length of paper first; this is usually the length positioned immediately next to the head wall. Work up the stairs from this length before hanging the shorter lengths over the foot of the stairs. Paper the head wall last of all.

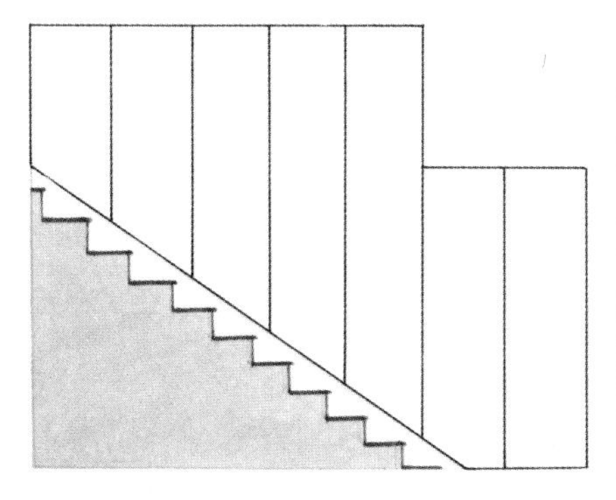

## 375 Measuring thickness of floorboards

To find the thickness of a boarded floor, bend the end of a nail, or piece of wire, at right angles and insert it into a gap between the floorboards. Twist the nail so the bent piece catches on the underneath of the floorboard when the nail is pulled up. Mark the nail where it emerges from the floor and remove it. Measure from the mark to the bent end to establish the thickness of the floor.

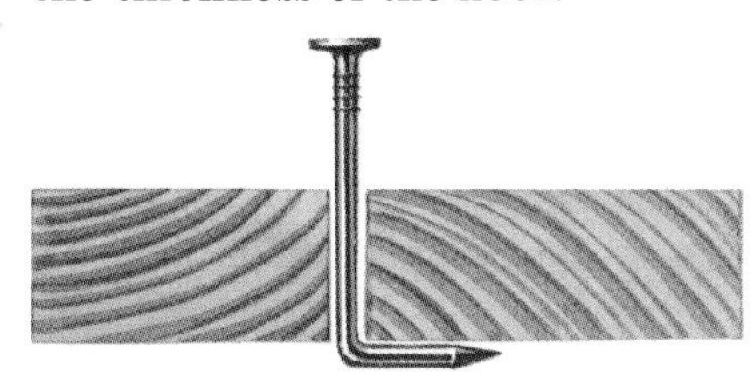

## 376 Sawing metal in awkward positions

Reversing a hacksaw blade may make it easier to saw metal that is positioned awkwardly. Fit the blade with the teeth facing towards the handle so it cuts when the hacksaw is pulled rather than pushed. Alternatively, fit the blade upside down into the saw.

## 377 Preventing a door from catching

Adjusting the hinges of a door can prevent it catching on the jamb or the floor as it opens and closes. If the door is catching near the top, pack the hinge out at the bottom by inserting a strip of card between the hinge and the framework. This will raise the door and push the bottom over slightly while moving the top of the door back. If the door is catching near the bottom of the jamb, pack out the top hinge with card in the same way.

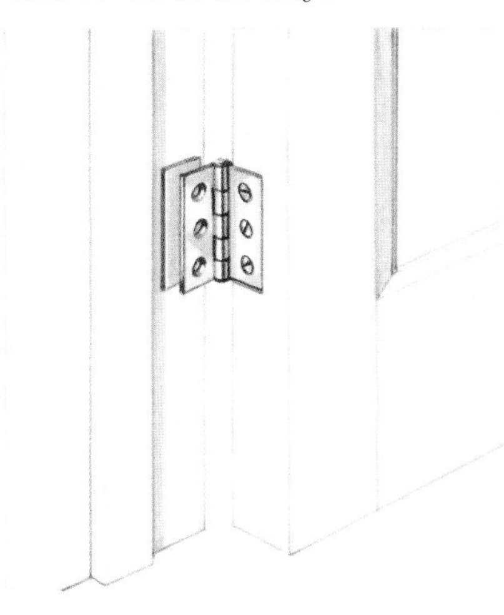

## 378 Making grooves in dowels

Ready-grooved wooden dowels are preferable when making strong fixings into timber, such as for a dowelled or mortised joint. If they are unavailable, however, it is easy to make them from plain dowels. Hold the dowel between the jaws of a pair of pliers and grip the pliers with enough pressure to indent shallow grooves in the opposite sides. Move the pliers down the dowel, repeating the process each time, until the entire dowel is covered. The grooves will allow air and excess glue to escape when the dowel is positioned.

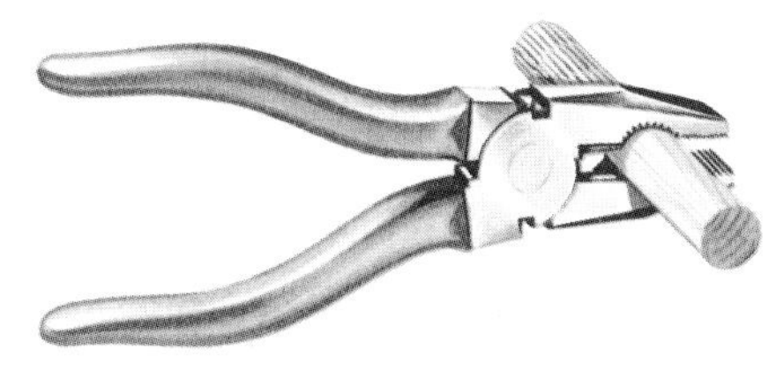

## 379 Protecting gullies while cleaning gutters

Place a shallow tin under the bottom of a downpipe while cleaning gutters. This prevents dirt and rubbish dropping into the gully underneath it and blocking the drain. Remember to remove the tin when the job is complete.

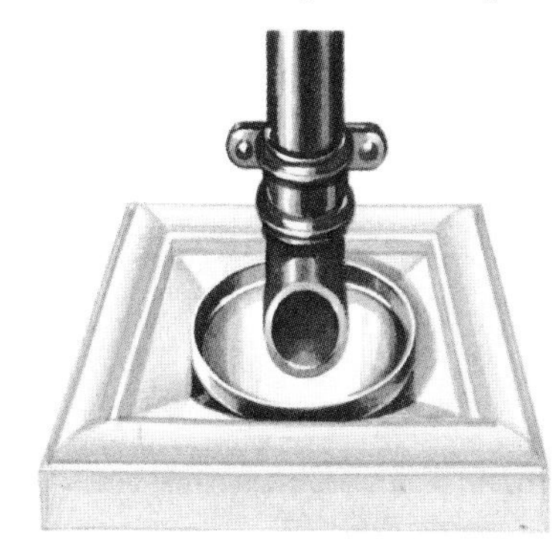

## 380 Cutting plasterboard quickly and cleanly

The right way to cut plasterboard is to score the papered side of the board deeply with a trimming knife. Bend the board along the cut to break it open and then make a cut from the reverse side. This prevents the edges along the cuts from crumbling.

## 381 Strengthening a mitred joint

Glue a strip of thin plywood within the joints to make an exceptionally strong mitred joint. Use a tenon saw to cut a slot in each mitre; each slot should be deep enough to take half the width of the ply strip and wide enough to take its thickness. Finally, glue the strip into position. Save time by using ply the exact thickness of the saw cut.

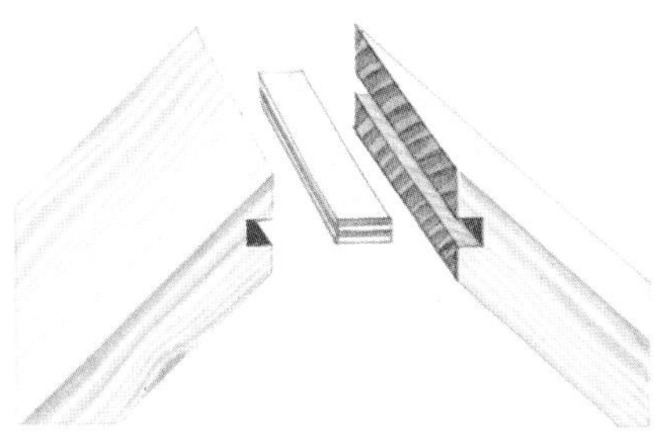

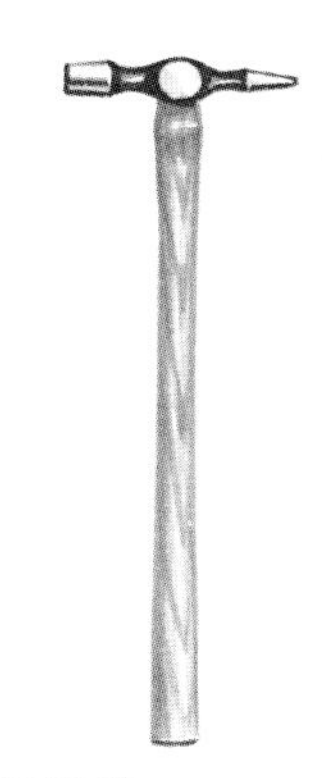

## 382 Pin hammer

The lightest version of a cross-peen hammer, a pin hammer is useful for hammering pins and small nails, which a heavier hammer would bend. Preserve the handle, which is usually made of wood, by occasionally rubbing it with linseed oil. Allow the oil to soak into the wood for at least thirty minutes before wiping the handle dry.

## 383 Safety on stairs

Always fit safety gates at the head and foot of flights of stairs if there are small children in the house.

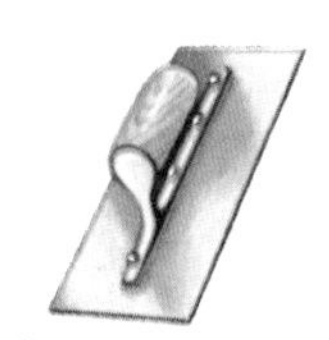

## 384
**Metal float**

Used to apply plaster to large areas of wall, and for giving a smooth finish to a final plaster coat.

## 385
**Working with a power saw**

Never try to clear a blocked blade in a power saw without first turning off the electricity supply at the socket.

## 386 Nailing mitred corners in softwood

When nailing mitred corners together, make sure that the two lengths of timber are firmly held together in a vice. This stops the joint being pushed out of line by the force of the blows of the hammer.

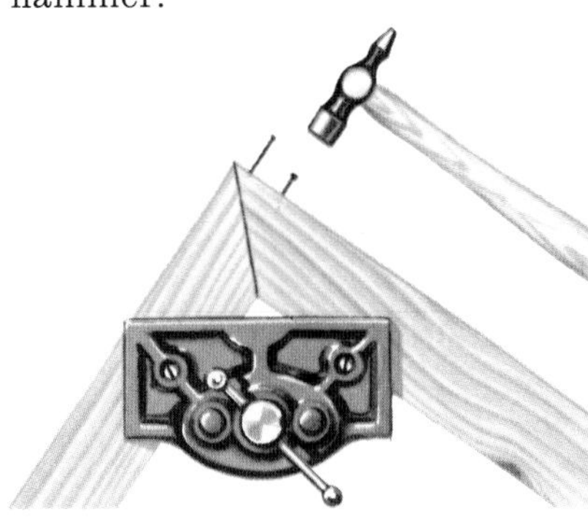

## 387 Mitring the edges of ceramic tiles

Mitre the edges of ceramic tiles either on an abrasive wheel fitted to a bench grinder or with a rasp-plane. Work the tile against the rasp or wheel rather than the rasp or wheel against the tile to lessen the risk of the tile breaking during the mitring process.

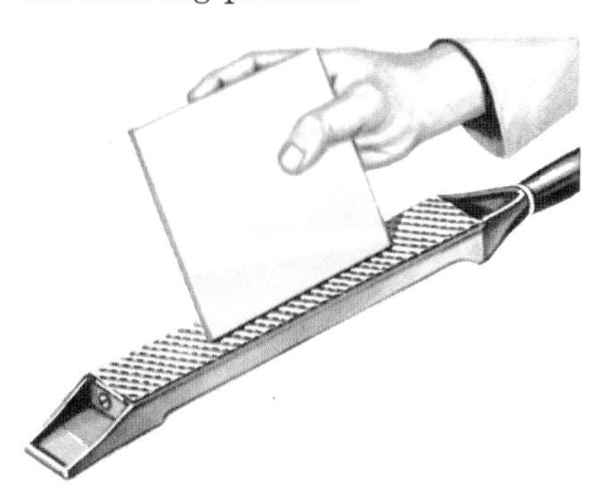

## 388 Preparing metals for soldering

Before soldering metals, always thoroughly clean their surfaces by rubbing them down with abrasive paper. After this, wipe them with a cloth dipped in methylated spirit just before applying the solder. This removes all traces of grease, and any of the inevitable grit left by the paper. It also helps the solder to adhere properly.

## 389 Stopping concrete becoming slippery

The best way of preventing a concrete path becoming slippery in wet weather is to roughen it by brushing the surface with an acid solution.

Wet the concrete and then, using an old soft-bristled broom, brush on two or three coats of hydrochloric acid, diluted with eight parts water. Leave the last coat of the solution on the path for a few minutes, then hose down the path thoroughly to remove all traces of the solution.

Hydrochloric acid is dangerous —it is essential therefore to wear protective rubber gloves and old clothes during the job.

## 390 Butt-jointing lengths of polystyrene sheeting

When lining a wall with polystyrene sheeting, overlap the edges of adjacent sheets by about 25 mm/1 in. Using a metal straight-edge as a guide and a sharp trimming knife, cut through the centre of the overlap, taking care to cut both thicknesses of sheeting. Peel off the top strip, then gently lift the cut edge and peel off the bottom strip. Spread adhesive under the raised edges and press them down carefully with a wall-paper brush.

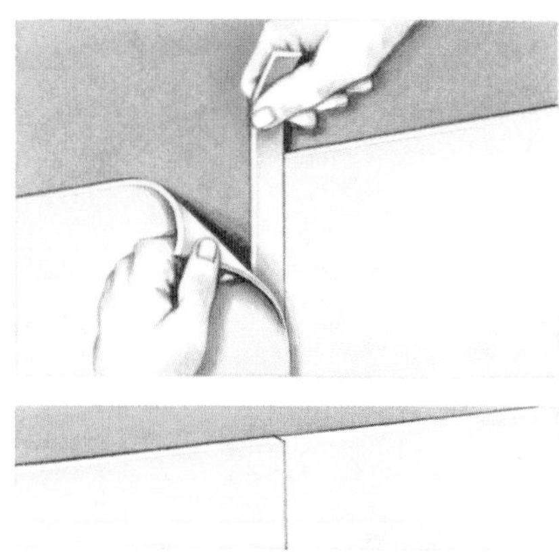

## 391 Preventing the tops of stake ends splitting

To avoid splitting the top ends of narrow stakes when they are being driven into heavy soil, protect them with blocks of hardwood. Cramp blocks on opposite sides of each stake flush with the top. Tighten the cramp to its maximum extent to make sure that the blocks do not slip while being hammered.

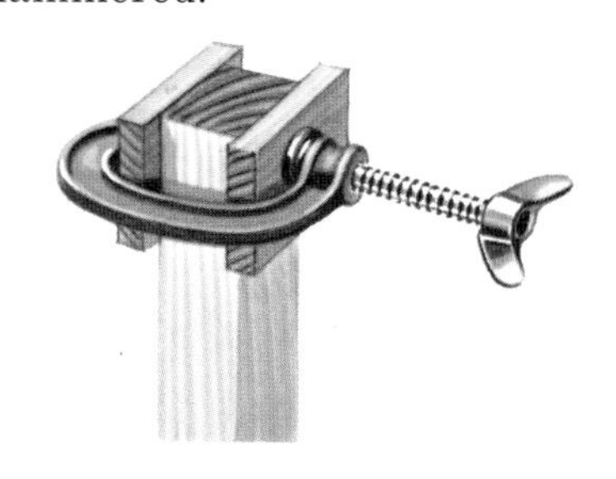

## 392 Repairing dents and holes in vinyl tiles

Unsightly dents and holes in vinyl tiles can be invisibly repaired by using shavings scraped from a piece of tile of the same colour with a trimming knife. Chop the shavings up with a very sharp trimming knife to the consistency of rough sand and then mix them with a little clear varnish to form a paste. Fill the damaged hole with the mixture and, when it has thoroughly dried, glasspaper it smooth. Finally wax and polish the repaired area.

## 393 Avoiding splits near the end of wood

Avoid splitting wood when nailing near the end of a timber length by fitting the wood oversize and nailing as required. Trim off the surplus wood afterwards.

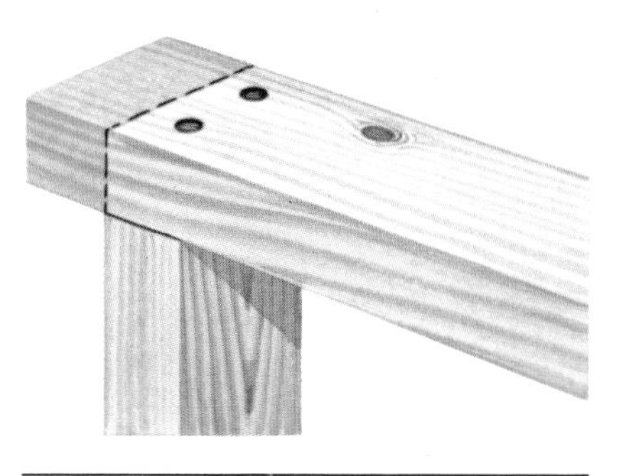

## 394 Concealing screws in veneered panels

Conceal screw-heads in veneered-surface panels with the aid of a short length of steel tube with a diameter slightly larger than the screw-head. Chamfer one end of the tube with a file to a sharp edge. Then take a scrap piece of panel and hammer the sharpened end of the tube into it, until the tube cuts below the surface of the veneer. Prise out the veneer circle and put it to one side.

Fit the screw into the panel, making sure the head of the screw is driven below the surface of the veneer, and then place the tube centrally over the screw head. Again hammer it below the veneer surface. Prise out the veneer and glue the veneer circle removed from the scrap into position to replace it.

## 395 Painting window sills for complete protection

Always apply two top coats of gloss paint to external window sills. Sills are exposed to more heat and dampness than any other external woodwork and the additional coat of paint should extend the life of the paintwork by at least two years.

## 396 Clench-nailing timber for a stronger join

Get a strong fixing when clench-nailing two pieces of timber together by hammering the nails from opposite sides and bending the points of the nails in opposite directions on either side.

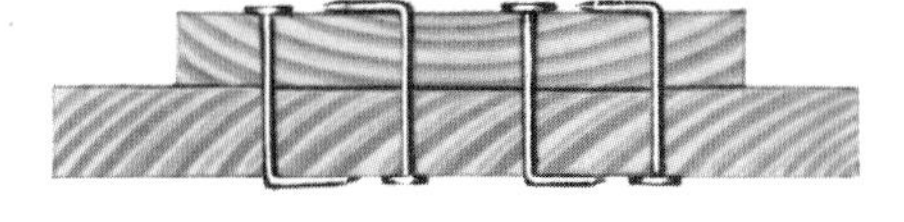

## 397 Refixing loose knots to make wood usable

Loose knots in a piece of wood need not make it unusable. To refix them, first push out the knot from one side and coat its edges and the inside edges of the knot hole with a clear adhesive. Then replace the knot in the hole and, after the adhesive has dried, smooth off any excess glue.

## 398 Repairing the front edge of concrete steps

Renew a broken edge of a concrete step by first chipping away all the loose concrete. Chip out about 25-37 mm/1-1½ in of the step, undercutting the edges with a bolster. Place a board against the front face of the step and hold it in place with bricks—making sure that the top of the board is flush with the top of the step. Coat the edge with a PVA bonding agent to stop the existing concrete absorbing too much moisture from the new mix.

Mix one part of cement with three parts of coarse sand and, using a trowel, apply the mortar, forcing the mix into the undercut edge. Smooth off the surface with a wooden float, so that the concrete will dry out to a slightly roughened finish.

Remove the board after about six hours, but avoid stepping on the repair for at least a week. If the weather is hot, cover the repair with damp sacking.

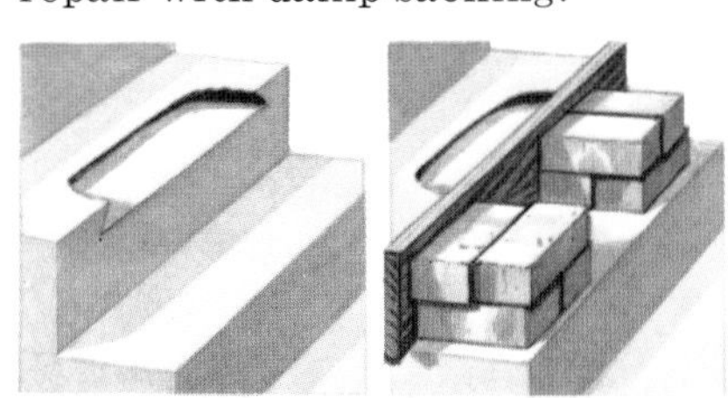

## 399 Strengthening bolts set in concrete

Help anchor bolts set into concrete by bending the bolt just below the point at which it will protrude above the surface. This gives a very firm fixing.

## 400 Reinforcing joints with fasteners

The simplest way of reinforcing timber joints—where appearance is secondary to function—is to use corrugated fasteners. Place the sharpened edge of the corrugations across the joints and hammer in place. Use two fasteners for extra strength if necessary.

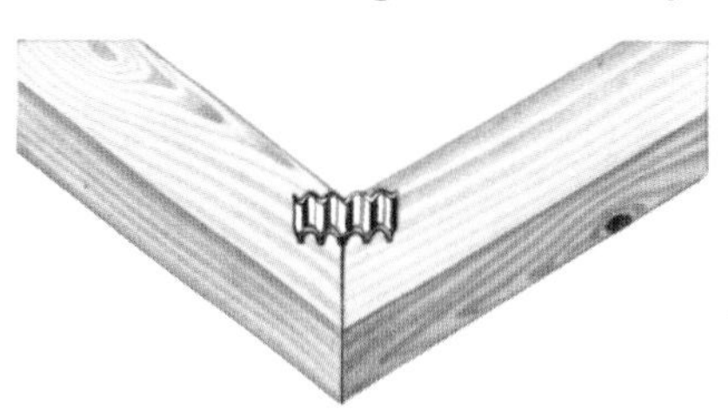

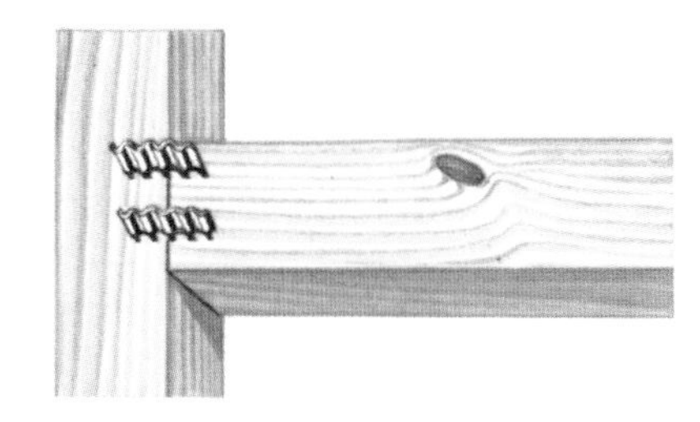

## 401 Preventing dampness in timber floors

As a precaution against damp, regularly check that the airbricks fitted above the damp-course level on the outside walls of a house are not blocked by leaves, soil or other debris. Without the ventilation provided by the bricks, dampness will eventually cause timber floors to start to rot.

## 402 Plumb line

A small weight and string can be used as a plumb line to find the true vertical when wallpapering. Use a suction pad with a screw hook attachment if the line is awkward to fix.

## 403 Connecting electric cable

Never extend an electric cable by wiring the ends of two pieces of cable together and taping them with insulation tape. Always use a proper connector with screw fixings.

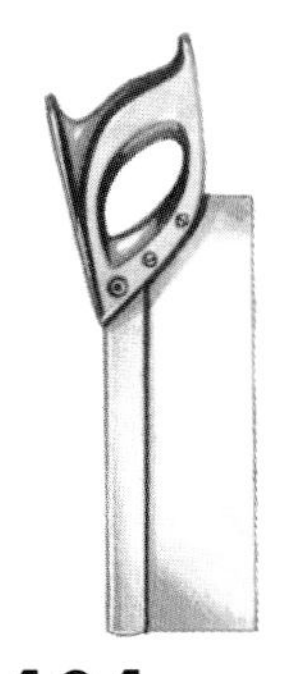

## 404
### Tenon saw

The rigid-backed blade of a tenon saw makes it ideal for cutting woodwork joints accurately. The best saw to buy has between fourteen and sixteen teeth per 25 mm/1 in. This ensures a fine cut on a joint.

## 406 Fitting a vinyl floor tile round a pipe

When fitting a vinyl floor tile round an obstacle, such as a pipe, always make sure that the tile is accurately positioned during the marking-up process. First, place the tile to be fitted over the tile in front of the pipe. Rest a ruler up against the pipe's side and, using a set square to ensure accuracy, draw a line from the pipe on to the tile. Without moving the tile, draw a line from the other side of the pipe.

Keeping the new tile facing in the same direction, move it so that it covers the tile immediately to the right, or left, of the pipe. Again using a set square and ruler, mark the lines from the front and back of the pipes to intersect the first two lines and form a square. Draw the diagonals to find the centre of the square, and, using a compass, draw a circle with the same diameter as the width of the square. Cut a line from the back of the tile and cut out the circle with a trimming knife. Apply adhesive to the back of the tile and then fit it into place around the pipe.

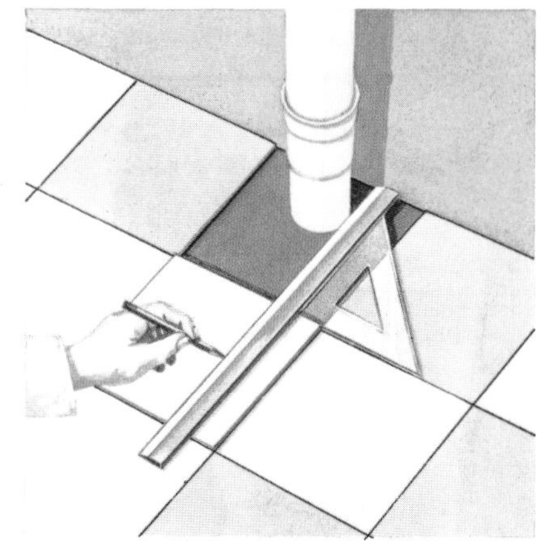

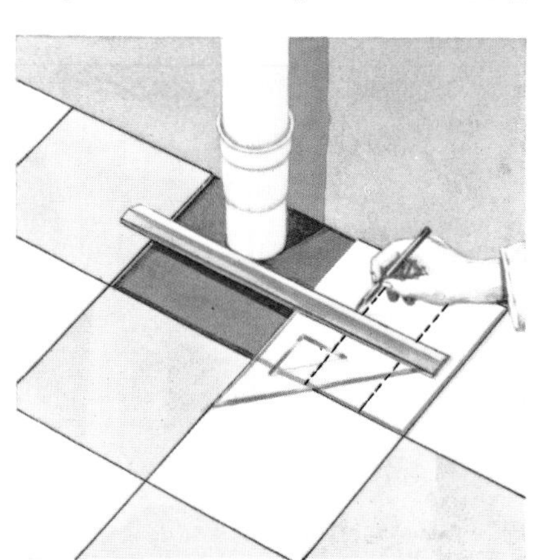

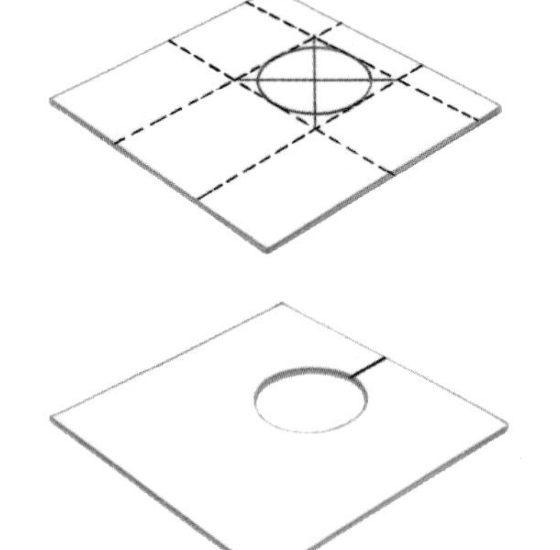

## 405
### Replacing a fuse

Never replace a burnt-out fuse with anything other than the correctly rated fuse wire, or the cause of the overloading may be concealed and a serious fire may start.

## 407 Wallpapering around a corner

When papering round a corner, trim the paper so that 13 mm/½ in turns the corner. Paste in position and then cover the overlap with the next piece.

## 408 Cutting a sheet of hardboard correctly

Always cut from the face side and use a fine-toothed saw, such as a tenon saw, when cutting a sheet of hardboard. Mark a cut line, saw carefully, as forcing the saw may tear the sheet, and support both ends of the sheet.

## 409 Estimating paint for woodwork

One coat of paint on one side of a door takes about $\frac{1}{20}$ litre/$\frac{1}{10}$ pint of paint; use this value to estimate the amount of paint needed to decorate a room's woodwork.

Visualize how much skirting is equivalent to the area of a door—and the same with window frames, cornices, door mouldings and so on—to get a fairly accurate idea of the amount of paint for one coat only. Double this to estimate for the two coats needed for proper coverage of the entire room.

## 410 Polishing a short length of metal tube

When polishing a short length of metal tube, insert a dowel of matching diameter into each end. The dowels will serve as hand grips, making it easier to turn the tube against a polishing wheel fitted to a grinder.

## 411 Preparing very hard putty for use

If putty is too hard to use, soften it by kneading in turpentine or turpentine substitute. The liquid should be added in small quantities to shallow indentations in the putty, kneading well each time. Continue adding liquid and kneading until the right dough-like consistency has been reached.

## 412 Insulating gaps in exposed floorboards

To prevent heat loss and draughts between floorboards, fill gaps larger than 6mm/¼in with offcut strips of wood. For smaller gaps, home-made papier mâché is one of the best alternatives.

To make the papier mâché filler, use a white unprinted, uncoated paper, cut or torn into pieces about the size of a postage stamp. A bucketful of these pieces is sufficient for a floor area of about 7sq m/75sq ft. Pour small quantities of boiling water over the pieces, while pounding them with a piece of wood, to make a thick paste. Allow it to cool for about two hours, then pour in a packet of cellulose-based wallpaper paste and mix thoroughly.

Using a scraper, force the mixture between the gaps in the floorboards. After three days, rub down with a fine-grade glasspaper block. Finally, colour the filler with a proprietary wood stain to blend in with the floor.

## 413 Filing aluminium speedily and easily

Use a coarse single-cut file to file aluminium. When filing, occasionally dip the file into paraffin. This stops the teeth clogging.

## 414 Choosing hacksaw blades for metalwork

Use a hacksaw blade with 32 teeth per 25mm/1in if a particularly smooth cut is needed. For general work, use a blade with 18 teeth per 25mm/1in.

## 415 Joining timber with a scarf joint

To make a scarf joint, used to join two lengths of timber to form a long span, cramp together the lengths of wood being joined, allowing for an overlap of twice the proposed joint length. Saw across the lengths from side to side to create an angle that will give an exact fit.

Glue and screw the timbers to secure the joint. This provides a stronger fixing than nailing.

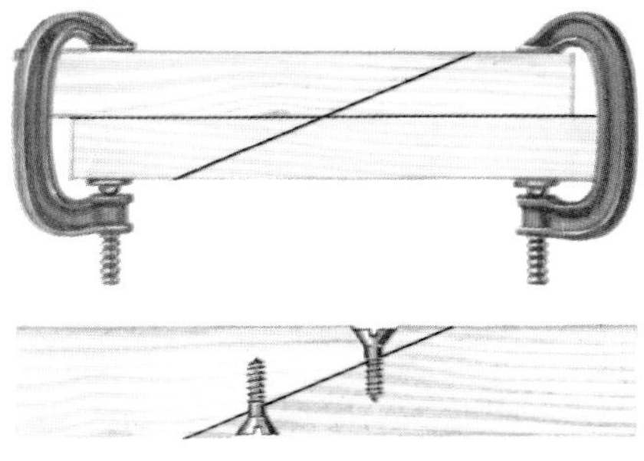

## 416 Laying cork floor tiles

Before laying cork tiles prepare the surface and check for adequate underfloor ventilation. When laying the tiles on a wooden floor always nail them in position as well as applying adhesive. First nail a headless pin in the centre of the tile and then one in each corner. If the floor is not wooden, place heavy weights on the tiles until the glue sets. This can take between two to six hours, depending on the adhesive used. Check with the supplier for suitability.

## 417 Handling a cold chisel safely

Fit a scrap piece of expanded metal, or thin transparent plastic sheet, round the shaft of a cold chisel when hammering it into brickwork or concrete. This prevents chippings flying into the face. Also, always hold the chisel with the thumb against its side; if the hammer slips during the job, it will be less painful.

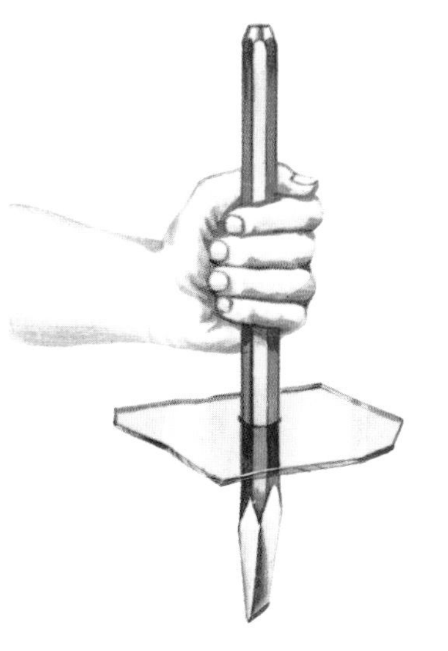

## 418 Cutting bevelled edges in wood

When cutting a bevelled edge on a piece of wood, cramp a length of spare timber to the wood as a guide for the saw blade. Mark the required cutting angle on the wood and, using a straight-edge, extend the angle to line up with the top of the guide. Keep the saw blade against this top edge to maintain the correct angle. After completing the cut, smooth the edges down with glasspaper.

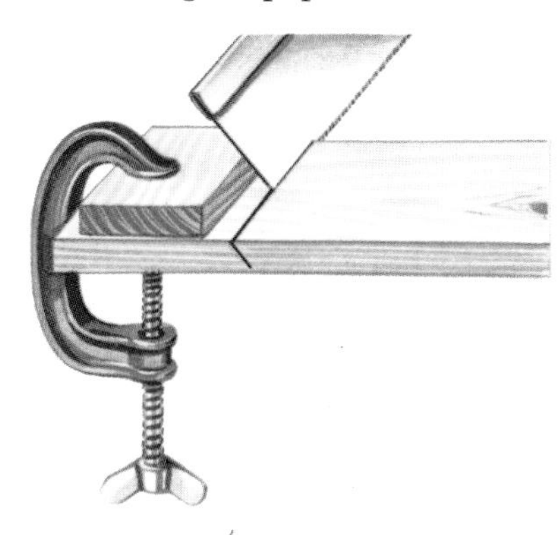

## 419 Pincers

Pincers are mainly used to remove stubborn nails that cannot be extracted with a claw hammer. Always work the pincers down the nail, pulling it clear in a series of short movements. Otherwise the nail may bend over and leave a large hole as it is prised clear.

## 420 Spray painting

Never use a paint spray near a naked flame or fire. Some types of paint, when atomized, create highly combustible mixtures.

## 421
### Surveyor's tape

A surveyor's tape is an essential tool for measuring long distances, such as foundations for walls. Remember, however, that the "give" in the linen of the tape makes it unsuitable for measurements which have to be accurate to less than 25 mm/1 in.

## 422
### Rewiring a plug

When rewiring a plug, make sure there are no whiskers of wire protruding from the casing. When the power is switched on, anyone who touches them will get a shock.

## 423 Securing chair rungs when regluing them

Always clamp chair legs in position when regluing rungs. After gluing the end of the rung and its socket, fit the rung back into position and then wrap a double length of cord around the chair legs, placing pieces of card between the legs and the cord to stop the cord marking the wood's surface. Insert a length of wood through the cords at the front of the chair and twist it—tourniquet fashion—to tighten the cord and pull the legs into position. Jam the wood against the rung to prevent the cord unwinding before the glue has set. Leave the cord in place for at least twelve hours.

## 424 Testing the soundness of a grinding wheel

Before attaching a grinding wheel to its mounting on a power grinder hang it from a cord and tap it lightly with the end of a spanner or a similar small tool. If the tone sounds flat, do not use the wheel. It is almost certainly fractured and will be extremely dangerous if it breaks apart while spinning. The wheel should give a clear "ring"—in much the same way as a crystal glass "rings" when its rim is flicked with a finger-nail.

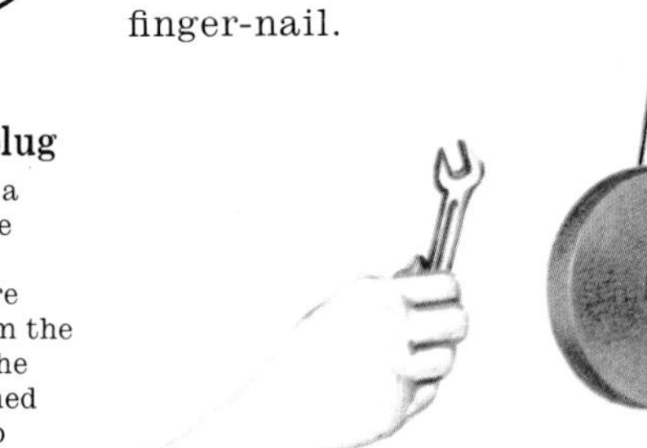

## 425 Tightening a loose-fitting chair rung

Remove the rung and saw a slot in its end no deeper than the depth of the hole into which it will be inserted. Insert a wedge cut to the same length that projects approximately 6mm/¼in from the end. Before refitting the rung, scrape off all old glue from the rung and from the hole into which it fits. Apply new glue to both the rung and the hole and hammer the chair leg on to the rung, using a block of wood to avoid damage to the leg's surface. The wedge will force the rung open as it is driven into the hole.

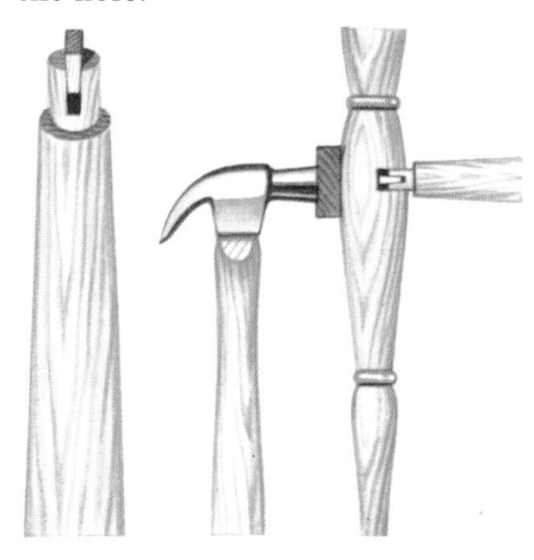

## 426 Making a concrete floor less slippery

A concrete floor in front of a workbench often becomes slippery through continuous wear. This could be dangerous, so brush plaster of Paris on to the surface to roughen it.

## 427 Washing and preserving exterior paintwork

Add a little proprietary brush-cleaning liquid to warm water when washing down paintwork. This removes dirt far better than detergent. Always wash the paintwork thoroughly with fresh water afterwards. Ideally, wash down exterior paintwork at least once and preferably twice a year, which makes it last longer. Dirt in the atmosphere, settling on the paintwork, is one of the main causes of paintwork breaking up.

## 428 Making a ceiling more soundproof

A simple way to soundproof a ceiling is to fit fireproof acoustic tiles to it. Either glue the tiles directly in place or glue and pin them to a series of battens nailed directly to the joists. Fill the gap between the tiles and the ceiling with glass wool insulating material as the job progresses.

## 429 Cutting thick paving slabs cleanly

Use a masonry cutting disc attached to a power drill to cut thick paving slabs. Scratch the cutting line with a nail and cut along its full length through half the thickness of the slab. Then place the slab over a block of wood, making sure that it runs the full length of the cut. Apply heavy and equal pressure to both sides of the cut to snap the slab. Alternatively, place the half-cut slab upside down on two blocks either side of the cut and split it with a bolster.

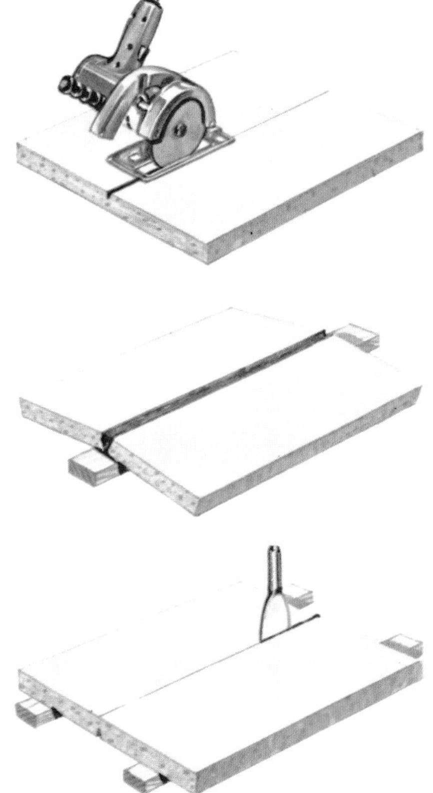

## 430 Locating the timber framework in a wall

Tap across the wall with the handle of a screwdriver to locate the timber framework behind it. High notes indicate woodwork; low notes the spaces in between. Alternatively, drill a horizontal line of holes about 25 mm/1 in apart with the smallest possible twist drill to locate the uprights. On walls where the skirting has been nailed to the uprights, mark a line between each row of nails and hold a plumb line so that the plumb bob lines up with the mark. This will indicate the approximate centre of each upright.

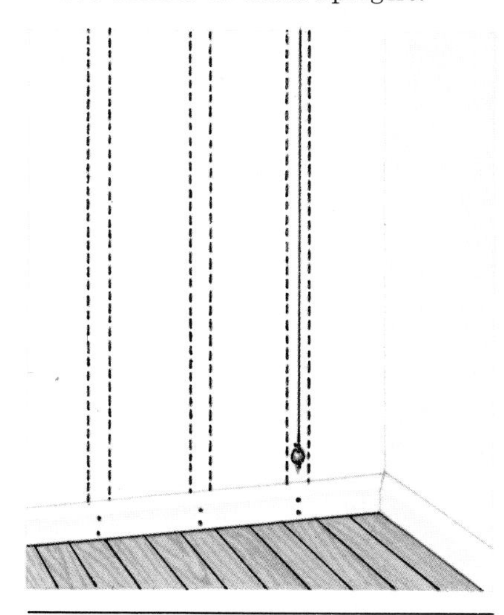

## 431 Concealing scratches in mahogany

Use iodine as a way of staining and concealing scratches in dark surfaces, such as mahogany. Apply the iodine with either a fine water-colour brush or with cotton wool wrapped around the end of a cocktail stick.

## 432 Removing a shattered light bulb easily

Removing the metal base of a shattered light bulb from a socket can be difficult. Switch off the electricity at the mains and then press and twist a suitably sized rubber ball against the base to free it. Alternatively, use a pair of pliers to grip and turn the inside surfaces of the base.

## 433 Checking the position of a thermostat

Always check the position of the thermostat when having a central-heating system installed or moving into a house or flat where central heating is already fitted. To work efficiently, the thermostat must be fitted on an internal wall, at least 1½ m/5 ft above the floor. It should not be in a draughty area, which could mean that the system would be operating almost constantly, or near a heat source, such as a cooker, which would cause it to cut off the heat while other parts of the house are cold.

## 434 Removing light scratch marks from glass

Rubbing with a piece of dampened felt dipped in jeweller's rouge will remove light scratches from glass. Jeweller's rouge is available from hardware shops.

## 435 Repainting sash window frames

Before repainting a sash window, push a piece of thin card around the edges of the window to check on the amount of clearance between the window and the frame. If the card becomes difficult to slide at any one point, strip off the old paint back to the woodwork at that point. An additional coat of paint could prevent the window sliding properly. If stripping paint back to the original woodwork, remember to prime the bare wood with a wood primer before repainting. Take care not to get paint on the sash cords—this will weaken them.

## 436 Sanding floors with a sanding machine

When using a sanding machine, always wear a belt fitted round the back of the waist and attached to the handle to combat the powerful pulling action of the machine.

Prepare the room for sanding by removing all furniture. Remember also to remove any projecting nails and tacks, or to punch them below the surface. One exposed nail or tack is enough to rip the abrasive sheet on the machine, or even damage the machine's roller. Carry out the first sanding at an angle of 45° across the boards, using coarse paper, and the second at the same angle, but working in the opposite direction. This will help eliminate any high spots in the floor's surface. Make the third and the fourth sandings down the length of the boards, working with the grain and using medium paper and fine paper respectively. Overlap each sanding slightly.

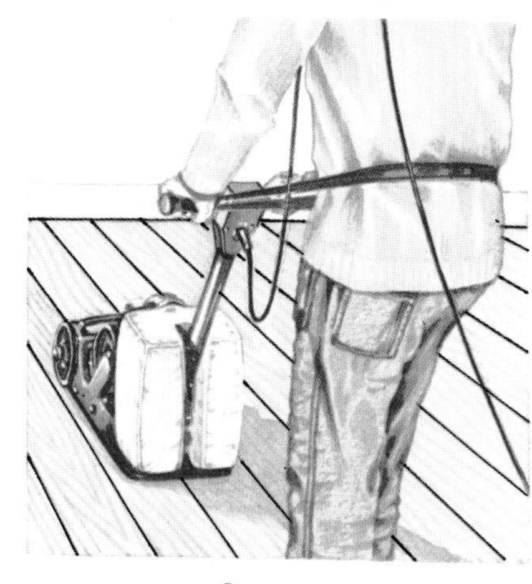

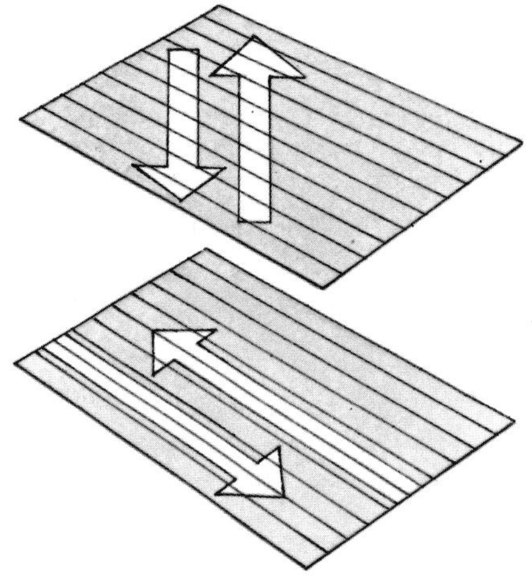

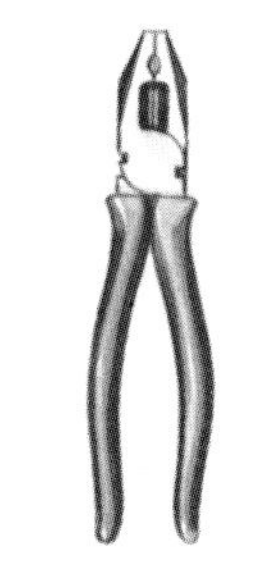

## 437 Pliers

Always buy pliers with rubber grips insulating the handles. This means that they can be used for electrical repairs as well as for general work.

## 438 Working with cutting tools

Keep cutting tools sharp at all times—forcing a blunt tool can easily lead to it slipping and causing a serious cut.

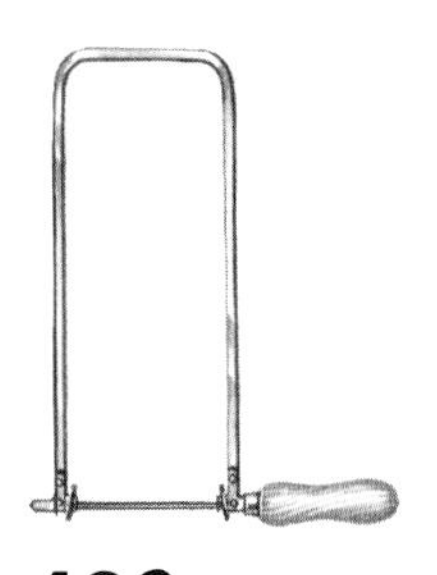

## 439
### Fretsaw

The frame of a fretsaw gives it manoeuvrability, making it ideal for cutting intricate shapes and curves over a large area. Only cut in downward strokes and make sure that the blade is fitted with the teeth facing forwards.

## 440
### Cutting timber with a power saw

Never push the end of a length of timber through a power saw with the fingers. It could result in serious injury. Use a scrap length of wood to push the timber past the blade.

## 441 Repairing small burns in woven carpets

Small burns in woven carpets can often be repaired by using a thread taken from the edge of the carpet, or, preferably, from an offcut. Trim off the burned edges around the hole. Then wind the thread around a large knitting needle and squeeze it tight so that it will fit compactly into the hole. Apply rubber latex adhesive to the base of the hole. Wait until it becomes tacky and then slide the thread from the needle into the hole. Allow the adhesive to dry for a few hours and then trim the loops flush with the carpet.

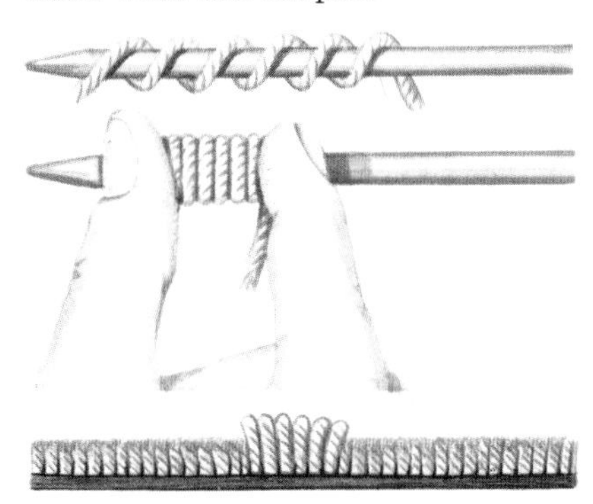

## 442 Cleaning rusty saw and chisel blades

Rusty saw and chisel blades should be cleaned by rubbing them with wire wool dipped in turpentine substitute.

## 443 Regrinding a badly worn oilstone

If frequent use has worn a hollow in an oilstone, regrind the stone flat, using silver sand and an old piece of glass, about 45cm/18in square. Lay the glass on a flat surface and sprinkle a thin layer of silver sand over it. Wet the stone and, keeping it damp, rub it in circular movements over the sand until the stone is flat.

If working on a very smooth surface, such as laminate, lay sheets of newspaper beneath the glass, dampening the top sheets. Otherwise, the pressure being exerted on the stone may cause the glass to slide about.

## 444 Hanging unpatterned wallpapers

Reverse alternate lengths when hanging unpatterned wallpaper. For example, paste the top of the first length to the top of the wall, but paste the top of the next length to the bottom. This procedure helps disguise the slight variations in colour that can occur within a roll. When cutting the wallpaper into lengths mark the top of each one for easy reference.

## 445 Disguising chipped fixing holes in mirrors

Chipped edges around the fixing holes in a mirror are often the result of not centralizing the screw when securing the mirror to a wall. To disguise the edges, fit a decorative rosette and dome-headed screw to cover the damage. Rosettes are manufactured with a chromium-plated finish, in plain "white" silver and in various colours.

Place a washer behind the mirror and fit a rubber grommet in the hole. Place the rosette over the hole and fit the screw through it, the grommet and the washer into a wall plug. Screw the dome-head cap into the screw head.

## 446 Ensuring that interior paintwork lasts longer

When painting areas subject to sunlight and condensation inside the house—such as window ledges and french window frames—use gloss paint for the top coat. This gives a harder and longer-wearing surface than matt paint.

## 447 Cutting a tile to fit around a corner

To cut a floor tile so that it will fit around a corner, first place the tile to be fitted over the nearest whole tile on one side of the corner. Place another tile over it and hard up against the skirting. Use it as a straight-edge to mark a cut line on the first tile.

Without turning the tile, slide it on to the nearest whole tile around the other side of the corner. With the second tile again in position, mark another line. Cut down the lines to their intersection to complete the job.

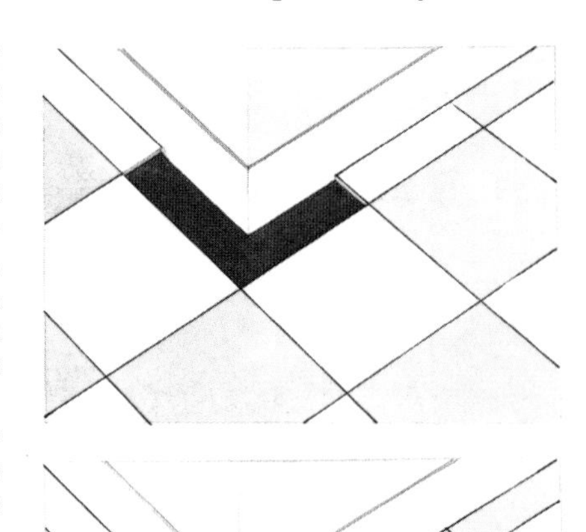

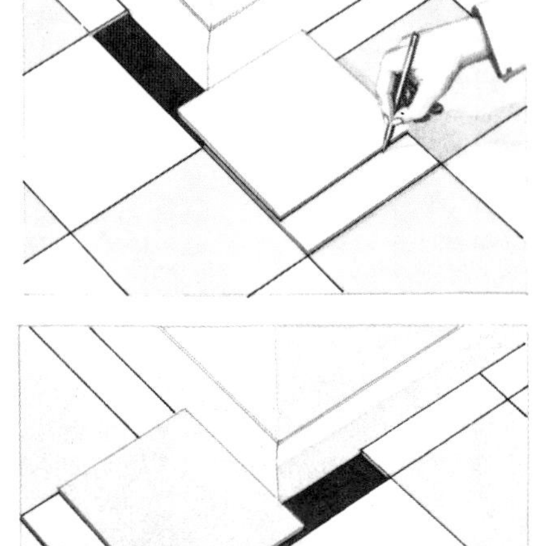

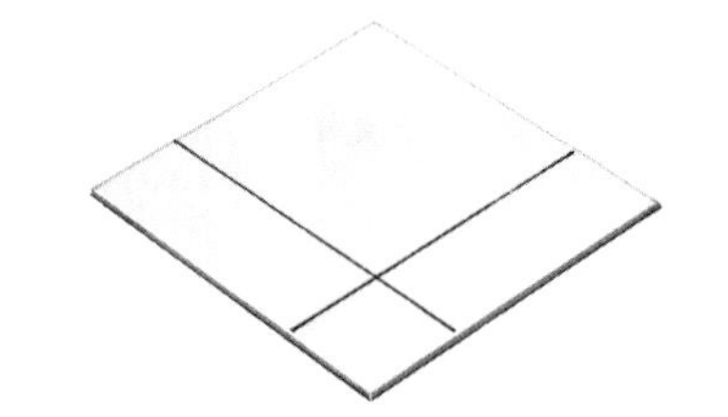

## 448 Preserving timber used outside

When preparing timber for outside use, soak it in creosote or proprietary preservative rather than simply brushing on preservative. This will prolong the timber's life. First make a trough in soft, deeply dug soil that has been raked level. Lay out four rows of bricks, set on edge, to form a rectangle slightly longer in length than that of the timber. Cover the bricks with a polythene sheet, making sure that the sheet overlaps them by at least 45cm/18in, and hold it in place by resting a brick on each corner. Press the sheet down in the middle to form a V-shaped trough and dig a hole deep enough to take a bucket for eventual drainage.

Pour in the creosote or proprietary preservative and then immerse the timber, using bricks to hold it beneath the surface. Allow the timber to soak for at least two hours, and preferably longer. To empty the trough, remove the bricks keeping the polythene in place at each corner and drain the liquid into the bucket.

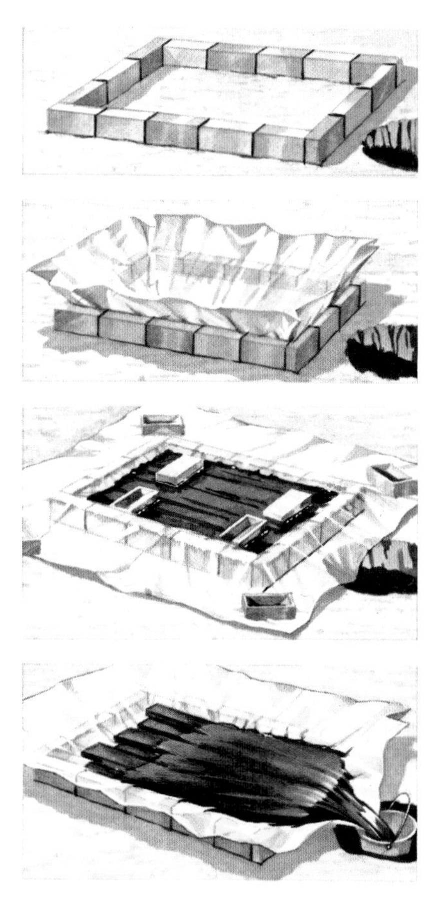

## 451 Working with an orbital sander

Never press down on an orbital sander. The weight of the tool in itself is sufficient to remove any blemishes from a surface.

## 452 Giving clear glass an opaque finish

Opaque glass—particularly suitable for diffusing the glare of a fluorescent light—can easily be made by grinding the surface of clear glass. Use a square of glass 12mm/½in thick as a rubbing block, and an abrasive powder, such as carborundum powder.

Grind the edges of the rubbing block and lay the clear glass on a level surface covered with a piece of felt or old blanket. Wearing protective gloves, spread a little powder on the glass and add a few drops of water. Rub this in a circular movement, applying even pressure. Take care not to press down too heavily, or the glass may crack. Add more powder and water as required until the whole surface has a greyish opaque finish.

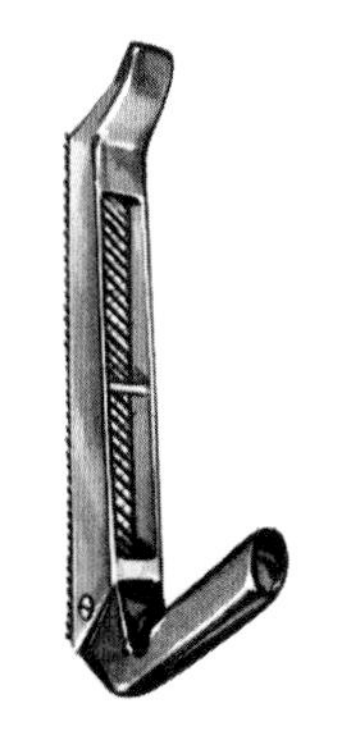

## 454 Rasp plane

Use a rasp plane to plane off strips of wood quickly. For a smoother finish always hold the plane in line with the wood, which means that the teeth, set at 45° to the body of the plane, will be cutting at an angle.

## 449 Repairing damaged or scuffed wallpaper

To repair a damaged area of wallpaper, first lay a matching piece of wallpaper over the damaged area. Cut through both the new and the old piece of paper with a trimming knife. Remove the damaged section and stick the new paper in its place.

## 450 Using a chalk line to mark out straight lines

The simplest way to mark out a straight line over a long distance on a wall or a floor is to "snap" a chalk line. Take a piece of string that is slightly longer than the distance to be marked out and rub it with chalk along its entire length. Attach each end to a nail, making sure that the string is taut, and pluck it like a bowstring. The string will snap back to leave a clear chalk line. When "snapping" exceptionally long distances, press the centre of the string firmly down on the wall or floor and snap each half of the length of string in turn.

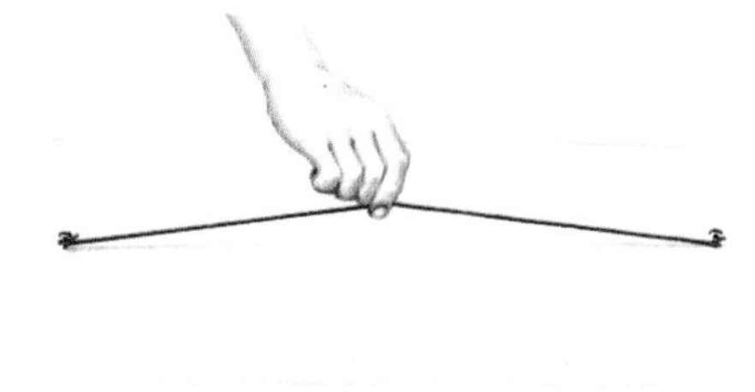

## 453 Applying plaster to plasterboard

When applying a skim-coat of plaster to plasterboard, wet the grey face of the plasterboard slightly before starting the job. The water helps to slow down the plaster's setting process and thus gives more time to finish the job.

## 455 Major rebuilding on roofs

Never attempt major rebuilding work on a roof—such as the task of dismantling a damaged chimney stack. Apart from the hazards involved, specialized scaffolding is required, as well as expert techniques to prevent falling brickwork damaging the roof.

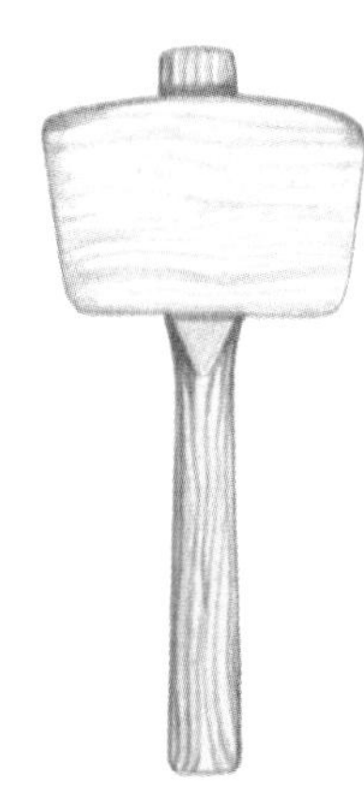

## 456 Mallet

Always use a beech mallet to hit chisels when making cuts in timber. A hammer will quickly split the handle of a chisel.

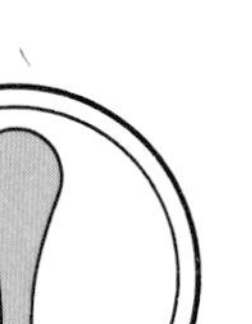

## 457 Storage heaters

Never cover a storage heater with material. If the heat is prevented from escaping the heater may be damaged.

## 458 How to bend timber to an even curve

Bend a length of timber to a curve—a technique known as kerfing—by making a series of parallel cuts across the timber to a depth not exceeding three-quarters of the timber's thickness. The amount of curve will depend on the pliability of the wood, the depth and width of each cut, and the distance between each cut. Where possible practise the cuts on a scrap piece of the wood.

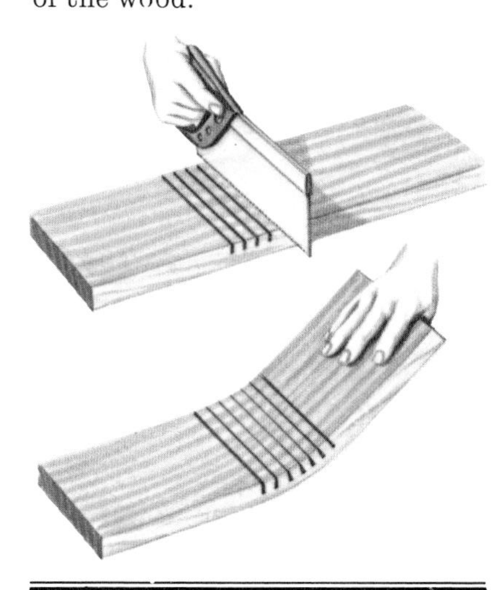

## 459 Smoothing the edges of a laminated surface

Always smooth the edges of a piece of wood which has a glued laminated surface from the laminated side, working downwards. If the edges are smoothed in the normal way the laminate may split.

## 460 Bonding aluminium without soldering

Bond aluminium surfaces together with a two-part epoxy-resin glue as an alternative to soldering them. First, clean the surfaces being joined with turpentine substitute, if necessary, and roughen them with a coarse grade of emery paper to provide a good "key" for the glue. After this, mix the necessary amount of glue and spread it over the two surfaces. Allow the glue to dry for a few minutes and then cramp the surfaces together. Leave the glue to harden for at least six hours.

## 461 Cleaning clogged abrasive papers

Clean abrasive papers clogged with sawdust or metal filings by working the paper—abrasive side up—rigorously over the corner of a piece of timber.

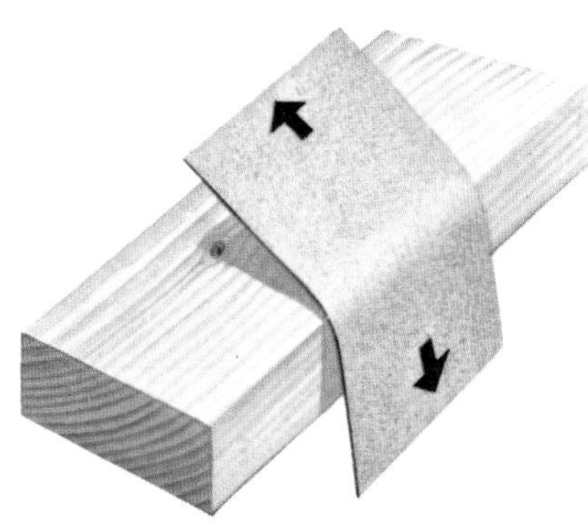

## 462 Cutting ceramic tiles quickly and cleanly

Simplify the cutting of ceramic tiles by using a wooden base board slightly larger than the size of the tiles to be cut. Secure a taut length of galvanized wire across the board with nails or screws. Score through the glazed surface of the tile and place it—glazed surface uppermost—on the board with the scored line over the wire. Press firmly on each side of the scored line to snap the tile cleanly.

When cutting off a narrow strip of tile, place a piece of wood on the narrow strip and press down on it. This ensures that pressure is evenly applied along the complete length of the cut. For a very narrow strip, use pincers to nibble off the waste material and smooth down the cut edge with glasspaper or a file if necessary.

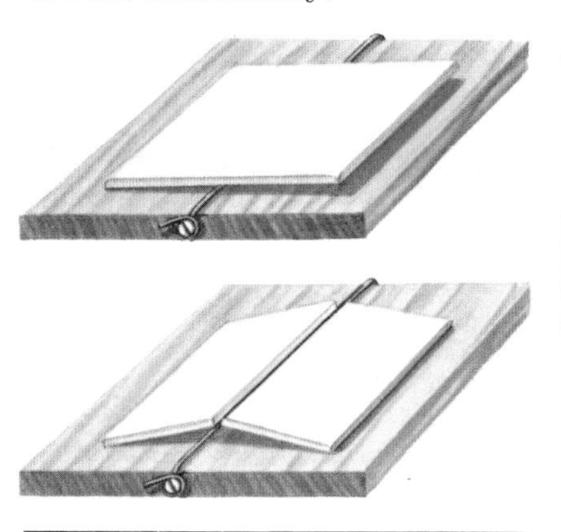

## 463 Fitting a platform to a step-ladder

Fit a small extension platform to a step-ladder for paint, brushes and tools to stand on. Make the platform by gluing and screwing two strips of wood underneath a 12mm/½in piece of blockboard. The strips project beyond the platform to slot into two brackets fitted under the top tread of the step-ladder. Finally nail a narrow moulding around the edges of the platform to prevent the brushes and tools rolling off.

Also, an S-hook is a useful tool for hanging cans of paint safely.

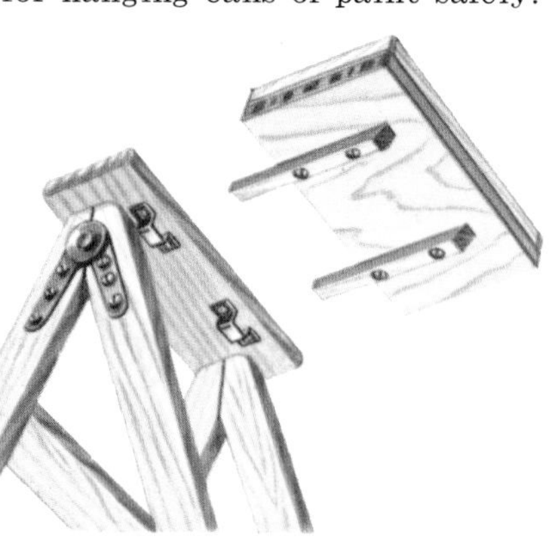

## 464 Fitting a support block in a corner joint

Strengthen butt-jointed corners by gluing small triangular-shaped blocks of softwood along the length of the joint. Space the blocks the length of a block apart. If there is sufficient access space, cramp a scrap of wood to the outside of the joint to act as a stop, and nail the blocks to help them grip tightly.

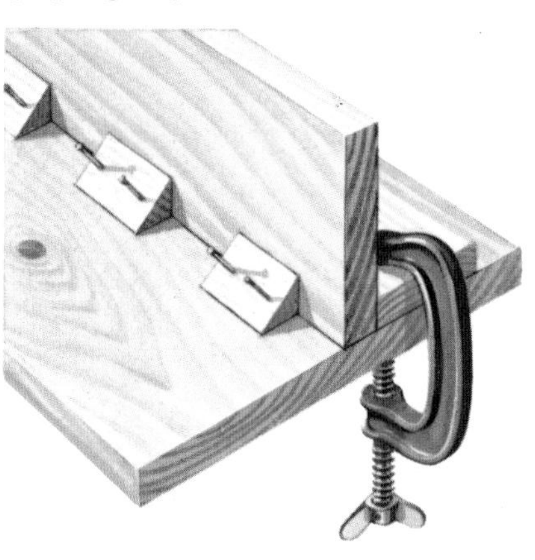

## 465 Ensuring a brick wall remains weatherproof

The mortar between bricks, called pointing, often needs replacing to preserve the weathering qualities of the wall.

A masonry cutting disc fitted to a power drill removes pointing much more quickly than the tedious alternative of using a cold chisel and hammer. Since it is a dusty job, always wear protective glasses and keep the windows closed. To complete the job, brush the joints down to remove the dust and loose mortar.

## 466 Making accurate drill holes for dowels

To ensure that holes for dowels are drilled exactly vertically make a jig from a scrap piece of hardwood, approximately 25mm/1in wide and 38mm/1½in deep. Drill two vertical holes with the same diameter and spacing as the holes to be drilled for the dowels. Double-check that the holes are vertical and then score lines on the sides of the jig to indicate the centre of the holes for use as marking guides.

To use the jig cramp it in place on the timber being drilled and start to drill directly down through the holes. Remove the jig and finish drilling.

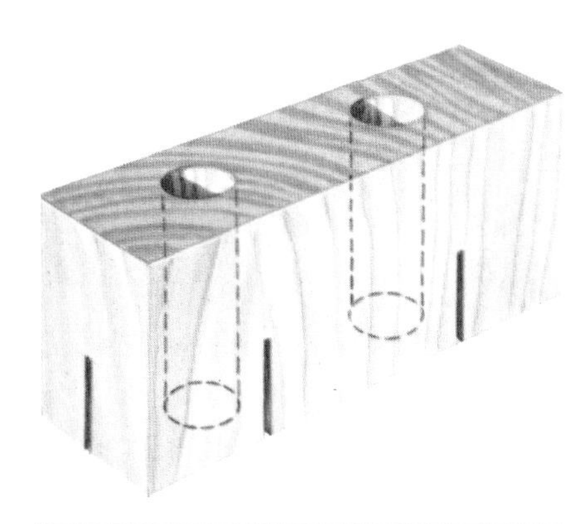

## 467 Suitable screws for aluminium

Always use aluminium nails or chromium-plated or cadmium-plated screws in aluminium. These materials do not corrode.

## 468 Fixing heavy felt to walls

Felt wall coverings come in wide rolls—measuring as much as 1.85m/6ft across. To help support the roll when fixing the felt to the pasted wall, insert a batten through the roll and suspend it between two step ladders. This makes the felt easy to unroll.

## 469 The order of painting exterior walls

If exterior painting has to be spread over a period of time, treat each side of a house as a separate, but complete, part of the job. Any weathering or shade changes between new tins of paint will then be effectively disguised.

## 470 Cutting a ceramic quadrant tile

Use a hacksaw to cut a quadrant tile. First, cut halfway through the tile from the back. Then, resting the tile on a level surface, tap the back sharply with the handle of a cold chisel on either side of the cut lines to complete the cut.

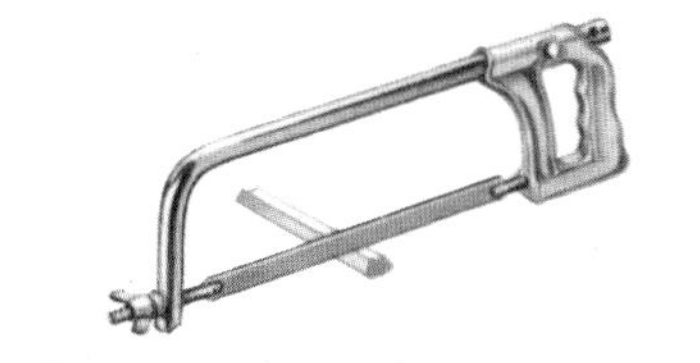

## 471 Preventing a nut working loose

To stop a nut working loose, make two cuts in an X-shape in the exposed end of the bolt with a hacksaw. Insert the blade of a cold chisel in the cuts and hammer them open slightly. Alternatively, if there is room, grip the nut with a spanner and fit a second nut tightly on top.

## 472 Fitting self-adhesive plastic sheeting

To avoid trapping air bubbles when fitting long lengths of self-adhesive plastic sheeting to a work-top or any other surface, peel away one end of the backing paper and staple the backing paper to a length of broom handle.

Place the sheeting in position on the surface. Roll the broom handle to remove more of the backing paper, at the same time smoothing down the sheet with a cloth to remove any air bubbles.

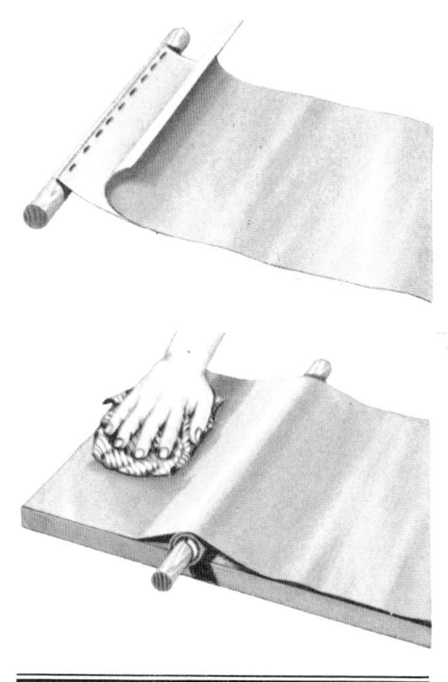

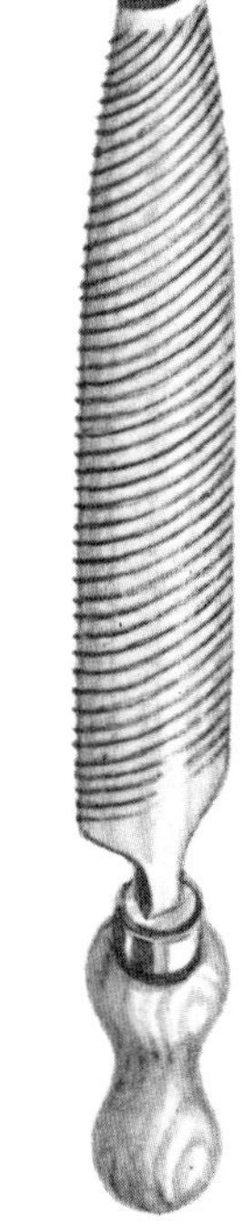

## 473 Rasp

Use a half-round rasp to smooth the edges of wood, ply, plastic, hardboard and soft metals. The finer the teeth in the rasp, the smoother the finish will be.

## 474 Lifting heavy weights

When lifting heavy weights, bend at the knee and not at the waist. Keep the legs together and the back as straight as possible. This lessens the risk of back strains or ruptures.

# 475-482

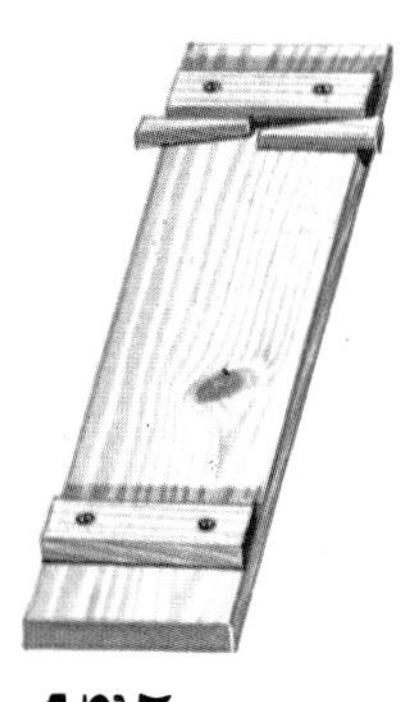

## 475
**Cramping block**

Make a cramping block from scrap timber to hold wood in place while it is being glued. Screw a length of batten to a timber base to act as a "stop". Position a second batten cut to the same size alongside the wood being glued, leaving gaps for wedges to be inserted.

## 476
**Heaters and blowlamps**

Never carry a paraffin or bottled-gas heater—or a blowlamp—around when it is alight. Turn it off first.

## 477 Making window pelmets removable

When fitting wooden pelmets over windows, always arrange that they can easily be removed when redecorating. One way is to use the interlocking type made from a top board that has a batten screwed beneath it. Screw two widths of timber to the window frame into which the batten can slot. When redecorating, simply lift out the top board.

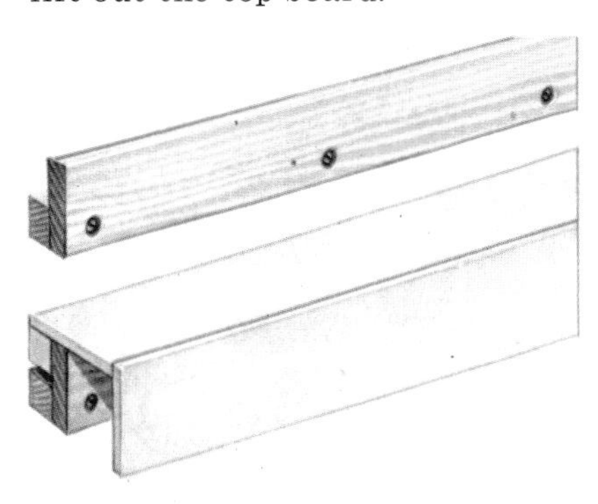

## 478 Pinning timber joints together invisibly

Timber joints can be fixed together invisibly and extremely firmly by nailing panel pins into one of the pieces of wood and then snipping off the heads at an angle. Glue both surfaces of the joint and hammer the timbers together.

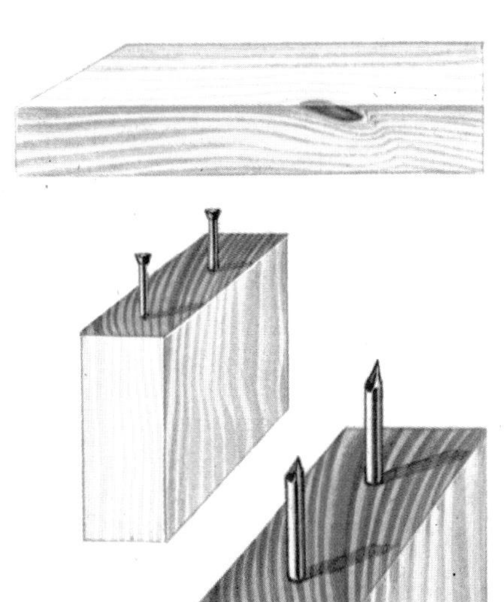

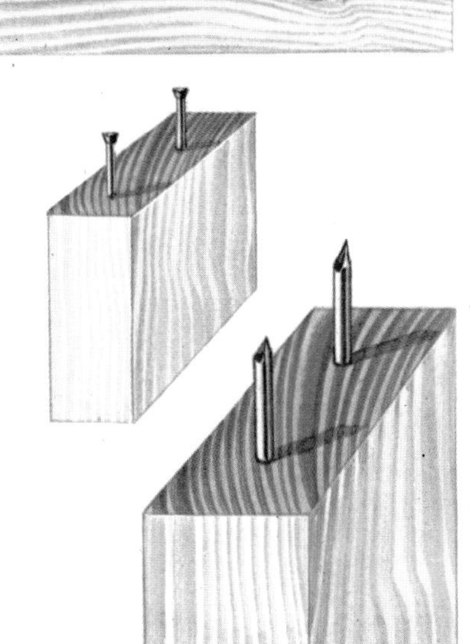

## 479 Dealing with loose skirting when papering

The usual method for covering any gaps between the skirting board and wall when wallpapering is to turn the bottom edge of the paper on to the top of the skirting. However, if the paper is knocked or if the skirting pulls farther away from the wall the paper can tear.

To avoid this—if the skirting cannot be fitted back into position—fill the gap before papering. Use a proprietary plaster filler mixed with a PVA adhesive; the adhesive stops the filler cracking away from the skirting as it dries out. Paint over the filler and cut the wallpaper to fit flush with the bottom of the wall and the top of the filled skirting board.

## 480 Installing a glazed door or French window

When hanging a new door that is to be fitted with glass, do not glaze the door until after it has been hung. Apart from its extra weight, fitting the glass first blocks up hand holds that make positioning the door easier.

## 481 Spacing ceramic tiles before grouting

When fixing ceramic tiles that are not manufactured with fitted spacers—lugs on their edges used to separate the tiles in preparation for jointing or grouting—use spacers cut from a sheet of card about 1.5 mm/$\frac{1}{16}$in thick, or use matchsticks. Fit two spacers below each tile to ensure it remains horizontal, and two in each vertical join. Remove the spacers before grouting the joins.

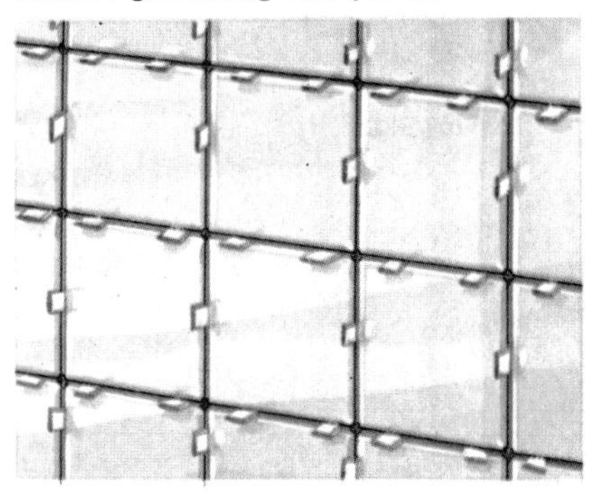

## 482 Dealing with gaps under skirting boards

If a gap develops between the edge of the floor and skirting boards—caused, especially in newly built houses, by wood drying out—use a moulding to cover it. Nail the moulding to the floor, not to the skirting, as this allows for further movement of the skirting without it directly affecting the butted edges of any carpeting or tiles laid tight up against the moulding.

If the moulding length butts up against a door frame, curve it for a neater appearance. Mark the shape of the curve on the moulding with a pencil and chisel off the corner along this line, smoothing down any rough edges with glasspaper. Pin the moulding to the floor at 200 mm/8 in intervals, being careful not to split the moulding when hammering the pins home into position.

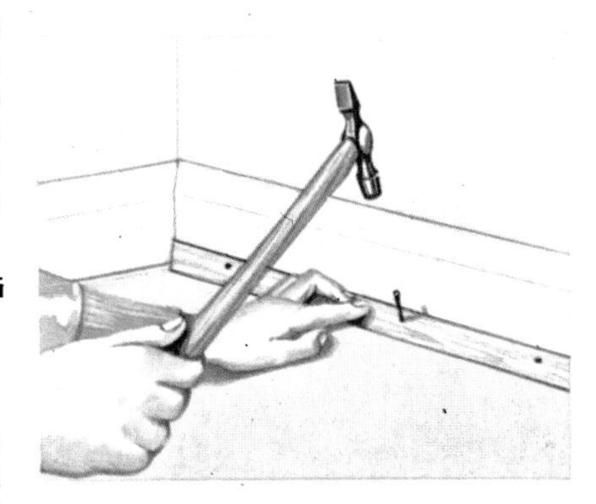

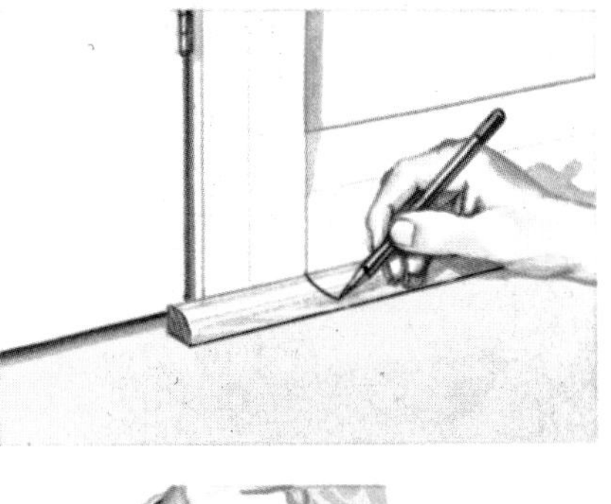

## 483 Curing badly worn drawer runners

If a drawer has to be lifted into its fully closed position because the runners are badly worn, there is a simple way of dealing with the problem. Insert two or three drawing pins into the top of the runners near the front edge of the drawer to remedy the fault.

## 484 Preparing wood for priming

When painting new woodwork, stop up the holes with wood filler before the wood is primed. Normal practice is to seal any knots with shellac, fill the holes and then prime the wood. Tackle any holes that have been missed, or not filled properly, before undercoating the wood.

## 485 When to use rapid-hardening cement

If laying concrete out of doors in cold weather, use rapid-hardening cement. This dries twice as quickly as ordinary cement and so reduces the chances of a sudden frost causing the surface to crack or crumble. Never, however, lay this over ordinary cement.

## 486 Preparing surfaces for emulsion

Never use wire wool to rub down surfaces that are to be painted with emulsion paint. As emulsion is water-based, rust spots may appear if small strands of the wool become embedded in it.

## 487 Fitting wallpaper around a door frame

To fit wallpaper around a door frame, first paste a full length of paper and make two folds; one of these, when unfolded, should be the height of the door. Unfold the smaller fold and fit it at the top of the wall.

Make a rough cut, using the inside of the door frame as a guide, finishing off with a diagonal cut at the corner. The double thickness of paper not only simplifies these initial cuts but also prevents paste getting on to the door. Unfold the trimmed paper and smooth it down with a hanging brush. Score the edges around the door frame and cut away the excess.

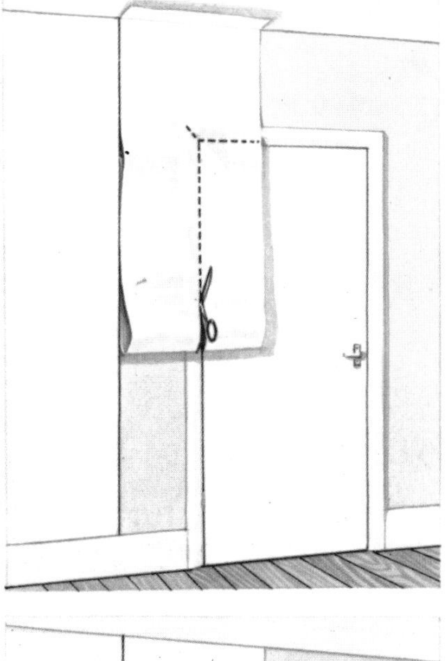

## 488 Smoothing curved timber surfaces

The best way to smooth large curved surfaces is to make a mitten out of a length of glass-paper approximately 100 mm/4 in wide, with the ends stapled together. The palm and fingers can follow the shape of the curve more easily, and so the surface will be smoothed much more evenly.

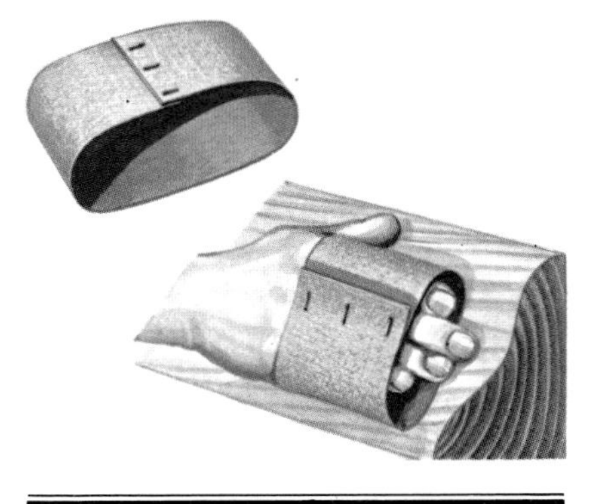

## 489 Lightening or removing stains in wood

Use an oxalic acid solution to lighten dark stains on wooden surfaces and to remove ink stains from white wood furniture. Dissolve 28 g/1 oz of oxalic acid crystals in 0.3 litres/½ pint of hot water and, wearing protective gloves, rub the surface with a lint-free cloth dipped in the solution.

Continue until the stain is bleached out or the wood is bleached to the required finish. Finally, wipe the surface with vinegar, wash it thoroughly with clean water to counteract the acid and dry it. Store any excess solution out of the reach of children.

## 490 Cutting awkward shapes in foam rubber

Foam rubber is extremely difficult to cut cleanly and accurately because it is so spongy and pliable, especially if intricate shapes are involved. The way round the problem is to soak the piece of foam in water and then to deep-freeze it in a freezer. The resultant block can be sawn, drilled or turned on a lathe; one useful cutting tool for foam is an electric bread knife.

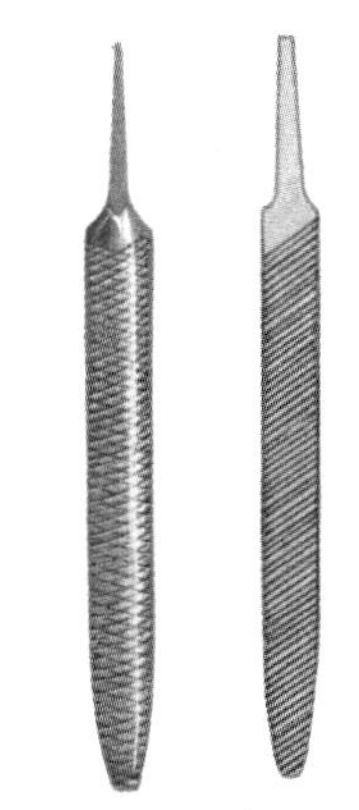

## 491 Files

The general-purpose metal-working files are the flat file for level surfaces and the half-round file with a rounded face for concave curves. The more teeth on either file the smoother the cut. A file with teeth arranged in single diagonal rows is called single cut; a second row of teeth criss-crossing the first makes it a double cut.

## 492 Nails in wood

If scrap pieces of wood have nails protruding from them, never leave them lying about on the floor when doing carpentry work. Hammer the sharp ends of the nails over, or remove the nails with pincers.

# 493-501

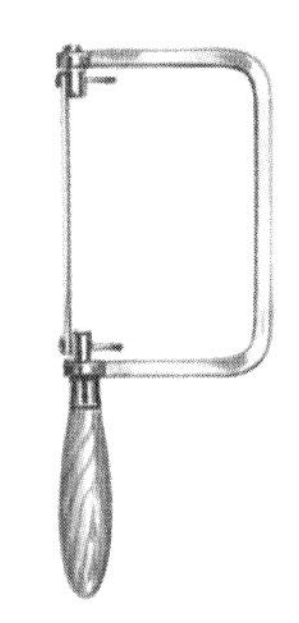

## 493
**Coping saw**

When cutting a curve with a coping saw, make the cut in one complete operation where possible. This ensures a smoother finish than stopping the cut halfway and starting the curve again from the other end.

## 494
**Electric flex and carpets**

Never run an electric flex under a carpet. The constant pressure caused by people treading on the carpet will eventually wear down the protective coating of the flex, creating the risk of a short circuit with a danger of fire.

## 495 Preparing a new paint brush before use

An inexpensive new paint brush should be soaked in linseed oil for at least a day before use. This helps soften the bristles and lengthen its life. All brushes should be broken in by first using them to apply undercoating. This helps remove any loose bristles, which may otherwise work free during top-coating and spoil the finish.

## 496 Positioning laminate for easy gluing

When gluing laminate to a surface with contact adhesive, lay three or four strips of hardwood across the surface once the glue has become dry to the touch. Make sure that the glued surface of the laminate is also touch dry and place it in position on top of the hardwood strips. Align it carefully—once the laminate is in contact with the surface it cannot be moved. Withdraw the strips one at a time, at the same time pressing the laminate down firmly.

## 497 Testing chisel and plane blades

To test the sharpness of a newly ground chisel or plane blade, hold a sheet of paper in one hand and lightly run the cutting edge of the blade down the paper. If the blade has been correctly sharpened, it will slice the paper cleanly—if not, it will leave a ragged edge down the sheet.

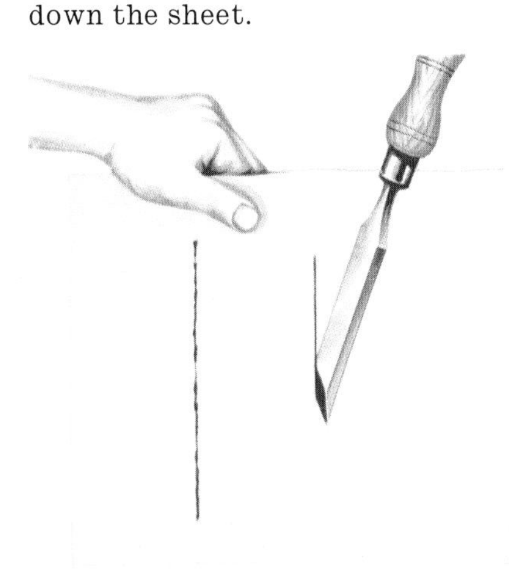

## 498 The correct way to use a paint brush

A paint brush should always be held by the handle—never by the metal band around the brush. This can make all the difference between ending up with a smooth finish or a rough one.

Apply gloss paint in vertical strokes and emulsion in horizontal ones. Then—without recharging the brush—criss-cross lightly across the surface. Finally brush back into the paint to lay it off. When cutting-in along edges, hold the brush between the thumb and forefinger. Keep it well charged with paint and work it slowly downwards.

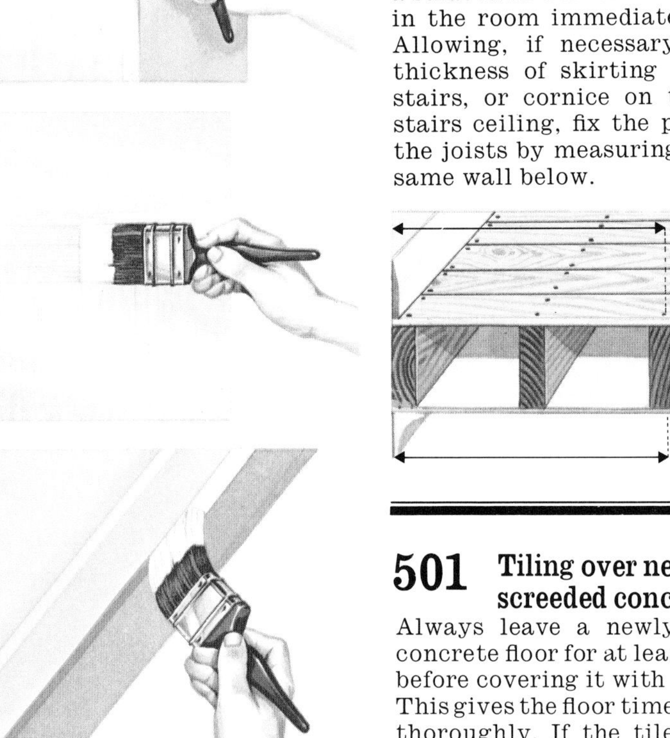

## 499 Fitting edging strips to laminated surfaces

When fitting laminate to the top and edge of a work-top surface, always fit the edging strip first. This ensures that the top surface overlaps the edge.

If fitted the other way round, the joint-line between the two laminates will be unprotected, whether it is chamfered or not, and so can be damaged more easily.

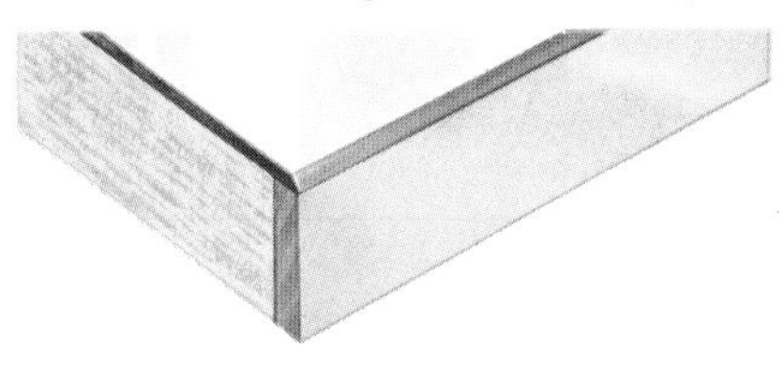

## 500 Locating joists for fixing into ceilings

Always screw direct into joists when fixing into ceilings—fixings screwed into plasterboard will not hold. To avoid unnecessary damage to the ceiling, first try to locate the joists by tapping the ceiling. If this fails, measure from a structural wall to the joist nails in the room immediately above. Allowing, if necessary, for the thickness of skirting board upstairs, or cornice on the downstairs ceiling, fix the position of the joists by measuring from the same wall below.

## 501 Tiling over newly screeded concrete

Always leave a newly screeded concrete floor for at least a month before covering it with floor tiles. This gives the floor time to dry out thoroughly. If the tiles are laid before this, the mortar bedding which is used as a "key" for the tiles may fail.

## 502 Wallpapering window recesses

Always wallpaper a window recess before the wall into which the window is recessed. This makes the overlapping joint less conspicuous, as it faces out towards the window.

## 503 Avoiding damage drilling sheet metal

Cramp soft or thin sheets of metal very firmly between two pieces of hardwood when drilling the metal. Cramping the metal ensures accuracy, while the wood not only gives the drill head a start (it can often slip before biting into the metal) but also eliminates the risk of denting the metal and of leaving rough, burred edges.

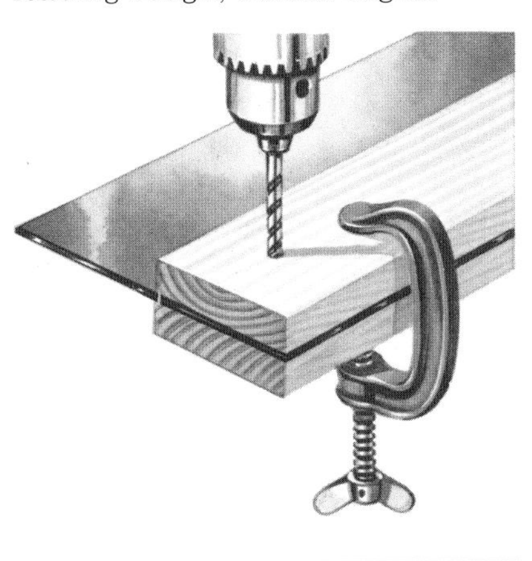

## 504 Cleaning a badly clogged oilstone

Frequent use of an oilstone can lead to it becoming clogged with oil. The best way to remove this is to place the stone in an old biscuit tin or baking tray and leave it in an oven set at around 149°C/300°F for two hours. At the end of this, the oil will have drained out of the stone. Remove and wipe it clean.

## 505 Removing burn marks on polished surfaces

To remove a superficial burn mark from a polished wood surface rub the damaged area lightly with a piece of fine wire wool. This leaves a dull patch on a polished surface that can be restored by rewaxing.

If the burn mark is too deep for this method, gently scrape it away using a razor blade held at a right angle to the surface. Fill the hollow with a proprietary wood filler stained to the required shade. Again, restore the lustre of the polished surface by rewaxing.

## 506 Reducing the noise of a cistern and flush pipe

A noisy lavatory cistern can be a nuisance—especially at night. One way of silencing it is to fit a length of plastic or rubber pipe from the ball valve to within 6mm/¼in of the bottom of the cistern. As the cistern refills, the water will enter below the surface of the water instead of pouring down on to it.

With a high-level cistern, the sound of water running down the flush pipe can also be reduced by fitting felt or rubber pads between the pipe and the wall. Secure the pads in position with tape.

## 507 Checking sheet vinyl flooring for damp

Before laying sheet vinyl flooring on a solid ground floor, make sure that the floor on which the vinyl is being laid is level and dry and that the airbricks around the side of the house are not blocked. Even after taking this precaution, it is important to check for rising damp after laying the vinyl. This is because vinyl is impervious to damp and it could take as long as a year—when skirting boards become affected—before it becomes clear that damp is building up. Lift a section of the vinyl after about a month to check whether it is damp on the underside.

## 508 Removing blisters in veneered surfaces

Use a trimming knife to remove a blister in a veneered surface. Cut the blister down its centre. Press down on one side of the blister and work a wood glue into the raised side with a flexible knife or a piece of thin card. Press the raised side down, wiping off any excess glue, and repeat the procedure with the other side. If the repair has been made near the edge of the surface, cramp a block over it for at least twelve hours to allow the glue to set. Cover the repair with waxed paper to prevent the wood block sticking to the surface. If a cramp cannot be fitted, cover the waxed paper with a flat block and a suitable heavy weight.

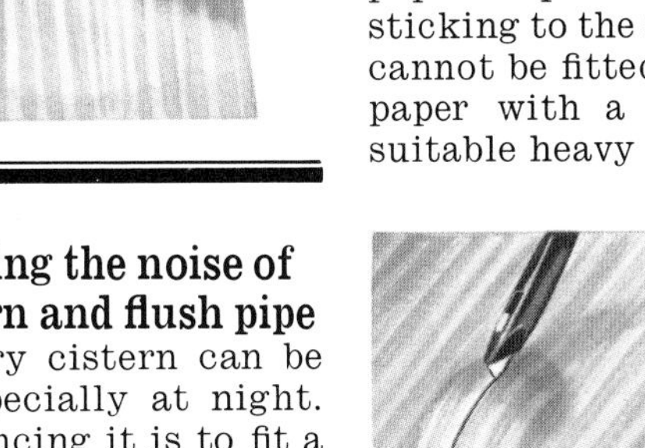

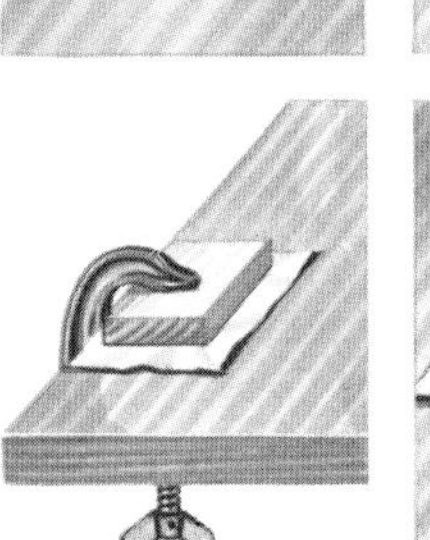

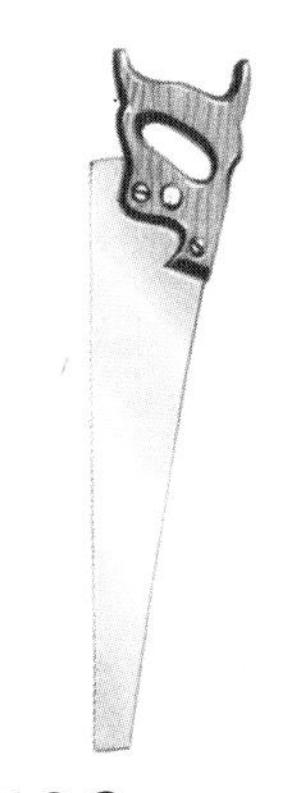

## 509 Panel saw

A panel saw is a good general-purpose saw, as it cuts both with the grain and across it. The best saw to buy is one between 560mm/22in and 600mm/24in long with ten teeth every 25mm/1in.

## 510 Using paint stripper

Never use chemical paint stripper near a naked flame under any circumstances. The stripper gives off a highly inflammable vapour.

# 511-520

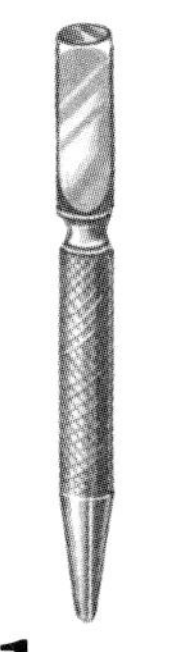

## 511
**Nail punch**

Always discard a nail punch if the head has split around the edges. It can be dangerous if a piece snaps off while hammering. If the point is chipped it can be reground to its original shape.

## 512
**Making windows child-proof**

Always make sure that window catches are fitted out of the reach of children, especially on upper floors.

## 513 Marking out a dowelled joint accurately

A simple way of marking the position for the dowels when making a dowelled joint is to tape round-head nails on one piece of wood, with the heads of the nails at the position for the dowels. Tap the nailheads into the wood until the shank of the nail itself is flush with it. Rest the second piece of wood in position over the nails and strike it firmly with a wooden mallet. The indentations left by the nail heads will show exactly where the holes should be drilled for the dowels.

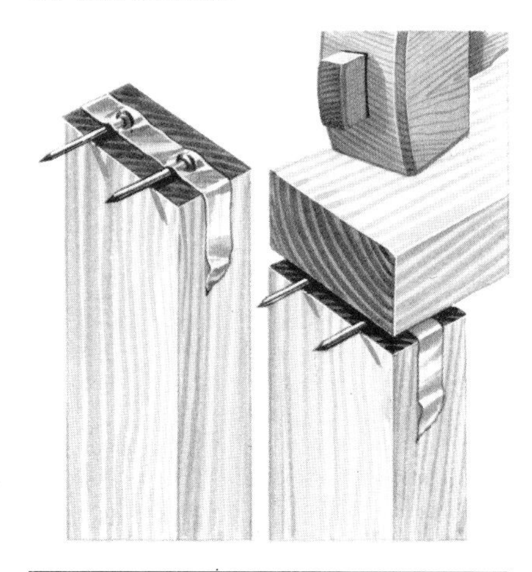

## 514 Saving time when fixing fittings to a wall

Where a large number of fixings, such as clothes hooks, have to be secured to a wall, it is often simpler to attach a softwood batten to the wall first. This means that fewer fixings have to be made directly into the wall, thus saving a considerable amount of drilling and plugging. The same method can be used for fixing a curtain rail.

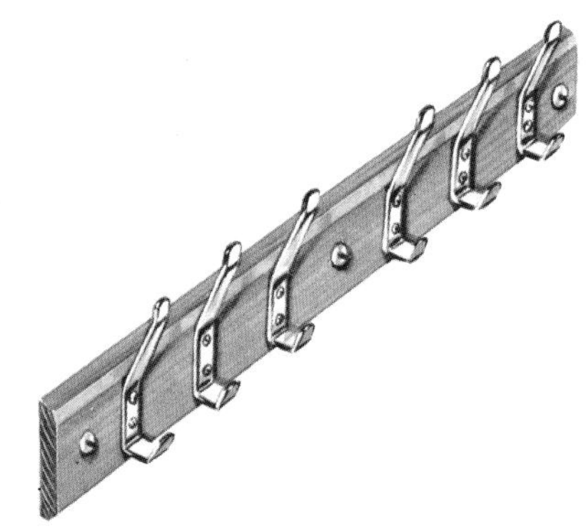

## 515 Assessing if a saw can be sharpened

To decide whether or not a saw can be sharpened, check the teeth in the middle of the blade for wear. If there is a hollow along the edge of the blade, it is unlikely that the blade can be successfully re-sharpened.

## 516 Making screws burglar-proof

Ordinary screws can be adapted to make them burglar-proof—a particularly necessary precaution when screwing down timber-framed rooflights. First drill pilot holes for the screws and insert them into the holes in the normal way, stopping just short of the final tightening turns.

Remove the screws, noting the edges of the screw slots which take the pressure. File these edges off, then reinsert the screws and tighten them fully. Because there is no edge for the screwdriver to bite on in an anticlockwise direction, the screws can never be undone once they have been fixed.

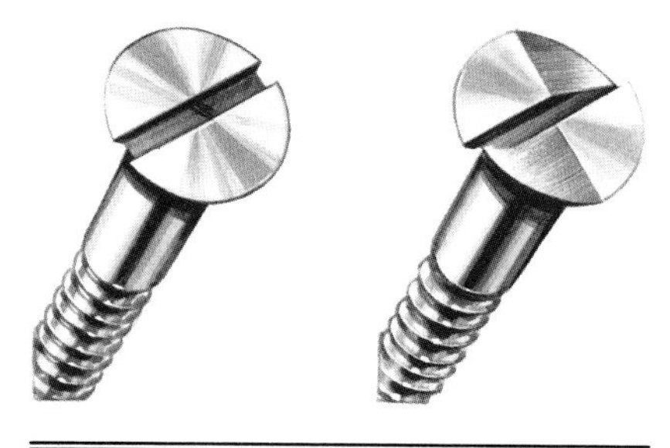

## 517 Stripping sheathing from electric cable

Strip the sheathing from electric cable by first bending it to form a tightly compressed "U" shape. Score the outer bend of the "U" lightly with a sharp trimming knife and remove the sheathing. The stress created by the bend is enough to split the sheathing without any danger of cutting through the wires.

## 518 Choosing glasspaper for different jobs

Use a medium-grade glasspaper for general rubbing-down work when painting walls or wood, and a fine paper for the final smoothing. Use a coarse paper only when a surface is badly flaked.

## 519 Maintaining the tip of a screwdriver

Occasionally regrind the tip of a screwdriver blade to ensure that it is perfectly square. Make sure that the thickness of the blade matches the slot of a standard-size screwhead. It should be thick enough to hold the screw in a horizontal position.

## 520 Marking up timber and metal accurately

Whenever possible, place the material to be cut in its intended position and mark it up direct. This eliminates the errors that can occur when transferring measurements.

When marking up timber, always use a trimming knife. It is not only more accurate than a pencil but, as it cuts into the wood, it also helps the initial saw cuts. Finally scribble pencil lines on the waste material as a reminder that the cut should be made on that side.

To mark up a piece of metal, first rub the surface with chalk. The score mark made with a nail or trimming knife will then be clearly seen.

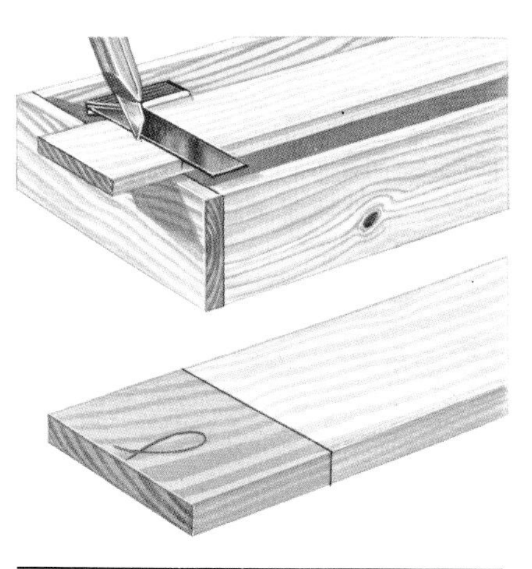

## 521 Ensuring a tight fit between floorboards

To lay square-edged floorboards tightly against each other, make three pairs of wedges, each about 45 cm/18 in long and 50 mm/2 in wide at one end, tapering to 25 mm/1 in at the other.

First, lay three floorboards in position across the joists, hand-tight against the walls. Place the wedges against the last board—one pair in the centre and a pair near each end. Immediately in front of each pair of wedges, nail a scrap length of timber to the joists, leaving the heads of the nails protruding so that they can be withdrawn easily later. Using two hammers, drive the wedges simultaneously from each side to jam the three floorboards against each other. Nail the boards to the joists before removing the wedges. Continue in this way to cover the floor.

One board may have to be cut to a smaller size to complete the coverage of the floor area. Since filling a small gap immediately in front of a wall can be difficult, use a full-width board against the wall and leave the small space between it and the remainder of the boards. Place the last board against the wall—do not nail it. Cut a floorboard that is slightly wider than the gap and chamfer the edges slightly with a plane. Drive the board into position, protecting it with an off-cut of wood. Finally, nail this filler piece and the last board to the joists.

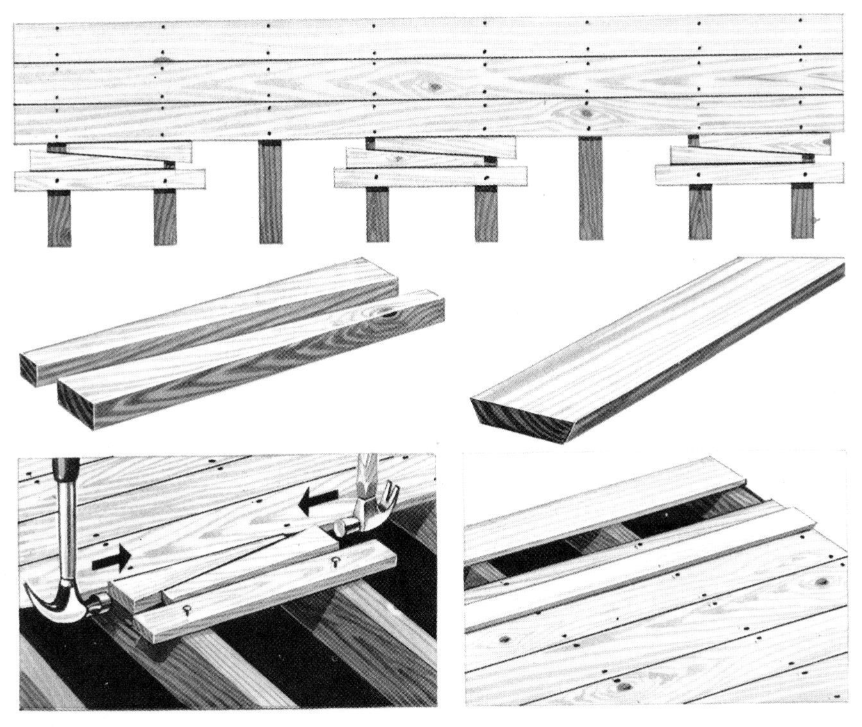

## 522 Bringing out the grain of timber surfaces

Use water, chemical or spirit stains to bring out the grain of a timber surface. Always work with the grain, using a soft cloth or brush. If a less prominent grain effect is required, lightly wet the surface with water and, when dry, rub it down with glasspaper. When the stain is applied the grain will not be brought out as much.

## 523 Priming wood for painting

An undercoat paint can be used as a primer when mixed with raw linseed oil. For unpainted wood use a mix of undercoat paint containing 10 per cent of linseed oil, preferably adding a little red lead powder to the mixture. Where paint has been stripped back to the surface, use a mix with 5 per cent of linseed oil.

## 524 Securing loose wallpaper joints

If part of a butt joint between adjacent lengths of wallpaper does not stick down properly, ease back both edges of the paper from the wall and, with a small brush or cotton swab, paste the wall beneath the joint, using as little paste as possible. Carefully brush the paper back into position, cover it with a sheet of blotting paper and press down the joint with a soft pad of cloth.

## 525 Drilling through a glazed ceramic tile

To prevent a twist-bit slipping when drilling a hole in a glazed ceramic tile, use a felt pen to mark the point at which the hole is to be drilled and stick a strip of clear adhesive tape over the mark before drilling.

## 526 Preparing and painting a cement-rendered wall

Before painting a cement-rendered finish for the first time, the lime in the cement must be neutralized, or the paint will be washed off by rain. Paint the surface with a masonry sealer—made up by dissolving $\frac{1}{2}$ kg/1 lb of zinc sulphate into 6 litres/$1\frac{1}{4}$ gallons of water—or a zinc chromate primer, obtainable from a builders' merchant. Leave the sealer or primer to dry before starting to paint. Any excess solution can be stored for future use. Complete the job with a masonry paint. This can be either emulsion or cement-based; the former is more hard-wearing.

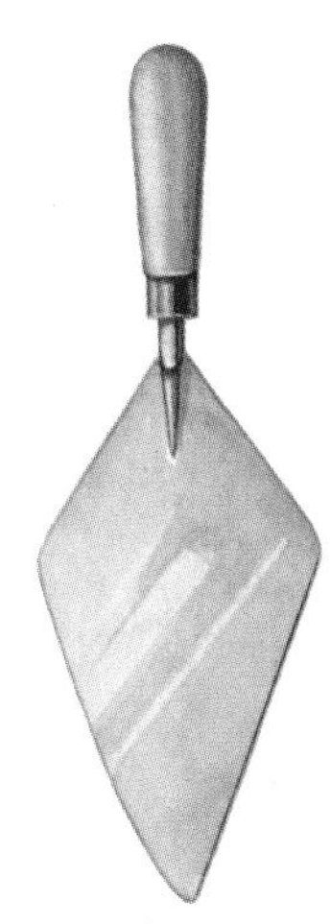

## 527 Trowel

A brick trowel has a straight edge for scooping up the mortar and a rounded edge for cleaning a roughly cut brick. A "right-handed" trowel has the straight edge on the left, looking from the handle.

## 528 Height and ladders

Standing on the top rungs of a ladder can be extremely dangerous. The highest rung that can be used with safety is the fourth rung from the top.

## 529 Paraffin blowlamp

Layers of paint can be burnt off more quickly with a paraffin blowlamp than a pressurized gas-fired blow-torch. Avoid playing the flame on glass when stripping paint off window frames or glazing bars—the glass may crack.

## 530 Handling insulation

Always wear as much protective clothing as possible when laying fibrous insulating material in a loft—otherwise the fibres can irritate the skin.

## 531 Finding the centre of a room's floor area

To find the centre of a room, regard it as a uniform rectangle, ignoring any recesses and projections such as fireplaces and hearths. Measure the full length of each wall and mark the centre points.

Rub a length of string with chalk and secure it with nails at the two centre points of two opposite walls. Keeping the string taut, snap it sharply to leave a chalk line against the floor. Mark a second chalk line between the two centre points of the other two walls; where the two lines intersect is the centre of the floor area.

If the room is L-shaped, treat it as two imaginary rectangles, regarding the centre of the larger as being the centre of the whole floor area, and snap the chalk lines accordingly.

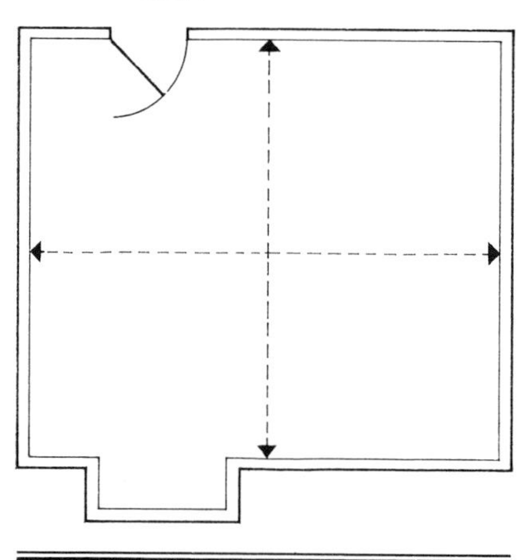

## 532 Coping with cracks in plaster

Sizeable cracks can often appear at the weakest points in plaster—where walls and ceilings meet. Treat the problem either by using a proprietary filler or fitting coving over the area.

## 533 Decorating newly applied plaster

New plaster can take at least six months to dry out, so only decorate it with water-based emulsion. The paint will not seal the surface and therefore will not affect the drying process.

## 534 Laying ceramic or vinyl floor tiles

Always start from the centre of the room when laying ceramic or vinyl floor tiles. Prepare the surface first and then work from the point where two chalk guidelines bisect the room and intersect at right angles.

Lay one row of tiles—without adhesive—at right angles to one of the guidelines. If the gap between the last tile and the wall is less than half the width of a tile—by 25mm/1in or more—move the whole row away from the wall to leave a half-width tile gap; mark a new chalk line accordingly.

Repeat the procedure to establish the second row of tiles at right angles to the first, this time moving both rows back by half a tile width if the gap between the last tile and the wall is too small. Mark the second guideline, checking the right angle most carefully. With the two guidelines established on the floor, lay the tiles, covering one half of the room and then the other. Remember to leave a 3mm/⅛in gap between ceramic tiles to allow for grouting. Apply the adhesive stage by stage.

To ensure that the rows are not distorted and will compact better, lay the tiles in the shape of a triangle. Having laid one complete row against one of the guidelines fit the next row one tile shorter at each end, and so on until no more rows can be laid. Then start again in one quarter of the room, working outwards from one edge of the triangle, starting with the shortest possible row and progressing to the longest.

Repeat the procedure in the opposite corner and then on the other side of the guideline. Leave those border tiles that need cutting to the end.

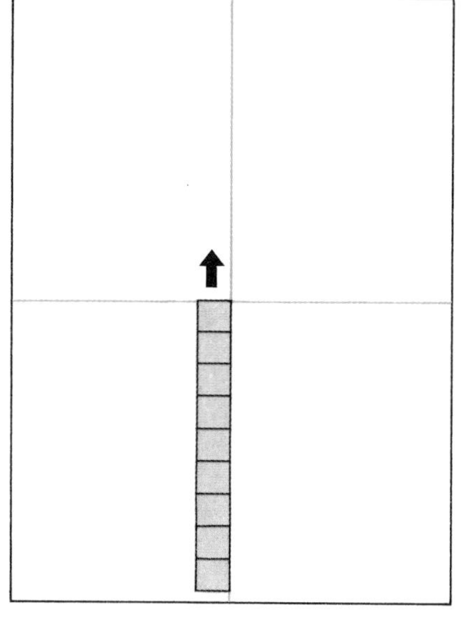

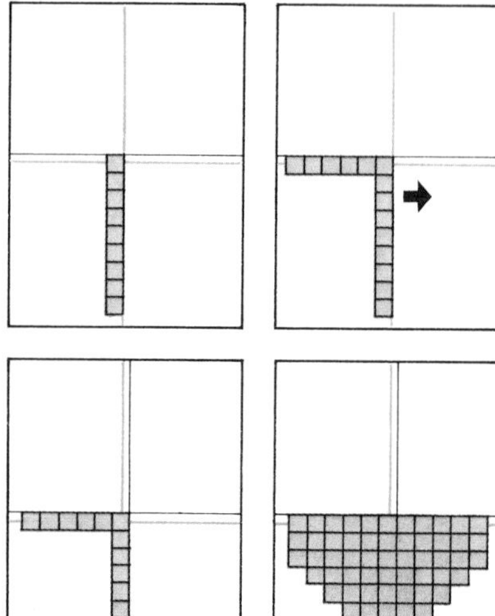

## 535 Cleaning and polishing tarnished brass

The best way to clean tarnished brass is to first wash off any surface dirt by scrubbing the brass with a soft brush dipped in a mixture of warm soapy water and a little ammonia. Then make up a solution of vinegar and salt, and apply this with a cloth, rubbing vigorously. Rinse with water, dry, and finally polish the brass with a proprietary metal cleaner.

## 536 Improving a varnish finish on wood

To obtain an extra high gloss on a varnish finish, rub down the penultimate coat of varnish with the back of a sheet of glasspaper wrapped round a cork block and then brush down the surface before applying the top coat. The "buffing" action smooths the surface even better than the commonly used alternative of flour paper—an extremely fine abrasive paper.

## 537 Fitting coving in a wallpapered room

Preferably fit coving before papering a room. If, however, the room is already papered, first remove the paper on the walls and ceiling which will be covered by the coving. This is because coving cannot be securely stuck to wallpaper.

Polystyrene coving is more frequently used today than plaster coving, but both can be fixed by the same method. Hold a length of the coving in position in the angle of the wall and ceiling and measure how far the top edge projects on to the ceiling. Cut a batten, 3mm/⅛in less than this distance in width and 91cm/3ft in length, and use it as a straight-edge. Place it against the ceiling, flush into the corner and, working round the room, cut away the paper on the ceiling with a trimming knife.

Repeat this procedure to remove the paper at the top of the wall. Then roughen the exposed plaster surfaces with a stripping knife.

When cutting the coving to fit, use a fine-toothed saw and cut from the front of the coving to ensure a clean front edge. Use a mitre block to cut the 45° angles for the corners; in the case of polystyrene coving, however, these can be bought pre-cut.

Apply the recommended adhesive to the top and bottom edges of the coving and press the coving into position. If the walls or ceiling are uneven enough to prevent the coving sticking firmly, hammer small nails at 30cm/12in intervals, punching the nail heads below the surface. Scrape away the adhesive that has been squeezed from the edges of the coving and use this surplus to fill any small gaps at the top and bottom of the coving, and the holes left by the sunken nails.

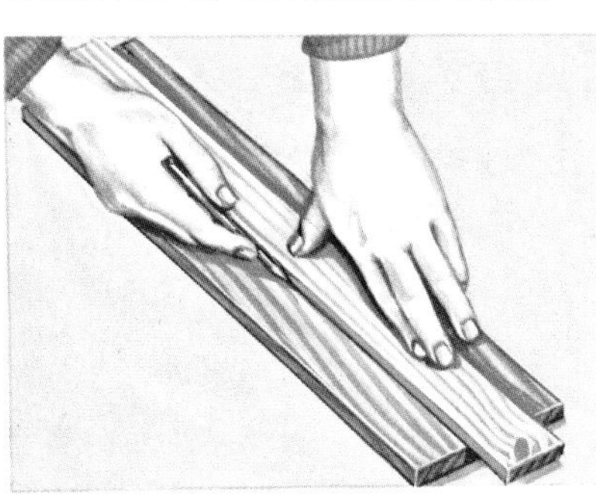

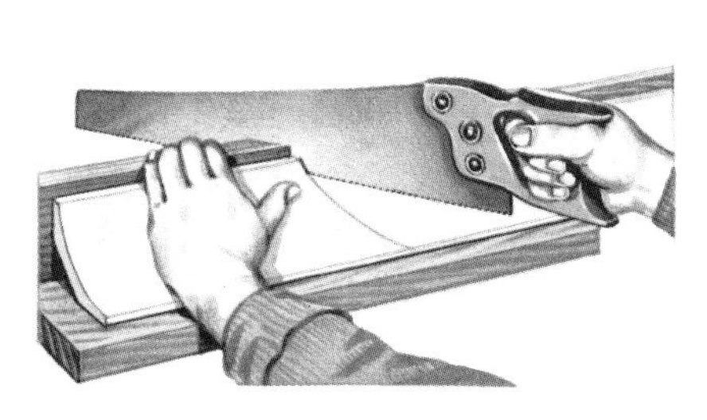

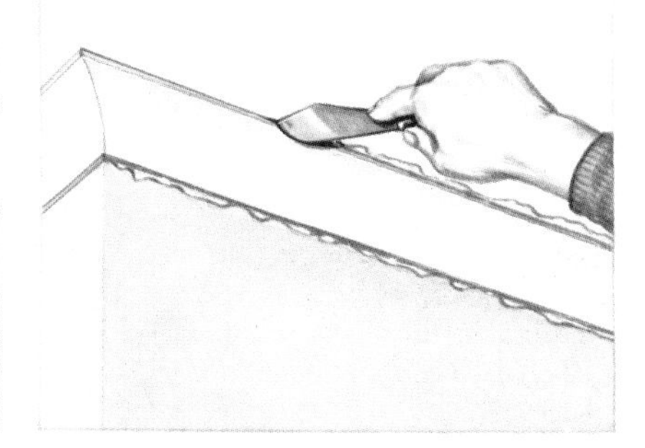

## 538 Clearing blocked pipes without damage

To avoid twisting a lead drainage pipe when clearing a blocked outlet in a basin or sink, place a length of wood within the "U" bend. When unscrewing the cap at the bottom of the outlet, push the wood firmly in the direction opposite to that in which pressure is being applied to the cap.

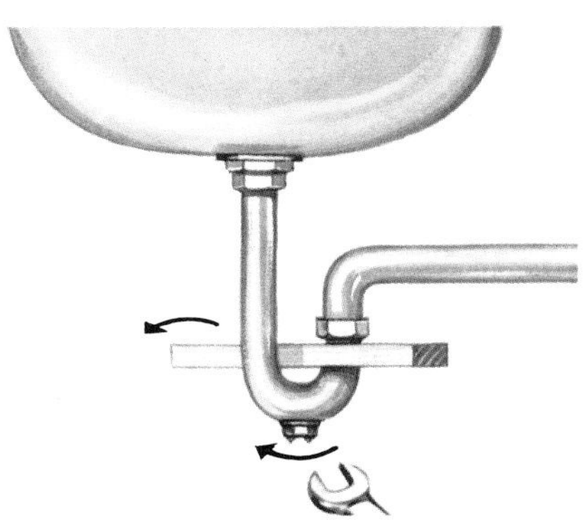

## 539 Taking care of two-part adhesives

Never mix the caps on two-part adhesivés. If this is done, the caps will seal up, and it will be impossible to remove them.

## 540 Fitting round-edge tiles inside reveals

RE (round-edge) tiles fitted inside reveals cover the cut edges of tiles on the adjoining wall surface. Always lay the tiles with the round edge facing the outside of the reveal. Some tiles are not manufactured with round edges, but instead have two glazed edges.

As with any tiling job, plan the work in advance. In particular, if it is necessary to trim the length of any of the tiles, decide where this will look the most attractive.

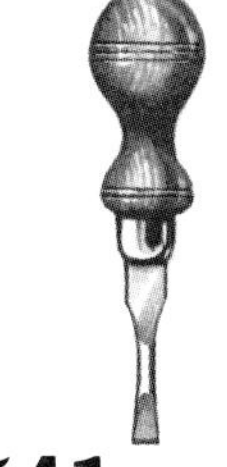

## 541 Miniature screwdriver

Screws often have to be fitted at an angle when working in a confined area, leaving insufficient space to use a conventional screwdriver. A miniature screwdriver can make it easier to fit awkwardly positioned screws.

## 542 Adjusting thermostats

Never adjust the thermostat of an immersion heater while the heater is in operation. Always switch it off first.

# 543-549

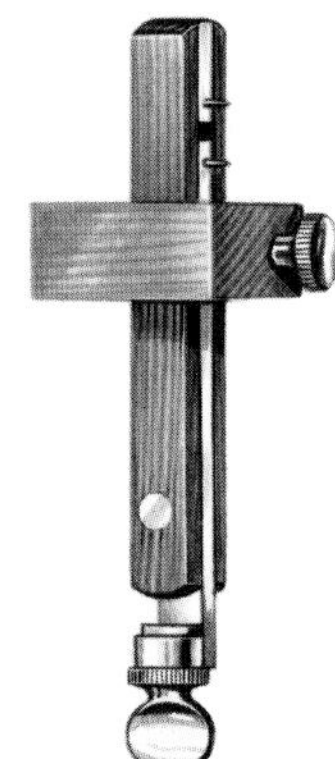

## 543
### Mortise gauge
When cutting a mortise set the two pins in a mortise gauge to the width of the chisel being used, and position the head of the gauge so that the pins mark the mortise lines centrally on the timber. When using any marking gauge, always pull rather than push the gauge to give a clearer and more accurate cutting line.

## 544
### Storing inflammable liquids
Never store inflammable liquids, such as petrol or paraffin, in the house—keep them in a garage or outside, under cover. In addition, always store them in cans or containers purpose-made for the job.

## 545 Cutting out a mortise for a tenon
If possible, use a chisel the exact width of the mortise—the slot in a mortise-and-tenon joint. The width should not exceed one-third the complete width of the wood being cut.

Set a mortise gauge to the chisel width and mark out the cut on the face side. Drive the chisel into the centre of the mortise to a depth of about 5mm/$\frac{3}{16}$in with a wooden-headed mallet, and, working backwards, make more chisel cuts every 3mm/$\frac{1}{8}$in. Stop 3mm short of the end of the final cutting line.

Reverse the chisel so that its bevelled edge is facing in towards the centre of the mortise and make similar cuts from the middle in the opposite direction, again stopping 3mm short. Chop out the cuts with the bevelled edge of the chisel facing downwards, and continue as before with vertical cuts to the required depth. Finally, cut away the 3mm of timber left at each end of the mortise.

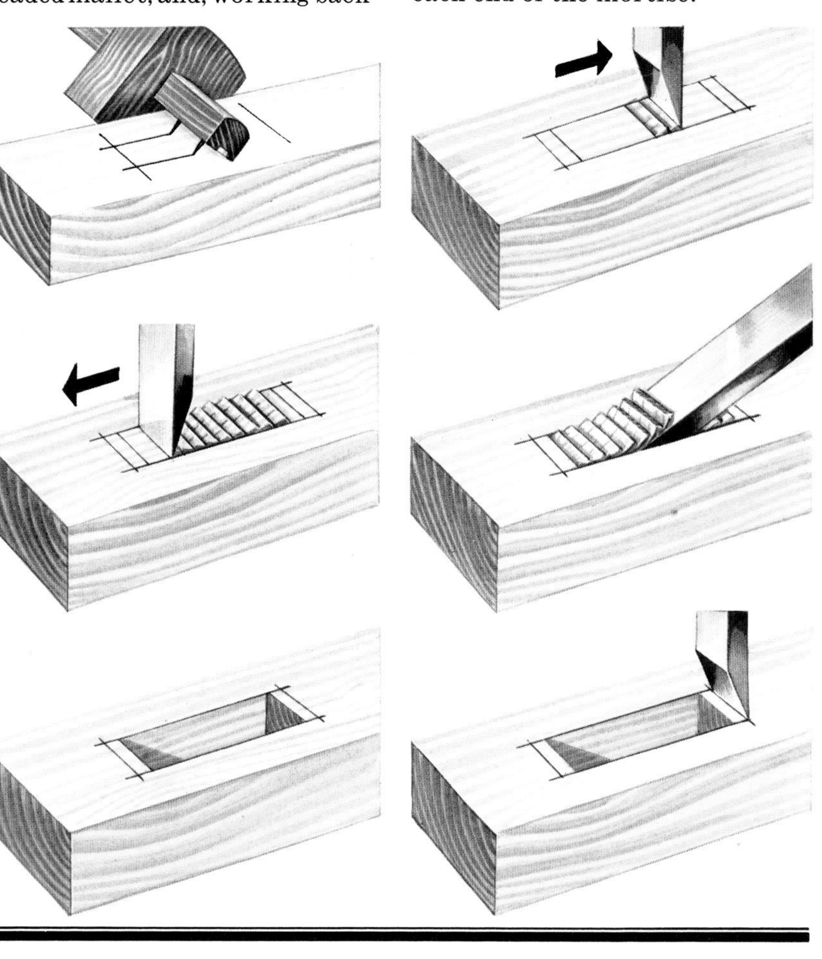

## 546 Giving ceilings a stippled appearance
To create a stippled effect on ceilings, first paint the ceiling with a proprietary plastic compound. Then wrap a plastic bag tightly around a sponge and, while the compound is still wet, bounce the bag gently on the ceiling. On each bounce the bag pulls at the compound and leaves an attractive stippled effect.

## 547 Repairing small holes in a garden hosepipe
Pinhole leaks in a hosepipe can be a nuisance. The easiest way to repair small holes in a plastic garden hose is to heat a soldering iron, or the end of an old screwdriver, and gently work it across the hole and around its edges. Spread the melted plastic around to seal the hole, being careful not to buckle the pipe.

## 548 Making a cylinder lock turn smoothly
Always use a graphite powder lubricant to ease the pin mechanism of a cylinder lock at six-month intervals. If oil is used it will attract dust and eventually clog the moving parts. A simple method is to rub the lead of a pencil over the blade of the key. Work the key in and out of the lock several times, applying more of the graphite to the key until the lock mechanism turns smoothly.

## 549 Making a tenon for a mortise
Mark up the tongue—the tenon of a mortise-and-tenon joint—with the mortise gauge pre-set to the width of the mortise, to ensure an exact fit. The width should not exceed one-third the thickness of the wood being cut. Having marked the width and depth of the proposed tenon on the timber, place the wood at a 45° angle in a vice. With a tenon saw cut down just on the waste side of both the tenon lines. Reverse the wood to cut down the opposite edges. Then, cramp the wood upright in the vice and saw vertically through the cuts to the depth required. Finally, lay the wood flat and complete the cut by sawing off the outside waste pieces. Check the fit.

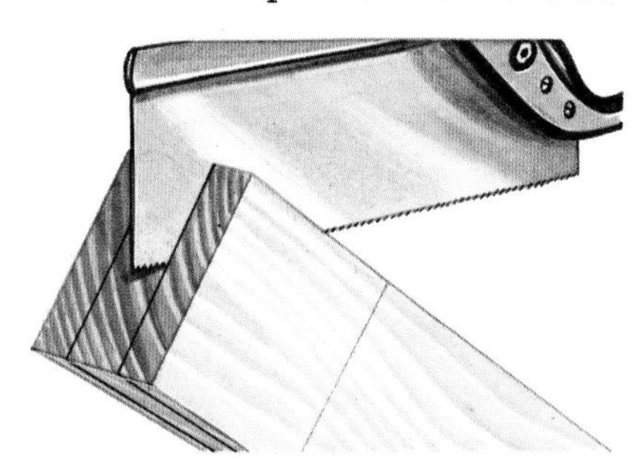

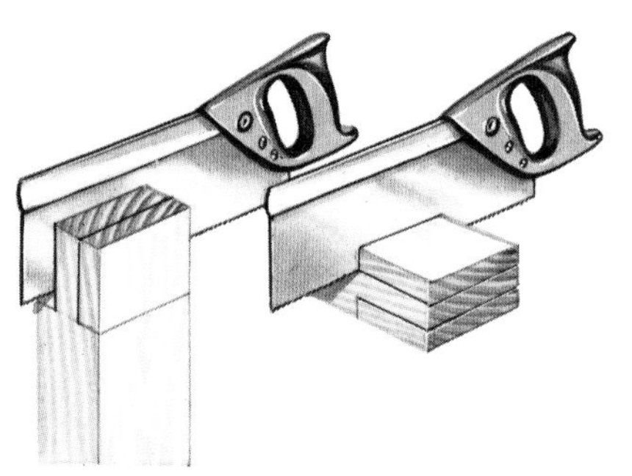

## 550 Making a through mortise-and-tenon

The through mortise-and-tenon joint is the strongest T-joint. To make the joint, first mark up the mortise in the usual way, but continue the top and bottom lines round to the opposite edge. Mark this edge as the outer edge of the joint and extend the length of the mortise by 3mm/⅛in at both top and bottom. This additional length will be used to take the wedges to secure the joint. Mark up the tenon, but extend its length so that it will protrude slightly through the mortise. Chisel out the mortise, cutting back for the wedges on the outer edge. Saw the tenon and cut finely tapered wedges to fit part-way into the mortise slots.

Apply adhesive to both the tenon and the inside of the mortise and assemble the joint. Apply adhesive to the wedges and, striking them alternately to keep the tenon straight, hammer them into the slots. Cramp the joint and, when the glue has dried, smooth down the protruding tenon end and wedges.

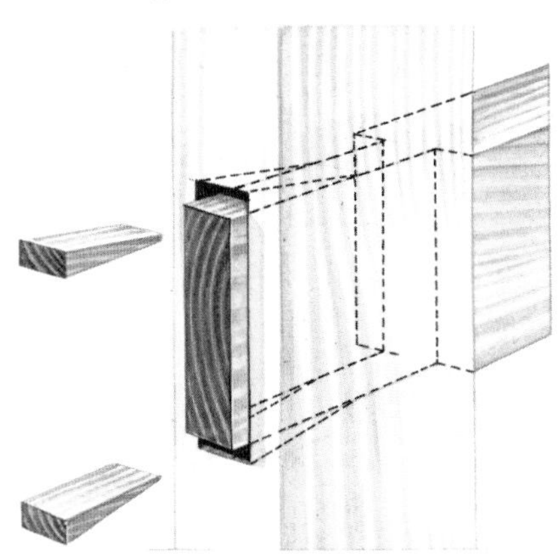

## 551 Heights for work-tops, tables and wall units

The ideal height of a work-top is the point where a person's outstretched hand reaches the wall when they are standing 45cm/18in from the wall. Fit shelves and cupboards at least 30cm/1ft above this height. When constructing a table allow for at least 100mm/4in clearance above the knee of a seated person.

## 552 Making it easier to cut thick timber

To gain more power and control when cutting thick pieces of timber, stand behind the saw's cutting edge and push the blade down vertically with both hands.

First make the timber secure by cramping it to the side of the workbench and fitting a stop at the far end of the timber. Start the initial cuts in the timber in the orthodox way, guiding the strokes with the thumb. Then move round to the back of the saw. Position the blade upright and work the saw up and down vertically through the timber. Provided the saw does not bind, the use of this method should ensure that the cutting line is exactly true.

## 553 Painting exterior pipes without marking walls

When painting drainpipes or waste pipes on outside walls, hold a piece of cardboard at the back of the pipes to prevent paint marking the walls.

## 554 Giving shelving a professional finish

To conceal the sandwich construction in manufactured boards when finishing off shelving, glue and pin half-round or flat strips of hardwood to the front edges. The mouldings can be painted, or stained and varnished to give the shelves the look of hardwood.

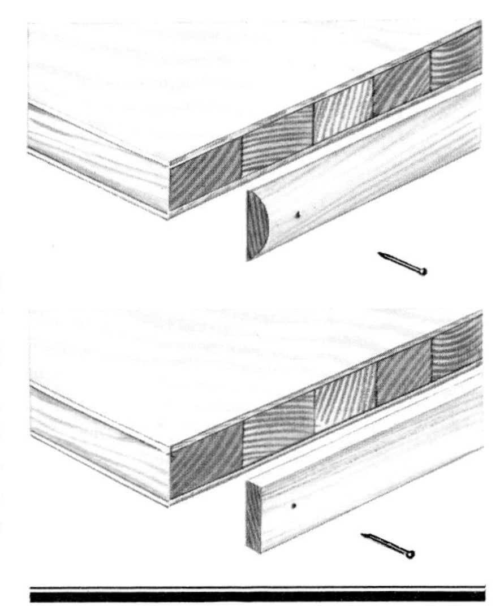

## 555 Removing a stubborn screw

Remove a stubborn screw by heating the head of the screw with a soldering iron to make it expand. Expansion enlarges the screw hole so that when the screw cools and contracts it can be loosened.

## 556 Reducing condensation on walls and ceilings

Fitting sheets of expanded polystyrene to walls and ceilings before papering helps reduce the effects of condensation that often occurs in kitchens and bathrooms. Use sheets of 2mm/$\frac{1}{16}$in thickness polystyrene, and hang them in a similar way to wallpaper.

## 557 Dealing with badly worn hinge holes

Loose hinges are the commonest cause of a door or a window not shutting properly. If, on examination, the holes for the hinge screws prove to be badly worn, remove the hinges and hammer wooden dowels into the screw holes. Cut the dowels off flush and refix the screws into the dowels.

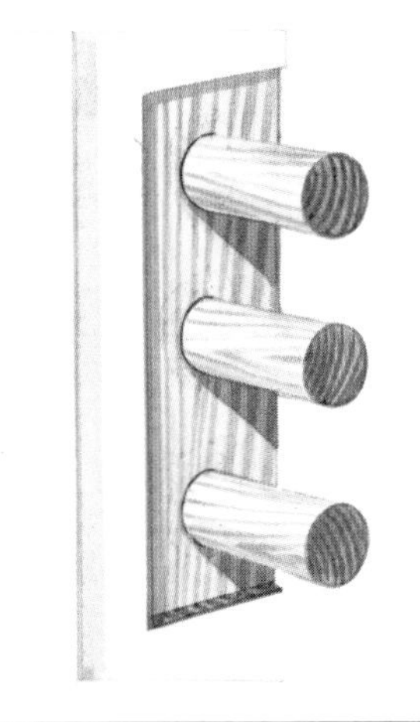

## 558 A precaution when insulating an attic

Never insulate underneath the cold water tank in an attic. Although it reduces heat loss in a room below, the tank is more liable to freeze up in cold weather, because heat cannot reach it.

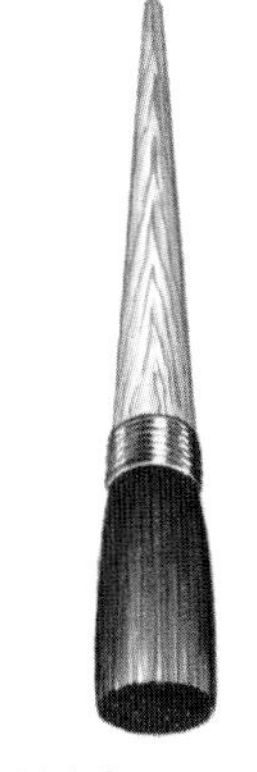

## 559 Sash brush

Use a sash brush to paint pipes and rounded mouldings. The brush is easier to use and it also lasts longer than a flat brush, which wears itself down unevenly on rounded surfaces.

## 560 Working at high levels

Always use a step-ladder—never chairs or boxes—when reaching up to a high level to, say, change a light bulb or put objects on high shelves.

# 561-566

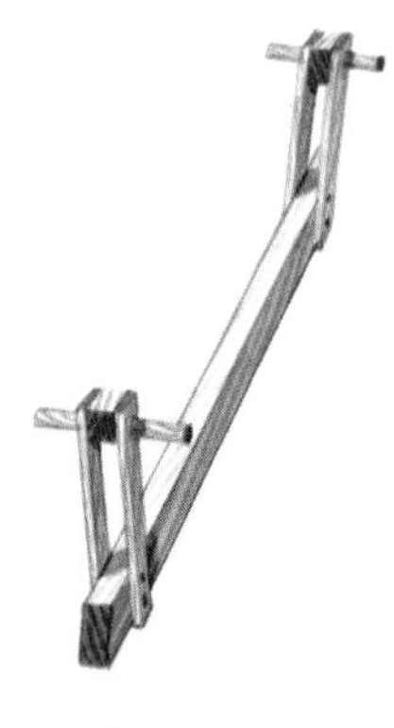

## 561
**Tamping beam**

Use a tamping beam to level the surface of newly laid cement. Make the beam from a length of timber at least 25mm/1in thick and 150mm/6in wide and fit it with a handle at each end. Drill a hole in the top of each handle to take a length of dowel as a hand grip, and bolt them in position.

## 562
**Rugs and polished surfaces**

Never lay rugs on highly polished floors without sewing or sticking patches of non-slip material to the underside. Thin rubber discs glued to each corner are perfectly adequate.

## 563 Saving time when trimming wallpaper

Use a pencil to mark off 75mm/3in and 300mm/12in intervals along both sides of a pasting table. These marks will be a useful and permanent guide and will save a great deal of repetitive work with a straight-edge, particularly when identical lengths of paper have to be trimmed.

## 564 Cutting large circular holes in tiles

Because of the crumbly nature of ceramic tiles, it is impossible to cut a large circular hole without breaking the tile. The best way to overcome the problem is to first select a coin that is nearest to the size required, and, placing it in position on the glazed surface, score round it with a tile cutter. Make a clean cut across the full width of the tile, bisecting the circle, and with a pair of pincers gnaw out each of the semicircles. Finally fit the tile in place, re-joining it along the cut line. Provided that the cut is clean, the join will hardly show.

## 565 Fitting screws the professional way

To finish off a job professionally, always tighten screws so that the slots are all aligned. Slots at varying angles look unattractive and detract from the finish.

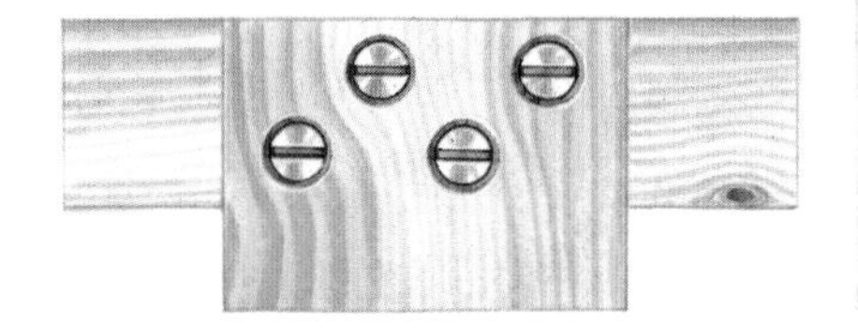

## 566 Replacing broken cords in a sash window

Always use a purpose-made pre-stretched wax cord when replacing a broken cord in a sash window and use clout nails to fix it. As the window has to be completely dismantled to deal with one broken cord, take the opportunity to replace the other cords in the window at the same time.

To remove the sashes from the frame, first carefully prise away the interior cover beadings, using an old chisel or a screwdriver. Lift out the bottom sash and cut the intact cord or cords. Lower the weights carefully to the bottom of the frame. Prise away the centre beadings and remove the top sash in the same way. Remove the remnants of the cords attached to each side of the sashes by pulling out the securing nails with pincers.

Lever out the wooden flaps that cover the sash traps at the bottom of the framework and remove the weights. If it is difficult to locate the flaps, because the framework has been painted a number of times, tap the bottom of the framework gently with a hammer until the paint cracks around the edges of the flaps.

Undo the cords from the weights, taking care not to mix them up—they are each specially balanced for either the top or lower sash windows. Next lubricate the pulley wheels to prevent the new sash cord from sticking and wearing down.

To rethread the new cord into the frame, tie one end of a length of string to a bent nail or small piece of lead, slightly curved to help it slip over the pulley wheel or a screw eye, and tie the other end to the new length of sash cord, knotted at the opposite end to prevent it slipping over the wheel. Feed the nail or lead over the pulley, and lower it down into the sash trap, drawing the cord over the pulley wheel. Tie the bottom end of the cord to the weight, using a figure-of-eight knot. Repeat this procedure until all four weights have been attached to the new cords.

Replace the top sash first by pulling the weights up and wedging them in position about 25mm/1in from the pulley. Stand the sash at the bottom of the window and, pulling the cord tight, nail the cord into the groove. Replace the bottom sash in the same way and refit the flaps and centre and interior cover beadings.

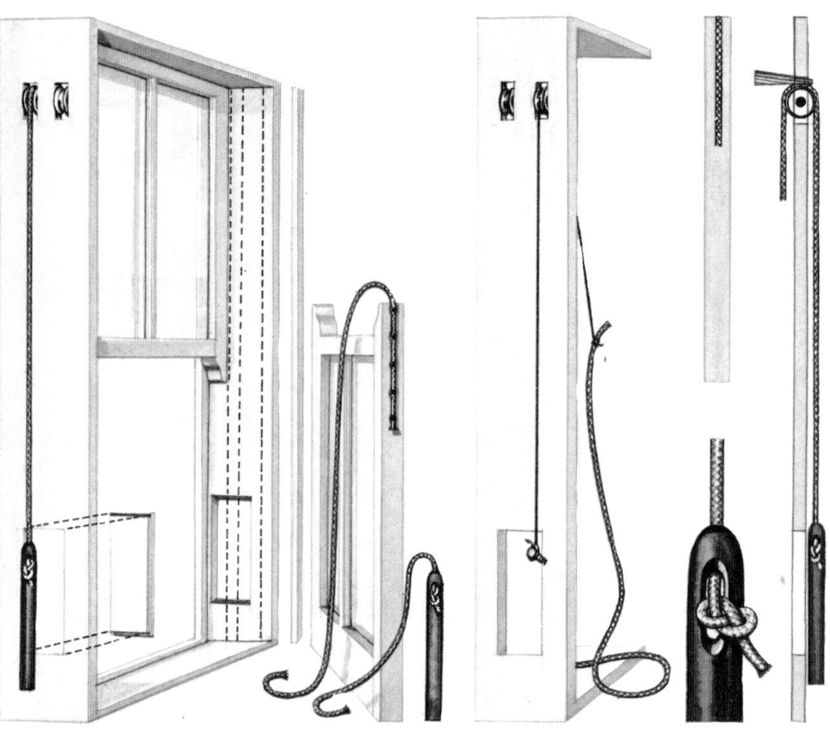

## 567 Gluing wedge-shaped timbers without mess

Always use two cramps when gluing wedge-shaped timbers to prevent the join slipping out of position. Insert waxed paper between the cramping block of the cramp, covering the join line and the joint. This will prevent the glue that will be squeezed from the joint sticking to the block.

## 568 Dealing with moss stains on stonework

Green moss stains on stonework can be removed with a wet scrubbing brush occasionally dipped in hydrated lime. Rinse off all traces of the lime afterwards.

## 569 Laying pipes and cables under floors

When cutting notches in joists to take pipes or electric cables beneath floorboards, saw the notches so that they are centred in the middle of the floorboards. This means that the boards can be nailed each side of the notches. At the same time—provided that the position of the pipes or cables is noted—the procedure reduces the chance of the pipes or cables being pierced when nailing hardboard or a similar covering to the floor.

## 570 Supporting a ladder on concrete surfaces

If a ladder is being used on a concrete or a paved surface, try to position it so that it is in front of a window. Fit a batten across the inside of the opening and rope it to the ladder to anchor it in position. This makes the support secure. If the ladder is to be used in this position for any length of time, screw the batten to supports fitted to the wall inside the window for additional safety.

## 571 Sawing wood at an angle in a vice

The rule to follow when cutting wood at an angle in a vice is to adjust the timber—not the saw. Place the wood within the vice so that the line of the angle being cut is positioned vertically. Not only is it easier to saw—as the saw can be used vertically—but it is also easier to cut accurately.

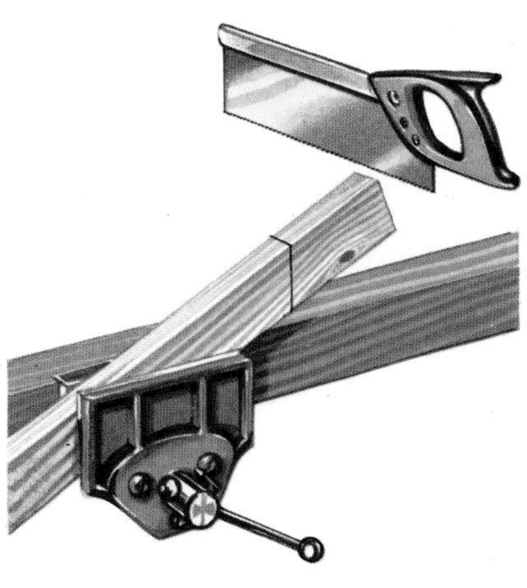

## 572 Temporarily sealing a broken window

To temporarily seal a broken window, place a sheet of polythene against the window frame and secure it by nailing a thin strip of wood along each of its sides. Polythene fixed without the strips of wood will rip more easily in a strong wind. When nailing the battens, make sure that the polythene sheet is stretched taut, sink the end and centre nails only, and leave the heads of the remaining nails protruding so that they can be easily removed.

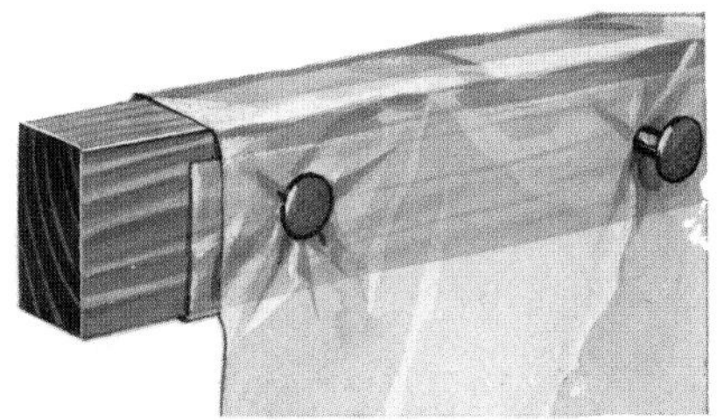

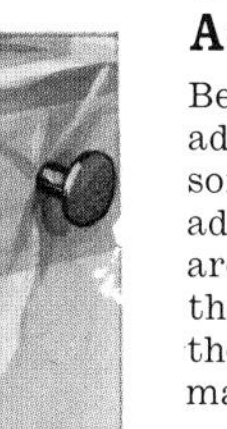

## 573 Testing if a wall needs sizing before papering

Before papering a wall, test whether it needs to be sized by moistening a finger and pressing it on the wall. If the mark disappears quickly, the wall surface is "hot" and size should be applied to it. The reason for applying size is to prevent the wall absorbing the water from the paste too quickly, thus stopping the paper sticking properly. It should always be applied to newly plastered walls before papering.

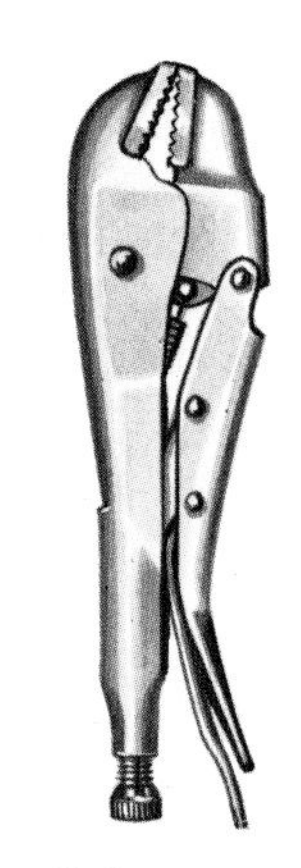

## 574 Adjustable grips

Before using adjustable grips on soft metals, wind adhesive tape around the teeth of the grips. This stops the serrations marking the metal.

## 575 Overhead glass

When fitting glass overhead in a greenhouse or lean-to, always use wire reinforced glass. If the glass is broken it will still splinter, but will be held together by the wire.

# Decorative finishes/1

A fitted kitchen is in essence no more than a series of boxes arranged in such a way as to provide adequate storage and work space and finished so that any awkwardly shaped corners and spaces are disguised. The problem that defeats most people who want to fit their own kitchen is not in making the boxes, which are relatively simple to construct, but in devising an attractive finish for them that is within the capabilities of a handyman. Each of these four distinctive designs provides a solution to that problem.

Using a wide-angled hinge, that enables a row of doors to butt directly against each other, hiding the frames, it is possible to build a rudimentary cupboard unit and yet complete it with an attractive and well-finished door.

A simple cupboard can be built from 15mm/⅝in laminated chipboard with a hardboard back. Butt-joint the structure, gluing and pinning from the outside. Support the shelves and top and bottom of each unit with battens, screwed through from the inside where appropriate. Screw the top batten, of the topmost unit, into the wall. Position the chosen worktop and doors in place and fix in position.

**Tongued-and-grooved board**
Build up the frame for each door by dowelling together lengths of 75mm/3in by 19mm/¾in timber. Cut strips of 12mm/½in by 100mm/4in tongued-and-grooved matching and pin the strips to the frame. Choose a vertical, diagonal or horizontal pattern, as desired. Coat the strips with clear matt polyurethane, but leave the edges unpainted. Cut edging strips, mitring the corners, and paint. Glue the strips and fit handles.

Use mitred joints for the worktop's wooden frame. Position strips of narrow, square beading around its inside edges; these are to support a chipboard panel covered with plastic laminate, so check that this will fit flush. Finish and seal (or varnish) the frame, and then fit the panel, screwing and gluing through the battens from underneath.

**Laminated chipboard**
Cut the doors from a sheet of 12mm/½in chipboard and cover both sides with plastic laminate. Fit laminate edges.

Glue and pin together three pieces of 19mm/¾in quadrant beading to form the handles. Punch the pins home, fill the holes and smooth and paint the handles before pinning and gluing them to the doors. Touch up the pin holes.

The worktop shown is postformed, but laminated chipboard could also be used. The gap between the top and door is filled by a Scotia moulding. Finish and paint the moulding and fix it by gluing and screwing into a batten.

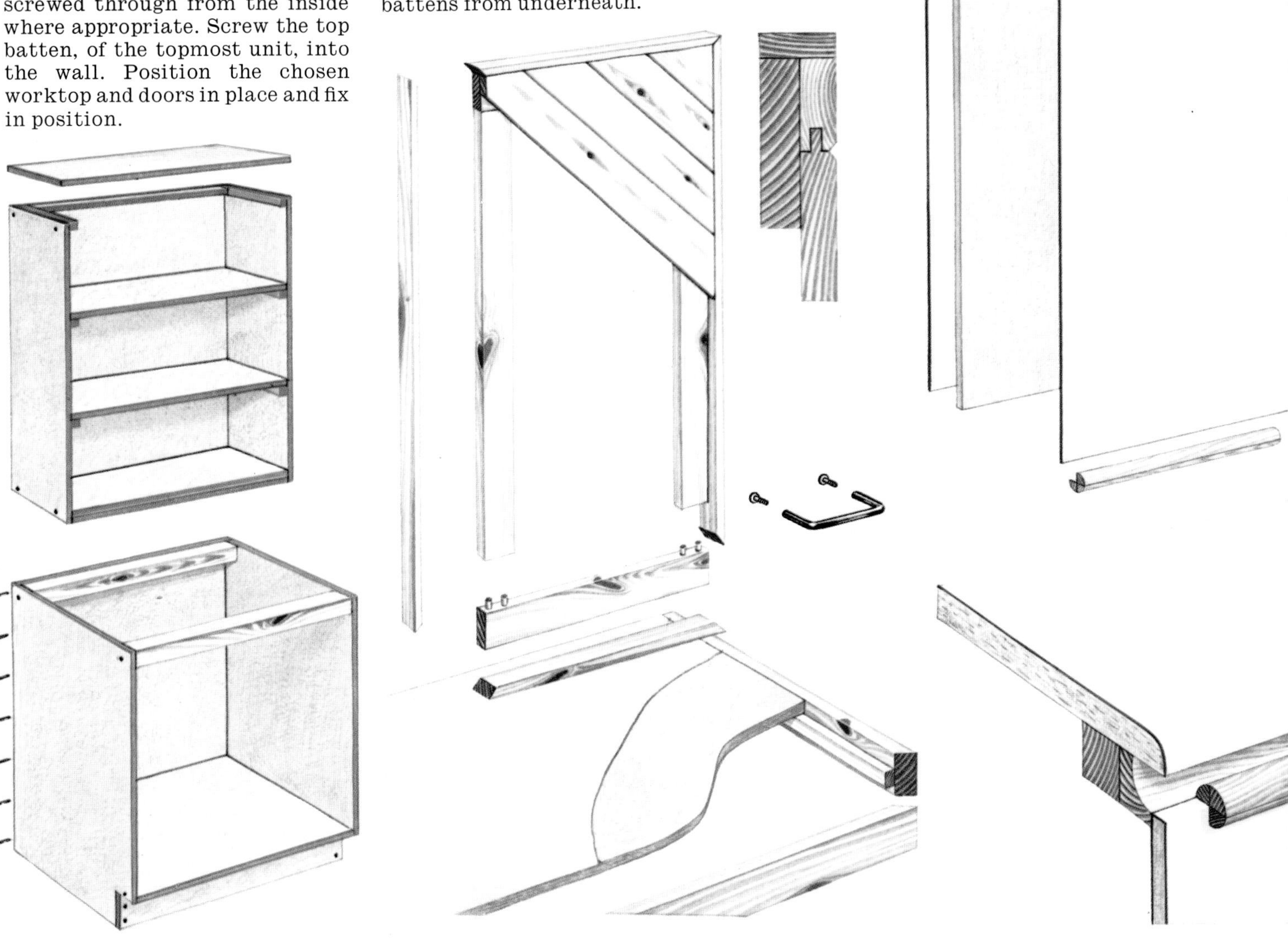

**Plywood panelling**

Make up a wooden frame for each cupboard door by dowelling together lengths of timber; 75 mm/3 in by 25 mm/1 in timber gives the most satisfactory proportions. Finish and paint.

Next, mitre the corner of four strips of 15 mm/⅝ in by 37 mm/1½ in panel moulding and glue them together to form an inner frame. Pin a pre-finished and pre-painted plywood panel to this frame and glue the completed unit to the door frame, supporting it at the back with square beading, glued and pinned to the outer frame.

Use a thick sheet of chipboard supported on a timber frame to form the base for the worktop; the front edging is also of chipboard and should be deep enough to take the width of half a tile. Finish by sticking tiles in position; if using quarry tiles, always seal them.

**Glass panelling**

Mitre four pieces of 50 mm/2 in by 19 mm/¾ in wood and pin and glue them together to form a wooden frame for the doors. Finish and paint except for the outside edges. Mitre the corners of four lengths of 12 mm/½ in by 25 mm/1 in parting beading; this will form the outside edging strips. Finish and paint the strips, except for their inside edges, and then glue them in place on the frame, with their rounded edges projecting forwards.

Cut strips of 12 mm/½ in by 9 mm/⅜ in glass beading to hold the glass in place on the front side of the door. Finish, paint and glue into place. To support the glass on the inside, fit a square bead around the edges.

The bottom doors can be constructed from a sheet of laminated chipboard, edged with 12 mm/½ in by 25 mm/1 in parting beading.

The worktop is a sheet of 18 mm/¾ in thick chipboard, strengthened with a timber frame and fitted with an edging strip of laminated chipboard or ordinary laminate. Glue and pin 12 mm/½ in by 25 mm/1 in parting beading to the upper and lower edges, rounded ends forwards. Lay tiles straight on to the chipboard.

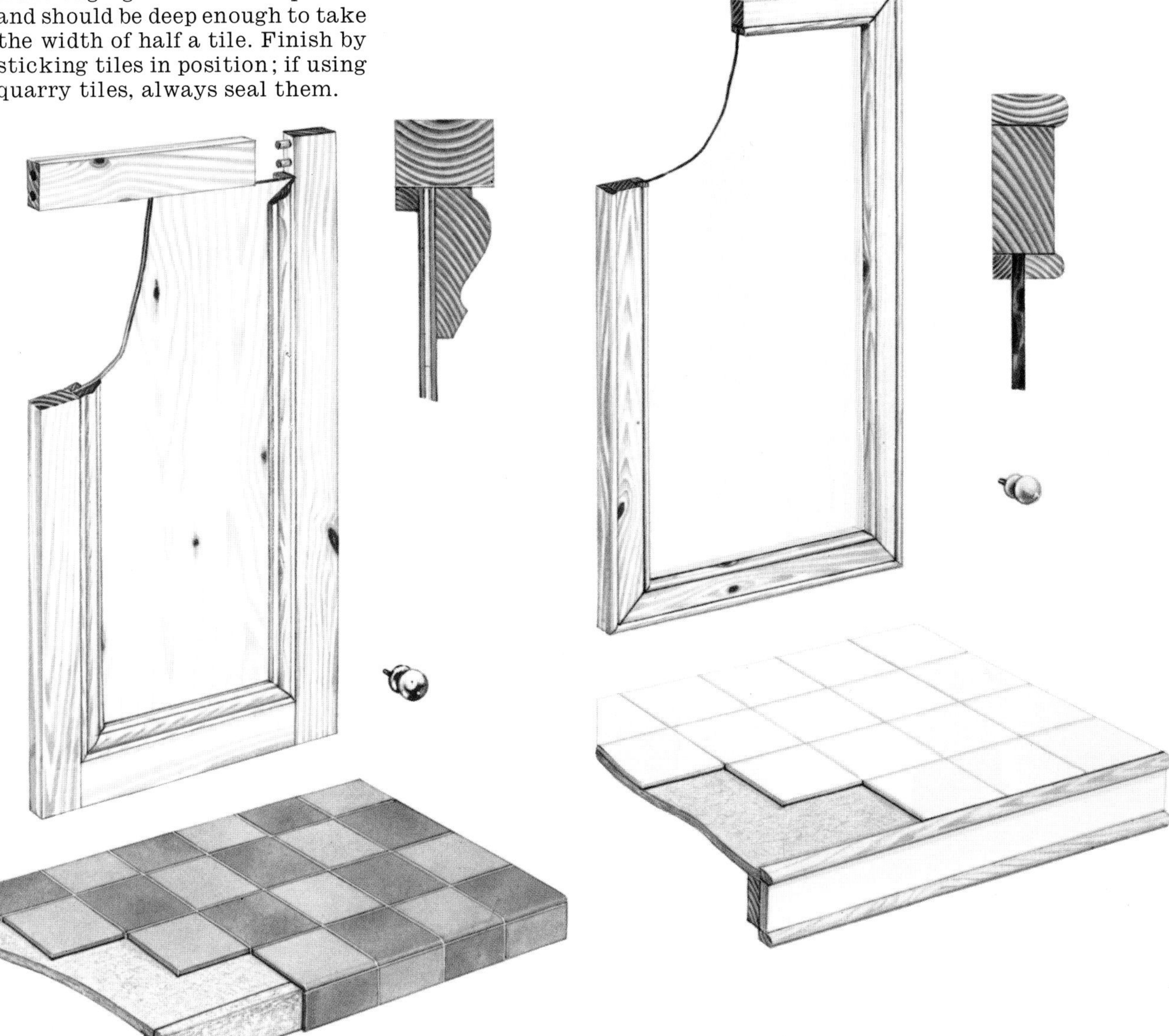

*See also Tips on*
Marking up 520
Adhesives 81, 496
Cutting 112
Dowelling 466, 513
Joints 381
Finishing 18, 499

It took no more than thoughtful selection, arranging, and careful finishing to bring a unified look to these pieces of furniture. Plan the purpose and appearance of the unit and simply build it up on a plinth. The trick is to judge the proportions so that the end product looks attractive and to work hard at the finish.

# 577

The Source
JAMES A. MICHENER
GOODBYE, COLUMBUS PHILIP ROTH
ANOTHER COUNTRY JAMES BALDWIN
GOING TO MEET THE MAN JAMES BALDWIN

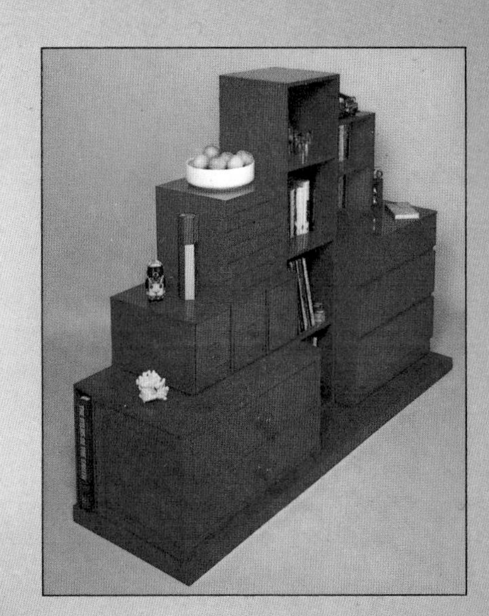

THE TOWN AND THE CITY
KEROUAC
PHILIP ROTH
OUR GANG

KENT STATE WHAT HAPPENED AND WHY
THE GOLDEN APPLES OF THE SUN RAY BRADBURY
THE ILLUSTRATED MAN RAY BRADBURY
GOING TO MEET THE MAN JAMES BALDWIN
the american mind
NO NAME IN THE STREET JAMES BALDWIN
TELL ME HOW LONG THE TRAIN'S BEEN GONE JAMES BALDWIN

GOODBYE BABY & AMEN DAVID BAILEY PETER EVANS
THE INVENTING OF AMERICA

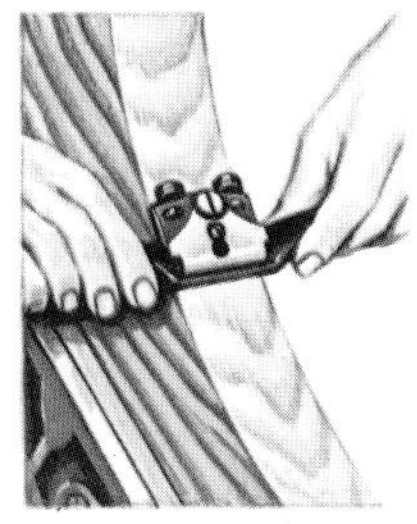

## 578
### Spokeshave

When smoothing inside curved surfaces, pull a spokeshave—do not push it like a plane. Always cut along the grain to avoid splitting the wood and damaging the blade.

## 579
### Central heating

Never switch on a boiler after a central-heating system has been drained, or the cylinder will explode. The system must be properly refilled first.

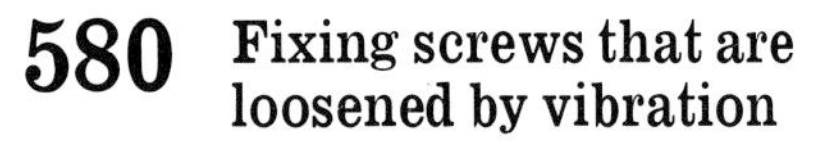

## 580 Fixing screws that are loosened by vibration

Screws that continually work themselves loose through vibration can be securely locked into place by driving a staple across the slot in the head of the screw.

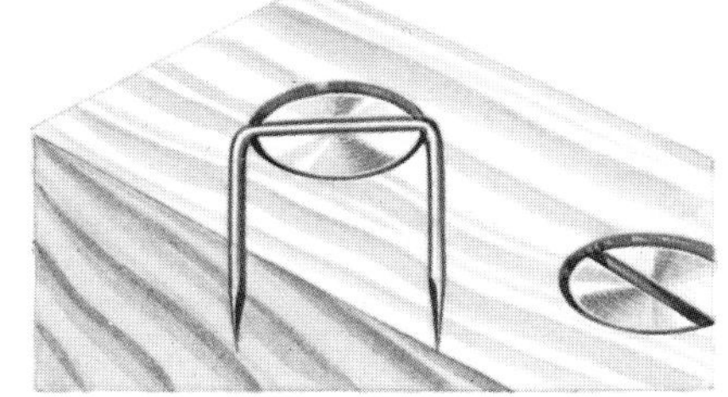

## 581 Decorating behind a wall-mounted radiator

First turn off the central heating system and drain a radiator before moving it to gain access to the wall behind. Place rags under the retaining nuts on each side of the radiator as a safeguard against possible leakage, and loosen the nuts. Remove the radiator from the wall brackets and swing it down on to a wooden block. Tighten the retaining nuts.

When the decorating has been completed, fix the radiator back in position. Take care, however, not to tighten the nuts too much; otherwise the packing in the joints will be damaged and the radiator may start to leak.

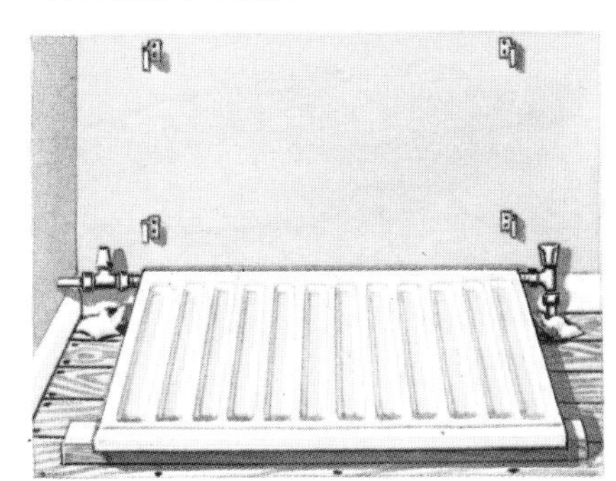

## 582 Smoothing the edge of a piece of glass

There are three stages to smoothing the edge of a piece of glass—arrissing, grinding and polishing. Arrissing eliminates the sharp edges of the glass, grinding gives the edge a smooth finish and polishing puts the final shine on the grinding. A ground or smooth edge is generally adequate for such articles as table tops, shelving and sliding doors for cabinets.

Carry out the arrissing stage by rubbing the sharp edges of the glass with a slightly wetted smooth abrasive stone. Hold the stone at an angle of 45° and work downwards away from the sheet of glass to avoid "shelling" on the edges. This is the name given to the minute flakes of glass that can splinter away from the surface, leaving the edges looking ragged. When both sharp edges along one length have been arrissed, use a medium abrasive stone, again wetted, to start the grinding process. Work the stone backwards and forwards along the edge until all the shiny glass patches have disappeared. Finish off with a smooth stone to get a smooth finish.

If a polished edge is required, rub the smoothed finish with a block of hardwood, about 150mm/6in long, 60mm/2½in wide and 40mm/1⅝in thick. Alternatively, squeeze a drop of oil on to a cloth and rub it along the smooth edge. This removes any loose and finely ground particles of glass and, at the same time, adds a brighter finish to the glass. However, it should be noted that the polishing process requires a lot of time and patience, so it may be preferable to leave this final stage of polishing to glass merchants, who have special machines for the job.

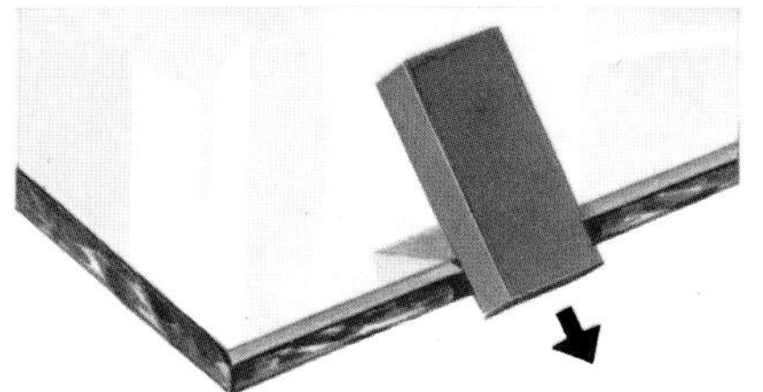

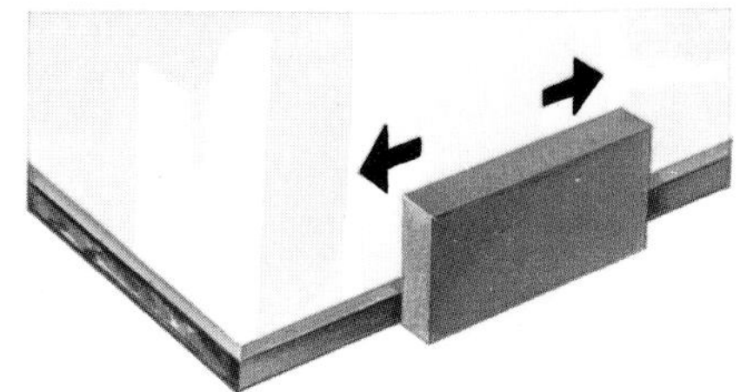

## 583 Securing timbers of different thicknesses

Always nail or screw a thinner piece of timber to a thicker piece. This ensures a firm fixing.

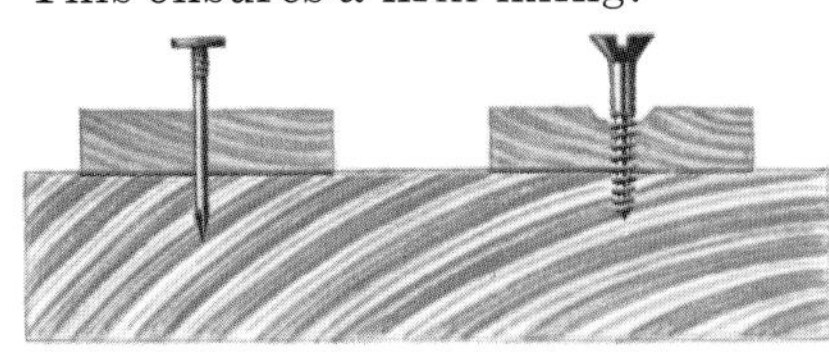

## 584 Making it easier to lay floor tiles

When tiling a floor—or working on any job involving a considerable amount of kneeling—prevent the knees from becoming sore by tying protective pads around them. Make the pads from two pieces of thick foam rubber. Pierce holes in each corner and thread string through them. Tie the string behind the knees.

## 585 Supporting the paper when papering ceilings

Use a length of batten at least 50mm/2in wider than the paper to take the weight of the folded paper while the paper already in position is being brushed down. To make it easier to hold, attach a short rod of at least 25mm/1in diameter as a handle.

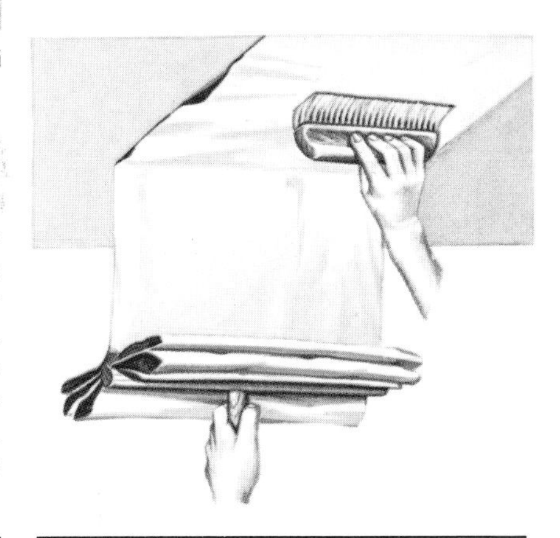

## 586 Fitting a stopper to a drawer

To prevent drawers being pulled out accidentally, fit a block of wood to the back of the drawer so that it catches on the front inside edge of the drawer unit to hold the drawer in place. Remove the drawer and fix the block with a screw, so that the block can pivot to reach approximately 12mm/½in above the top of the drawer.

Pivot the block upright and fit a second screw in position. Then remove the second screw, pivot the block down and slide the drawer back into position. Once the drawer is in place, turn the block upright again and reinsert the screw in the block.

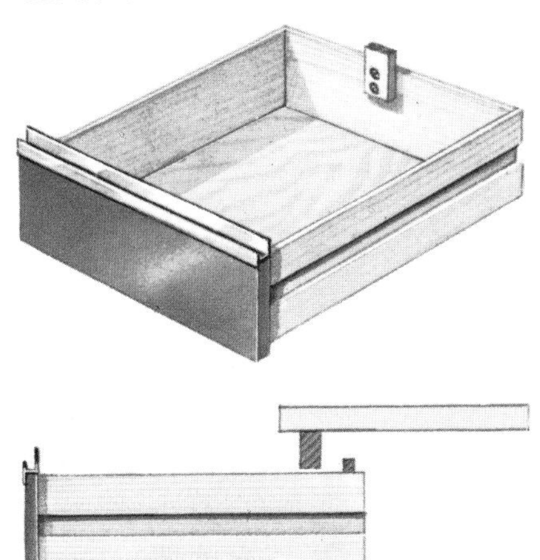

## 587 Making it easier to repair a cistern

To keep the valve of a cistern closed while working on the inside, tie the ball-valve arm to a length of wood placed across the top of the cistern.

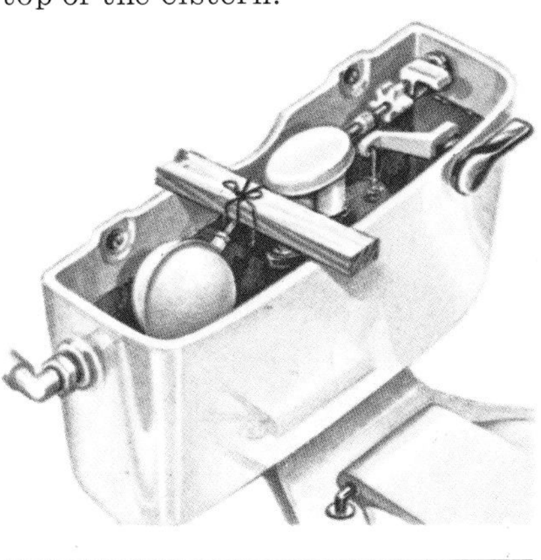

## 588 Making glass doors and French windows safer

Stick coloured self-adhesive strips across the full width of glass doors at a child's eye-level. This safety precaution will reduce the danger of children not seeing the glass and running into it. The tape is easily adjustable.

## 589 Repairing water channels in sills

Window sills and door sills have a groove cut into the underside to prevent rainwater being drawn back to the wall of the house by capillary attraction. If, over the years, this groove has become blocked by numerous coats of paint, so making it difficult to clean out easily, a simple alternative is to fit a strip of hardwood under the sill.

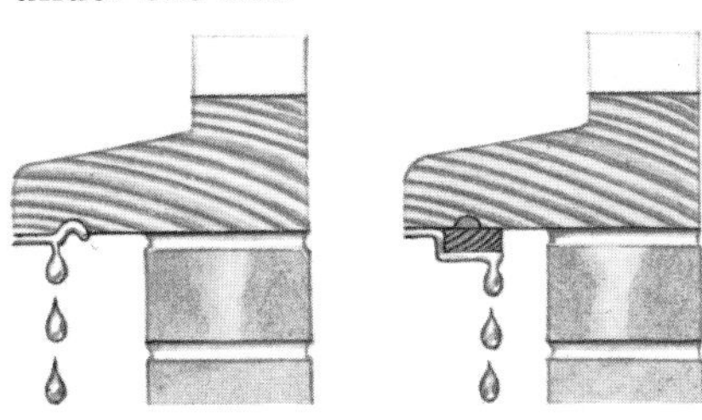

## 590 Marking out a curve for a garden path

Use a length of garden hosepipe as a guide for cutting out the curves for a garden path. Lay the hosepipe to within 50mm/2in of the required shape and fit 150mm/6in nails either side of it to hold the hose in position. Maintain a 50mm/2in gap from the hose when cutting out the curves.

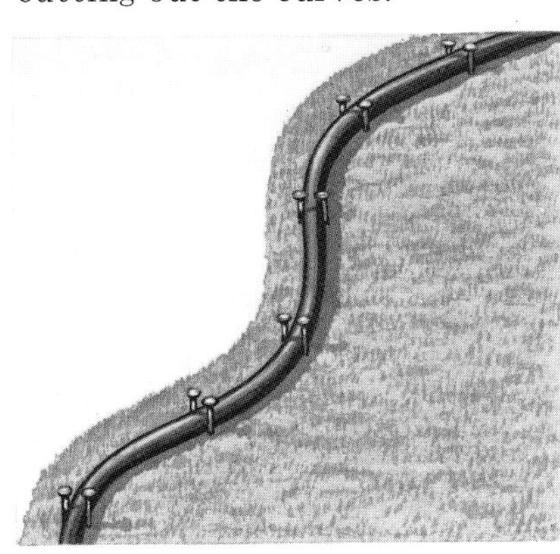

## 591 Maintaining a disused chimney

To keep a disused chimney dry and ventilated, bed a ridge tile in mortar over the top of the stack.

## 592 Sharpening tools on a grinding wheel

Tools being sharpened on a grinding wheel should be frequently dipped into cold water. Too great a build-up of heat will ruin the cutting edge. When sharpening only use light pressure.

## 593 Dowelling into mitred corners

First mark the positions of the dowels by tapping pins into one mitred face, snipping the heads off and pressing them into the other face. Remove the pins. Then clamp the wood in a vice, check that the edge to be drilled is horizontal and drill the holes.

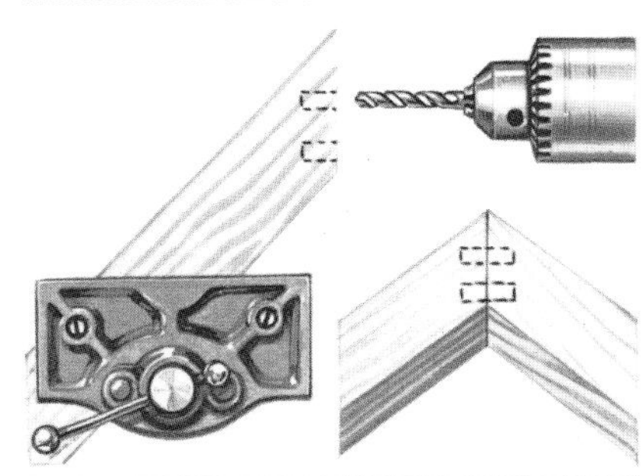

## 594 Sawing aluminium with a hacksaw

When cutting aluminium with a hacksaw, always use a hacksaw blade with fairly large teeth. A fine-toothed blade will quickly clog with aluminium filings, making sawing difficult.

## 595 "S" hook

Essential when painting from a ladder, an "S" hook can be hung on the ladder rungs or from guttering to hold a paint tin or kettle.

## 596 Gas leaks

Never try to trace a gas leak with a naked flame.

# Decorative finishes/3

The fibreglass feet used on all these pieces of furniture not only provide attractive mountings but also give style to what would otherwise be rather ordinary furnishings. They also bring unity to the unmatched pieces. The idea is simple but effective—and a very inexpensive way of transforming a room.

Fibreglass is an unusual material for the home handyman to use in quantity; however, the techniques involved in moulding it are far simpler than they appear and are well within the scope of any do-it-yourself enthusiast.

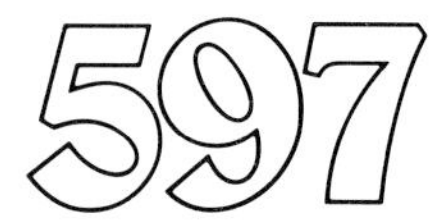

### Making the template

The basic requirement for making a set of fibreglass feet is the shaping of a plaster plug on to which layers of fibreglass matting can be built up.

Work out the final fibreglass shape required in cross-section on tracing paper. To make it possible to remove the fibreglass from the plug without damaging it, the shape should taper from the base to the top, with no undercuts.

Transfer one-half of the shape to a thin metal sheet, preferably aluminium, leaving a sizeable margin around the edge. Cut the shape out with tinsnips. Smooth the shaped edge down with a file and emery paper.

### Assembling the cutting blade

Use the metal template as a cutting blade to shape the plaster plug. Mount the template on a 12mm/½in thick copper pipe. Do this by cutting a slot in the top of the pipe and drilling two holes. Drop the top of the template in place and drill two holes through the holes in the pipe. Fasten the two together with nuts and bolts. Next cut a wooden baseboard. Use wooden blocks to hold the pipe in position and to form a core to reduce the build up of plaster. Glue the blocks together and drill through the centre of both to take the pipe. Assemble the blade and blocks, gluing the bottom block to the baseboard.

### Making the plaster plug

Because plaster of Paris dries fairly quickly, it is important to work speedily when building up the plug. Make up the plaster to the consistency of wet cement and then start building up a mound of it around the wooden blocks. As the plaster subsides outwards into the path of the blade, begin rotating the blade to scrape away excess plaster to create the outline of the shape required. Keep adding more plaster and rotating the blade until a perfect outline is achieved. Leave the plaster to harden for a few hours and then remove the blade. Fill in the hole left by the pipe with a few dabs of plaster.

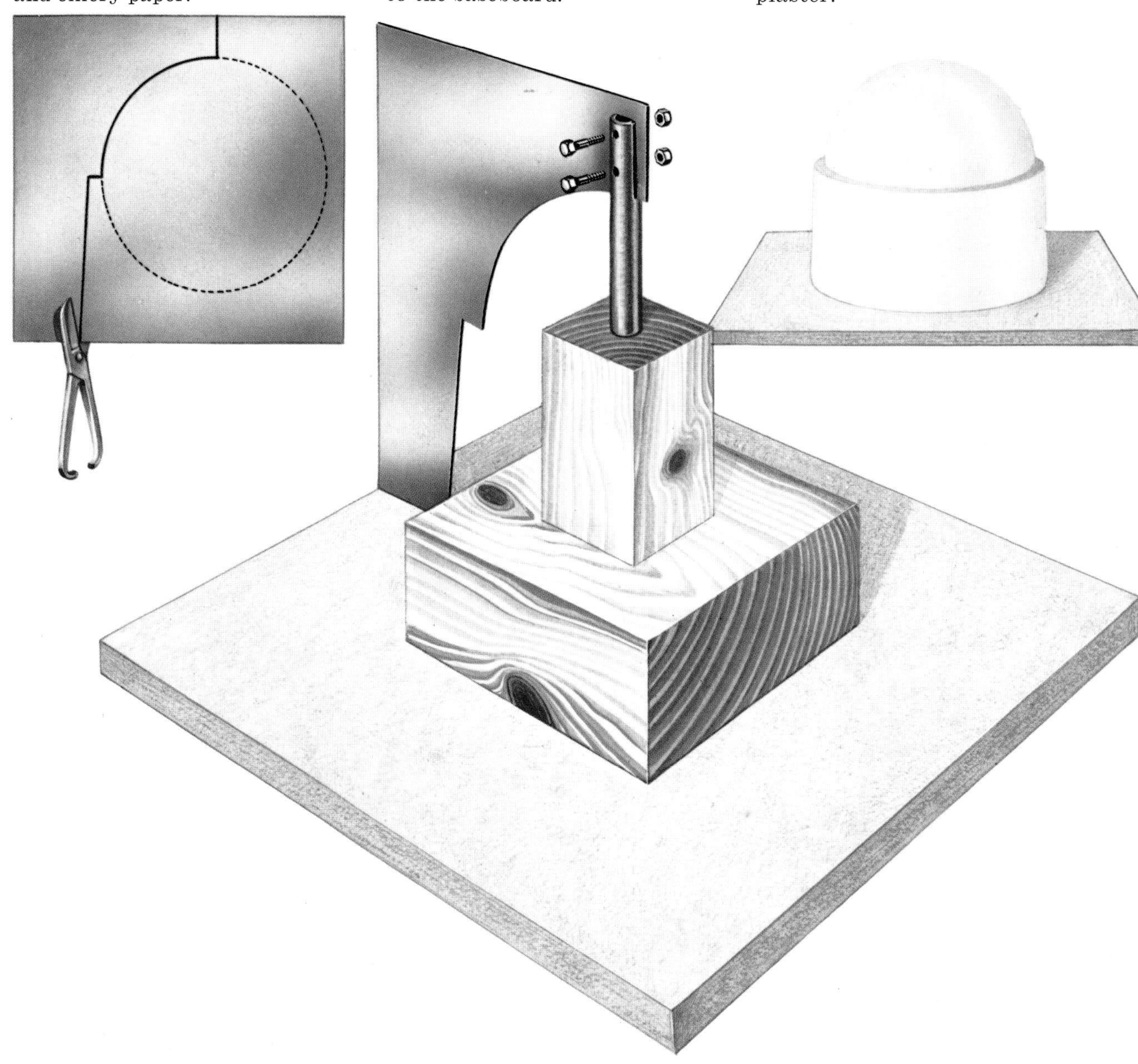

**Fibreglass finishes**
To achieve the best finish on the fibreglass feet, a fibreglass mould must be made first. This mould is then used to build up the feet to achieve a smooth outer finish.

**Making the fibreglass mould**
First seal the plug and board with shellac, and coat with two layers of non-silicone wax; then polish. Brush on a proprietary releasing agent. Leave to dry. Mix a gel coat resin and add hardener, following the manufacturer's instructions, mixing only a small amount at a time.

At this stage a pigment can be added. By making the mould in a contrasting colour to the finished object it is possible to see at a glance if the mould is transferring itself to the object, or if part of the object has been left on the mould. Brush on the gel coat resin and leave to dry for the time specified by the manufacturer.

When handling fibreglass matting always wear rubber gloves, taped at the wrists, and work in a well ventilated room. Cut the fibreglass matting into manageable strips. Mix a quantity of the basic resin with hardener, and brush over the gel coat. Place the fibreglass strips on the plug, dabbing in the resin mixture, until the whole plug is covered. Repeat, brushing on a second coat of mat and resin. Before the mould is thoroughly dry, trim it along the edge of the board. Once dry remove it from the plug. Fill any blemishes on the inside with polyester filler and finish off with wet-and-dry paper.

**Making the fibreglass feet**
Follow the same procedure used in making the mould. Apply the releasing agent to the inner surface of the mould and, once dry, brush on the gel coat resin with pigment and allow to dry. Apply the two layers of fibreglass matting and resin mixture with pigment added. Again, before it has completely dried, trim along the edges of the mould. Once dry remove the finished object. Drill screw holes along the edges so that the feet can be attached.

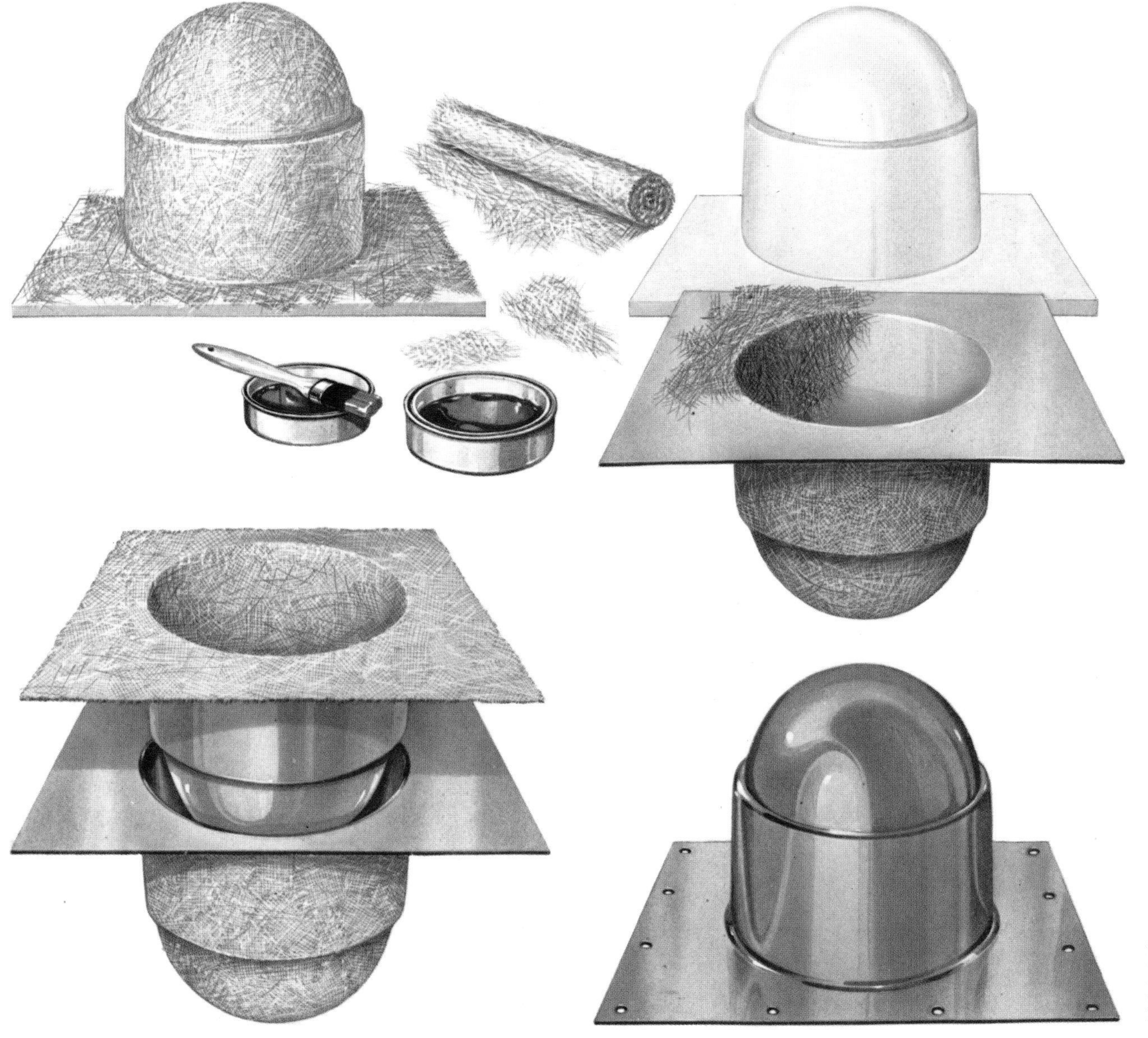

*See also Tips on*
Marking up 520
Adhesives 81
Cutting 113, 353
Drilling 239, 503

# Decorative finishes/4

A professional finish counts for so much, whether on projects built for the home or on existing pieces of furniture. The examples illustrated, ranging from this carefully stained cupboard to a chest decorated with newspaper, are typical of the transformation that can be achieved. Stencilling and marquetry—used so effectively on the screen and the back of the chair—are both simple skills to practice and acquire.

# 598

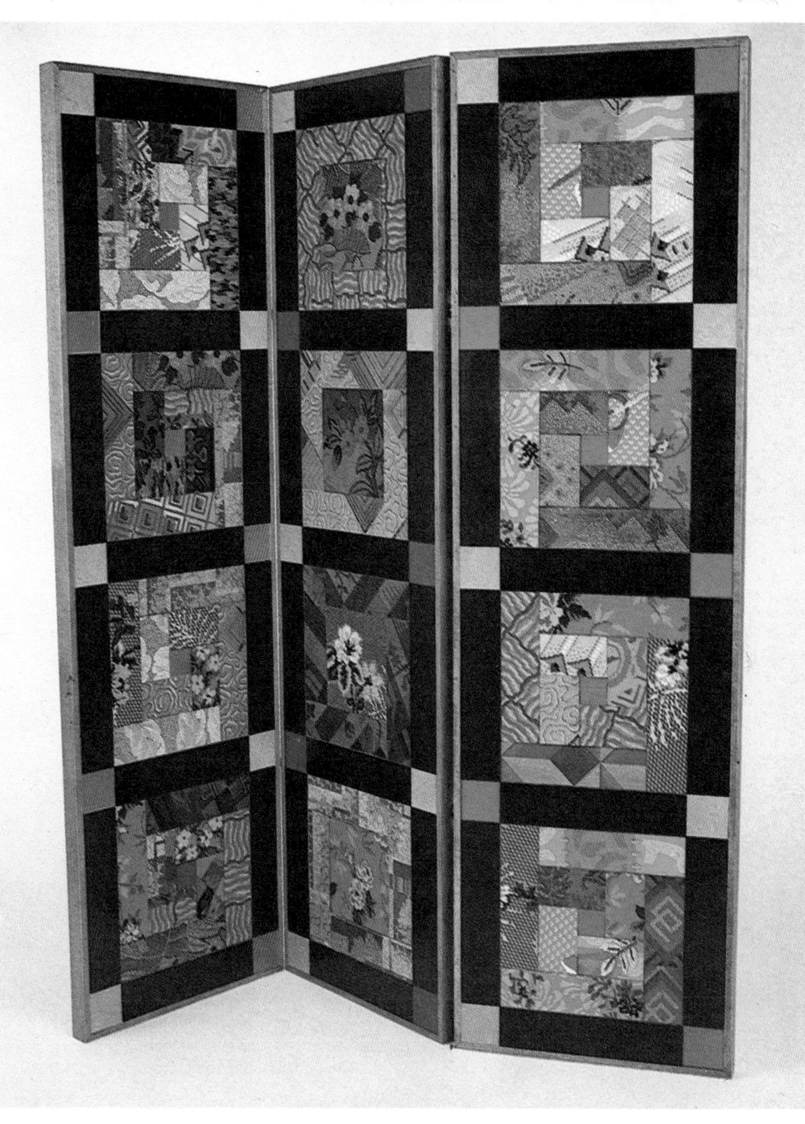

### Display mirror

This unusual mirror can be used to display various collectors' items, such as postcards. Its construction is extremely simple. An outer and inner frame are individually butt-jointed together and then combined.

To make the outer frame—this will hold the items intended for display—use a length of 12mm/½in thick softwood slightly wider than the items involved. Cut two pieces to the overall height required and two pieces to the required length. Square off the ends and butt the lengths against the two side pieces.

To make the inner frame—this will support the mirror—use another four lengths of 12mm/½in thick softwood approximately two-thirds the width of the first piece. Cut the side and horizontal pieces so that the joins of the two frames overlap—thus the two horizontal pieces extend the complete length of the outer frame.

Glue and screw the two frames together. Insert the mirror into the inner frame and secure it.

Glue the display items in position around the outer margin of the frame and then decorate it with beading. On the outer edge two half-rounds are combined—on the inner edge one half-round and one quarter-round. Mitre the ends of each piece of beading and glue and pin as illustrated. Stain or varnish.

### Newsprint decoration

Unusual and eye-catching finishes can be given to a range of objects by using newspaper to decorate them.

First, make sure that the surface to be decorated is smooth and clean; if necessary, size it with a thinned-down coat of heavy-duty wallpaper paste. Cut out the newspaper as whole sheets or as arbitrary shapes. Depending on the finish required, the paper can be torn to leave ragged edges or cut cleanly with sharp scissors. Coat the newspaper thoroughly with paste and stick it down, overlapping the edges as desired. Then varnish it, making sure to use acrylic glaze; wood varnish makes newsprint transparent.

To enhance the effect, note that attachments, such as the castors on a chest, look especially attractive if they are painted in a colour picked out from the covering.

### Colour staining wood

Prepare the wood by using paint stripper, a scraper and glasspaper to get its surface as clean as possible. If the object is badly stained, bleach it—preferably using genuine wood bleach. Bleaching is also useful when trying to match lighter with darker woods; it can be used as well to give added brightness to the dye.

Before applying the dye, clean the stripped surface with turpentine substitute. Also test for colour on a matching offcut first, as dyes can dry to different shades.

On large objects use a soft, dry, clean, lint-free cloth; for crevices, use a brush. Apply one even coat, working quickly and with the grain. Wipe off any excess with a clean, dry cloth and then leave the surface to dry for at least six hours. Then apply further coats. Finish with coloured varnish or polyurethane wood sealer.

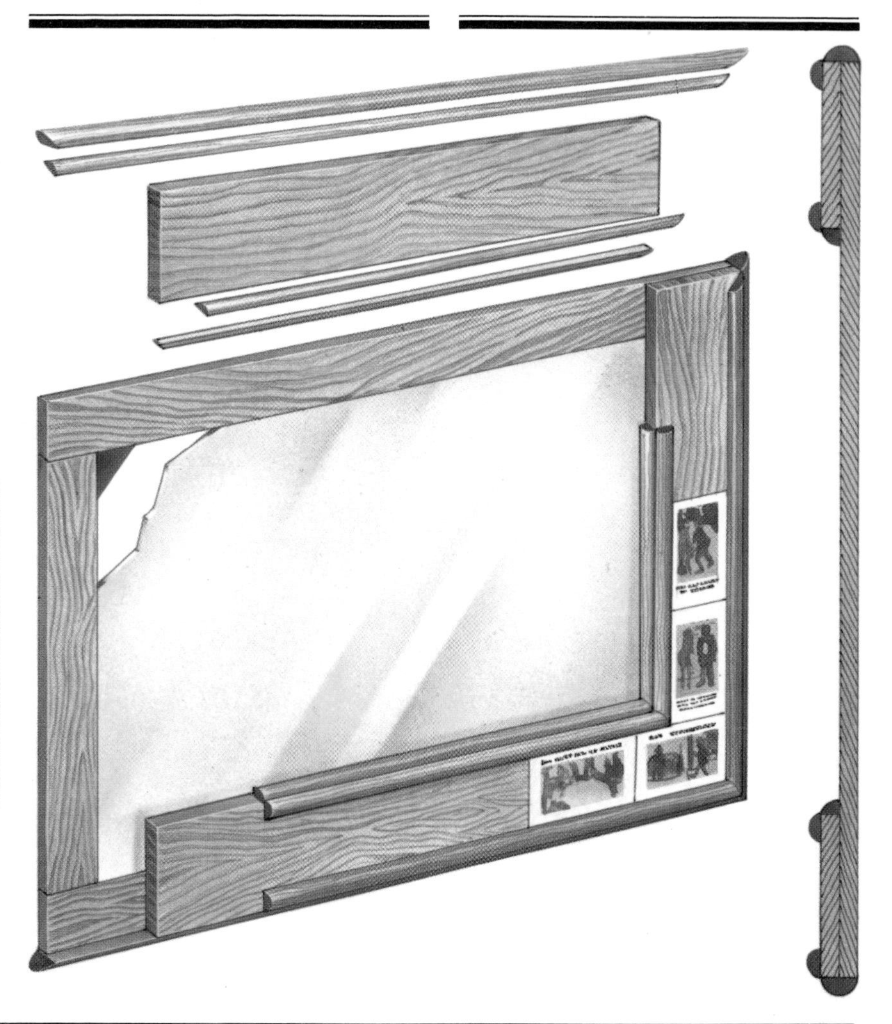

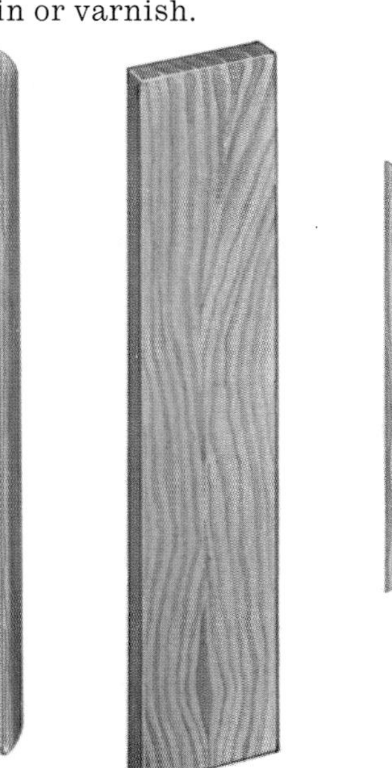

**Mosaics**
Objects around the home can be simply decorated with mosaic patterns, using pieces of broken pottery. These can be glazed or unglazed, according to choice. Mount the pieces on the chosen base with tile cement and then fill the cracks with grouting.

If using a flower pot for the base, build up the mosaic and then paint the rim with two coats of white emulsion. Next, take some artist's oil paint of the same colour as the mosaic and mix a dab of it with polyurethane varnish. Paint the rim with the mixture to give it the look of real glazed pottery. The white line on the pot illustrated was added freehand as a final decorative touch.

**Marquetry**
Ordinary floor tiles can be used to make appealing marquetry patterns. The results are visually attractive and far easier to make than the traditional alternative, using wood veneers.

The trick to making marquetry is to plan the pattern on paper first. The process is much simplified by drawing up a grid and standardizing the widths of material to be used as far as possible. A useful guide is to remember that domestic vinyl floor tiles are usually 228 mm/9 in or 304 mm/12 in square, while cork tiles are usually 304 mm/12 in square.

Select the tiles from which the pieces are to be cut in accordance with the colour scheme required. Cut out the pieces, using a trimming knife and a straight-edge. Mount them with contact adhesive, using one which allows the pieces to be moved around into final position. Finish by coating with floor sealer. Polish.

**Stencilling**
To cut a stencil plate, preferably use genuine stencilling paper or film, obtainable from art and papercraft shops. Some of these have ready-printed patterns, but otherwise trace on the desired pattern.

If stencilling paper is unobtainable, coat ordinary paper—of medium weight or thicker—with a half-and-half mixture of boiled linseed oil and turpentine to make it tough and impervious to moisture. Apply this with a rag to both sides of the paper until it is saturated. Hang and leave it to dry.

Cut out the pattern with a stencilling knife or a scalpel, holding it pencil-fashion. Work on an even, hard surface, holding the paper firmly in position.

To minimize weakening of the plate, cut out details before tackling larger areas. Apply even pressure—frequent lifting of the knife will cause jagged edges. Punch out small circles and dots with various sizes of needle. Smooth the edges of larger, tricky shapes with fine glasspaper.

Prepare wood carefully before stencilling it. Prime and undercoat raw wood; over areas of topcoat where stencilled patterns are to lie, apply a coat of matt paint. A "grained" effect can be achieved, if desired, by thinning the matt paint slightly with turpentine, brushing it on to a gloss surface and then dragging a piece of crumpled-up netting over it. Make sure that the paint is bone dry before starting to stencil.

If lines are to feature as part of the decoration as well as the stencilled pattern, paint them on first with a good-quality sable brush. If the pattern is to lie within a border, find the centre of the border and of the pattern and make sure that they match up exactly.

Tape the stencil plate into position. Block off areas which are to be painted in different colours with masking tape. Each colour must be allowed to dry completely before another colour is applied.

The paint should be either water- or turpentine-based, and of a fairly thick consistency. Acrylics are excellent, as they are fast-drying and easy to clean off. Use a proper stencilling brush; this is cylindrical, with its bristles cut to form a flat surface.

To prevent paint running under the stencil plate, never overload the brush and work the paint well into the bristles on old newspaper before starting work. When they leave an even speckling of paint, start on the stencil. Hold the brush vertically and dab, rather than brush, the paint into the openings of the plate.

After the stencilling has been completed and the paint has completely dried, apply at least three coats of varnish as a finishing touch. Satin-finish polyurethane varnish provides an attractive and not too glossy finish when used as a topcoat.

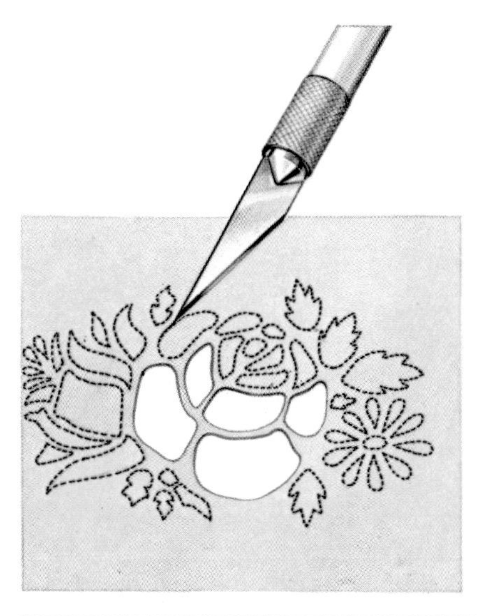

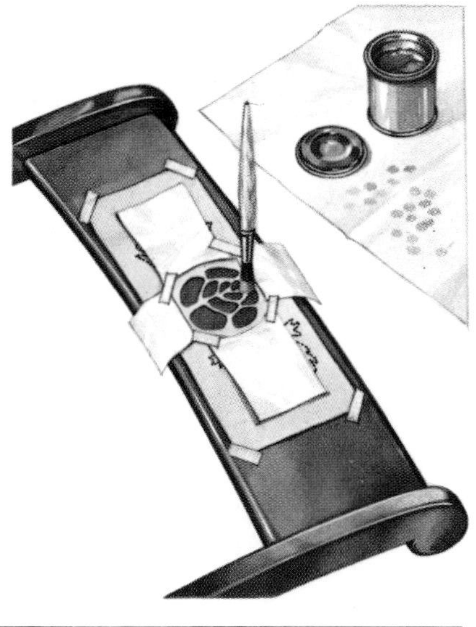

*See also Tips on*
Murals and enlargements 3
Picture framing 599
Marking up 520
Adhesives 81
Joints 243
Beading 331
Finishing 107, 518

# Picture framing

Good picture framing will enhance the appearance of the image itself. Even though the basic techniques involved are conventional, the frames illustrated make use of unusual materials and finishes, carefully chosen to complement the subject in mood and style and so forming a pleasing aesthetic whole. Bamboo, for example, perfectly sets off the oriental picture, while the fan shows how unconventional objects can be framed.

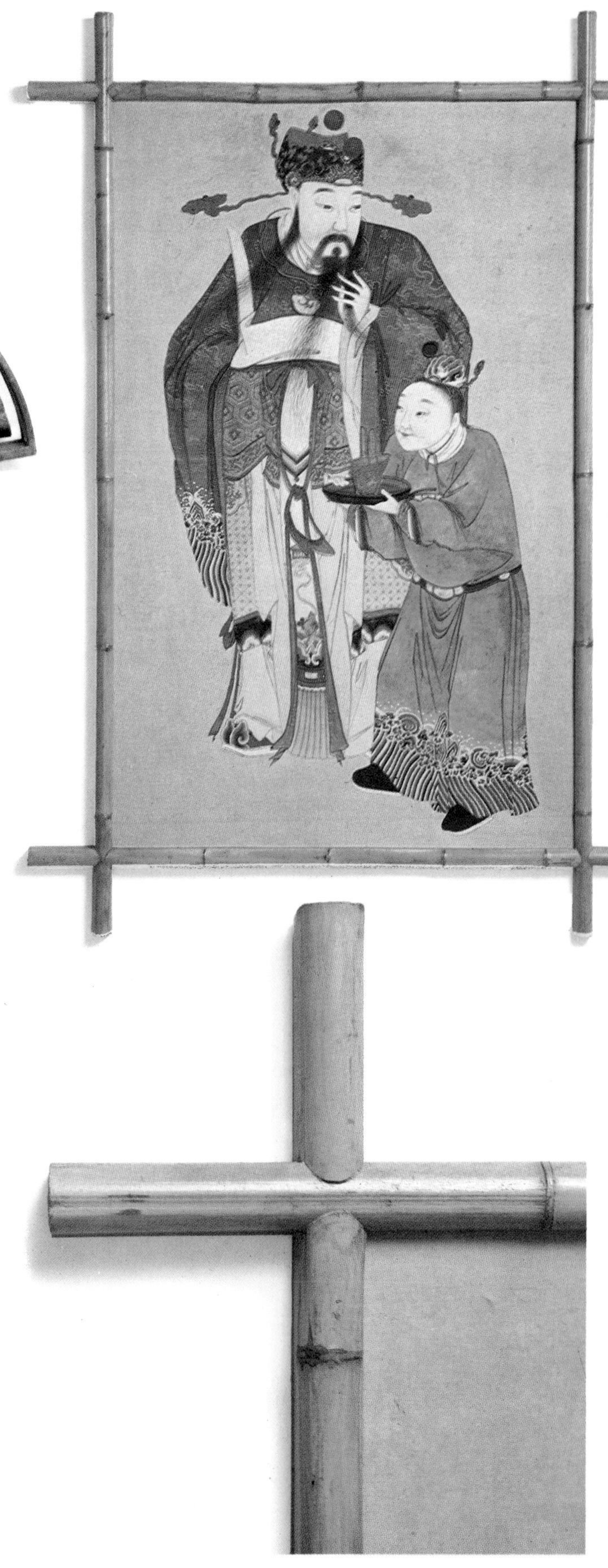

599

Commercial picture moulding

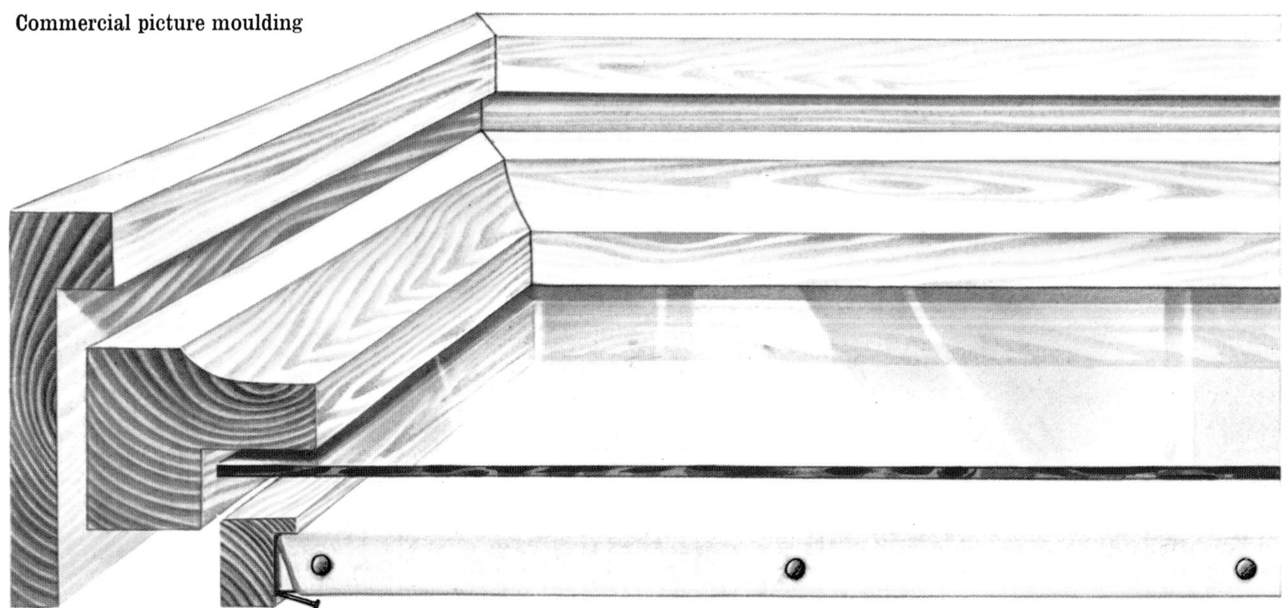

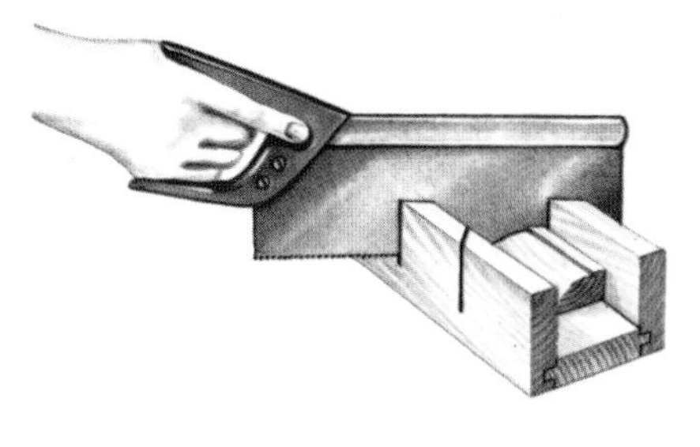

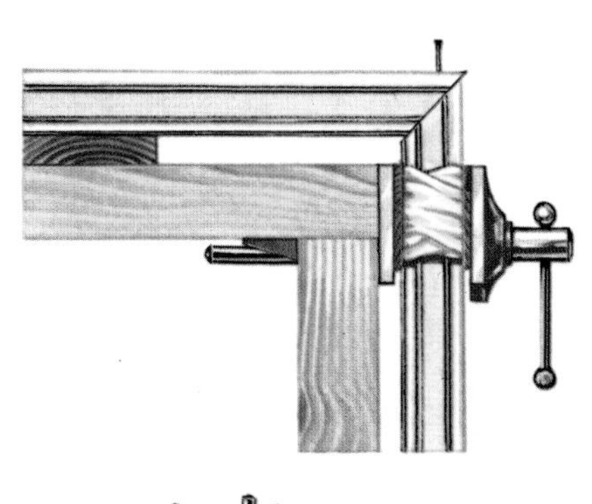

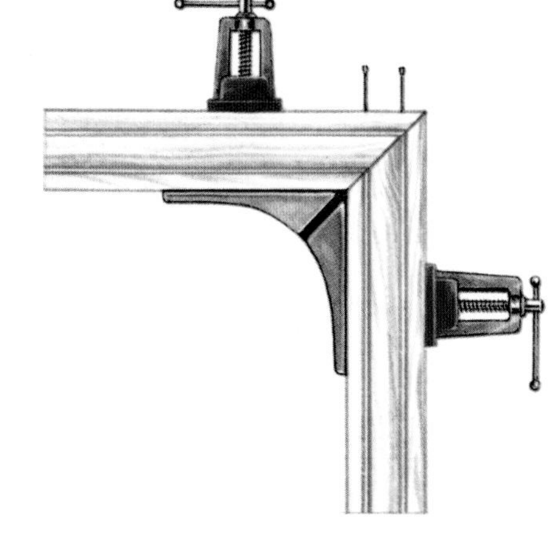

**Aesthetics of picture framing**

The art of good picture framing is to design and build a frame that both enhances and complements the picture it surrounds. The three main considerations to bear in mind are colour, proportion and profile. Within each of these there are three basic approaches; those of a contrast or analogy with the subject—or pure decoration.

Where appropriate, the eventual position the picture will occupy should also be considered. Modern paintings are often more attractive unframed than framed, but they still require a backing to prevent them from being lost against their surroundings.

A general guideline is to avoid duplicating the colours and proportions of the picture in the frame. To repeat either will result in an exaggerated emphasis. Equally, do not use a totally unrelated colour or proportion as this again will detract from the desired effect.

Colours used as shadows in the picture are often suitable for the frame. They not only relate it to the picture but also tend to give the picture depth. When deciding the proportions and colours it is best to experiment.

The profile of the frame involves three basic shapes used individually or as combinations of each other—flat, concave and convex. The golden rule is to keep it simple and flowing.

**Basic construction of a frame**

Having measured and marked off the frame, mitre the ends of each piece, using a mitre block and sharp tenon saw. Combine the pieces in sections.

When using a woodworking vice, cramp one piece with its mitred edge flush with the sides of the jaws, glue the other piece and hold it in position, supporting it on a block at the opposite end. Offset the position of its mitred end as illustrated, leaving a difference of 1.5mm/$\frac{1}{16}$in for the smallest frame to 2mm/$\frac{3}{32}$ in for the largest. This allows for the movement of the pieces as the pins are hammered home. Glue the joint with white wood glue. On mouldings up to 12mm/$\frac{1}{2}$in wide use two or more 25mm/1in pins, according to the depth of moulding. On larger mouldings use fine pins to locate the joint and then tap a heavier one in place. On the largest mouldings—up to 75mm/3in—pin the joint and then drill through the corner diagonally to take a screw. If a wider frame is desired, build it up from a series of smaller interlocking pieces, pinned together.

When using a double cramp, as illustrated, position the mitred edges flush and glue and pin.

Check the completed frame for alignment before the glue has set. If necessary, the mitre can be forced open and wedged square. Disguise any inaccuracies in the fit with fine-grain wood filler.

Builders' moulding

## Mounts

Most water-colours need a mount. Cutting one and getting a clean bevelled edge takes practice.

Using stiff card or artists' tinted board, mark up the opening to take the picture. Place the card face up on a piece of scrap card on a level surface. With a very sharp trimming knife or scalpel against a steel straight-edge, cut through the board with two or three strokes, leaving a margin of about 3 mm/⅛ in at the corners. Trim these after removing the waste and finish off with glass-paper, if necessary.

Untinted mounts can either be painted or covered with any choice of material. When painting board or other material, always thin the paint and apply more than one coat. For a stippled effect, first brush the paint on generously and quickly and then dab it with part of a sawn-off broom head with medium stiff bristles.

When covering a mount with material, cut it to 25 mm/1 in more overall than the area of the mount. Before gluing the material in position, allow it to partially dry. Smooth the material down, one side at a time, as illustrated. Cut out the centre, leaving a sufficient overlap, and finally turn the material under, avoiding building up glue along the bevel. If the material is to be painted, use thinned emulsion. Work carefully to ensure full coverage.

## The profile

The profile can be built up using either proprietary picture mouldings or builders' mouldings. With the former, assemble the individual mouldings as separate frames and combine. Assemble builders' mouldings—such as cornices and door panel mouldings—by first making a basic flat frame and then gluing and pinning the moulding strips individually to it.

The moulding can be given a wood finish, painted, or covered with material, according to choice. For a wood finish, fill pinholes with fine-grain filler, stain the surfaces and finish with beeswax or polyurethane.

The colouring of commercial mouldings can be altered by rubbing them down with wire wool and brushing on an emulsion base. The brassy look of a gilded edge can be toned down with spirit and wood stain.

Builders' mouldings can be prepared for painting with white emulsion or, preferably, gesso—a mixture of size and whitening. Brush on one coat, leave to dry and then rub down with glass-paper. Apply two or three more coats and rub down—or use the broom head for a stippled effect, if desired. Colour with emulsion.

When using material to cover a curved section, cover the various pieces separately before assembly.

Follow the illustrations above for final assembly.

*See also Tips on*
Marking up 253, 520
Adhesives 81, 352
Fixing 245

# Chess and draughts

Shiny smooth metal is both pleasant to the touch and pleasing to the eye and therefore ideal for chess and draughts pieces. These chessmen, with their unusual modernistic shape, are made from sections of high-grade copper and aluminium alloy tubes.

Aluminium is also used for the white squares on the board, acrylic for the black. The draughts are simply copper sealing rings filled with polyester resin.

Because of the precision involved in this project, it is essential to work in metric measurements throughout. Consult the supplier about pipe sizes.

### Board materials

**Base:** One 351 mm square of blockboard, 12 mm thick. Four strips of 351 mm long hardwood lipping, 10 mm by 12 mm. Two 354 mm square hardwood veneers.

**Squares:** Four strips of 320 mm by 40 mm aluminium alloy and four of 320 mm by 40 mm black acrylic. All 2.5 mm thick.

### Construction

Square up the edges of the blockboard to take the lipping. Mitre the lipping and glue, cramping it until dry. Plane the edges of the lipping so that it is flush with the top and bottom of the blockboard. Glue and cramp the slightly oversized veneers to the surfaces. Trim and plane the excess veneer to size. Finish with polyurethane varnish.

Tape the two sets of strips together and finish off the edges with a file and wet-and-dry paper. Cut out 40 mm squares with a hacksaw and finish the sawn edges in the same way. Polish the aluminium with a damp cloth and scouring powder and the acrylic with an acrylic polish. Mark up, leaving a 5 mm gap around the edge and a 3 mm gap between each square. Glue in position with epoxy resin.

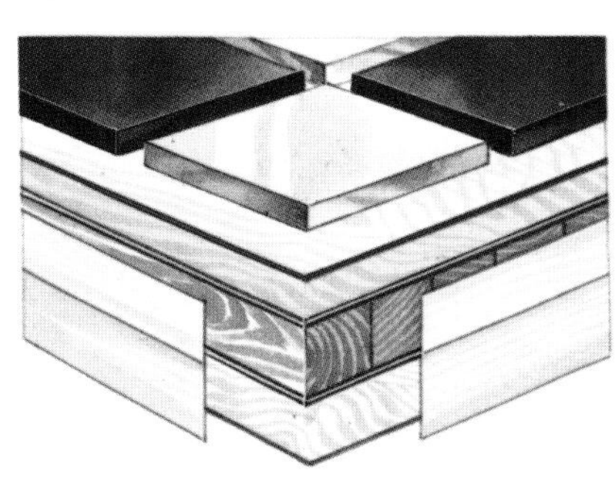

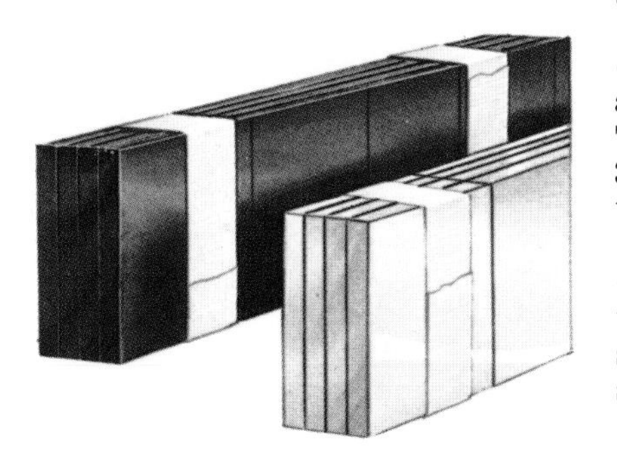

*See also Tips on*
Marking up 520
Cutting 353, 594
Finishing 520

### Draughtsmen

Each piece is made from a 35 mm/1⅜ in diameter copper sealing ring, the bore of which is built up with polyester gel coat resin, hardener and pigment.

For a good finish, fit the rings tightly along a length of timber and polish them against a buffing wheel. Complete by washing them in hot water and detergent.

Thoroughly clean and polish two pieces of glass, using a non-silicone wax. Lay the rings on one piece. Mix the polyester resin and pigment and add the hardener. Pour the mixture into the rings, taking care to stop when they are one-third full to avoid any possibility of the resin warping. Leave the resin to harden and then fill up another third. Free the rings from the glass by tapping them with a piece of softwood.

Paint the sides of the rings with a PVA releasing agent and replace on the glass. Pour in the final layer of resin until it stands just proud of the rim of each ring. Place the second piece of glass on top of the rings to spread the resin and so give an even finish. Leave until hard. Free the rings from the glass in the same way.

Scrape off any surplus resin and wipe clean with a damp cloth. Finish with a metal polish.

### Chessmen

Cut and shape the chessmen from 300 mm lengths of copper and aluminium alloy tubes. Make sure that both metals are of a bendable grade. Three diameter sizes are required of each type—16 mm/⅝ in, 22 mm/¾ in and 28 mm/1 in.

Polish with emery cloth and wet-and-dry paper.

Mark out the positions for the decorative grooves and the overall heights of the pieces. The positions for the two grooves, measuring from the bottom up, are 3 mm and 19 mm on the rook, bishop and knight. The pawns are 16 mm/⅝ in diameter tubes and require no additional cutting or shaping. Their proportionate height is 31 mm with the two grooves positioned at 3 mm and 17 mm.

Make the grooves with a pipe cutter. Experiment then cut out the pieces with the cutter or hacksaw. File the ends smooth and square, and finish with fine wet-and-dry paper.

Mark the setting with a paint spot on the adjustment screw thread and tape the rollers.

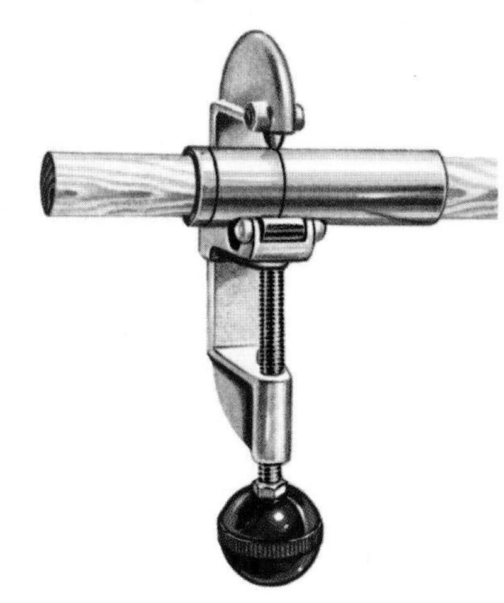

**Rook:** Cut from 22 mm/¾ in diameter tubes. Height 38 mm. Mark four notches with dividers and file.

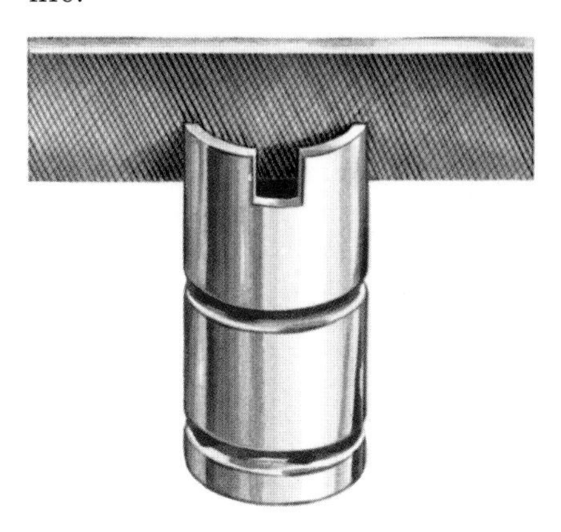

**Bishop:** Cut from 22 mm/¾ in diameter tubes. Height 38 mm. Set each piece at 55° against a scrap block. Size a block to hold a scriber at the desired height and mark out the slot. Cut with a hacksaw and file.

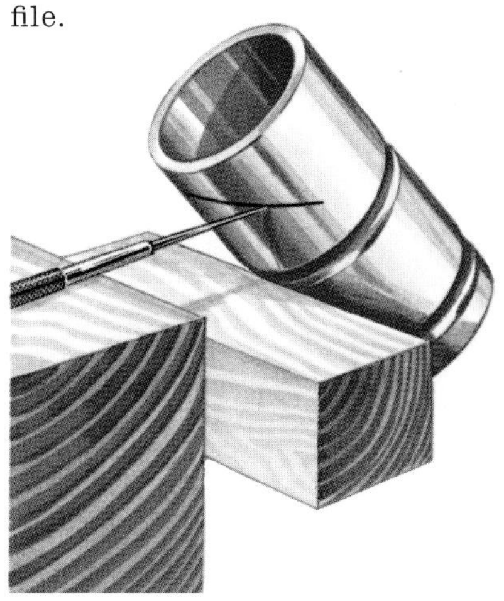

**Knight:** Cut from 22mm/⅞in diameter tubes. Height 59mm—before bending; 42mm—finished. Mark out four equidistant verticals with dividers. Saw down to 2mm above the top groove. File out two of the four strips with a fine needle file. Using a pair of flat-nose pliers, bend as illustrated to form the horse's head. If necessary, trim off the ends of the strips with a hacksaw for final positioning.

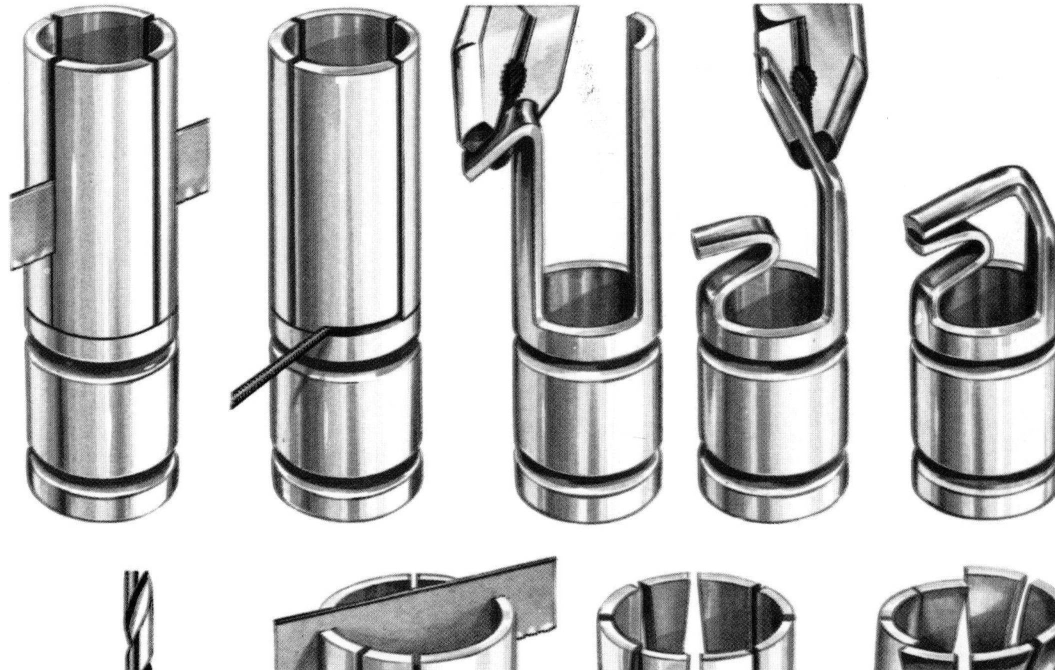

**Queen:** Cut from 28mm/1in diameter tubes. Height 50mm. Upper groove 25mm from the base. Mark a line around circumference 8mm from the top groove. Mark the positions for ten equidistant holes with dividers. Using the appropriate bit, drill out the holes. Cut vertically down to the centre of each hole with a hacksaw and shape each slot with a flat file as illustrated. Using a pair of flat-nose pliers, bend the full length of each section inwards until all the top edges touch. Complete the shaping by bending the upper halves of each section upwards.

**King:** Cut from 28mm/1in diameter tubes. Height 74mm—before bending; 70mm—finished. Upper groove 25mm from the base. Mark out four equidistant verticals with dividers. Saw down to 18mm above the upper groove. File out two of the four strips with a small needle file. Mark up the shape of the crown as illustrated; the suggested width of the upright is 9mm, with a 6mm deep crosspiece set 4mm from the top. With a hacksaw and round needle file, remove the waste. To make the operation easier, wedge each piece on to the end of an appropriate-sized dowelling rod, held in a vice. Bend the two crosses together, using a pair of flat-nose pliers, and tap them into the final position with a soft-faced hammer.

# Glove puppets

Harder-wearing than conventional papier mâché puppets, this exciting cast of characters for a traditional Punch and Judy puppet show will appeal to children of all ages. The basic techniques involved in moulding and decorating the fibreglass heads of the various glove puppets are relatively simple and can be used to make any character desired.

To achieve the finish of the glove puppets illustrated requires careful working with clay and handling of paint. Once mastered, the method of forming the fibreglass heads is simple.

**Modelling the clay**

Start by mounting a cardboard tube, of about 37 mm/1½ in diameter, in some plasticine on a wooden board. Using modellers' clay, form a ball approximately the size of the head and push it on to the top of the tube.

With a spatula, mould the outline of the face, working the clay about 37 mm/1½ in down the tube for the neck. Add the eyelids, eyebrows and ears separately.

Finish off the clay surface by covering it with an even layer of soft soap, using a brush or the fingers. Finally, carefully insert thin metal strips behind the ears in a line from one side of the neck to the other to form a solid wall, thus making it possible to separate the plaster moulds.

**Making the plaster moulds**

Because plaster of Paris sets fairly quickly, it is important to work rapidly when building up the moulds. First fix a clay collar around the base of the neck to control the build up of plaster. Mix the plaster with water to the consistency of custard, making sure that it is runny enough to cover more detailed areas.

Flick the plaster on to the clay until it is completely covered, taking care not to create any air bubbles. As the plaster hardens, start applying it in lumps and continue until a 25 mm/1 in thick layer has been built up. Then leave the plaster to dry. Once dry, separate the moulds from the clay, wash them in cold water and leave to dry. Seal with shellac.

**Starting the fibreglass head**

First coat the two plaster moulds with a releasing agent, using two layers of non-silicone wax and one layer of PVA adhesive for a smoother finish. Leave to dry for about thirty minutes.

When handling the fibreglass matting, wear rubber gloves, taped at the wrists, and work in a well-ventilated room. Use a layer of thin fibreglass tissue to fill the finer details on the moulds and two layers of thicker matting to complete the head.

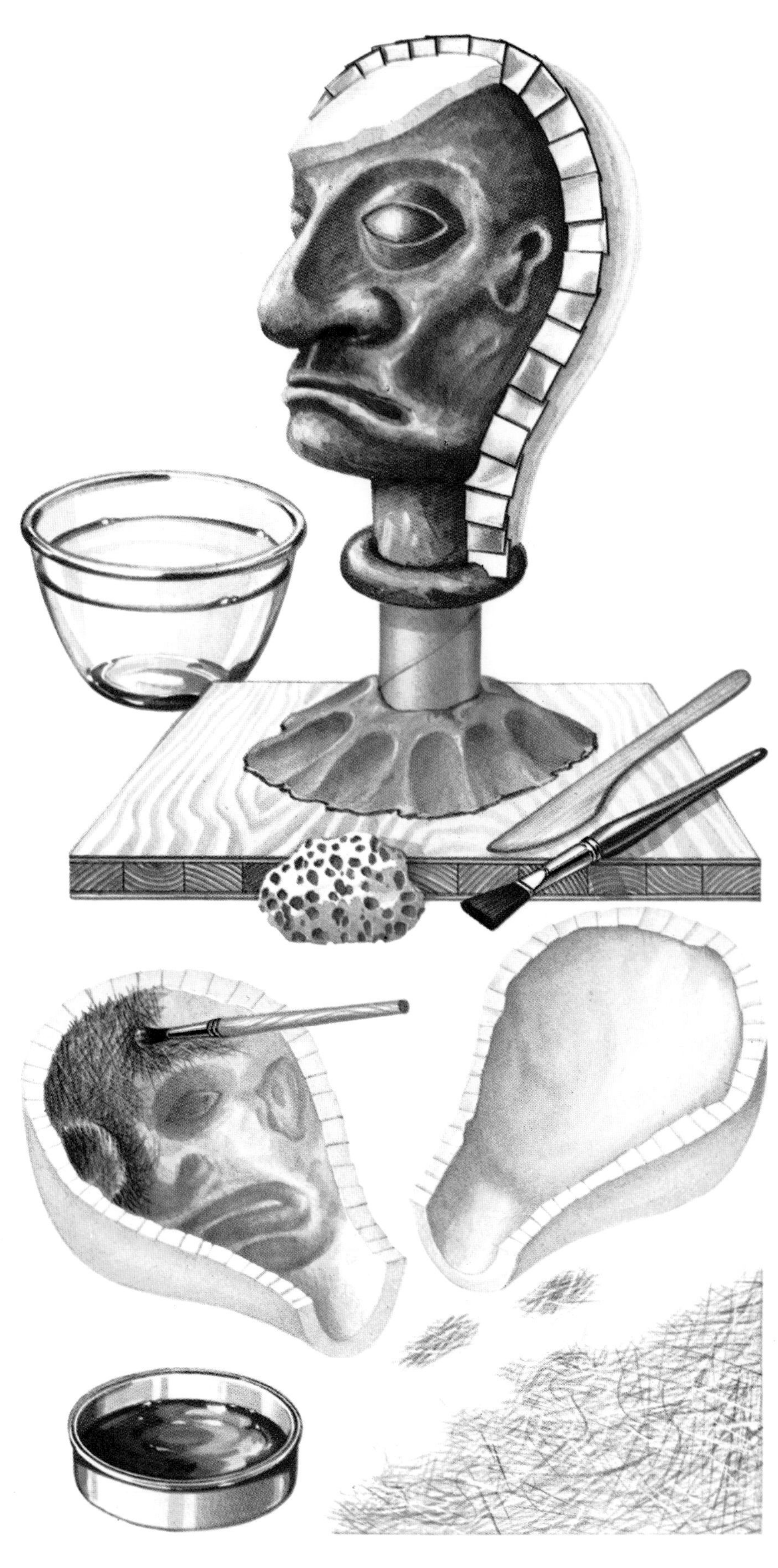

*See also Tip on* Adhesives 81

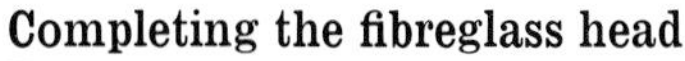

**Completing the fibreglass head**
Prepare the fibreglass by cutting it into suitably sized pieces. Mix a gel coat resin and add hardener.

Cover both moulds with the tissue, overlapping the various pieces. Press it in place with a stiff brush coated in resin, avoiding any air bubbles. Once covered, immediately apply a second coat of resin mixture and then the first layer of thick matting, again dabbing it in place with the resin mixture. Repeat the procedure for the final layer of matting. Leave to dry thoroughly.

Remove the fibreglass heads from the moulds, cleaning off any traces of the wax and PVA adhesive. Join the two halves with strips of matting, brushed in place with the resin mixture. Make sure that the bond between them is strong; leave to dry. Fill any blemishes with polyester filler and finish off with slightly dampened wet-and-dry paper.

**Painting and finishes**
To make painting easier, attach the completed fibreglass head to the cardboard tube supported on the wooden block. First undercoat the heads with white emulsion or poster paint. Then paint the features as desired with poster or with emulsion paint, and seal with a strong clear varnish. Finally add hair as required, gluing in place with contact adhesive.

**Making the glove body**
First size a piece of fabric so that it covers the full length of the arm, from the elbow to the outstretched hand, and is approximately twice the width of the thickest part of the arm. Lay the right or left hand on the fabric in the position required to manipulate the puppet. The thumb and the third and fourth fingers control the arms, and the index and second fingers the head. Mark up the positions on the fabric, allowing for the width of the cardboard tube—approximately 37 mm/1½ in. Cut out the body shape and use it as a template for the back piece. Combine the two pieces by sewing up the sides and shoulders.

Position the cardboard tube in the head and neck, mark up to the required size, remove and cut to fit. Replace and fix permanently.

Make the hands from wood or felt and glue or sew them to the arm openings. Make the feet from wood, and glue and pin them to lengths of dowel for the legs. Glue strips of leather to the top of the dowels and stitch the strips to the glove below a skirt or flap of a jacket.

Sew up a 12 mm/½ in seam at the bottom of the glove and pass a wire through to keep the bottom open. Attach a wire hook to the back edge, so that the puppet can be hung upside down.

# Modular toy kit

Based on the principle of interchangeability of parts—the parts used for the lorry cab double as the cab for the engine and the catwalk on the tanker serves as the cockpit of the racing car, for example—the carefully crafted pieces illustrated below can be built up into a surprising number of fascinating and realistic toys. Only some of the possibilities are shown. Once the basic construction of the individual components has been completed, the toy and its design is a matter of choice. This gives a child scope for creative construction of his or her own—making the toy educational as well as a source of amusement.

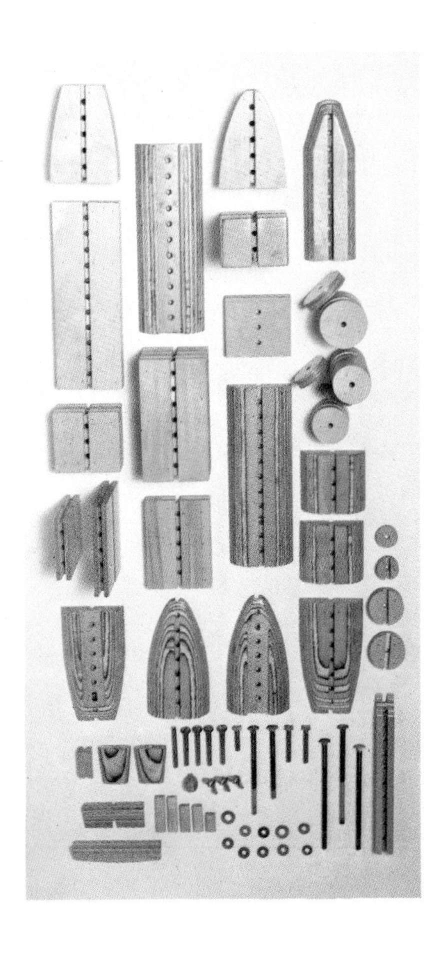

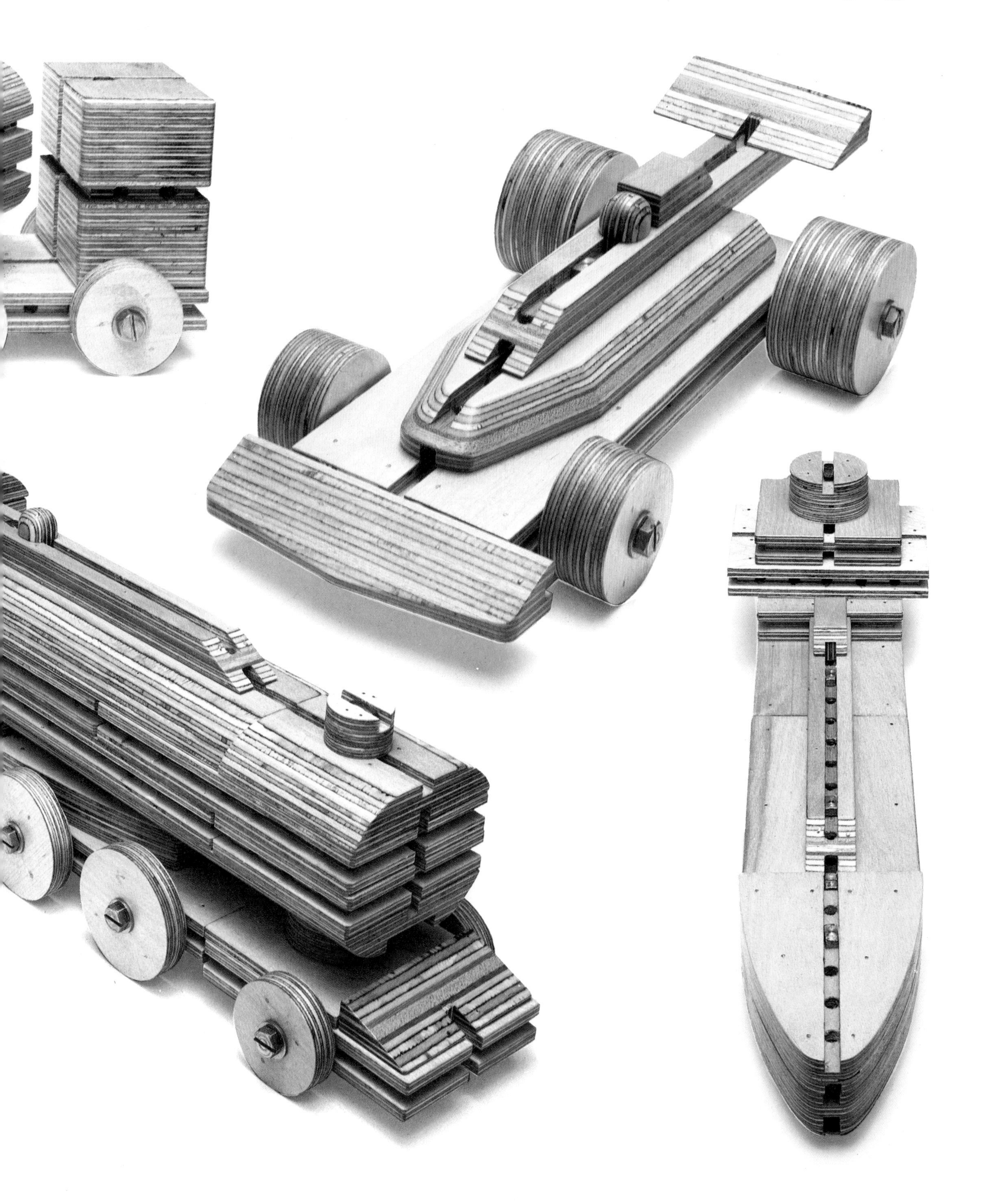

The twenty-four components (A to X) of this modular toy are cut from one 6mm thick sheet of 1.83m by 1.22m plywood. Each component is illustrated to scale in perspective, end and side views; two or more side views of one perspective represent the additional sizes needed of the component concerned. Where more than one of a particular component is required, the component is referred to by its letter, followed by the amount, thus: C (Four). Components are further defined by the 6mm slots (i) or 30mm slots (ii) cut along the top face—thus E (Two i).

**Cutting, drilling and finishing**

Components A to J have the same overall width of 86mm and are made from three layers of ply. Two drilled flats are also required, two 80mm by 86mm (X).

Having marked up each piece, cut them out and plane down the line, working from each end towards the centre. Glue and pin, avoiding the outer edges of the curved components. When shaping the curved components, bolt them together to ensure a uniform curve and smooth with a rasp plane and glasspaper.

Through vertical holes, 6mm in diameter, with centres 20mm apart, take the bolts on all components—except M, O, P and V. These four components are slotted into place. Components A to D and K also have equally spaced side holes, each 5.5mm in diameter and 32mm deep. Make a template and use a drill stand to simplify drilling. Finish with two coats of varnish.

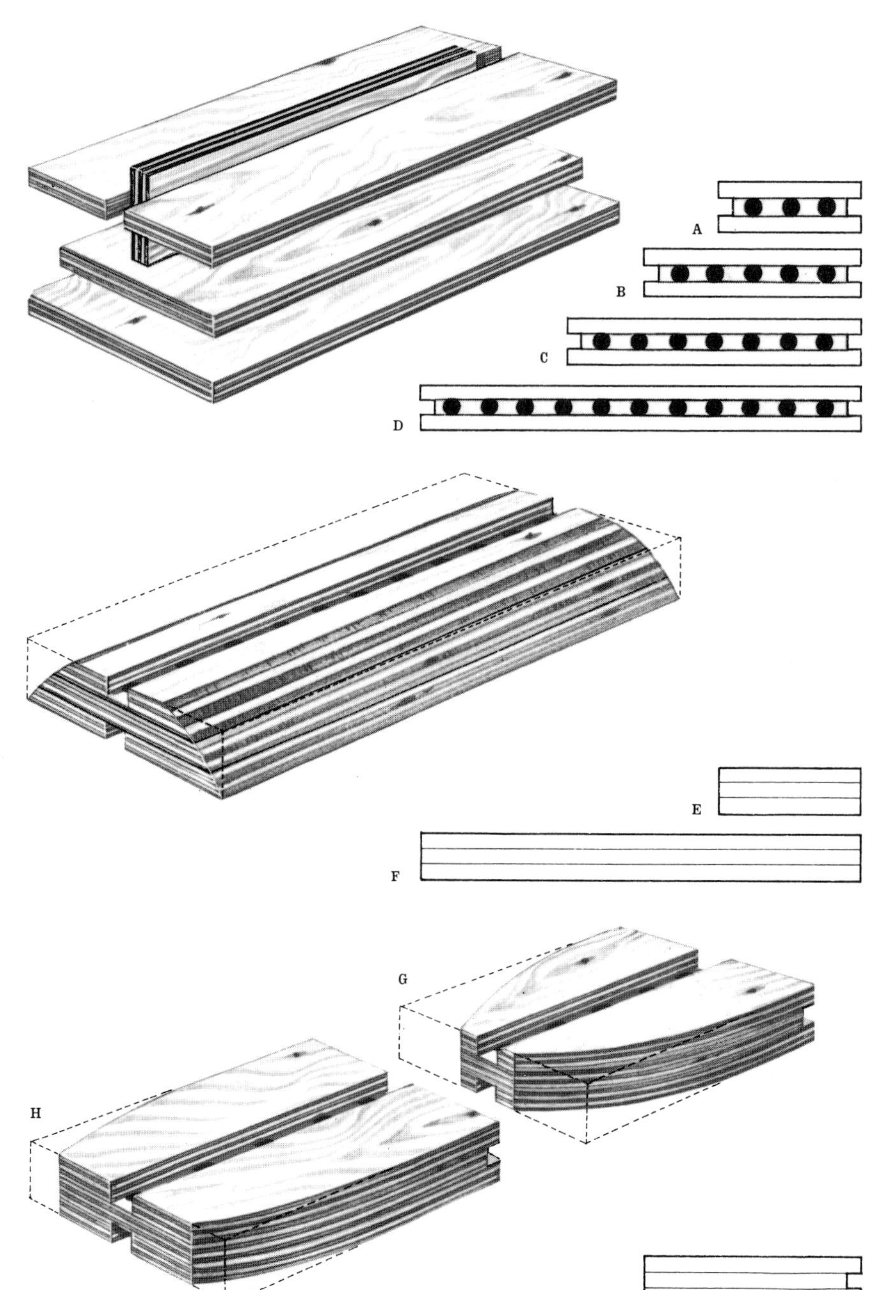


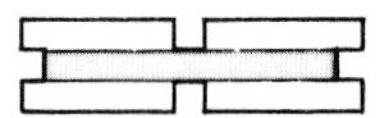

A (Four): Overall length 80mm
B (Two): Overall length 120mm
C (Four): Overall length 160mm
D: Overall length 240mm
The middle layer is 74mm wide and 12mm shorter than the overall length. The outer layers consist of two pieces each 40mm wide. Draw a centre line on each side of the middle layer, centre a spacer of 6mm ply on the line, and glue the outer pieces alongside it. Cut, drill and finish as above.

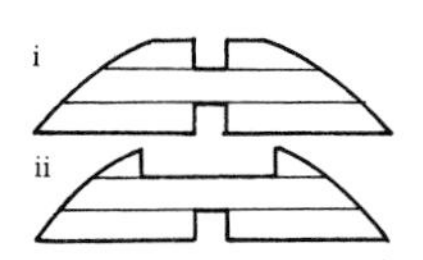


E (Two i): Length 80mm
F (i and ii): Length 240mm
Cut the three layers so that all edges are flush. Mark up the shape of the curve for Ei and Fi at each end, leaving a 20mm flat surface either side of the centre line on the top face. Use this shape to mark up the ends for Fii. Cut, drill and finish as described above.

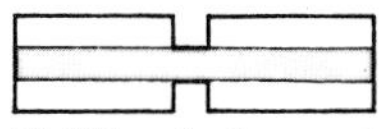

G (Two): Length 120mm
H (Two): Length 120mm
The middle layer of each component is 114mm long to allow for a 6mm slot at the squared end. To ensure that both sets of curved pieces are uniform in shape, make a template for each set. G is shaped to a rounded point and H has a blunt end 50mm wide. Bolt together in pairs and smooth down with a rasp plane and glasspaper.

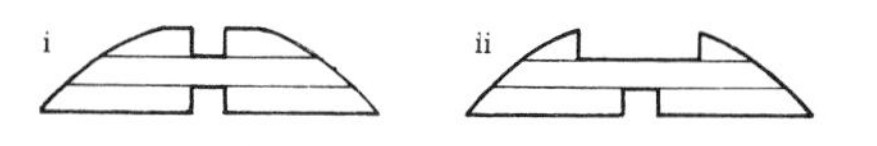


I (i and ii): Length 160 mm
J (i and ii): Length 160 mm
Size the three layers so that all edges are flush. Use the template from G to shape one end of J, and the template from H to shape one end of I. Bolt together in pairs and smooth down as before. Use the curved shape from Fi and ii to mark up the squared ends and smooth down, aligning F with I and J.

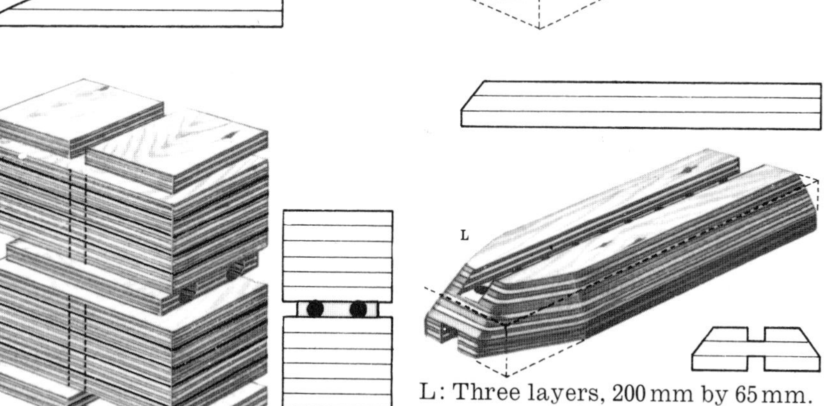


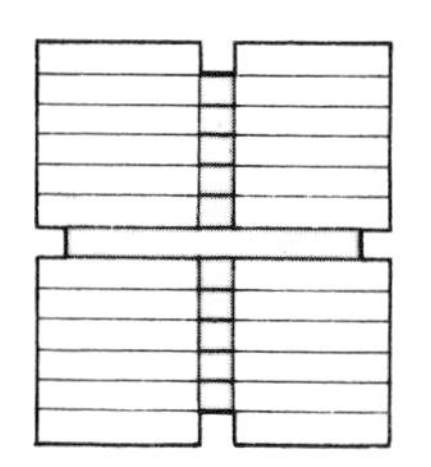

K: Two blocks, each five layers thick, 86 mm by 60 mm, sandwiching a middle layer, 80 mm by 54 mm, and capped top and bottom by four pieces, 38 mm by 40 mm. Chisel down dotted lines either side to complete 6 mm slots.

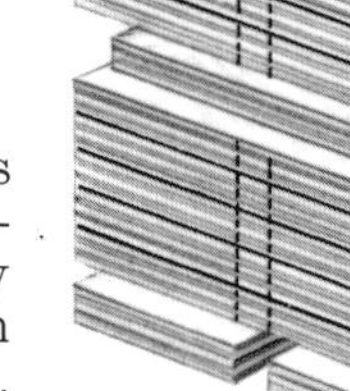

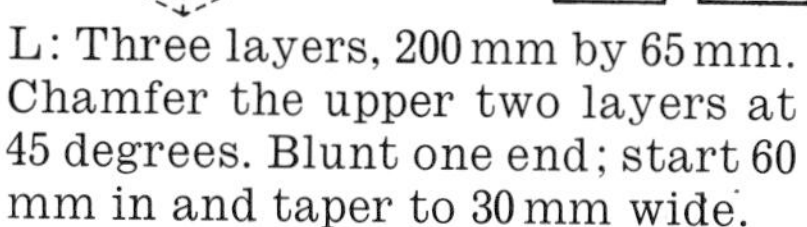

L: Three layers, 200 mm by 65 mm. Chamfer the upper two layers at 45 degrees. Blunt one end; start 60 mm in and taper to 30 mm wide.

All bolts 6 mm diameter coach bolts.
Ten 50 mm long bolts with heads slotted with a hacksaw for the axles. All other bolts cut to size with heads filed to a T-shape.
One 140 mm, 132 mm, 102 mm, 96 mm and 86 mm long.
One 55 mm long sawn off head.
Two 108 mm and 55 mm long.
Three 126 mm long.
Five 48 mm long.
Six 66 mm long.
Six hexagonal nuts.
Six wing nuts.
Twenty washers.

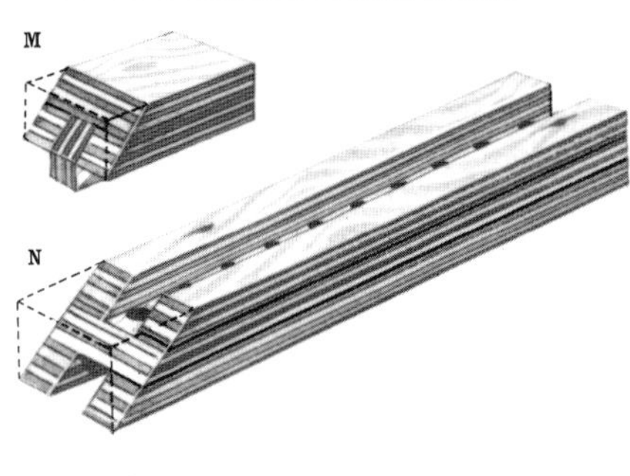


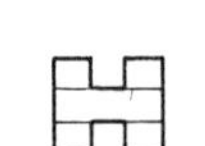

M: Two layers, 45 mm by 20 mm, with 45 mm by 12 mm tongue. Bevel 10 mm in.
N: Three layers, 220 mm by 24 mm. Bevel 24 mm in from one end.

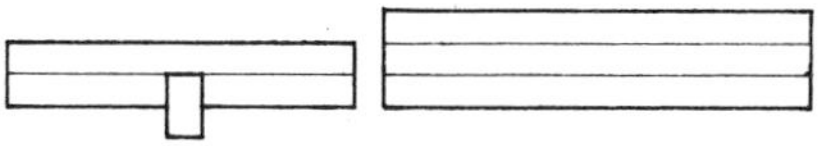

O: Two layers, 82 mm by 36 mm, with 36 mm × 12 mm tongue: bevel.
P: Three layers, middle 26 mm by 120 mm for tongue, 86 mm by 12 mm; outer 32 mm by 120 mm. Bevel and shape.

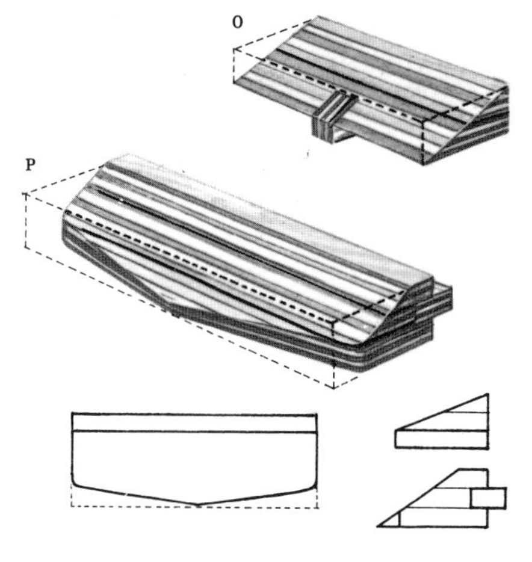


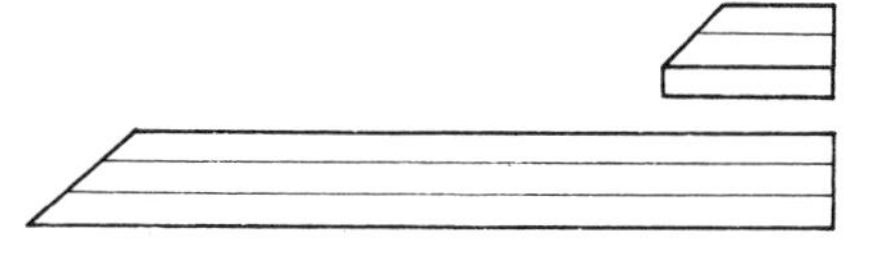

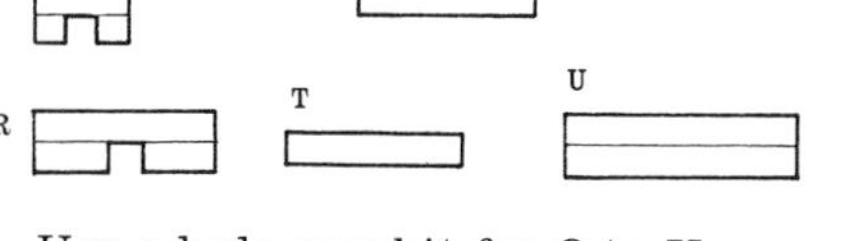


Use a hole saw bit for Q to U.
Q: Three layers, slot, 32 mm bit.
R (Two): Two layers, one slot, 51 mm bit.
S (Nine): Two layers, 51 mm bit.
T (Five): One layer, 51 mm bit.
U (Six): Two layers, 63 mm bit.
V: Three layers, middle 22 mm by 22 mm, outer 16 mm by 22 mm.

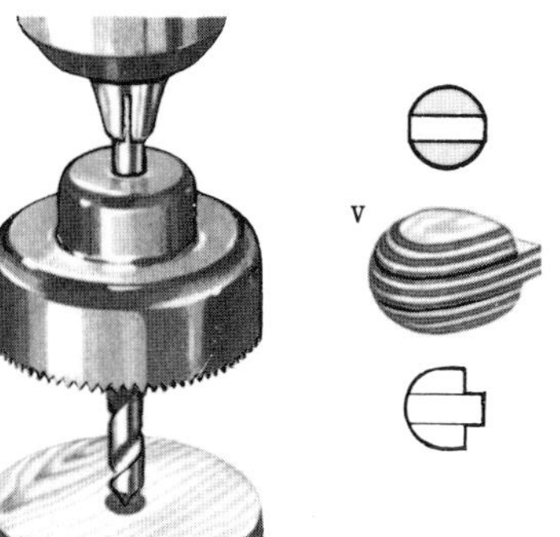

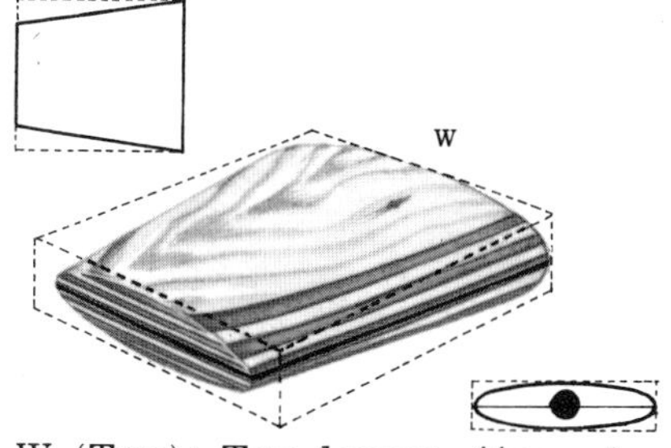


W (Two): Two layers, 44 mm by 51 mm, shape one end to 32 mm; drill one 5.5 mm centre hole to take a bolt with the head sawn off.

*See also Tips on*
Marking up 520
Smoothing 98, 171, 175, 203, 488
Finishing 77, 536

**P**
**Project**

The components for each toy are referred to by their key letter and number required, thus:
Truck: A (Four). Bolts: Two 108mm. Sixteen washers.

**Racing car**
D. L. M. N. O. P. S (Four). U (Six). V. Bolts: Two 55mm. Four 50mm. Eight washers. Two wing nuts.

**Truck**
A (Four). B. C (Three). D. Ei (Two). Fi. Fii. K. N. S (Nine). T (Five). Bolts: One 126mm and 96mm. Two 108mm. Eight 50mm. Sixteen washers. Five wing nuts.

**Train**
A (Four). B. C (Four). D. Ei (Two). Fi. Fii. G. K. N. O. Q. S (Five). T. U (Six). V. X (Two). Bolts: One 140 mm, and 132mm. Three 126mm. Ten 50mm. Twenty washers. Five wing nuts.

**Ship**
A (Two). B. C (Two). Fii. G (Two). H (Two). Ii. Ji. M. N. R. T. Bolts: One 102mm, five 48mm. Six hexagonal nuts.

**Submarine**
A (Two). C (Three). Ei (Two). Fi. Fii. G (Two). H (Two). Ii. Iii. Ji. Jii. W (Two). Bolts: One 86mm. Six 66mm. One 55mm headless. Seven hexagonal nuts.

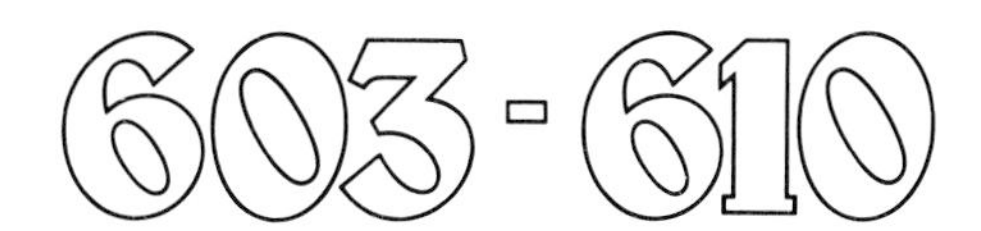

## 603 Laying foundations for a wall in clay

When planning to build a garden wall, always check the type of soil in the garden before starting work. If the soil is clay, a long spell of dry weather will inevitably cause the clay to shrink and the wall to crack or even collapse. The only satisfactory solution is to lay the foundation on miniature concrete "piles"—the system used to support buildings where there is a risk of soil movement.

Dig the trench for the foundation, and then use a hand auger to bore holes into the sub-soil to a depth of 1 m/3 ft, spacing the holes at about 2.5 m/8 ft intervals. Make sure that the diameter of the auger's bore is at least equal to the width of the foundation being laid across the piles.

As ordinary cement will be attacked by the sulphates in the clay, thus weakening the foundation, use a sulphate-resistant cement to fill the holes and for the foundation concrete. When laying this, insert two 12 mm/½ in diameter mild-steel reinforcing rods along the length of the foundation. Cover the rods with a minimum thickness of 38 mm/1½ in of concrete or surface rusting may occur.

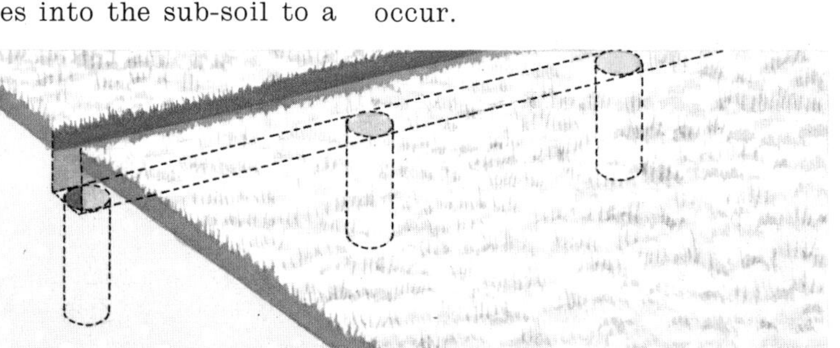

## 607 Locating a blown fuse quickly

Labelling the fuses in a fuse box will save considerable time in identifying a fuse that has failed. The simplest way to do this is to turn on all the lights and power points in the house. Then switch off the electricity, remove a fuse, and then switch the electricity back on. Note which lights are out of action when a fuse has been removed and check individual points by plugging in table lights. Label each fuse accordingly. Replace the fuse and repeat the procedure with another fuse.

Alternatively, draw a diagram of the fuse circuits, noting which circuit each fuse controls. Stick the diagram on the inside cover of the fuse box, or on a wall nearby.

In addition, keep a torch and a selection of fuse wire handy by the box.

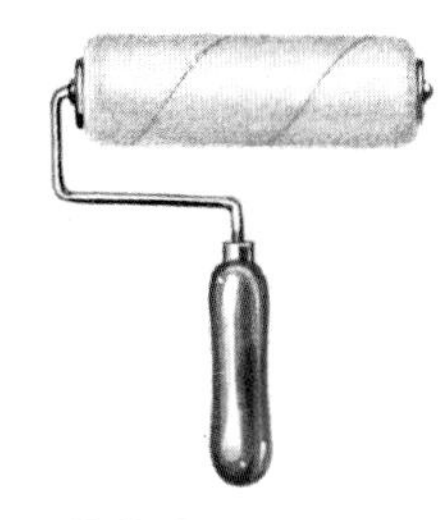

## 609 Paint roller

Although paint rollers use more paint than a brush, they cover large areas more quickly and efficiently. Use a foam-rubber or a mohair sleeve when working with gloss paint; for all other paints, use a felt or lamb's-wool sleeve.

## 604 Using a paint roller from a ladder

The biggest problem when using a paint roller from a ladder is where to stand the paint tray. To avoid having to climb up and down the ladder, empty the paint into a clean bucket and stand a short length of board on it. Hang the bucket from an "S" hook attached to a rung of the ladder. Make sure that the bucket is big enough to take the full width of the roller and use the board to roll out the excess paint.

Never hold the paint tray; this will leave you without a hand free to steady yourself.

## 605 Storing an assortment of screws conveniently

A convenient way of keeping an assortment of screws, nails and hooks ready to hand is to keep them in a scrap of corrugated paper. This can save time searching for the odd fitting for a minor repair job.

## 606 Working safely with bleaches

Bleaches burn, so always wear gloves and old clothes when using them. If any splashes do get on the skin, wash them off immediately with cold water. Because bleaches also destroy the bristles of natural fibre brushes, always use a nylon-fibre brush to apply them.

## 608 Measuring a pipe's circumference

It is easier—and far more accurate—when measuring the circumference of a pipe to overlap the tape and take the measurement from a given point. For instance if the tape is overlapped by 50 mm/2 in, deducting the 50 mm will give the actual circumference of the pipe.

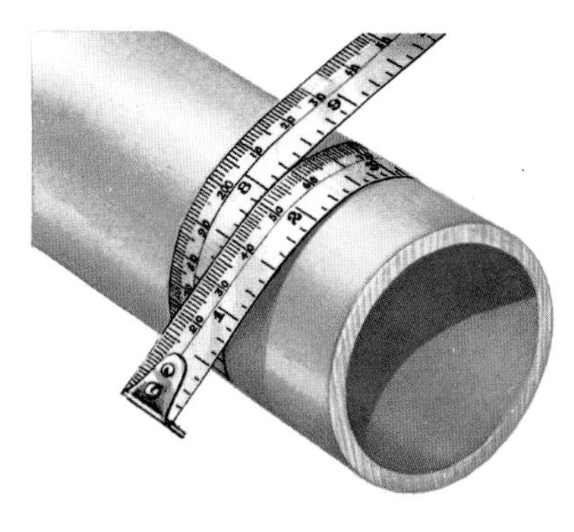

## 610 Nailing

Always hold a nail as near the head as possible when starting to hammer it home. This lessens the chance of striking the fingers if the hammer slips.

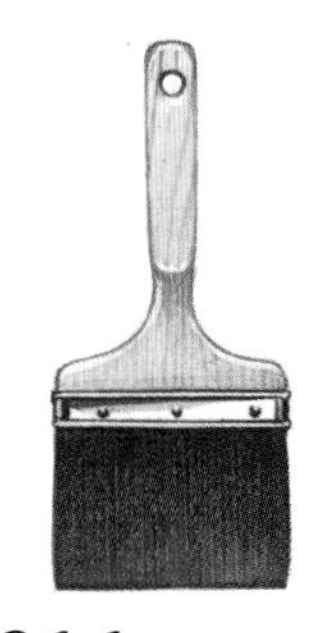

## 611
**Pasting brush**

Use the 150mm/6in brush especially made for the job when applying adhesive to wallpaper. Always wash the brush in clean warm water after use, making sure that all traces of paste have been removed.

## 612
**Electric cable and damp**

Never fit electric cables in a position where they can be attacked by wet or damp.

## 613 Estimating the amount of wallpaper needed

To estimate the amount of wallpaper needed to paper a room, measure the height of the room, add on an allowance for trimming, and calculate how many lengths can be cut from one roll; the usual length of a roll is 10m/33ft.

Multiply the width of the paper, usually 520mm/20½in, by the number of lengths that can be cut from one roll. Ignoring doors and windows, unless they are extremely large, measure the perimeter of the room, divide this figure by the first figure to calculate the number of rolls required. Remember that fractions must be made up to the next whole number.

If the room has different ceiling heights, such as a stairwell, measure those areas with the same height and add the totals together.

## 614 Preparing paper for pasting

As most modern wallpapers are rolled with the pattern on the outside, problems can arise when pasting the paper. This is because, when the paper is laid on a table for pasting, the ends roll back into the length, which can result in paste getting on to the surface of the pattern.

Deal with this by planning the job in advance, so that all the lengths of paper required are rough cut to size and left lying on the pasting table overnight, with the patterned side downwards. Hold the ends down by loosely looping a length of string round the pasting table legs and over the combined lengths of paper.

Next day, the paper will no longer curl, making it much simpler to paste individual lengths.

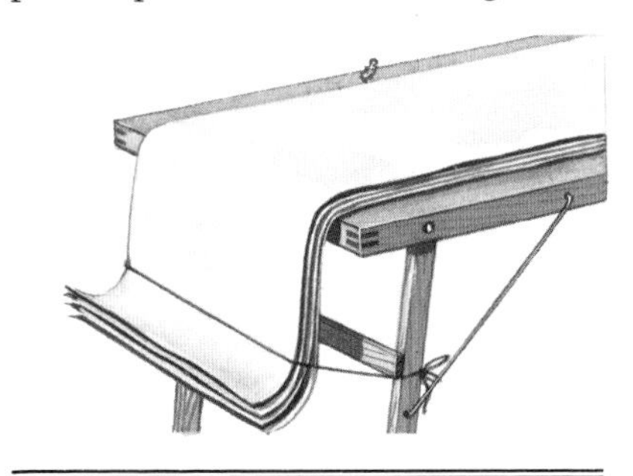

## 615 Pasting sheets of wallpaper

The correct way to paste wallpaper is to work from the centre of the paper outwards. Align the top of the length of paper to be pasted with one end of the pasting table, allowing one side of the paper to overhang the back edge of the table. Spread paste down the centre of the paper and then, working outwards from the centre, along the back edge. Reposition the paper so that there is a slight overhang at the front of the table and again brush from the centre. Always work facing the light to make it easier to check for unpasted patches.

## 616 Maintaining asphalt paths and driveways

Coat an asphalt surface every four years with a proprietary sealer to improve the surface. Weed the asphalt, if necessary, and then pour the sealer over the asphalt directly from the can, spreading it with an old stiff-bristled broom. The process will also fill any small cracks that may have appeared in the surface.

## 617 Folding pasted ceiling paper

When pasting long lengths of ceiling paper, paste the first length and then fold the first 60cm/2ft in half, pasted sides together. Then fold the next two feet of paper concertina-fashion, doubling the pasted paper over on to itself. Make a further concertina fold. Then move the folded paper to one end of the pasting table. Paste the remainder and, if necessary, make further folds. Fold the last 60cm/2ft over on itself.

When papering, brush this 60cm/2ft length into place first. Then gradually unfold and brush the concertina of paper into place.

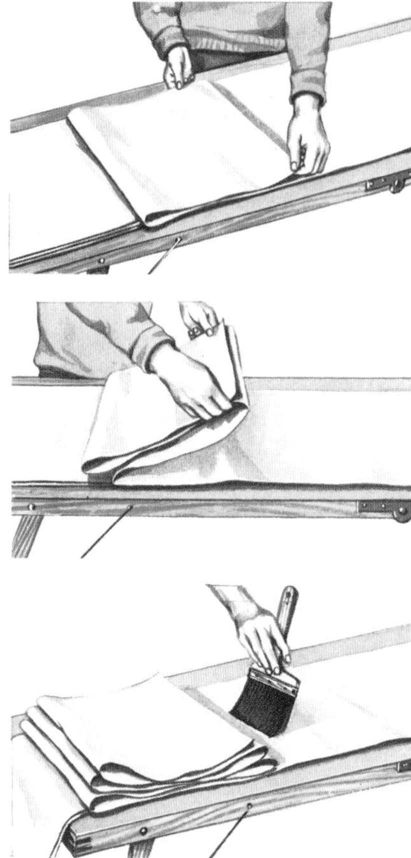

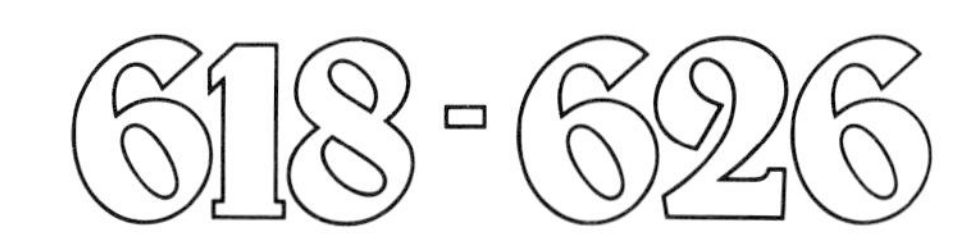

## 618 Folding sheets of pasted wallpaper

If a sheet of wallpaper is too long for a pasting table, paste about a third of the sheet first. Then fold this in two with the pasted sides together, making sure that the edges of the folded paper are aligned with each other. Move the folded paper to the end of the table and paste the remainder of the length. Fold this to within 75mm/3in of the piece that has been previously folded.

To carry the paper to the wall, rest it over an arm, making sure that the top end of the paper faces downwards. Paste this end against the wall first.

## 619 Making paint and papering estimates

When painting and papering a room for the first time, make a note of the quantities used. Next time the room has to be redecorated there will be no need to repeat the laborious task of estimating the quantities.

## 620 Fixing the vertical for wallpapering

When wallpapering a room, a vertical should be established with a plumb line every time a corner is turned. Start with the wall containing the main window. Use a plumb line to check whether the frame of the window is vertical or not. If it is, then the first length of wallpaper should be aligned exactly with it.

If, however, the frame is out of square, a guide line will be needed. Measure the width of the wallpaper, subtracting at least 12mm/½in (more if the frame is far out of square) to allow for trimming. Mark this measurement with a pencil on the wall at a point adjacent to the window frame.

Hang a plumb line from a nail near the ceiling, making sure that the line hangs over the pencil mark. Carefully mark a dotted line down the length of the plumb line. Remove the plumb line and use a straight-edge to join the dotted line up. Use this guide line to hang the first length of paper.

## 621 Planning the pasting of wallpaper

When using a cellulose-based paste on a medium or lightweight wallpaper, be sure to allow enough time for the paste to soak into the paper properly before hanging it. Aim to have a pasted piece soaking while pasting or hanging another sheet. Paste one complete length of paper first and put it to one side. Paste another length, put this to one side and hang the first length. Continue alternating between lengths in this way until the entire wall is covered.

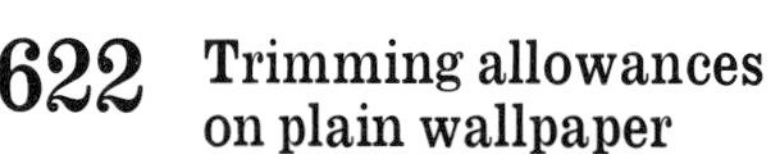

## 622 Trimming allowances on plain wallpaper

When cutting plain wallpaper, always allow an extra 50mm/2in on each length for trimming at ceiling and skirting levels.

## 623 Making pull-switches easy to find in the dark

Pull-switches in bathrooms and toilets can be made easier to find in the dark by dipping the knob of the switch in luminous paint.

## 624 Decorating the top of a garden wall

As a cheaper alternative to using expensive coping stones to decorate the top of a garden wall, use a two-tier row of old roofing tiles. Using the standard mix of mortar, lay the tiles lengthways across the brickwork and cap them with bricks laid across the full width of the wall.

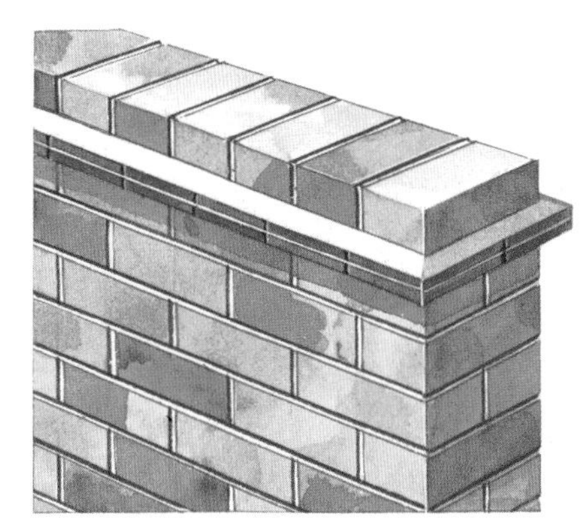

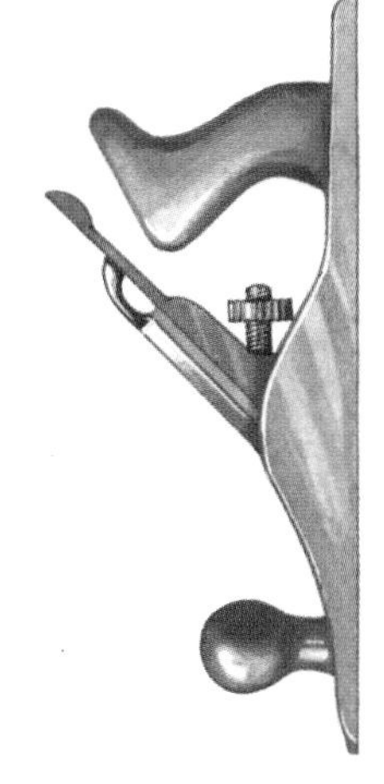

## 625 Plane

The best all-purpose plane for the handyman is a jack plane, which is especially suited for smoothing most coarse or fine wood surfaces. Always stand the plane on edge when resting it on a work bench. This reduces the chance of accidentally damaging the cutting blade.

## 626 Bending electric cable

Never bend an electric cable sharply when fitting around a corner. The radius of any bend should be at least four times the diameter of the cable, or the insulation could be damaged.

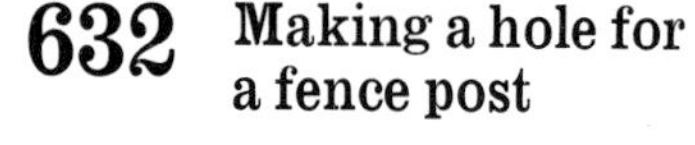

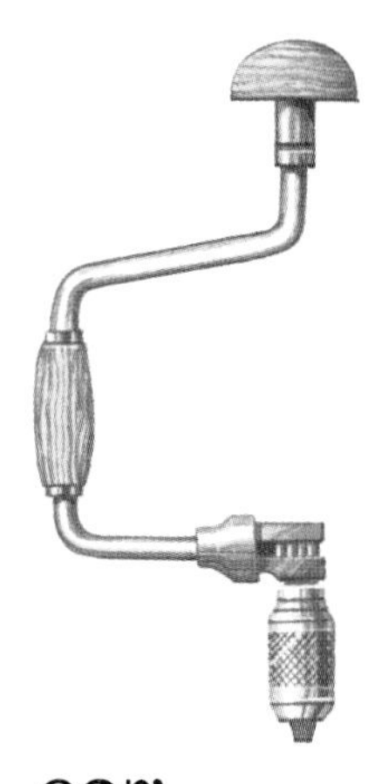

## 627
### Swingbrace drill

Use a swingbrace for drilling large holes quickly. To prevent the wood splitting as the drill head emerges, drill through the wood from one side until the tip just emerges and then complete the drilling from the other. Alternatively, fit a block to the underside of the wood and continue drilling into it.

## 628
### Polystyrene and gloss paint

Never paint polystyrene tiles or sheeting with gloss paint. This creates the risk of fire.

## 629 Repairing the corner of a concrete step

The easiest way of replacing a small corner that has broken away from a concrete step is to glue it back into position. Ask a builders' merchant to recommend a suitable adhesive. Clean out the damaged area thoroughly and then replace the damaged piece. Wedge two pieces of timber to hold the concrete in position until the adhesive has dried.

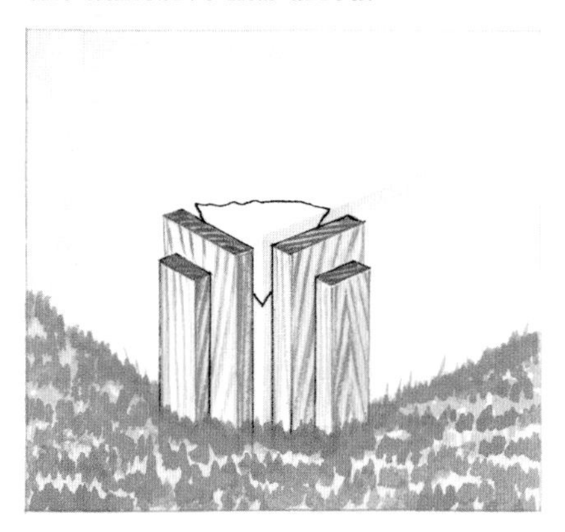

## 630 Removing hammer dents from wood

A common fault when hammering is to misdirect the blow so that the wood is dented—"bruised", as it is known in the trade. However, bruises can often be removed by ironing over the dent with a cloth dipped in boiling water. The wood swells with the moisture and rises to fill the bruise.

## 631 Avoiding dye and paint runs on a door

The easiest way of avoiding disfiguring runs and drips when painting a door is to remove the door from its hinges and paint it laying flat. Place the door across a pair of small trestles, or similar supports. Paint one side of the door and then the other.

Always follow this procedure if staining a door with wood dye, as it is important that the dye is applied to the door in one operation only. This is because rescuing splashes or drips of dye will lead to areas of the door being stained darker than others.

## 632 Making a hole for a fence post

When setting a fence post directly into soil, use a length of iron piping of 25 mm/1 in diameter to make a series of holes to a depth of about 450 mm/18 in. Hammer the pipe down into the soil to force earth into it, clearing the earth from the pipe each time by hitting the side of the pipe sharply with a hammer or pushing a strip of moulding through the pipe.

If a post is being set in concrete, however, dig the hole with a spade, making sure that it is large enough to contain sufficient concrete to hold the post securely. Start by digging out a circle of over 300 mm/12 in diameter and then dig down at an angle to the required depth. Spread a layer of concrete in the bottom of the hole. With the aid of a helper, stand the post in position, checking the vertical with a spirit level. Shovel concrete around the post, pressing the mix well down and shaping it at ground level so that rainwater will drain away from the post. Allow the concrete to dry for six hours and then fill in the remainder of the hole.

In both cases, always coat the post with preservative before fitting it.

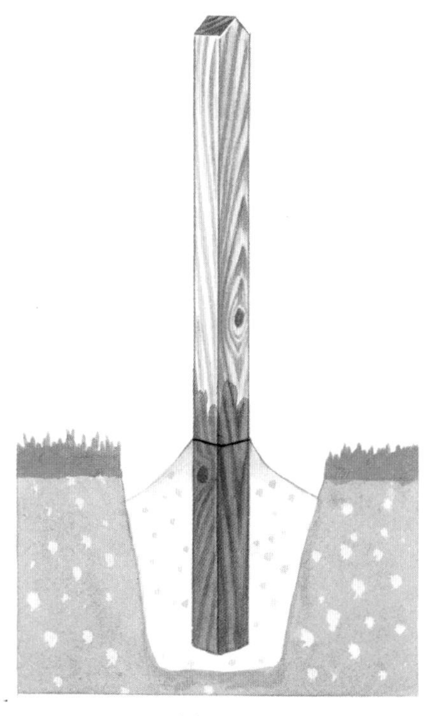

## 633 Stacking bricks to avoid damage

Always stack bricks on edge, making a retaining wall by turning the end bricks sideways on every other row. Otherwise bricks may topple from the stack and their edges may be damaged.

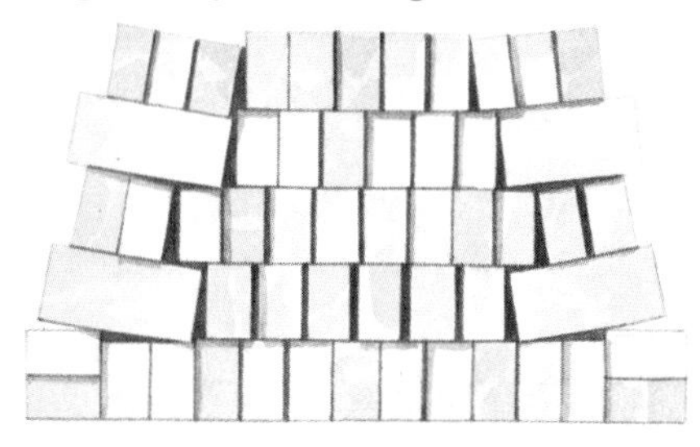

## 634 Utilizing plywood offcuts on joints

Plywood offcuts, cut into right-angled triangles, add considerable strength to a butt joint. They also make crude, but very rigid, shelf supports when used to brace two short lengths of wood. Nail and glue the ply in position against the wood.

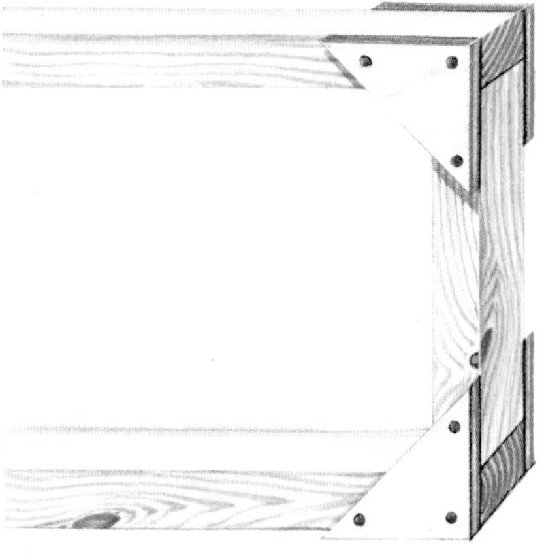

## 635 Removing stains from brickwork

Brickwork both inside and outside the house can be disfigured by white, powdery stains—known as efflorescence. The easiest way to remove them is to apply at about fifteen-minute intervals two or three brush coats of a neutralizing liquid, available from builders' merchants. Use a stiff-bristled scrubbing brush.

## 636 Sizing glass for sliding doors

When sizing glass for a sliding door, remember that the top channel is cut deeper than the lower one to allow the glass to be easily lifted in and out. Make a hardboard template to ensure that the glass will be cut to the correct height and depth. Fit the template in the tracks and run it along them to check it does not bind at any point.

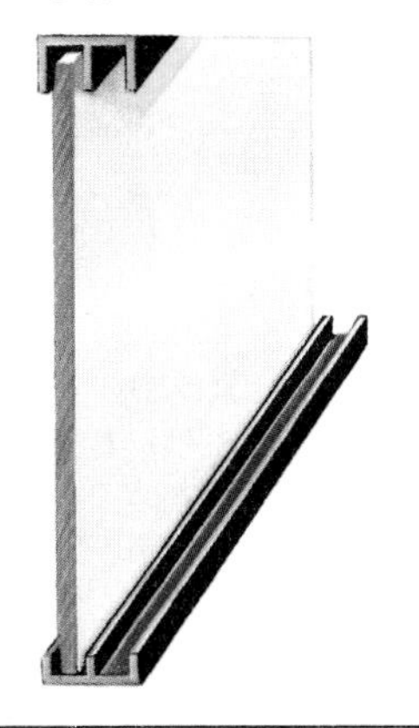

## 637 Tidying the painted edges of glazing bars

The most effective way of straightening up crooked paint lines along the edges of newly painted glazing bars—which can happen even if a plastic or metal shield is used—is to use a trimming knife blade fitted to a holder. With a corner of the blade cut the line marking the edge of the paint. Then go along this line working the blade sideways and outwards. Never cut straight up and down, or the blade will catch and leave a ragged edge.

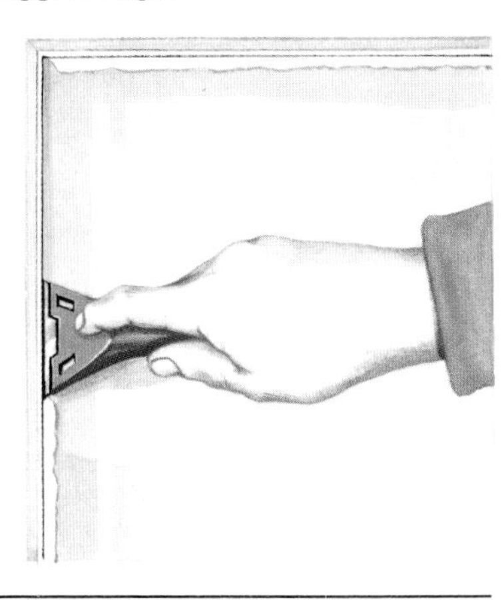

## 638 Sinking wall plugs in ceramic tiles

When inserting fixings into ceramic wall tiles, always make sure that the plastic or fibre plug in the hole is sunk completely below the thickness of the tile. Even if only a small part of the plug sticks up into the tile when the screw is tightened, the expansion of the plug will crack the tile.

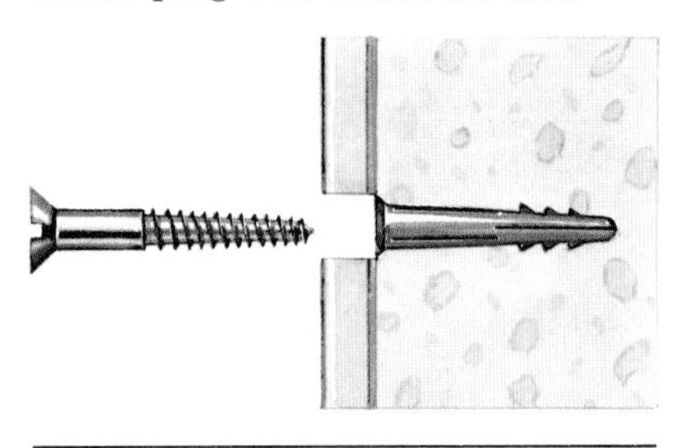

## 639 Adapting a scraper to fill cracks in plaster

Using a half-round file, make a slightly concave curve in the middle of a scraper blade and use it to fill cracks in plaster. The curve ensures that even the smallest cracks are covered; these are usually extremely difficult to fill.

After completing the job, allow the filler to dry thoroughly and then use glasspaper to rub it down flush with the surface.

## 640 Temporarily repairing a cracked window

Use clear nail varnish to seal a cracked window pane. Apply two coats on each side of the crack, allowing one to dry before applying the second.

## 641 Avoiding splitting wood when nailing

Always use oval wire nails if there is a risk of the wood splitting down the grain when nailing into it. Drive the nails home with the axis of the head following the grain—not across it.

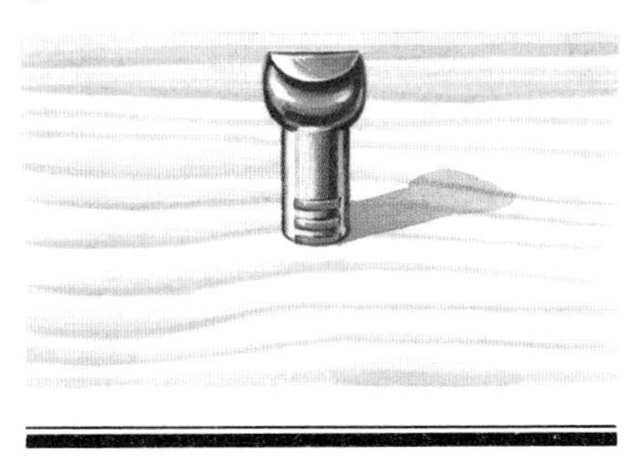

## 642 Maintaining a square edge when smoothing

Use an L-shaped sanding block, rather than a normal one, if it is important to keep the edges of a piece of timber square when smoothing them. Otherwise there is a risk that the edges will be rounded.

Make the block from two scrap lengths of wood about 150 mm/6 in long, cutting a 1.5 mm/$\frac{1}{16}$ in deep slot in the bottom piece and then screwing both pieces together at right angles. Feed a strip of glasspaper—abrasive side downwards—through the slot, and then simply slide the block backwards and forwards along the edge being smoothed. To get a perfectly flat and square finish, make sure that the block is held firmly against the timber.

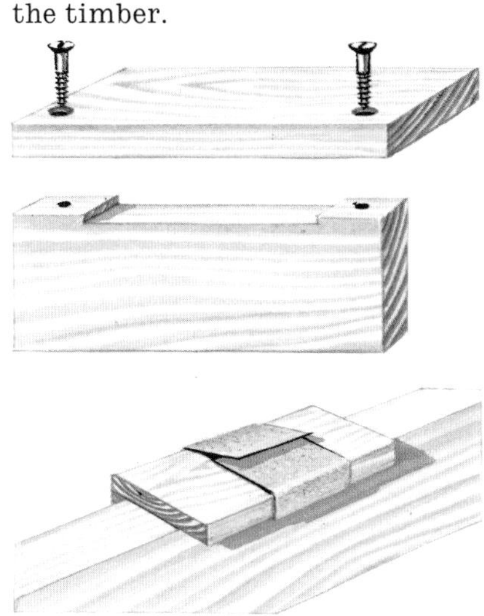

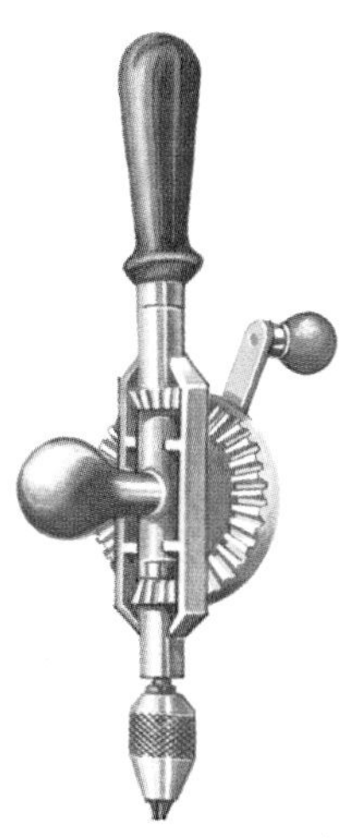

## 643 Wheelbrace drill

Use a wheelbrace for drilling small holes in awkward places. Only use the detachable side handle when more control is required.

## 644 Insulation and power tools

When buying a power tool, always, if possible, choose one with double insulation. The double insulation means that it is impossible to come into contact with the live parts of the tool.

# 645-654

## 645
**Frenchman**

Use a Frenchman to cut back pointing in brickwork. The tool can be made from an old kitchen knife. Cut the end of the knife square with a hacksaw and file off any burrs. Then heat the tip and bend the last 12mm/½in at a right angle.

## 646
**Storing paint-stained cloths**

Cloths that have been used to mop up oil or paint should never be stored in a drawer. Spontaneous combustion can occur and cause a fire.

## 647 Laying mosaic tiles on floors speedily

When laying mosaic tiles, follow the same basic procedure as that for laying ordinary floor tiles. Remember, however, that the side of the mosaic sheet that is not covered with paper is the back—not the front—of the mosaic.

Apply adhesive to the floor and, before laying the tiles, grout the backs of the sheets well. Clean off any excess grout and lay the tiles—grouted face down—tamping them firmly into position. Be sure to leave a gap between the sheets the same as that between the individual tiles. Remove excess adhesive and then fill any gaps around the edges of the floor. After the sheets have set, soak the paper and then peel it off. Finally, grout the gaps between the sheets.

## 648 Sawing a long cut in a length of timber

When sawing a long cut in timber, wedge the timber open as soon as possible after starting the cut. This will prevent the saw from binding in the cut.

## 649 Using felt paper as underlay for carpet

When carpeting a room, always lay felt paper on old floorboards if there is any possibility of damp rising to affect the carpet. Leave a 50mm/2in gap round the edges of the room and fix the paper with double-sided tape, making sure that the tape covers the gap as well. Since carpets tend to shrink, the tape will help to hold them firmly in position.

## 650 Preparing hardboard before using it

To avoid the possibility of hardboard warping, condition the boards first before laying them. Place the boards rough side uppermost on the floor and wet them, using about one glass of water to each board. Leave them to dry for two or three days.

## 651 Resurfacing a bath with enamel paint

When resurfacing a bath, always use the paint manufactured for the purpose. The job will take about five days, during which the bath must not be used.

Rub down the surface thoroughly—first with glasspaper and then with wet-and-dry paper. Clean the bath and wipe it dry. Fit tins or plastic beakers under the taps to catch any drips. Then brush on a thin layer of undercoat. When this has dried, brush on the first top coat—as thinly as possible—and leave it for a day. Work from the bottom up. Then apply a second top coat, this time leaving it for two days. Keep the bathroom well ventilated, as the fumes of the paint can be dangerous.

Finally, fill the bath up to the overflow with cold water and leave it for a further forty-eight hours.

## 652 Storing blockboard and hardboard

Always store sheets of blockboard and plywood so that air can circulate between the boards. This prevents the boards warping. Lay evenly spaced battens under each board.

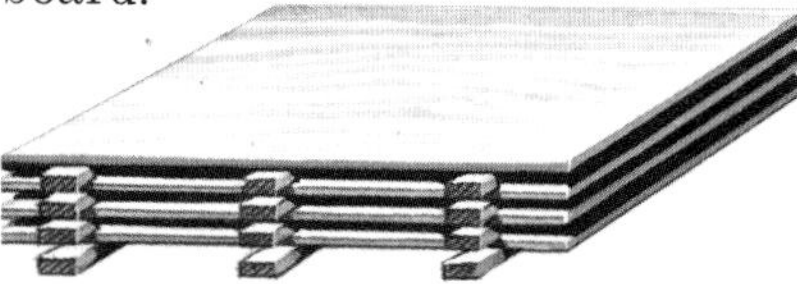

## 653 Covering a floor with sheets of hardboard

When levelling a floor with hardboard, always lay the sheets with their textured side upwards. The textured face provides a better "key" for the adhesive when laying vinyl tiles.

Start laying the sheets from the centre of the room, staggering the rows so that there will be no overlap between the joints of the hardboard and the tiles. Fix the sheets securely in position, starting from their centres, by nailing them at 150mm/6in intervals across their complete areas.

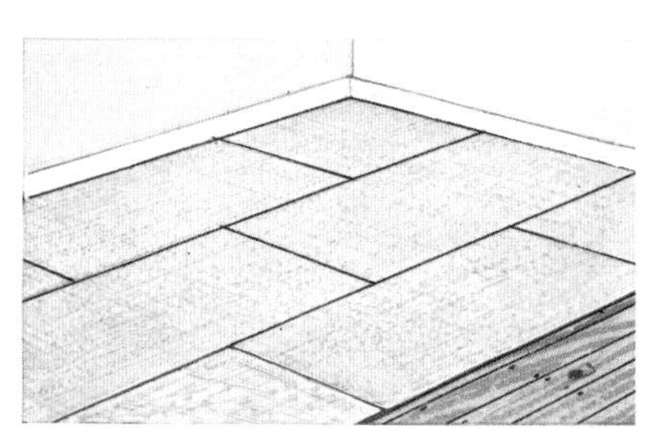

## 654 Dealing with cracks in plaster

When filling cracks in plaster which is to be painted, mix a little of the chosen colour with the filler to help it blend in with the paint.

## 655 Preventing an iron drainpipe rusting

If the back of an iron drainpipe is not fully covered when painting, rust will form. This can cause leakage problems around the joints in the pipe, and could eventually spread to affect the paint at the front of the pipe. A convenient way of checking that the back has been properly painted is to tape a mirror to a square of hardboard and insert it behind the pipe.

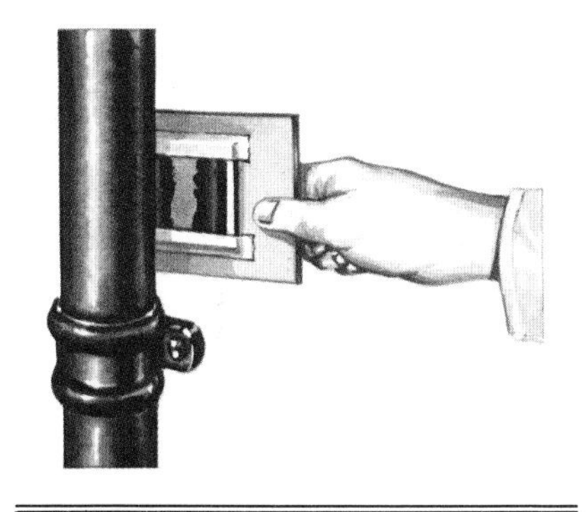

## 656 Stopping floorboards from creaking

Creaking floorboards can often be cured by removing the boards and nailing battens to the sides of the joists. Make sure that the battens protrude slightly above the joists so the underside of the boards fit tightly against it.

## 657 Foundations for gate posts in soft soil

When setting gate posts into soft soil, fit them on a single-strip foundation to link both posts together. If the posts are fitted separately, the slightest settlement of the soil can throw one post out of true. If this happens, the gate may jam or not shut properly.

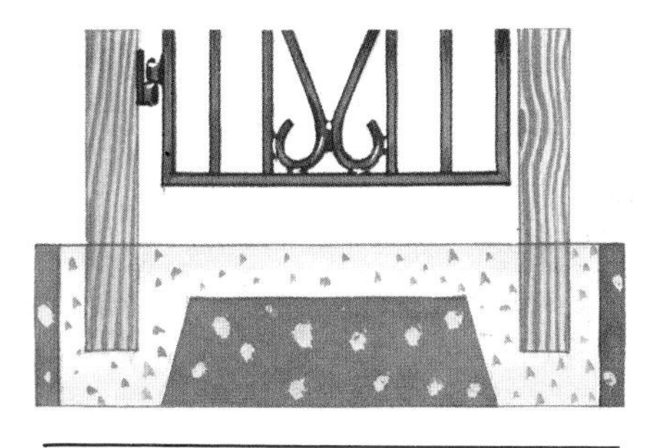

## 658 Using epoxy resin on a mortise-and-tenon

When gluing mortise-and-tenon joints with an epoxy resin, apply the hardener to the mortise and the adhesive to the tenon. This procedure is particularly useful if a number of joints are being glued at the same time. As the setting process begins only when the two parts of the glue are mixed together, it allows more time to fit the joints.

## 659 Bending plywood without splitting it

Plywood is much easier to bend if what will be the outside surface of the ply is wetted first. Always bend with the grain running across the curve. If plywood is bent against the grain, it will only bend slightly before it splits. Afterwards, leave it to dry overnight.

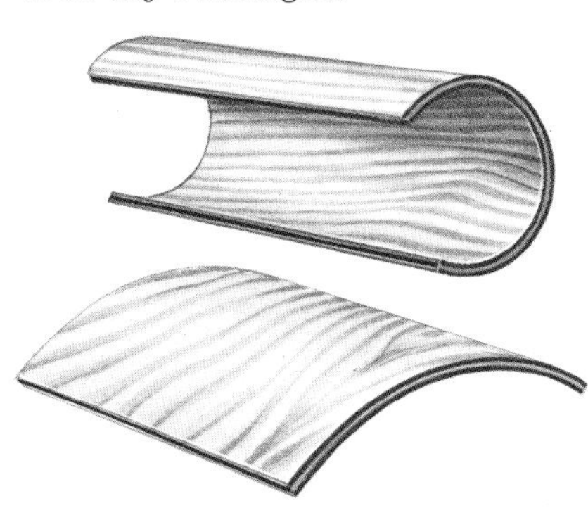

## 660 Dealing with damp walls

One hint to remember if dampness appears along a stretch of wall above a skirting board is that it may be caused by the plaster simply having come away from the wall. The moisture-content of the air in the gap created—which need be only the thickness of a cigarette paper—condenses when the heat of the room works its way through the plaster.

Cut back a 60 cm/2 ft square area of damp wall and apply a new coat of plaster. Leave it for a few weeks. If it stays dry, cut back the remainder of the damp wall surface, and replaster. If not, call in a professional to check the damp course.

## 661 Fitting a new broom handle firmly in place

Unless the end of a new broom handle is slightly chamfered, it will not fit properly into the head of the broom. When doing this job, always remember to mark the exact depth to be trimmed—too much chamfering may make it difficult to get a tight fit and cause the head to wobble on the broom.

The easiest way of marking the depth is to insert a pencil into the broom-head hole and mark the depth on it with your thumb. Keeping the thumb against the pencil, transfer the depth to the handle and mark its position.

Chamfer the handle up to this mark by filing it with a rasp. Fit the handle in the hole and secure it with a nail or a screw.

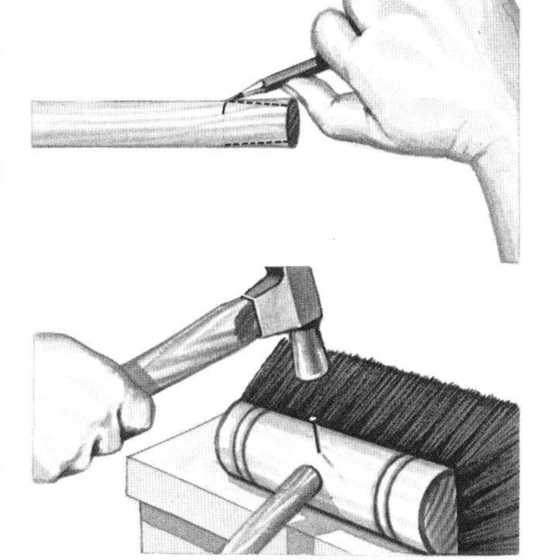

## 662 Removing ballpoint ink stains on carpet

Remove ballpoint ink stains from a carpet or similar absorbent surface by dabbing them with a cloth dipped in methylated spirit, turpentine substitute or petrol. Sponge down with cold water.

## 663 Spirit level

To check the accuracy of a spirit level, first place it on a flat surface that gives a level reading. Then turn it through 360°. If the spirit level is accurate the reading will be in exactly the same position.

## 664 Cutting holes in glass

Never cut holes in glass without wearing protective glasses. Small splinters can otherwise fly upwards into the eyes when the glass is tapped out from below.

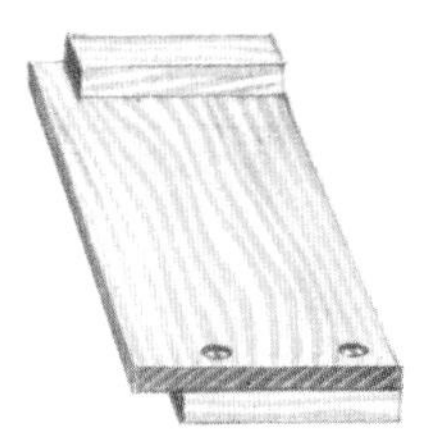

## 665 Bench hook

Timber being cut with a tenon saw can be held steady with a bench hook. When making the bench hook, cut both stops 50 mm/2 in shorter than the width of the base and make sure that the cutting sides of the stops are exactly square to guide the saw blade accurately.

## 666 Grinding tools

Always wear protective glasses when grinding a tool on a grinding wheel. Even a small particle of flying grit or dirt can seriously damage the eye.

## 667 Sharpening knives and scissors

Use a slipstone—a small hand version of an oilstone—to sharpen scissors. Lightly oil the stone and rub it backwards and forwards along the cutting edge of the scissor blade until the edge is sharpened. Turn the blade round and, keeping the slipstone flat against the blade, rub it again to remove any slight burrs along the cutting edge. Repeat the process on the other blade.

Use an oilstone to sharpen knives. Rub the knife blade backwards and forwards along the length of the stone, turning it on each stroke to follow the existing angle of the cutting edge. Finish off the job by holding a slipstone almost flat against the cutting edge and, working away from the sharpened edge, lightly rub down each side of the blade. This will remove any small burrs in the metal and hone the cutting edge.

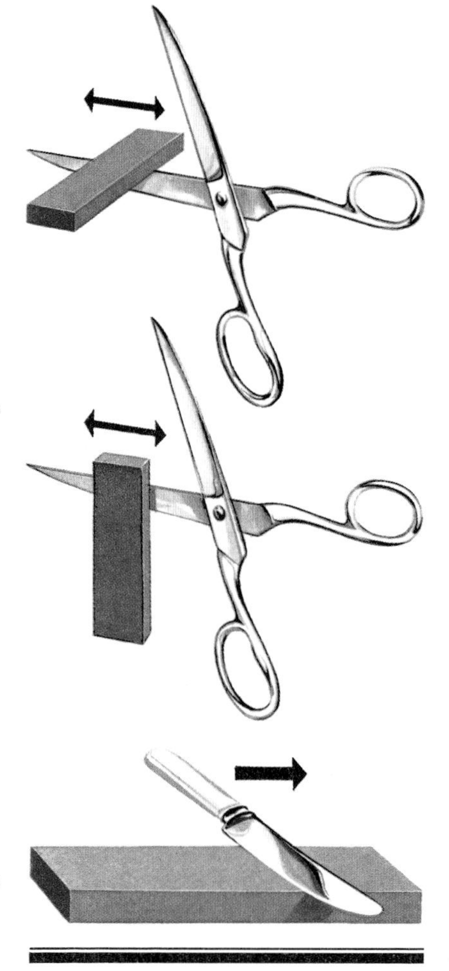

## 668 Filling cracks in cement-rendered walls

Mix equal parts of cement and fine sand to fill small cracks in cement-rendered walls. Work the mix with water until it has the consistency of a thick paste, and then work it into the cracks with a firm brush. Smooth down, if necessary.

## 669 Selecting ceramic tiles for exterior use

When buying ceramic tiles for use outside, make sure the tiles have been treated to make them frost-resistant. This process, which is usually carried out during manufacture, seals the porosity of the clay so that any moisture within the tiles cannot expand when frozen and crack the glazed surface.

## 670 Disguising uprights on bookshelves

Long rows of books on shelving look attractive, but their appearance is often spoiled by uprights inserted between the shelves to prevent them sagging. The way to deal with this problem is to cut each upright so that it can be positioned 6 mm/¼ in back from the front of the shelves. Buy an old book for each upright—approximately the same height—and carefully remove the cover. Glue the inside of the cover and carefully fit it in position around the upright so that it completely conceals it. When other books are placed on each side of the dummy, the line will appear unbroken.

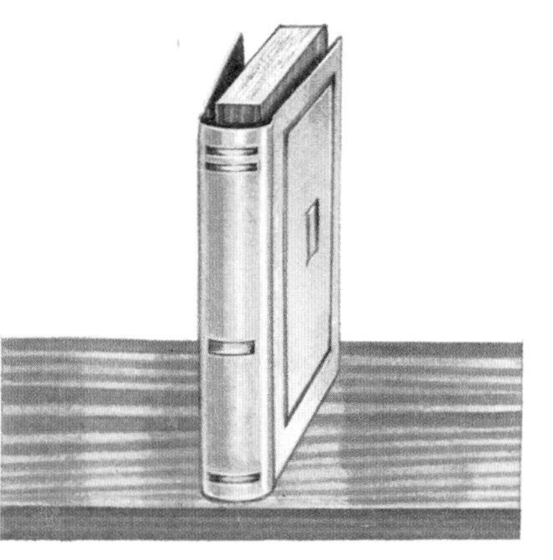

## 671 Repairing vinyl and linoleum flooring

To repair a worn or damaged area of linoleum or vinyl sheet flooring patch a new piece into the old. Lay a square of the replacement material over the damaged area. Allow for a generous overlap and make sure that any pattern is matched exactly.

Tape the square to the floor covering and, using a trimming knife and a straight-edge, cut through both the patch and the floor covering. Remove the cut pieces and scrape away any old adhesive from the floor.

Check that the patch fits the space, trimming it with the knife or glasspapering the edges, if necessary. Then apply adhesive to the underside of the patch and, to help the patch adhere, weight it down while the glue is drying.

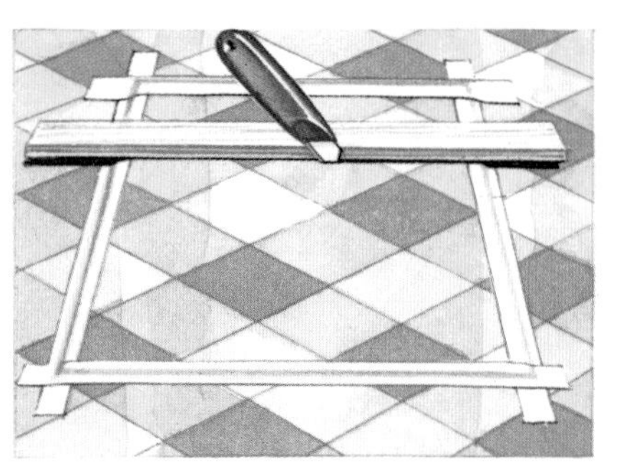

## 672 Removing grease from walls before repainting

When washing a wall before repainting it, remove any patches of grease by rubbing them with a cloth dipped in turpentine substitute. If the wall surface is too porous, run a hot iron over a sheet of blotting paper to draw out most of the grease. Then seal the area with an aluminium primer.

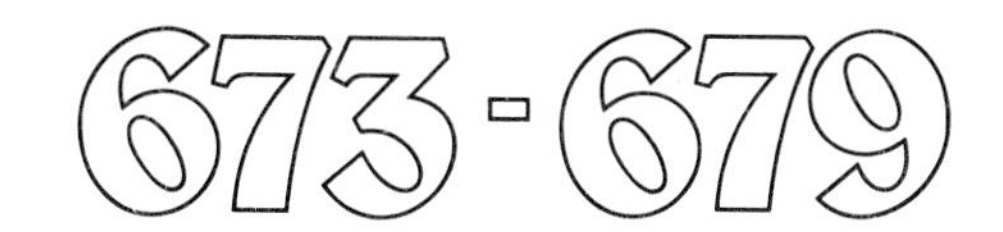

## 673 Keeping courses level when laying bricks

When building a brick wall, it is vital that bricks are laid both level horizontally and evenly vertically. Start laying the courses by building both ends up first and then infilling. During the first stage, regularly check that the vertical alignment is exact by holding a spirit level against the bricks, or, if the wall is too high for this to be accurate, use a plumb line.

When infilling, use two L-shaped corner blocks and a line to check the horizontal alignment. To make each block, screw two small 50mm/2in cubes of softwood on to one side of a larger block of the same thickness, leaving a gap between the two smaller blocks. Hammer a nail halfway home in the back of the larger block.

To use the line, tie one end to the nail on one of the blocks. Pass the line through the gap. Position this block at one end of the wall, pull the line taut and attach it to the other block at the opposite end, again passing the line through the gap and winding any excess line around the nail to keep it taut. By doing this the tension of the line will hold the blocks in position.

Lay the bricks so that they are approximately 19mm/$\frac{3}{4}$in away from the line. If the line is any nearer the brickwork, it can snag on the surface and cause even a short course of bricks to be as much as 6mm/$\frac{1}{4}$in out of line. Repeat the procedure, course by course, up the wall.

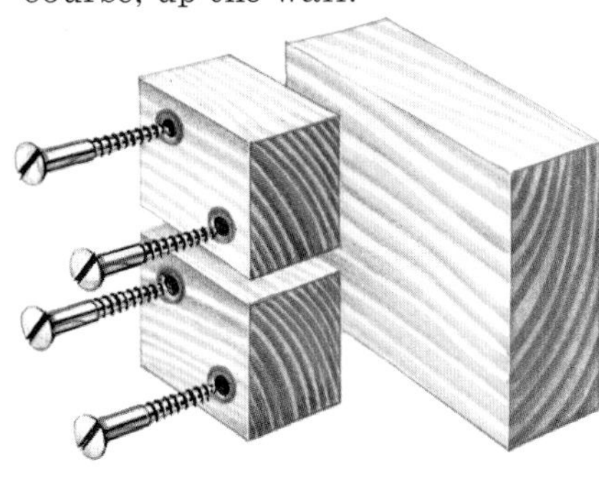

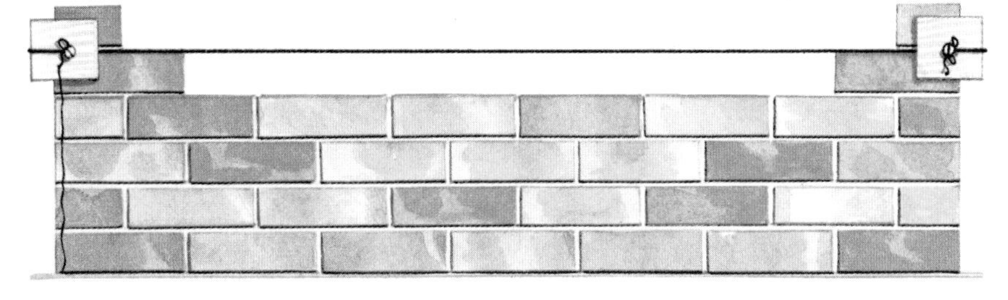

## 674 Removing self-adhesive tiles

Some mirror and aluminium tiles are self-adhesive—fixed to a surface by sticker pads, usually positioned behind each corner of the tile. To remove such tiles without damaging the surface or leaving part of the pads behind, drop lighter fuel behind the tile and over the pads. Allow the fuel to soak into the pads for two or three minutes before removing them. Then clean the surface.

## 675 Painting putty in filled holes in wood

If using putty to fill holes in wood, always wait for at least two days before painting the filled surface. This allows a thin crust to form over the putty, and for it to dry out slightly. Without this crust, a paint brush will not only leave bristle marks across the surface of the putty, but it can also drag the putty away from one side of the filled hole, making the filling useless.

## 676 The right way to burn off paintwork

The quickest way to strip paintwork is to burn it off with a blowlamp or blowtorch, but there is a right and a wrong way of tackling the job. The right way is to always strip minor areas, such as mouldings and rebates, before tackling the major areas around them. The aim is to remove the paint without damaging the surface beneath it, but if the main areas are stripped first, the exposed wood can be badly scorched when trying to deal with the smaller ones.

When stripping mouldings, always work from the top downwards. As the paint melts, remove it with a scraper or—in awkward places—with a shave hook. Collect the melted paint in a container on the ground, taking care not to let any fall on the hand.

## 677 Repairing worn or damaged wooden steps

A worn wooden step outside a door can be dangerous. Either replace the step or screw a metal tread over it.

Apply a layer of mastic along the top of the step before fitting the tread into position. The mastic prevents rainwater from seeping underneath the metal. This dampness would quickly lead to the step itself rotting.

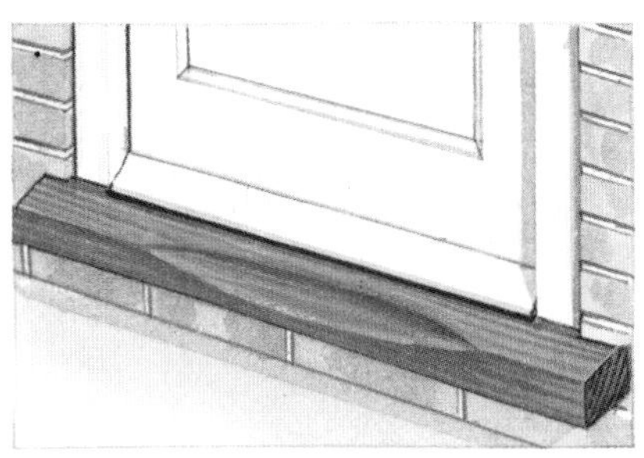

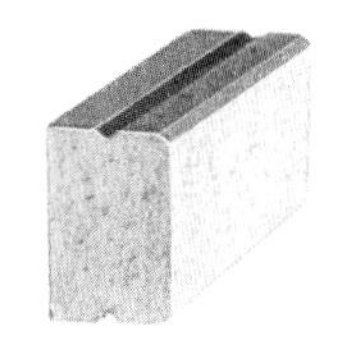

## 678 Glasspaper block

For a good finish always use a glasspaper block made from cork, to avoid applying too great a pressure when smoothing flat surfaces. If large areas require extensive smoothing, save time by fitting three blocks with rough, medium, and fine glasspaper.

## 679 Safety with chuck keys

When fitting an attachment to a power drill, remember to remove the chuck key after the chuck has been tightened. Otherwise the key will fly out when the drill is started, with the risk of serious injury.

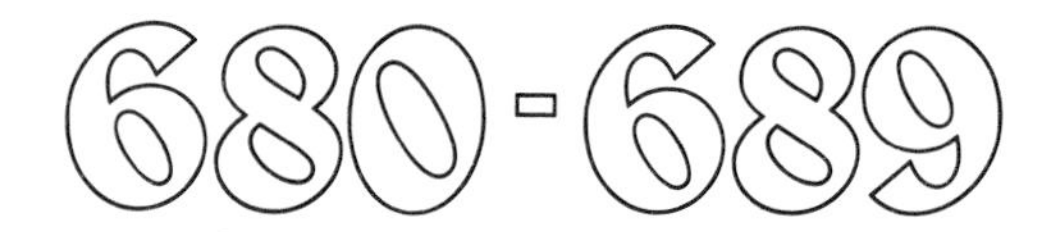

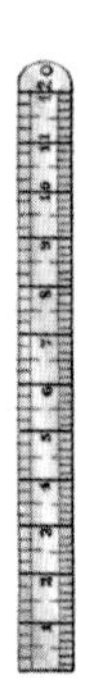

## 680 Straight-edge

The markings on a straight-edge often become difficult to read after the rule has been used for some time. To restore them, rub the surface with a black crayon, then lightly wipe over the face of the rule with a soft cloth.

## 682 Preventing a shelf from bowing

When a batten cannot be fitted to support the length of a shelf—where, for instance, it would take up valuable space or look unsightly—support the length invisibly by plugging screws into the back wall.

Start by placing the shelf against the wall and scribing the positions for the screws on both shelf and wall at 225 mm/9 in intervals. Then fit the screws into the wall, leaving about 19 mm/¾ in of their length exposed. Cut off the heads with a hacksaw.

Check the marks on the shelf against the final position of the screws and then drill holes in the shelf to a depth of 25 mm/1 in at each marked point. When the shelf is placed in position, the sheared-off screws will fit into the holes, providing an extremely rigid fixing along the shelf's length. Screw battens, or other supports, to the side wall to take the main weight of the shelf.

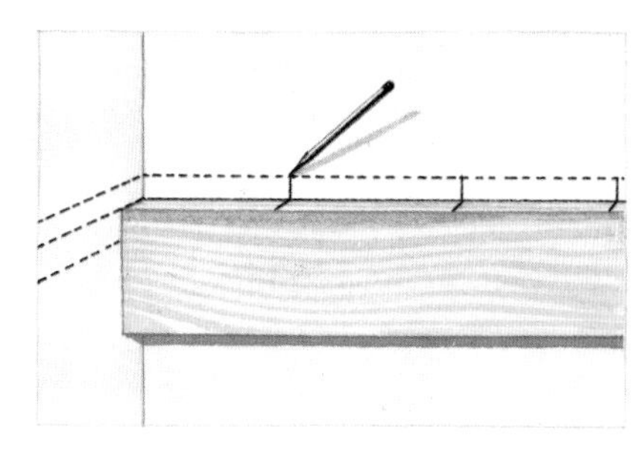

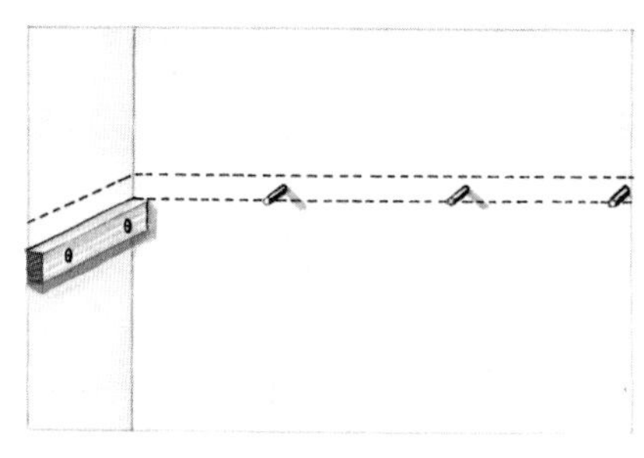

## 686 Tongued-and-grooved board for a floor finish

To achieve the best finish on wood floors, use tongued-and-grooved boarding laid over existing floorboards. Because the fixings are concealed, the final appearance of the floor is much neater and the interlocking boards keep out any draughts.

Nail through the tongue of each board. Use lost head nails and drive them at an angle every 300 mm/12 in along the tongue. Make sure that the head of the nail is punched just below the surface. If left protruding, the head will prevent the groove of the next board fitting tightly.

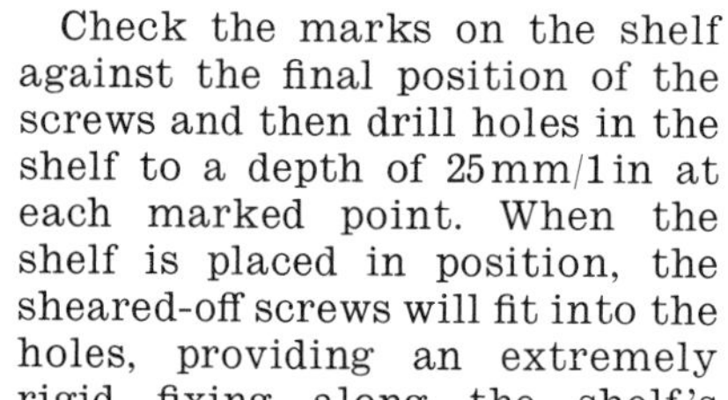

## 683 Hanging unbacked fabrics on walls

Always hang unbacked fabrics, such as hessian or decorative felt, on a surface that has been lined—never on a bare surface. Then apply the recommended adhesive to the lining paper, and not to the fabric, when hanging it. This prevents stretching and avoids the danger of overlapped edges soiling the fabric underneath. Overlap the edges by 25 mm/1 in, and when the adhesive has partially dried make a butt joint by cutting along a straight-edge through both pieces of fabric down the centre of the overlap.

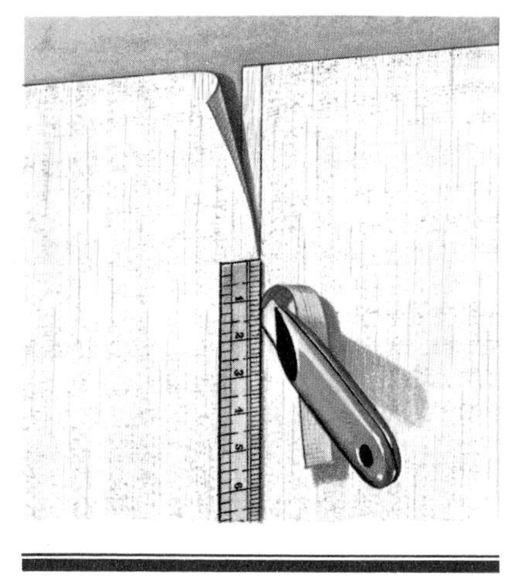

## 684 Increasing the life of wooden posts

The life of wooden fence posts can easily be prolonged. At a point just above ground level drill a 10 mm/⅜ in diameter hole angled downwards and reaching the centre of the post. Pour creosote into the hole about once every nine months. This will slowly spread through the bottom of the post and help prevent it from rotting. Plug the hole with a cork.

## 685 Selecting electric light bulbs

Any ordinary electric light bulb that is fitted so that it points upwards will often produce a bright circle of light on the ceiling above, especially if it is fitted to a light with a dense fabric shade.

To avoid this effect, replace the bulb with a crown silver bulb. This is a bulb which has a special coating across the top. The light from the bulb is reflected downwards and outwards only. Because it is softer and warmer the wattage of the crown silver bulb will have to be higher than that of an ordinary bulb if the same degree of brightness is required.

## 687 Fixing a loose or cracked slate

The simplest way of fixing a loose slate is to renail it with aluminium alloy nails. Alternatively, bend a strip of lead into the shape of a Z and position it so that one end secures the edge of the slate and the other is fitted tightly around a roofing batten. If a slate is cracked, seal it with a proprietary bituminous mastic, obtainable from builders' merchants.

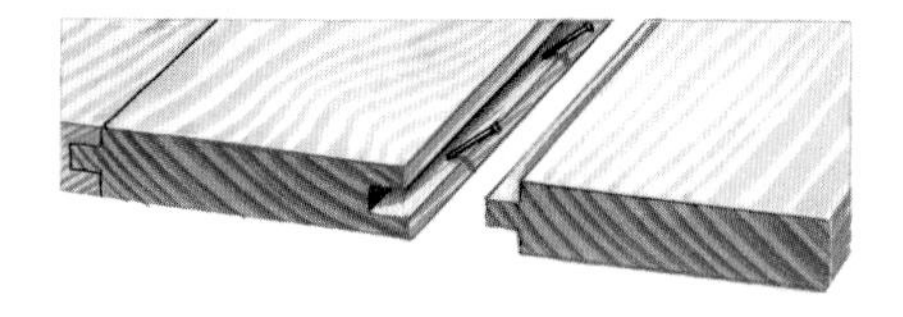

## 688 Preparing blockboard for painting

Allow four weeks for blockboard to dry out where it is to be used before painting it. This reduces the risk of the paint cracking.

## 689 Closing newly painted windows

If newly painted windows have to be closed overnight, use matchsticks to prevent the painted edges coming into contact. Insert the matches at the top and bottom of the frame, on the hinged side of casement windows, and above and below sash windows.

## 681 Electric plugs

Always change a cracked plug on an electric appliance immediately. If the plug is touched with a moist hand there is a risk of electric shock.

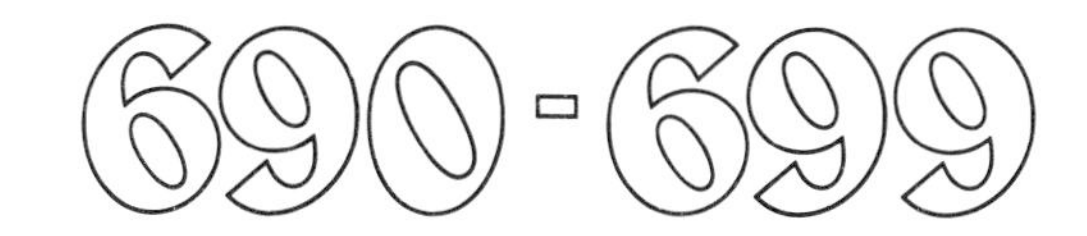

## 690 Gluing a broken vase

A sand box can be a help when rebuilding a vase that has broken into a number of pieces. The weight and fluidity of sand makes it an ideal medium for this job.

Use a box large enough to give sufficient space in which to work. Stand the base of the vase in the box and pour dry sand, both inside and outside the base, to a point just below where the first fragment is to be glued. Make sure there are no grains of sand on the edge being glued.

Fit the first fragment in place, using a slow-drying two-part epoxy-resin glue. Allow at least twenty minutes for the glue to develop a hard outside skin, which will prevent sand sticking to it. Then pour more sand into the box —again both inside and outside the vase—to a level just below where the next piece is to be glued. Apply the glue and leave it as before to form a skin before pouring the next layer of sand into the box.

Continue the process until the vase is completely buried in the sand. Because air cannot reach the joins, allow at least a week for the glue to harden before carefully emptying out the sand and removing the vase. Clean off excess glue and sand carefully.

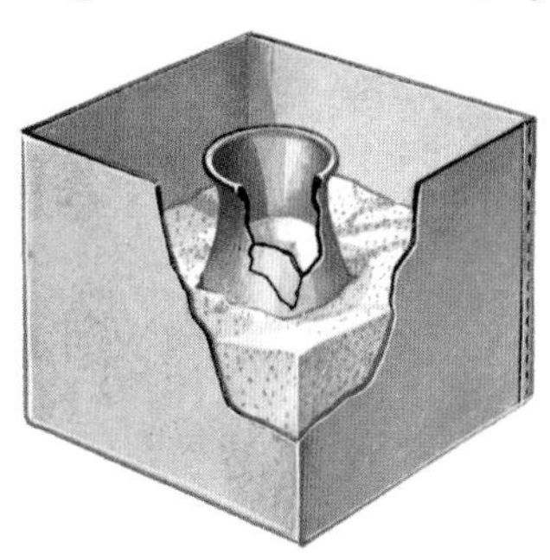

## 691 Making a strong glued and nailed joint

When making a glued and nailed joint, be sure to use the correct type and size of nail punch and punch the nail head below the surface of the timber before the glue has dried. This will avoid the necessity of disturbing the freshly glued joint when finishing.

## 692 Wiring up electric terminals correctly

Always fit the wire clockwise around the screw threads when wiring a screw-type electric terminal. This ensures that, when the screws are tightened, the wires will not unwind but will be tightened around the screws.

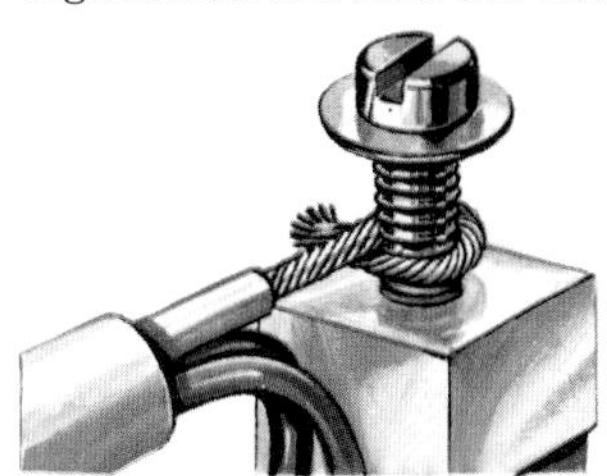

## 693 Preparing plaster surfaces for tiling

Before tiling over a porous plaster surface, always apply a coat of a solvent-based primer to it. Otherwise, the tile adhesive will dry out too quickly, weakening the bond between the tiles and the plaster.

## 694 Making non-vinyl paper waterproof

Vinyl is the best paper to use in kitchens and bathrooms because it is extremely resistant to water and steam. If non-vinyl paper is used, it may bubble from the wall after hot water has been running. This is the result of steam getting through the porous paper and softening the paste behind it.

Cure this by applying two coats of varnish to the paper when it is dry to make it waterproof. Remember, however, that if the colour of the paper is important, the coats of varnish will tend to darken it.

## 695 Filing metal edges without scratching

Use a smooth-grade file to finish off metal. To avoid the danger of the file's teeth scratching the surface, rub a stick of chalk over the file as required during the smoothing process. Use a single-cut file for hard metals and a rasp-cut file for soft ones.

## 696 Thawing a frozen waste outlet

If the waste outlet of a sink has frozen, pour some salt down the pipe to help thaw it out. To help speed up the thawing process, wrap cloths that have been wrung out in hot water around the U-bend underneath the sink.

## 697 Securing heavy glass on doors and windows

Heavy glass fitted to a door or to a large hinged window should be tightly secured, or its weight will eventually cause the framework of the door or window to drop and so prevent it from closing properly.

Overcome this by inserting two blocks of wood of the same thickness as the glass within the rebate, making sure that they fit tightly between the glass and the edge of the frame. This is known in the glazing trade as "toeing and heeling". Fit the first block at the bottom on the hinged side of the frame and the second block, slightly tapered if necessary, at the top of the frame on the side opposite the hinges. Because the glass is now securely wedged, the framework itself cannot sag.

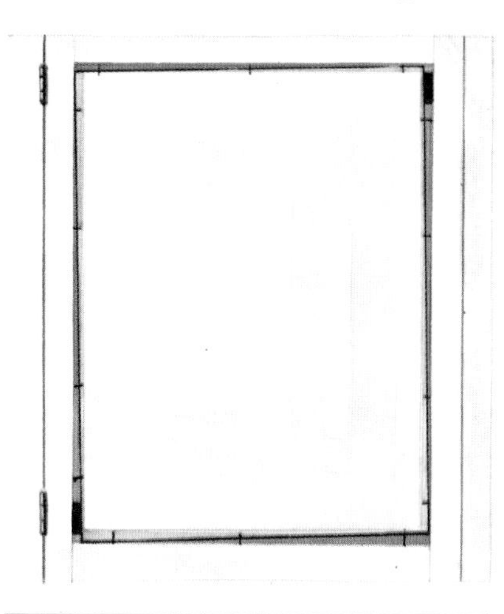

## 698 Folding rule

Because of the thickness of a folding rule, inaccuracies can occur when lining up the measurement mark with the surface. Stand the rule on edge so that the measurements touch the surface at the point where they are to be marked.

## 699 Storage safety

Keep medicines, dangerous substances (such as bleach or weed-killer), tools and other materials in a locked cupboard, well out of the reach of children.

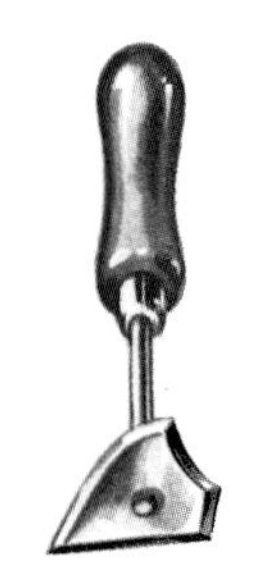

## 700 Shavehook

Use a shave hook on frames or mouldings to remove paint or varnish that has been burned off with a blow lamp or stripped with chemical stripper. The combination shave hook, which has four different edges, is also ideal for scraping lead piping before soldering.

## 701 Demolishing walls

Never demolish a wall in a house without making sure that it is not structural, that is supporting another part of the structure. If uncertain, consult an expert to help identify which wall is which.

## 702 Making a slow-drying plaster mix

When making up plaster for the finishing coat, mix cellulose filler with the plaster powder. Adding the filler not only makes the plaster mix much easier to work with—giving it a creamy consistency that dries out very smoothly—but also retards the setting process for half an hour or so. This allows more time to complete the job which is particularly helpful when handling plaster for the first time.

Add about 225g/½lb of cellulose filler to every 6kg/14lb of plaster. Dissolve the filler in water before adding it to the plaster powder.

## 703 Fitting uprights to support shelving

To ensure that shelving uprights are fitted correctly, first draw a horizontal line to mark where the top of each upright is to be fixed. Then place the first upright in position and check its vertical alignment with a plumb line. Screw it to the wall.

Next, cut a piece of wood to the same length as the proposed distance between the first and second uprights. Square off its ends and use it as a spacer bar to establish the distance between the two uprights and the vertical alignment of the second. Do this by placing the bar at right angles first to the top and then to the bottom of the fitted upright and fix the second accordingly. Repeat as necessary.

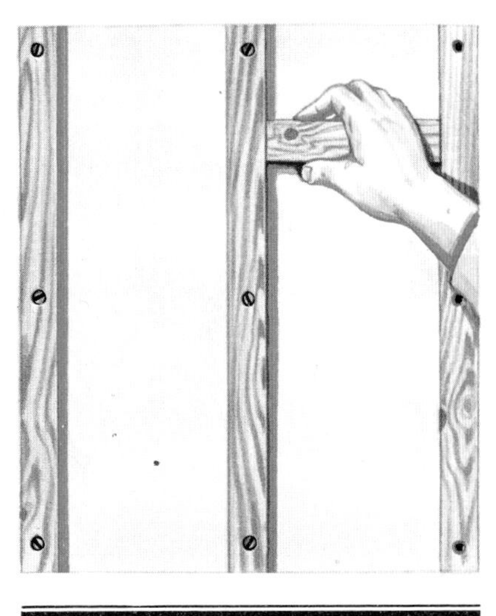

## 704 Fitting carpet around a projecting wall

When cutting a carpet to fit around a projecting wall, always allow a little extra so that the carpet will fit tightly around the obstacle. If the carpet is cut exactly to the line of the side walls, a gap will almost certainly appear.

Using a trimming knife, start the cuts at the corners of the projection and slant the cuts inwards at a slight angle to the vertical. Then fold the carpet back and, using the back of the blade, press the carpet firmly into the angles of the wall and floor. Cutting through the pile, trim off the surplus carpet around the projection and finally along the main wall.

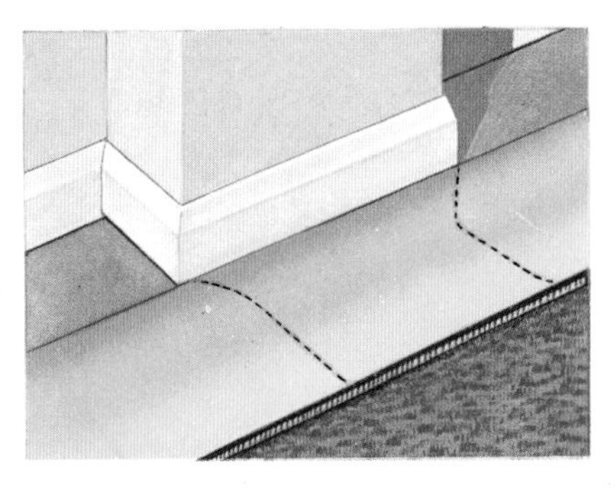

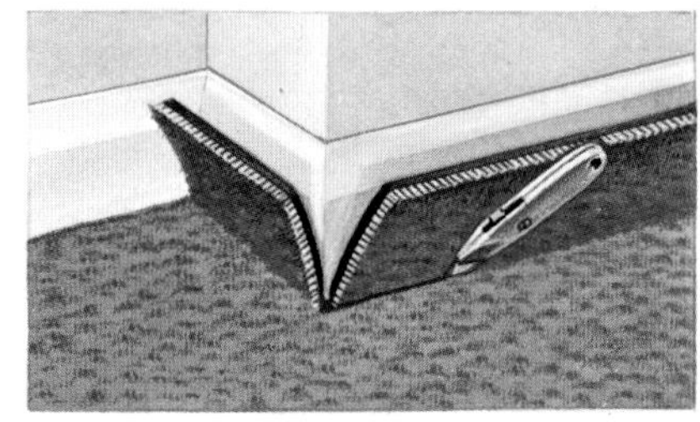

## 705 Dealing with a radiator that fails to heat up

If the top of a radiator fails to heat up properly it is usually because there is air trapped inside it. Deal with this by opening the air vent at the top of the radiator with a "bleeder" key—one is usually provided by the manufacturer. However, if the radiator remains cool, it could be that it is too level for the air to be able to escape. Check with a spirit level to see if this is the case; if it is, free the radiator from its mounting and adjust it so that it is angled at a very slight tilt to the wall.

## 706 The right way to use a spray gun

Using a spray gun is one of the most convenient ways of painting large areas. Before starting, mask off any area that is not to be painted and thin down the paint.

Always wear a face mask and work with the gun no less than 300mm/12in away from the surface. Never swing the gun in an arc from side to side, as this will lead to an uneven finish. Instead, keep the gun moving in a straight line and work across the surface.

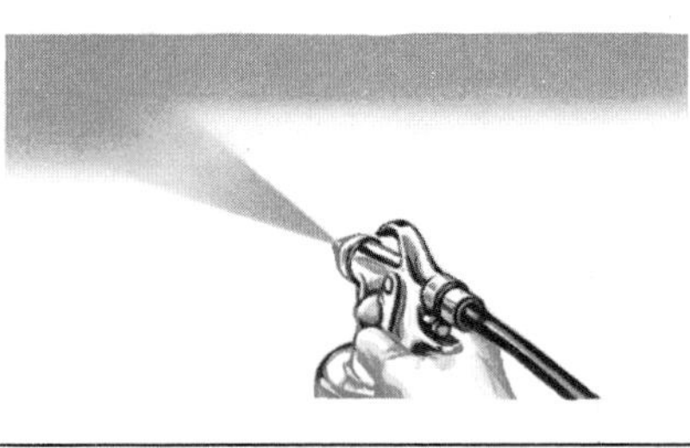

## 707 Preparing a surface to take plaster

Before plastering a surface, always apply a plaster undercoat or a mortar rendering to it. Make sure to check with the supplier that the undercoat is the correct type for the plaster.

When applying a plaster undercoat to a small area use a wooden float and work in thin layers of plaster—about 3mm/⅛in thick at a time. Build these up to a maximum thickness of about 12mm/½in, though this will depend on the type of plaster being used. Never try to apply this thickness in one operation; this will cause the plaster to fall from the surface under its own weight as fast as it is applied. On larger areas work between two 12mm/½in thick uprights and level the plaster with a straight-edge pressed against the uprights.

When using a mortar mix, make the mix weak—one part of cement, one part of lime and six parts of sand is perfectly adequate. A stronger mix will prevent moisture being absorbed and lead to damp patches on the wall.

Before the undercoat dries, roughen up the surface slightly with a scratcher. This provides a "key" for the final coat.

## 708 Applying plaster to a wall or ceiling

Only tackle small areas when plastering; leave complete walls or ceilings to the professionals. Having prepared the surface, make up the mix by pouring plaster powder into a clean bucket and adding water until the mix has the consistency of whipped cream. Heap some of the mix on a hawk. Then, using a metal float—or a wooden float if applying a plaster undercoat—slice off enough mix to fill about half the float's blade. Hold the float level and shake it gently so that the plaster settles evenly.

Apply the plaster with the leading edge of the float at an angle of 30° to the wall's surface. Do not hold the float flat, or the mix will stick to it. Spread the plaster by sweeping the float backwards and forwards across the surface, making sure that the float is thoroughly wetted before picking up more plaster. Use a firm pressure to level the plaster at the point of application, reducing the pressure as the plaster spreads.

When finishing off, lightly brush the plaster with water to help even out the drying time of the whole surface. Finally, smooth across it with the float.

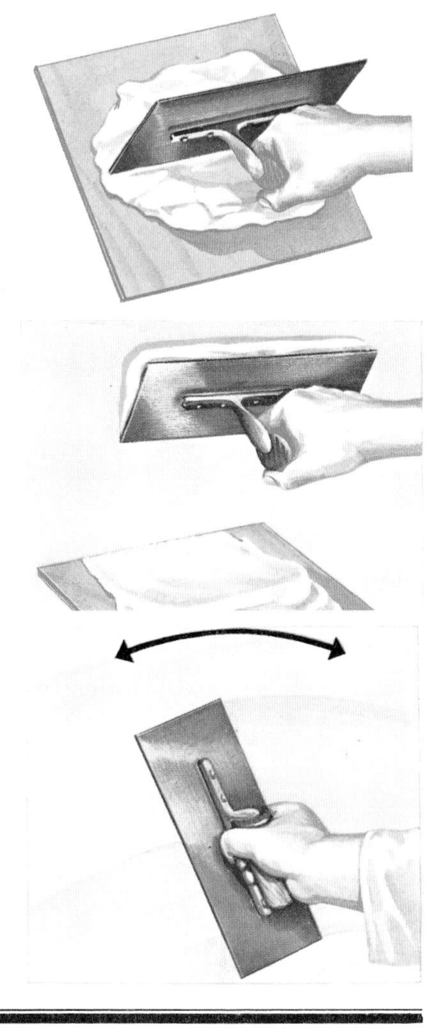

## 709 Avoiding smears when painting skirting

The finished surface of a painted skirting board can be easily smeared if the brush picks up dirt from the floor. To avoid this, first sweep the floor. Then stick masking tape flush against the bottom of the skirting to protect the brush.

## 710 Repairing faulty putty in leaking gutters

Stains down an outside wall of a house are usually a sign that a gutter is leaking—either because debris has accumulated in it causing a blockage or because the putty in the joint between two lengths of guttering has deteriorated. This is a common fault with cast-iron gutters.

If faulty putty is the cause, repair the gutter by unscrewing the nut and bolt at the joint and raising the top gutter section enough for the old putty to be scraped away. Spread a layer of metal casement putty, about 6mm/¼in thick, within the joint. Bolt the two sections together again and, after cleaning off the excess putty squeezed from the joint, apply a coat of bitumous paint to both the inside and outside of the joint.

## 711 Stopping veneers splitting when sawing

To cut veneered wood without splitting the veneer, mark up the cut line on both sides of the wood and stick adhesive tape along the line on the underside. Cut through the wood with a tenon saw. Peel off the tape, working towards the cut to avoid removing the veneer.

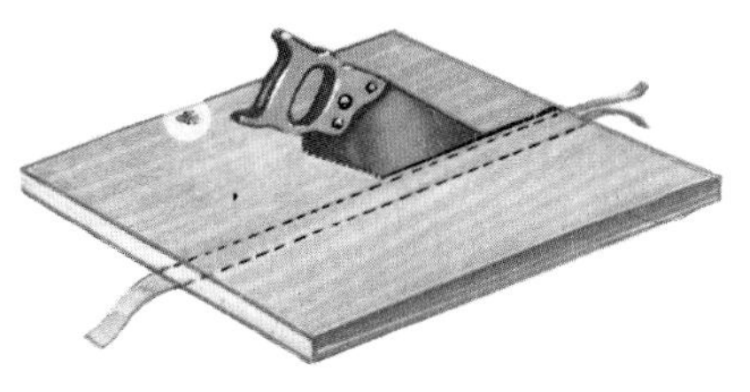

## 712 Strengthening a butt joint with a bolt

Butt joints linking cross rails to the legs of a wooden table or bench should always be strengthened if it is intended that they should take heavy weights. Do this by fitting a bolt through each leg, secured by a nut recessed into the cross rail.

First, measure the length of the bolt from the washer to the threaded end. Add 3mm/⅛in to this figure and mark this measurement with a crayon on the bit being used to drill the hole for the bolt. Drill through the centre of the leg and into the cross rail until the mark is reached.

Transfer the measurement to the cross rail and, working from the mark towards the leg, chisel out a slot measuring three times the thickness of the nut and half its width. Insert the nut into the slot and the bolt into the hole, turning the bolt head to tighten the nut. Fill the slot with a proprietary wood filler.

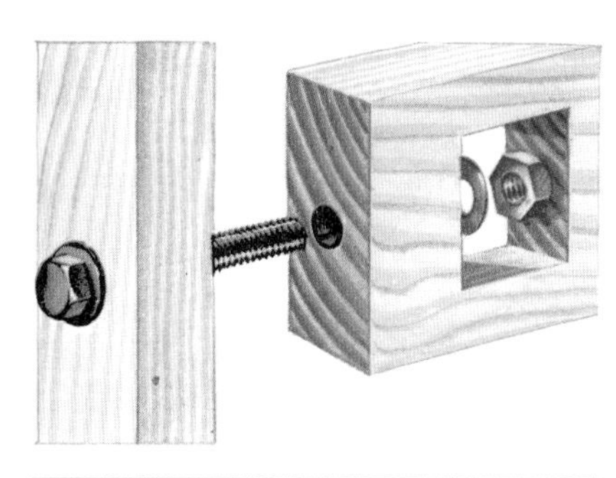

## 713 Trimming knife

Before storing a trimming knife always push the blade into a cork or an india rubber—both for safety and the protection of the blade.

## 714 Drilling into ceilings

When drilling into a ceiling, always wear glasses to protect the eyes from falling grit and dust.

## 715
### Seam roller
Used to ensure a good butt joint between wallpaper lengths, a seam roller can sometimes cause excess paste to be squeezed out of the joint. Lightly sponge off this paste from the paper and make sure that the head of the roller is thoroughly clean so that paste is not transferred to the next butt joint.

## 717 Laying strip carpet on a staircase
If a fully fitted stair carpet is required always leave the planning and laying to an experienced carpet layer.

When laying strip carpet, which is easier to lay and costs less than a fitted carpet, always lay the pile facing down the stairs to ensure longer wear. If the tread feels smoother to the touch when rubbed towards the nose of the stair, it is facing the correct way.

For the neatest and safest finish use tackless fitting strips to secure the carpet. Either use right-angled tackless fittings or, for a very secure fixing, two separate fittings for each stair.

If using separate fittings leave a gap, equal to the thickness of the carpet when doubled over, between the tackless strip on the tread and the tackless strip on the riser. Make sure that the points on the tread's fitting face up the stairs, and down the stairs on the riser's fitting.

Work can be started from the top or bottom of the stairs. Always fix an extra pleat to the last riser covered to allow the carpet to be moved up or down when it is worn. Use a blunt bolster or similar tool to hammer the carpet firmly into the gap between each pair of tackless fittings. Pull the carpet taut to the next step and continue the length of the stairs fitting in the same way.

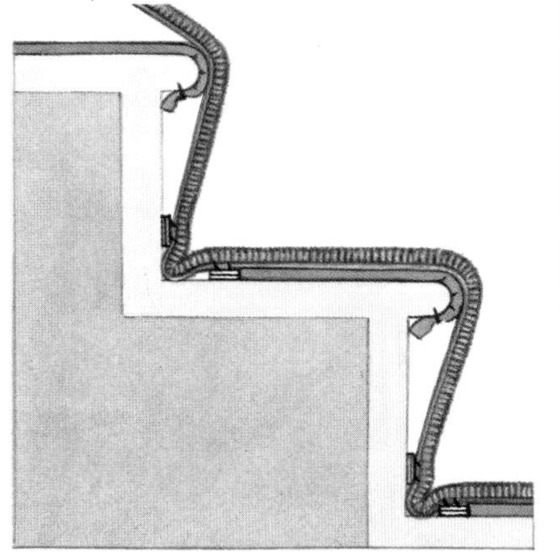

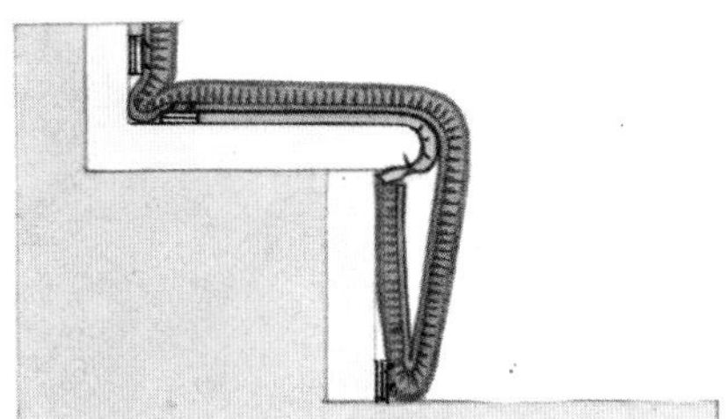

## 721 Making drawers easy to slide
If rubbing candlewax along the runners does not prevent a drawer from sticking, it may be possible to fix strips of plastic laminate along the top edges of the runners and into the bottom grooves of the sliding tracks.

Use a contact adhesive to stick the strips on the drawer runners, and either cramp the strips into place until the glue hardens, or cut 3mm/⅛in thick battens slightly longer than the depth between the top of the drawer and the top of the runners and "spring" them into position.

If the drawer runs on blocks fitted within the drawer unit, glue the laminate strips to the bottom of the drawer.

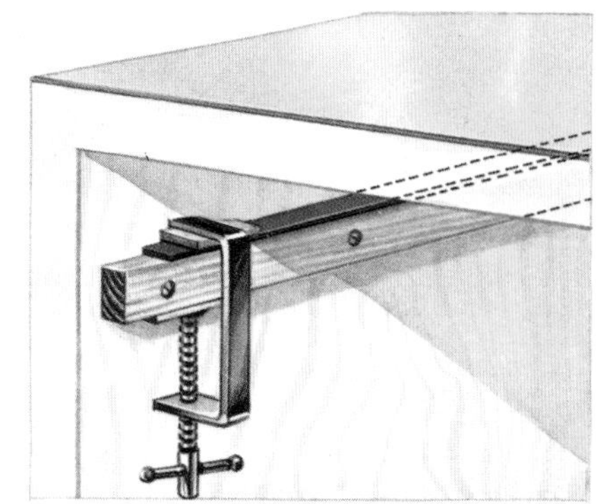

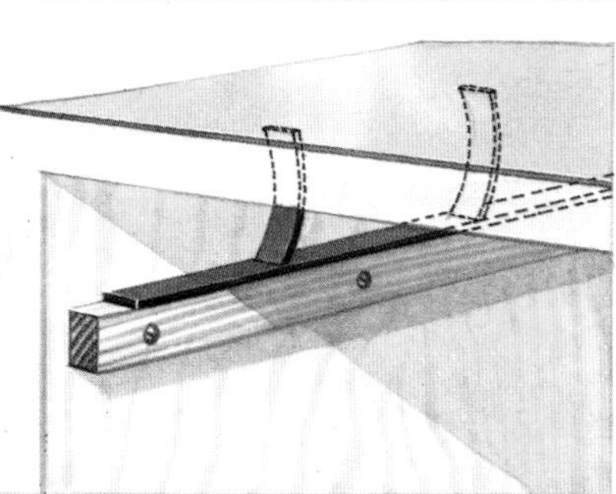

## 716
### Electric sockets
Never run more appliances from an electric socket than the maximum number permitted by its rating. Too many appliances run off the socket will overload it, causing it to fuse or start a fire.

## 718 Drilling large holes in narrow wood lengths
Before drilling a large hole in a narrow piece of wood, fit a cramp across the width of the wood at the point where the hole is to be drilled. Keeping the sides of the wood under pressure should prevent them from splintering.

## 719 Smoothing wood with an abrasive disc
When using an abrasive disc on a drill to smooth wood, tilt the drill slightly so that about 25mm/1in of the disc is in contact with the wood. Work in long sweeping movements. Avoid stopping in mid-sweep or deep ridges will be scored into the surface. These are almost impossible to remove.

## 720 Dealing with stains on walls and ceilings
Stains on a ceiling or a wall can often be caused by dampness. First, the source of the dampness must be traced and eliminated.

With ceilings always check the loft. Once the dampness is cured and the ceiling has dried out remove any damaged paper, if necessary. Then seal the stains with two coats of aluminium sealer. Allow the sealer to dry, then repaint or repaper the area.

Follow the same procedure with walls. Points to check include the damp course and external air bricks. Once the source of damp has been removed, seal the walls—inside and out—with sealer before repainting. If the trouble persists, however, always call in a professional for advice.

## 722 Levelling concrete for woodblocks or tiles

A cracked and slightly uneven concrete floor can be made suitable for wood-block flooring or tiles by smoothing it with a 3mm/⅛in layer of screeding. Various compounds are available and are normally sold in powder form to which water has to be added. Always follow the manufacturer's instructions to make up the mix.

Wash the floor with water and detergent to remove any dirt and grease and pour the mix over it. Work from a corner of the room towards a door and spread the compound with a metal float to a thickness of about 3mm/⅛in. Do not worry if slight trowel marks are left in the surface—these will disappear as the compound settles and dries. Allow at least two hours of drying time before walking on the surface, and at least twenty-four hours before starting to lay wood blocks or tiles.

## 723 Estimating stair carpet requirements

Always allow for an additional length equal to the depth of the bottom stair riser when estimating for stair carpet. Add this length to the combined length of one tread and riser multiplied by the number of stairs. Turn the extra length against the last riser covered and, when wear occurs, move the carpet and turn the surplus against the riser at the opposite end. This considerably lengthens the life of the carpet.

If the staircase includes winding stairs each winding tread must be measured separately at its widest point to get an accurate estimate.

## 724 Matching strips of carpet for joining

Always make sure that the pile of each strip of matching carpet is facing in the same direction. Any strip with the pile facing in another direction will look completely different in colour and texture. To find the direction, rub a palm along the carpet. If it feels smoother rubbing from left to right, the pile is facing right—and vice versa.

## 725 Fitting underlay pads for stair carpeting

Proprietary underlay pads are the most convenient form of underlay for stair carpeting. Make sure that the pads extend at least 50mm/2in beyond the edge of each tread nosing of the staircase. If the pad is fitted flush with the nosing, the carpet will quickly wear along the edges of each tread. Align the pads below each nosing, and secure them with tacks or staples on the treads and risers.

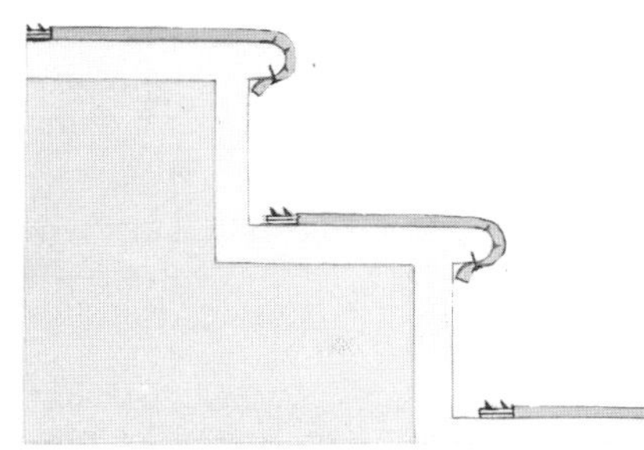

## 726 Concealing the joins when papering ceilings

Where the width of a room makes it economical, hang ceiling paper parallel to the main window, working away from it. This will make butt joints less visible.

## 727 Laying carpet down a winding staircase

Always ensure that the pile on a stair carpet faces down the stairs on a winding stair (or "winder").

Secure the carpet on the winder with tacks, or, if the carpet is not too bulky, fit tackless fitting strips. If using the latter and working upwards, first secure a strip on the tread below the first winder in the normal way. Pull the carpet up over the tread of the winder and position the pile. Fold the resulting surplus up against the riser and, holding the fold in position, pull the carpet away from the winder sufficiently to position a strip against the fold at the foot of the riser. Keeping the carpet taut on the tread below tack the strip and the folded double thickness of carpet to the riser. Pull the carpet back on to the tread of the winder, and continue the operation.

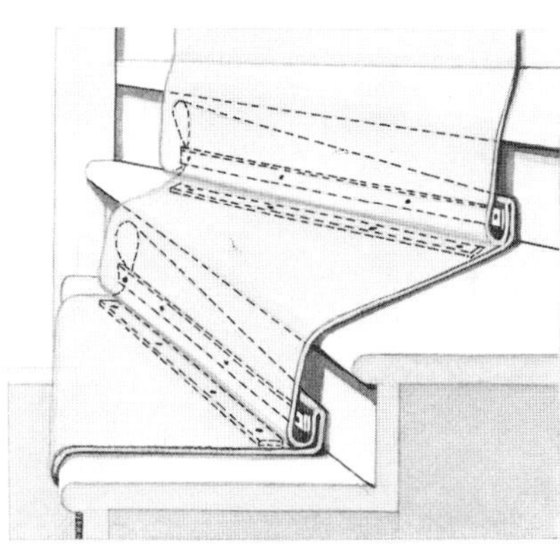

## 728 Joining stair and landing carpet

Always make the join between stair and landing carpets under the tread nosing of the top stair. A join made elsewhere on the landing could work itself loose and become dangerous.

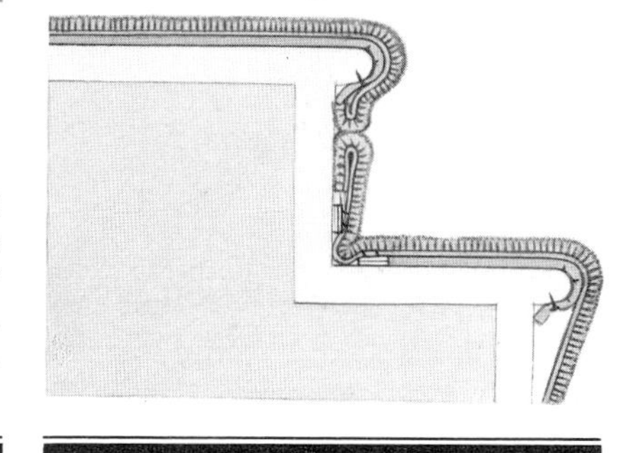

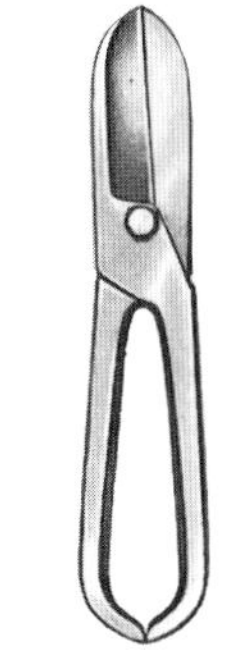

## 729 Tinsnips

Always keep snips as straight as possible when cutting thin sheet metal. If the snips are twisted over, the cutting jaws can be forced open and ruined.

## 730 Working with acids and alkalis

Always wear rubber gloves, protective glasses and old clothes when using acids and alkalis, or acid and alkaline-based fluids. Keep a quantity of clean fresh water on hand as an additional safeguard in case of splashing.

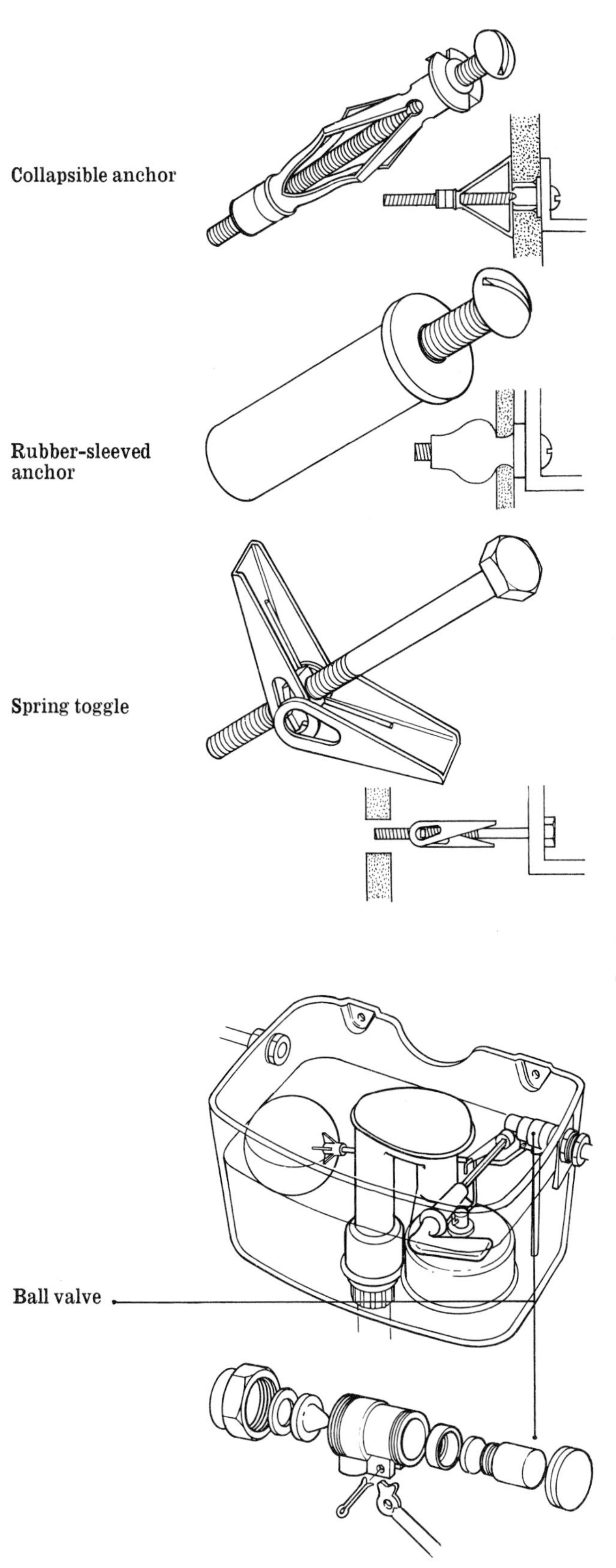


**Adhesives**
Five all-purpose adhesives will cope with most D-I-Y jobs:

*Contact adhesives* Economical and strong adhesives, mainly used for gluing timber veneers, plastic laminates and ceramic tiles. Their chief advantage is that they provide instant bonding, so avoiding the need to cramp materials for long periods. The adhesive is applied to both surfaces and left to become touch-dry before they are bonded together, using a firm pressure.

*Epoxies* Very strong and versatile adhesives, used when a permanent bond is needed. They are heat-resistant and waterproof and adhere well to glass, china, stone, concrete, rubber and many plastics. However, their expense makes it uneconomic to use them on large jobs.

Epoxies are made up of two compounds—a hardener and a resin—which must be mixed in equal quantities. Setting time is up to six hours, but, in some cases, this can be accelerated by gentle heat.

*General-purpose type adhesives* Although general-purpose adhesives are not permanent in all circumstances, they are excellent for small and light household repairs. They are moderately waterproof, heat resistant and have the advantage of being quick-drying and transparent.

*Natural latex* This has a strong, flexible bond and is excellent for fixing carpets and fabrics. It dries quickly and can be washed.

*PVA* The most practical and frequently used adhesive for general indoor work and household repairs. It has the advantage of being clean and easy to use—but the surfaces being glued must be cramped together during bonding. It is not waterproof and so should not be used outdoors.

There is also a wide variety of proprietary special-purpose adhesives for fixing perspex, tiles and wallpaper, etc. As the range is so wide, ask the supplier's advice.

**Adjustable grips** *See* Tip 574

**Aggregate**
Crushed stone, gravel and sand, which, when mixed with cement, give bulk and strength to concrete. Aggregate consists of fine and coarse particles, whose proportions should be calculated according to the strength of concrete required. "All-in" aggregate can be obtained from builders' merchants, made up in the correct proportions for specific jobs.

**Anchors and toggles**
Used for fastening into a hollow wall where there is no backing timber to provide a fixing for screws or nails.

*Collapsible anchors* Insertion of the screw draws the metal gripping shoulders against the inner wall surface; these will remain in place if the bolt is removed.

*Rubber-sleeved anchors* Can be used in solid walls or for fixing plastic or metal sheeting. The bolt compresses a rubber sleeve against the surface of the wall.

*Spring toggles* Two spring-loaded arms expand to grip the wall.

**Arrissing**
Glaziers' term for the first stage of smoothing the edges of newly cut glass with a slightly wet and smooth abrasive stone.

**Asphalt**
Consisting of bitumen and crushed stone, or aggregate, its uses include surfacing driveways, lining gutters and waterproofing flat roofs, basement walls and floors. Amateurs should limit themselves to repair work—using sacks of cold asphalt, obtainable from builders' merchants and intended specifically for D-I-Y use.

**Ballast**
Gravel, grit, sand and shingle, used as aggregate for cement.

**Ball valve**
A valve, containing a rubber, fibre or nylon washer, that controls the flow of water into a cistern. It is operated by a lever with a copper or plastic ball-float on the end. As the water rises, so does the float; when the cistern is full, the valve shuts off the flow of water.

**Beading**
A strip of hardwood or plastic half-round moulding used as a decoration or a finish.

**Bench hook** *See* Tip 665

**Bending spring** *See* Tip 38

**Blockboard**
Strips of softwood up to 25 mm/1 in wide are glued and sandwiched together between two sheets of veneer under high pressure to make blockboard. The boards are suitable for cladding or carvassing work. The usual sheet size is 2440 mm/8 ft by 1220 mm/4 ft, with thickness varying from 12.5 mm/½ in to 32 mm/1¼ in.

**Bolster** *See* Tip 212

**Bolts**
Fastenings used to secure most materials together, or fixings into walls and ceilings.

*Coach bolts* Used in light and heavy construction, a coach bolt has a round head with a square collar, which prevents the nut from working loose when fully tightened.

*Machine bolts* These have square or hexagonal shaped heads and are used in light construction.

*Masonry bolts* Used for fixing to building blocks, aggregate or concrete. A plastic or steel anchor expands as the bolt is tightened to grip the side of the hole.

*Rag bolts* These have ragged ends, which hold firmly when bedded in concrete. They are used whenever a firm fixing is needed, such as when fixing a handrail in position against a wall.

**Bond**
Varied arrangements of bricks in a wall, designed to give both strength and a good appearance. The principal bonds are English, English garden wall, stretcher, open and Flemish.

**Brackets and fasteners**
Metal brackets are either L- or T-shaped and are used for reinforcing joints or as supports.

Corrugated fasteners—strips of corrugated metal, sharpened along one edge—provide a quick and easy way of reinforcing T-joints. The fasteners are simply hammered into the joint. Both types should only be used on light work, where appearance is secondary to strength.

**Bradawl** *See* Tip 233

**Bricks**
Fired clay blocks used for building. Almost all conform to various international standards, but always seek the supplier's advice when choosing bricks for a particular job. Four basic types in common use are:

*Air brick* Perforated brick used in wall construction to allow for ventilation.

*Commons (or Flettons)* Economical general-purpose bricks, which can be used for building both internal and external walls. Because they are prone to frost damage, they should usually be covered with rendering or plaster.

*Engineering* Hard bricks which do not absorb water easily and have a high load-bearing capacity. They are normally used only in underground structures.

*Facings* Durable and weather-resistant bricks, used chiefly for their decorative qualities.

**Bruising**
Indentations left in a wood surface after it has been struck.

**Builder's square** *See* Tip 269

**Building blocks**
Building blocks have the advantage of being quicker to lay than bricks. They fall into two main categories. Common blocks are excellent for most domestic building purposes. The most popular for D-I-Y use are aerated blocks, which have a high thermal insulation value and take both nails and screws. They come in load-bearing and non-load-bearing grades, both of which have to be rendered. Facing blocks are produced in a range of finishes suitable for use in external walls. Unlike the aerated blocks, these blocks do not need rendering.

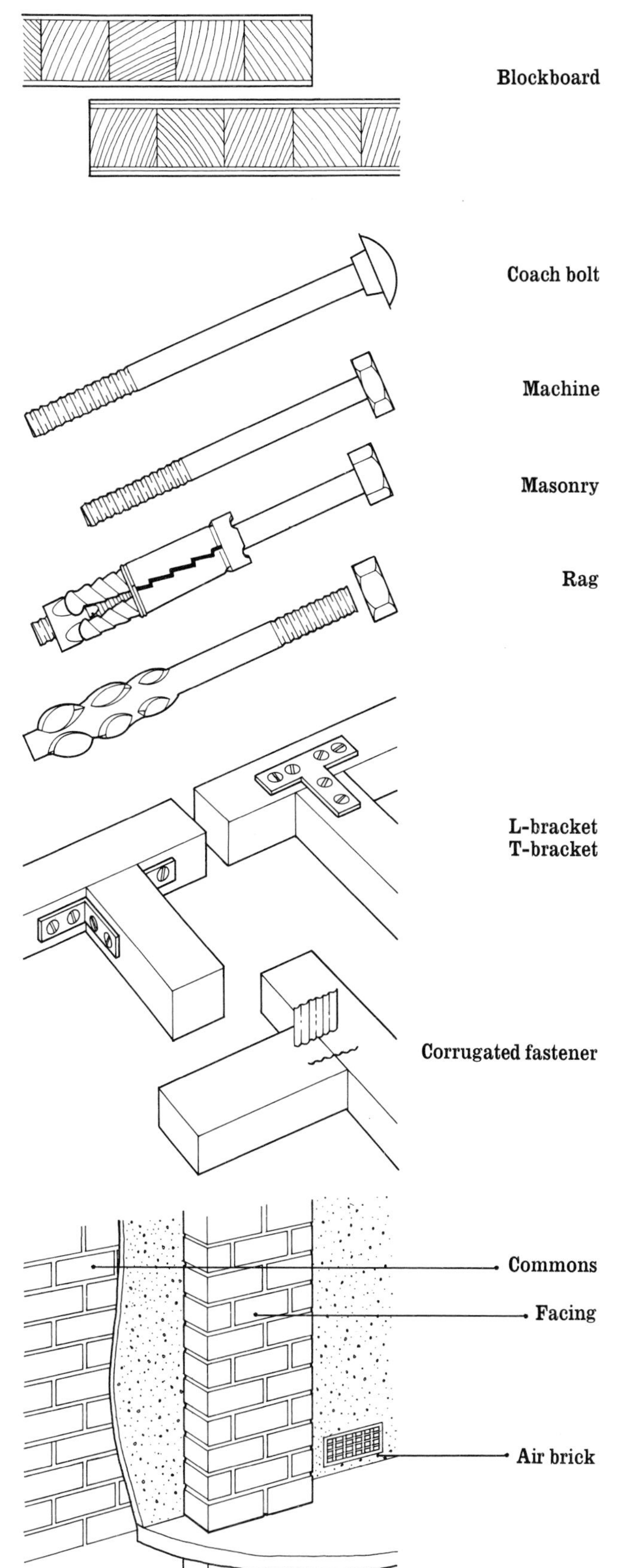

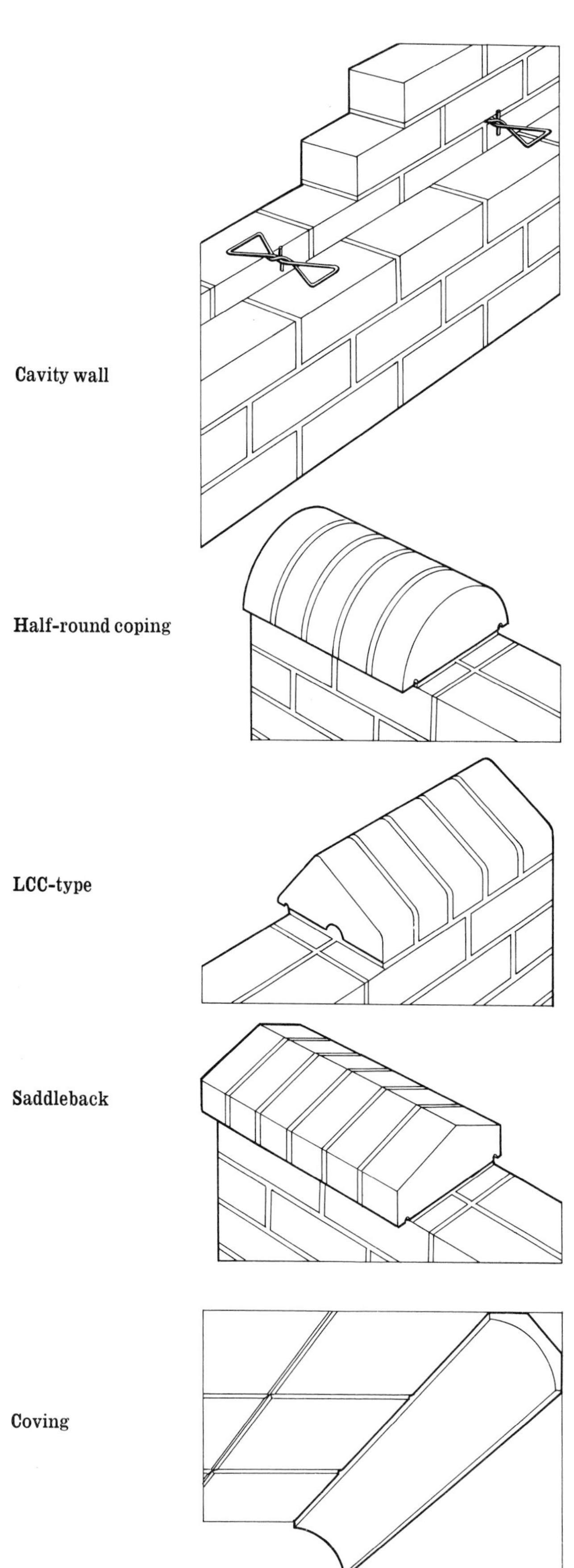


**Carbon tetrachloride (CTC)**
Liquid solvent used as a cleaning agent to remove oil and grease—in particular to degrease some woods, such as teak, before gluing, so that the glue will stick well. It should never be used in poorly ventilated areas.

**Cavity wall**
Damp-proof wall, consisting of two sections of bricks or blocks with a gap of about 50mm/2in between them to prevent moisture reaching the inner wall. .Metal ties give it strength.

**Cellulose lacquer**
Furniture finish recognizable by its glossy appearance. It is not heat-resistant, and moisture should be wiped off immediately.

**Cement**
A powder which, when combined with water, sets hard to bond the aggregate in concrete and mortar. Ordinary Portland cement, obtainable from builders' merchants, is suitable for most jobs requiring concrete, mortar or grout—the filling between individual wall and floor tiles.

Masonry cement is used for pointing brickwork, as bedding mortar for wall tiles and for interior and exterior finishes. White Portland cement provides an attractive finish for rendering, or when used with coloured slabs.

**Chamfer**
Angled face made by paring off the corner of a piece of wood or stone.

**Chase**
A groove cut into a brick or blockwork wall, or a concrete floor, so that conduits can be concealed beneath the finished surface.

**Chipboard**
Board made from chips of softwood bonded together under high pressure and temperature. Chipboard is normally made up of alternating layers of fine and coarse chips. Standard chipboard is suitable for interior use only; for outside work, use the specified special-quality board.

**Chisel** *See* Tip 135

**Claw hammer** *See* Tip 251

**Clench-nailing**
Procedure in nailing wood to wood. The nails are driven home from opposite directions and the points are bent over and hammered flat.

**Compass** *See* Tip 40

**Concrete**
Mixture of cement, aggregate and water. The ingredients are mixed together in different proportions, according to the strength required.

Concrete has two forms—*in situ* and precast. The former is the wet mixture, prepared by hand or machine, and poured into specially prepared formwork. It is normally used for laying foundations, paths and drives. Precast concrete comes ready-made as paving slabs, beams or lintels.

**Coping**
Capping, made from hard brick, stone, concrete, metal or terracotta, used to finish the tops of walls as a protection against bad weather. Copings are either double-weathered (sloping two ways) or single-weathered (sloping one way). They project beyond each face of the wall and have drips on the underside to prevent water running back on to the wall.

**Coping saw** *See* Tip 493

**Cove/coving**
Ready-made covings, which form a curved join between ceiling and wall, are frequently used to disguise cracks and provide a decorative finish. Plaster covings have a smoother texture than polystyrene covings, but polystyrene covings must always be used when fitting ceiling tiles.

**Cramping block** *See* Tip 475

**Creosote**
General-purpose wood preservative, used on external timber and fence posts to protect the wood from the weather and to prevent the growth of fungus. Gate posts and tall weight-carrying fence posts should be pressure-impregnated with preservative by the supplier before purchase.

**Crevice brush** *See* Tip 54

**Crosscut saw** *See* Tip 309

**Curing**
Procedure of covering newly laid concrete with damp sacking or plastic sheeting to prevent the surface drying out too quickly and subsequently cracking.

**Cutting-in brush** *See* Tip 122

**Damp-proof course**
A layer of impervious material built into walls between two courses of bricks to prevent damp rising. It must be a minimum of 150mm/6in above ground level.

Damp-proof courses are also used in parapets and chimneys, and round door and window openings. Layers of similar material, used beneath concrete floors, are known as damp-proof membranes. The most common damp-proofing materials are made from bituminous felt and toughened polythene; both can be bought in rolls.

**Dividers** *See* Tip 271

**Double glazing**
Two panes of glass with a gap between them which helps to keep heat in and noise out. The simplest D-I-Y fitting is a removable pane which is fitted into a plastic channel and fixed to the frame.

A gap of 19mm/¾in reduces heat loss by half. A wider gap of 100mm/4in to 200mm/8in will provide effective sound insulation. Note that a good seal around the panes is important if double glazing is to be efficient.

**Dry mix**
A mortar or concrete mix in which little water is used; the drier the mix, the stronger the mortar or concrete will be.

**Dry rot**
A fungus which attacks damp and poorly ventilated woodwork and is often a symptom of structural defects. Its presence is indicated by the "dry" condition of the wood, a red rusty dust and a musty "mushroomy" smell. Small areas can be dealt with by the amateur, but large areas require thorough specialist treatment. If in doubt, always seek expert advice.

**Dusting brush** *See* Tip 307

**Efflorescence**
White powdery substance which appears as patches on walls. It is the result of the salts in the bricks crystallizing on the surface as a result of evaporation.

**Expanded polystyrene**
Lightweight insulating material, bought in blocks, sheets or tiles, used to insulate walls and ceilings.

**Fasteners** *See* Brackets

**Felt paper**
Light economical underlay that is used to cover floors if dust rises between the floorboards.

**Fibreboard**
Board or sheet made of wood pulp or other fibres. Common types are known as hardboard, wallboard or insulating board.

**Files** *See* Tip 491

**Filler**
Usually cellulose-based, used for filling holes and cracks in walls, ceilings and other plaster or wood surfaces. There is a variety of special-purpose fillers that should be selected according to suitability for a particular job.

Ordinary cellulose filler is suitable for most indoor plaster repairs. A ready-mixed filler is often more convenient and easy to use and will give an extra smooth finish. A special-purpose filler is also available for filling cracks in walls and ceilings—flexible enough to keep cracks covered even if movement occurs. It is "self-texturing" and one coat is enough to give a good decorative finish. Another special-purpose filler is designed for use on chipped or scratched paintwork.

Exterior fillers are specially formulated to give extra strength and resistance to wear. They can be used for a wide range of outdoor repairs, including work on concrete, stone, brickwork, cement screeding and rendering.

The specified type of wood filler should be used for interior and exterior repairs. Exterior wood filler will withstand bad weather and is particularly suited for repairs in and around woodwork where the material is subject to a degree of movement.

Damp-proof course

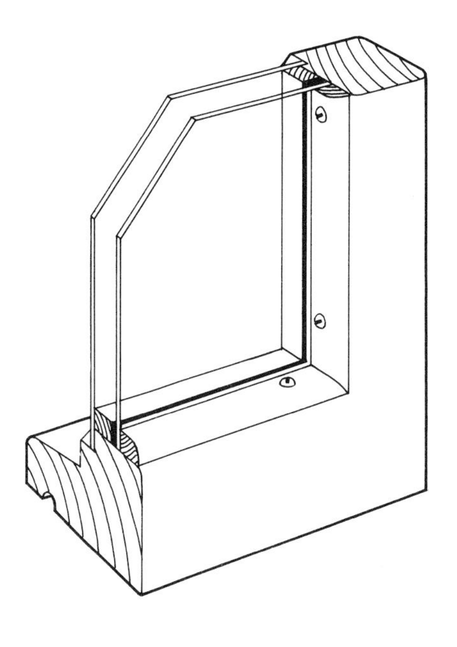

Double-glazing

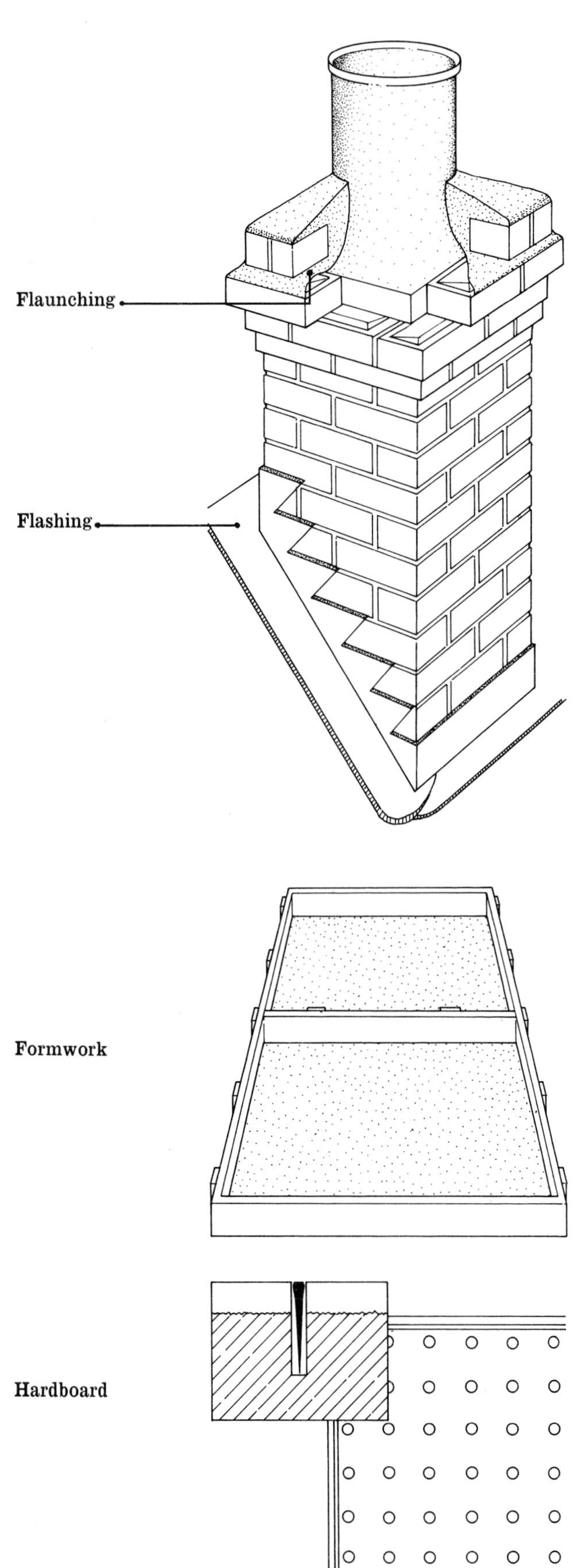


**Fine-gauge drill** *See* Tip 214

**Flashing**
Strips of metal or bituminized felt used to weatherproof the junctions between different materials in different planes, as, for example, the junction between chimney stack and surrounding roof.

**Flaunching**
Cement mortar surrounding the base of chimney pots to seal the chimney stack against rain.

**Flux**
Substance with which metals being soldered together are coated. It prevents the surface of the metals oxidizing and aids the flow of the solder. All-purpose proprietary fluxes are suitable for most jobs, but note that, generally speaking, resin should be used for electrical connections, tallow for pewter and lead and borax for hard soldering.

**Folding rule** *See* Tip 698

**Formwork**
Timber construction used as a frame for casting concrete.

**Frenchman** *See* Tip 645

**Fretsaw** *See* Tip 439

**G-cramp** *See* Tip 231

**Gimlet** *See* Tip 366

**Glasspaper**
The most commonly used abrasive paper, ranging in quality from coarse to fine, and used on its own, around a hand-held block or on a power tool. The finish that glasspaper will give to a surface depends on the type of paper used. For a fine finish, start with a coarse grade and end with a fine one. Always keep it dry.

**Glasspaper block** *See* Tip 678

**Glaze**
Thin wash of colour, usually over graining or marble, to give additional depth, colour and transparency to the surface.

**Glazing bars**
Metal or wooden bars, which form the framework of window panes.

**Grout**
Cement-based material, used for filling gaps between ceramic or clay floor tiles. It can be bought in powder form and mixed with water, or as a ready-mixed compound. Always use water-resistant grout on exterior work or where tiles will be exposed to running water, as on the floor and walls of shower units. Note, in addition, that some proprietary grouts contain white pigment, which gives a better decorative finish than ordinary grout.

**Hacksaw** *See* Tip 288

**Hammer** *See* Tip 327

**Hardboard**
High-density material, made from softwood pulp compressed into sheets under heat and high pressure. It is obtainable in standard, medium and tempered grades.

Standard hardboard has one smooth surface and one rough one. It can also be bought in a vàriety of decorative embossed finishes. Unfinished hardboard should always be sealed before papering or painting.

Double-faced hardboard, when both surfaces are finished, is used when both sides of the board will be visible. Enamelled hardboard is coated with a plastic-based paint, and, as a consequence, is very hard-wearing. Plastic laminate-faced hardboard has one surface coated with melamine or PVC, which is both decorative and easily cleaned. It is ofted used for sliding doors. Tempered hardboard is impregnated with oil to make it hard and water-resistant. It can be used as finished flooring or as a lining for walls and ceilings in outside buildings.

**Hardcore**
Broken bricks, rubble or stone, used as a base for paths, drives, foundations and concrete floors.

**Hardwood**
Although usually more expensive than softwood, hardwood is more durable and hard-wearing, as its finished surface is more resistant to marking. Examples include oak, beech, cherry, chestnut, elm, mahogany, rosewood, walnut and teak.

**Hawk** *See* Tip 179

**Hinges**
Hinges must be able to support the full weight of the fitting when open. Types in common use include:

*Concealed or "soss" hinge* Used on cabinets to make doors flush with cabinet frame or for screens.

*Fixed-pin butt hinge* Used mainly for doors and windows.

*Joint stay* Used on cabinets for opening door to angle of 90°.

*Rising-butt hinge* Causes a door to rise slightly on opening so as to clear carpet on other side.

*Spring-loaded hinge* Used on heavy screen doors so that they close automatically.

*Wide-angled hinge* Enables a door to fit flush with the outside of the cupboard frame.

**Honing**
The process of sharpening tools on an oilstone to give them a razor-sharp edge.

**Insulating board**
Lightly compressed in manufacture, it has a low density and good thermal insulation and sound-absorption qualities. Often used as a pinboard.

*Medium hardboard* Known as wall board, it has a medium density and is most frequently used for partitioning.

**Joints**
There is a large variety of carpentry joints, but the average handyman need only be concerned with a few of the basic ones:

*Butt joint* Simplest of joints, which can be made straight or right-angled. It is secured by nails, corrugated fasteners, brackets, screws or glue.

*Dovetail joint* A very strong joint, as its angled sides make it impossible to pull apart. The through dovetail is both the strongest and most decorative version, and is frequently used when making drawers. However, all forms of joint require skill to make.

*Halving joint* A simple joint to make, it is neat in appearance and very strong. Glue is the fixing medium. Halving joints can be L-shaped, T-shaped or X-shaped. T-shaped halving joints are used in the construction of simple framework, and the X-shaped joint when two pieces of timber have to cross each other without increasing the thickness of one piece.

*Housing joint* The through housing joint is a frequently used T-joint, particularly for shelving because it resists a downward thrust well.

*Lapped joint* Full- and half-lap joints are strong and neat, and are frequently used in panelling.

*Mitre joint* Used for picture framing and larger jobs, such as bookcases, it has a neat appearance because the end grain of the wood is concealed. Joints are usually glued and pinned, but, for extra strength, dowels or loose-tongue mitres can be used.

*Mortise-and-tenon joint* One of the strongest T-joints. The through mortise-and-tenon is an even stronger version, used in heavy framing and furniture work.

**Key**
Roughening of a smooth surface to provide a bond or grip for materials such as paint, plaster, rendering, adhesive or cement.

**Keyhole saw** *See* Tip 162

**Knot** *See* Timber

**Knotting**
Shellac and methylated spirit solution, used to seal the surface of knots in new timber, preventing the resin from bleeding through the paint.

**Laminate**
All plastic laminates are made from layers of paper or fabric impregnated with synthetic resin and bonded together under heat and pressure into a rigid sheet. They are hard wearing and have good resistance to heat. Standard grade thickness is 1.5 mm/$\frac{1}{16}$ in.

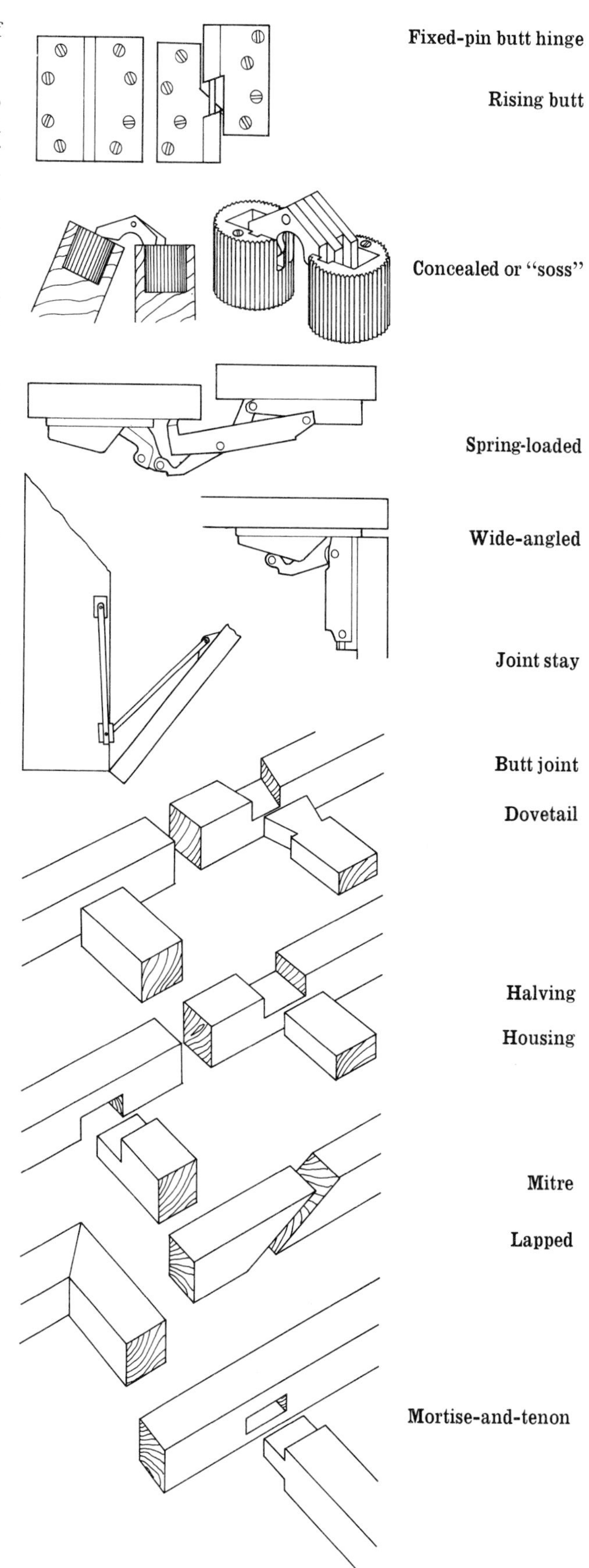

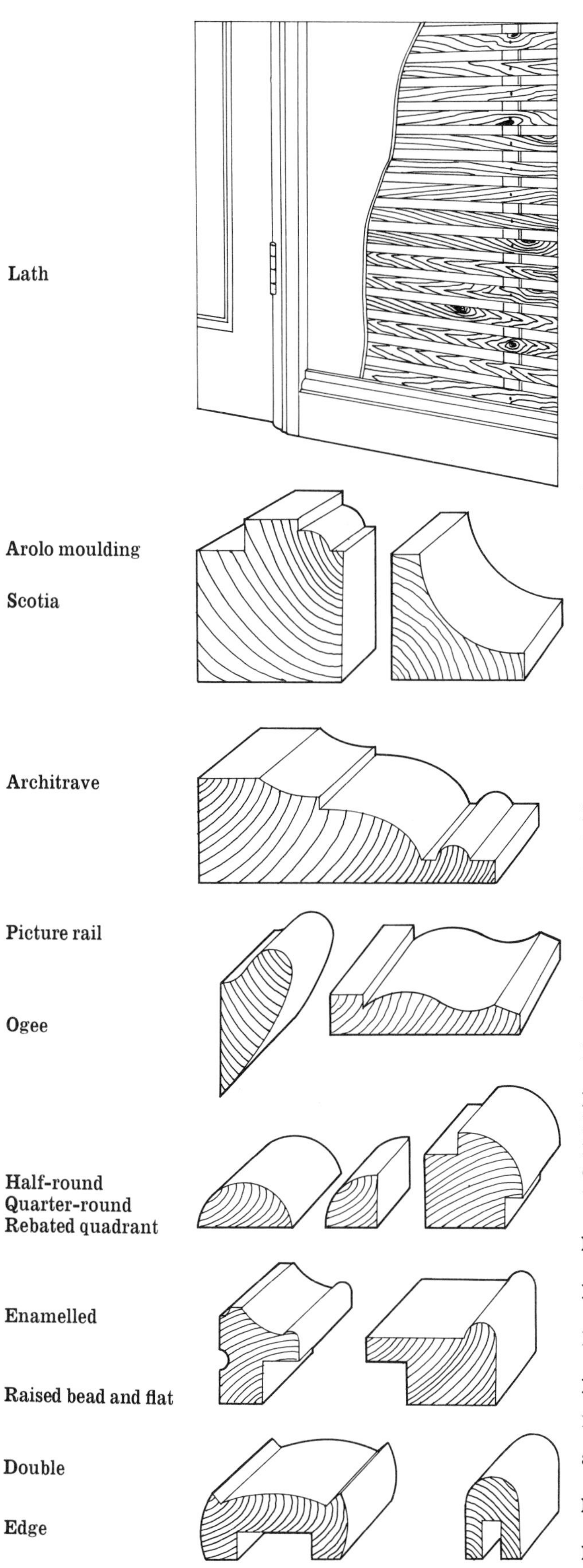


**Lath**
Strips of wood used as a fixing surface for wall and ceiling plaster. The laths are nailed to the joists, or uprights in the wall, separated by 8 mm/⅜ in gaps to provide a key for plaster. Lath and plaster was the traditional way of constructing an internal wall or ceiling, but has since been discontinued in favour of other methods.

**Lime**
Normally sold as hydrated lime or quicklime. Used in mortar it reduces drying shrinkage, so enabling the mortar to retain water, making the mix more workable.

**Lining paper**
Used to improve adhesion for heavier wallpapers, or as a base for paint, lining paper is available in light and medium weights. It should always be used when papering a surface that has been treated with an oil-based paint. A special "finished" lining paper—incorporating small chips of wood—can be used to cover poor plaster work before painting with emulsion. It provides a textured finish.

**Linseed oil**
Cheap and easy to use wood finish. It darkens timber to give a tough water-resistant non-gloss finish. Linseed oil is normally used on teak, rosewood and mahogany. It should not be applied to light-coloured timbers and softwoods as it will discolour them.

**Mallet** *See* Tip 456

**Marble**
Hard stone that polishes well and is available in several different colours. It is suitable for table tops, fireplaces, hearthstones.

**Marking gauge** *See* Tip 349

**Masonry punch** *See* Tip 195

**Metal float** *See* Tip 354

**Methylated spirit**
Alcohol with wood spirit additive. Used for stripping French polish and water-based paints.

**Miniature screwdriver** *See* Tip 541

**Mitre block** *See* Tip 87

**Mortar**
Cement and fine aggregate mix, used to joint brickwork. The mix should be neither much stronger nor much weaker than the type of brick being laid.

**Mortise gauge** *See* Tip 543

**Mouldings**
Decorative ornamental fittings. Architraves are used on doors, double astragal mouldings cover joints and edge mouldings can be used on hardboard or ply—but there are many different varieties.

**Nail punch** *See* Tip 511

**Nails**
A wide range of nails varying in shape, size, metal and finish is available; choose according to suitability for a particular job. Nails can be made of mild steel, brass, aluminium alloy, copper, or they can be galvanized. The following nails are the most commonly used in general-purpose D-I-Y jobs.

*Annular nail* Used for nailing sheet material, such as plywood, to wood. Its teeth give a strong grip.

*Chair nail* Used for concealing tacks when upholstering; the nails come in various finishes, such as bronze, copper and chrome.

*Clout nail* A galvanized nail with an extra large head, used primarily for fixing roof felt or plasterboard.

*Cut tack* Used for nailing linoleum and carpets.

*Duplex head nail* Used for temporary fixing, its double head makes it easy to remove.

*Floor brad* Used for fixing floorboards to joists.

*Lost head nail* Used in general carpentry and flooring work when there is no risk of splitting the wood. The head can be punched below the surface and the hole filled.

*Masonry nail* The purpose-made nail for driving into concrete and brick. It is made from hard steel and provides a very strong fixing.

*Oval wire nail* Used in carpentry work where the head of the nail has to be sunk below the surface. It is unlikely to split wood.

*Panel pin* Used for fixing hardboard or thin plywood to timber frames. It has a small head and fine gauge and is barely visible when driven below the surface.

*Roofing nail* Galvanized roofing nails are used for fitting corrugated roofing to rafters.

*Round wire nail* Used for general all-purpose nailing. It has a strong gripping power.

*Sprig* Small wire nail with little or no head. A glazing sprig is used to hold a pane of glass in its frame.

*Staples* Provide quick and easy anchorage for fence wire and upholstery.

**Notched spreader** *See* Tip 21

**Nuts**
The thread of the nut should always match the thread of the bolt; if these do not match, then the threads may be stripped when the nut is tightened. Hexagonal and square-headed nuts are the most common. Lock nuts, such as the split-pin lock and the fibre lock, are so-called because they are self-locking; use them if there is a risk of vibration loosening the fitting. Wing nuts are suitable for use when the fitting only needs to be hand-tight and easily removable. T-nuts are a specialized furniture bolt.

**Oilstone**
Used for sharpening tools. Although natural stones, such as Washita or Arkansas, can be bought, the artificial stones such as India, Carborundum and Aloxite are more easily obtainable and have the advantage of constant quality. There are three grades of oilstone—coarse, medium and fine. A coarse stone is used for removing a chipped cutting edge, medium-grade stone for the intermediate sharpening stage and a fine-grade stone for the final cutting edge (*see also* Tip 249).

**Oxalic acid**
A poisonous and highly dangerous acid mainly used in a dilute solution as a woodwork bleach and for removing stains. Always wear rubber gloves when handling it.

**Paint brushes** *See* Tip 56

**Paint pad** *See* Tip 89

**Paint roller** *See* Tip 609

**Paint**
There are two basic types of paint used in household painting—emulsion, a water-based paint generally used on walls and ceilings, and gloss paint, an oil-based paint used on woodwork and metalwork. A high proportion of paints now sold are "gel-type"—known as thixotropic—which are non-drip. They adhere well to a brush or roller, minimize splashing and have good covering power.

Proprietary brands of exterior wall finishes are available for outdoor work. Both water-based and oil-based paints can be used, depending on the finish required; both are specially formulated to provide a weather-resistant finish.

*Emulsions* Conventional emulsion dries to a matt finish. It has the disadvantage of a dull surface, which tends to show up marks. It cannot be washed and can only be lightly wiped. Emulsions of the non-drip variety are generally more durable, moisture resistant and washable than conventional emulsions. Some proprietary emulsions have special additives that enable them to cover woodwork and metalwork as well as walls and ceilings. They are available in a wide range of finishes, ranging from matt through to various stages of sheen and gloss. Brands containing vinyl will be tough and washable.

*Gloss paints* Generally used on surfaces requiring a tough finish that can withstand frequent cleaning. Unless using a non-drip variety, an undercoat should always be applied first. Many gloss paints today contain additives to increase toughness; some brands are made up so that brushes only need to be washed out in soap and water after use.

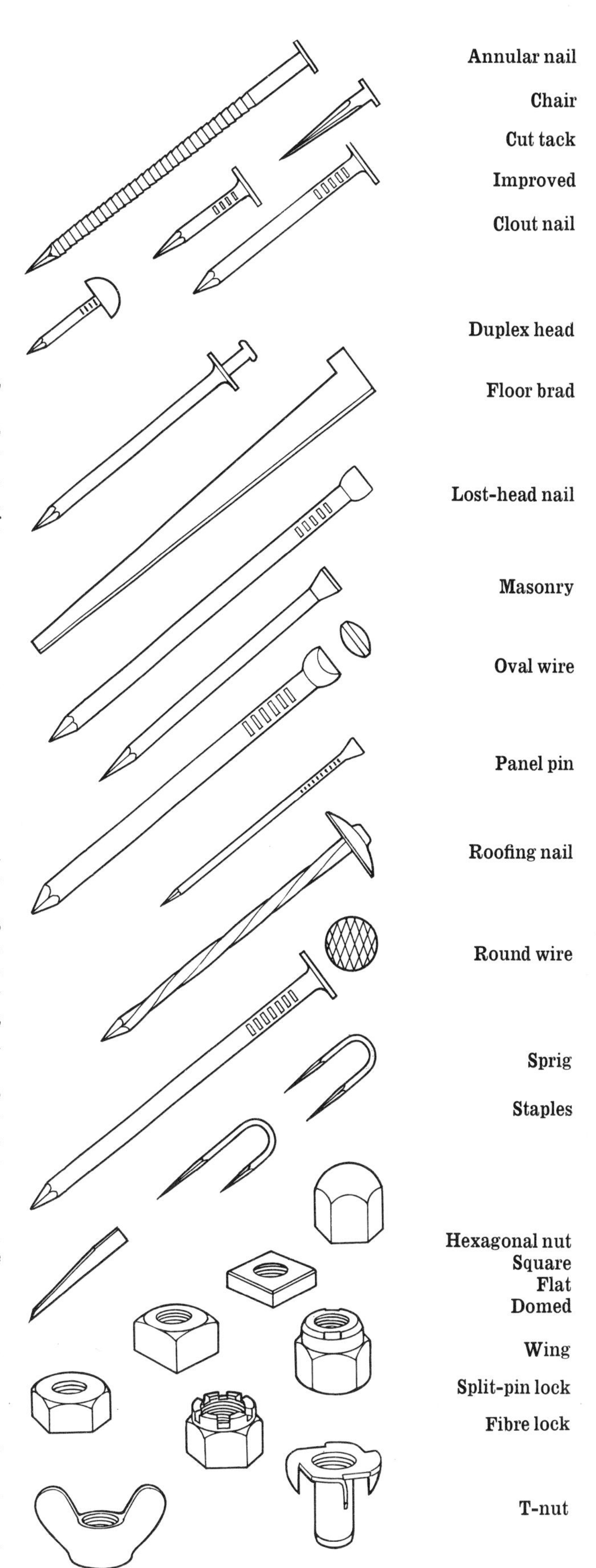

Annular nail
Chair
Cut tack
Improved
Clout nail
Duplex head
Floor brad
Lost-head nail
Masonry
Oval wire
Panel pin
Roofing nail
Round wire
Sprig
Staples
Hexagonal nut
Square
Flat
Domed
Wing
Split-pin lock
Fibre lock
T-nut

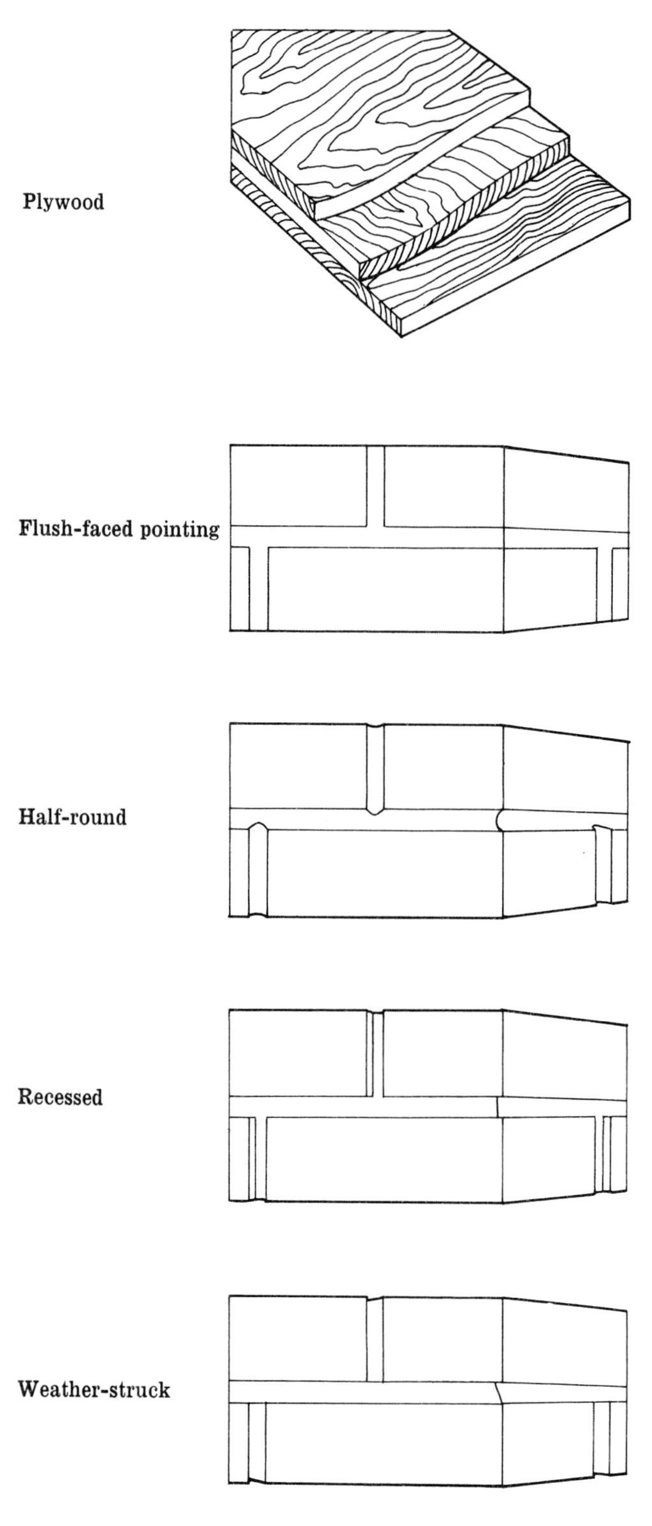


**Paint stripper**
Liquid chemical used for removing paint. Strippers can be used on metal and plaster as well as wood. Brands vary in suitability for different jobs, so always ask the retailer's advice. Stripper contains strong chemicals, which can burn, so always wear gloves when using it. If necessary, lay paper on the floor beneath the item being stripped—the paint that peels off will be impregnated with the stripper and may affect existing paintwork, as well as being a hazard to children or pets.

**Panel saw** *See* Tip 509

**Paraffin blowlamp** *See* Tip 529

**Pare**
Trimming the outer surface or edge of an object with a cutting or shaving action.

**Pasting brush** *See* Tip 611

**Paving slab**
These can be home-cast or ready-cast. Home-cast slabs are made using the same mixing technique as for laying concrete paths. However, use them only for paths and garden walls, as they have no structural strength. When buying ready-cast slabs, add an additional 5 per cent to requirements to take care of breakages.

**Pebble dash**
Decorative finish given to an exterior wall, and frequently used to disguise irregular wall surfaces. Fine pebbles or crushed stone are scattered on to a cement-rendered wall while the cement is still wet. The pebble dash should be painted with a protective waterproof paint to give added protection against erosion.

**Pelmet**
Wood or fabric covering at the top of a window, which conceals the curtain fittings.

**Pincers** *See* Tip 419

**Pin hammer** *See* Tip 382

**Plane** *See* Tip 625

**Plaster**
Modern plasters are based on gypsum, and ready-mixed brands can be bought for undercoats and finishing coats. The type of plaster required will vary, depending on the condition of the surface, so always ask the advice of the retailer. When mixing plaster, always follow the manufacturer's instructions carefully, as it is vital to achieve the right consistency to get the correct finish.

Plastering is a skilled job, so large areas such as complete walls and ceilings should be left to a professional, but repairs and small areas are well within the scope of the handyman.

**Plasterboard**
Fire-resistant material with a smooth surface; it is made up of a core of plaster of Paris sandwiched between two sheets of heavy paper. Plasterboard is easy to cut and decorate. It is used for lining walls and ceilings and should be sealed before painting or papering. Some types can be bought with an aluminium foil backing; use them when additional insulation is needed.

**Pliers** *See* Tip 437

**Plugs** *See* Wallplugs

**Plumb line**
Machine-made brass or lead weight tied to a builder's line and used for establishing true verticals (*see also* Tip 402).

**Plywood**
Sheet material made up of an odd number of veneers glued together under pressure with the grain in each veneer at right angles to the next layer for strength and stability. The greater the number of veneers, the stronger the sheet of plywood. Plywood sheets range from 3-ply to 11-ply and are made in both hardwood and softwood. Plywood can also be bought with plastic laminate or a hardwood veneer surface. Since wet or heat can cause plywood to warp, use exterior quality for exterior work.

**Pointing**
Term used for finishing off the mortar in brickwork. In time the pointing in a wall may deteriorate, so enabling dampness to get into a wall; in these circumstances

always repoint the brickwork. In addition, note that mortar joints should never be finished so that they slope inwards—from the top down—or water will collect on the top edges of the bricks and hasten deterioration. The following types of joints should be used:

*Flush-faced* This is formed by cutting the mortar off flush with the face of the brick. On old brickwork, where the bricks are badly chipped, an effective finish can be achieved by converting the flush-faced joint into a "bagged" joint. This is done by rubbing the mortar over the face of the brick with a piece of sackcloth. The ultimate effect, when the wall is painted a single flat colour, is effective and weatherproof.

*Half-round* This is a good weatherproof joint and can be formed by using an old bucket handle.

*Recessed* A joint largely favoured for its aesthetic appearance—it causes strong shadows, which are cast on the joint line. It is best used on hard engineering bricks, which are better able to resist the effects of frost, but is unsuitable for use in coastal regions, where the effects of weathering are extreme. The joint is formed by waiting until the mortar is almost dry and then scraping it out with a flat strip of hardwood moulding to form the recess.

*Weather-struck* Its sloping surface makes for very good protection against rain. The joint is recessed under the top brick and slightly overhangs the lower brick. Use a pointing trowel to fill the joints with mortar and the same tool to form the overhangs, working along a straight-edge lined up with the top of the lower brick.

**Polyurethane**

Polyurethane lacquer, which has good heat- and water-resistant properties, gives a tough finish to timber. It is easy to apply and can be bought in a proprietary pack. Coloured polyurethane lacquers are transparent stains that allow the grain of wood to show through. Before applying it, make sure that all traces of previous finishes have been removed.

**Power tools**

Power tools take the hard work out of many D-I-Y jobs involving drilling, sawing, sanding, smoothing and polishing. The basic and most useful tool is the electric drill, which can be bought with a single- or variable-speed motor. The latter works either through a mechanical gearbox or an electric change. With a mechanical gearbox, the turning force, or torque, of the drill is increased at a lower speed, but with an electric change the torque is reduced. A drill with a mechanical gearbox is therefore a better buy if a really low drilling speed is required; the chief advantage of the electric change is that it increases physical control of the drill.

The size of a drill is classified by the largest drill size that its chuck—the part that grips the attachments—can take. The larger the chuck, the wider the range of attachments that can be used.

*Twist bits* A set of bits, ranging in diameter from small to large, will cope with most drilling jobs.

*Special bits* These include masonry bits, designed for drilling into bricks and concrete; countersunk bits, for countersinking screws; a combination bit, designed to both drill a screw hole and to countersink it at the same time; and a spearpoint bit, designed for drilling glass. A hole saw bit is useful for cutting holes in plywood, hardboard and timber—but note that it should not be used on material more than 6mm/¼in thick. For larger holes, use a power bore bit.

After completing any drilling job, always rub down the bits that have been used with steel wool and then wipe them with a rag dipped in thin oil. Make sure that all waste wood is removed from the grooves; otherwise the bits will clog, overheat and be ruined.

*Sanding and polishing* Basic attachments are a rubber backing pad and a selection of abrasive discs, ranging from coarse to fine; a wire brush for cleaning bare metal; and a lamb's-wool bonnet for polishing.

*Saws* A circular saw attachment is invaluable. Different types of

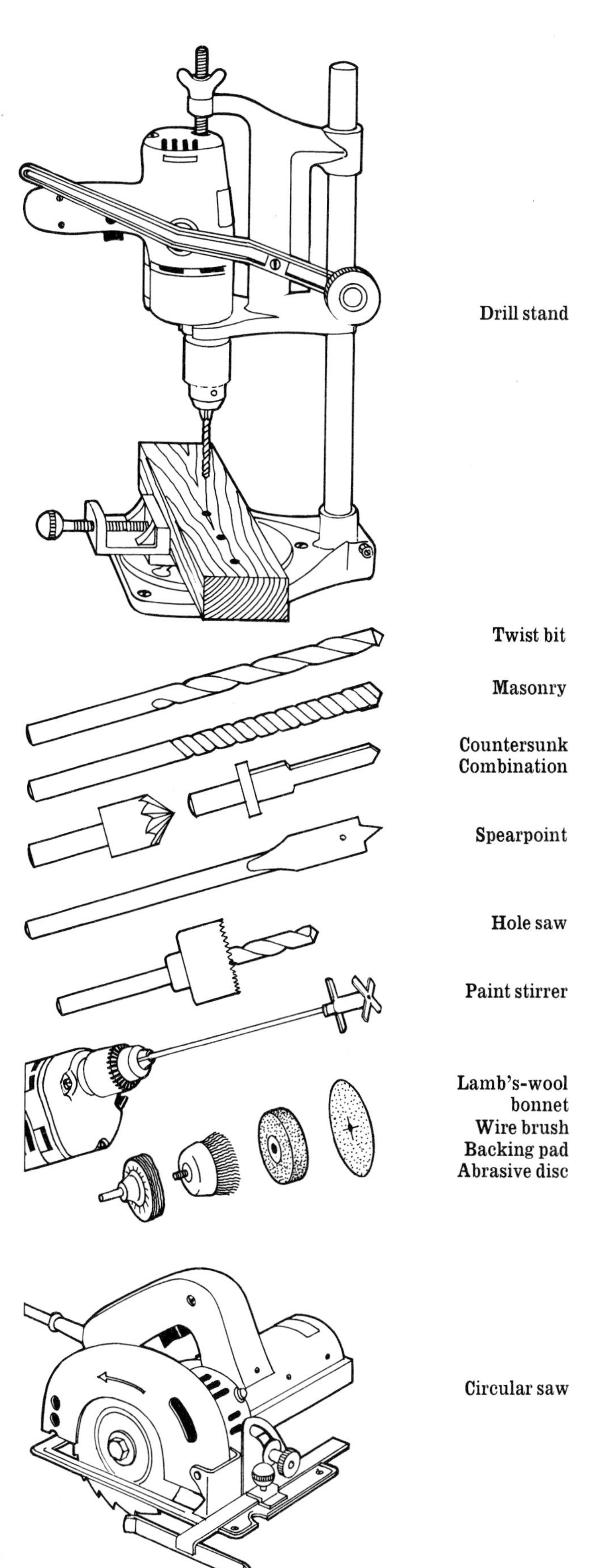

Drill stand

Twist bit

Masonry

Countersunk
Combination

Spearpoint

Hole saw

Paint stirrer

Lamb's-wool bonnet
Wire brush
Backing pad
Abrasive disc

Circular saw

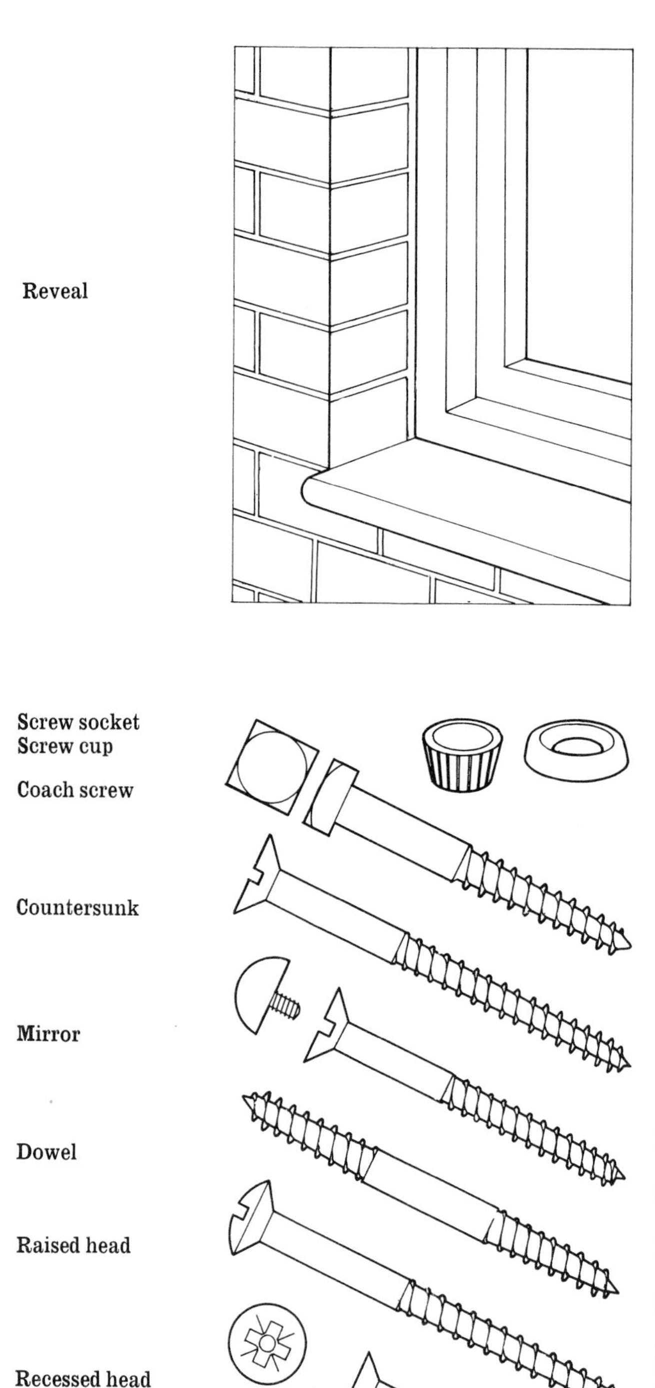


blade can be bought for coarse or fine sawing. Jig saw attachments are also available.

In addition, a drill stand is a useful purchase, so that drilling can be carried out accurately.

Before buying any extra attachments, however, always check that they can be used with the drill. Many accessories will only fit a drill made by the same manufacturer.

**Primer**
First coat of paint or specially formulated liquid, used to provide a good key for subsequent coats of paint or as a protective base. It seals the surface and prevents paint from soaking into it.

A primer should always be used on all new unpainted surfaces—both externally and internally—that are to be painted with an oil-based paint; it is not normally necessary, however, when finishing with a water-based paint inside the house. Acrylic primer also acts as undercoat. All-surface primers are available, but it is preferable, whenever possible, to use the primers designed specifically for use on wood, metal, building boards, plaster or concrete.

**Putty**
Used in glazing to seal glass. Linseed oil putty is used for wooden frames, and metal casement putty for metal frames.

**Putty knife** *See* Tip 105

**Rasp** *See* Tip 473

**Rasp plane** *See* Tip 454

**Ratchet screwdriver** *See* Tip 19

**Rebate**
Rectangular recess along a piece of timber to receive another piece of material.

**Render**
To apply cement mortar or plaster to the face of a wall.

**Riser** *See* Stair

**Reveal**
Vertical side of an opening in a wall, such as a window or arched opening, usually set at right angles to it.

**Sash brush** *See* Tip 559

**Sash cramp** *See* Tip 146

**Scratcher** *See* Tip 193

**Screed**
Sand and cement layer over a concrete sub-floor to provide a smooth surface suitable for laying tiles, linoleum and so forth.

**Screw cups and sockets**
Function similarly to washers; they simplify dismantling.

**Screwdriver** *See* Tip 4

**Screws**
Screws are classified by their gauge—the diameter of their shanks—and their overall length. Lengths may differ, but the gauge number does not vary; the thinner the screw, the lower the gauge. They are normally made of steel or brass. Common types are:

*Coach screw* Used for strong fixing in heavy construction.

*Countersunk* Used in general woodwork. It has a flat head which can be driven flush with the surface or slightly below it.

*Mirror screw* Used when the screwhead would detract from appearance, as in fixing mirrors. A chrome-capped head threads into the screwhead.

*Dowel screw* Used in invisible woodwork joining.

*Raised head* Also used in general woodwork, this has a neater appearance than the countersunk screw. Nickel- or aluminium-plated versions can be used for fixing door handle plates.

*Recessed head* Also used in woodwork, it has the advantage of being easier to fit in confined spaces. However, a special screwdriver is needed to fit the screws.

*Round head* Used primarily for fitting metal to timber; the head protrudes from the surface.

*Self-tapping* Used to fix thin plastic, metal sheets, etc. As the screw is tightened it cuts its own thread.

**Scriber** *See* Tip 347

**Sealant**
Material used for making water-tight repairs outdoors and in bathrooms and kitchens. Sealants are flexible materials that are able to adhere to the adjacent surfaces and still expand and contract with structural movements.

Soft mastics are the most commonly used sealants. They are applied with a trowel, mastic gun or straight from the tube. Sealing tape is generally used on surfaces that have a hole or leak—for example, when temporarily sealing a lean-to roof.

**Sealer**
Coat of paint or other material applied to a surface to seal it in preparation for finishing. Special sealers are available for different surfaces, such as wood and floors.

**Seam roller** *See* Tip 715

**Shave hook** *See* Tip 700

**Shellac**
Type of resin found in trees. It forms the basis of varnish and most types of polish.

**"S" hook** *See* Tip 595

**Smoothing brush** *See* Tip 368

**Soil pipe**
A pipe that conveys waste material from a water closet to the drainage system.

**Soldering**
Joining metals by using a soldering iron to heat the solder until it melts and then, with a flux, running the solder between them. Solder generally comes in strip or wire form. Soft solder is a mixture of tin and lead. Soldering with soft solder is a low-temperature process, which is suitable for joints that will not take a lot of weight or heat. Alloys for hard soldering are made from copper, silver and zinc. The process gives a stronger join, but requires more heat than soft soldering.

**Spigot**
Projection at the end of a pipe that is inserted in the socket of another pipe to form a joint.

**Spirit level** *See* Tip 663

**Spokeshave** *See* Tip 578

**Spot board** *See* Tip 72

**Sprig** *See* Nails

**Stair**
The upright board is known as the riser, while the horizontal part is known as the tread.

**Stipple**
Textured finish achieved by dabbing with a brush.

**Stop cock**
A valve used to cut off the supply on a gas or water supply pipe.

**Straight-edge** *See* Tip 680

**Stripping knife** *See* Tip 120

**Surveyor's tape** *See* Tip 421

**Swingbrace drill** *See* Tip 627

**Tackless fitting**
Convenient fitting for fixing carpets. It consists of a length of wooden batten or metal strip with numerous spikes projecting at a 60° angle on one side. Fittings are nailed to the floor around the skirting with the spikes facing towards the wall. Where the fittings are being used on concrete or stone floors, they have to be glued to the floor.

**Tamping beam** *See* Tip 561

**Template**
A thin plate of any material cut to an outline of a surface for use as a cutting guide.

**Tenon**
End of a piece of wood cut so that it can be inserted into a recess or mortise. It can be secured by wedging or gluing.

**Tenon saw** *See* Tip 404

**Thinner**
Liquid used to regulate the thickness of paint or varnish. Methylated spirit can be used to thin French polish; however, always use a recommended proprietary thinner when thinning paint or lacquer.

Soil pipe

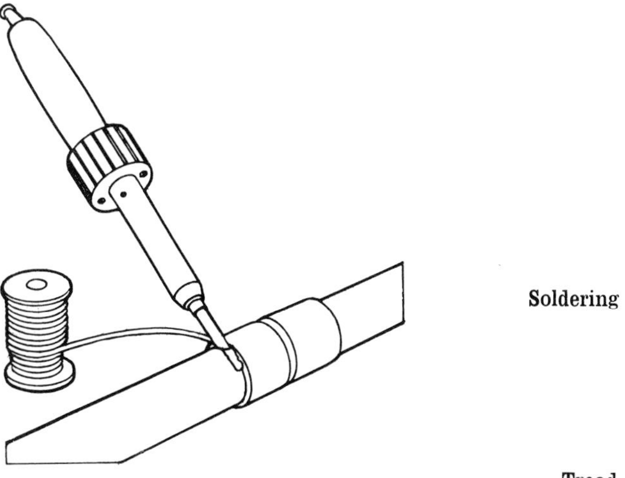

Soldering

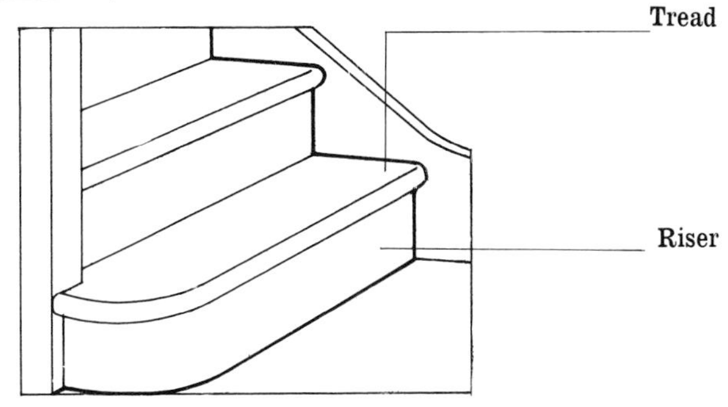


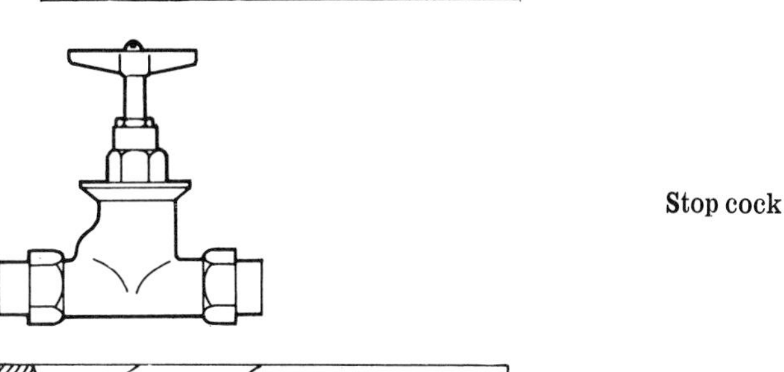

Stop cock

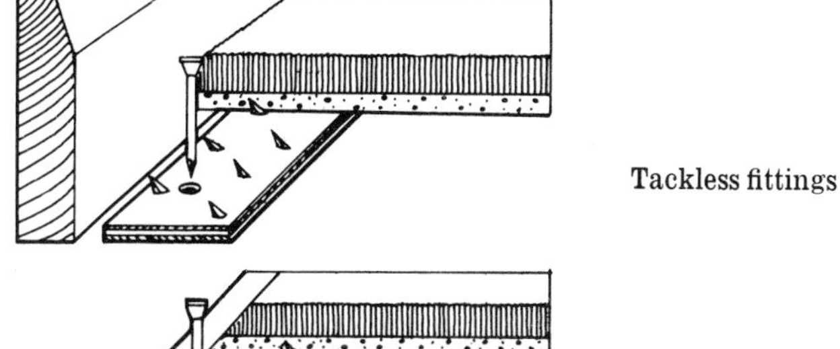

Tackless fittings

Dead knot

Live knot

Brittle heart

Cup shakes

End shakes

Tongued-and-grooved

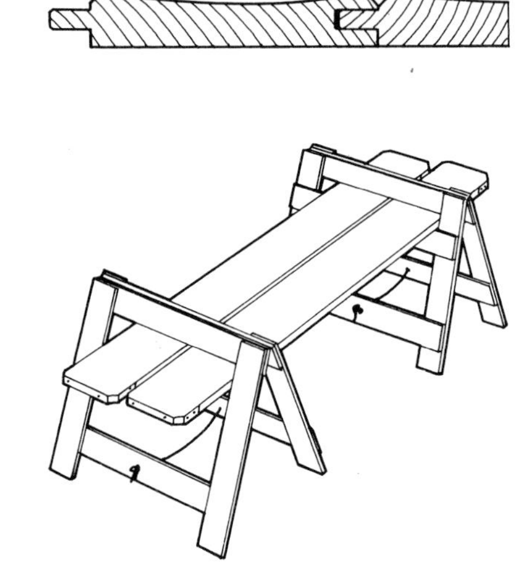

Trestle

**Tiles**

*Ceramic tiles* One of the most popular decorative tiles, ranging from Field tiles, with square edges for normal tiling, to RE tiles, with one rounded edge for finishing off the edge of a tiled area, and REX tiles with two rounded edges for use in corners.

*Cork tiles* Popular floor covering. They have to be laid on a firm, level surface and should be coated with a sealant and a hard wax polish. They are especially suitable for bathrooms, as they are warm to the touch.

*Mosaic tiles* Sold in sheets in varying mosaic patterns.

*Polystyrene tiles* Lightweight insulation tiles, frequently used on ceilings. They should never be coated with gloss paint and should be fixed with special adhesive.

*Quarry tiles* Unglazed hard-wearing tiles. They are either machine-made or man-made. Man-made tiles tend to vary slightly in size and shape and absorb more water than machine-made ones. The normal colours are red, buff or brown, but others are also available.

*Vinyl tiles* Hard-wearing grease-resistant tiles, usually used on floors. Some types are self-adhesive. Vinyl tiles should be covered with a sealant for long-lasting wear. Vinyl asbestos tiles are more brittle; they can be used in damp conditions.

**Timber**

Always ask for timber that has been seasoned—that is, that the timber has dried out naturally after being felled and cut into planks. Also always check that the colour of the wood is even throughout its length and that it has been stored level. Common faults to watch for in timber are:

*Brittle heart* Cracks across the grain of timber. Normally only found in hardwood, these cracks weaken the wood, which should not be used for structural work unless the faulty area is removed.

*Cup shakes* Splits in timber that has been cut mainly from the heartwood of the tree. The whole affected area should be sawn off.

*End shakes* Splits in the ends of boards caused by the ends drying out more quickly than the rest of the wood. When buying timber, make sure that the affected ends are cut off at least 25mm/1in in from the end of the longest split.

*Knots* Dead knots are usually star-shaped and surrounded by a black ring. When the timber dries out, they are likely to shrink and drop out of the wood. As a precaution, always remove them and then patch them back into place with glue. Live knots—without the black ring—do not normally shrink, but, as a safeguard, they should be coated with knotting.

**Tinning**

Name given to the process of covering metal with solder.

**Tinsnips** *See* Tip 729

**Toggles** *See* Anchors

**Tongued and grooved**

Interlocking boards that fit together to present a sound, gap-free surface. Each board has a groove on one edge and a projection on the other.

**Tread** *See* Stair

**Trestle**

A support for a horizontal platform acting as a work surface.

**Trimming knife** *See* Tip 713

**Trowel** *See* Tip 527

**Try square** *See* Tip 74

**T-square** *See* Tip 177

**Undercoat**

High-opacity paint, which dries quickly to form a base for the finishing coat.

**Underlay**

Sheet material used on flooring as a base for carpet. It is essential to use underlay for satisfactory carpeting, as it acts as a shock absorber between the carpet and the floor. However, some carpets now have their own foam-backing bonded to them, which makes underlay unnecessary.

A good-quality underlay will always give a better finish to the carpet than a poorer quality one. Paper felt is an inexpensive underlay, but is suitable only for rooms such as bedrooms, which are not in constant use. Underfelt is a more popular underlay; it consists of felt layers bonded together to give a cushion effect. Rubber underlays made of foam or natural rubber are also popular. They should not be used, however, where there is underfloor heating.

**Varnish**
Preservative, such as polyurethane, used chiefly on wood.

**Vice** *See* Tip 103

**Wallpaper**
There is a wide range of wallpaper types, some of which are ready pasted.

*Anaglypta* A strong embossed wallpaper; its variant—Supaglypta—is even stronger and more deeply embossed. Both aré suitable for covering crazed plaster.

*Common* Normally machine-printed and available in a variety of weights and qualities.

*Embossed* Available in light, medium or heavy weights. Heavy embossed wallpaper—called duplex—is a two-layer laminate.

*Flock paper* Silk, nylon or wool cuttings are glued to the surface of the paper during manufacture to give it a velvety texture.

*In-grain* Contains wood chips and has a rough texture.

*Mica print* Has a satin-like look.

*Moiré* Has a watered silk look.

*Textured paper* Often used to cover badly cracked ceilings and walls. The surface can be painted.

*Vinyl paper* A paper-backed PVC paper, which is very tough and washable and often selected for use in bathrooms and kitchens.

*Washable paper* Has a specially treated surface, which makes it water-resistant and easy to clean.

A fairly wide range of hand-printed wallpapers is also available. These tend to be more expensive, but of a high quality with a large variety of patterns.

**Wallplugs**
When fixing to a solid wall, it is essential to insert a suitable plug for the nail or screw to grip on. Plugs can be cut from offcuts of softwood; alternatively, wood, fibre or plastic dowels can be bought to match the screws.

**Washers**
Used with nuts and bolts to enable them to be turned easily and to avoid tearing the wood. The normal washer used for woodwork is a plain washer; use single coil, internal and external tooth washers for metal.

**Waste pipe**
A pipe that conveys waste water from a sink, basin or bath to the drainage system.

**Wax polish**
Good proprietary brands are available for protecting and improving a wood-finished surface. Unlike varnishing, wax polishing a newly stained surface is a treatment that has to be repeated when the shine wears off.

**Wet-and-dry paper**
Silicone-carbide abrasive paper which can be used in two ways—dry like glasspaper, or wet (damp) to smooth down and clean off paint on metal or woodwork—to give a very fine finish. After rubbing down with wet paper, always wash a surface before repainting.

**Wet rot**
Occurs in timber containing 20 per cent or more moisture. Wood becomes spongy when wet and brittle when dry. Infected wood should be cut out and the surrounding area treated with a fungicidal preservative. If decay is severe, consult a specialist.

**Wheelbrace** *See* Tip 643

**Wheel cutter** *See* Tip 164

**Wooden float** *See* Tip 329

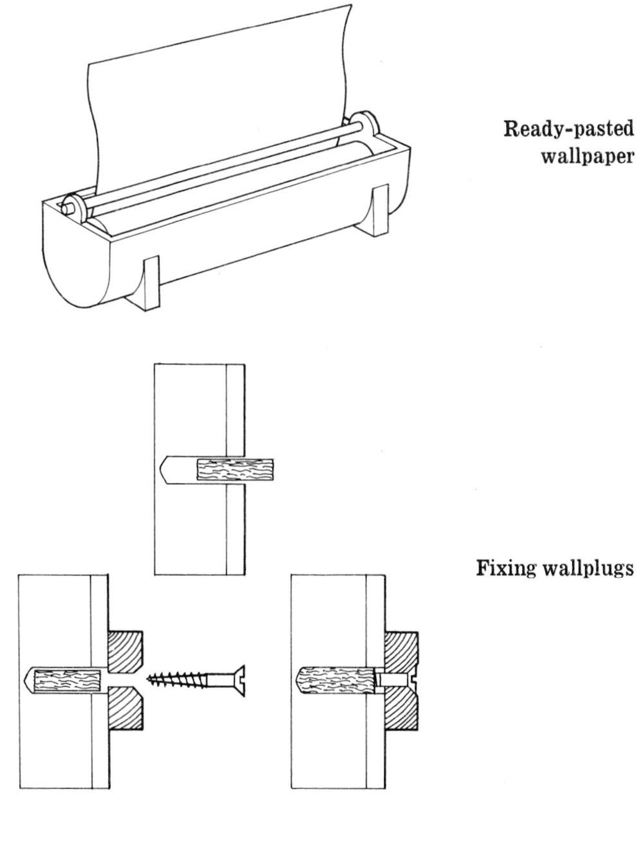

**Ready-pasted wallpaper**

**Fixing wallplugs**

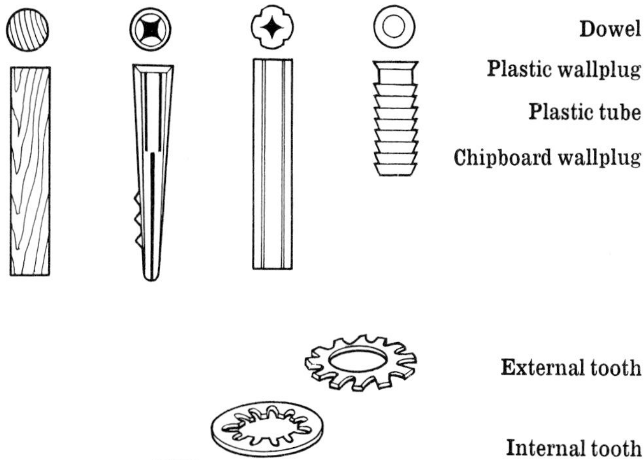

**Dowel**

**Plastic wallplug**

**Plastic tube**

**Chipboard wallplug**

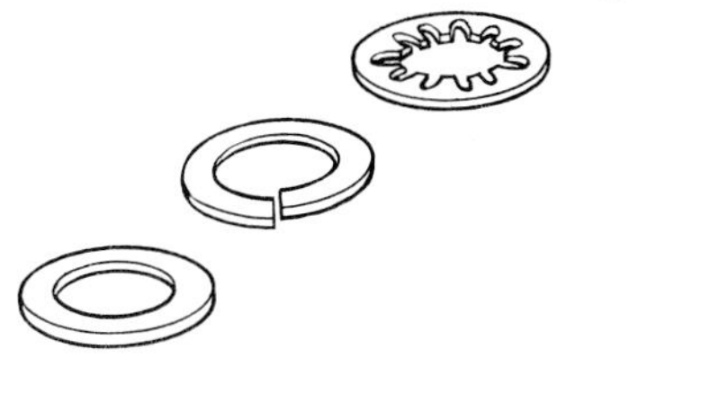

**External tooth**

**Internal tooth**

**Single coil**

**Plain washer**

# Acknowledgements

The publishers gratefully acknowledge the assistance of the following individuals and organizations:

Andrew Duncan; Peter Parkinson (designer, chess and draughts set); John Pennicott (modular toy kit); Amanda Webb (fibreglass puppets). Nick Hawker (picture framing), Clancy de Roe (artist, "Eating My Heart Out"), Benita Armstrong (portrait). For the Sampson/Fether designs, the prototypes were built by Hans Bromwich (tiled tables); Barry Caldecott (upholstered sofa, outdoor lounger, fabric light, room-in-one kit/1, decorative finishes/2); Sally Caldecott (jigsaw cushions, outdoor lounger); Alan Clarke (storage screen/2); John Coleman (tiled furniture); Angela Coles (canvas drawer unit); Adrian Corry and Nevill Taylor (storage screen/1); Albert Fether (workbench); Rae Fether and Deborah Morrel (decorative finishes/4); Murray Hunter (hi-fi speakers); Ed Mathews and Peter Walker Taylor (decorative finishes/3); Colin Murray (room-in-one kit/2); Neville Pryke (prototype co-ordinator); Alex Roberts (hi-fi rack, decorative finishes/1); Tony Rostron (wall painting); Richard Thorn (unit shelving/1, unit shelving/3, panels); Craig Tomlinson (tiled plinths); Jim Warren (sculptured bed).
Chinacraft Catering Supplies at William Page & Co. Ltd., London W1; Selwyn Davidson, London W1; P. Denny & Co. Ltd., London W1; Earlspin, London W1; Habitat Designs Ltd., London SW3; Knight Games, London W1; Laskys, London W1; The Neal Street Shop, London WC2; The New Neal Street Shop, London WC2; William Page & Co. Ltd., London W1; Stanley Tools Limited, Sheffield; Christopher T. Strangeways, London SW10; B. and T. Waller, London WC2.

The tools illustrated on the cover and in the opening pages of the book were designed and made by Matthew Wurr.